Nonlinear Dynamics in Complex Systems via Fractals and Fractional Calculus

Nonlinear Dynamics in Complex Systems via Fractals and Fractional Calculus

Editor

Viorel-Puiu Paun

MDPI • Basel • Beijing • Wuhan • Barcelona • Belgrade • Manchester • Tokyo • Cluj • Tianjin

Editor
Viorel-Puiu Paun
University Politehnica of
Bucharest
Bucharest, Romania

Editorial Office
MDPI
St. Alban-Anlage 66
4052 Basel, Switzerland

This is a reprint of articles from the Special Issue published online in the open access journal *Fractal and Fractional* (ISSN 2504-3110) (available at: https://www.mdpi.com/journal/fractalfract/special_issues/complex_system).

For citation purposes, cite each article independently as indicated on the article page online and as indicated below:

LastName, A.A.; LastName, B.B.; LastName, C.C. Article Title. *Journal Name* **Year**, *Volume Number*, Page Range.

ISBN 978-3-0365-8336-5 (Hbk)
ISBN 978-3-0365-8337-2 (PDF)

© 2023 by the authors. Articles in this book are Open Access and distributed under the Creative Commons Attribution (CC BY) license, which allows users to download, copy and build upon published articles, as long as the author and publisher are properly credited, which ensures maximum dissemination and a wider impact of our publications.

The book as a whole is distributed by MDPI under the terms and conditions of the Creative Commons license CC BY-NC-ND.

Contents

About the Editor vii

Preface to "Nonlinear Dynamics in Complex Systems via Fractals and Fractional Calculus" . . ix

Viorel-Puiu Paun
Special Issue: Nonlinear Dynamics in Complex Systems via Fractals and Fractional Calculus
Reprinted from: *Fractal Fract.* 2023, 7, 412, doi:10.3390/10.3390/fractalfract7050412 1

Marius Mihai Cazacu, Iulian-Alin Roșu, Luminița Bibire, Decebal Vasincu, Ana Maria Rotundu and Maricel Agop
Theoretical and Experimental Designs of the Planetary Boundary Layer Dynamics through a Multifractal Theory of Motion
Reprinted from: *Fractal Fract.* 2022, 6, 747, doi:10.3390/10.3390/fractalfract6120747 7

Jiahui Wang, Chengwei Dong and Hantao Li
A New Variable-Boostable 3D Chaotic System withHidden and Coexisting Attractors: Dynamical Analysis, Periodic OrbitCoding, Circuit Simulation, and Synchronization
Reprinted from: *Fractal Fract.* 2022, 6, 740, doi:10.3390/10.3390/fractalfract6120740 25

Maria-Alexandra Paun, Vladimir-Alexandru Paun and Viorel-Puiu Paun
Spatial Series and Fractal Analysis Associated with Fracture Behaviour of UO_2 Ceramic Material
Reprinted from: *Fractal Fract.* 2022, 6, 595, doi:10.3390/10.3390/fractalfract6100595 51

Chengwei Dong
Dynamic Analysis of a Novel 3D Chaotic System with Hidden andCoexisting Attractors: Offset Boosting, Synchronization, and CircuitRealization
Reprinted from: *Fractal Fract.* 2022, 6, 547, doi:10.3390/10.3390/fractalfract6100547 71

Yuxing Li, Bingzhao Tang, Bo Geng and Shangbin Jiao
Fractional Order Fuzzy Dispersion Entropy and Its Application in Bearing Fault Diagnosis
Reprinted from: *Fractal Fract.* 2022, 6, 544, doi:10.3390/10.3390/fractalfract6100544 93

Yijun Zhu and Huilin Shang
Global Bifurcation Behaviors and Control in a Class of Bilateral MEMS Resonators
Reprinted from: *Fractal Fract.* 2022, 6, 538, doi:10.3390/10.3390/fractalfract6100538 111

Maria-Alexandra Paun, Vladimir-Alexandru Paun and Viorel-Puiu Paun
Fractal Analysis and Time Series Application in ZY-4 SEM Micro Fractographies Evaluation
Reprinted from: *Fractal Fract.* 2022, 6, 458, doi:10.3390/10.3390/fractalfract6080458 133

Maria-Alexandra Paun, Mihai-Virgil Nichita, Vladimir-Alexandru Paun and Viorel-Puiu Paun
Minkowski's Loop Fractal Antenna Dedicated to Sixth Generation (6G) Communication
Reprinted from: *Fractal Fract.* 2022, 6, 402, doi:10.3390/10.3390/fractalfract6070402 151

Yuxing Li, Lingxia Mu and Peiyuan Gao
Particle Swarm Optimization Fractional Slope Entropy: A New Time Series Complexity Indicator for Bearing Fault Diagnosis
Reprinted from: *Fractal Fract.* 2022, 6, 345, doi:10.3390/10.3390/fractalfract6070345 167

Yongxi Jiang, Xiaofang Yang and Tianxiu Lu
Sensitivity of Uniformly Convergent Mapping Sequences in Non-Autonomous Discrete Dynamical Systems
Reprinted from: *Fractal Fract.* 2022, 6, 319, doi:10.3390/10.3390/fractalfract6060319 185

Chengwei Dong and Jiahui Wang
Hidden and Coexisting Attractors in a Novel 4D Hyperchaotic System with No Equilibrium Point
Reprinted from: *Fractal Fract.* **2022**, *6*, 306, doi:10.3390/10.3390/fractalfract6060306 . . . . **195**

Dragos-Constantin Nica, Marius-Mihai Cazacu, Daniel-Eduard Constantin, Valentin Nedeff, Florin Nedeff, Decebal Vasincu, et al.
Boundary Layer via Multifractal Mass Conductivity through Remote Sensing Data in Atmospheric Dynamics
Reprinted from: *Fractal Fract.* **2022**, *6*, 250, doi:10.3390/10.3390/fractalfract6050250 . . . . **219**

Chengwei Dong
Dynamics, Periodic Orbit Analysis, and Circuit Implementation of a New Chaotic System with Hidden Attractor
Reprinted from: *Fractal Fract.* **2022**, *6*, 190, doi:10.3390/10.3390/fractalfract6040190 . . . . **241**

About the Editor

Viorel-Puiu Paun

Viorel-Puiu Paun is full university professor of Physics at "Politehnica" University of Bucharest, Faculty of Applied Sciences, Physics Department, and a titular member of Academy of Romanian Scientists. The main areas of his scientific interest are nonlinear dynamics and chaos theory, with their applications in different physico-chemical systems (nanostructures, composites), biological systems and in human organs such as the brain, lungs and stomach. More precisely, he is an expert in fractal interpretation of common diagnostic medical imaging tests (X-rays, CT scan, MRI, etc.). He is furthermore interested in the knowledge and use of new composite materials in oral rehabilitation. He is interested in material properties, compatibility with human tissue and their validity over time, in surgery. He has carried out extensive research in all the above-mentioned fields, including, in particular, time series methods, fractal analysis and diffusion processes. Viorel-Puiu Paun has published more than 150 papers in national and international journals, 117 ISI journal papers, 50 communications in national and international meetings (more than 30 on invitation), 577 citations without self-citations, and 20 books, chapters and monographs. His Hirsch factor value is currently 23. He was a guest/visiting professor at nine prestigious universities in Europe, including University of Cambridge, UK (2015), École Polytechnique Fédérale de Lausanne (EPFL), Switzerland (1996-1997, 2014), University of Florence, Italy (2011), ENSICA Toulouse, France (2007), and School of Physical Sciences, Kent University, Canterbury, UK (2004, 2006), among others.

Preface to "Nonlinear Dynamics in Complex Systems via Fractals and Fractional Calculus"

The use of fractal analysis and fractional-order partial differential equations in real complex systems is commonly encountered today in the fields of theoretical science and engineering applications. This means that the productive, efficacious computational tools required for analytical and numerical estimations of such physical complex models, and our reliance on their development, have been welcome. This book discusses the use of fractional calculus and novel algorithms to solve fractional-order derivatives of classic problems, including chaotic instabilities in theories of mathematical physics, fractal-type spatiotemporal behaviors in field theory and nonlinear dynamic processes in plasma complex structures. This volume collects some important advances in the fields of fractal curves, fractal analysis and fractional calculus, as well as new solutions of fractal differential equations. In addition, it assembles some novel insights and extraordinary perceptions into nonlinear complex systems theory, proving to be an important and representative book in the field, and a valuable reference in the specialized literature.

Viorel-Puiu Paun
Editor

Editorial

Special Issue: Nonlinear Dynamics in Complex Systems via Fractals and Fractional Calculus

Viorel-Puiu Paun [1,2]

[1] Physics Department, Faculty of Applied Sciences, University Politehnica of Bucharest, 060042 Bucharest, Romania; viorel.paun@physics.pub.ro
[2] Academy of Romanian Scientists, 050094 Bucharest, Romania

Citation: Paun, V.-P. Special Issue: Nonlinear Dynamics in Complex Systems via Fractals and Fractional Calculus. *Fractal Fract.* **2023**, *7*, 412. https://doi.org/10.3390/fractalfract7050412

Received: 10 May 2023
Accepted: 18 May 2023
Published: 20 May 2023

Copyright: © 2023 by the author. Licensee MDPI, Basel, Switzerland. This article is an open access article distributed under the terms and conditions of the Creative Commons Attribution (CC BY) license (https://creativecommons.org/licenses/by/4.0/).

Advances in our knowledge of nonlinear dynamical networks, systems and processes (as well as their unified repercussions) currently allow us to study many typical complex phenomena taking place in nature, from the nanoscale to the extra-galactic scale, in an comprehensive manner. Thus, systems generally deemed dynamical systems, chaotic systems or fractal systems clearly have something essential in common, and can be considered to belong to the same class of complex phenomena discussed herein. In other words, the physical, biological and financial data of complex systems, as well as the technological data (observed using mechanical or electronic devices), available today can be managed using same unique conceptual approach; this approach works both analytically and through computer simulations, using effective nonlinear dynamics procedures. The works presented in this technical publication are those that have appeared in the *Fractal and Fractional* journal in a Special Issue of the same name, which included the thirteen individually published papers plus an Editorial signed by the editor of this book.

In the first work introduced in this volume, the authors affirmed that the accurate determination of atmospheric temperature using telemetric platforms is an active issue, and one that can also be tackled with the aid of multifractal theory to observe the fundamental behaviors of the lower atmosphere. These observations can then be used to facilitate such determinations [1]. Thereby, within the framework of the scale relativity theory, PBL dynamics can be analyzed with the aid of a multifractal hydrodynamic scenario. Considering the PBL as a complex system that is assimilated into mathematical objects of a multifractal type, its various dynamics exert a multifractal tunnel effect. Such a treatment allows one to define both a multifractal atmospheric transparency coefficient and a multifractal atmospheric reflectance coefficient. These products are then used to create theoretical temperature profiles, which lead to correlations with real results obtained using radiometer data (RPG-HATPRO radiometer), with favorable results. Such methods could be further used and refined in future applications to efficiently produce theoretical atmospheric temperature profiles.

In the reference [2], the authors consider that the study of hidden attractors plays a very important role in the engineering applications of nonlinear dynamical systems. Thus, in this paper, a new three-dimensional (3D) chaotic system is proposed, in which hidden attractors and self-excited attractors appear as the parameters change. Meanwhile, asymmetric coexisting attractors are also found as a result of the system's symmetry. The complex dynamical behaviors of the proposed system were investigated using various tools, including time series diagrams, Poincaré first return maps, bifurcation diagrams, and basins of attraction. Moreover, unstable periodic orbits within a topological length of 3 in the hidden chaotic attractor were calculated systematically using the variational method, which required six letters to establish suitable symbolic dynamics [2]. Furthermore, the practicality of the hidden attractor chaotic system was verified using circuit simulations. Finally, offset boosting control and adaptive synchronization were used to investigate the utility of the proposed chaotic system in engineering applications.

The third selected work refers to the fractal analysis of some nuclear ceramic materials. SEM micrographs of the fracture surface of UO2 ceramic materials have been analyzed. In this paper, some algorithms were introduced, and a computer application based on the non-linear time series method was developed. Utilizing the embedding technique of phase space, the attractor is reconstructed. In addition, the fractal dimension, lacunarity, and autocorrelation dimension average value have been calculated [3].

To further understand the dynamical characteristics of chaotic systems with a hidden attractor and coexisting attractors, we refer readers to the fourth work. Here, the fundamental dynamics of a novel three-dimensional (3D) chaotic system, derived by adding a simple constant term to the Yang–Chen system, were investigated under different parameters; these include the bifurcation diagram, Lyapunov exponents spectrum, and basin of attraction [4]. Additionally, an offset-boosting control method is presented to the state variable, and a numerical simulation of the system is also introduced. Furthermore, the unstable cycles embedded in the hidden chaotic attractors are extracted in detail, which shows the effectiveness of the variational method and the one-dimensional symbolic dynamics. Finally, the adaptive synchronization of the novel system is successfully designed, and a circuit simulation is implemented to illustrate the flexibility and validity of the numerical results. Theoretical analysis and simulation results indicate that the new system has complex dynamical properties, and can be used to facilitate engineering applications [4].

The fifth work is dedicated to fuzzy dispersion entropy (FuzzDE), a very recently proposed non-linear dynamical indicator which combines the advantages of both dispersion entropy (DE) and fuzzy entropy (FuzzEn) to detect dynamic changes in a time series. However, FuzzDE only reflects the information of the original signal, and is not very sensitive to dynamic changes. To address these drawbacks, a fractional order calculation on the basis of FuzzDE was proposed; it is referred to as FuzzDEα. The calculation may be used as a tool for signal analysis and the fault diagnosis of bearings [5]. In addition, other fractional order entropies were introduced, including fractional order DE (DEα), fractional order permutation entropy (PEα), and fractional order fluctuation-based DE (FDEα); a mixed-features extraction diagnosis method was also proposed. Both simulated as well as real-world experimental results demonstrated that the FuzzDEα, at different fractional orders, is more sensitive to changes in the dynamics of the time series. The proposed mixed-features bearing fault diagnosis method achieves a 100% recognition rate with only three features, among which the mixed-feature combinations with the highest recognition rates all include FuzzDEα. FuzzDEα also appears most frequently [5].

Investigating global bifurcation behaviors, the vibrating structures of micro-electromechanical systems (MEMS) received substantial attention in the sixth work of this collection. This paper considers the vibrating system of a typical bilateral MEMS resonator containing fractional functions and multiple potential wells. By introducing new variations, the Melnikov method is applied to derive the critical conditions for global bifurcations. By engaging in the fractal erosion of the safe basin to intuitively depict the phenomenon of pull-in instability, the point-mapping approach is used to present numerical simulations that are in close agreement with analytical predictions, showing the validity of the analysis. It is found that chaos and pull-in instability, two initially sensitive phenomena of MEMS resonators, may be due to homoclinic bifurcation and heteroclinic bifurcation, respectively [6]. On this basis, two types of delayed feedback are proposed to control the complex dynamics successively. Their control mechanisms and effects are then studied. It follows that under a positive gain coefficient, delayed position feedback and delayed velocity feedback can both reduce pull-in instability; nevertheless, in suppressing chaos, only the former is effective. The results may have some potential value in broadening the application fields of global bifurcation theory, and in improving the performance reliability of capacitive MEMS devices [6].

In the seventh paper presented in this book, SEM microfractographies of Zircaloy-4 are studied using fractal analysis and the time series method. First, a computer application that associates a fractal dimension and lacunarity with each SEM micrograph picture was developed; the application also produced a nonlinear analysis of the data acquired from the quantitatively evaluated time series. Utilizing the phase space-embedding technique to reconstruct the attractor and to compute the autocorrelation dimension, the fracture surface of the Zircaloy-4 samples was investigated. The fractal analysis method manages to highlight damage complications, and provides a description of the morphological parameters of various fractures by calculating the fractal dimension and lacunarity [7].

In the eighth study presented herein, the authors discuss the engineering and construction of a special sixth-generation (6G) antenna based on the fractal known as Minkowski's loop. The antenna has the shape of this known fractal, set at four iterations, to obtain maximum performance. The frequency bands for which this 6G fractal antenna was designed are 170 GHz to 260 GHz (WR-4) and 110 GHz to 170 GHz (WR-6), respectively. The three resonant frequencies, optimally used, are equal to 140 GHz (WR-6) for the first, 182 GHz (WR-4) for the second, and 191 GHz (WR-4) for the third. The electromagnetic behaviors of the fractal antennas and their graphical representations are highlighted at these frequencies [8].

In the next work, the ninth of the thirteen, it is established that slope entropy (SlEn) is a time series complexity indicator proposed in recent years that has shown excellent performance in the fields of medicine and hydroacoustics. In order to improve the ability of SlEn to distinguish between different types of signals and solve the problem of selecting two threshold parameters, a new time series complexity indicator is proposed on the basis of SlEn. This was achieved by introducing fractional calculus and combining particle swarm optimization (PSO) in an indicator named PSO fractional SlEn (PSO-FrSlEn). Then, PSO-FrSlEn is applied to the field of fault diagnosis, and a single-feature extraction method and a double-feature extraction method based on PSO-FrSlEn are proposed for rolling bearing faults [9]. The experimental results illustrated that only PSO-FrSlEn can classify ten kinds of bearing signals with 100% classification accuracy (by using double features), which is at least 4% higher than the classification accuracies of the other four fractional entropies [9].

In the tenth work, it is shown that the metric of H may be denoted by d when H is a compact metric space. Then, we can let $(H, f_{1,\infty})$ be a non-autonomous discrete system, where $f_{1,\infty} = \{f_n\}_{n=1}^{\infty}$ is a mapping sequence. This paper discusses the infinite sensitivity, m-sensitivity, and m-cofinite sensitivity of $f_{1,\infty}$. It proves that if $f_n (n \in \mathbb{N})$ are feebly open and uniformly converge to $f:H \to H$, $f_i \circ f = f \circ f_i$ for any $i \in \{1, 2, \ldots\}$, and $\sum_{i=1}^{\infty} D(f_i, f) < \infty$, then (H, f) has the above sensitive property if and only if $(H, f_{1,\infty})$ has the same property, where $D(\cdot, \cdot)$ is the supremum metric [10].

The investigation of chaotic systems containing hidden and coexisting attractors has attracted extensive attention. The eleventh paper presents a four-dimensional (4D) novel hyperchaotic system that is advanced by adding a linear state feedback controller to a three-dimensional chaotic system with two stable node focus points [11]. The proposed system has no equilibrium point, or two lines of equilibria, depending on the value of the constant term. Complex dynamical behaviors, such as hidden chaotic and hyperchaotic attractors and the five types of coexisting attractors within the simple four-dimensional autonomous system, are investigated and discussed, and they are numerically verified through the analysis of phase diagrams, Poincaré maps, the Lyapunov exponent spectrum, and its bifurcation diagram. The short unstable cycles in the hyperchaotic system are systematically explored using the variational method, and symbol codings of cycles with four letters are produced based on the topological properties of the trajectory's projection onto the two-dimensional phase space. The bifurcations of the cycles are explored through a homotopy evolution approach. Finally, the novel four-dimensional system is implemented using an analog electronic circuit, and is found to be consistent with the numerical simulation results [11].

In the twelfth manuscript, multifractal theories of motion based on scale relativity theory are considered in the description of atmospheric dynamics. It is shown that these theories have the potential to highlight the nondimensional mass conduction laws that describe the propagation of atmospheric entities [12]. Then, using special operational procedures and harmonic mappings, these equations may be rewritten and simplified so that their plotting and analysis may be performed. The inhomogeneity of these conduction phenomena was analyzed, and the study found that it can fluctuate and increase at certain fractal dimensions, leading to the conclusion that certain atmospheric structures and phenomena of either atmospheric transmission or stability can be explained by atmospheric fractal dimension inversions. Finally, this hypothesis is verified using the ceilometer data found throughout the atmospheric profiles [12].

This Special Issue, which is the subject of our editorial, also collates some new insights into the theory of hidden attractors and multistability phenomena, which have considerable application prospects in engineering [13]. Thus, in the final work, the thirteenth, by modifying a simple three-dimensional continuous quadratic dynamical system, a new autonomous chaotic system with two stable node foci that can generate double-wing hidden chaotic attractors is reported. The rich dynamics of the proposed system were discussed; said system has some interesting characteristics in terms of its different parameters and initial conditions, which were found through the use of dynamic analysis tools such as the phase portrait, the Lyapunov exponent spectrum, and bifurcation diagrams. The topological classification of the periodic orbits of the system was investigated using a recently devised variational method. The symbolic dynamics of four and six letters have been successfully established under two sets of system parameters, including hidden and self-excited chaotic attractors [13]. The system was implemented using a corresponding analog electronic circuit to verify its realizability.

This volume gathers together information on some important advances in the fields of fractal curves, fractal analysis and fractional calculus [14,15]. Thereby, the Special Issue which is the subject of our editorial also collates some novel insights into the theory of complex systems; it is a significant and relevant volume for our field of study, and will be appreciated as a useful reference within the specialized literature.

Conflicts of Interest: The authors declare no conflict of interest.

References

1. Cazacu, M.M.; Ros, U.I.-A.; Bibire, L.; Vasincu, D.; Rotundu, A.M.; Agop, M. Theoretical and Experimental Designs of the Planetary Boundary Layer Dynamics through a Multifractal Theory of Motion. *Fractal Fract.* **2022**, *6*, 747. [CrossRef]
2. Wang, J.; Dong, C.; Li, H.A. New Variable-Boostable 3D Chaotic System with Hidden and Coexisting Attractors: Dynamical Analysis, Periodic Orbit Coding, Circuit Simulation, and Synchronization. *Fractal Fract.* **2022**, *6*, 740. [CrossRef]
3. Paun, M.-A.; Paun, V.-A.; Paun, V.-P. Spatial Series and Fractal Analysis Associated with Fracture Behaviour of UO2 Ceramic Material. *Fractal Fract.* **2022**, *6*, 595. [CrossRef]
4. Dong, C. Dynamic Analysis of a Novel 3D Chaotic System with Hidden and Coexisting Attractors: Offset Boosting, Synchronization, and Circuit Realization. *Fractal Fract.* **2022**, *6*, 547. [CrossRef]
5. Li, Y.; Tang, B.; Geng, B.; Jiao, S. Fractional Order Fuzzy Dispersion Entropy and Its Application in Bearing Fault Diagnosis. *Fractal Fract.* **2022**, *6*, 544. [CrossRef]
6. Zhu, Y.; Shang, H. Global Bifurcation Behaviors and Control in a Class of Bilateral MEMS Resonators. *Fractal Fract.* **2022**, *6*, 538. [CrossRef]
7. Paun, M.-A.; Paun, V.-A.; Paun, V.-P. Fractal Analysis and Time Series Application in ZY-4 SEM Micro Fractographies Evaluation. *Fractal Fract.* **2022**, *6*, 458. [CrossRef]
8. Paun, M.-A.; Nichita, M.-V.; Paun, V.-A.; Paun, V.-P. Minkowski's Loop Fractal Antenna Dedicated to Sixth Generation (6G) Communication. *Fractal Fract.* **2022**, *6*, 402. [CrossRef]
9. Li, Y.; Mu, L.; Gao, P. Particle Swarm Optimization Fractional Slope Entropy: A New Time Series Complexity Indicator for Bearing Fault Diagnosis. *Fractal Fract.* **2022**, *6*, 345. [CrossRef]
10. Jiang, Y.; Yang, X.; Lu, T. Sensitivity of Uniformly Convergent Mapping Sequences in Non-Autonomous Discrete Dynamical Systems. *Fractal Fract.* **2022**, *6*, 319. [CrossRef]
11. Dong, C.; Wang, J. Hidden and Coexisting Attractors in a Novel 4D Hyperchaotic System with No Equilibrium Point. *Fractal Fract.* **2022**, *6*, 306. [CrossRef]
12. Nica, D.-C.; Cazacu, M.-M.; Constantin, D.-E.; Nedeff, V.; Nedeff, F.; Vasincu, D.; Ros, U.I.-A.; Agop, M. Boundary Layer via Multifractal Mass Conductivity through Remote Sensing Data in Atmospheric Dynamics. *Fractal Fract.* **2022**, *6*, 250. [CrossRef]
13. Dong, C. Dynamics, Periodic Orbit Analysis, and Circuit Implementation of a New Chaotic System with Hidden Attractor. *Fractal Fract.* **2022**, *6*, 190. [CrossRef]

14. Agop, M.; Paun, V.P. *On the New Perspectives of Fractal Theory. Fundaments and Applications*; Romanian Academy Publishing House: Bucharest, Romania, 2017.
15. Paun, V.P.; Agop, M.; Chen, G.R.; Focsa, C. Fractal-Type Dynamical Behaviors of Complex Systems. *Complexity* **2018**, *2018*, 8029361. [CrossRef]

Disclaimer/Publisher's Note: The statements, opinions and data contained in all publications are solely those of the individual author(s) and contributor(s) and not of MDPI and/or the editor(s). MDPI and/or the editor(s) disclaim responsibility for any injury to people or property resulting from any ideas, methods, instructions or products referred to in the content.

Article

Theoretical and Experimental Designs of the Planetary Boundary Layer Dynamics through a Multifractal Theory of Motion

Marius Mihai Cazacu [1], Iulian-Alin Roșu [2,*], Luminița Bibire [3], Decebal Vasincu [4], Ana Maria Rotundu [2] and Maricel Agop [1,5,*]

[1] Department of Physics, "Gheorghe Asachi" Technical University of Iasi, 700050 Iași, Romania
[2] Faculty of Physics, "Alexandru Ioan Cuza" University of Iasi, 700506 Iași, Romania
[3] Department of Environmental Engineering and Mechanical Engineering, Faculty of Engineering, Vasile Alecsandri University of Bacau, 600115 Bacău, Romania
[4] Department of Biophysics, Faculty of Dental Medicine, "Grigore T. Popa" University of Medicine and Pharmacy, 700115 Iași, Romania
[5] Academy of Romanian Scientists, 050044 Bucharest, Romania
* Correspondence: alin.iulian.rosu@gmail.com (I.-A.R.); m.agop@yahoo.com (M.A.)

Abstract: The accurate determination of atmospheric temperature with telemetric platforms is an active issue, one that can also be tackled with the aid of multifractal theory to extract fundamental behaviors of the lower atmosphere, which can then be used to facilitate such determinations. Thus, in the framework of the scale relativity theory, PBL dynamics are analyzed through the aid of a multifractal hydrodynamic scenario. Considering the PBL as a complex system that is assimilated to mathematical objects of a multifractal type, its various dynamics work as a multifractal tunnel effect. Such a treatment allows one to define both a multifractal atmospheric transparency coefficient and a multifractal atmospheric reflectance coefficient. These products are then employed to create theoretical temperature profiles, which lead to correspondences with real results obtained by radiometer data (RPG-HATPRO radiometer), with favorable results. Such methods could be further used and refined in future applications to efficiently produce atmospheric temperature theoretical profiles.

Keywords: PBL dynamics; multifractality; scale relativity theory; radiometer data

1. General Considerations: From Differentiability to Non-Differentiability in Atmospheric Process Dynamics

The PBL (planetary boundary layer) dynamics remain a subject of great interest due to the many consequences regarding atmospheric behavior on both a local and a global scale. Because of the effects of buoyancy, tropospheric temperature profiles limits the motion verticality of atmospheric entities, and therefore the PBL appears as a principal stable factor in atmospheric dynamics [1]. The PBL is often turbulent, and because turbulence causes mixing, the bottom part of the standard atmosphere homogenizes, while the area above is commonly known as the "free atmosphere". Therefore, the PBL plays a tremendous role in aerosol and humidity transport and in the stratification and complex dynamic interplay of the atmosphere; its existence is commonly determined by inversions of various physical parameters, especially temperature [1]. However, while its common behavior patterns can be somewhat anticipated from a phenomenological perspective, the exact description of the atmospheric parameter inversions is not fully known.

Most models employed in the study of PBL dynamics assume, which can be unjustified, physical variables' differentiability. The successful applications of such models have to be understood on a sequential level, which means that differentiability would mostly be valid for larger domains. Classically, any and all dynamic variables that are dependent on spatiotemporal coordinates also become dependent on the scale resolution [1–5]. Thus, instead of employing dynamical variables through non-differentiable functions, we must use certain approximations of that function derived through its averaging at different scale resolutions. As a consequence, all dynamic variables must then act as the limit of a family of functions, these being non-differentiable for a null scale resolution and differentiable for a nonzero scale resolution.

In general, non-differential methods are considered suitable in the field of complex systems, where real measurements are conducted at a finite scale resolution. The implication is that a new physical theory for such systems is developed, and in this theory, motion laws, which are invariant to coordinate transformations, must be integrated with scale laws that are similarly invariant. The present assumptions lead to a theory that was first developed in the framework of the scale relativity theory, which defines fractal physical models [4–6].

In the following, the PBL dynamics in the framework of the scale relativity theory are analyzed, assimilating it with a mathematical object of multifractal type (PBL dynamics considered through the multifractal tunnel effect). The rationale for this assimilation lies in the fact that the stratification of the lower atmosphere resembles the structure of a tunneling barrier scenario. The intent of this development is to continue the theoretical and practical advances into atmospheric physics using multifractality and to elaborate the basis of a multifractal theoretical model, which could be used to study the evolution of many types of parameters, most relevantly temperature. Starting with main theoretical aspects, the atmosphere is considered from a multifractal perspective, with all the mathematical consequences that this entails. Then, a multifractal tunnel effect in an external scalar potential configuration is seen to produce a multifractal barrier object, which plays the role of the PBL. This barrier entity and its properties are explained, and a variable is chosen which can function as an iterative parameter in order to implement the resulting equations as a model of atmospheric temperature. Finally, ceilometer and radiometer data are employed as experimental data, and theoretical atmospheric temperature data is contrasted with atmospheric temperature experimental data.

Regarding the usage of the multifractal tunnel effect as a theoretical implement in atmospheric studies, to the best of our knowledge, this is a novel application; however, this effect was previously employed in a study explaining the "chameleon effect" of cholesterol [7]. In terms of merely applying multifractal theories to the atmosphere, a number of studies have been elaborated, such as one that deals with developing a multifractal random-walk description of turbulence itself, another study that analyzes the multifractal long-term characteristics of local temperature fluctuations, and a recent study that seeks to multifractally characterize atmospheric particular matter pollution [8–10]. It is noteworthy, however, that given the theoretical complexity of using multifractal techniques, especially in a scientific field such as atmospheric studies, which is already marked by added difficulties in the form of chaos and scaling issues, there are not many current works that explore the connections between multifractality and atmospheric fluid dynamics. This is the case even though the formation of turbulence through strange attractors, which are fractal in nature, has been both experimentally and theoretically established decades ago [11,12]. Therefore, it is also our hope that this study will not only present a functional application of theory to practice but will also broaden the field of multifractal atmospheric study.

2. Theoretical Design: Non-Differentiability Calibrated on PBL Dynamics in the Form of the Multifractal Hydrodynamic Model

Considering the PBL's complexity, which can be assimilated with a mathematical object of multifractal type, in such conjecture, the PBL dynamics can be explained through the scale relativity theory (the PBL structural units occur on continuous but non-differentiable multifractal curves), dynamics that can be described through the scale covariance derivative [5,13–16]:

$$\frac{\hat{d}}{dt} = \partial_t + \hat{V}^l \partial_l + \frac{1}{4}(dt)^{\left[\frac{2}{f(\alpha)}\right]-1} D^{lp} \partial_l \partial_p \tag{1}$$

where:
$$\hat{V}^l = V_D^l - iV_F^l, \tag{2a}$$
$$D^{lp} = d^{lp} - i\hat{d}^{lp}, \tag{2b}$$
$$d^{lp} = \lambda_+^l \lambda_+^p - \lambda_-^l \lambda_-^p, \tag{2c}$$
$$\hat{d}^{lp} = \lambda_+^l \lambda_+^p + \lambda_-^l \lambda_-^p, \tag{2d}$$
$$\partial_t = \frac{\partial}{\partial t},\ \partial_l = \frac{\partial}{\partial x^l},\ \partial_l \partial_p = \frac{\partial}{\partial x^l}\frac{\partial}{\partial x^p},\ i = \sqrt{-1},\ l,p = 1,2,3. \tag{2e}$$

The meanings of the above parameters are explained in greater detail in one of our previous works [16].

There exist many types of ways to define the notion of fractal dimension: Kolmogorov fractal dimension, Hausdorff–Besikovitch fractal dimension, and many others [17–20]. For such studies, it is necessary to select just one of these definitions, and for the meaning of fractal dimension to be constant, given the fact that the dimension directly dictates whether or not the process is correlative or not [17–20]. Thus, through the singularity spectrum, $f(\alpha)$, it is possible to identify not only dynamic spaces in the PBL that are characterized by just one fractal dimension but also dynamic spaces whose fractal dimensions are situated in an interval of values, implying multifractality. It is possible to employ the singularity spectrum in order to identify universality classes in PBL dynamics, even considering the regularity of the attractors involved.

If the PBL dynamics are described by Markovian stochastic processes [21–23]:
$$\lambda_+^i \lambda_+^l = \lambda_-^i \lambda_-^l = 2\lambda \delta^{il} \quad i,l = 1,2,3, \tag{3}$$

where λ is a specific coefficient of the multifractal–non-multifractal scale transition and δ^{il} is Kronecker's pseudotensor, the scale covariant derivative in Equation (1) becomes:
$$\frac{d}{dt} = \partial_t + \hat{V}^l \partial_l - i\lambda(dt)^{(\frac{2}{f(\alpha)})-1}\partial_l \partial^l. \tag{4}$$

Thus, if one accepts the principle of the scale covariance, which is by applying Equation (1) to Equation (2a), without constraints, the PBL's motion equations of the structural units dynamics become:
$$\frac{d\hat{V}^i}{dt} = \partial_t \hat{V}^i + \hat{V}^l \partial_l \hat{V}^i + \frac{1}{4}(dt)^{[\frac{2}{f(\alpha)}]-1} D^{lk} \partial_l \partial_k \hat{V}^i = 0. \tag{5}$$

In this manner, acceleration, $\partial_t \hat{V}^i$, convection, $\hat{V}^l \partial_l \hat{V}^i$, and dissipation, $D^{lk}\partial_l \partial_k \hat{V}^i$, are all balanced at every point of any multifractal curve of the PBL structural units dynamics. Particularly, for Equation (3), the motion Equation (5) becomes:
$$\frac{\hat{d}\hat{V}^i}{dt} = \partial_t \hat{V}^i + \hat{V}^l \partial_l \hat{V}^i - i\lambda(dt)^{[\frac{2}{D_F}]-1}\partial_l \partial^l \hat{V}^i = 0. \tag{6}$$

Now, through the separation of PBL structural units dynamics on scale resolution (differentiable and non-differentiable scale resolutions), Equation (5) becomes:
$$\partial_t V_D^i + V_D^l \partial_l V_D^i - V_F^l \partial_l V_F^i + \frac{1}{4}(dt)^{[\frac{2}{f(\alpha)}]-1}D^{lk}\partial_l \partial_k V_D^i = 0, \tag{7a}$$
$$\partial_t V_F^i + V_F^l \partial_l V_D^i + V_D^l \partial_l V_F^i - \frac{1}{4}(dt)^{[\frac{2}{f(\alpha)}]-1}D^{lk}\partial_l \partial_k V_F^i = 0, \tag{7b}$$

while Equation (6) takes the form:
$$\partial_t V_D^i + V_D^l \partial_l V_D^i - \left[V_F^l + \lambda(dt)^{[\frac{2}{f(\alpha)}]-1}\partial^l\right]\partial_l V_F^i = 0, \tag{8a}$$

$$\partial_t V_F^i + V_D^l \partial_l V_F^i + \left[V_F^l + \lambda(dt)^{[\frac{2}{f(\alpha)}]-1} \partial^l \right] \partial_l V_D^i = 0. \tag{8b}$$

For the non-rotational motions of the PBL structural units dynamics, the complex velocity fields in Equation (2a) take the form:

$$\hat{V}^i = -2i\lambda(dt)^{[\frac{2}{f(\alpha)}]-1} \partial^i \ln \Psi, \tag{9}$$

where Ψ is the states function. From here, for:

$$\Psi = \sqrt{\rho} e^{is}, \tag{10}$$

where $\sqrt{\rho}$ is the amplitude and s is the phase, the complex velocity fields in Equation (9) become explicitly:

$$\hat{V}^i = 2\lambda(dt)^{[\frac{2}{f(\alpha)}]-1} \partial^i s - i\lambda(dt)^{[\frac{2}{f(\alpha)}]-1} \partial^i \ln \rho, \tag{11}$$

which enable the definition of the real velocity fields:

$$V_D^i = 2\lambda(dt)^{[\frac{2}{f(\alpha)}]-1} \partial^i s, \tag{12}$$

$$V_F^i = i\lambda(dt)^{[\frac{2}{f(\alpha)}]-1} \partial^i \ln \rho. \tag{13}$$

Through Equations (12) and (13) and using the mathematical procedures from [21–23], Equation (8) reduces to the multifractal hydrodynamic equations:

$$\partial_t V_D^i + V_D^l \partial_l V_D^i = -\partial^i Q, \tag{14}$$

$$\partial_t \rho + \partial_l \left(\rho V_D^l \right) = 0, \tag{15}$$

with Q, the multifractal specific potential:

$$Q = -2\lambda^2 (dt)^{[\frac{4}{f(\alpha)}]-2} \frac{\partial^l \partial_l \sqrt{\rho}}{\sqrt{\rho}} = -V_F^i V_F^i - \frac{1}{2} \lambda (dt)^{[\frac{2}{f(\alpha)}]-1} \partial_l V_F^l. \tag{16}$$

Equation (14) gives the multifractal specific momentum conservation law of the PBL dynamics, while Equation (15) produces the multifractal state density conservation law of the same dynamics. The multifractal specific potential in Equation (16) implies the multifractal specific force:

$$F^i = -\partial^i Q = -2\lambda^2 (dt)^{[\frac{4}{f(\alpha)}]-2} \partial^i \frac{\partial^l \partial_l \sqrt{\rho}}{\sqrt{\rho}}, \tag{17}$$

which shows the multifractality of the motion curves of the PBL dynamics.

We note that for external constraints, for example, the external scalar potential, U, the multifractal hydrodynamic equations take the form:

$$\partial_t V_D^i + V_D^l \partial_l V_D^i = -\partial^i (Q + U), \tag{18}$$

$$\partial_t \rho + \partial_l \left(\rho V_D^l \right) = 0. \tag{19}$$

It is possible to extrapolate the following theoretical results using the equations previously mentioned:

I. The existence of a multifractal specific force implies that all PBL structure units must be considered through a multifractal medium;
II. This medium can be considered a multifractal fluid whose dynamics are characterized by the hydrodynamic model presented previously;

III. Since the velocity field, V_F^i, is absent from the multifractal states density conservation laws, it induces the possibility of non-manifest PBL dynamics, meaning that it facilitates the transmission of multifractal specific momentum and multifractal energy;

IV. All potential issues regarding reversibility and existence of the eigenstates are solved by the conservation of multifractal energy and multifractal momentum;

V. When using the tensor:

$$\hat{\tau}^{il} = 2\lambda^2 (dt)^{[\frac{4}{f(\alpha)}]-2} \rho \partial^i \partial^l \ln \rho, \qquad (20)$$

the multifractal specific potential (Q) equation can be defined as a multifractal equilibrium equation:

$$\rho \partial^i Q = \partial_l \hat{\tau}^{il}. \qquad (21)$$

The multifractal tensor $\hat{\tau}^{il}$ can now be written in the form:

$$\hat{\tau}^{il} = \eta \left(\partial_l V_F^i + \partial_i V_F^l \right), \qquad (22)$$

with:

$$\eta = \lambda (dt)^{[\frac{2}{f(\alpha)}]-1} \rho. \qquad (23)$$

Then, this is a multifractal linear constitutive equation that must be employed for a multifractal "viscous fluid".

3. PBL Dynamics Mimed as a Multifractal Atmospheric Tunnel Effect

Let us describe the PBL dynamics through the following assumptions:

I. The PBL, as a complex system both in a structural and functional perspective, can be assimilated with a mathematical object of multifractal type;

II. PBL dynamics can be described through the scale relativity theory in the form of multifractal hydrodynamic equations;

III. The PBL works as a multifractal atmospheric tunnel effect described through the external scalar potential (see Figure 1):

$$U(x) = \begin{cases} 0 & -\infty < x < 0 \\ U_0 & 0 \leq x \leq a \\ 0 & a < x < +\infty \end{cases}, \qquad (24)$$

where U_0 is the multifractal atmospheric barrier height and a is its width (the characteristics of PBL).

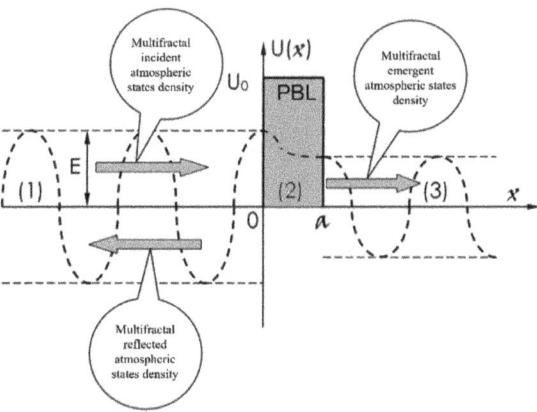

Figure 1. External scalar potential configuration (multifractal atmospheric barrier—PBL) for the tunnel effect of the multifractal (atmospheric) type.

Then, PBL dynamics are described through the multifractal energy conservation law of the form:

$$Q + U = E, \quad (25)$$

or explicitly:

$$2\lambda^2 (dt)^{[\frac{4}{f(\alpha)}]-2} \frac{\partial^l \partial_l \sqrt{\rho}}{\sqrt{\rho}} + U = E. \quad (26)$$

In Equation (26), ρ is the multifractal atmospheric state density, U is the external scalar potential, λ is the specific coefficient associated with the multifractal–non-multifractal transition, and E is the multifractal energy constant. We note that the results of Equation (26) are given by means of the functionality of the first Newton's principle applied to Equation (18) on multifractal manifolds.

Considering the one-dimensional case, Equation (26) through the substitution:

$$\sqrt{\rho} = \theta(x), \quad (27)$$

becomes:

$$\partial_{xx}\theta(x) + \frac{1}{2\lambda^2 (dt)^{[\frac{4}{f(\alpha)}]-2}} (E - U)\theta(x) = 0. \quad (28)$$

In the following, the above equations will be used to mime PBL dynamics through the multifractal atmospheric tunnel effect (any PBL structural unit with known energy penetrates a barrier of greater energy than the incident one).

As it is shown in Figure 1, we distinguish three zones denoted by (1), (2), and (3) as:

(1). the multifractal atmospheric incidence zone;
(2). the multifractal atmospheric barrier;
(3). the multifractal atmospheric emergence zone.

In such context, if θ_1, θ_2, and θ_3 are the multifractal functions corresponding to the above mentioned three zones, we have the following equations:

$$\frac{d^2\theta_1}{dx^2} + k^2\theta_1 = 0, \quad -\infty < x < 0 \quad (29a)$$

$$\frac{d^2\theta_2}{dx^2} - q^2\theta_2 = 0, \quad 0 \leq x \leq a \quad (29b)$$

$$\frac{d^2\theta_3}{dx^2} + k^2\theta_3 = 0, \quad a < x < +\infty \quad (29c)$$

where:

$$k^2 = \frac{E}{2\lambda^2 (dt)^{(4/f(\alpha))-2}}, \quad q^2 = \frac{U_0 - E}{2\lambda^2 (dt)^{(4/f(\alpha))-2}} \quad (30)$$

Now, through integration, the following solutions of the above equations are obtained:

$$\theta_1(x) = A_1 e^{ikx} + B_1 e^{-ikx}, \quad -\infty < x < 0 \quad (31a)$$

$$\theta_2(x) = A_2 e^{qx} + B_2 e^{-qx}, \quad 0 \leq x \leq a \quad (31b)$$

$$\theta_3(x) = A_3 e^{ikx}, \quad a < x < +\infty \quad (31c)$$

where A_1, B_1, A_2, B_2, and A_3 are constants. We note the following:

I. e^{ikx} corresponds to the multifractal incident atmospheric states density (from $-\infty$) in the multifractal zone (1) and to the multifractal emergent atmospheric states density (to $+\infty$) in the multifractal zone (3);
II. e^{-ikx} corresponds to the multifractal reflected atmospheric states density, which exists only in the multifractal zone (1), passing from $x = 0$ to $x = -\infty$ since in the multifractal zone (3), the external scalar potential is uniformly null.

Since the general expression of the multifractal atmospheric current of the states density in the one-dimensional case has the form [5,24]:

$$J_x = i\lambda(dt)^{(2/f(\alpha))-1}\left(\overline{\theta}\frac{d\theta}{dx} - \theta\frac{d\overline{\theta}}{dx}\right) \quad (32)$$

then the following currents can be defined:

- The multifractal atmospheric current density of the multifractal atmospheric incident states density in zone (1):

$$J_i = 2\lambda(dt)^{(\frac{2}{f(\alpha)})-1}k|A_1|^2 \quad (33)$$

- The multifractal atmospheric current density of the multifractal atmospheric emergent states density in zone (3):

$$J_e = 2\lambda(dt)^{(2/f(\alpha))-1}k|A_3|^2 \quad (34)$$

- The multifractal atmospheric current density of the multifractal reflected atmospheric states density:

$$J_r = -2\lambda(dt)^{(2/f(\alpha))-1}|B_1|^2 \quad (35)$$

These results give the possibility of a univocal characterization of the multifractal atmospheric tunnel effect through the multifractal atmospheric transparency:

$$T = \frac{J_e}{J_i} = \left|\frac{A_3}{A_1}\right|^2 \quad (36)$$

and the multifractal atmospheric reflectance:

$$R = \frac{J_r}{J_i} = \left|\frac{B_1}{A_1}\right|^2 \quad (37)$$

Imposing now the coupling conditions (in $x = 0$ and $x = a$), both for the functions θ_i and their derivates, i.e.,

$$\theta_1(0) = \theta_2(0) \quad (38a)$$

$$\frac{d\theta_1}{dx}(0) = \frac{d\theta_2}{dx}(0) \quad (38b)$$

$$\theta_2(a) = \theta_3(a) \quad (38c)$$

$$\frac{d\theta_2}{dx}(a) = \frac{d\theta_3}{dx}(a) \quad (38d)$$

the multifractal algebraic system is obtained:

$$A_1 + B_1 = A_2 + B_2 \quad (39a)$$

$$ik(A_1 - B_1) = q(A_2 - B_2) \quad (39b)$$

$$e^{qa}A_2 + e^{-qa}B_2 = e^{iqa}A_3 \quad (39c)$$

$$q(e^{qa}A_2 - e^{-qa}B_2) = ike^{iqa}A_3 \quad (39d)$$

Following the same mathematical procedure from [24], the multifractal atmospheric transparency takes the form:

$$T = \frac{4q^2k^2}{4q^2k^2 + (q^2 + k^2)^2 \text{sh}^2(qa)} \quad (40)$$

while the multifractal atmospheric reflectance becomes:

$$R = \frac{(k^2 + q^2)^2}{(q^2 - k^2)^2 + 4q^2k^2 \cdot \text{cth}^2(qa)} \tag{41}$$

Moreover, in the old notations (30), it is obtained:

$$R = \frac{U_0^2 \text{sh}^2\left\{\left[\frac{(U_0-E)}{2\lambda^2(dt)^{(4/f(\alpha))-2}}\right]^{1/2} a\right\}}{U_0^2 \text{sh}^2\left\{\left[\frac{(U_0-E)}{2\lambda^2(dt)^{(4/f(\alpha))-2}}\right]^{1/2} a\right\} + 4E(U_0 - E)} \tag{42}$$

$$T = \frac{4E(U_0 - E)}{U_0^2 \text{sh}^2\left\{\left[\frac{(U_0-E)}{2\lambda^2(dt)^{(4/f(\alpha))-2}}\right]^{1/2} a\right\} + 4E(U_0 - E)} \tag{43}$$

For graphical dependencies, it is preferable to use the dimensionless coordinate system:

$$X = ka = \left[\frac{E}{2\lambda^2(dt)^{(\frac{4}{f(\alpha)})-2}}\right]^{\frac{1}{2}} a \tag{44a}$$

$$Y = qa = \left[\frac{(U_0 - E)}{2\lambda^2(dt)^{(4/f(\alpha))-2}}\right]^{\frac{1}{2}} a \tag{44b}$$

Then, the multifractal atmospheric transparency and multifractal atmospheric reflectance become:

$$R = \frac{(X^2 + Y^2)^2}{(Y^2 - X^2)^2 + 4X^2Y^2\text{cth}^2(Y)} \tag{45}$$

$$T = \frac{4X^2Y^2}{4X^2Y^2 + (X^2 + Y^2)^2\text{sh}^2(Y)} \tag{46}$$

The 3D variations of the multifractal atmospheric transparency, T, on the dimensionless coordinates, X and Y, are depicted in Figure 2a,b:

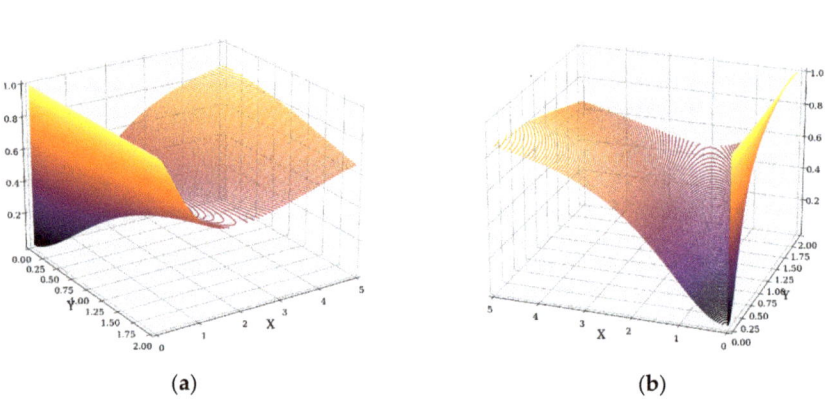

Figure 2. The 3D variations of the multifractal atmospheric transparency, T, of the dimensionless coordinates, X and Y: (**a**,**b**) the dependence T = T (X, Y).

The 2D variations of the multifractal atmospheric transparency, T, on the dimensionless coordinates, X and Y, are depicted in Figure 3a,b:

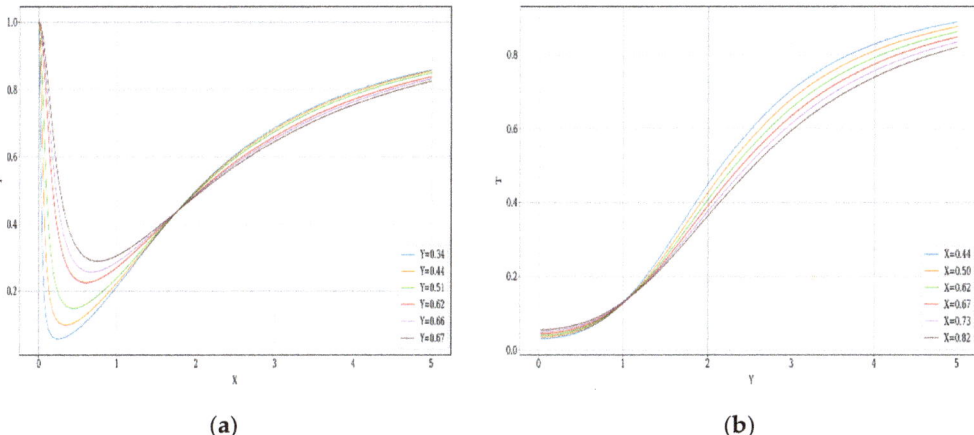

Figure 3. The 2D variations of the multifractal atmospheric transparency, T, of the dimensionless coordinates, X and Y: (**a**) the dependence T = T (X, Y = constant); (**b**) the dependence T = T (X = constant, Y).

In Figure 4a,b, the 3D variations of the multifractal–atmospheric reflectance, R, on the dimensionless coordinates, X and Y, are given.

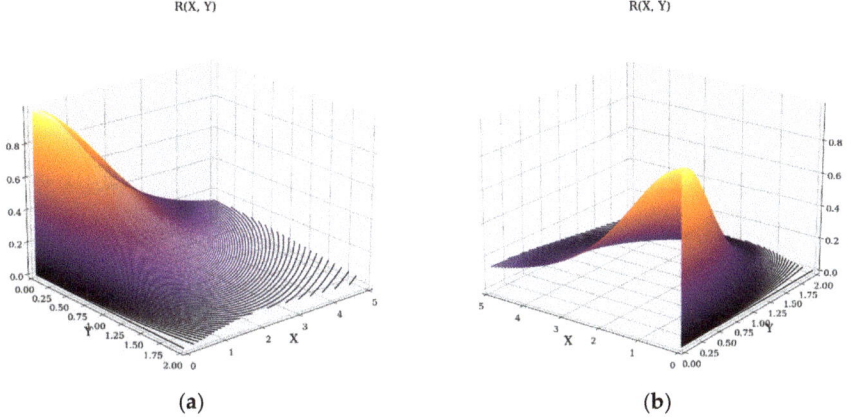

Figure 4. The variation of the multifractal atmospheric reflectance, R, of the dimensionless coordinates, X and Y: (**a**,**b**) the dependence R = R (X, Y).

The dependence that T manifests with regards to X involves both minimal and asymptotic positive variations of the multifractal atmospheric transparency, while the dependence of T with regards to Y shows only asymptotic positive variations of this transparency. In the case of R, the behavior is exactly opposite, with the dependence that R manifests with regards to X involving maximal and asymptotic negative variations of the multifractal atmospheric reflectance, while the dependence of R with regards to Y involves only asymptotic negative variations of the multifractal atmospheric reflectance.

In Figure 5a,b, the 2D variations of the multifractal–atmospheric reflectance, R, on the dimensionless coordinates, X and Y, are given.

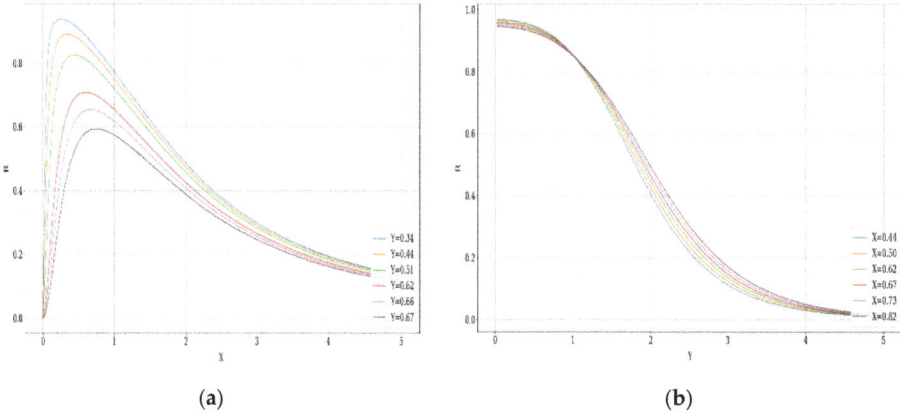

(a) (b)

Figure 5. The 2D variations of the multifractal atmospheric reflectance, R, of the dimensionless coordinates, X and Y: (**a**) the dependence R = R (X, Y = constant); (**b**) the dependence R = R (X = constant, Y).

In such a frame, since X is proportional with a minimal dimension relevant to the PBL, namely the potential barrier width a, and T has a proportionality relation with the atmospheric PBL temperature, Figure 3a can be transformed into Figure 6.

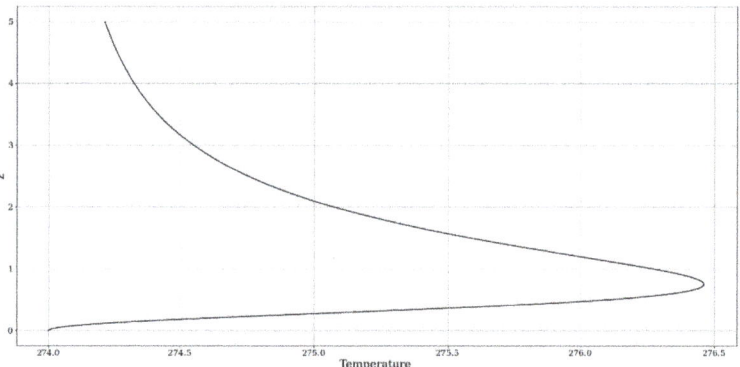

Figure 6. Example of a theoretical atmospheric temperature profile.

The theoretical results imply a temperature inversion, thus showing a good accord with a common understanding of the atmospheric temperature profile. Furthermore, with the decrease in transparency, a confined multifractal environment is created in the barrier, which then leads to a greater states density and an increase in temperature, which is in correspondence with the experimental results.

4. Experimental Design

For the purpose of confirming the reflectance and transparency results obtained so far, real atmospheric profiles are required. This profiling is justified by the fact that our analysis considers the PBL, and other atmospheric boundary layers, as multifractal barriers whose lengths represent their thickness relative to an atmospheric profile perpendicular to the ground level. Indeed, the fact that the non-dimensional parameters, X and Y, are proportional to the parameter a points to the fact that vertical atmospheric profiles represent the transport phenomena of multifractal atmospheric parameters through multifractal barriers. Ideally, to test the theories of transparency, an atmospheric parameter with a high degree of predictability and whose profile behaviors are relatively well known must be chosen, and atmospheric temperature proves itself to be an ideal candidate. When verifying the inversion behavior of such a parameter, it is important to note that temperature has a natural connection to the states density in all non-degenerated-type systems. In addition, in our context, all multifractal physical measures are, in one way or another, proportional or inversely proportional to the transparency in the multifractal barrier. However, what also must be considered is that the equations for transparency and reflectance are non-dimensional, in which case the proportionality or inverse proportionality can vary in the way that it must be considered, and instead of perfect proportionality, patterns of behavior must be identified.

In order for our theoretical results to be compared to real data, theoretical temperature profiling must be achieved, and thus the transparency equation must be iterated as a model for the theoretical modeling of the atmospheric temperature, as in Figure 6. The control parameter of such a model, since we have considered the proportionality of X and Y to a, is the PBLH, which in this case can be considered synonymous with a itself. To obtain the PBLH, ceilometer data has been used, and temperature data has been obtained through radiometer data. The ceilometer platform utilized in this study is a CHM15k ceilometer operating at a 1064 nm wavelength, and the radiometer platform is an RPG-HATPRO radiometer platform. Both are positioned in Galați, Romania, at the UGAL–REXDAN facility found at coordinates 45.435125N, 28.036792E, 65 m ASL, which is a part of the "Dunărea de Jos" University of Galați. These instruments have been chosen and set up to conform to the standards imposed by the ACTRIS community. From a computational perspective, the necessary calculations are performed through code written and operated in Python 3.6. Four instances are chosen for this study: all four are time series taken on the 5th, 6th, 7th, and 8th of May 2022 (Figures 7–18). Static profiles are also shown, and all of them are extracted from the beginning of the time series (Figures 19–22).

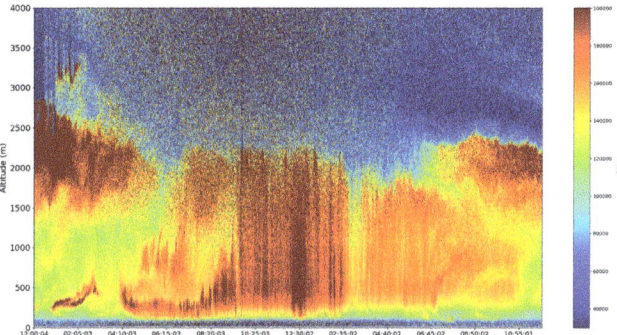

Figure 7. Time series of atmospheric RCS profiles; ceilometer data; Galati, Romania, 5 May 2022.

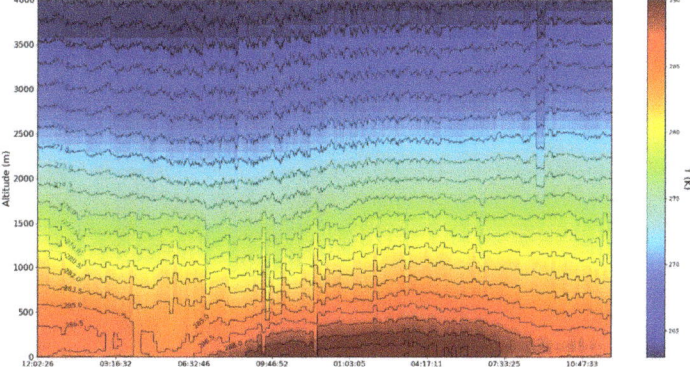

Figure 8. Time series of atmospheric temperature profiles; radiometer data; Galati, Romania, 5 May 2022.

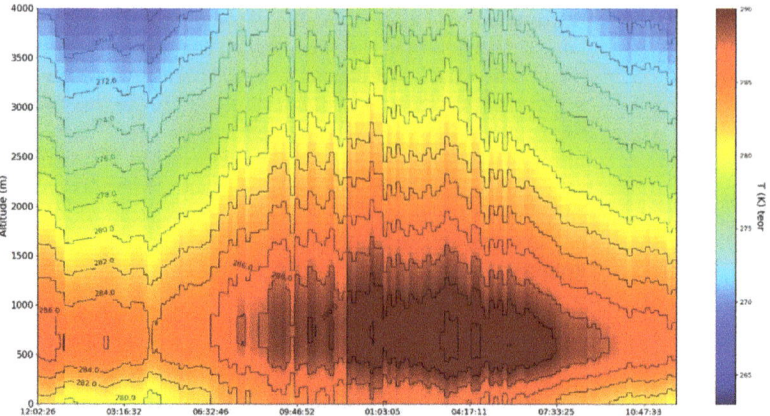

Figure 9. Time series of atmospheric temperature profiles; theoretical model data; Galati, Romania, 5 May 2022.

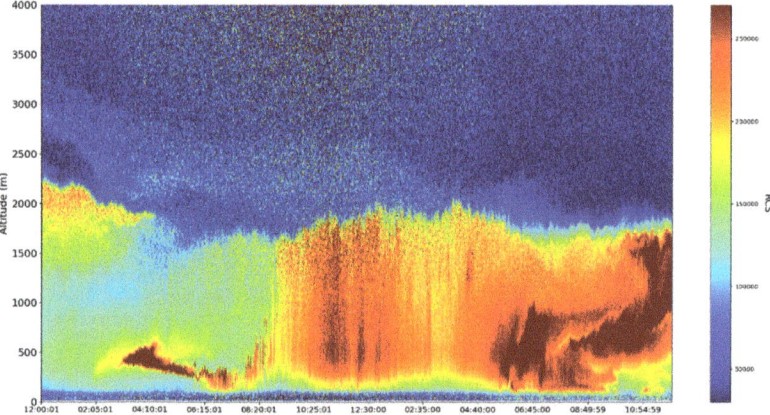

Figure 10. Time series of atmospheric RCS profiles; ceilometer data; Galati, Romania, 6 May 2022.

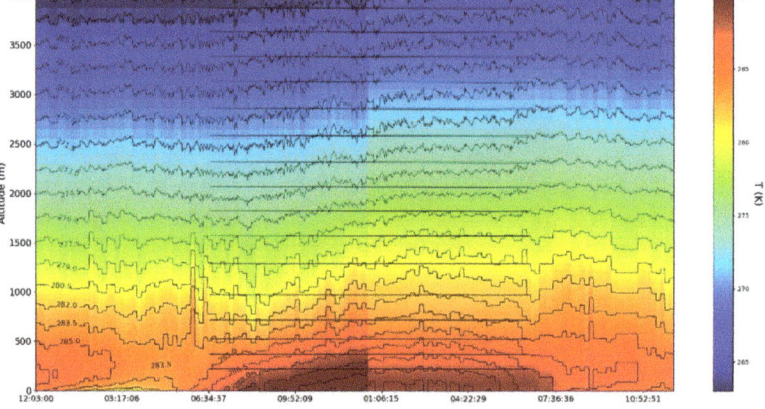

Figure 11. Time series of atmospheric temperature profiles; radiometer data; Galati, Romania, 6 May 2022.

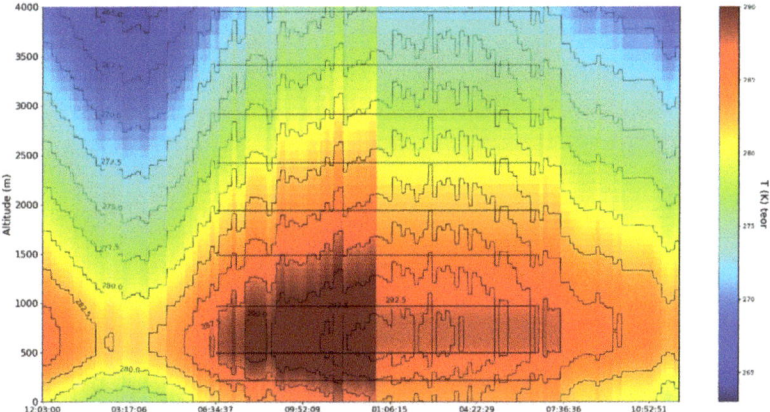

Figure 12. Time series of atmospheric temperature profiles; theoretical model data; Galati, Romania, 6 May 2022.

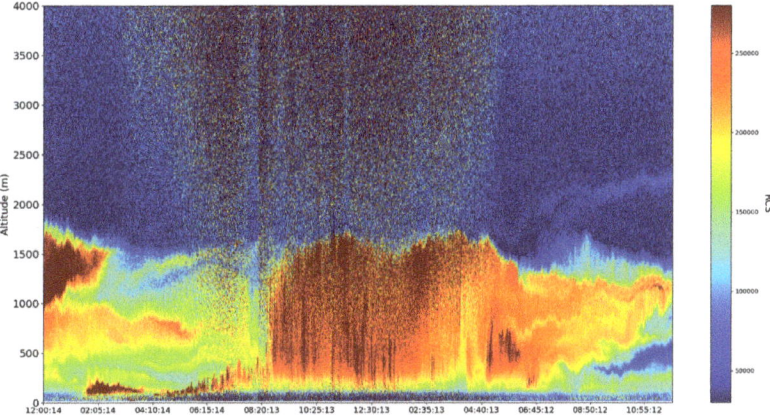

Figure 13. Time series of atmospheric RCS profiles; ceilometer data; Galati, Romania, 7 May 2022.

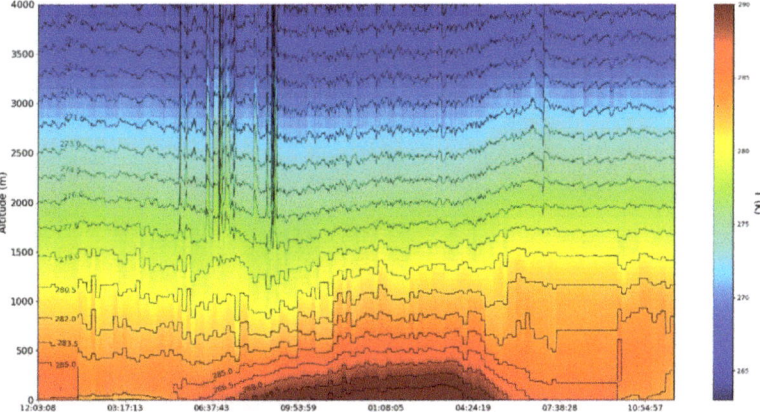

Figure 14. Time series of atmospheric temperature profiles; radiometer data; Galati, Romania, 7 May 2022.

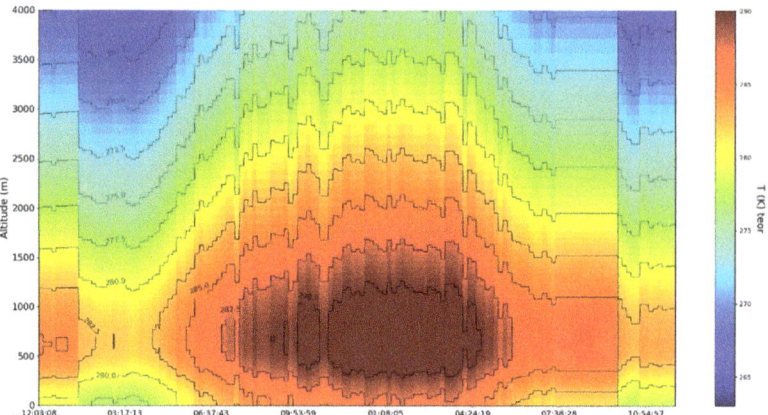

Figure 15. Time series of atmospheric temperature profiles; theoretical model data; Galati, Romania, 7 May 2022.

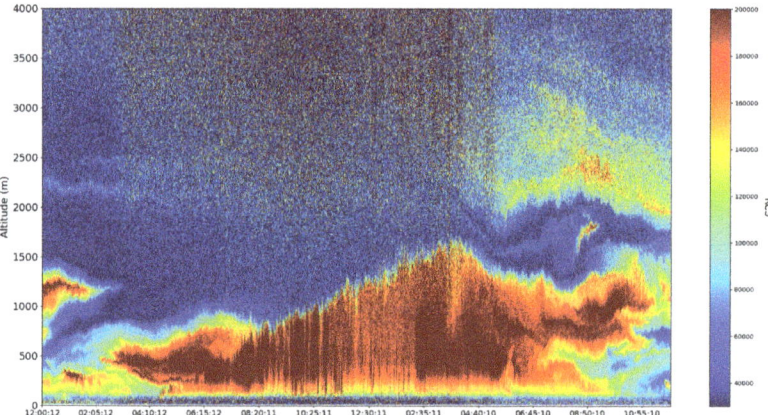

Figure 16. Time series of atmospheric RCS profiles; ceilometer data; Galati, Romania, 8 May 2022.

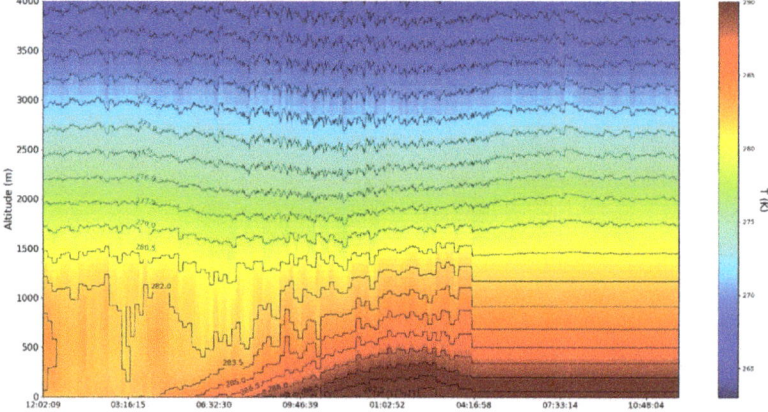

Figure 17. Time series of atmospheric temperature profiles; radiometer data; Galati, Romania, 8 May 2022.

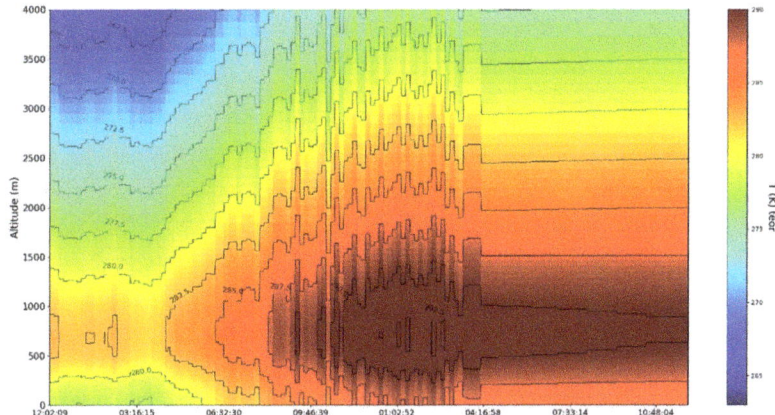

Figure 18. Time series of atmospheric temperature profiles; theoretical model data; Galati, Romania, 8 May 2022.

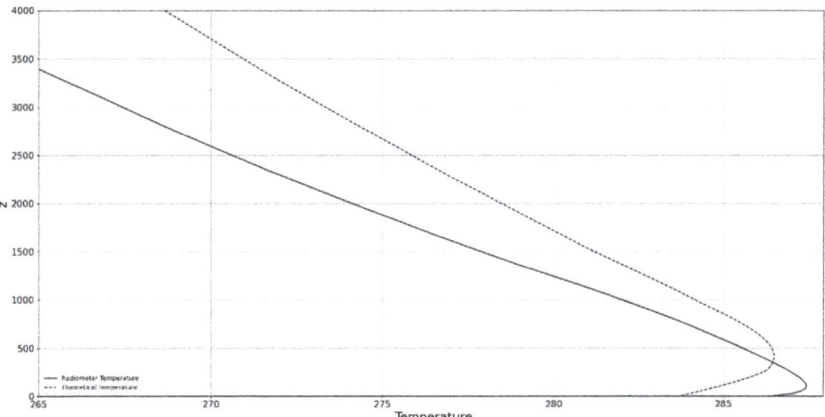

Figure 19. Profile of atmospheric temperature; radiometer data and theoretical model data; Galati, Romania, 5 May 2022; straight line: radiometer temperature; dotted line: theoretical temperature.

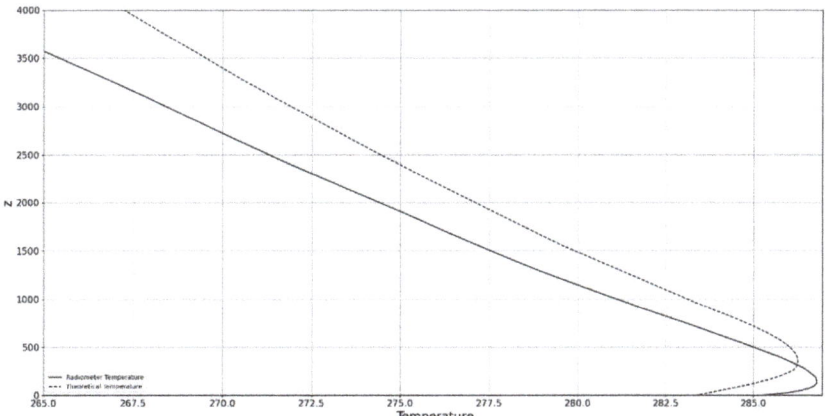

Figure 20. Profile of atmospheric temperature; radiometer data and theoretical model data; Galati, Romania, 6 May 2022; straight line: radiometer temperature; dotted line: theoretical temperature.

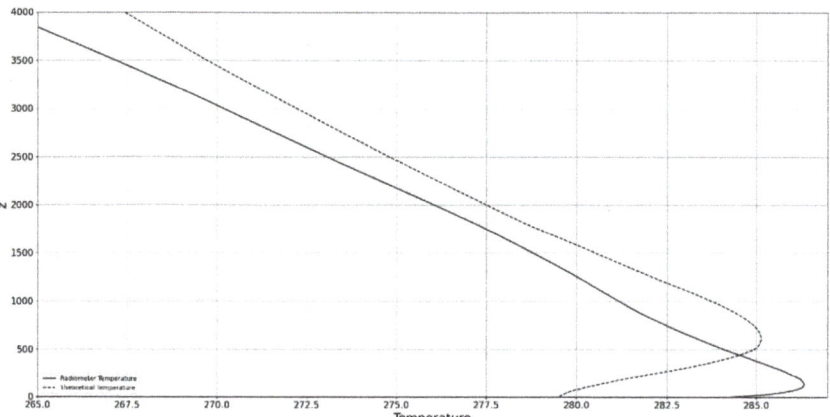

Figure 21. Profile of atmospheric temperature; radiometer data and theoretical model data; Galati, Romania, 7 May 2022; straight line: radiometer temperature; dotted line: theoretical temperature.

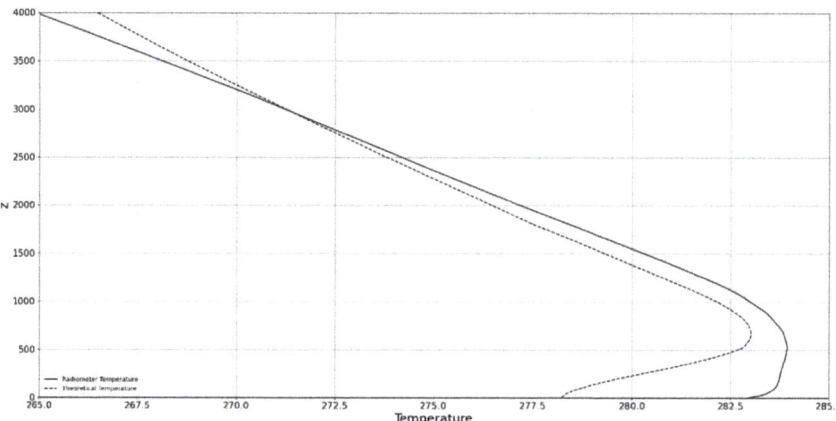

Figure 22. Profile of atmospheric temperature; radiometer data and theoretical model data; Galati, Romania, 8 May 2022; straight line: radiometer temperature; dotted line: theoretical temperature.

As can be seen in the timestamps of the time series, they all represent datasets taken for the entirety of each day, starting from midnight (Figures 7–18). The temporal resolution of the ceilometer data is one profile every minute, and the spatial resolution is 3.5 m. From the ceilometer profiles, typical low atmosphere behaviors are readily available, and the diurnal–nocturnal cycle of the PBL can be observed (Figures 7, 10, 13 and 16). To determine PBLH, a vertical spatial derivative algorithm was applied to the profiles—this well-established method, called the "gradient method", has also been compared in past studies with more current algorithms [25–27]. This PBLH is then iterated in order to produce the theoretical temperature time series as previously explained (Figures 9, 12, 14 and 18). It is found that while the theoretical time series seems to slightly overestimate the inversion and slightly underestimate the temperature lapse at higher altitudes, they are a close match to the behavior of the experimental time series (Figures 8, 9, 11–14, 17 and 18). These results point towards the fact that our multifractal interpretation has merits, meaning that the model does predict the temperature inversion and subsequent lapse throughout the atmosphere. Considering the fundamental capability of the model to properly assess the general behavior and evolution of the experimental data, it can be used in future studies as a theoretical predictor of atmospheric temperature if further adjustments are performed. For a more precise analysis of the order differences between the experimental and theoretical temperature datasets to be performed, static profiles are shown next.

A discussion regarding the nature of temperature profiles is in order; it is known that for diurnal profiles, there exists a slightly greater decrease in temperature in the SL, and for nocturnal profiles, there is an inversion at the SL [1,28–31]. Otherwise, inversions also mark the occurrence of the PBLH [1]. In this case, solely nocturnal profiles have been chosen from the beginning of the time series. As can be seen in the temperature profile figures, the theoretical model predicts the inversion at the boundary layer, although once again, it does not always accurately predict the altitude at which the inversion takes place (Figures 19–22). This is because the model has not been adjusted to account for any surface radiative effects, merely taking into consideration the effects of the boundary layer. That being said, maximal differences between the theoretical and the experimental temperature profiles are on the order of degrees throughout the entirety of the profile; thus, it is possible to state that the model shows success in approximating both the order and the spatial evolution of the atmospheric temperature profile and iterating it with PBLH data produces satisfactory results. The slight differences between Figures 19 and 22, Figures 20 and 21 must also be highlighted—even though the order of the differences between the theoretical and real profiles seems to remain the same, the theoretical profile in Figure 22 might show a more favorable shape because of the slightly lower temperature gradient that can be found in the early segment of the dataset represented by Figure 17.

5. Conclusions

In conclusion, by employing a multifractal interpretation of atmospheric dynamics, wherein the laws that govern atmospheric motions are reliant on the notion of scale resolution, it is possible to construct the framework for atmospheric parameter behavior inversion. By considering the atmosphere from a multifractal states density perspective, the PBL, or any other atmospheric boundary layer, can be stated as a potential barrier with associated transparencies and reflectance, which directly govern the fluctuations of all multifractal atmospheric parameters. This is then found, through the use of non-dimensional plotting, to imply inversions in such parameters, including temperature. Finally, radiometer data offers various examples of atmospheric temperature inversions, wherein theoretical products made by iterating the model with PBLH data given by a ceilometer platform agree with experimental data.

Author Contributions: Conceptualization, M.M.C., I.-A.R. and M.A.; methodology, M.M.C., I.-A.R. and M.A.; software, M.M.C., I.-A.R. and M.A.; validation, M.M.C., I.-A.R. and M.A.; formal analysis, M.M.C., I.-A.R., M.A. and A.M.R.; investigation, M.M.C., I.-A.R., M.A., A.M.R. and D.V.; resources, M.M.C., I.-A.R., M.A., L.B. and D.V.; data curation, M.M.C., I.-A.R. and M.A.; writing—original draft preparation, M.M.C., I.-A.R., M.A., L.B and D.V.; writing—review and editing, M.M.C., I.-A.R. and M.A.; visualization, M.M.C., I.-A.R. and M.A.; supervision, M.M.C. and M.A.; project administration, M.M.C., I.-A.R. and M.A.; funding acquisition, M.M.C. All authors have read and agreed to the published version of the manuscript.

Funding: This work was supported by a grant from the Romanian Ministry of Education and Research, CNCS-UEFISCDI, project number PN-III-P1-1.1-TE-2019-1921, within PNCDI III.

Institutional Review Board Statement: Not applicable.

Informed Consent Statement: Not applicable.

Data Availability Statement: The raw data supporting the conclusions of this article will be made available by the authors without undue reservation.

Acknowledgments: The authors acknowledge the UGAL–REXDAN cloud remote sensing facility, part of ACTRIS–RO (Aerosol, Clouds and Trace gases Research InfraStructure—Romania), for providing radiometer data used in this study. In addition, the authors acknowledge the RADO (Romanian Atmospheric 3D research Observatory).

Conflicts of Interest: The authors declare no conflict of interest.

References

1. Roland, S. *Practical Meteorology: An Algebra-Based Survey of Atmospheric Science*; The University of British Columbia: Vancouver, BC, Canada, 2015.
2. Badii, R.; Politi, A. *Complexity: Hierarchical Structures and Scaling in Physics*; Cambridge University Press: Cambridge, UK, 1997.
3. Mitchell, M. *Complexity: A Guided Tour*; Oxford University Press: Oxford, UK, 2009.
4. Notalle, L. *Fractal Space-Time and Microphysics*; World Scientific Publisher: Singapore, 1993.
5. Merches, I.; Agop, M. *Differentiability and Fractality in Dynamics of Physical Systems*; World Scientific Publisher: Singapore, 2015.
6. Nottale, L. *Scale Relativity and Fractal Space-Time: A New Approach to Unifying Relativity and Quantum Mechanics*; Imperial College Press: London, UK, 2011.
7. Agop, M.; Buzea, C.; Vasincu, D.; Timofte, D. Dynamics of Biostructures on a Fractal/Multifractal Space-Time Manifold. In *Progress in Relativity*; IntechOpen: London, UK, 2019; p. 117.
8. Liu, L.; Hu, F.; Huang, S. A Multifractal Random-Walk Description of Atmospheric Turbulence: Small-Scale Multiscaling, Long-Tail Distribution, and Intermittency. *Bound. Layer Meteorol.* **2019**, *172*, 351–370. [CrossRef]
9. Kalamaras, N.; Tzanis, C.G.; Deligiorgi, D.; Philippopoulos, K.; Koutsogiannis, I. Distribution of Air Temperature Multifractal Characteristics Over Greece. *Atmosphere* **2019**, *10*, 45. [CrossRef]
10. Plocoste, T.; Carmona-Cabezas, R.; Jiménez-Hornero, F.J.; de Ravé, E.G. Background PM10 atmosphere: In the seek of a multifractal characterization using complex networks. *J. Aerosol Sci.* **2021**, *155*, 105777. [CrossRef]
11. Ruelle, D.; Takens, F. On the nature of turbulence. *Les Rencontres Phys. Mathématiciens Strasbg. RCP25* **1971**, *12*, 1–44.
12. Takens, F. Detecting Strange Attractors in Turbulence. In *Dynamical Systems and Turbulence. Warwick 1980*; Springer: Berlin/Heidelberg, Germany, 1981; pp. 366–381.
13. Nottale, L. Scale relativity and fractal space-time: Applications to quantum physics, cosmology and chaotic systems. *Chaos Solitons Fractals* **1996**, *7*, 877–938. [CrossRef]
14. Nottale, L.; Auffray, C. Scale relativity theory and integrative systems biology: 2 Macroscopic quantum-type mechanics. *Prog. Biophys. Mol. Biol.* **2008**, *97*, 115–157. [CrossRef] [PubMed]
15. Chavanis, P.-H. Derivation of a generalized Schrödinger equation from the theory of scale relativity. *Eur. Phys. J. Plus* **2017**, *132*, 286. [CrossRef]
16. Roșu, I.-A.; Nica, D.-C.; Cazacu, M.M.; Agop, M. Cellular Self-Structuring and Turbulent Behaviors in Atmospheric Laminar Channels. *Front. Earth Sci.* **2022**, *9*, 801020. [CrossRef]
17. Baker, G.L.; Gollub, J.P. *Chaotic Dynamics: An Introduction*; Cambridge University Press: New York, NY, USA, 1996.
18. Ott, E. *Chaos in Dynamical Systems*; Cambridge University Press, University of Maryland: College Park, MD, USA, 2002; pp. 160–182. [CrossRef]
19. Van den Berg, J.C. *Wavelets in Physics*; Cambridge University Press: Cambridge, UK, 2004; pp. 143–147.
20. Cristescu, C.P. *Nonlinear Dynamics and Chaos Theoretical Fundaments and Applications*; Romanian Academy Publishing House: Bucharest, Romania, 2008.
21. Agop, M.; Ochiuz, L.; Tesloianu, D.; Buzea, C.; Irimiciuc, S. *Non-Differentiable Dynamics in Complex Systems*; Nova Science Publishers: New York, NY, USA, 2018.
22. Mandelbrot, B. *The Fractal Geometry of Nature*; W.H. Freeman Publishers: New York, NY, USA, 1982.
23. Barnsley, M.F. *Fractals Everywhere*; Morgan Kaufmann Publisher: San Francisco, CA, USA, 1993.
24. Bujoreanu, C.; Irimiciuc, Ș.; Benchea, M.; Nedeff, F.; Agop, M. A fractal approach of the sound absorption behaviour of materials. Theoretical and experimental aspects. *Int. J. Non-Linear Mech.* **2018**, *103*, 128–137. [CrossRef]
25. Flamant, C.; Pelon, J.; Flamant, P.H.; Durand, P. Lidar determination of the entrainment zone thickness at the top of the unstable marine atmospheric boundary layer. *Bound. Layer Meteorol.* **1997**, *83*, 247–284. [CrossRef]
26. Haeffelin, M.; Angelini, F.; Morille, Y.; Martucci, G.; Frey, S.; Gobbi, G.P.; Lolli, S.; O'Dowd, C.D.; Sauvage, L.; Xueref-Rémy, I.; et al. Evaluation of Mixing-Height Retrievals from Automatic Profiling Lidars and Ceilometers in View of Future Integrated Networks in Europe. *Bound. Layer Meteorol.* **2011**, *143*, 49–75. [CrossRef]
27. Rosu, I.-A.; Cazacu, M.-M.; Prelipceanu, O.S.; Agop, M. A Turbulence-Oriented Approach to Retrieve Various Atmospheric Parameters Using Advanced Lidar Data Processing Techniques. *Atmosphere* **2019**, *10*, 38. [CrossRef]
28. Orlanski, I.; Ross, B.B.; Polinsky, L.J. Diurnal Variation of the Planetary Boundary Layer in a Mesoscale Model. *J. Atmospheric Sci.* **1974**, *31*, 965–989. [CrossRef]
29. Hu, X.-M.; Nielsen-Gammon, J.; Zhang, F. Evaluation of Three Planetary Boundary Layer Schemes in the WRF Model. *J. Appl. Meteorol. Clim.* **2010**, *49*, 1831–1844. [CrossRef]
30. Seidel, D.J.; Ao, C.; Li, K. Estimating climatological planetary boundary layer heights from radiosonde observations: Comparison of methods and uncertainty analysis. *J. Geophys. Res. Atmos.* **2010**, *115*, 1–15. [CrossRef]
31. Wyngaard, J.C. Structure of the PBL. In *Lectures on Air Pollution Modeling*; American Meteorological Society: Boston, MA, USA, 1988; pp. 9–61.

Article

A New Variable-Boostable 3D Chaotic System with Hidden and Coexisting Attractors: Dynamical Analysis, Periodic Orbit Coding, Circuit Simulation, and Synchronization

Jiahui Wang, Chengwei Dong * and Hantao Li *

Department of Physics, North University of China, Taiyuan 030051, China
* Correspondence: dongchengwei@tsinghua.org.cn (C.D.); lihantao@nuc.edu.cn (H.L.)

Abstract: The study of hidden attractors plays a very important role in the engineering applications of nonlinear dynamical systems. In this paper, a new three-dimensional (3D) chaotic system is proposed in which hidden attractors and self-excited attractors appear as the parameters change. Meanwhile, asymmetric coexisting attractors are also found as a result of the system symmetry. The complex dynamical behaviors of the proposed system were investigated using various tools, including time-series diagrams, Poincaré first return maps, bifurcation diagrams, and basins of attraction. Moreover, the unstable periodic orbits within a topological length of 3 in the hidden chaotic attractor were calculated systematically by the variational method, which required six letters to establish suitable symbolic dynamics. Furthermore, the practicality of the hidden attractor chaotic system was verified by circuit simulations. Finally, offset boosting control and adaptive synchronization were used to investigate the utility of the proposed chaotic system in engineering applications.

Keywords: hidden attractor; unstable periodic orbit; circuit simulation; coexisting attractors; offset boosting; adaptive synchronization

1. Introduction

Chaos theory has grown tremendously in recent decades and holds great promise for practical applications [1,2]. The study of chaotic systems began with the discovery of strange attractors by Lorenz in 1963 [3], when he constructed a three-dimensional (3D) quadratic chaotic system that exhibited the famous butterfly effect. Many other chaotic systems have since been presented, some of which satisfy the Šil'nikov theorem [4], such as the Chen system [5], Qi system [6], Lü system [7], and Rössler system [8]. Recently, two types of attractors were classified by Leonov and Kuznetsov [9], namely self-excited attractors and hidden attractors, and the difference between them is reflected in whether the attractor intersects a neighborhood of any unstable fixed points. The Lorenz system and the systems mentioned above are all referred to as self-excited attractors, while others that do not satisfy the Šil'nikov theorem are referred to as hidden attractors. Owing to the unique features of hidden attractors, they are difficult to locate and thus play a vital role in encryption and communication [10–12]. However, hidden attractors also bring disadvantages and present difficulties in the simulation of drilling systems and phase-locked loops [13].

Based on this, the study of hidden attractors has become an attractive research direction and has received considerable attention from researchers. There are three main types of hidden attractors, which are systems with no equilibria [14–17], only stable equilibria [18–20], and infinitely many equilibria [21,22]. The types of hidden attractors with infinite numbers of equilibria can be divided into various systems, including systems with line equilibria, ellipsoidal equilibria, and circular equilibria. Currently, for hidden attractors with infinite equilibria, researchers have primarily focused on systems with line equilibria [23–25]. By using a computer search, Jafari et al. discovered nine chaotic flows with line

equilibria, all of which were hidden attractor chaotic systems [26]. Some new systems with hidden chaotic attractors were constructed by introducing perturbations or nonlinear terms into existing hidden attractor chaotic systems [27,28], while many new systems have also been obtained on the basis of modifying the Sprott system and Jafari system [29,30]. The existence of multi-stability can be found in hidden attractor chaotic systems, as reflected by the fact that coexisting attractors have been discovered, and thus, performance flexibility can be achieved [31,32]. In addition, researchers have also concentrated on studying hidden chaotic attractors in fractional-order systems [33–36], memristor systems [37–40] and jerk systems [41,42]. Hyperchaotic systems with planes or surfaces of equilibrium points that have hidden attractors are of particular interest, as they exhibit more complex dynamical behaviors than low-dimensional chaotic systems [43,44]. Multiscroll chaotic systems have exceptional benefits in the areas of digital image encryption and private communication [45]. The multi-stability in asymmetric systems, conditional symmetric systems, and self-reproducing systems also have attracted widespread attention [46–48]. In Ref. [49], the complex dynamic behaviors and hidden attractors in delayed impulsive systems were explored by means of various bifurcation analyses.

In this paper, we constructed a new hidden attractor chaotic system and explored its dynamical behavior using attraction basins, power spectra, bifurcation diagrams, and other nonlinear analysis tools. Our motivation was to develop an effective method to devise a novel chaotic system with hidden and coexisting attractors based on the existing ones, enabling us to further understand the properties of hidden attractors and multi-stability. The main difficulties in constructing such a system is that there is no general method to clarify which form of feedback controller can be added to produce a new variable-boostable system with both hidden attractors and coexisting attractors. The application of the proposed design lies in the new system being easy to control and synchronize, and the variable can be boosted to any level, so it can reduce the number of components required for signal conditioning. Moreover, offset boosting can be combined with amplitude control to achieve the full range of linear transformations of the signal. Furthermore, the existence of coexisting attractors can also make the system more flexible without adjusting parameters, and it can be used with suitable control strategies to cause switching between various coexisting states. Therefore, it has potential application prospects in the engineering field.

The main contributions and novelty of this work are summarized as follows. (1) We proposed a new 3D chaotic system and explored the adaptive synchronization of the new system. Compared to the above contributions in the literature, the prominent feature of the new system is that it belongs to the variable-boostable chaotic flow, which indicated that it is convenient for chaotic applications. (2) We found self-excited attractors and hidden attractors with two stable equilibrium points in this dissipative system when the parameters were varied. In addition, we investigated the existence of various coexisting asymmetric attractors. To the best of our knowledge, this combination of novel characteristics has rarely been reported. (3) We developed a topological classification method and built complicated symbolic dynamics with six letters instead of four, encoding the unstable periodic orbits embedded in the hidden chaotic attractor, which allowed one to perform a more comprehensive analysis of the periodic orbits.

The rest of the paper is organized as follows. A new hidden attractor chaotic system is proposed, and its fundamental properties and dynamical characteristics under parameter variations are explored in Section 2. In Section 3, a numerical method for calculating periodic orbits, the variational method, is introduced. Section 4 uses the variational method to systematically calculate the periodic orbits of the new system. In Section 5, a corresponding circuit is designed to verify its practicality. Offset boosting control and adaptive synchronization of the novel system are investigated in Section 6. Finally, Section 7 presents the conclusions.

2. New Hidden Chaotic System with Two Stable Equilibria

In retrospect, Wei and Yang introduced the generalized Sprott C system with three real parameters [50]:

$$\begin{aligned}
\frac{dx}{dt} &= a(y-x), \\
\frac{dy}{dt} &= -cy - xz, \\
\frac{dz}{dt} &= y^2 - b.
\end{aligned} \quad (1)$$

When $a = 10$, $b = 100$, and $c = 0.4$, there is a hidden chaotic attractor in system (1), which is characterized by two stable fixed points.

With the use of the Bendixson theorem, a hidden attractor was found in a complex variable Lorenz chaotic system [51]. In this work, we discovered the hidden attractor by adding a disturbance term to the existing chaotic system, which could lead to the generation of a new system, but there is no universal method. We first found that the construction of hidden attractor chaotic systems cannot be realized by adding a constant or linear term to the generalized Sprott C system. Therefore, we attempted to add a nonlinear term to the system, and it was further confirmed that adding it to the third equation of Equation (1) could generate hidden chaotic attractors. Inspired by system (1), we propose a new system by adding the kxy term to the third equation as follows:

$$\begin{aligned}
\frac{dx}{dt} &= a(y-x), \\
\frac{dy}{dt} &= -cy - xz, \\
\frac{dz}{dt} &= y^2 - b + kxy,
\end{aligned} \quad (2)$$

where x, y, z are the state variables, and a, b, c, k are positive constant parameters. When we select the parameter values of $a = 12$, $b = 100$, $c = 10$, and $k = 4.6$, the three Lyapunov exponents of system (2) can be estimated. To avoid transient chaos, we extended the time, and the Lyapunov exponents after 20,000 s were $L_1 = 0.9861$, $L_2 = 0$, and $L_3 = -22.9857$. The largest Lyapunov exponent was greater than 0, which confirmed the existence of chaos, as shown in Figure 1. Meanwhile, according to the Kaplan–Yorke formula,

$$D_{KY} = j + \frac{1}{|L_{j+1}|} \sum_{i=1}^{j} L_i = 2 + \frac{L_1 + L_2}{|L_3|} = 2.0429, \quad (3)$$

the fractal dimension also further verifies that the new system is chaotic.

2.1. Basic Properties of New Chaotic System

The basic properties of the new chaotic system are described as follows.
(1) Symmetry about the z-axis: When the coordinates are transformed, $(x, y, z) \to (-x, -y, z)$, the form of system (2) remains unchanged.
(2) Dissipativity:

$$\nabla \cdot V = \frac{\partial \dot{x}}{\partial x} + \frac{\partial \dot{y}}{\partial y} + \frac{\partial \dot{z}}{\partial z} = -a - c. \quad (4)$$

Since a and c are positive constants, the new system (2) is dissipative. Based on the equation,

$$\frac{dV}{dt} = e^{-a-c}, \quad (5)$$

the system converges to a set of measure zero exponentially as the volume of the phase space is contracted, $V = V_0 e^{-a-c}$. Therefore, the system will end up fixed to an attractor.

(3) Equilibrium: The new system has two fixed points:

$$
\begin{aligned}
E_1 &= (\sqrt{\tfrac{b}{k+1}}, \sqrt{\tfrac{b}{k+1}}, -c), \\
E_2 &= (-\sqrt{\tfrac{b}{k+1}}, -\sqrt{\tfrac{b}{k+1}}, -c).
\end{aligned}
\qquad (6)
$$

The Jacobi matrix can be obtained as follows:

$$
J = \begin{pmatrix} -a & a & 0 \\ -z & -c & -x \\ ky & 2y+kx & 0 \end{pmatrix}. \qquad (7)
$$

The characteristic equation is

$$
f(\lambda) = \lambda^3 + (a+c)\lambda^2 + (ac + 2xy + kx^2 + az)\lambda + 2axy + akx^2 + akxy. \qquad (8)
$$

By substituting the coordinates of the two fixed points separately, we obtain the same characteristic equation:

$$
f(\lambda) = a_3\lambda^3 + a_2\lambda^2 + a_1\lambda + a_0, \qquad (9)
$$

where

$$
\begin{aligned}
a_3 &= 1, \\
a_2 &= a+c, \\
a_1 &= b + \frac{b}{k+1}, \\
a_0 &= 2ab.
\end{aligned}
\qquad (10)
$$

From the Routh–Hurwitz criterion, the two fixed points are stable if the following conditions are satisfied: $a_i > 0, (i = 0, 1, 2, 3), a_2 a_1 - a_3 a_0 > 0$. The condition that needs to be satisfied for this system to have hidden attractors is $(c - a)k > -2c$. For the current parameters $(a, b, c, k) = (12, 100, 10, 4.6)$, the Routh–Hurwitz stability criterion can be satisfied. As a result, the two fixed points E_1 and E_2 are both stable node-focus points. The new system is a chaotic system in which a strange attractor is hidden.

(4) Power spectrum: The power spectrum of the chaotic state is almost fully covered with background and broad peaks, as shown in Figure 2.

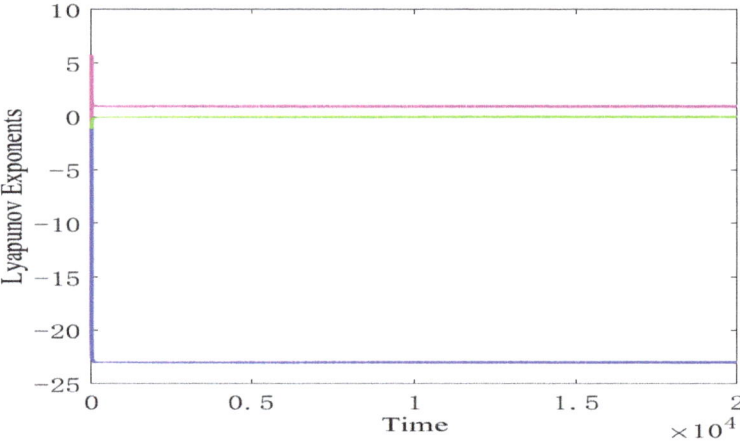

Figure 1. Lyapunov exponent spectrum of the new system (2) for $(a, b, c, k) = (12, 100, 10, 4.6)$.

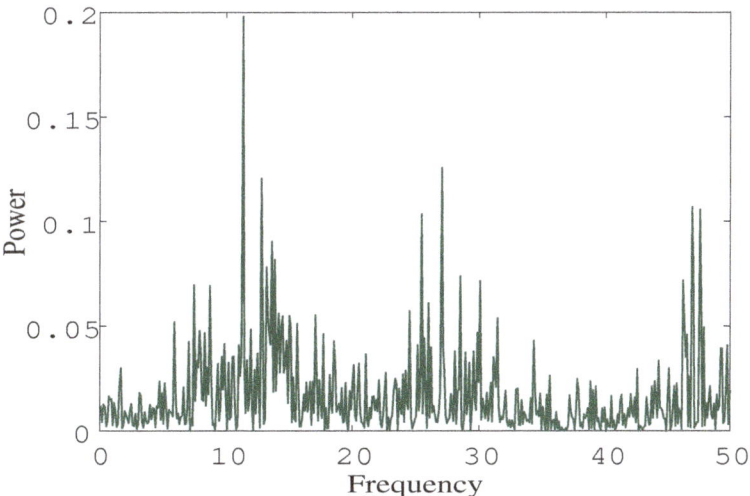

Figure 2. Continuous broadband power spectrum of the new chaotic system for $(a, b, c, k) = (12, 100, 10, 4.6)$.

(5) Phase portraits: Using the fourth-order Runge–Kutta numerical integration method, the 2D phase diagrams of the chaotic system for a time-length of 200 s with $a = 12$, $b = 100$, $c = 10$, and $k = 4.6$ were obtained from the initial conditions $(x_0, y_0, z_0) = (1, 1, 1)$, as shown in Figure 3.

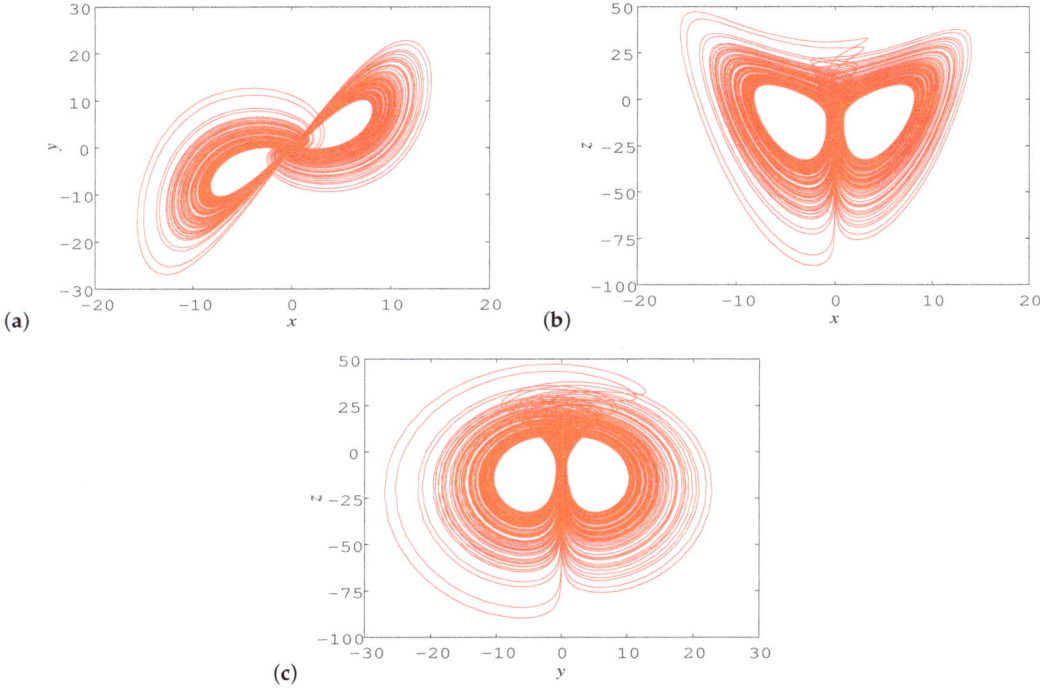

Figure 3. Projection in different two-dimensional (2D) phase spaces of system (2) for $(a, b, c, k) = (12, 100, 10, 4.6)$: (**a**) x-y plane, (**b**) x-z plane, and (**c**) y-z plane.

In addition, based on the definition of a hidden attractor, we checked the basins of attraction to determine whether a chaotic attractor of the new system could be found from the initial conditions near the equilibrium points. A cross-section at $z = -10$ was selected, and the basins of attraction were captured in three regions, as shown in Figure 4a, in which the blue dots represent the crossing trajectories of the chaotic attractor. The initial values in the red and yellow regions converged to the fixed points E_1 and E_2, respectively. The orange region represents chaos. In simple terms, the initial values in this region result in a chaotic state. Therefore, it can be clearly observed from the basins of attraction that system (2) contains a hidden chaotic attractor.

The exact correspondence is illustrated in Figure 4b, where the phase diagram trajectory finally converges to the fixed point E_1 for the initial value $I_1 = (12, -5, -10)$ in the red attraction basin and to the fixed point E_2 for the initial value $I_2 = (-12, 5, -10)$ in the yellow attraction basin, while the initial value $(1, 1, -10)$ in the orange region finally evolves to chaos. In Figure 4c, coexisting time series for different initial values are also shown, which indicates the multi-stability in system (2).

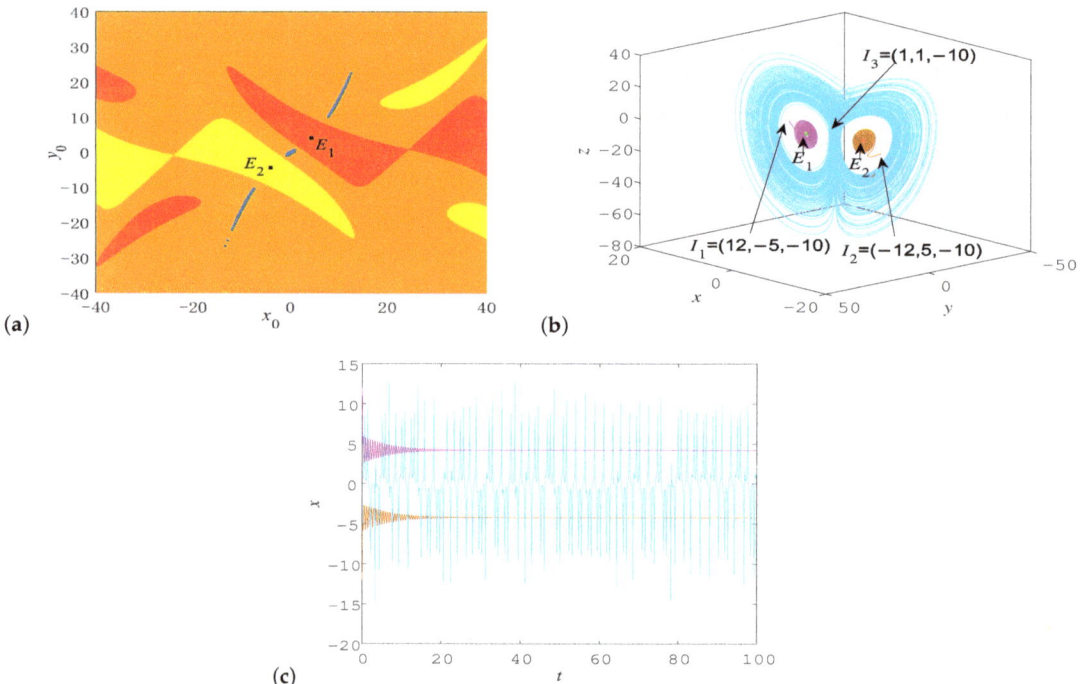

Figure 4. (a) Three colored basins of attraction at $z = -10$ on (x, y) plane. (b) Three-dimensional (3D) views of the chaotic attractor and two fixed point attractors. (c) Coexisting time-series diagram of $x(t)$.

2.2. Observation of Chaotic and Complex Dynamics

The system parameters change to enrich the dynamical behaviors of the new system (2). In order to completely explore the diverse dynamical behaviors, we investigated the bifurcations under parameter variations and verified the complicated dynamical behaviors with the aid of bifurcation diagrams, largest Lyapunov exponent spectra, and division diagrams of two parameters.

2.2.1. Fix $b = 100$, $c = 10$, and $k = 4.6$ and Vary a

We fixed the parameters as $b = 100$, $c = 10$, and $k = 4.6$ while letting a vary in the region $[0, 30]$. A summary of the results of the bifurcation diagram and the corresponding largest Lyapunov exponent spectrum are shown in Figure 5. When a increased, the new system converged to a fixed point and then transitioned to chaos, after which the solution became periodic through an inverse period-doubling bifurcation, then evolved to chaos, and finally degenerated to periodic solutions again.

Different types of coexisting attractors can also be found in system (2), which shows that the multi-stability of the new system is very rich. As the 2D phase portraits show in Figure 6a,b, system (2) included two coexisting chaotic attractors for the parameter $a = 27.35$ when different initial values $(x_0, y_0, z_0) = (1, 1, 1)$ and $(x_0, y_0, z_0) = (-1, -1, 1)$ were selected. Moreover, when the parameter was set at $a = 29$, the system entered a periodic state, and due to the symmetry of the system, the coexistence of two periodic attractors appeared, as depicted in Figure 6c,d. A periodic attractor whose tip faced right or left was obtained depending on the initial values.

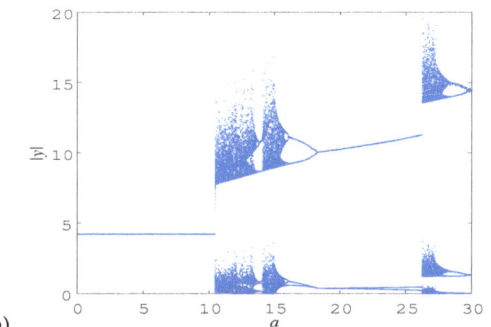
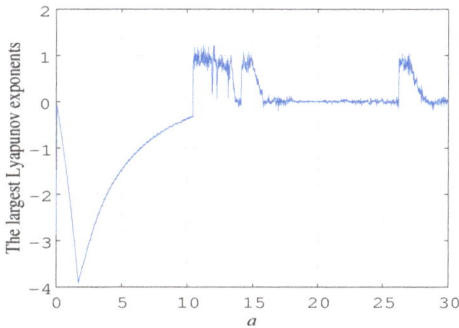

Figure 5. (a) Bifurcation diagram and (b) largest Lyapunov exponent spectrum versus a, where $b = 100, c = 10$, and $k = 4.6$.

2.2.2. Fix $a = 12$, $c = 10$, and $k = 4.6$ and Vary b

Keeping the parameters $a = 12$, $c = 10$, and $k = 4.6$ constant, we let b vary from 40 to 140. Figure 7 shows the bifurcation diagram and the maximum Lyapunov exponent diagram versus b. The system went through a process of period-doubling bifurcations to chaos, transitioning from a periodic to a chaotic solution. The solution was chaotic over a large range, from 68 to 140, which was accompanied by periodic windows. In Figure 8, we present the exact details of the various periodic solutions that occur when b varies. It is worth noting that asymmetric periodic attractors coexist when $b = 47$ with the initial values of $(x_0, y_0, z_0) = (1, 1, 1)$ and $(x_0, y_0, z_0) = (-1, -1, 1)$.

2.2.3. Fix $a = 12$, $b = 100$, and $k = 4.6$ and Vary c

We varied c from -10 to 20 while keeping $a = 12$, $b = 100$, and $k = 4.6$. The bifurcation diagram and largest Lyapunov exponent spectrum are shown in Figure 9. The system exhibited intriguing dynamical behaviors in this case, undergoing a pitchfork bifurcation followed by a period-doubling bifurcation route to chaos, interspersed with several periodic windows, and finally, it converged to the equilibrium point. Rich dynamical behaviors can also be observed from the phase diagrams with different parameter values, as displayed in Figure 10. The complexity of the chaos varied when parameter c was changed, and there was a significant difference, which can also be reflected by the size of the largest Lyapunov exponent. Compared with the strange attractor when $c = 8$ (see Figure 10c), we conclude that the chaotic behavior of the system was more complex when $c = -2$ (see Figure 10b).

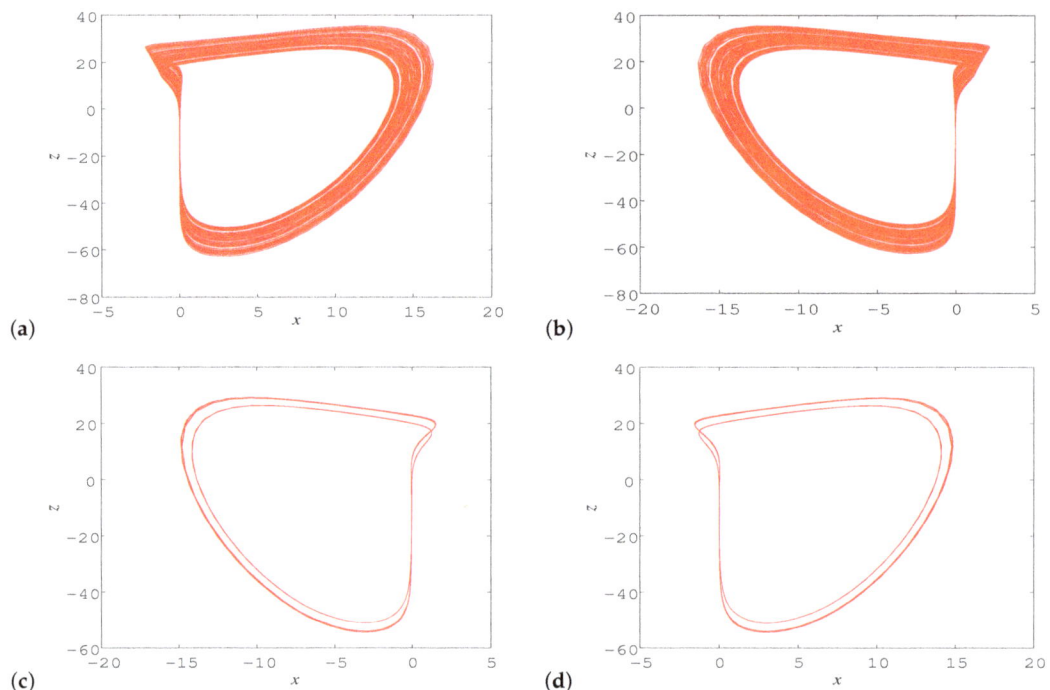

Figure 6. Two-dimensional views of coexisting chaotic attractors and periodic attractors in system (2) with parameters $b = 100$, $c = 10$, and $k = 4.6$: (**a**) $a = 27.35, (x_0, y_0, z_0) = (1, 1, 1)$, (**b**) $a = 27.35$, $(x_0, y_0, z_0) = (-1, -1, 1)$, (**c**) $a = 29, (x_0, y_0, z_0) = (1, 1, 1)$, and (**d**) $a = 29, (x_0, y_0, z_0) = (-1, -1, 1)$.

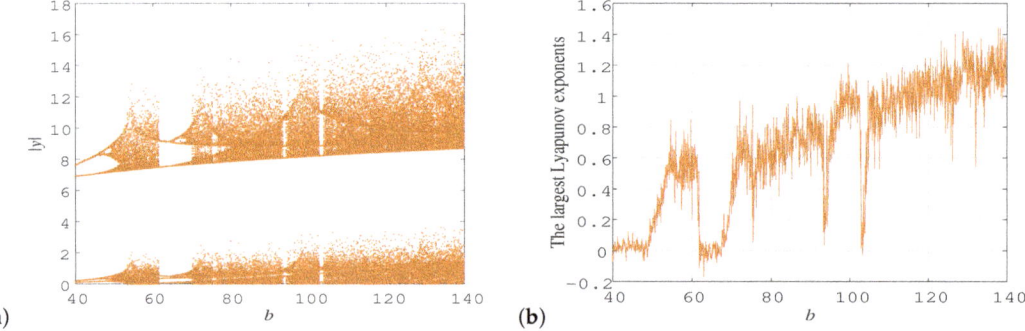

Figure 7. (**a**) Bifurcation diagram of $|y|$ with b as the varied parameter and (**b**) the largest Lyapunov exponent spectrum, where $a = 12$, $c = 10$, and $k = 4.6$.

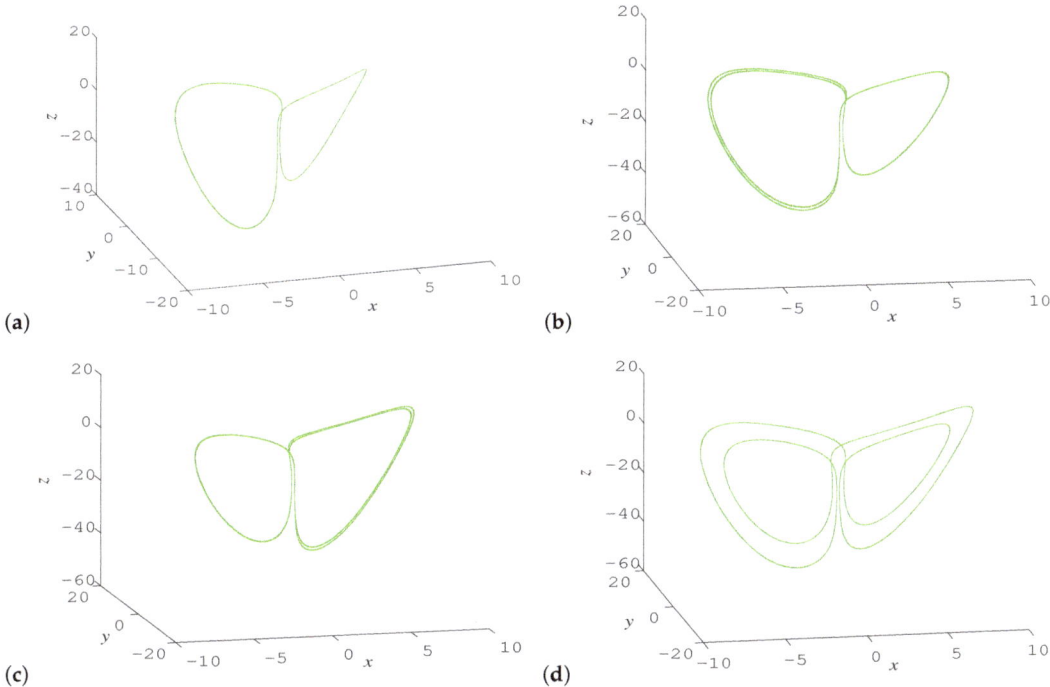

Figure 8. Three-dimensional views of various limit cycles with parameters $a = 12$, $c = 10$, and $k = 4.6$: (**a**) $b = 45, (x_0, y_0, z_0) = (1, 1, 1)$, (**b**) $b = 47, (x_0, y_0, z_0) = (1, 1, 1)$, (**c**) $b = 47$, $(x_0, y_0, z_0) = (-1, -1, 1)$, and (**d**) $b = 65, (x_0, y_0, z_0) = (1, 1, 1)$.

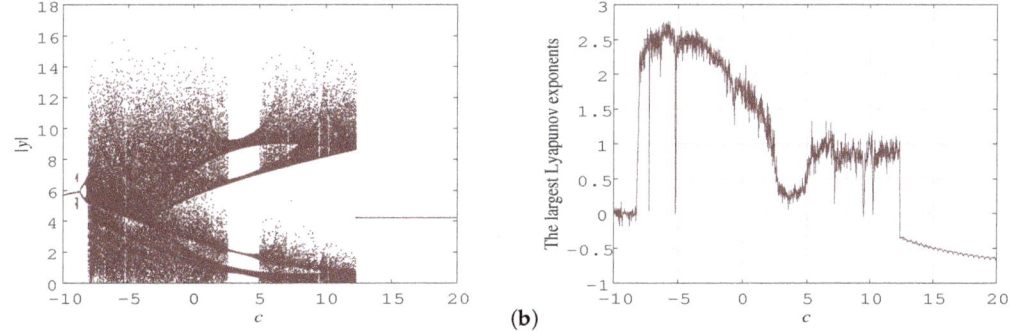

Figure 9. (**a**) Bifurcation diagram of $|y|$ with c as the varied parameter and (**b**) the largest Lyapunov exponent spectrum, where $a = 12$, $b = 100$, and $k = 4.6$.

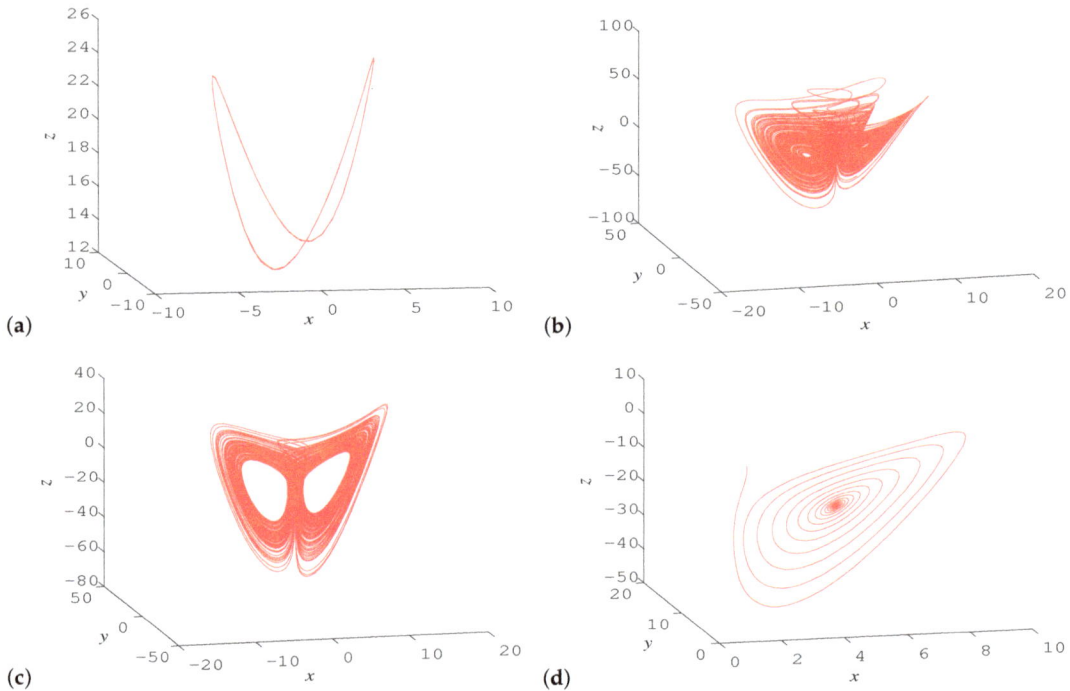

Figure 10. Three-dimensional views of rich dynamical behaviors with parameters $a = 12$, $b = 100$, and $k = 4.6$: (**a**) $c = -10$, (**b**) $c = -2$, (**c**) $c = 8$, and (**d**) $c = 15$. The initial values of $(x_0, y_0, z_0) = (1, 1, 1)$ were selected.

2.2.4. Fix $a = 12$, $b = 100$, and $c = 10$ and Vary k

We varied k from 0 to 20, again keeping the other parameters constant at $a = 12$, $b = 100$, and $c = 10$. From the results in Figure 11, it is evident that the system transitioned from convergence to a fixed point into chaos, which was accompanied by periodic windows in between. Table 1 lists the Lyapunov exponents and Kaplan–Yorke dimensions for the different parameter values, demonstrating the diverse dynamical behaviors with the change of the k value.

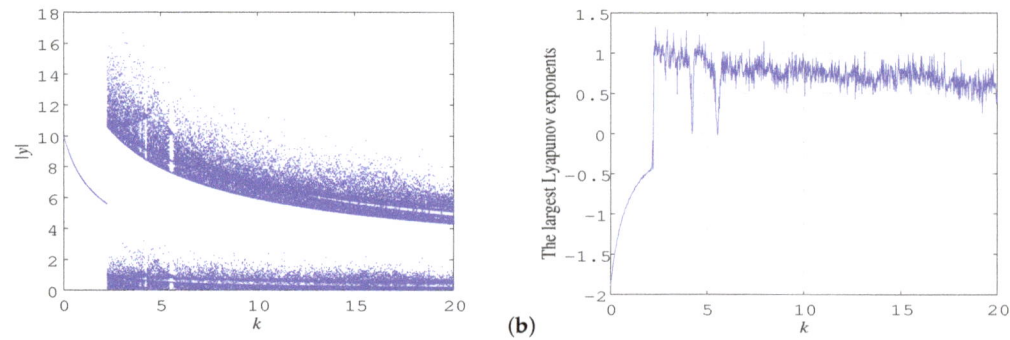

Figure 11. (**a**) Bifurcation diagram of $|y|$ with k as the varied parameter and (**b**) the largest Lyapunov exponent spectrum, where $a = 12$, $b = 100$, and $c = 10$.

Table 1. Lyapunov exponents and Kaplan–Yorke dimension of system (2): $(a, b, c) = (12, 100, 10)$ and $(x_0, y_0, z_0) = (1, 1, 1)$.

k	L_1	L_2	L_3	D_{KY}	Dynamics
1	−0.794149	−0.795286	−20.4107	0	Equilibrium
3	0.961912	0	−22.9613	2.0419	Chaos
4.225	0	−0.0340439	−21.9686	1.0	Period
5	0.920123	0	−22.9146	2.0399	Chaos
5.54	0	−0.0956672	−21.9091	1.0	Period
13	0.742037	0	−22.7375	2.0324	Chaos

2.2.5. Division of Different Parameters

The division diagram for the parameters c and k is shown to investigate the characteristics of the dynamical behaviors of the new system when the other parameters remained constant at $a = 12$ and $b = 100$. The parameter c was set to vary between −10 and 30, whereas the parameter k was altered between 0 and 25. Figure 12a shows the division of this region by a pseudo-colored map, which was obtained by computing the largest Lyapunov exponents. There are a variety of colors in the division diagram, corresponding to rich variations. The different colors represent different dynamical behaviors. Red, orange, yellow, and green represent chaotic states, cyan corresponds to a periodic state, and blue indicates an equilibrium state. The complexity of the chaos increased as the color became redder. The division diagram of the parameters c and k coincides well with the different dynamical behaviors for the individual parameters shown in Figures 9 and 11. Similarly, we fixed $c = 10$ and $k = 4.6$, and the division diagram for parameters a and b was obtained, as shown in Figure 12b, in which most regions are periodic. The division diagrams in Figure 12 indicate that the dynamical behaviors of the new system were very rich.

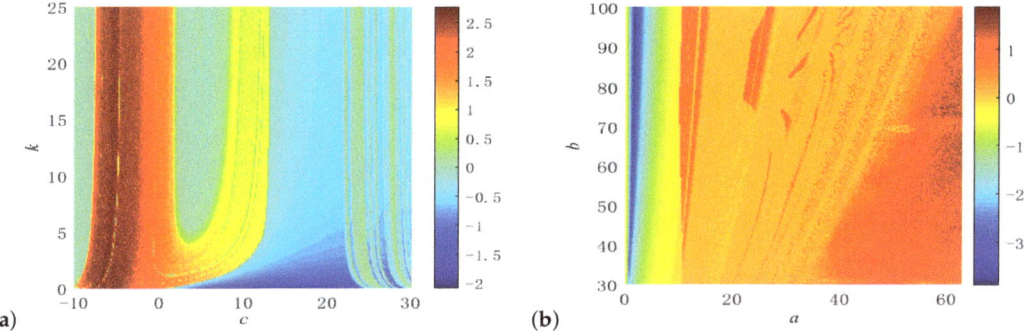

Figure 12. Diagram of largest Lyapunov exponents with different parameters: (**a**) division for parameters c and k ($a = 12$ and $b = 100$) and (**b**) division for parameters a and b ($c = 10$ and $k = 4.6$).

3. Variational Method

Chaotic motion consists of multiple unstable periodic orbits embedded in the strange attractor [52]. The study of periodic orbits gives us a better understanding of the chaotic properties of dynamical systems. If the system is high-dimensional or strongly chaotic, many existing methods for finding unstable periodic orbits will become inefficient or even fail. Here, we use the new method proposed by Lan and Cvitanović, namely the variational method [53]. This method is robust and converges at a fast rate. The variational method employs the logical limit of the multi-point shooting method. First, we have to make an initial loop guess for the overall topology of the unstable periodic orbit and then drive it toward the evolution of the real periodic orbit. The following partial differential equation dominates the loop evolution toward the cycle:

$$\frac{\partial^2 \tilde{x}}{\partial s \partial \tau} - \lambda A \frac{\partial \tilde{x}}{\partial \tau} - v \frac{\partial \lambda}{\partial \tau} = \lambda v - \tilde{v}. \tag{11}$$

In Equation (11), λ is used to control the period, the deformation of the loop is described by the fictitious time τ, the intrinsic coordinate used to parameterize the loop is $s \in [0, 2\pi]$, $A_{ij} = \frac{\partial v_i}{\partial x_j}$ denotes the gradient matrix of the velocity field, v is the dynamic flow vector field, defined by the derivative of x, and $\tilde{v}$ represents the tangential velocity of the loop.

The stability of the numerical method can be achieved using the Newton descent method. At this point, the cost function obtained by the evolution of the loop toward the cycle is monotonically decreasing:

$$F^2[(\tilde{x})] = \frac{1}{2\pi} \oint_{L(\tau)} d\tilde{x} [\tilde{v}(\tilde{x}) - \lambda v(\tilde{x})]^2. \tag{12}$$

Through iteration, the tangential velocity direction of the loop is continuously brought closer to the velocity direction of the dynamical flow. When $\tau \to \infty$, the two directions become consistent, and thus, the loop converges to the true periodic orbit defined by the dynamical system flow. Consequently, the period of the periodic orbit can be calculated from the following equation:

$$T_p = \int_0^{2\pi} \lambda(\tilde{x}(s, \infty)) ds. \tag{13}$$

Discretization of the loop derivatives is required to ensure numerical stability:

$$\tilde{v}_n \equiv \frac{\partial \tilde{x}}{\partial s} \Big|_{\tilde{x} = \tilde{x}(s_n)} \approx (\hat{D}\tilde{x})_n. \tag{14}$$

A five-point approximation is used for the numerical calculations, and the matrix is

$$\hat{D} = \frac{N}{24\pi} \begin{pmatrix} 0 & 8 & -1 & & & & & 1 & -8 \\ -8 & 0 & 8 & -1 & & & & & 1 \\ 1 & -8 & 0 & 8 & -1 & & & & \\ & & & & \cdots & & & & \\ & & & & 1 & -8 & 0 & 8 & -1 \\ -1 & & & & & 1 & -8 & 0 & 8 \\ 8 & -1 & & & & & 1 & -8 & 0 \end{pmatrix}. \tag{15}$$

Thus, Equation (11) can be changed to the following form with a fictitious time Euler step $\delta \tau$:

$$\begin{pmatrix} \hat{A} & -\hat{v} \\ \hat{a} & 0 \end{pmatrix} \begin{pmatrix} \delta \tilde{x} \\ \delta \lambda \end{pmatrix} = \delta \tau \begin{pmatrix} \lambda \hat{v} - \tilde{v} \\ 0 \end{pmatrix}, \tag{16}$$

where $\hat{A} = \hat{D} - \lambda \text{diag}[A_1, A_2, ..., A_N]$, $\hat{v} = (v_1, v_2, ..., v_N)^t$, $\tilde{v} = (\tilde{v}_1, \tilde{v}_2, ..., \tilde{v}_N)^t$, and $\hat{a}$ is an Nd-dimensional row vector, which restricts the change of the coordinates. By inverting the matrix on the left of Equation (16), we can solve for $\delta \tilde{x}$ and $\delta \lambda$ to acquire the deformation of the loop coordinates and period. The banded lower–upper decomposition method can be used to accelerate the computation, and the Woodbury formula can be employed to deal with periodic and boundary terms [54]. The variational method can be effectively used to calculate the unstable periodic orbits of various chaotic systems [55–57]. In the next section, we utilize the variational method to locate the unstable periodic orbits in the hidden chaotic attractor of system (2).

4. Symbolic Encoding of Unstable Periodic Orbits in the Hidden Chaotic Attractor with Six Letters

Periodic orbit theory can be used to calculate many physical quantities, such as the fractal dimension and topological entropy [58,59]. In most cases, the theory is acquired by performing calculations for the required unstable short-period orbits. Here, we explore the unstable periodic orbits in the hidden chaotic attractor of system (2) for the parameter values of $(a, b, c, k) = (12, 100, 10, 4.6)$. When the Poincaré section $z = -10$ is chosen, the first return map can be plotted, which contains a large number of dense points with a certain hierarchical structure, as shown in Figure 13. There were five branches, and thus, it was necessary to build complex symbolic dynamics to encode the periodic orbits of the new system (2) for the current parameters [60]. Taking this into account, we used the variational method to locate the cycles of the new system, and six cycles with simple topological structures were found, as shown in Figure 14. The symbolic encoding rules of these periodic orbits are as follows:

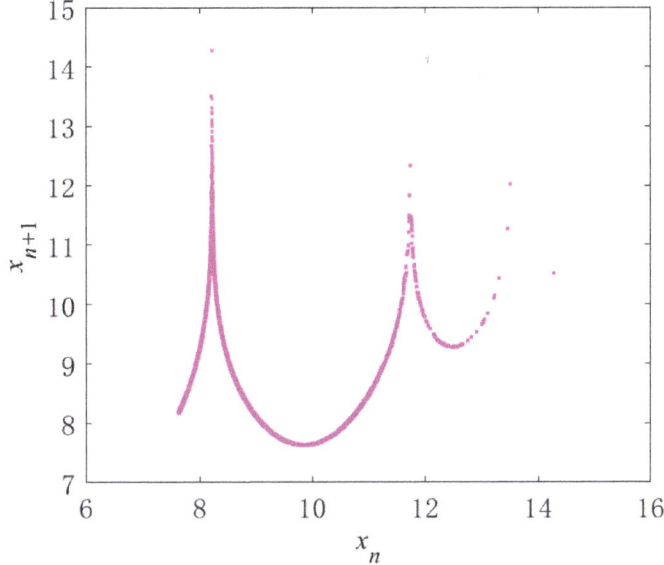

Figure 13. Poincaré first return map with a section $z = -10$ for $(a, b, c, k) = (12, 100, 10, 4.6)$.

(1) For a cycle with a smooth ellipse shape around a fixed point, the symbol 0 is used to denote the cycle around the left and the symbol 1 is used to denote the cycle around the right.

(2) For an irregular cycle around a fixed point with a smaller extension on the z-axis around 100, which has a blunt fold, in the shape of a raised wing, the symbol 2 is used to denote the cycle around the left and the symbol 3 is used to denote the cycle around the right.

(3) For an irregular cycle around a fixed point with a larger extension on the z-axis around 140, which has a very sharp fold, forming the shape of a ginkgo leaf, the symbol 4 is used to denote the cycle around the left and the symbol 5 is used to denote the cycle around the right.

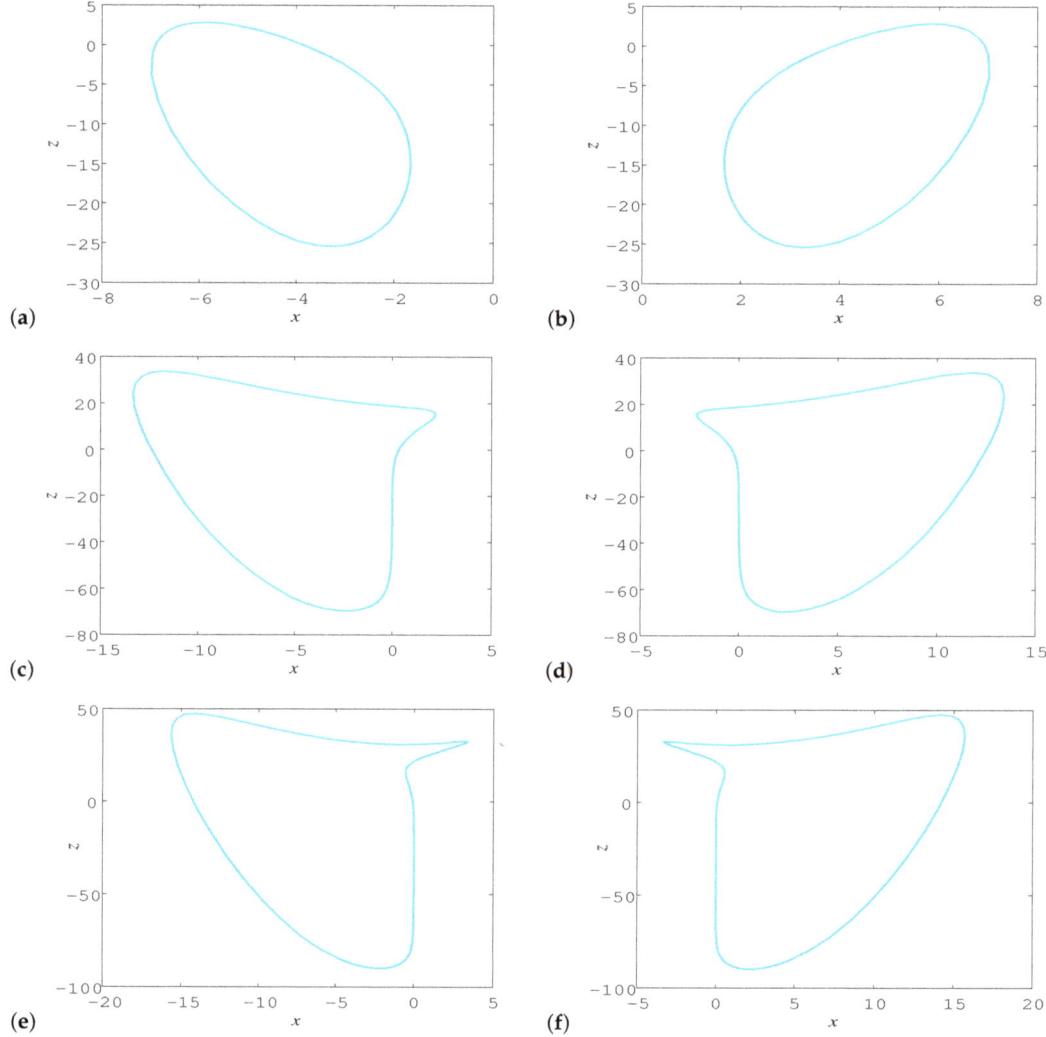

Figure 14. Six building block cycles for system (2), $(a, b, c, k) = (12, 100, 10, 4.6)$: (**a**) cycle 0, (**b**) cycle 1, (**c**) cycle 2, (**d**) cycle 3, (**e**) cycle 4, and (**f**) cycle 5.

The six cycles presented above are the building blocks that make up the orbits of the new system, and the other complex long-period orbits are composed of them. Thus, we can calculate the cycles systematically by utilizing the six-letter symbolic dynamics. It can be clearly seen that cycles 0 and 1 were symmetric to each other, as were cycles 2 and 3 and cycles 4 and 5. They were cycles with a topological length of 1, while cycles had a topological length of 2 when they rotated once around each of the left and right fixed points or twice around a fixed point. Since there was z-axis symmetry in the system, we could likewise find symmetric and asymmetric cycles with a topological length of 2, as shown in Figure 15.

The cycles could be classified into two types: self-conjugated and mutually conjugated. The periods of the cycles that were conjugated to themselves were not equal to those of the other cycles, such as cycles 01, 23, and 45. Two mutually conjugated cycles had equal periods and symmetry, e.g., cycles 03 and 12. We discovered that several cycles with topological length 2 were pruned, which means that they did not exist, such as cycles 02, 13, and 04. We also found that building blocks with symbols 0 or 1 could not be combined with the building blocks with symbols 4 or 5 to form a periodic orbit. Therefore, for example, for the cycles of topological length 3, there would not be cycles 045 and 124. After some attempts, we found that cycles 012, 123, 002, and 022 were also pruned. To obtain a clear picture of the periodic orbits of the new system, we show the 2D phase diagrams of nine cycles with topological length 3 in Figure 16. All the cycles and their periods T_p within a topological length 3 are tabulated in Table 2.

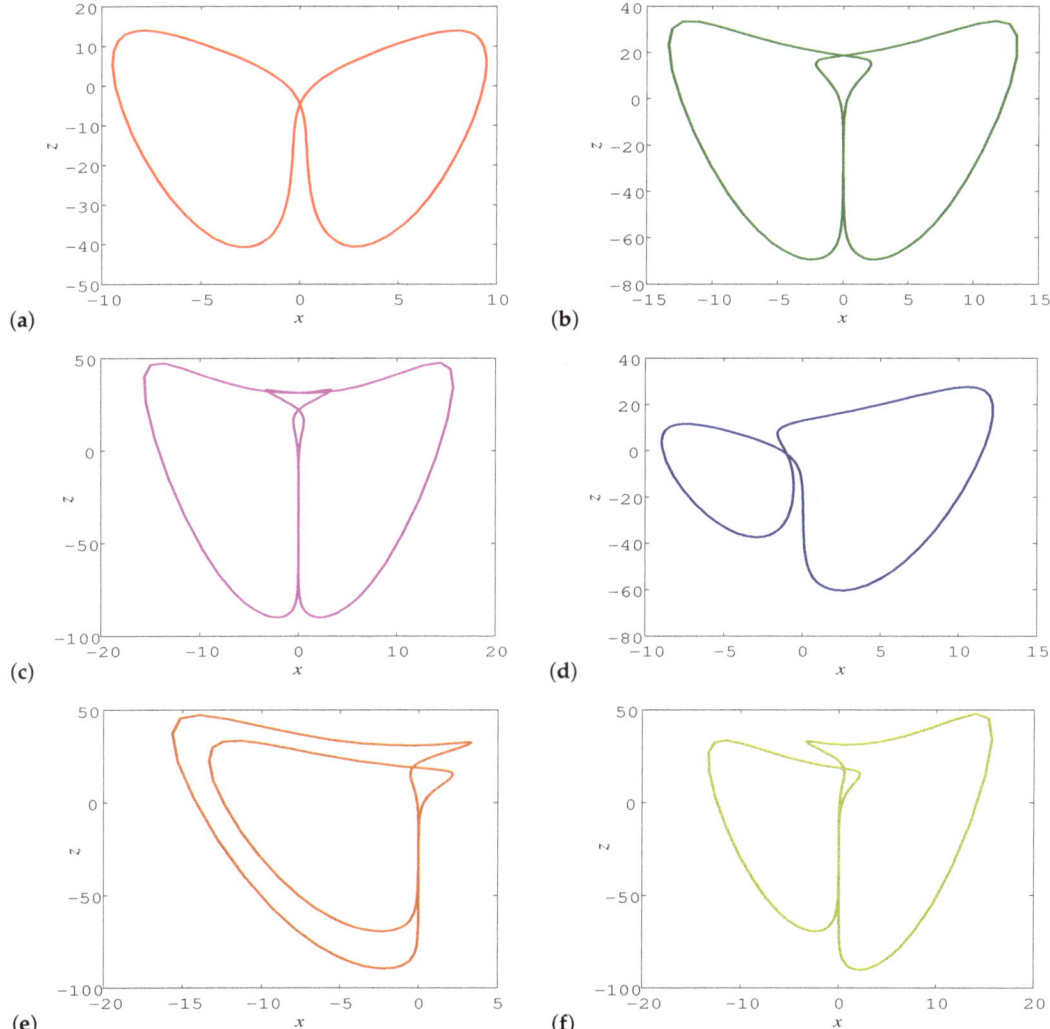

Figure 15. Unstable periodic orbits with topological length of 2 in the new system: (**a**) cycle 01, (**b**) 23, (**c**) 45, (**d**) 03, (**e**) 24, and (**f**) 25.

Figure 13 shows that the multi-branch structure of the first return map created some difficulties for the analysis of the unstable periodic orbits. The establishment of the symbolic encoding approach based on the topological structure of the trajectory and its circuiting property with respect to different equilibrium points showed the effectiveness of the analysis of the cycles in the hidden chaotic attractors. It is hoped that this method can also be used to encode periodic orbits embedded in hidden hyperchaotic attractors.

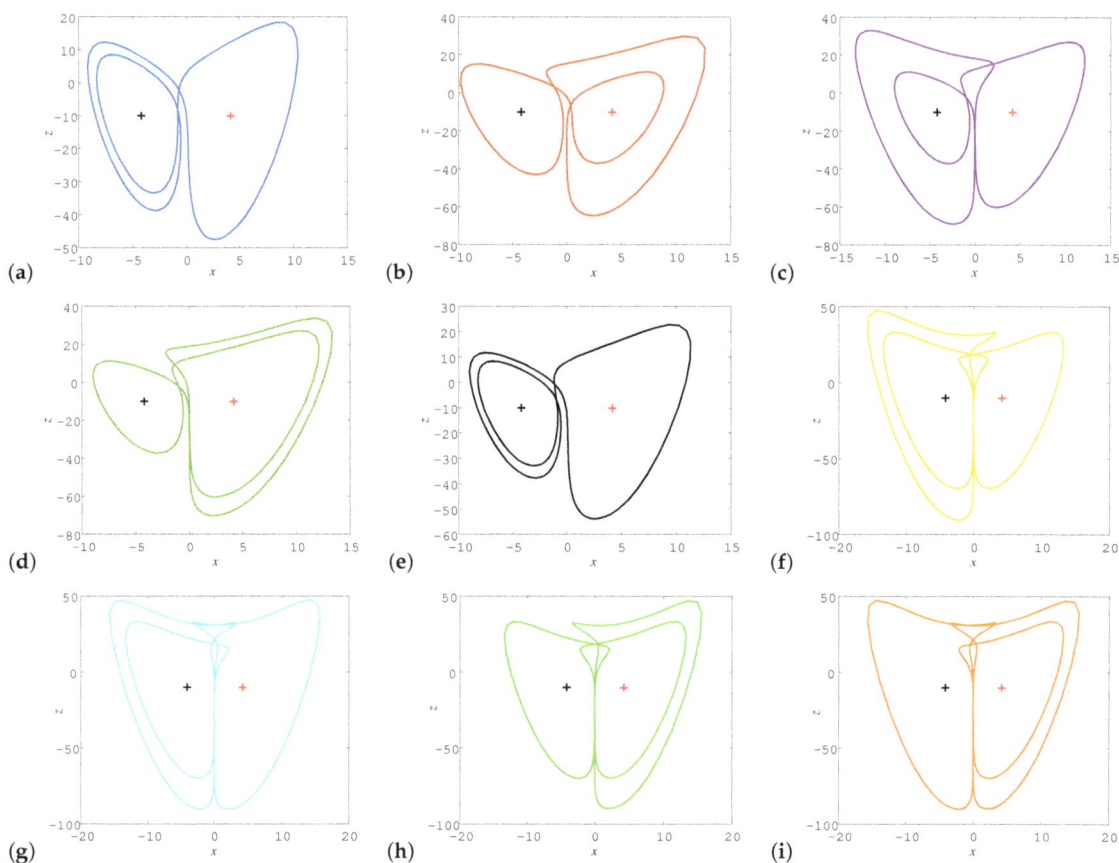

Figure 16. Unstable periodic orbits with a topological length of 3 in the new system, where the two stable equilibria are marked with "+": (a) cycle 001, (b) 013, (c) 023, (d) 033, (e) 003, (f) 243, (g) 245, (h) 253, and (i) 345.

Table 2. Unstable cycles in the new system within a topological length of 3.

Length	Itineraries	Periods	Length	Itineraries	Periods	Length	Itineraries	Periods
1	0	0.645509	3	223	3.552630	3	001	2.324411
	1	0.645509		233	3.552630		011	2.324411
	2	1.186404		033	2.981070		123	—
	3	1.186404		122	2.981070		032	—
2	01	1.559290		021	2.653639		003	2.401931
	23	2.366105		013	2.653639		112	2.401931
	12	1.792160		031	—		113	—
	03	1.792160		012	—		002	—
	02	—		132	2.962501		022	—
	13	—		023	2.962501		133	—
1	4	1.515729	3	445	4.815813	3	354	4.221816
	5	1.515729		455	4.815813		234	3.878345
2	24	2.695403		344	4.221765		325	3.878345

Table 2. Cont.

Length	Itineraries	Periods	Length	Itineraries	Periods	Length	Itineraries	Periods
3	35	2.695403		255	4.221765		225	3.892262
	25	2.706161		335	3.881997		334	3.892262
	34	2.706161		224	3.881997		254	4.211233
	45	3.031718		244	4.211320		345	4.211233
	235	3.889210		355	4.211320			
	324	3.889210		245	4.221816			

5. Circuitry of Proposed System

Multi-scroll chaotic systems often use current–feedback operational amplifiers (CFOAs) to implement the circuit, which helps to enhance the frequency bandwidth [61]. FPGA implementation has strong universality and is less limited by hardware resources [62], while circuit simulation has the characteristics of simple debugging and a low cost. To verify the correctness and feasibility of the new proposed system, circuit simulations were performed in this study, and we selected the NI Multisim 14 software (accessed on 1 May 2015 and website address https://www.ni.com/zh-cn/suppot/downloads) to simulate the circuit. The state variables x, y, and z were reduced by a factor of 10 to avoid the state variables being out of the dynamic range of the device. Therefore, system (2) is rewritten as

$$\begin{aligned}\dot{X} &= a(Y-X),\\ \dot{Y} &= -cY - 10XZ,\\ \dot{Z} &= 10Y^2 - 0.1b + 10kXY,\end{aligned} \quad (17)$$

where $X = 0.1x$, $Y = 0.1y$, and $Z = 0.1z$.

By performing a time-scale transformation of Equation (17), in which the time-scale factor is set to $\tau_0 = \frac{1}{R_0 C_0} = 1000$ and $t = \tau_0 \tau$, we obtain

$$\begin{aligned}\dot{X} &= 1000a(Y-X),\\ \dot{Y} &= -1000cY - 10,000XZ,\\ \dot{Z} &= 10,000Y^2 - 100b + 10,000kXY.\end{aligned} \quad (18)$$

Based on Kirchhoff's law, the following equation can be obtained from the circuit diagram in Figure 17:

$$\begin{aligned}\dot{X} &= \frac{R_3}{R_2 R_4 C_1}Y - \frac{R_3}{R_1 R_4 C_1}X,\\ \dot{Y} &= -\frac{R_9}{R_7 R_{10} C_2}Y - \frac{R_9}{R_8 R_{10} C_2}0.1XZ,\\ \dot{Z} &= \frac{R_{16}}{R_{13} R_{17} C_3}0.1Y^2 + \frac{R_{16}}{R_{15} R_{17} C_3}V_1 + \frac{R_{16}}{R_{14} R_{17} C_3}0.1XY.\end{aligned} \quad (19)$$

The circuit consisted of three functional modules: addition, integration, and inversion, and the three channels corresponded to the three variables of the system. As shown in Figure 17, the circuit included nineteen resistors, three capacitors, nine TL082CP operational amplifiers, and three analog multipliers (the output gain was 0.1). The power supply voltage was ± 17 V. The coefficients of system (2) were $a = 12$, $b = 100$, $c = 10$, and $k = 4.6$, and the values of the circuit components were $C_1 = C_2 = C_3 = 100$ nF, $R_1 = R_2 = 8.333$ kΩ, $R_3 = R_9 = R_{16} = 100$ kΩ, $R_4 = R_5 = R_6 = R_7 = R_{10} = R_{11} = R_{12} = R_{15} = R_{17} = R_{18} = R_{19} = 10$ kΩ, $R_8 = R_{13} = 1$ kΩ, $R_{14} = 0.217$ kΩ, and $V_1 = -1$ V.

The designed circuit was successfully implemented in Multisim, and the results are reported in Figure 18. The results of the circuit implementation agreed with the numerical simulation results, which validated the realizability of the proposed new system (2).

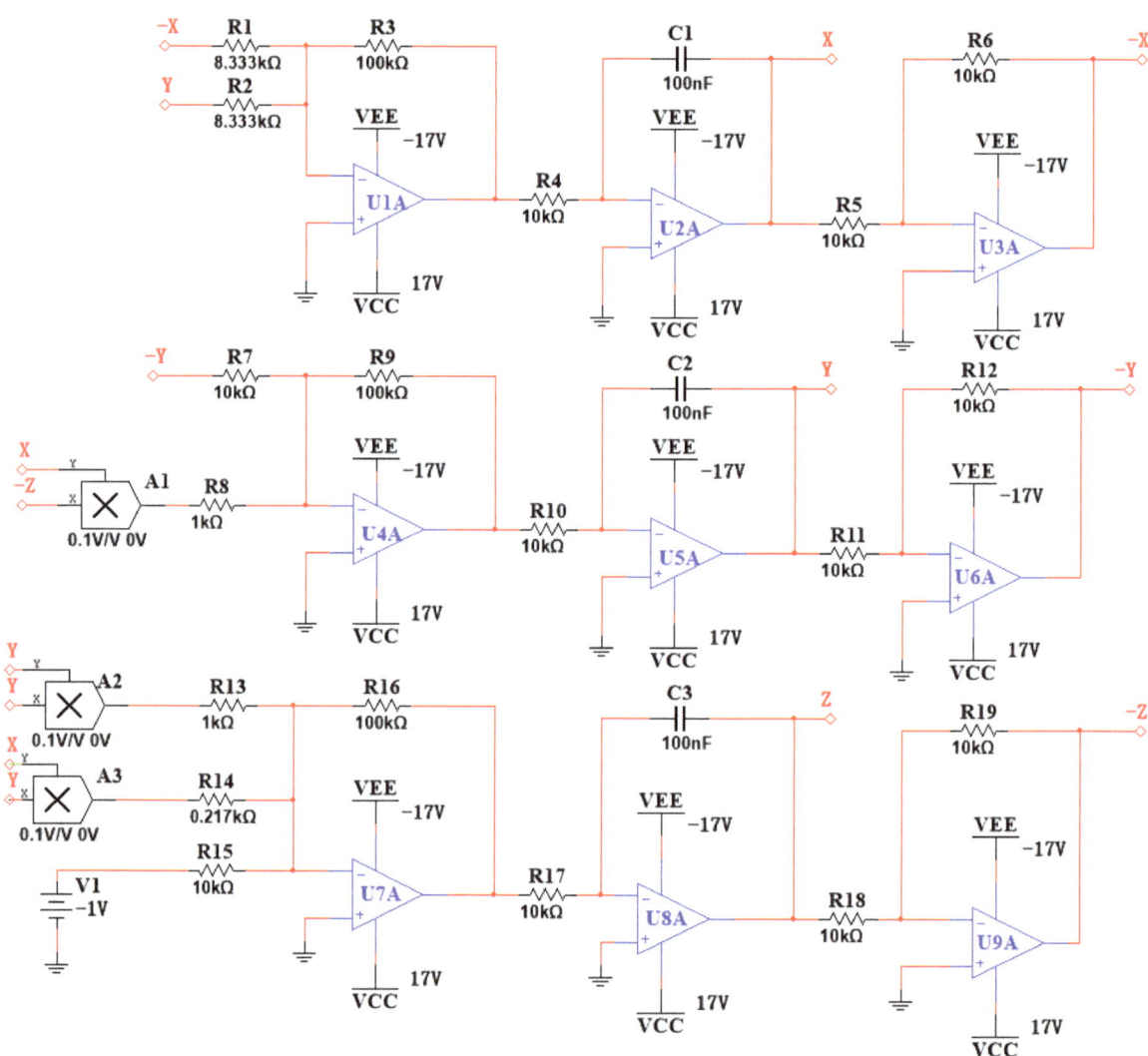

Figure 17. Circuit diagram of the new hidden attractor chaotic system.

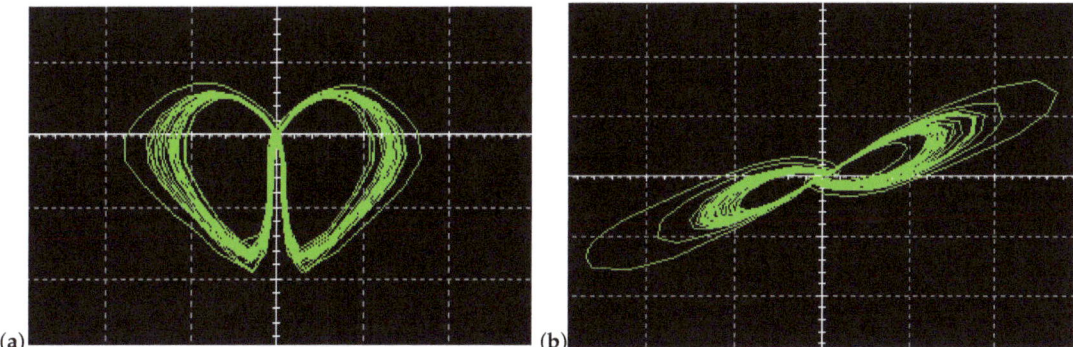

(a) (b)

Figure 18. Phase portraits of the circuit from Multisim: (**a**) X-Z plane and (**b**) X-Y plane.

6. Offset Boosting Control and Adaptive Synchronization of New System

Engineering applications for variable-boostable systems show considerable promise, and they are simple to control once offsets are added [63,64]. As the offset changes, bipolar or unipolar signals may be produced. We select z as the state variable, since it only occurs once in system (2). The control parameter w has the ability to boost the state variable z. As a result, the offset-boosted system can be written as

$$\begin{aligned} \frac{dx}{dt} &= a(y-x), \\ \frac{dy}{dt} &= -cy - x(z+w), \\ \frac{dz}{dt} &= y^2 - b + kxy, \end{aligned} \quad (20)$$

where the control parameter w is a constant.

We select parameter values of $a = 12$, $b = 100$, $c = 10$, and $k = 4.6$, and the initial values of the variables were all set to 1. As shown in Figure 19, it is evident from the attractors with various offsets into the y-z phase space and the time sequence diagram that a chaotic signal could change from being a bipolar signal to a unipolar signal. As the value of the control parameter w changed, the attractor moved up and down along the z-axis. For example, when w was taken as 0, a bipolar signal existed. When the value of w was taken as -75, a positive unipolar signal appeared, while a negative unipolar signal appeared when w was taken as 40.

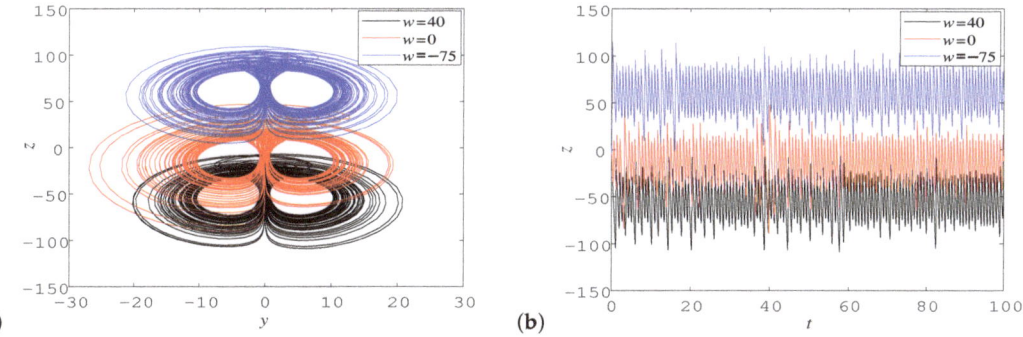

(a) (b)

Figure 19. (**a**) Chaotic attractors with different offsets w in the y-z plane; (**b**) State z with different values of the offset boosting controller w.

It can be seen from the above discussion that our new proposed system has an easy-to-control nature, and the adjustment of the overall signal can be achieved simply by changing a single parameter, i.e., adding an offset w to the variable z to achieve a shift in the z-direction, which has potential in engineering applications.

Chaotic synchronization is the key to achieving chaotic and confidential communication. There are various schemes for synchronization [65], and in this section, we take an adaptive synchronization approach to realize the chaotic synchronization of two identical systems with unknown parameters due to its robustness and simple implementation.

The following master system is the new hidden attractor chaotic system we introduced:

$$\begin{aligned} \dot{x}_m &= a(y_m - x_m), \\ \dot{y}_m &= -cy_m - x_m z_m, \\ \dot{z}_m &= y_m^2 - b + kx_m y_m, \end{aligned} \quad (21)$$

and the slave system adopts the following form by adding adaptive controls u_x, u_y, and u_z for each of the three directions:

$$\begin{aligned} \dot{x}_s &= a(y_s - x_s) + u_x, \\ \dot{y}_s &= -cy_s - x_s z_s + u_y, \\ \dot{z}_s &= y_s^2 - b + kx_s y_s + u_z. \end{aligned} \quad (22)$$

The synchronization error is set to

$$\begin{aligned} e_x &= x_s - x_m, \\ e_y &= y_s - y_m, \\ e_z &= z_s - z_m. \end{aligned} \quad (23)$$

Then, the error dynamics of the slave system (22) and master system (21) can be written as

$$\begin{aligned} \dot{e}_x &= a(e_y - e_x) + u_x, \\ \dot{e}_y &= -ce_y - x_s z_s + x_m z_m + u_y, \\ \dot{e}_z &= y_s^2 - y_m^2 + kx_s y_s - kx_m y_m + u_z. \end{aligned} \quad (24)$$

The examination of the stability of the error system is based on the transformation of the synchronization issue between the master and slave systems. The adaptive controller selected in this scheme is

$$\begin{aligned} u_x &= -\hat{a}(t)(e_y - e_x) - k_1 e_x, \\ u_y &= \hat{c}(t)e_y + x_s z_s - x_m z_m - k_2 e_y, \\ u_z &= -y_s^2 + y_m^2 - \hat{k}(t)x_s y_s + \hat{k}(t)x_m y_m - k_3 e_z, \end{aligned} \quad (25)$$

in which k_1, k_2, and k_3 are positive gain constants and $\hat{a}(t), \hat{b}(t), \hat{c}(t)$, and $\hat{k}(t)$ are parameter estimates. Therefore, substituting Equation (25) into Equation (24) and simplifying it yields

$$\begin{aligned} \dot{e}_x &= (a - \hat{a}(t))(e_y - e_x) - k_1 e_x, \\ \dot{e}_y &= -(c - \hat{c}(t))e_y - k_2 e_y, \\ \dot{e}_z &= (k - \hat{k}(t))x_s y_s - (k - \hat{k}(t))x_m y_m - k_3 e_z. \end{aligned} \quad (26)$$

The parameter estimation error is set to

$$\begin{aligned} e_a(t) &= a - \hat{a}(t), \\ e_b(t) &= b - \hat{b}(t), \\ e_c(t) &= c - \hat{c}(t), \\ e_k(t) &= k - \hat{k}(t). \end{aligned} \quad (27)$$

Then, we obtain

$$\begin{aligned} \dot{e}_a &= -\dot{\hat{a}}, \\ \dot{e}_b &= -\dot{\hat{b}}, \\ \dot{e}_c &= -\dot{\hat{c}}, \\ \dot{e}_k &= -\dot{\hat{k}}. \end{aligned} \quad (28)$$

The error dynamics can be rewritten as follows:

$$\begin{aligned} \dot{e}_x &= e_a(e_y - e_x) - k_1 e_x, \\ \dot{e}_y &= -e_c e_y - k_2 e_y, \\ \dot{e}_z &= e_k x_s y_s - e_k x_m y_m - k_3 e_z. \end{aligned} \quad (29)$$

The quadratic Lyapunov function can be constructed as follows:

$$V = \frac{1}{2}(e_x^2 + e_y^2 + e_z^2 + e_a^2 + e_b^2 + e_c^2 + e_k^2). \quad (30)$$

Differentiating V along the trajectories of the system yields

$$\dot{V} = -k_1 e_x^2 - k_2 e_y^2 - k_3 e_z^2 - e_a(\dot{\hat{a}} - e_x(e_y - e_x)) - e_b \dot{\hat{b}} - e_c(\dot{\hat{c}} + e_y^2) - e_k(\dot{\hat{k}} + e_z x_m y_m - e_z x_s y_s). \quad (31)$$

Thus, the parameter estimates can be set as

$$\begin{aligned} \dot{\hat{a}} &= e_x(e_y - e_x) + k_4 e_a, \\ \dot{\hat{b}} &= k_5 e_b, \\ \dot{\hat{c}} &= -e_y^2 + k_6 e_c, \\ \dot{\hat{k}} &= e_z x_s y_s - e_z x_m y_m + k_7 e_k, \end{aligned} \quad (32)$$

where k_4, k_5, k_6, and k_7 are positive gain constants.

We obtained a negative definite Lyapunov function:

$$\dot{V} = -k_1 e_x^2 - k_2 e_y^2 - k_3 e_z^2 - k_4 e_a^2 - k_5 e_b^2 - k_6 e_c^2 - k_7 e_k^2. \quad (33)$$

According to Lyapunov stability theory, under the adaptive controller, all the synchronization errors e_x, e_y, and e_z and parameter estimation errors e_a, e_b, e_c, and e_k globally and exponentially converge to 0 when the initial values are chosen at random. Therefore, through the above theoretical analysis, it is known that the master system and the slave system can be fully synchronized.

The effectiveness of the proposed approach was verified by numerical simulations, which are described as follows. The parameters were set as $(a, b, c, k) = (12, 100, 10, 4.6)$, which resulted in a hidden chaotic attractor. The gain constants were selected as

$k_i = 3$ $(i = 1, 2, 3, 4, 5, 6, 7)$. The initial values of the master system, slave system, and parameter estimates were taken as

$$(x_m(0), y_m(0), z_m(0)) = (-1, 2.5, -4), (x_s(0), y_s(0), z_s(0)) = (-0.5, -0.5, -5), (\hat{a}(0), \hat{b}(0), \hat{c}(0), \hat{k}(0)) = (2, 113, 15, 10) \quad (34)$$

Figure 20 displays the full synchronization of the respective states of the master and slave systems. It can be seen that after a short time, the state trajectories of the master system x_m, y_m and z_m gradually overlapped with the slave system x_s, y_s and z_s. The time-histories of the synchronization errors and parameter estimation errors are also shown in Figure 21, which indicate that all the errors asymptotically converged to zero with time. In summary, the simulation results of this new hidden chaotic system demonstrated the operability of the chaotic circuit and adaptive synchronization control.

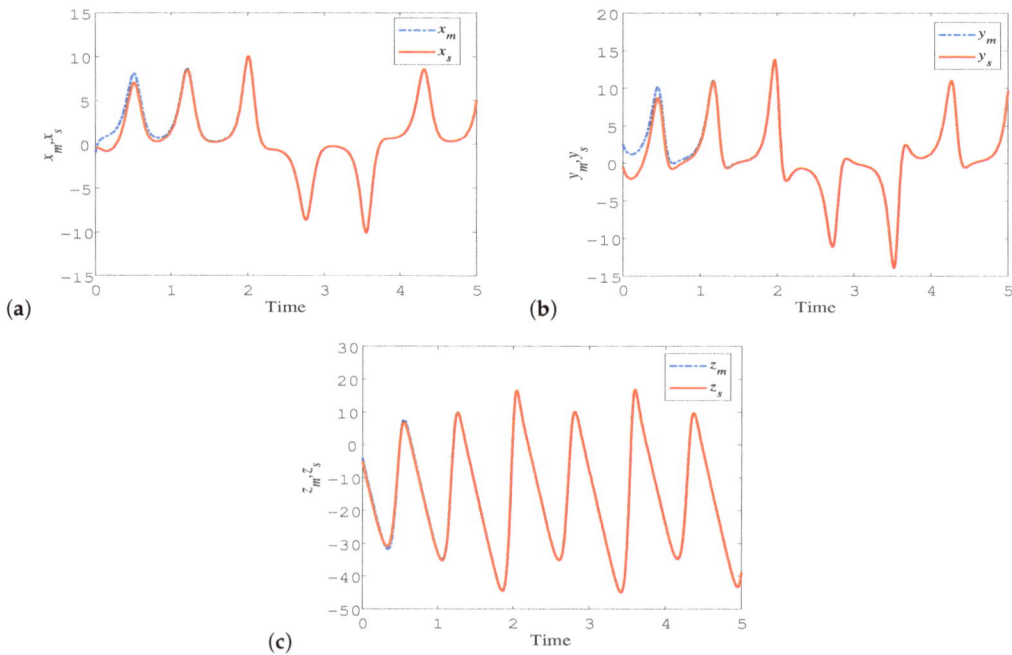

Figure 20. Time evolution diagrams of the master and slave systems showing results of the complete synchronization of the respective states: (**a**) x variable, (**b**) y variable, and (**c**) z variable.

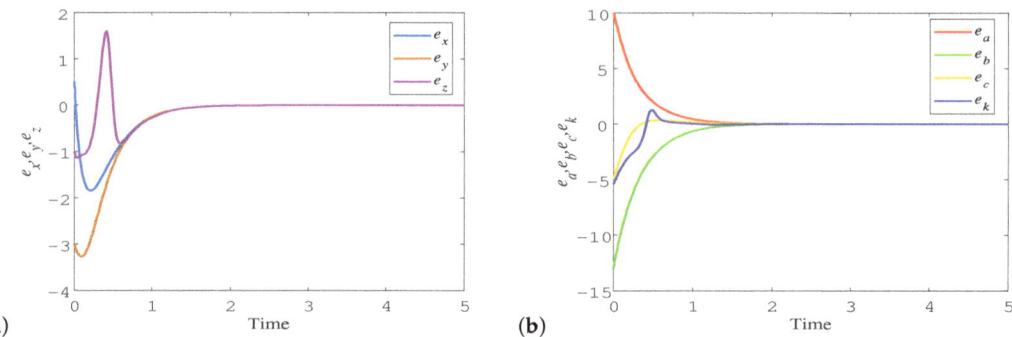

Figure 21. Time evolution of (**a**) synchronization errors e_x, e_y, and e_z, and (**b**) parameter estimation errors e_a, e_b, e_c, and e_k.

7. Conclusions

On the basis of the generalized Sprott C system, we added a nonlinear cross-term to the third equation to construct a new hidden attractor chaotic system that has two stable equilibria. To quantitatively examine its chaotic properties, several tools, including the Lyapunov exponent spectrum, power spectrum, and the Poincaré first return map, were applied. The influences of four parameters on the dynamical behaviors of the system were explored by means of bifurcation diagrams, maximum Lyapunov exponent spectra, and division diagrams of two parameters, and the rich and complex dynamical behaviors of the system were also presented in combination with the phase portraits. Meanwhile, the existence of various coexisting attractors was discovered, which indicated a multi-stability phenomenon. Furthermore, we calculated the unstable periodic orbits embedded in the hidden chaotic attractor with the help of the variational method, and we encoded and classified the cycles using six-letter symbolic dynamics. Finally, a circuit simulation, offset boosting control, and adaptive synchronization linked this hidden attractor chaotic system to physical experiments and verified the practicality of the system.

We believe that the periodic orbit coding method used in this paper can provide a reference for analyzing periodic orbits in other hidden attractor chaotic systems. More results from studies on the applications of the proposed hidden attractor chaotic system will be revealed in future research. Moreover, the hidden attractors in fractional-order systems have also attracted extensive attention in recent years. When a single parameter changes, self-excited, hidden, or nonhyperbolic chaotic attractors will appear in a new fractional-order chaotic system with different families of hidden and self-excited attractors [66]. In a new fractional-order chaotic system without any equilibrium points based on a fracmemristor, the hidden chaotic attractors are propagated infinitely using a trigonometric function [67]. We can investigate the fractional-order system corresponding to this hidden attractor chaotic system to gain a better grasp of the complexity of chaotic systems and their variety of practical applications. To present the multi-stability of coexisting attractors, memristor chaotic systems can also be introduced. Attention should also be paid to the FPGA implementation of chaotic systems, which will be the focus of our subsequent work.

Author Contributions: J.W.: software, methodology, formal analysis, validation, investigation, writing–original draft preparation, writing–review and editing. C.D.: conceptualization, methodology, software, investigation, supervision, project administration, writing–original draft preparation, writing–review and editing, funding acquisition. H.L.: supervision, project administration, funding acquisition. All authors have read and agreed to the published version of the manuscript.

Funding: This work is supported by National Natural Science Foundation of China (Grant Nos. 11647085, 11647086, and 12205257), Shanxi Province Science Foundation for Youths (Grant No. 201901D211252), the Scientific and Technological Innovation Programs of Higher Education Institutions in Shanxi (Grant Nos. 2019L0505 and 2019L0554), and the Graduate Innovation Project of Shanxi Province (Grant No. 2022Y635).

Institutional Review Board Statement: Not applicable.

Informed Consent Statement: Not applicable.

Data Availability Statement: The data used to support the findings of this study are available from the corresponding author upon request.

Acknowledgments: We thank the anonymous reviewers for their many insightful comments and suggestions, which substantially improved the manuscript.

Conflicts of Interest: The author declares no conflict of interest.

References

1. Altan, A.; Karasu, S.; Bekiros, S. Digital currency forecasting with chaotic meta-heuristic bio-inspired signal processing techniques. *Chaos Solitons Fractals* **2019**, *126*, 325–336. [CrossRef]
2. Cvitanović, P.; Artuso, R.; Mainieri, R.; Tanner, G.; Vattay, G. *Chaos: Classical and Quantum*; Niels Bohr Institute: Copenhagen, Denmark, 2012; pp. 131–133.

3. Lorenz, E.N. Deterministic nonperiodic flow. *J. Atmos. Sci.* **1963**, *20*, 130–141. [CrossRef]
4. Šil'nikov, L.P. A case of the existence of a denumerable set of periodic motions. *Sov. Math. Dokl.* **1965**, *6*, 163–166.
5. Chen, G.; Ueta, T. Yet another chaotic attractor. *Int. J. Bifurc. Chaos* **1999**, *9*, 1465–1466. [CrossRef]
6. Qi, G.; Chen, G.; Du, S.; Chen, Z.; Yuan, Z. Analysis of a new chaotic system. *Phys. A* **2005**, *352*, 295–308. [CrossRef]
7. Lü, J.; Chen, G. A new chaotic attractor coined. *Int. J. Bifurc. Chaos* **2002**, *12*, 659–661. [CrossRef]
8. Rössler, O.E. An equation for continuous chaos. *Phys. Lett. A* **1976**, *57*, 397–398. [CrossRef]
9. Leonov, G.A.; Kuznetsov, N.V. Hidden attractors in dynamical systems. From hidden oscillations in Hilbert-Kolmogorov, Aizerman, and Kalman problems to hidden chaotic attractor in Chua circuits. *Int. J. Bifurc. Chaos* **2013**, *23*, 1330002. [CrossRef]
10. Wang, S.; Wang, C.; Xu, C. An image encryption algorithm based on a hidden attractor chaos system and the Knuth-Durstenfeld algorithm. *Opt. Lasers Eng.* **2020**, *128*, 105995. [CrossRef]
11. Khalaf, A.J.M.; Abdolmohammadi, H.R.; Ahmadi, A.; Moysis, L.; Volos, C.; Hussain, I. Extreme multi-stability analysis of a novel 5D chaotic system with hidden attractors, line equilibrium, permutation entropy and its secure communication scheme. *Eur. Phys. J. Spec. Top.* **2020**, *229*, 1175–1188. [CrossRef]
12. Lai, Q.; Wang, Z.; Kuate, P.D.K. Dynamical analysis, FPGA implementation and synchronization for secure communication of new chaotic system with hidden and coexisting attractors. *Mod. Phys. Lett. B* **2022**, *36*, 2150538. [CrossRef]
13. Leonov, G.A.; Kuznetsov, N.V.; Kuznetsova, O.A.; Seledzhi, S.M.; Vagaitsev, V.I. Hidden oscillations in dynamical systems. *Trans. Syst. Contr.* **2011**, *6*, 54–67.
14. Jafari, S.; Pham, V.T.; Kapitaniak, T. Multiscroll chaotic sea obtained from a simple 3D System without equilibrium. *Int. J. Bifurc. Chaos* **2016**, *26*, 1650031. [CrossRef]
15. Pham, V.T.; Jafari, S.; Volos, C.; Wang, X.; Golpayegani, S. Is that really hidden? The presence of complex fixed-points in chaotic flows with no equilibria. *Int. J. Bifurc. Chaos* **2014**, *24*, 1450146. [CrossRef]
16. Jafari, S.; Sprott, J.C.; Golpayegani, S. Elementary quadratic chaotic flows with no equilibria. *Phys. Lett. A* 2013, *377*, 699–702. [CrossRef]
17. Dong, C.; Wang, J. Hidden and coexisting attractors in a novel 4D hyperchaotic system with no equilibrium point. *Fractal Fract.* **2022**, *6*, 306. [CrossRef]
18. Wang, X.; Chen, G. A chaotic system with only one stable equilibrium.Commun. *Nonlinear Sci. Numer. Simul.* **2012**, *17*, 1264–1272. [CrossRef]
19. Bao, B.; Li, Q.; Wang, N.; Xu, Q. Multistability in Chua's circuit with two stable node-foci. *Chaos* **2016**, *26*, 043111. [CrossRef]
20. Molaie, M.; Jafari, S.; Sprott, J.C.; Golpayegani, S. Simple chaotic flows with one stable equilibrium. *Int. J. Bifurc. Chaos* **2013**, *23*, 1350188. [CrossRef]
21. Wang, X.; Chen, G. Constructing a chaotic system with any number of equilibria. *Nonlinear Dyn.* **2013**, *71*, 429–436. [CrossRef]
22. Gotthans, T.; Petržela, J. New class of chaotic systems with circular equilibrium. *Nonlinear Dyn.* **2015**, *81*, 1143–1149. [CrossRef]
23. Feng, Y.; Rajagopal, K.; Khalaf, A.J.M.; Alsaadi, F.E.; Alsaadi, F.E.; Pham, V.T. A new hidden attractor hyperchaotic memristor oscillator with a line of equilibria. *Eur. Phys. J. Spec. Top.* **2020**, *229*, 1279–1288. [CrossRef]
24. Zhang, X.; Wang, C. Multiscroll hyperchaotic system with hidden attractors and its circuit implementation. *Int. J. Bifurc. Chaos* **2019**, *29*, 1950117. [CrossRef]
25. Bao, J.; Chen, D. Coexisting hidden attractors in a 4D segmented disc dynamo with one stable equilibrium or a line equilibrium. *Chin. Phys. B* **2017**, *26*, 080201. [CrossRef]
26. Jafari, S.; Sprott, J.C. Simple chaotic flows with a line equilibrium. *Chaos Solitons Fractals* **2013**, *57*, 79–84. [CrossRef]
27. Dong, C. Dynamics, periodic orbit analysis, and circuit implementation of a new chaotic system with hidden attractor. *Fractal Fract.* **2022**, *6*, 190. [CrossRef]
28. Cang, S.; Li, Y.; Zhang, R.; Wang, Z. Hidden and self-excited coexisting attractors in a Lorenz-like system with two equilibrium points. *Nonlinear Dyn.* **2019**, *95*, 381–390. [CrossRef]
29. Wei, Z. Dynamical behaviors of a chaotic system with no equilibria. *Phys. Lett. A* **2011**, *376*, 102–108. [CrossRef]
30. Pham, V.T.; Volos, C.; Jafari, S.; Wei, Z.; Wang, X. Constructing a novel no-equilibrium chaotic system. *Int. J. Bifurc. Chaos* **2014**, *24*, 1450073. [CrossRef]
31. Huang, L.; Wang, Y.; Jiang, Y.; Lei, T. A novel memristor chaotic system with a hidden attractor and multistability and its implementation in a circuit. *Math. Probl. Eng.* **2021**, *2021*, 7457220. [CrossRef]
32. Jafari, S.; Ahmadi, A.; Khalaf, A.J.M.; Abdolmohammadi, H.R.; Pham, V.T.; Alsaadi, F.E. A new hidden chaotic attractor with extreme multi-stability. *AEU-Int. J. Electron. Commun.* **2018**, *89*, 131–135. [CrossRef]
33. Goufo, E.F.D. On chaotic models with hidden attractors in fractional calculus above power law. *Chaos Solitons Fractals* **2019**, *127*, 24–30. [CrossRef]
34. Cui, L.; Lu, M.; Ou, Q.; Duan, H.; Luo, W. Analysis and circuit implementation of fractional order multi-wing hidden attractors. *Chaos Solitons Fractals* **2020**, *138*, 109894. [CrossRef]
35. Clemente-López, D.; Tlelo-Cuautle, E.; de la Fraga, L.G.; de Jesús Rangel-Magdaleno, J.; Munoz-Pacheco, J.M. Poincaré maps for detecting chaos in fractional-order systems with hidden attractors for its Kaplan-Yorke dimension optimization. *AIMS Math.* **2022**, *7*, 5871–5894. [CrossRef]
36. Almatroud, A.O.; Matouk, A.E.; Mohammed, W.W.; Iqbal, N.; Alshammari, S. Self-excited and hidden chaotic attractors in Matouk's hyperchaotic systems. *Discret. Dyn. Nat. Soc.* **2022**, *2022*, 1–14. [CrossRef]

37. Yuan, F.; Wang, G.; Wang, X. Extreme multistability in a memristor-based multi-scroll hyper-chaotic system. *Chaos* **2016**, *26*, 073107. [CrossRef]
38. Bao, B.; Bao, H.; Wang, N.; Chen, M.; Xu, Q. Hidden extreme multistability in memristive hyperchaotic system. *Chaos Solitons Fractals* **2017**, *94*, 102–111. [CrossRef]
39. Wang, L.; Zhang, S.; Zeng, Y.; Li, Z. Generating hidden extreme multistability in memristive chaotic oscillator via microperturbation. *Electron. Lett.* **2018**, *54*, 808–810. [CrossRef]
40. Mezatio, B.A.; Motchongom, M.T.; Tekam, B.R.W.; Kengne, R.; Tchitnga, R.; Fomethe, A. A novel memristive 6D hyperchaotic autonomous system with hidden extreme multistability. *Chaos Solitons Fractals* **2019**, *120*, 100–115. [CrossRef]
41. Wang, Z.; Sun, W.; Wei, Z.; Zhang, S. Dynamics and delayed feedback control for a 3D jerk system with hidden attractor. *Nonlinear Dyn.* **2015**, *82*, 577–588. [CrossRef]
42. Li, P.; Zheng, T.; Li, C.; Wang, X.; Hu, W. A unique jerk system with hidden chaotic oscillation. *Nonlinear Dyn.* **2016**, *86*, 197–203. [CrossRef]
43. Bao, B.; Jiang, T.; Wang, G.; Jin, P.; Bao, H.; Chen, M. Two-memristor-based Chua's hyperchaotic circuit with plane equilibrium and its extreme multistability. *Nonlinear Dyn.* **2017**, *89*, 1157–1171. [CrossRef]
44. Singh, J.P.; Roy, B.K.; Jafari, S. New family of 4-D hyperchaotic and chaotic systems with quadric surfaces of equilibria. *Chaos Solitons Fractals* **2018**, *106*, 243–257. [CrossRef]
45. Lin, Y.; Wang, C.; Xu, H. Grid multi-scroll chaotic attractors in hybrid image encryption algorithm based on current conveyor. *Acta Phys. Sin.* **2012**, *61*, 240503. [CrossRef]
46. Sprott, J.C.; Li, C. Asymmetric bistability in the Rössler system. *Acta Phys. Pol. B* **2017**, *48*, 97. [CrossRef]
47. Li, C.; Sprott, J.C.; Zhang, X.; Chai, L.; Liu, Z. Constructing conditional symmetry in symmetric chaotic systems. *Chaos Solitons Fractals* **2022**, *155*, 111723. [CrossRef]
48. Li, C.; Sprott, J.C.; Hu, W.; Xu, Y. Infinite multistability in a self-reproducing chaotic system. *Int. J. Bifurc. Chaos* **2017**, *27*, 1750160. [CrossRef]
49. Wang, X.; Kuznetsov, N.V.; Chen, G. (Eds.) *Chaotic Systems with Multistability and Hidden Attractors; Emergence, Complexity and Computation*; Springer: Cham, Switzerland, 2021; Volume 40.
50. Wei, Z.; Yang, Q. Dynamical analysis of the generalized Sprott C system with only two stable equilibria. *Nonlinear Dyn.* **2012**, *68*, 543–554. [CrossRef]
51. Munoz-Pacheco, J.M.; Volos, C.; Serrano, F.E.; Jafari, S.; Kengne, J.; Rajagopal, K. Stabilization and synchronization of a complex hidden attractor chaotic system by backstepping technique. *Entropy* **2021**, *23*, 921. [CrossRef]
52. Strogatz, S.H. *Nonlinear Dynamics and Chaos: With Applications to Physics, Biology, Chemistry, and Engineering*; Perseus Books: Reading, MA, USA, 1994.
53. Lan, Y.; Cvitanović, P. Variational method for finding periodic orbits in a general flow. *Phys. Rev. E* **2004**, *69*, 016217. [CrossRef]
54. Press, W.H.; Teukolsky, S.A.; Veterling, W.T.; Flannery, B.P. *Numerical Recipes in C*; Cambridge University Press: Cambridge, UK, 1992.
55. Dong, C.; Liu, H.; Jie, Q.; Li, H. Topological classification of periodic orbits in the generalized Lorenz-type system with diverse symbolic dynamics. *Chaos Solitons Fractals* **2022**, *154*, 111686. [CrossRef]
56. Lan, Y.; Cvitanović, P. Unstable recurrent patterns in Kuramoto-Sivashinsky dynamics. *Phys. Rev. E* **2008**, *78*, 026208. [CrossRef]
57. Dong, C.; Liu, H.; Li, H. Unstable periodic orbits analysis in the generalized Lorenz-type system. *J. Stat. Mech. Theory Exp.* **2020**, *2020*, 073211. [CrossRef]
58. Artuso, R.; Aurell, E.; Cvitanović, P. Recycling of strange sets: I. Cycle expansions. *Nonlinearity* **1990**, *3*, 325–359. [CrossRef]
59. Lan, Y. Cycle expansions: From maps to turbulence. *Commun. Nonlinear Sci. Numer. Simul.* **2010**, *15*, 502–526. [CrossRef]
60. Hao, B.L.; Zheng, W.M. *Applied Symbolic Dynamics and Chaos*; World Scietic: Singapore, 1998; pp. 11–13.
61. Munoz-Pacheco, J.M.; Tlelo-Cuautle, E.; Toxqui-Toxqui, I.; Sanchez-Lopez, C.; Trejo-Guerra, R. Frequency limitations in generating multi-scroll chaotic attractors using CFOAs. *Int. J. Electron.* **2014**, *101*, 1559–1569. [CrossRef]
62. Sayed, W.S.; Roshdy, M.; Said, L.A.; Herencsar, N.; Radwan, A.G. CORDIC-based FPGA realization of a spatially rotating translational fractional-order multi-scroll grid chaotic system. *Fractal Fract.* **2022**, *6*, 432. [CrossRef]
63. Li, C.; Sprott, J.C. Variable-boostable chaotic flows. *Optik* **2016**, *127*, 10389–10398. [CrossRef]
64. Zhang, X.; Li, C.; Dong, E.; Zhao, Y.; Liu, Z. A conservative memristive system with amplitude control and offset boosting. *Int. J. Bifurc. Chaos* **2022**, *32*, 2250057. [CrossRef]
65. Dong, C. Dynamic analysis of a novel 3D chaotic system with hidden and coexisting attractors: Offset boosting, synchronization, and circuit realization. *Fractal Fract.* **2022**, *6*, 547. [CrossRef]
66. Munoz-Pacheco, J.M.; Zambrano-Serrano, E.; Volos, C.; Jafari, S.; Kengne, J.; Rajagopal, K. A new fractional-order chaotic system with different families of hidden and self-excited attractors. *Entropy* **2018**, *20*, 564. [CrossRef] [PubMed]
67. Munoz-Pacheco, J.M. Infinitely many hidden attractors in a new fractional-order chaotic system based on a fracmemristor. *Eur. Phys. J. Spec. Top.* **2019**, *228*, 2185–2196. [CrossRef]

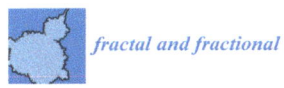

Article

Spatial Series and Fractal Analysis Associated with Fracture Behaviour of UO₂ Ceramic Material

Maria-Alexandra Paun [1,2,*], Vladimir-Alexandru Paun [3] and Viorel-Puiu Paun [4,5]

[1] School of Engineering, Swiss Federal Institute of Technology (EPFL), 1015 Lausanne, Switzerland
[2] Division Radio Monitoring and Equipment, Section Market Access and Conformity, Federal Office of Communications OFCOM, 2501 Bienne, Switzerland
[3] Five Rescue Research Laboratory, 75004 Paris, France
[4] Department of Physics, Faculty of Applied Sciences, University Politehnica of Bucharest, 060042 Bucharest, Romania
[5] Academy of Romanian Scientists, 050094 Bucharest, Romania
* Correspondence: maria_paun2003@yahoo.com

Abstract: SEM micrographs of the fracture surface for UO_2 ceramic materials have been analysed. In this paper, we introduce some algorithms and develop a computer application based on the time-series method. Utilizing the embedding technique of phase space, the attractor is reconstructed. The fractal dimension, lacunarity, and autocorrelation dimension average value have been calculated.

Keywords: ceramics; SEM micrographs; fractal analysis; time series; fractal dimension; lacunarity; autocorrelation dimension

Citation: Paun, M.-A.; Paun, V.-A.; Paun, V.-P. Spatial Series and Fractal Analysis Associated with Fracture Behaviour of UO₂ Ceramic Material. *Fractal Fract.* **2022**, *6*, 595. https://doi.org/10.3390/fractalfract6100595

Academic Editors: Zine El Abiddine Fellah and António Lopes

Received: 17 August 2022
Accepted: 10 October 2022
Published: 14 October 2022

Publisher's Note: MDPI stays neutral with regard to jurisdictional claims in published maps and institutional affiliations.

Copyright: © 2022 by the authors. Licensee MDPI, Basel, Switzerland. This article is an open access article distributed under the terms and conditions of the Creative Commons Attribution (CC BY) license (https://creativecommons.org/licenses/by/4.0/).

1. Introduction

The uranium chemical element has the capital letter U as its symbol, and its atomic number is 92. Statistically speaking, it constitutes three important isotopes that may definitely be found in nature: ^{238}U (99.28% abundance), ^{235}U (0.71% abundance), and ^{234}U (0.0054% abundance). Classified in the periodic table as an actinide, uranium is generally a solid body at room temperature [1]. Uranium is a naturally radioactive element, from the physics viewpoint. It powers nuclear reactors in the form of nuclear fuel and helps to make atomic bombs (still improperly called), but more precisely, named nuclear bombs, because fission is a nuclear process.

Uranium-235 is an isotope of uranium that makes up about 0.71% of naturally existing uranium in nature. Unlike the predominant isotope uranium-238 (fertile material), uranium-235 is a fissile material; that is, they can support a nuclear chain reaction and a nuclear fission, respectively. Moreover, uranium-235 is the only fissile isotope that exists in nature as a primordial nuclide.

At first sight, real ceramic materials may be interpreted as inorganic and non-metallic materials. They are typically crystalline in nature (but may also contain a combination of glassy and crystalline phases) and are compounds formed among metallic and non-metallic elements. Chemically speaking, they are materials with atomic and ionic bonds, of which the complex hyaline structure is obtained by sintering. This is basically responsible for many of the properties of ceramics [2–4]. The word ceramic comes from the Greek word keramicos, which in direct translation, means burnt clay. In conclusion, being typically a crystalline construction, it can be considered traditionally as a mixed compound mostly made of metallic and non-metallic elements, so a composite material.

Ceramic materials are usually fabricated by the application of heat (at high temperatures) upon processed clays and other natural crude materials (especially in powder form) to shape a rigid solid product. Ceramic final products that reasonably utilize rocks and minerals as a starting point must endure certain processing in order to command the particle size; potion purity; particle size repartition; and finally, the heterogeneity of the mixture. These important characteristics play a major role in the total properties of the completed ceramics. From a chemical point of view, ceramic materials are mainly metallic and non-metallic oxides. In conclusion, the clays from which they are obtained are part of the large category of alumino-silicates, substances present in a high percentage in the Earth's crust [2]. Combustion results in a crystalline internal structure, with covalent and electrovalent (ionic) chemical bonds between the constituent atoms and molecules, but we do not wish to go into such details here.

Worth knowing is also the fact that, when uranium dioxide (UO_2), recognized as nuclear fuel, is stuffed with supplementary ions of oxygen in the meshes of the network, it can form nonstoichiometric compounds (e.g., UO_{2+x}), of which the composition may change with the function of exterior environmental conditions, among which we enumerate temperature itself and the partial pressure of oxygen. The fracture comportment of a sintered ceramic UO_2 substance has been studied in light of microstructural (micro porosity, grain size, etc.) parameters, with everything being in the function of the most adequate composition delivered and the final architecture. Utilizing SEM images as an investigation method, the fracture properties have been evaluated and compared for different microstructural conditions present in the same sample of solid ceramic materials and in a sintered UO_2 pellet specimen. As a general conclusion, we can consider that the fracture strength in the low-density area was superior in contrast to the that of the high-density area. Among other things, this was assigned to fissure-type deflection and bifurcation at the grain boundary, expected as owed to the porosity presence. This paper realizes an investigation of the uranium dioxide SEM pictures by utilizing the time series evaluation procedures and fractal analysis, a natural prolongation of a usual research executed before but on ductile materials [5–8].

Being justified by recent developments in inferential statistical analysis procedures for chaotic modular processes and by the new concept of spatial chaos, we introduce a continuation of deterministic boarding of the structural microscopic study of ceramic integral materials.

The work in this paper is highlighted in four sections. The first section introduces the background of the use of uranium dioxide (UO_2) as nuclear fuel and ceramic materials in general. The second section focuses on providing theoretical support regarding the fractal dimension, lacunarity, and time (spatial) series. The third section introduces the results obtained and elaborates on them in a discussion. Finally, the paper concludes in the fourth and last section devoted to the conclusions.

2. Theoretical Background in Brief

2.1. Fractal Dimension and Lacunarity

The fractal-image-specific feature highlighted here is the fractal dimension, conditioned by the following formula:

$$D = \lim_{\varepsilon \to 0}\left(\frac{\ln N}{\ln \varepsilon}\right) \quad (1)$$

where N is the cell number and ε is the cell size [9,10].

The lacunarity numerical value is computed in accordance with the following formula:

$$\Lambda = \left(\frac{\sigma}{\mu}\right)^2 \quad (2)$$

when σ is the standard deviation of the mass and μ is also the mass average value out of the total picture [11,12]. To estimate the fractal dimension, it is necessary to compose a graphic and afresh; to calculate the lacunarity, the graphical algorithm of least squares must be utilized [13,14].

2.2. Time (Spatial) Series

Let T be a dynamic system in the classical sense. More precisely, T is said to be such a mathematical object (in fact a system) if there exists a map $f: X \rightarrow X$, such that

$$T: N \times X \rightarrow X, \ T(n,x) = (f \circ f \circ \ldots \circ f)(x) = f^n(x) \tag{3}$$

Let $F: X \rightarrow R$ be a map with real determinations, which can be considered a mathematical measure of physical state space in Lagrange sense. If the variables $t, \tau \in S$ can be appreciated as being fixed (τ is named time delay) and $x \in X$ is a stationary state, then a repeated measurement succession

$$F(x), F(T(t+\tau,x)), F(T(t+2\tau,x)), \ F(T(t+3\tau,x)), \ldots, F(T(t+(d-1)\tau,x)) \tag{4}$$

can be named as a time series (beginning with (t, x)) correlated to T [15,16].

For the determined state $x \in X$, a correlated time (spatial) series with the discrete dynamical system (see definition above) is written as

$$F(x), F(f(x)), \ldots, F\left(f^{n-1}(x)\right) \tag{5}$$

By definition, we call being an attractor (or attraction group) for the system T a mathematical object that has the following qualities:

(1) $K \subset X$ is a nonempty set;
(2) K is closed;
(3) K is invariant, i.e., $T(x) \subset X$, for all $x \in K$.

Moreover, it is stated that there is a vicinity such that

$$\lim_{t \rightarrow \infty} d(T(t,x), K) = 0, \ \text{for all } x \in U \tag{6}$$

Takens Embedding Theorem [17] is the principal outcome that theoretically permits attractor reconstruction for a physical dynamical system, which begins from the numerical data of one algebraic time series. Thus, if K is a dense invariant set of T and if b is the box-counting fractal dimension of K, then the map

$$H: K \rightarrow R^{2b+1} \tag{7}$$

is described by

$$H(x) = F(T(t,x)), F(T(t-\tau,x)), \ldots, F(T(t-2b\tau,x)) \tag{8}$$

The function defined above is generically injective. Analytically speaking, a property is called generic if the mentioned quality on a set that comprises a countable intersection of open dense sets is true [18,19]. A spatial series is, by definition, a suite of observations made on an orderly variable with regard to two structural coordinates. However, in such data, usually, the necessary statistical independence is absent. Regarding spatial series in statistics, we must think about random spatial series and how such a data series works mathematically. A spatial series, but mostly a random spatial series, is an assembly of casual variables $F(x^1, x^2, \ldots, x^n)$, called random variables, a set of functions depending on certain spatial coordinates $(x^1, x^2, \ldots, \underline{x}^n)$.

We try to construct a statistical series of the second order, in other words, a series for which $(x^1, x^2, \ldots, \underline{x}^n)$ argument fluctuates only on an ordinary Cartesian grid/lattice. Utilizing the appropriations of the linear (Hilbert) space connected to the series of data, the notions of novelty and a complete nondeterministic series are highlighted [15].

Regarding the comportment of a time (spatial) series (in other words, the quality of randomness), this one can be investigated by calculating the autocorrelation function value, which is an estimate of the influence of past states on the future state [16,17]. As far as that goes, a discrete dynamical system T interpreted by the map $f: X \to X$, the autocorrelation function formula associated with the spatial series $F(x), F(f(x)), \ldots, F(f^p(x))$ is determined as follows:

$$C(n) = \frac{\sum_{i=0}^{p-n} (F \circ f^i - m)(x) \cdot (F \circ f^{i+n} - m)(x)}{\sum_{i=0}^{p-n} (F \circ f^i)^2 (x)} \qquad (9)$$

where m is the time-average function:

$$m = \frac{\sum_{i=0}^{p} (F \circ f^i)(x)}{p+1} \qquad (10)$$

2.3. SEM Picture Exploration

Chaotic statistical comportment has been proven in numerous physical, chemical, economic, and biological natural processes. Today, just two statistical chaos physics concepts are unanimously accepted. The primal conception is the temporal chaos for which any function of variables in phase space are time-dependent. The second conception, the spatial statistical chaos concept, indicates a chaos state of these data with respect to spatial coordinates. This philosophical vision opens the way for accession to nonlinear deterministic procedures/technics of spatiotemporal phenomena [16].

Even though fundamental elements of ceramic thermo-mechanical comportment are recognized, the nature, interplay, and multitude of physical, chemical, and ambient variables implicated in the engendering of a true microstructure cannot be exactly defined. Therefore, it seems legitimate to adopt a viable viewpoint and to consider the micro fractures as various textures, in fact veritable 'black boxes', which have been caused by two independent processes, respectively, a stochastic process (in a large sense) or another process related to matter manifestation in the format of deterministic spatial chaos [20]. As a primary check, if the studied sample could be an expression of deterministic chaos, we can be mastering methods of classical time series analysis found at disposition, which refer to an estimation of the power spectrum and autocorrelation function, in principle. To come into possession of particular characteristics of the system, it is necessary for the attractor reconstruction techniques to be applied, which allows for estimations of the Lyapunov exponent and of the correlation dimension.

For the study of UO_2 SEM pictures, we used computer programming initially created for metallic or alloy materials but subsequently excellently adapted to ceramic materials, a software application that generates a time series associated with the image, then reconstructs the associated attractor, and finally computes its autocorrelation dimension [21]. The procedure for investigating a SEM picture (micrograph) is debuted by loading an image bitmap version in the computer software application used. The first step in our consideration is to generate the weighted fractal dimensions map (WFDM) through which the potential modified structures themselves are revealed (conformable to a precedent article [15]). The second step to follow is to produce a real spatial series for a picture-selected zone, as follows: the initial picture is cut into slices that are approximatively 12–16 pixels deep; by placing all these fragments/pieces together, we procure an entire tape/strip. The spatial series $s(t)$ is acquired by calculating the mean value of the grey level for every pixel column within the tape. The investigation of these nonlinear data suites starts with the attractor reconstruction by embedding the spatial series in an upper dimensional phase space. We establish a reasonable time delay $\tau > 0$ from the beginning and then, continuing, for a determined embedding dimension d, we take into account the collection/set

$$s(t), s(t+\tau), s(t+2\tau), \ldots, s(t+(d-1)\tau) \qquad (11)$$

which is assimilated to a formal point in a pseudo phase space and immediately constructed (the series sampling procedure).

In the end, we obtain the attractor by connecting these points that are conformable to their succession. The attractor integral correlation $C(r)$, as a distance function, is the expectation that any two points from a phase space is separated by a Euclidian interval/distance less than or equal to r. It can now be assumed that $C(r)$ is a power-type function of r, of which the exponent designated by D is mostly assimilated with the autocorrelation dimension. The value of D is close to the regression line slope related to autocorrelation function $C(r)$. This method of calculation is reiterated for different embedding dimension values. We close this routine action with the autocorrelation dimension plot; with a function of the embedding dimension value; and finally, by calculating its regression line slope [22–27].

3. Results and Discussion

Further on, we offer an example of the procedure to investigate the SEM pictures of a UO_2 ceramic material [23]. We emphasise/mention that the sorting of the micrographs with the referenced areas was executed as stated by the WFDM method [15]. Conforming to the mentioned procedure, three sets of characteristic images are studied as much as possible [25,26].

Step 1. Study of the entire picture.

We study the images enclosed in a yellow rectangle, practically the entire picture. In Figure 1, the original SEM image and an entire selected area are presented, while in Figure 2, the graphical attractor reconstruction, in two and three dimensions, is shown.

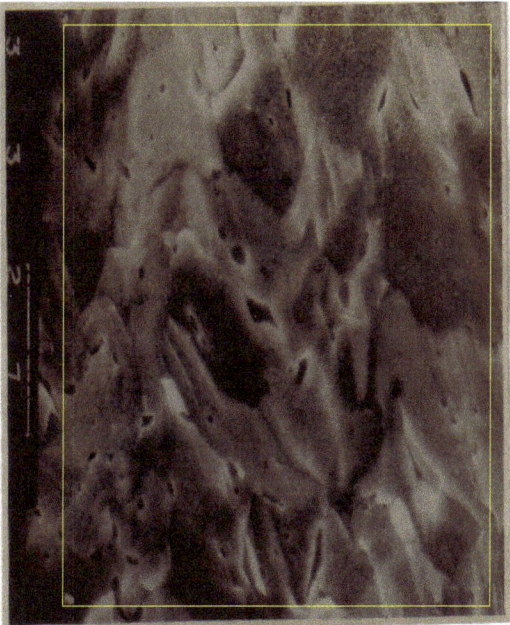

Figure 1. Original image and a selected area.

Figure 2 shows the attractor reconstruction [20] for the rectangle with yellow sides of normal area along with a considerable area with microcracks and prominent breakage, conformable to Figure 1. Both attractor reconstructions are presented. In embedding dimension 2, some points are observed, and in embedding dimension 3, some broken lines are noticed [16,17].

First, we survey the spatial series generated by the entire picture (Figure 3).

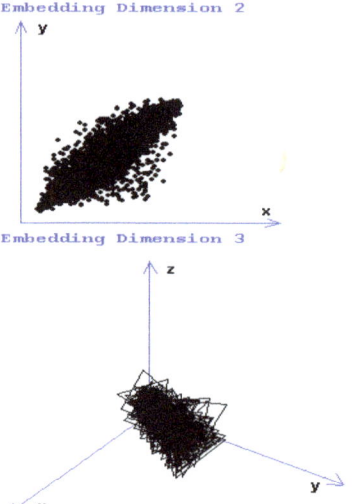

Figure 2. Attractor reconstruction.

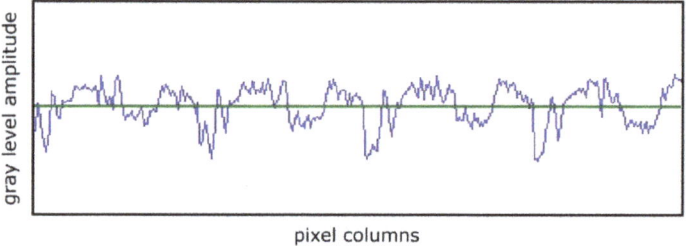

Figure 3. The time series generated by the selected area in Figure 1.

In Figure 3, the continuous green line placed horizontally represents the series average value over the entire time considered.

According to the algorithm, further on, we will study a modified area (Figure 4) and gravity poles are determined (Figure 5).

Figure 4. The selection of the modified area (according to WFDM).

Figure 5. The gravity poles of the modified area.

From Figure 6, we can determine the slope of the autocorrelation dimension versus the embedding dimension for the modified area.

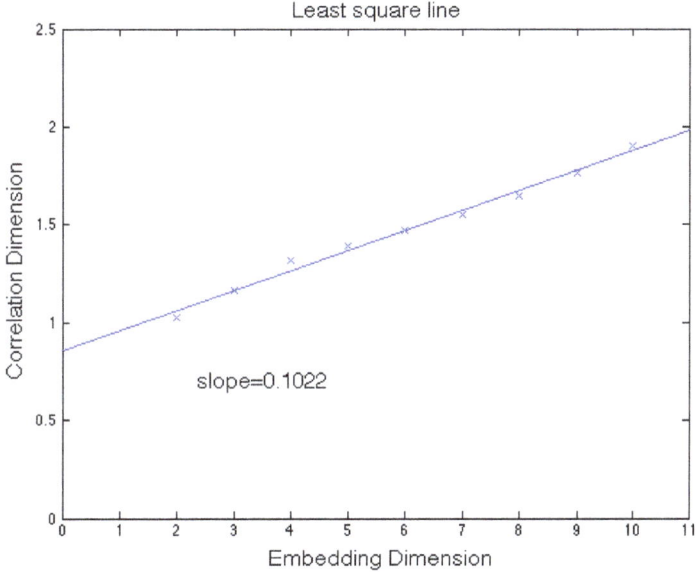

Figure 6. The autocorrelation dimension versus the embedding dimension for the modified area.

The graphic of the entire area autocorrelation, in Figure 6, representing the correlation dimension versus the embedding dimension, shows the slope computation. The correlation dimension versus the embedding dimension slope is 0.1022.

In Figure 7, the primary processing of the selected image 1 is depicted. This suite contains a set of three images, more specifically, from left to right, the original image (the portion in the yellow border), the grayscale version, as well as the grayscale version without luminance.

In Figure 8, the secondary processing of the selected image 1, including the binarized version and the application of the mask, are presented.

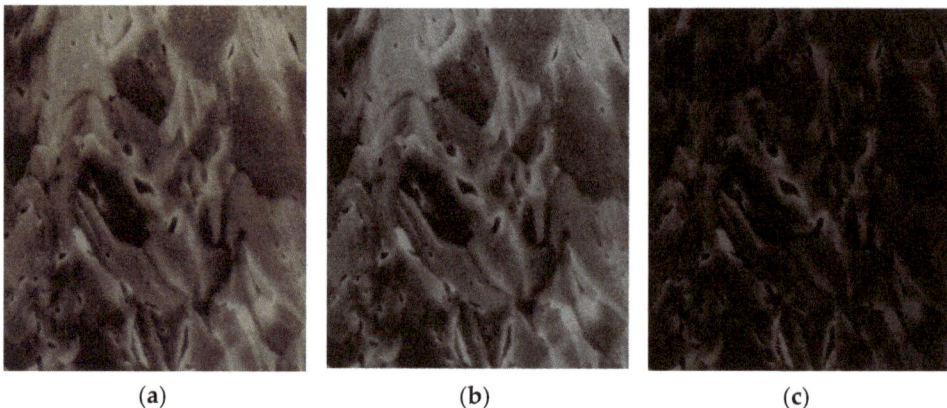

Figure 7. Primary processing of the selected image 1: (**a**) original image (the portion in the yellow border); (**b**) the grayscale version; and (**c**) the grayscale version without luminance.

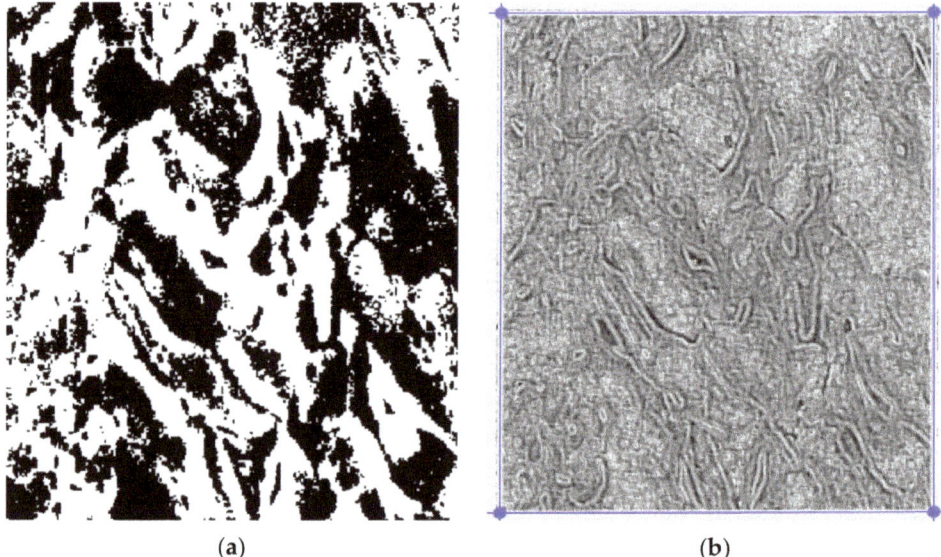

Figure 8. Secondary processing of the selected image 1: (**a**) binarized version; (**b**) application of the mask. A threshold of 25 was used for binarization.

Following the numerical evaluations with the appropriate software of the selected image, the values of fractal dimension $D = 1.8220$, standard deviation $s = \pm\sqrt{\sigma^2} = \pm 0.3440$, and lacunarity $\Lambda = 0.0357$ were obtained, as in Table 1.

Table 1. Calculation of fractal parameters.

Name	Fractal Dimension	Standard Deviation	Lacunarity
Image 1	1.8220	±0.3440	0.0357

Figure 9 (see below) represents the three-dimensional graph of the voxel representation for image 1.

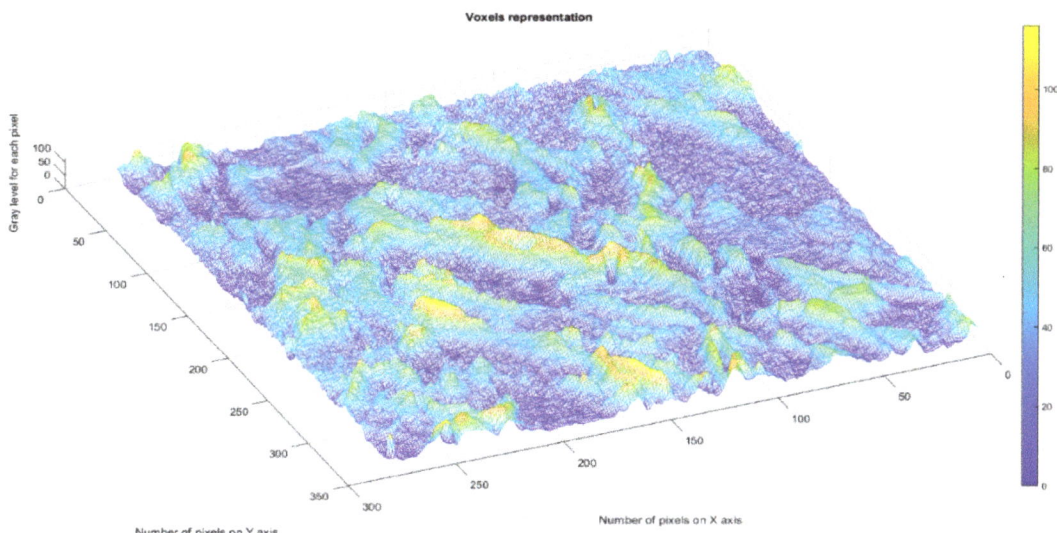

Figure 9. Voxels representation for image 1.

Step 2. The study of the selected zones images from the entire picture (according to Figure 10).

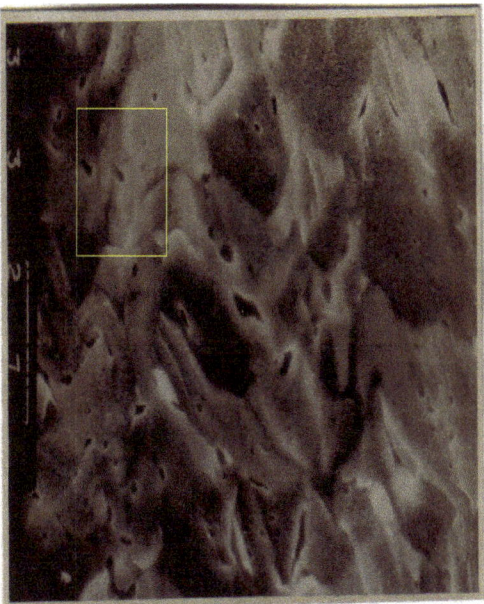

Figure 10. The first distinct zone selection.

In Figure 10, we selected one distinct zone, the yellow rectangular frame zone, considered with different structures from a first visual analysis.

Figure 11 shows the attractor reconstruction [20] for the rectangle with yellow sides of normal area along with a considerable area with microcracks and prominent breakage, conformable to Figure 10. Both attractor reconstructions are presented. In embedding dimension 2, some points are observed, and in embedding dimension 3, some broken lines are noticed [16,17].

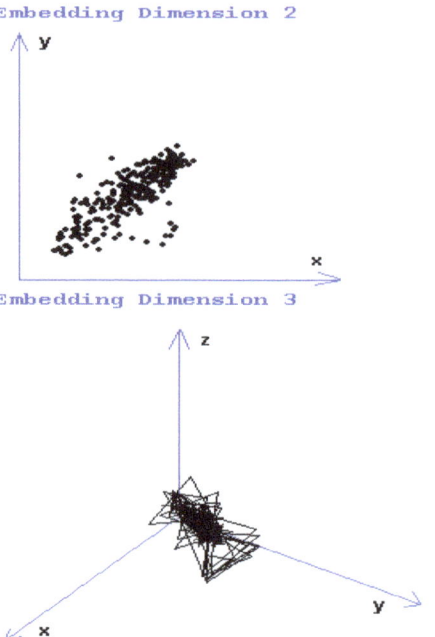

Figure 11. Attractor reconstruction.

Further on, in Figure 12, the selection of the modified area with the application of WFDM for Figure 10 is presented. Staying on the same subject, the gravity poles of the modified area for Figure 10 are showcased in Figure 13.

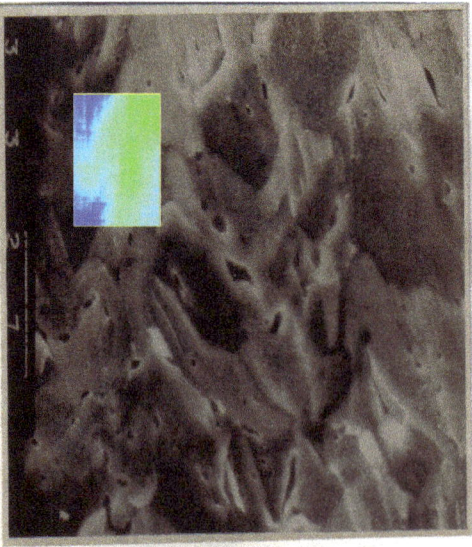

Figure 12. The selection of the modified area (WFDM) for Figure 10.

Figure 13. The gravity poles of the modified area for Figure 10.

Second, we study the time series generated by the picture associated with the selected modified area in Figure 14.

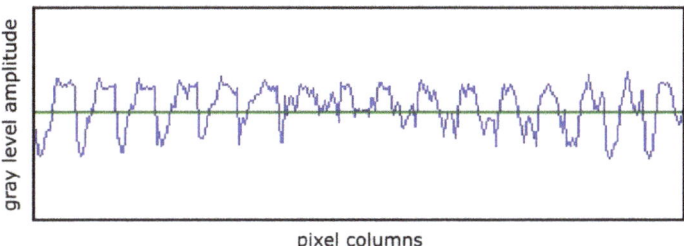

Figure 14. The time series generated by the selected modified area for Figure 10.

In Figure 14, the continuous green line placed horizontally represents the series average value over the entire time considered.

From Figure 15, we can determine the slope of the autocorrelation dimension versus the embedding dimension for the modified area (WFDM for Figure 10).

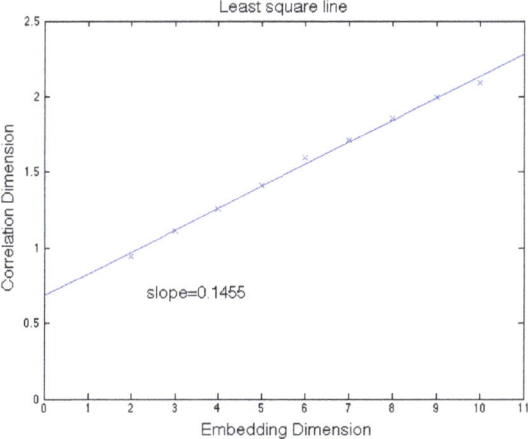

Figure 15. The autocorrelation dimension versus the embedding dimension for the modified area.

The graphic of the modified area (WFDM for Figure 10) autocorrelation, in Figure 15, representing the correlation dimension versus the embedding dimension, shows the slope computation. The correlation dimension versus the embedding dimension slope is 0.1455.

In Figure 16, the primary processing of the selected image 2 is depicted. This suite contains a set of three images, more specifically, from left to right, the original image (the portion in the yellow border), the grayscale version, as well as the grayscale version without luminance.

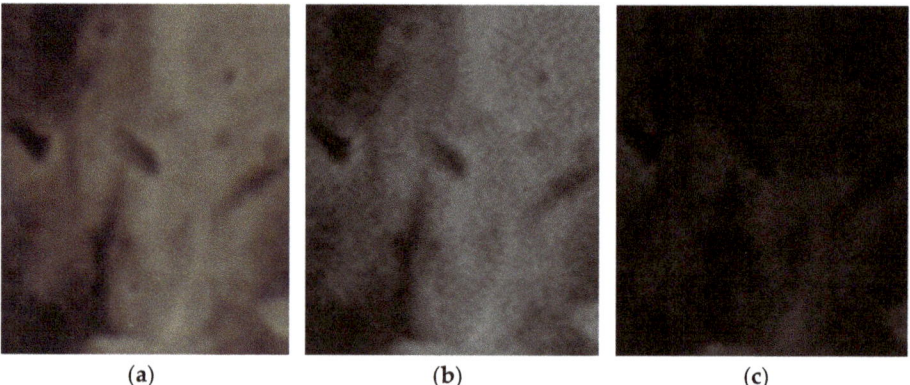

Figure 16. Primary processing of the selected image 2: (**a**) original image (the portion in the yellow border); (**b**) the grayscale version; and (**c**) the grayscale version without luminance.

In Figure 17, the secondary processing of the selected image 2, including the binarized version and the application of the mask, are presented.

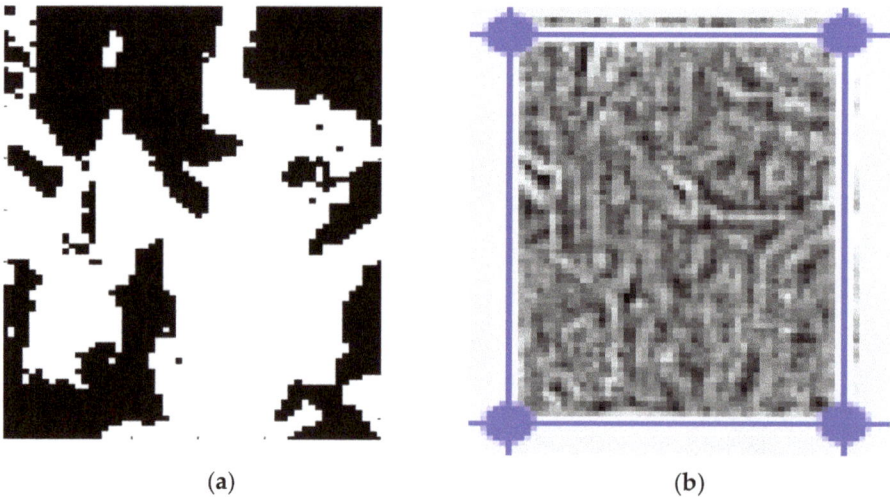

Figure 17. Secondary processing of the selected image 2: (**a**) binarized version; (**b**) application of the mask. A threshold of 25 was used for binarization.

Following the numerical evaluations with the appropriate software of the selected image, the values of fractal dimension $D = 1.7751$, standard deviation $s = \pm\sqrt{\sigma^2} = \pm 0.3363$, and lacunarity $\Lambda = 0.0359$ were obtained, as in Table 2.

Table 2. Calculation of fractal parameters.

Name	Fractal Dimension	Standard Deviation	Lacunarity
Image 2	1.7751	±0.3363	0.0359

Figure 18 (see below) represents the three-dimensional graph of the voxel representation for image 2.

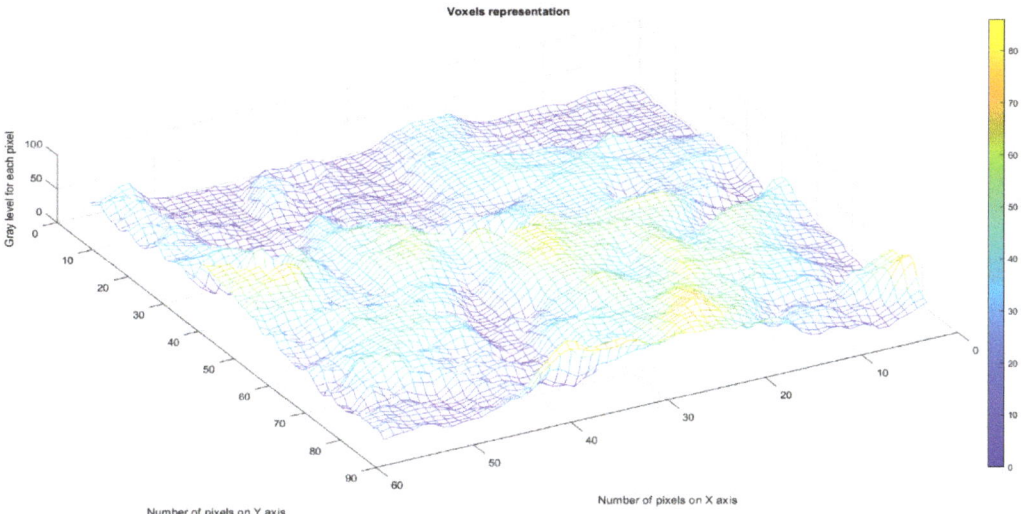

Figure 18. Voxels representation for image 2.

Step 3. The study of the second chosen zone image according to Figure 19.

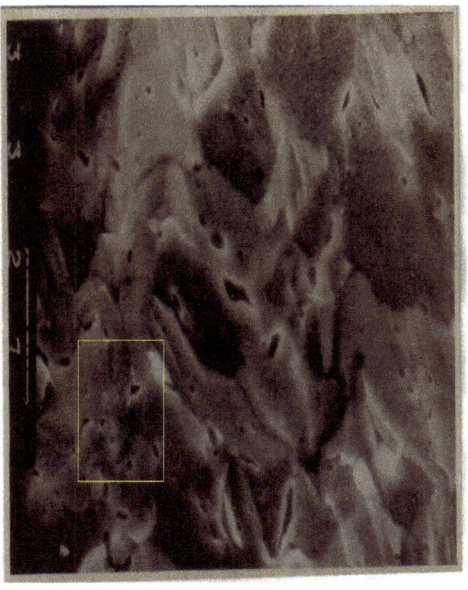

Figure 19. Image and a selected area for the second distinct zone.

Figure 20 shows the attractor reconstruction [20] for the rectangle with yellow sides of a normal area along with a considerable area with microcracks and prominent breakage, conformable to Figure 19. Both attractor reconstructions are presented. In embedding dimension 2, some points are observed, and in embedding dimension 3, some broken lines are noticed [16,17].

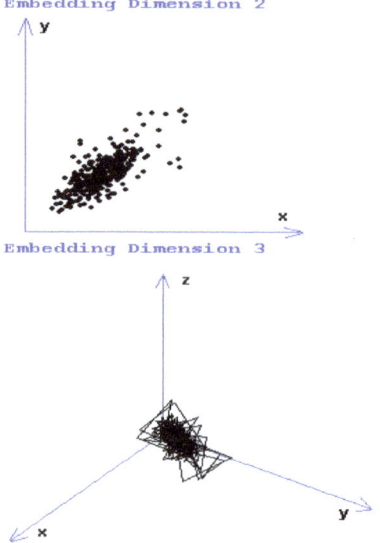

Figure 20. Attractor reconstruction.

Further on, in Figure 21, the selection of the modified area with the application of WFDM for Figure 19 is presented. Staying on the same subject, the gravity poles of the modified area for Figure 19 are showcased in Figure 22.

Second, we study the time series generated by the picture associated with the selected modified area in Figure 23.

From Figure 23, we can determine the slope of the autocorrelation dimension versus the embedding dimension for the modified area (WFDM for Figure 19).

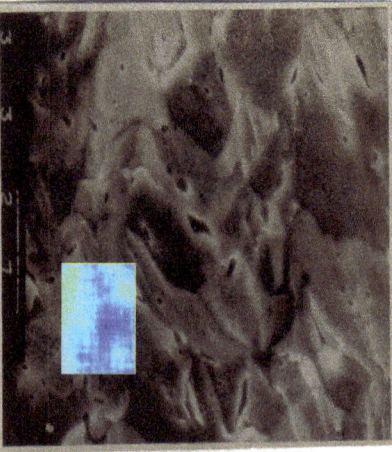

Figure 21. The selection of the modified area (WFDM) for Figure 19.

Figure 22. The gravity poles of the modified area for Figure 19.

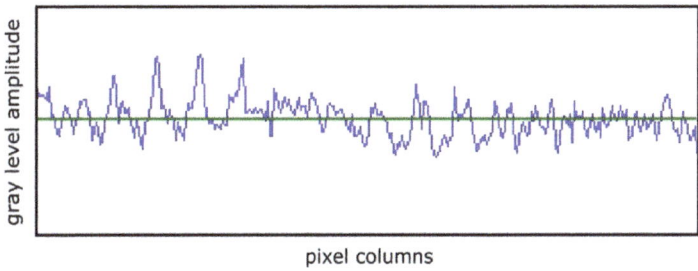

Figure 23. The time series generated by the selected modified area for Figure 19.

In Figure 23, the continuous green line placed horizontally represents the series average value over the entire time considered.

The graphic of the modified area (WFDM for Figure 19) autocorrelation, in Figure 24, representing the correlation dimension versus the embedding dimension, shows the slope computation. The correlation dimension versus the embedding dimension slope is 0.1304.

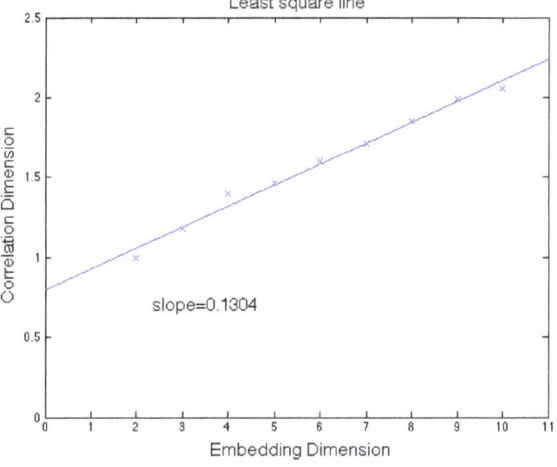

Figure 24. The autocorrelation dimension versus the embedding dimension for the modified area.

In Figure 25, the primary processing of the selected image 3 is depicted. This suite contains a set of three images, more specifically, from left to right, the original image (the portion in the yellow border), the grayscale version, as well as the grayscale version without luminance.

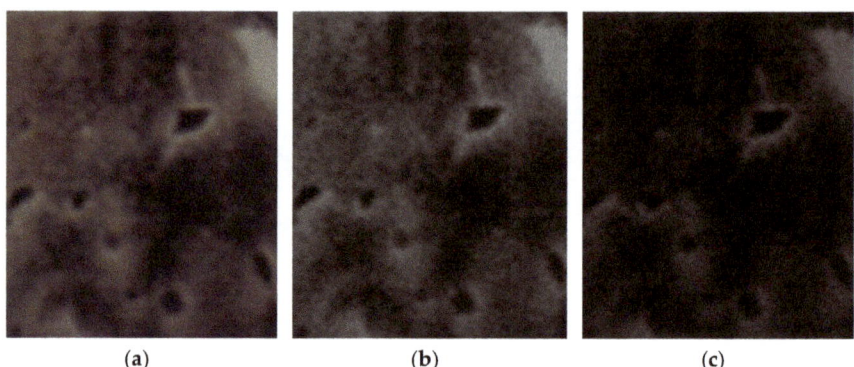

Figure 25. Primary processing of the selected image 3: (**a**) original image (the portion in the yellow border); (**b**) the grayscale version; and (**c**) the grayscale version without luminance.

In Figure 26, the secondary processing of the selected image 3, including the binarized version and the application of the mask, is presented.

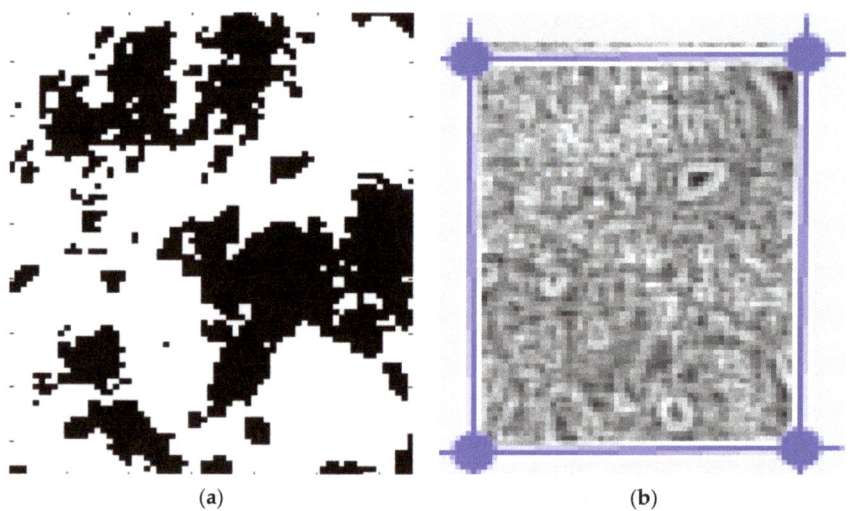

Figure 26. Secondary processing of the selected image 3: (**a**) binarized version; (**b**) application of the mask. A threshold of 25 was used for binarization.

Following the numerical evaluations with the appropriate software of the selected image, the values of fractal dimension $D = 1.8103$, standard deviation $s = \pm\sqrt{\sigma^2} = \pm 0.3508$, and lacunarity $\Lambda = 0.0375$ were obtained, as in Table 3.

Table 3. Calculation of fractal parameters.

Name	Fractal Dimension	Standard Deviation	Lacunarity
Image 3	1.8103	±0.3508	0.0375

Figure 27 (see below) represents the three-dimensional graph of the voxel representation for image 3.

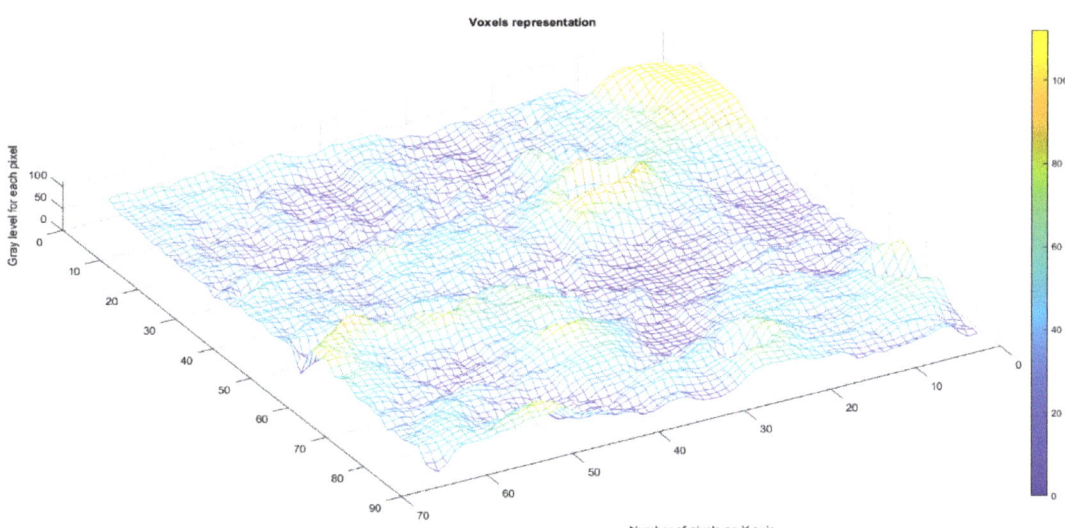

Figure 27. Voxels representation for image 3.

Final Discussions

The substance of the work refers to the fact that the deformation of ceramics is different from that of metals and alloys, being small compared to that of metals, which means that they are fragile substances, unlike metals and alloys, which are ductile substances, characterized by consistent deformation at the same stress. In addition, the break develops at different levels of the loading load (tension); that is, the break in ceramics is made at a high level of stress, with an order of magnitude higher than the break in metals and alloys. We will continue to detail the differences in deformation and fracturing behaviour for ceramics and their connection with the fractal dimension of the image and its lacunarity.

We will present a mini explanation of the writing of this study below. The paper proposes a quantitative analysis of the SEM images of the fracture surface of UO_2, using the fractal dimension of the image and its lacunarity. This information, obtained through the fractal analysis, is closely related to highlighting the type of fracture (brittle in our case) and the microcracks produced in the material. As can be seen, there is a direct connection with the microdeformations present on the image in the area without significant tearing of the material and a directly proportional increase in the lacunarity in the area with the rupture produced.

The method was explained above, but we also want to make a presentation of the things performed to put the method into operation. We have examined the fracture surfaces of two distinct areas with different microstructures to test for fractal behaviour. The zones are also differentiated by a simple visual observation, as they have distinct aspects due to the fact that one of the zones is unaffected by the breaking process, while the second zone is distinct due to the fact that it is a specific breaking zone.

A slit island analysis was used to determine the fractal dimension, D, of successively sectioned fracture surfaces. We found a correlation between increasing the fractional part of the fractal dimension and increasing toughness. In other words, as the toughness increases, the fracture surface increases in roughness. However, more than just a measure of roughness, the applicability of fractal geometry to a fracture implies a mechanism for generation of the fracture surface. The results presented here imply that brittle fracture is a fractal process; this means that we should be able to determine processes on the atomic scale by observing the macroscopic scale by finding the generator shape and the scheme for generation inherent in the fractal process. In addition, we attempt to relate the fractal dimension to fracture toughness. We also show that, in general, the fractal dimension increases with increasing fracture toughness.

4. Conclusions

The SEM micrographs of the fracture surface for a ceramic UO_2 material, using the fractal analysis technique and time (spatial) series, have been investigated.

For the SEM picture analysis, a software application that generates a time series associated with the image, and then reconstructs the attractor and computes its autocorrelation dimension was developed.

The present study was carried out on a statistically sufficient number of SEM micrographs, treated according to the procedure of modified areas. To avoid augmentation in the article size, only one integral SEM picture has been presented from which one normal area (first zone) and another one corresponding to a modified area (second zone) have been selected.

The fractal dimension of the entire picture is $D = 1.8220 \pm 0.3440$ and lacunarity is $\Lambda = 0.0357$, and for the first zone (normal area), fractal dimension is $D = 1.7751 \pm 0.3363$ and lacunarity is $\Lambda = 0.0359$. For the second zone (modified area), the fractal dimension $D = 1.8103 \pm 0.3508$ and lacunarity $\Lambda = 0.0375$ were obtained.

The average of the autocorrelation dimension for entire picture is 0.1023. The average of the autocorrelation dimension for the normal area of the first zone is 0.1455. The average of the autocorrelation dimension for the modified area of the second zone is 0.1304.

Author Contributions: Conceptualization, V.-P.P. and M.-A.P.; methodology, V.-P.P.; software, V.-A.P.; validation, V.-P.P., M.-A.P. and V.-A.P.; formal analysis, V.-P.P., M.-A.P. and V.-A.P.; investigation, V.-A.P. and M.-A.P.; resources, V.-A.P. and M.-A.P.; data curation, V.-A.P.; writing—original draft preparation, V.-P.P.; writing—review and editing, M.-A.P. and V.-P.P.; visualization, V.-A.P.; supervision, V.-P.P.; project administration, V.-P.P. All authors have read and agreed to the published version of the manuscript.

Funding: This research received no external funding.

Data Availability Statement: The data used to support the findings of this study cannot be accessed due to commercial confidentiality.

Acknowledgments: The co-authors M.A. Paun, V.A. Paun, and V.P. Paun thank Jenica Paun, for her continuous kind support.

Conflicts of Interest: The authors declare no conflict of interest.

References

1. Lounsbury, M. The Natural Abundances of the Uranium Isotopes. *Can. J. Chem.* **1956**, *34*, 259–264. [CrossRef]
2. Roberts, J.T.A.; Ueda, Y. Influence of Porosity on Deformation and Fracture of UO_2. *J. Am. Ceram. Soc.* **1972**, *55*, 117–124. [CrossRef]
3. Kapoor, K.; Ahmad, A.; Laksminarayana, A.; Hemanth Rao, G.V.S. Fracture properties of sintered UO_2 ceramic pellets with duplex microstructure. *J. Nucl. Mater.* **2007**, *366*, 87–98. [CrossRef]
4. Canon, R.F.; Roberts, J.T.A.; Beals, R.J. Deformation of UO_2 at High Temperatures. *J. Am. Ceram. Soc.* **2006**, *54*, 105–112. [CrossRef]
5. Moan, G.D.; Rudling, P. (Eds.) *Zirconium in the Nuclear Industry, 13th International Symposium, ASTM-STP 1423*; ASTM International: West Conshohocken, PA, USA, 2002; pp. 673–701.
6. Kaddour, D.; Frechinet, S.; Gourgues, A.F.; Brachet, J.C.; Portier, L.; Pineau, A. Experimental determination of creep properties of Zirconium alloys together with phase transformation. *Scr. Mater.* **2004**, *51*, 515–519. [CrossRef]
7. Brenner, R.; Béchade, J.L.; Bacroix, B. Thermal creep of Zr–Nb1%–O alloys: Experimental analysis and micromechanical modelling. *J. Nucl. Mater.* **2002**, *305*, 175–186. [CrossRef]
8. Olteanu, M.; Paun, V.P.; Tanase, M. Fractal analysis of zircaloy-4 fracture surface, Conference on Equipments, Installations and Process Engineering. *Rev. De Chim.* **2005**, *56*, 97–100.
9. Datseris, G.; Kottlarz, I.; Braun, A.P.; Parlitz, U. Estimating the fractal dimension: A comparative review and open source implementations. *arXiv* **2021**, arXiv:2109.05937v1.

10. Nichita, M.V.; Paun, M.A.; Paun, V.A.; Paun, V.P. Fractal Analysis of Brain Glial Cells. Fractal Dimension and Lacunarity. *Univ. Politeh. Buchar. Sci. Bull. Ser. A Appl. Math. Phys.* **2019**, *81*, 273–284.
11. Bordescu, D.; Paun, M.A.; Paun, V.A.; Paun, V.P. Fractal Analysis of Neuroimagistics. Lacunarity Degree, a Precious Indicator in the Detection of Alzheimer's Disease. *Univ. Politeh. Buchar. Sci. Bull. Ser. A Appl. Math. Phys.* **2018**, *80*, 309–320.
12. Peitgen, H.-O.; Jurgens, H.; Saupe, D. Chaos and Fractals. In *New Frontiers of Science*; Springer: Berlin/Heidelberg, Germany, 1992.
13. Mandelbrot, B.B.; Passoja, D.E.; Paullay, A.J. Fractal character of fracture surfaces of metals. *Nature* **1984**, *308*, 721–722. [CrossRef]
14. Mandelbrot, B. *Fractal Geometry of Nature*; Freeman: New York, NY, USA, 1983; pp. 25–57.
15. Paun, V.P. Fractal surface analysis of Zircaloy-4 SEM micrographs using the time-series method. *Cent. Eur. J. Phys.* **2009**, *7*, 264–269.
16. Takens, F. Detecting strange attractors in turbulence. *Lect. Notes Math.* **1981**, *898*, 366–381.
17. Takens, F. On the numerical determination of the dimension of an attractor. In *Dynamical Systems and Bifurcations*; Braaksma, B.L.J., Broer, H.W., Takens, F., Eds.; Springer: Berlin/Heidelberg, Germany, 1985; pp. 99–106.
18. Xu, L.; Shi, Y. Notes on the Global Attractors for Semigroup. *Int. J. Mod. Nonlinear Theory Appl.* **2013**, *2*, 219–222. [CrossRef]
19. Sauer, T.; Yorke, J.; Casdagli, M. Embedology. *J. Stat. Phys.* **1991**, *65*, 579–616. [CrossRef]
20. Passoja, D.E.; Psioda, J.A. *Fractography in Materials Science*; ASTM International: West Conshohocken, PA, USA, 1981; pp. 335–386.
21. Mattfeldt, T. Nonlinear deterministic analysis of tissue texture: A stereological study on mastopathic and mammary cancer tissue using chaos theory. *J. Microsc.* **1997**, *185*, 47–66. [CrossRef] [PubMed]
22. Thompson, J.M.T.; Stewart, H.B. *Nonlinear Dynamics and Chaos*; John Wiley and Sons: Hoboken, NJ, USA, 1986.
23. Horovistiz, A.; de Campos, K.A.; Shibata, S.; Prado, C.C.; de Oliveira Hein, L.R. Fractal characterization of brittle fracture in ceramics under mode I stress loading. *Mater. Sci. Eng. A* **2010**, *527*, 4847–4850. [CrossRef]
24. Falconer, K. *Fractal Geometry: Mathematical Foundations and Applications*, 3rd ed.; John Wiley & Sons, Ltd.: Chichester, UK, 2014.
25. Nichita, M.V.; Paun, M.A.; Paun, V.A.; Paun, V.P. Image Clustering Algorithms to Identify Complicated Cerebral Diseases. Description and Comparaisons. *IEEE Access* **2020**, *8*, 88434–88442. [CrossRef]
26. Postolache, P.; Borsos, Z.; Paun, V.A.; Paun, V.P. New Way in Fractal Analysis of Pulmonary Medical Images. *Univ. Politeh. Buchar. Sci. Bull. Ser. A Appl. Math. Phys.* **2018**, *80*, 313–322.
27. Scott, D.W. *Statistics: A Concise Mathematical Introduction for Students, Scientists, and Engineers*; John Wiley & Sons, Inc.: Hoboken, NJ, USA, 2020.

Article

Dynamic Analysis of a Novel 3D Chaotic System with Hidden and Coexisting Attractors: Offset Boosting, Synchronization, and Circuit Realization

Chengwei Dong

Department of Physics, North University of China, Taiyuan 030051, China; dongchengwei@tsinghua.org.cn

Abstract: To further understand the dynamical characteristics of chaotic systems with a hidden attractor and coexisting attractors, we investigated the fundamental dynamics of a novel three-dimensional (3D) chaotic system derived by adding a simple constant term to the Yang–Chen system, which includes the bifurcation diagram, Lyapunov exponents spectrum, and basin of attraction, under different parameters. In addition, an offset boosting control method is presented to the state variable, and a numerical simulation of the system is also presented. Furthermore, the unstable cycles embedded in the hidden chaotic attractors are extracted in detail, which shows the effectiveness of the variational method and 1D symbolic dynamics. Finally, the adaptive synchronization of the novel system is successfully designed, and a circuit simulation is implemented to illustrate the flexibility and validity of the numerical results. Theoretical analysis and simulation results indicate that the new system has complex dynamical properties and can be used to facilitate engineering applications.

Keywords: hidden attractor; coexisting attractors; offset boosting; symbolic dynamics; circuit simulation; adaptive synchronization

Citation: Dong, C. Dynamic Analysis of a Novel 3D Chaotic System with Hidden and Coexisting Attractors: Offset Boosting, Synchronization, and Circuit Realization. *Fractal Fract.* **2022**, *6*, 547. https://doi.org/10.3390/fractalfract6100547

Academic Editor: Viorel-Puiu Paun

Received: 1 September 2022
Accepted: 22 September 2022
Published: 27 September 2022

Publisher's Note: MDPI stays neutral with regard to jurisdictional claims in published maps and institutional affiliations.

Copyright: © 2022 by the author. Licensee MDPI, Basel, Switzerland. This article is an open access article distributed under the terms and conditions of the Creative Commons Attribution (CC BY) license (https://creativecommons.org/licenses/by/4.0/).

1. Introduction

Since the meteorologist Lorenz discovered chaos phenomena in 1963 [1], chaos has been widely and deeply studied. As such, with the development of computer science and technology, several continuous chaotic systems have been discovered, including the Chua, Sprott, and Jerk systems [2–6]. The shapes of chaotic attractors are various, and the two representative shapes are the wing shape and scroll shape. Chaos widely exists in three-dimensional (3D) or high-dimensional continuous nonlinear dynamical systems. It is considerably important to produce new chaotic systems based on existing chaotic attractors when studying chaos. A wide range of engineering problems can be investigated by applying the complexity of chaotic systems [7], including image encryption, secure communication, and control and synchronization. Thus, it is of significance to analyze the dynamics of new chaotic systems.

Recent research involves classifying periodic and chaotic attractors as self-excited attractors or hidden attractors [8]. The self-excited attractor has an attraction basin associated with the unstable equilibrium, while the attraction basin of a hidden attractor does not intersect with the small neighborhood of any equilibria. It has been found that attractors in a dynamical system with stable equilibria [9–11], an infinite number of equilibria [12–17], or no equilibrium points [18–21] are hidden attractors. Owing to the unique dynamic characteristics of the hidden attractor, it has become a research hotspot in recent years. Self-excited and hidden chaotic attractors can be separately observed in Matouk's hyperchaotic systems [22]. In Ref. [23], hidden attractors are put forward from an existing chaotic saddle through a boundary crisis. New 3D autonomous chaotic systems without linear terms, which have an infinite number of equilibrium points that display complex dynamics, have also been proposed [24,25]. In Ref. [26], a new inductor-free two-memristor-based chaotic circuit with three line equilibrium points was found. Synchronization and control of a chaotic system with a hidden attractor has been implemented by numerical simulation [27]. Zeng et al. investigated a special memristor-based Jerk system in which self-excited and hidden attractors can be introduced [28]. Based on the Jerk chaotic system, a multi-scroll hyperchaotic system with hidden attractors that can produce any number of scrolls was also devised [29].

Many nonlinear dynamical systems often exhibit coexisting attractors in their respective attraction basins [30,31], and it is thus of great significance to discuss coexisting attractors. In Ref. [32], a new 4D chaotic system with coexisting and hidden attractors was generated. A novel 5D system with extreme multi-stability and hidden chaotic attractors has been presented [33]. Coexisting hidden attractors were also constructed in a 4D segmented disc dynamo [34]. In Ref. [35], coexisting hidden attractors with complex transient transition behaviors were explored in a simple 4D system with only one control parameter. The dynamics of a novel 4D multistable chaotic system having a plane as the equilibria has been introduced [36], and several interesting dynamic characteristics, such as antimonotone bifurcations and offset boosting, are also revealed via common nonlinear analysis tools. In Ref. [37], a new 5D chaotic system with a hidden attractor and coexisting attractors was derived and its dynamical behavior analyzed numerically. Pham et al. also discovered coexisting attractors in a novel 3D system without equilibria [38].

In this work, we constructed a novel 3D system with a double-wing chaotic attractor and two stable equilibrium points. The prominent feature of the new system is that it belongs to the category of hidden attractors. We also illustrated that the system is variable-boostable and has various coexisting attractors for a determined range of parameters. To the best of our knowledge, this combination of novel characteristics has not yet been reported in such a hidden attractor chaotic system with stable equilibrium points. Finally, we established an electronic analog circuit of the new double-wing chaotic system through MultiSIM, demonstrating that the mathematical model has practical feasibility for circuit realization.

This rest of this paper is organized as follows. Section 2 presents the mathematical model of the system and its dynamic characteristics. In Section 3, the complex dynamical behaviors of the new double-wing chaotic system are analyzed numerically, and basins of attraction of various coexisting attractors are shown. To systematically locate the unstable cycles embedded in the hidden chaotic attractor, 1D symbolic dynamics is introduced in Section 4, which can be reliably utilized in calculations. Section 5 presents the MultiSIM electronic circuit simulation study. To stimulate interest in such systems and realize robust technological applications, Section 6 introduces adaptive synchronization with unknown parameters. Finally, several concluding remarks are given in Section 7.

2. Mathematical Model and Its Properties

Yang and Chen proposed a new 3D chaotic system with one saddle and two stable node-focus points [39] that connects the Lorenz and Chen systems and denotes a transition from one to the other. The form of the Yang–Chen system is given in Equation (1), and the complex dynamics and compound structure of the system were investigated and discussed with careful numerical simulations [39]:

$$\begin{aligned} \frac{dx}{dt} &= a(y-x), \\ \frac{dy}{dt} &= cx - xz, \\ \frac{dz}{dt} &= xy - bz. \end{aligned} \quad (1)$$

Based on this system, we added a simple constant term to the third equation and obtained a novel 3D chaotic system,

$$\begin{aligned}
\frac{dx}{dt} &= a(y-x), \\
\frac{dy}{dt} &= cx - xz, \\
\frac{dz}{dt} &= xy - bz - d,
\end{aligned} \quad (2)$$

where $a, b, c,$ and d are real parameters. Because Equation (2) is modified from Equation (1), and because Equation (1) is obtained from the classical Lorenz model without one dissipative term $-y$, the meanings of the parameters a, b, and c in Equation (2) should be the same as those in the classical Lorenz system, which are the Prandtl number, aspect ratio of the rolls, and Rayleigh number, respectively. d is chosen as a control parameter in order to observe the production of a hidden attractor in the system. When $a = c = 35, b = 3$, and $d = 0$, the system is the original Yang–Chen system. We take the values of parameters a, b, and c from the literature [39], and randomly take the newly introduced parameter d as 10. When $(a, b, c, d) = (35, 3, 35, 10)$ and the initial values are $(x_0, y_0, z_0) = (1, 1, 1)$, system (2) presents a strange attractor in the shape of a double wing, as shown in Figure 1. To further verify that system (2) is chaotic, the three Lyapunov exponents calculated by the Wolf algorithm [40] are expressed as follows:

$$LE_1 = 1.100, LE_2 = 0, LE_3 = -39.098.$$

The fractional dimension of the system can also be calculated, which indicates the complexity of the attractor. The Kaplan–Yorke dimension of system (2) is defined as follows:

$$D_{KY} = j + \frac{1}{|LE_{j+1}|} \sum_{i=1}^{j} LE_i,$$

where j denotes the largest integer satisfying $\sum_{i=1}^{j} LE_i \geq 0$ and $\sum_{i=1}^{j+1} LE_i < 0$. Therefore, the Kaplan–Yorke dimension for the parameters $(a, b, c, d) = (35, 3, 35, 10)$ is found to be

$$D_{KY} = 2 + (LE_1 + LE_2)/|LE_3| = 2.0281.$$

When the coordinates are transformed as $(x, y, z) \to (-x, -y, z)$, the form of system (2) remains unchanged, which implies that system (2) is rotationally symmetric about the z axis.

The fixed points of system (2) are determined by solving the following equation:

$$\begin{aligned}
a(y-x) &= 0, \\
cx - xz &= 0, \\
xy - bz - d &= 0,
\end{aligned} \quad (3)$$

and the two fixed points are then

$$\begin{aligned}
E_1 &: (-\sqrt{bc+d}, -\sqrt{bc+d}, c), \\
E_2 &: (\sqrt{bc+d}, \sqrt{bc+d}, c).
\end{aligned} \quad (4)$$

To analyze the stability of the two fixed points E_1 and E_2, we undertake the calculations for the Jacobian matrix of system (2):

$$J = \begin{pmatrix} -a & a & 0 \\ c-z & 0 & -x \\ y & x & -b \end{pmatrix}.$$

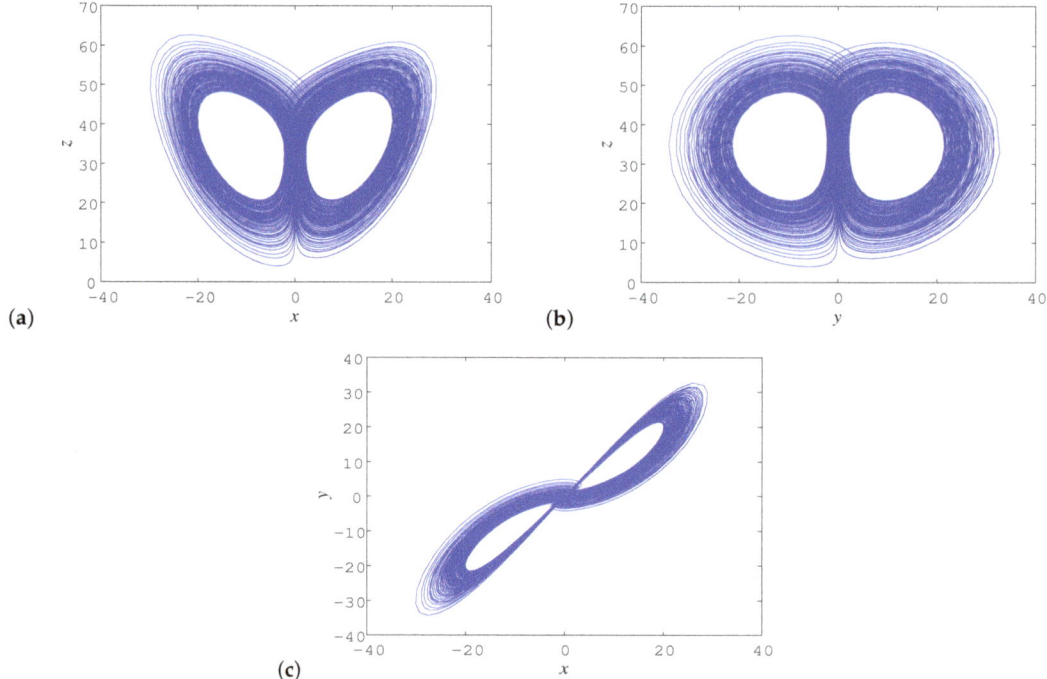

Figure 1. Two-dimensional projections of chaotic attractor onto various planes at time $t = 150$: (**a**) $x - z$, (**b**) $y - z$, and (**c**) $x - y$ planes.

We apply spectral stability theory to investigate the stabilities [41]. When the parameters are taken $(a, b, c, d) = (35, 3, 35, 10)$, the matrices $J(E_1)$ and $J(E_2)$ have the same spectral values $\lambda_1 = -37.812$, $\lambda_{2,3} = -0.094 \pm 14.591i$. Thus, the two fixed points are both stable node-focus points. System (2) possessing a chaotic attractor under current parameters means that the chaotic attractor is hidden.

The critical value of the Rayleigh parameter for a subcritical Hopf bifurcation that occurs in system (2) can also be obtained by using Routh–Hurwitz criterion. The characteristic equation is

$$f(\lambda) = \lambda^3 + (a+b)\lambda^2 + (ab - ac + x^2 + az)\lambda + ax^2 - abc + abz + axy.$$

By substituting the coordinates of the two fixed points in Equation (4) separately, we have the same characteristic equation:

$$f(\lambda) = a_3\lambda^3 + a_2\lambda^2 + a_1\lambda + a_0,$$

where

$$\begin{aligned} a_3 &= 1, \\ a_2 &= a + b, \\ a_1 &= ab + bc + d, \\ a_0 &= 2a(bc + d). \end{aligned}$$

From the Routh–Hurwitz criterion, the two fixed points E_1 and E_2 are stable if the following conditions are satisfied: $a_i > 0 (i = 0, 1, 2, 3)$ and $a_2 a_1 - a_3 a_0 > 0$. For the parameters $(a, b, d) = (35, 3, 10)$, system (2) yields a critical value of 38.229 for the Rayleigh parameter c for a subcritical Hopf bifurcation.

The dissipativity of system (2) can be examined by calculating $\nabla \cdot V$, which gives

$$\nabla \cdot V = \frac{\partial \dot{x}}{\partial x} + \frac{\partial \dot{y}}{\partial y} + \frac{\partial \dot{z}}{\partial z} = -a - b.$$

Therefore, system (2) exhibits dissipativity when $-a - b < 0$, and volumes in phase space will shrink to 0 exponentially fast as $t \to \infty$.

For clarity, we compare the new system (2) and the chaotic system proposed previously by Dong [10], as listed in Table 1. Moreover, we also summarize the similarities and differences in analysis methods used in the two chaotic systems and tabulate them in Table 2, from which it can be seen that an implementation of a circuit will be applied in both studies.

Table 1. Comparison with two chaotic systems with initial values $(1, 1, 1)$.

Systems	Equations	Parameters	Equilibria	Eigenvalues	Lyapunov Exponents	Fractional Dimensions	Attractor Type
This work	$\dot{x} = a(y - x)$ $\dot{y} = cx - xz$ $\dot{z} = xy - bz - d$	$a = 35$ $b = 3$ $c = 35$ $d = 10$	$(-10.7238, -10.7238, 35)$ $(10.7238, 10.7238, 35)$	-37.812 $-0.094 \pm 14.591i$	1.100 0 -39.098	2.0281	Hidden
Dong [10]	$\dot{x} = a(y - x) + kxz$ $\dot{y} = -cy - xz$ $\dot{z} = -b + xy$	$a = 10$ $b = 100$ $c = 11.2$ $k = -0.2$	$(-11.0634, -9.0387, -9.1503)$ $(11.0634, 9.0387, -9.1503)$	-18.7413 $-0.314 \pm 11.424i$	0.7457 -0.0057 -26.8144	2.0276	Hidden
		$a = 10$ $b = 64$ $c = 0$ $k = 0$	$(-8, -8, 0)$ $(8, 8, 0)$	-12.8068 $1.4034 \pm 9.8983i$	1.4456 0.001 -11.4473	2.1264	Self-excited

Table 2. Analysis methods used in investigating the two chaotic systems.

	This Work	Dong [10]
Establishment of mathematical model	Adding a simple constant term $-d$ to Yang-Chen system	Adding a nonlinear term of cross-product kxz to generalized Lorenz-type system
Dynamics	Yes	Yes
Coexisting attractors	Yes	No
Offset boosting control	Yes	No
Symbolic dynamics of unstable cycles	Two letters	Four letters for hidden attractor Six letters for self-excited attractor
Circuit implementation	Yes	Yes
Synchronization	Yes	No

3. Dynamics of Novel Double-Wing Chaotic System

3.1. Bifurcation Diagram and Lyapunov Exponents

We investigated the dynamics of system (2) under different parameters by means of the bifurcation diagram with the Lyapunov exponents spectrum. The parameter region of interest is specified as $a \in [10, 60]$ and $b \in [0, 5]$, and the initial values are chosen as $(1, 1, 1)$. Taking the parameters a and b as variables, the remaining parameters of the system were fixed. By changing the parameters a and b, various states of system (2) can be observed.

The bifurcation diagram and corresponding Lyapunov exponents spectrum of system (2) by altering a are obtained in Figure 2a,b, respectively. It can be seen that system (2) exhibits chaotic and stable state behaviors versus different a values. Explicitly, system (2) exhibits chaotic behavior when $a < 40.5$, where one of the three Lyapunov exponents is greater than zero, one is equal to zero, and one is less than zero, whereas system (2) converges to a stable equilibrium point when $a \geq 40.5$, where the three Lyapunov exponents are all less than zero. In Figure 2c,d, the 3D projections of the phase portraits of system (2) in different states are also presented.

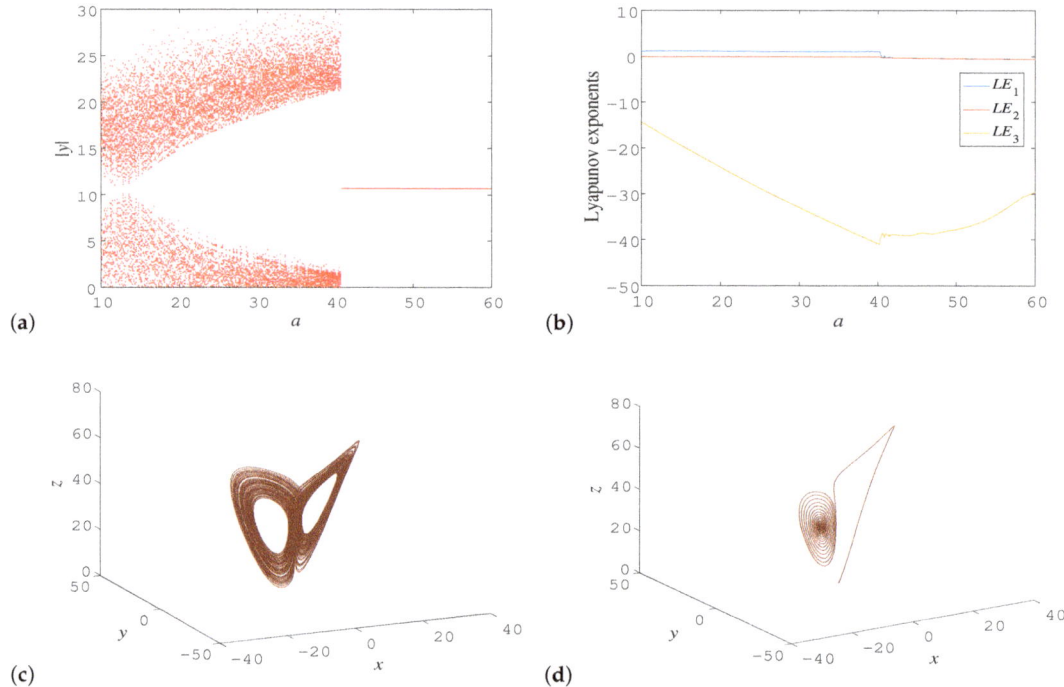

Figure 2. (**a**) Bifurcation diagram and (**b**) Lyapunov exponents spectrum of system (2) vs. a, where $b = 3, c = 35$, and $d = 10$. 3D view of phase portraits with (**c**) $a = 30$ and (**d**) $a = 50$.

Taking the parameter $b \in [0, 5]$, and letting $a = c = 35$ and $d = 10$, the bifurcation diagram and corresponding Lyapunov exponents spectrum are depicted in Figure 3. It is found that the system changes from periodic to chaotic through period-doubling bifurcations, and eventually becomes a stable state, indicating that the system has complicated dynamical characteristics. We note that diverse periodic attractors of the system appear with different parameters b, as shown in Figure 4.

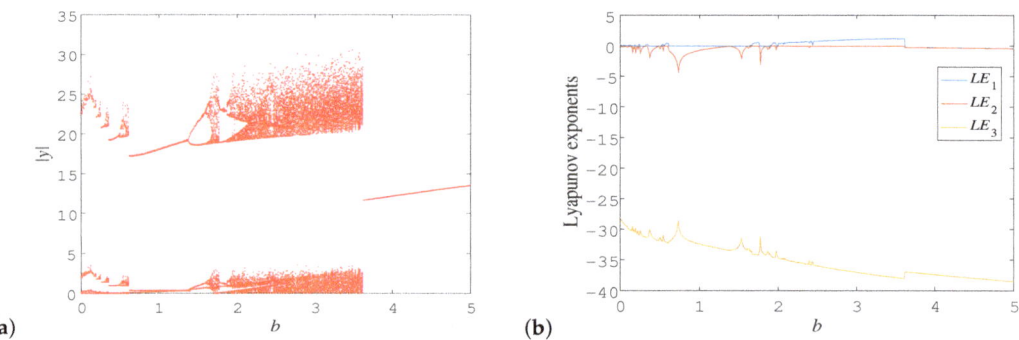

Figure 3. Parameter values $(a, c, d) = (35, 35, 10)$, (**a**) bifurcation diagram, and (**b**) Lyapunov exponents spectrum of system (2) for $b \in [0, 5]$.

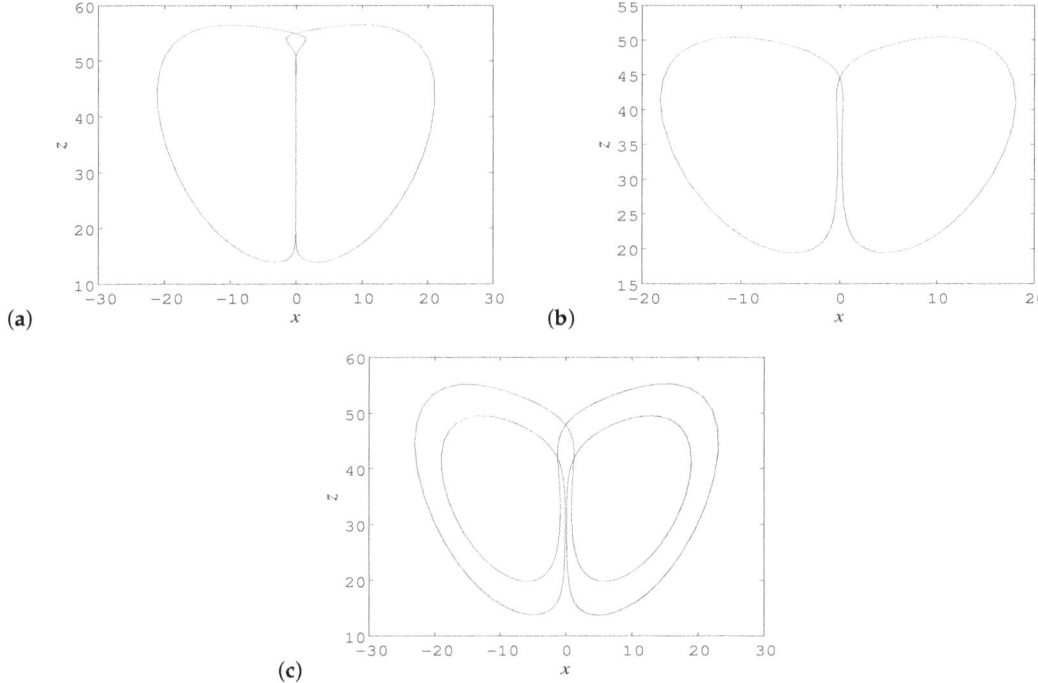

Figure 4. Two-dimensional view of different periodic attractors of system (2), $a = c = 35$ and $d = 10$: (**a**) $b = 0.3$; (**b**) $b = 1$; (**c**) $b = 1.8$.

3.2. Two-Parameter Lyapunov Exponents Analysis

We now explore the global dynamical behaviors by combining two-parameter Lyapunov exponents analysis. To better understand the intricate dynamics, we investigated the effects of two parameters c and d, for which a division diagram can be used to study different kinds of dynamical modes of system (2). Varying c and d within the interval of $c \in [0, 80], d \in [-40, 40]$, and the other parameters are unchanged ($a = 35, b = 3$), a pseudo-colored map on a 100×100 grid of parameters (c, d) was obtained by calculating the largest Lyapunov exponents; the initial conditions are set $(1, 1, 1)$, as shown in Figure 5. It can be observed in the figure that the magnitudes of the largest Lyapunov exponent values change with color. In particular, the red regions represent chaos, orange domains the periodic attractor, and the rest of the domains are related to stable equilibrium states. At the corresponding values of c and d, system (2) has distinct maximum Lyapunov exponents under different conditions, which further demonstrates that the rich dynamics of the proposed system is complex.

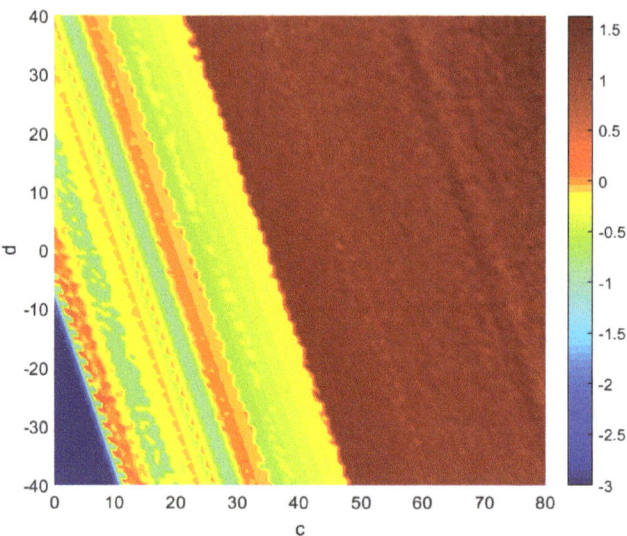

Figure 5. Two-parameter Lyapunov exponents diagram in (c, d) plane with initial values $(1, 1, 1)$.

3.3. Coexisting Attractors and Basins of Attraction

In this subsection, we discuss in detail an investigation into discovering multifarious coexisting attractors in system (2). In the following calculations, we take the parameter values $(a, c, d) = (35, 35, 10)$, and randomly choose various parameters b of the system. As system (2) remains invariant under the transformation $(x, y, z) \to (-x, -y, z)$, which means that any projection of the attractor has rotational symmetry about the z axis, consequently the proposed system may exhibit various coexisting attractors.

First, we explored the coexisting hidden chaotic attractor and stable equilibrium attractors of system (2); the 3D phase portraits are displayed in Figure 6a. Taking the parameters $(a, b, c, d) = (35, 3, 35, 10)$, for initial conditions $(x_0, y_0, z_0) = (1, 1, 1)$, a hidden chaotic attractor can be revealed (yellow color). For initial conditions $(x_0, y_0, z_0) = (-8, -8, 35)$, the trajectory of the system in the phase space converges to the stable equilibrium point E_1 (blue color). For initial conditions $(x_0, y_0, z_0) = (8, 8, 35)$, asymptotically converging behaviors toward another stable equilibrium point E_2 (red color) result.

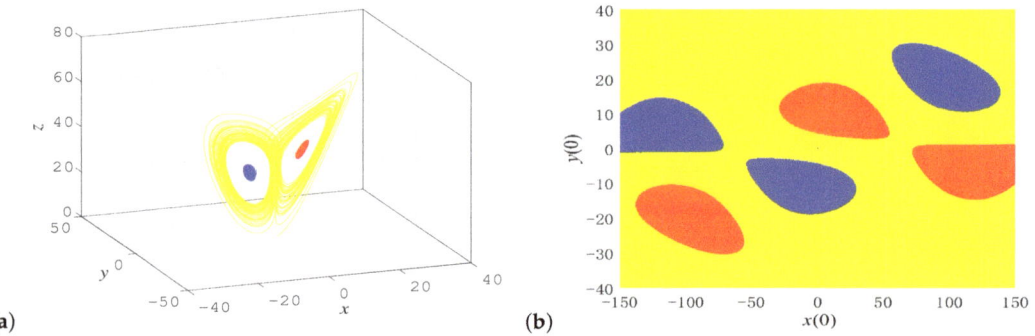

Figure 6. Coexisting hidden chaotic attractor and stable equilibrium state attractors of system (2); $(a, b, c, d) = (35, 3, 35, 10)$: (**a**) 3D phase portraits; (**b**) basins of attraction.

The basin of attraction, which is usually defined as the set of initial points to which the orbits converge for the specified attractor, can exhibit more information about the coexistence of attractions. Thus, the basins of attraction in the $x(0) - y(0)$ plane for

$z(0) = 35$ of the coexisting chaotic attractor and stable equilibrium attractors are displayed in Figure 6b. Three types of basins of attraction are shown in yellow, blue, and red, respectively. Yellow denotes a basin of a chaotic attractor, and blue and red basins represent attractors of two stable node-focus points E_1 and E_2, respectively. It can be observed from Figure 6b that the basins of attraction have the expected symmetry and a smooth boundary. In addition, according to the topological structure of the basin, the attraction basin of the chaotic attractor does not intersect with the small neighborhoods of the stable node-foci E_1 and E_2, which also indicates that the chaotic attractor is hidden.

Moreover, the parameters are set as $(a, b, c, d) = (35, 0.5, 35, 10)$, and two asymmetrical coexisting periodic attractors are illustrated in Figure 7a,b. We also plot the basins of attraction in the $x(0) - y(0)$ plane for $z(0) = 35$ of the two coexisting periodic attractors, as shown in Figure 7c, in which the yellow areas denote the attraction basin of the periodic attractor in Figure 7a and the blue areas the attraction basin of the periodic attractor in Figure 7b. Riddled basins of attraction are observed [42], which illustrates that the state of the system is very sensitive to the initial values. Coexisting periodic attractors of system (2) can also be observed under other parameters, as shown in Figure 8. Taking the parameters $(a, b, c, d) = (35, 0.42, 35, 10)$, there exists in system (2) a green limit cycle for initial values $(-1, -1, 1)$; system (2) also has a limit cycle (shown in purple) for initial values $(1, 1, 1)$. While taking parameters $(a, b, c, d) = (35, 1.5, 35, 10)$, system (2), a limit cycle (shown in blue) exists for initial values $(-1, -1, 1)$, and another limit cycle (shown in red) exists for initial values $(1, 1, 1)$. That system (2) has assorted coexisting periodic attractors proves that rich asymmetric multi-steady states exist in the new system.

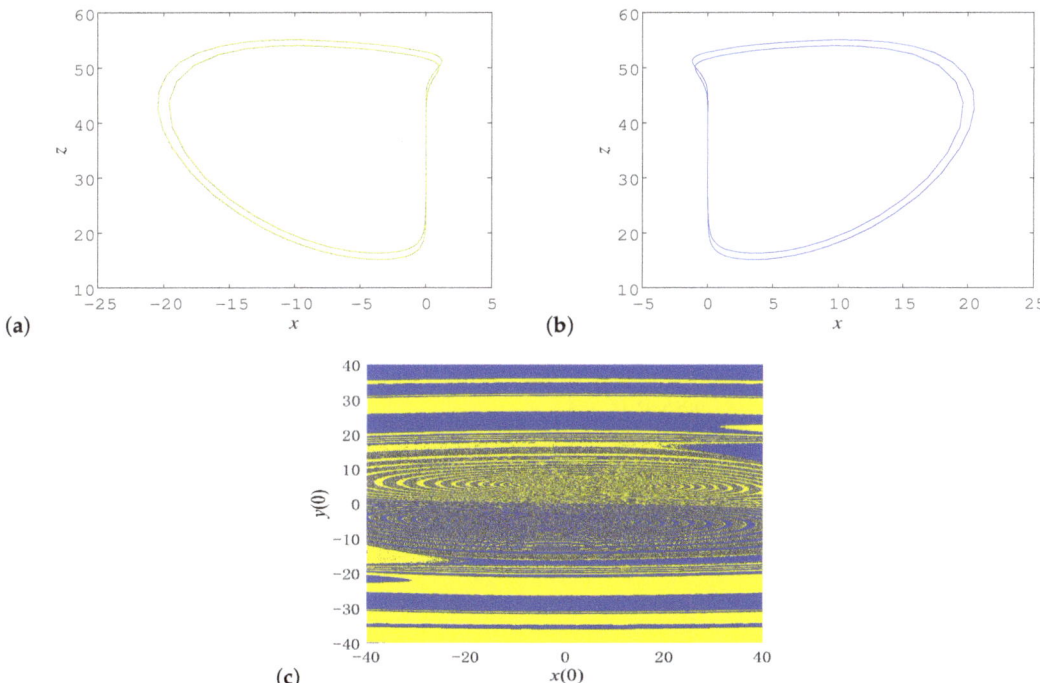

Figure 7. Two coexisting periodic attractors of system (2); $(a, b, c, d) = (35, 0.5, 35, 10)$: (**a**) periodic attractor with initial values $(-1, -1, 1)$; (**b**) another periodic attractor with initial values $(1, 1, 1)$; (**c**) basins of attraction.

Finally, we investigate coexisting chaotic attractors of system (2), and two asymmetrical chaotic attractors are illustrated in Figure 9. Fixing the parameters $(a, b, c, d) = (35, 0.53, 35, 10)$, if we choose initial conditions $(x_0, y_0, z_0) = (-1, -1, 1)$, system (2) has an asymmetrical chaotic attractor with projection onto the $x - z$ plane depicted in Figure 9a. The other asymmetrical chaotic attractor can also be revealed for initial values $(1, 1, 1)$ due to the symmetry about the z axis [see Figure 9b]; thus, the two chaotic attractors have the same Lyapunov exponents and fractal dimension.

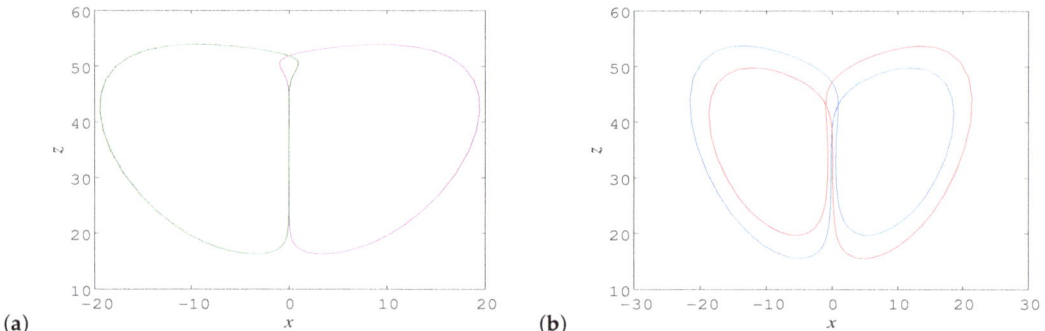

Figure 8. Coexisting periodic attractors of system (2) in (x, z) plane: (**a**) $(a, b, c, d) = (35, 0.42, 35, 10)$ and (**b**) $(a, b, c, d) = (35, 1.5, 35, 10)$.

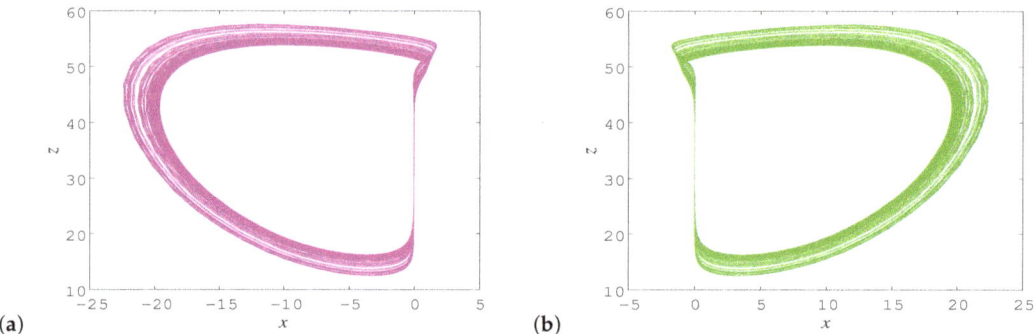

Figure 9. Coexisting chaotic attractors of system (2) in (x, z) plane; $(a, b, c, d) = (35, 0.53, 35, 10)$: (**a**) chaotic attractor with initial values $(-1, -1, 1)$ and (**b**) another chaotic attractor with initial values $(1, 1, 1)$.

3.4. Impact of Constant Term d

We now discuss the impact of the constant term d on the system's stability, including the disappearance of the saddle point at the origin. As the origin $(0, 0, 0)$ is no longer a fixed point when $d \neq 0$, system (2) may possess only two stable equilibria by introducing an additional constant term d. According to the Routh–Hurwitz criterion, it can be seen that the two equilibria are both stable under the conditions $-abc - ad + a^2b + ab^2 + b^2c + bd > 0$ and $2a(bc + d) > 0$. For the parameters $(a, b, c) = (35, 3, 35)$, it yields $-105 < d < 19.6875$. We further found that, when d is negative, system (2) converges to the stable equilibrium point under different initial conditions, and there is no chaotic state. Hence, when we take the parameters $(a, b, c) = (35, 3, 35)$ and $0 < d < 19.6875$, system (2) is able to produce a hidden chaotic attractor. When the parameter $d \geq 19.6875$, the two equilibrium points lose stability and become two saddle-focus points, and the chaotic attractor in system (2) is self-excited.

We also thoroughly examined the impact of the inclusion of the constant term d in the rest of Equation (1) (e.g., dx/dt or dy/dt), which may produce a similar or different impact. When the constant term d is added to the second equation of system (1), the new system no longer has rotational symmetry. By fixing the parameter values $(a, b, c) = (35, 3, 35)$ and changing the control parameter d, we find that three fixed points exist in the system, one of which is a stable node-focus point and two are saddle-focus points. Regardless of the value of d, the trajectory of the system eventually converges to the stable node-focus point under different initial values, so there is no hidden attractor in the system.

We now investigate the impact when the constant term d is added to the first equation of system (1). Taking the parameters $(a, b, c, d) = (35, 3, 35, 10)$, we found that the system has two stable node-foci coexisting with a chaotic attractor; thus, a hidden attractor also appears in this case. Figure 10 shows the basins of attraction for different initial conditions under current parameter values, in which yellow represents a basin of a chaotic attractor, and blue and red denote basins of stable equilibrium points E_1 and E_2, respectively. It can be seen that riddled basins of attraction arise here and that the basin of attraction no longer has symmetric similarity or a smooth boundary. Furthermore, when the parameter b changes, we also find that other types of coexisting attractors no longer exist. This is because the system has no z-axis rotational symmetry, which is the main difference between it and system (2). Therefore, we conclude that the new system obtained by adding the constant term d to the third equation of Equation (1) has both hidden attractors and coexisting attractors, and that its dynamic behaviors are more complex.

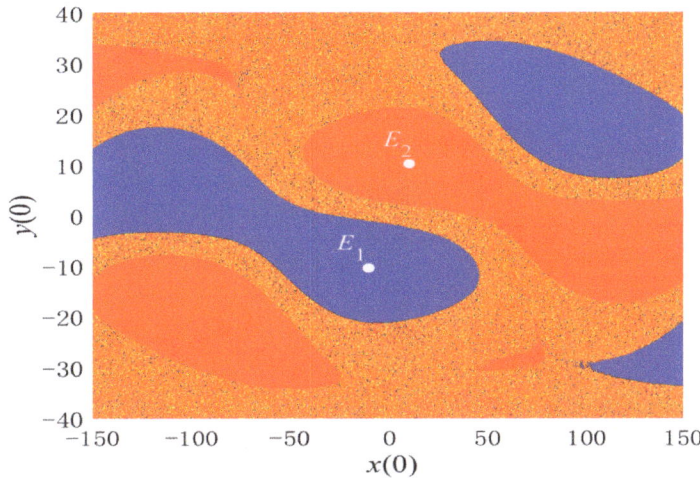

Figure 10. Riddled basins of attraction in $x(0) - y(0)$ initial plane with $z(0) = 35$.

3.5. Offset Boosting Control

Recently, a new category of chaotic systems called variable-boostable systems was proposed. In such a system, the variable can be boosted to any level and switched between a bipolar and unipolar signal, which is convenient for chaotic applications, as it can be used for amplitude control and reducing the number of components required for signal conditioning [43–46]. The state variable y appears twice in system (2), and thus it can be easily controlled. We offset-boost the state variable y by the transformation $y \to y + w$, where w denotes a constant. System (2) can be rewritten accordingly as

$$\begin{aligned}
\frac{dx}{dt} &= a(y + w - x), \\
\frac{dy}{dt} &= cx - xz, \\
\frac{dz}{dt} &= x(y + w) - bz - d.
\end{aligned} \quad (5)$$

To better illustrate this phenomenon, the offset-boosting of the chaotic attractor is shown in Figure 11 when the control parameter w is altered. The 2D projection of the attractor onto $y - z$ phase space is shown in Figure 11a and the corresponding time-sequence diagram given in Figure 11b. It can be observed that a bipolar signal is obtained for $w = 0$ (blue), a positive unipolar signal for $w = -35$ (green), and a negative unipolar signal for $w = 35$ (red). Therefore, we can transform the chaotic signal y from bipolarity to unipolarity when varying the control parameter w. Meanwhile, we also calculated the Lyapunov exponents spectrum versus w and found that the three Lyapunov exponents remain invariant, indicating that the state of system (5) does not undergo changes with the offset w.

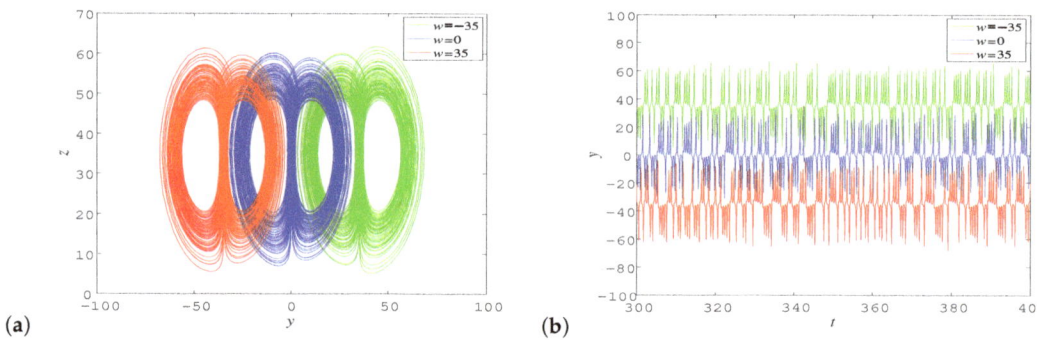

Figure 11. Offset boosting of chaotic attractor when varying control parameter w for $(a, b, c, d) = (35, 3, 35, 10)$: (**a**) in $y - z$ plane and (**b**) state y with different values of the offset boosting controller w. All computed for initial values $(1, 1, 1)$.

Through the above discussion, it is deduced that the new system (2) with a hidden double-wing chaotic attractor has potential chaos-based applications by selecting offset boosting control. In summary, the introduction of the offset w can flexibly shift the position of the chaotic attractor in the y direction in phase space, which has great application value in engineering.

4. One-Dimensional Symbolic Dynamics for Unstable Cycles Embedded in Hidden Chaotic Attractor

To systematically calculate all unstable cycles embedded in the hidden chaotic attractors, we must encode the orbits by means of symbolic dynamics [47]. By selecting an appropriate Poincaré cross-section, the continuous flow can be transformed into a discrete map. Figure 12 shows the first return map of system (2) for $(a, b, c, d) = (35, 3, 35, 10)$. When we choose a special Poincaré section $z = 35$, the initial values are $(1, 1, 1)$, where a dense point with a unimodal structure is presented, which implies that all cycles extracted can be encoded with two letters by 1D symbolic dynamics. Because only one critical point x_c for which $f(x_c)$ reaches the extremum value exists within the interval, a simple division of the phase space is whether a given orbit falls to the left or right of the critical point. If $x_i < x_c$, it is marked as symbol 0; if $x_i > x_c$, then it is marked as symbol 1. In the second iteration, we redefine each partition according to the two-step iteration of the points to obtain four partitions. In this way, we can partition the phase space into different regions, and mark each region with its own unique symbol.

In this work, the variational method [48] was adopted to perform the calculations. Two simplest periodic orbits, marked with symbols 0 and 1 (see Figure 13), can be considered as basic building blocks with which to construct the initial loop guess of more complex periodic orbits. Through 1D symbolic dynamics, we constructed the initial loop guess corresponding to each symbol sequence within the topological length of 5, and calculated the real periodic orbits. Their symbol sequences, periods, and coordinates of a point on the periodic orbits are tabulated in Table 3, from which the symmetry of the system can also be reflected. We also draw the cycles with different topological lengths in 3D phase space in Figure 14.

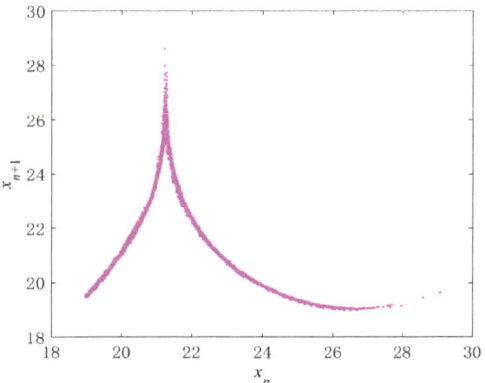

Figure 12. First return map of system (2) under parameters $(a, b, c, d) = (35, 3, 35, 10)$; the Poincaré section is taken as $z = 35$.

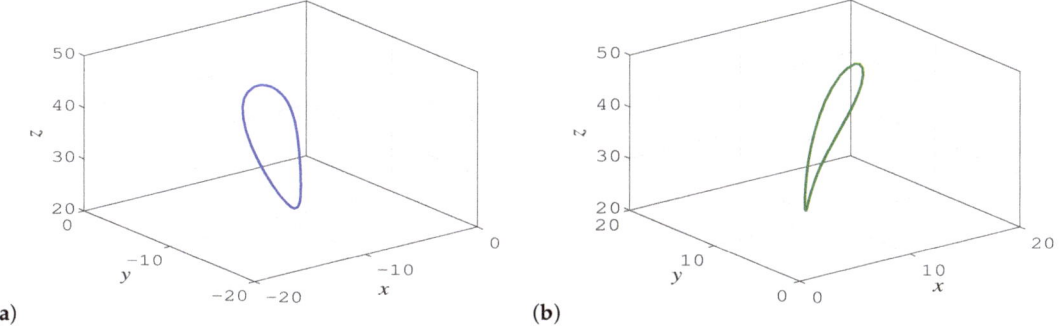

Figure 13. Two simplest periodic orbits as basic building blocks in system (2) for parameters $(a, b, c, d) = (35, 3, 35, 10)$: (**a**) cycle 0 and (**b**) cycle 1.

Table 3. Unstable cycles embedded in hidden chaotic attractor of system (2) up to topological length 5 for $(a, b, c, d) = (35, 3, 35, 10)$.

Length	Itineraries	Periods	x	y	z
1	0	0.468918	−10.393417	−7.216587	43.634264
	1	0.468918	10.393417	7.216587	43.634264
2	01	1.190901	−15.856545	−21.285817	21.799902
3	001	1.768396	−1.142202	0.192829	40.538631
	011	1.768396	1.142202	−0.192829	40.538631
4	0001	2.338366	−5.390366	−2.042326	44.498047
	0011	2.364638	8.016602	2.946163	47.893544
	0111	2.338366	5.390366	2.042326	44.498047
5	00001	2.975663	−0.259779	0.021441	36.277845
	00011	2.939762	−2.797000	−3.617918	20.432365
	00101	2.962243	−15.163685	−7.655255	52.919827
	00111	2.939762	2.797000	3.617918	20.432365
	01011	2.962243	15.163685	7.655255	52.919827
	01111	2.975663	0.259779	−0.021441	36.277845

When the parameters of the system change, the first return map of the system will also be altered accordingly, which may no longer be a 1D unimodal map, but have multiple branches, thus requiring more symbols to encode periodic orbits. In this case, it is more convenient and effective to establish symbolic dynamics based on the topological structure of orbits [49–51], such as the number of rotations between periodic orbits and equilibrium points. Furthermore, continuous deformation of the cycles with the change of parameters can also be explored by the variational method, which can help us judge the parameter values when the number of cycles or stability changes, and thus confirm the corresponding bifurcation phenomenon [52–54].

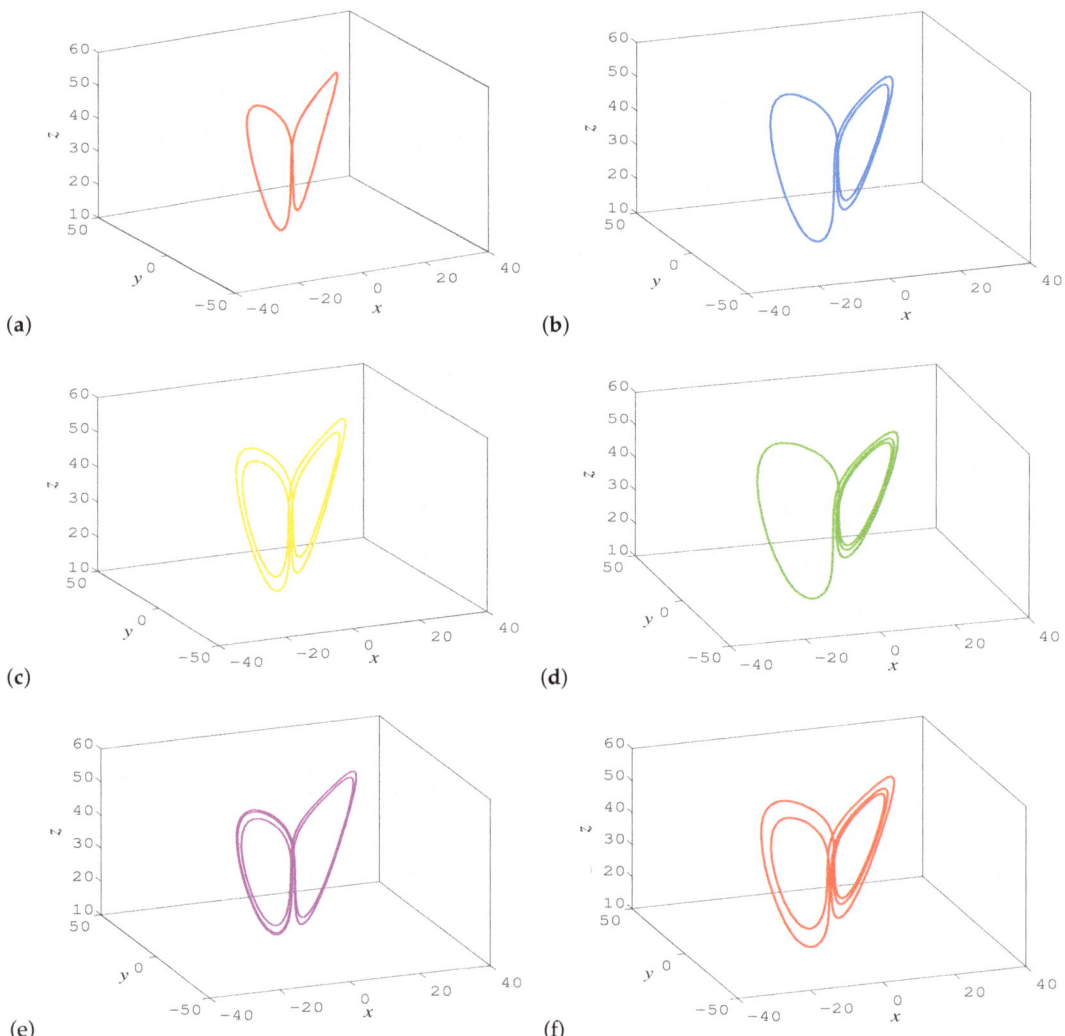

Figure 14. Unstable cycles in system (2) under parameters $(a, b, c, d) = (35, 3, 35, 10)$: Cycles (**a**) 01; (**b**) 011; (**c**) 0011; (**d**) 0111; (**e**) 00101; (**f**) 00111.

5. Circuit Implementation

To confirm the engineering feasibility of the new system, we designed an electronic circuit to verify the chaotic behaviors of the mathematical model. In Ref. [55], the circuit realization of a fractional chaotic system regarding capacitors and resistors was proposed to validate the theoretical results obtained via the numerical scheme. Here, the analog circuit of the new double-wing chaotic system (2) was executed in MultiSIM software. The circuit involves resistors, capacitors, operational amplifiers, and analog multiplier chips. A schematic of a circuit consisting of analog circuit components is illustrated in Figure 15, in which AD811AN units were selected as operational amplifiers. All the multipliers are chosen with an output coefficient of 0.1. When the circuit is executed, we fix the resistors $R_3 = R_9 = R_{16} = 350\text{ k}\Omega$, input the input signal $-X$ to the resistor R_1, and adjust the value of R_1; the linear dissipative term $-ax$ in the system equation can then be implemented in the circuit. We input the input signal X to the resistor R_7 and adjust the value of R_7; the linear forcing term cx can then be implemented. We adjust the values of $V1$ and R_{15}, implementing the constant term $-d$ in the system equation.

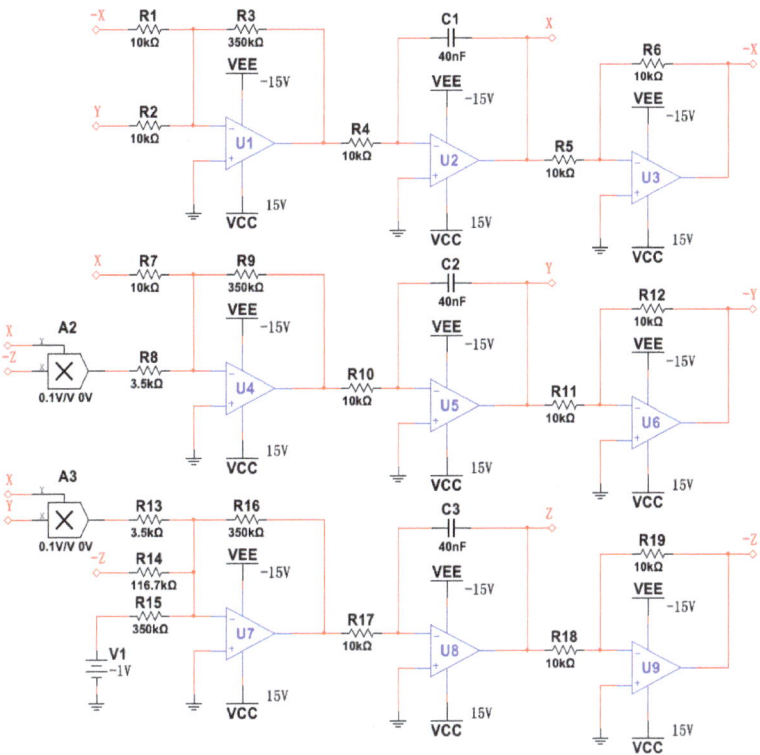

Figure 15. Circuit diagram of system (2).

Because the common power supply voltage is ± 15 V, the linear dynamic range of the operational amplifier is ± 13.5 V. As can be seen from the simulation results in Figure 1, all the values of state variables (x, y, z) in system (2) are out of the dynamic range, so they require scaling down. The state variables (x, y, z) of system (2) are re-scaled as $X = \frac{1}{10}x$, $Y = \frac{1}{10}y$, and $Z = \frac{1}{10}z$. We set the timescale factor $\tau_0 = \frac{1}{R_0 C_0} = 2500$ to better match the system, a new time variable τ is defined instead of t, and $t = \tau_0 \tau$. As a result, system (2) after scale transformation is described as

$$\begin{aligned} R_0 C_0 \dot{X} &= a(Y - X), \\ R_0 C_0 \dot{Y} &= cX - 10XZ, \\ R_0 C_0 \dot{Z} &= 10XY - bZ - \frac{d}{10}, \end{aligned} \qquad (6)$$

where $a = c = 35$, $b = 3$, and $d = 10$.

By introducing Kirchhoff's circuit laws into the circuit in Figure 15, the relationship between the circuit variables is expressed as

$$\begin{aligned}
\dot{X} &= \frac{R_3}{R_2 R_4 C_1} Y - \frac{R_3}{R_1 R_4 C_1} X, \\
\dot{Y} &= \frac{R_9}{R_7 R_{10} C_2} X - \frac{R_9}{R_8 R_{10} C_2} 0.1 XZ, \\
\dot{Z} &= \frac{R_{16}}{R_{13} R_{17} C_3} 0.1 XY - \frac{R_{16}}{R_{14} R_{17} C_3} Z + \frac{R_{16}}{R_{15} R_{17} C_3} V_1.
\end{aligned} \quad (7)$$

In Equation (7), X, Y, and Z correspond to the voltages on the integrators U2, U5, and U8, respectively, whereas the power supply is ± 15 V. Comparing Equation (6) with Equation (7), we selected $R_{14} = 116.7$ kΩ, $R_8 = R_{13} = 3.5$ kΩ, $R_i = 350$ kΩ ($i = 3, 9, 15, 16$), $R_j = 10$ kΩ ($j = 1, 2, 4, 5, 6, 7, 10, 11, 12, 17, 18, 19$), $C_1 = C_2 = C_3 = 40$ nF, $V1 = -1$ V.

The oscilloscope outputs showing 2D phase portraits of the circuit simulation are presented in Figure 16, which is very consistent with the numerical results plotted in Figure 1. Thus, the circuit experiment validated the feasibility of the proposed system.

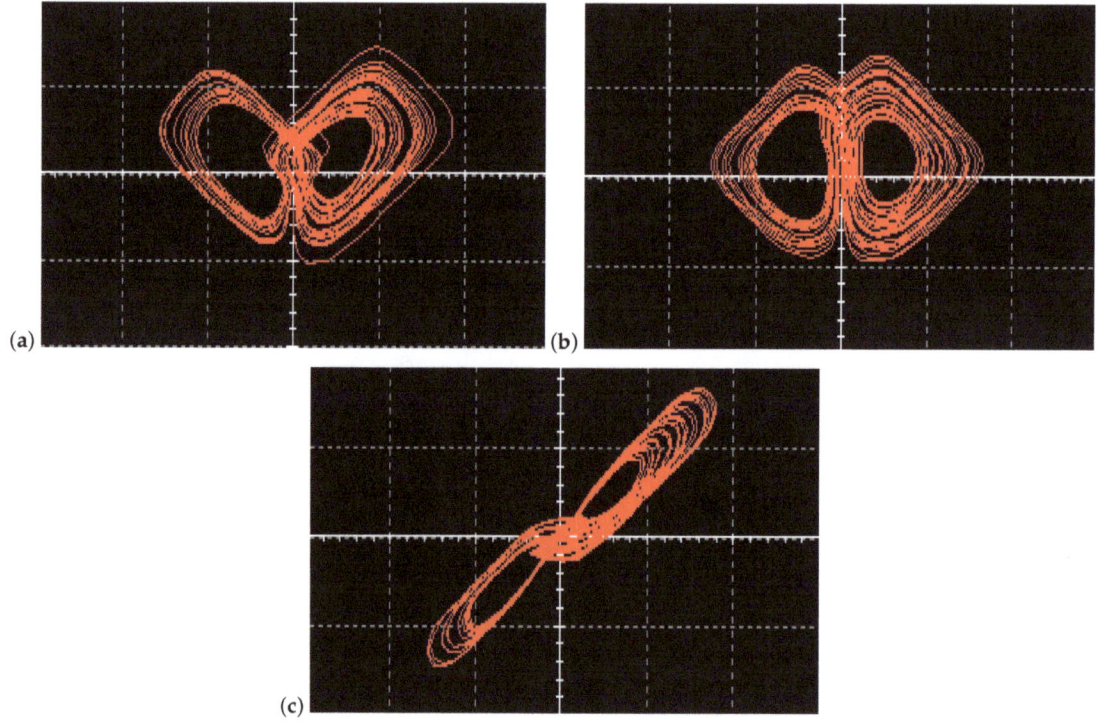

Figure 16. Chaotic behaviors of implemented electronic circuit with initial conditions $(X(0), Y(0), Z(0)) = (1V, 1V, 1V)$ in (**a**) $X - Z$, (**b**) $Y - Z$, and (**c**) $X - Y$ planes.

6. Adaptive Synchronization of Novel Three-Dimensional Chaotic System

To benefit from the rich dynamic characteristics provided by system (2) in chaos-based secure communication, the synchronization problem must be further explored. Hammouch et al. investigated numerical solutions and the identical synchronization of a variable-order fractional chaotic system [56]. Various synchronization methods have been put forward in the literature, including linear and nonlinear feedback, impulse control, and adaptive control. Among these synchronization schemes, adaptive control seems to be the most interesting due to its robustness and simple implementation [57,58]. Here, we employ the adaptive control method to achieve chaotic synchronization of two identical systems with unknown parameters.

The novel 3D system is considered the master system:

$$\begin{aligned} \dot{x}_m &= a(y_m - x_m), \\ \dot{y}_m &= cx_m - x_m z_m, \\ \dot{z}_m &= x_m y_m - bz_m - d, \end{aligned} \tag{8}$$

and the slave system is described as follows:

$$\begin{aligned} \dot{x}_s &= a(y_s - x_s) + u_x, \\ \dot{y}_s &= cx_s - x_s z_s + u_y, \\ \dot{z}_s &= x_s y_s - bz_s - d + u_z, \end{aligned} \tag{9}$$

in which $a, b, c,$ and d are unknown system parameters, and $u_x, u_y,$ and u_z are adaptive controls. We define the synchronization errors as follows:

$$\begin{aligned} e_x &= x_s - x_m, \\ e_y &= y_s - y_m, \\ e_z &= z_s - z_m. \end{aligned} \tag{10}$$

The error dynamics are easily calculated as

$$\begin{aligned} \dot{e}_x &= a(e_y - e_x) + u_x, \\ \dot{e}_y &= ce_x - x_s z_s + x_m z_m + u_y, \\ \dot{e}_z &= x_s y_s - x_m y_m - be_z + u_z. \end{aligned} \tag{11}$$

The designed adaptive controller is

$$\begin{aligned} u_x &= -\hat{a}(t)(e_y - e_x) - k_1 e_x, \\ u_y &= -\hat{c}(t)e_x + x_s z_s - x_m z_m - k_2 e_y, \\ u_z &= -x_s y_s + x_m y_m + \hat{b}(t)e_z - k_3 e_z, \end{aligned} \tag{12}$$

where $k_1, k_2,$ and k_3 are positive gain constants and $\hat{a}(t), \hat{b}(t), \hat{c}(t),$ and $\hat{d}(t)$ are parameter estimates. By substituting the expression of Equation (12) into Equation (11), we have

$$\begin{aligned} \dot{e}_x &= (a - \hat{a}(t))(e_y - e_x) - k_1 e_x, \\ \dot{e}_y &= (c - \hat{c}(t))e_x - k_2 e_y, \\ \dot{e}_z &= (\hat{b}(t) - b)e_z - k_3 e_z. \end{aligned} \tag{13}$$

The dynamic errors described by Equation (13) can be simplified by taking the parameter estimation errors as

$$\begin{aligned} e_a(t) &= a - \hat{a}(t), \\ e_b(t) &= b - \hat{b}(t), \\ e_c(t) &= c - \hat{c}(t), \\ e_d(t) &= d - \hat{d}(t). \end{aligned} \tag{14}$$

It follows that

$$\begin{aligned}
\dot{e}_a &= -\dot{\hat{a}}, \\
\dot{e}_b &= -\dot{\hat{b}}, \\
\dot{e}_c &= -\dot{\hat{c}}, \\
\dot{e}_d &= -\dot{\hat{d}}.
\end{aligned} \quad (15)$$

Therefore, Equation (13) can be re-expressed as

$$\begin{aligned}
\dot{e}_x &= e_a(e_y - e_x) - k_1 e_x, \\
\dot{e}_y &= e_c e_x - k_2 e_y, \\
\dot{e}_z &= -e_b e_z - k_3 e_z.
\end{aligned} \quad (16)$$

The synchronization condition can be established based on the Lyapunov criterion of stability. We consider the quadratic Lyapunov function defined by

$$V = \frac{1}{2}(e_x^2 + e_y^2 + e_z^2 + e_a^2 + e_b^2 + e_c^2 + e_d^2).$$

Differentiating V along the trajectories of the system gives

$$\dot{V} = -k_1 e_x^2 - k_2 e_y^2 - k_3 e_z^2 - e_a(\dot{\hat{a}} - e_x(e_y - e_x)) - e_b(\dot{\hat{b}} + e_z^2) - e_c(\dot{\hat{c}} - e_x e_y) - e_d \dot{\hat{d}}. \quad (17)$$

In view of Equation (17), we take the parameter update laws as

$$\begin{aligned}
\dot{\hat{a}} &= e_x(e_y - e_x) + k_4 e_a, \\
\dot{\hat{b}} &= -e_z^2 + k_5 e_b, \\
\dot{\hat{c}} &= e_x e_y + k_6 e_c, \\
\dot{\hat{d}} &= k_7 e_d,
\end{aligned} \quad (18)$$

where $k_4, k_5, k_6,$ and k_7 are positive gain constants. By substituting Equation (18) into Equation (17), we obtain

$$\dot{V} = -k_1 e_x^2 - k_2 e_y^2 - k_3 e_z^2 - k_4 e_a^2 - k_5 e_b^2 - k_6 e_c^2 - k_7 e_d^2, \quad (19)$$

which is a definite negative Lyapunov function. According to Lyapunov stability theory, all the synchronization errors $e_x, e_y,$ and e_z and parameter estimation errors $e_a, e_b, e_c,$ and e_d globally and exponentially converge to 0 for random initial values over time.

The effectiveness of the proposed scheme is verified by numerical simulation. The master system is defined as in Equation (8) with parameters $(a, b, c, d) = (35, 3, 35, 10)$ to ensure the chaotic behavior. The gain constants are selected as $k_i = 3$ for $i = 1, 2, 3, 4, 5, 6, 7$. The initial values of the master system, slave system, and parameter estimates are taken as

$$(x_m(0), y_m(0), z_m(0)) = (1, 0, -1), (x_s(0), y_s(0), z_s(0)) = (2, -0.5, -2), (\hat{a}(0), \hat{b}(0), \hat{c}(0), \hat{d}(0)) = (3, 1, 0.5, 12). \quad (20)$$

Thus, the initial values of the errors system (16) are $e_x(0) = 1, e_y(0) = -0.5,$ and $e_z(0) = -1$. Figure 17 describes the complete synchronization of the respective states of the master and slave systems, and Figure 18 illustrates the time-history of the synchronization errors and parameter estimation errors. It can be seen that all errors asymptotically converge to zero with time, indicating that the master and slave systems finally show the same dynamical behavior.

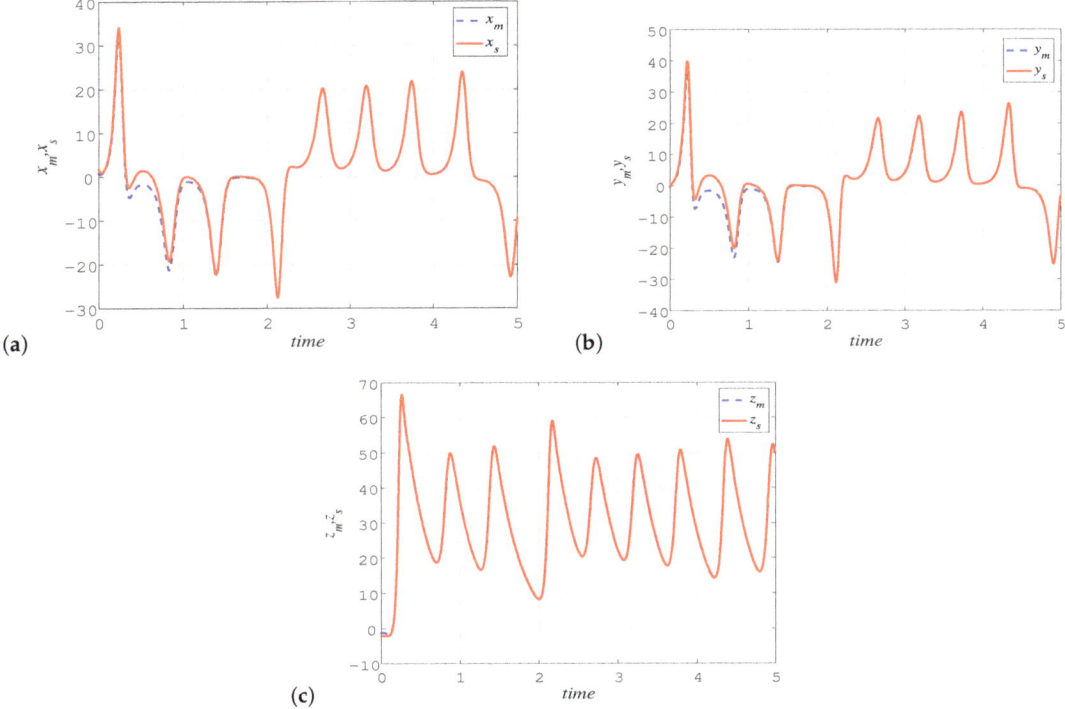

Figure 17. Time evolution sequence diagram of master and slave systems showing results of occurrence of adaptive synchronization. (**a**) x variable; (**b**) y variable; (**c**) z variable.

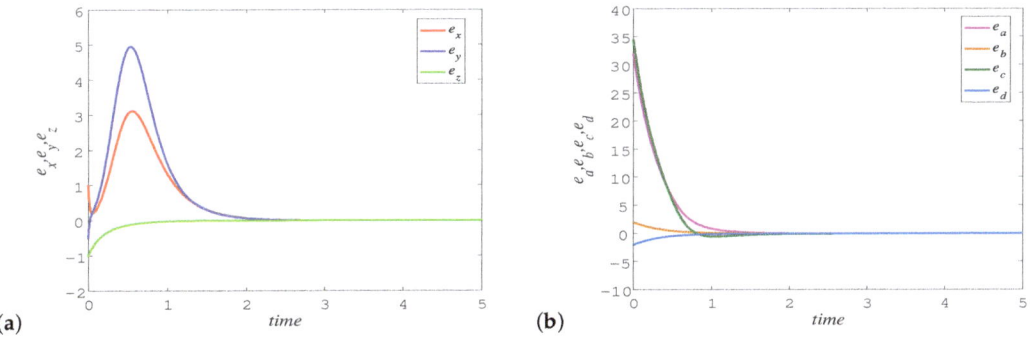

Figure 18. Time evolution of (**a**) synchronization errors e_x, e_y, and e_z, and (**b**) parameter estimation errors e_a, e_b, e_c, and e_d.

7. Conclusions

In this study, a new 3D double-wing chaotic system with two stable equilibrium points was constructed and explored. As the proposed system had only stable equilibria, it was a member of the family of hidden chaotic attractors. Dynamical characteristics, such as bifurcation diagram, basin of attractor, and offset boosting control, were investigated numerically. It was shown that the novel system with hidden attractors had very complex dynamical behaviors. One feature was that various attractors existed in the system, including equilibrium points and periodic and chaotic attractors. The other notable feature was that the system possessed a variety of different types of coexisting attractors. Unstable cycles embedded in the hidden chaotic attractors were systematically calculated by 1D symbolic dynamics, and circuit simulation for the novel double-wing chaotic system (2) was implemented to demonstrate its flexibility. A scheme for adaptive synchronization of the novel chaotic system with unknown parameters was also investigated. The new hidden attractor chaotic system has potential application prospects in the fields of secure communication, image encryption, and pseudo-random number generators.

As such, how to effectively construct the new system with multi-scroll hidden chaotic attractors is still an open problem; thus, a piecewise-linear or multi-saturated function must be employed to replace continuous functions. The mechanism of generating multi-scroll chaotic attractors is worth exploring. In this respect, the hidden bifurcation routes are considered good candidates. Furthermore, the symmetry of hidden bifurcation routes also warrants further study. The analysis method adopted in this work could promote further research of 3D autonomous chaotic systems and deepen the understanding of both hidden and coexisting attractors.

Funding: This work is supported by the National Natural Science Foundation of China (Grant Nos. 11647085 and 12205257), the Shanxi Province Science Foundation for Youths (Grant No. 201901D211252), and the Scientific and Technological Innovation Programs of Higher Education Institutions in Shanxi (Grant Nos. 2019L0505 and 2019L0554).

Institutional Review Board Statement: Not applicable.

Informed Consent Statement: Not applicable.

Data Availability Statement: The data used to support the findings of this study are available from the corresponding author upon request.

Acknowledgments: I thank the anonymous reviewers for their many insightful comments and suggestions, which substantially improved the manuscript.

Conflicts of Interest: The author declares no conflict of interest.

References

1. Lorenz, E.N. Deterministic nonperiodic flow. *J. Atmos. Sci.* **1963**, *20*, 130–141. [CrossRef]
2. Chua, L.O.; Itoh, M.; Kocarev, L.; Eckert, K. Chaos synchronization in Chua's circuit. *Int. J. Bifurcat. Chaos* **1993**, *3*, 93–108.
3. Sprott, J.C. Some simple chaotic flows. *Phys. Rev. E* **1994**, *50*, 647–650. [CrossRef] [PubMed]
4. Kuate, P.D.K.; Lai, Q.; Fotsin, H. Dynamics, synchronization and electronic implementations of a new Lorenz-like chaotic system with nonhyperbolic equilibria. *Int. J. Bifurcat. Chaos* **2019**, *29*, 1950197. [CrossRef]
5. Negou, A.N.; Kengne, J. Dynamic analysis of a unique jerk system with a smoothly adjustable symmetry and nonlinearity: Reversals of period doubling, offset boosting and coexisting bifurcations. *Int. J. Electron. Commun.* **2018**, *90*, 1–19. [CrossRef]
6. Ma, C.; Mou, J.; Xiong, L.; Banerjee, S.; Liu, T.; Han, X. Dynamical analysis of a new chaotic system: Asymmetric multistability, offset boosting control and circuit realization. *Nonlinear Dyn.* **2021**, *103*, 2867–2880. [CrossRef]
7. Strogatz, S.H. *Nonlinear Dynamics and Chaos: With Applications to Physics, Biology, Chemistry, and Engineering*; Perseus Books: Reading, MA, USA, 1994.
8. Wang, X.; Kuznetsov, N.V.; Chen, G. (Eds.) *Chaotic Systems with Multistability and Hidden Attractors*; Emergence, Complexity and Computation; Springer: Cham, Switzerland, 2021; Volume 40, p. 9.
9. Deng, Q.; Wang, C.; Wu, Y.; Lin, H. Hidden multiwing chaotic attractors with multiple stable equilibrium points. *Circuit World* **2022**, ahead-of-print. [CrossRef]
10. Dong, C. Dynamics, periodic orbit analysis, and circuit implementation of a new chaotic system with hidden attractor. *Fractal Fract.* **2022**, *6*, 190. [CrossRef]
11. Yang, Q.; Wei, Z.; Chen, G. An unusual 3d autonomous quadratic chaotic system with two stable node-foci. *Int. J. Bifurcat. Chaos* **2010**, *20*, 1061–1083. [CrossRef]
12. Jafari, S.; Sprott, J.C. Simple chaotic flows with a line equilibrium. *Chaos Soliton. Fract.* **2013**, *57*, 79–84. [CrossRef]
13. Ma, J.; Chen, Z.; Wang, Z.; Zhang, Q. A four-wing hyper-chaotic attractor generated from a 4-D memristive system with a line equilibrium. *Nonlinear Dyn.* **2015**, *81*, 1275–1288. [CrossRef]
14. Kingni, S.T.; Pham, V.T.; Jafari, S.; Woafo, P. A chaotic system with an infinite number of equilibrium points located on a line and on a hyperbola and its fractional-order form. *Chaos Soliton. Fract.* **2017**, *99*, 209–218. [CrossRef]
15. Pham, V.T.; Jafari, S.; Volos, C.; Kapitaniak, T. A gallery of chaotic systems with an infinite number of equilibrium points. *Chaos Soliton. Fract.* **2016**, *93*, 58–63. [CrossRef]

16. Huynh, V.V.; Khalaf, A.J.M.; Alsaedi, A.; Hayat, T.; Abdolmohammadi, H.R. A new memristive chaotic flow with a line of equilibria. *Eur. Phys. J. Spec. Top.* **2019**, *228*, 2339–2349. [CrossRef]
17. Nazarimehr, F.; Sprott, J.C. Investigating chaotic attractor of the simplest chaotic system with a line of equilibria. *Eur. Phys. J. Spec. Top.* **2020**, *229*, 1289–1297. [CrossRef]
18. Vaidyanathan, S.; Pham, V.T.; Volos, C.K. A 5-D hyperchaotic Rikitake dynamo system with hidden attractors. *Eur. Phys. J. Spec. Top.* **2015**, *224*, 1575–1592. [CrossRef]
19. Chowdhury, S.N.; Ghosh, D. Hidden attractors: A new chaotic system without equilibria. *Eur. Phys. J. Spec. Top.* **2020**, *229*, 1299–1308. [CrossRef]
20. Wang, N.; Zhang, G.; Kuznetsov, N.V.; Li, H. Generating grid chaotic sea from system without equilibrium point. *Commun. Nonlinear Sci. Numer. Simul.* **2022**, *107*, 106194. [CrossRef]
21. Dong, C.; Wang, J. Hidden and coexisting attractors in a novel 4D hyperchaotic system with no equilibrium point. *Fractal Fract.* **2022**, *6*, 306. [CrossRef]
22. Almatroud, A.O.; Matouk, A.E.; Mohammed, W.W.; Iqbal, N.; Alshammari, S. Self-excited and hidden chaotic attractors in Matouks's hyperchaotic systems. *Discrete Dyn. Nat. Soc.* **2022**, *2022*, 6458027. [CrossRef]
23. Yan, H.; Jiang, J.; Hong, L. The birth of a hidden attractor through boundary crisi. *Int. J. Bifurcat. Chaos* **2022**, *32*, 2230005. [CrossRef]
24. Pham, V.T.; Jafari, S.; Volos, C.; Fortuna, L. Simulation and experimental implementation of a line–equilibrium system without linear term. *Chaos Soliton. Fract.* **2019**, *120*, 213–221. [CrossRef]
25. Tapche, R.W.; Njitacke, Z.T.; Kengne, J.; Pelap, F.B. Complex dynamics of a novel 3D autonomous system without linear terms having line of equilibria: Coexisting bifurcations and circuit design. *Analog Integr. Circ. Sig. Process.* **2020**, *103*, 57–71. [CrossRef]
26. Tan, Q.; Zeng, Y.; Li, Z. A simple inductor-free memristive circuit with three line equilibria. *Nonlinear Dyn.* **2018**, *94*, 1585–1602. [CrossRef]
27. Tian, H.; Wang, Z.; Zhang, H.; Cao, Z.; Zhang, P. Dynamical analysis and fixed-time synchronization of a chaotic system with hidden attractor and a line equilibrium. *Eur. Phys. J. Spec. Top.* **2022**, *231*, 2455–2466. [CrossRef]
28. Zeng, D.; Li, Z.; Ma, M.; Wang, M. Generating self-excited and hidden attractors with complex dynamics in a memristor-based Jerk system. *Indian J. Phys.* **2022**, 1–15. [CrossRef]
29. Zhang, X.; Wang, C. Multiscroll hyperchaotic system with hidden attractors and its circuit implementation. *Int. J. Bifurcat. Chaos* **2019**, *29*, 1950117. [CrossRef]
30. Li, C.; Sprott, J.C. Multistability in the Lorenz system: A broken butterfly. *Int. J. Bifurcat. Chaos* **2014**, *24*, 1450131. [CrossRef]
31. Doubla, I.S.; Ramakrishnan, B.; Tabekoueng, Z.N.; Kengne, J.; Rajagopal, K. Infinitely many coexisting hidden attractors in a new hyperbolic-type memristor-based HNN. *Eur. Phys. J. Spec. Top.* **2022**, *231*, 2371–2385. [CrossRef]
32. Lai, Q.; Wang, Z. Dynamical analysis, FPGA implementation and synchronization for secure communication of new chaotic system with hidden and coexisting attractors. *Mod. Phys. Lett. B* **2022**, *36*, 2150538. [CrossRef]
33. Ahmadi, A.; Rajagopal, K.; Alsaadi, F.E.; Pham, V.T.; Alsaadi, F.E.; Jafari, S. A Novel 5D chaotic system with extreme multi-stability and a line of equilibrium and its engineering applications: Circuit design and FPGA implementation. *Iran. J. Sci. Technol. Trans. Electr. Eng.* **2020**, *44*, 59–67. [CrossRef]
34. Bao, J.; Chen, D. Coexisting hidden attractors in a 4D segmented disc dynamo with one stable equilibrium or a line equilibrium. *Chin. Phys. B* **2017**, *26*, 080201. [CrossRef]
35. Dang, X.Y.; Li, C.B.; Bao, B.C.; Wu, H.G. Complex transient dynamics of hidden attractors in a simple 4D system. *Chin. Phys. B* **2015**, *24*, 050503. [CrossRef]
36. Bayani, A.; Rajagopal, K.; Khalaf, A.J.M.; Jafari, S.; Leutcho, G.D.; Kengne, J. Dynamical analysis of a new multistable chaotic system with hidden attractor: Antimonotonicity, coexisting multiple attractors, and offset boosting. *Phys. Lett. A* **2019**, *383*, 1450–1456. [CrossRef]
37. Wen, J.; Feng, Y.; Tao, X.; Cao, Y. Dynamical analysis of a new chaotic system: Hidden attractor, coexisting-attractors, offset boosting, and DSP realization. *IEEE Access* **2021**, *9*, 167920–167927. [CrossRef]
38. Pham, V.T.; Volos, C.; Jafari, S.; Kapitaniak, T. Coexistence of hidden chaotic attractors in a novel no-equilibrium system. *Nonlinear Dyn.* **2017**, *87*, 2001–2010. [CrossRef]
39. Yang, Q.; Chen, G. A chaotic system with one saddle and two stable node-foci. *Int. J. Bifurcat. Chaos* **2008**, *18*, 1393–1414. [CrossRef]
40. Wolf, A.; Swift, J.B.; Swinney H.L.; Vastano J.A. Determining Lyapunov exponents from a time series. *Phys. D* **1985**, *16*, 285–317. [CrossRef]
41. Hislop, P.D.; Sigal, I.M. The general theory of spectral stability. In *Introduction to Spectral Theory*; Applied Mathematical Sciences; Springer: New York, NY, USA, 1996; Volume 113.
42. Zhou, L.; You, Z.; Tang, Y. A new chaotic system with nested coexisting multiple attractors and riddled basins. *Chaos Soliton. Fract.* **2021**, *148*, 111057. [CrossRef]
43. Sambas, A.; Vaidyanathan, S.; Zhang, S.; Zeng, Y.; Mohamed, M.A.; Mamat, M. A new double-wing chaotic system with coexisting attractors and line equilibrium: Bifurcation analysis and electronic circuit simulation. *IEEE Access* **2019**, *7*, 115454–115462. [CrossRef]

44. Zhang, Z.; Huang, L.; Liu, J.; Guo, Q.; Du, X. A new method of constructing cyclic symmetric conservative chaotic systems and improved offset boosting control. *Chaos Soliton. Fract.* **2022**, *158*, 112103. [CrossRef]
45. Li, C.; Sprott, J.C.; Liu, Y.; Gu, Z.; Zhang, J. Offset boosting for breeding conditional symmetry. *Int. J. Bifurcat. Chaos* **2018**, *28*, 1850163. [CrossRef]
46. Liu, X.C.; Tu, Q. Coexisting and hidden attractors of memristive chaotic systems with and without equilibria. *Eur. Phys. J. Plus* **2022**, *137*, 516. [CrossRef]
47. Hao, B.L.; Zheng, W.M. *Applied Symbolic Dynamics and Chaos*; World Scientic: Singapore, 1998; pp. 11–13.
48. Lan, Y.; Cvitanović, P. Variational method for finding periodic orbits in a general flow. *Phys. Rev. E* **2004**, *69*, 016217. [CrossRef]
49. Dong, C.; Lan, Y. Organization of spatially periodic solutions of the steady Kuramoto–Sivashinsky equation. *Commun. Nonlinear Sci. Numer. Simul.* **2014**, *19*, 2140–2153. [CrossRef]
50. Dong, C. Topological classification of periodic orbits in the Kuramoto–Sivashinsky equation. *Mod. Phys. Lett. B*, **2018**, *32*, 1850155. [CrossRef]
51. Dong, C. Periodic orbits of diffusionless Lorenz system. *Acta Phys. Sin.* **2018**, *67*, 240501. [CrossRef]
52. Dong, C.; Liu, H.; Li, H. Unstable periodic orbits analysis in the generalized Lorenz–type system. *J. Stat. Mech.* **2020**, *2020*, 073211. [CrossRef]
53. Dong, C.; Jia, L.; Jie, Q.; Li, H. Symbolic encoding of periodic orbits and chaos in the Rucklidge system. *Complexity* **2021**, *2021*, 4465151. [CrossRef]
54. Dong, C.; Liu, H.; Jie, Q.; Li, H. Topological classification of periodic orbits in the generalized Lorenz-type system with diverse symbolic dynamics. *Chaos Soliton. Fract.* **2022**, *154*, 111686. [CrossRef]
55. Sene, N. On the modeling and numerical discretizations of a chaotic system via fractional operators with and without singular kernels. *Math. Sci.* **2022**, 1–21. [CrossRef]
56. Hammouch, Z.; Yavuz, M.; Ödemir, N. Numerical solutions and synchronization of a variable-order fractional chaotic system. *Math. Model. Numer. Simul. Appl.* **2021**, *1*, 11–23. [CrossRef]
57. Gao, X.J.; Cheng, M.F.; Hu, H.P. Adaptive impulsive synchronization of uncertain delayed chaotic system with full unknown parameters via discrete-time drive signals. *Complexity* **2016**, *21*, 43–51. [CrossRef]
58. Azar, A.T.; Volos, C.; Gerodimos, N.A.; Tombras, G.S.; Pham, V.T.; Radwan, A.G.; Vaidyanathan, S.; Ouannas, A.; Munoz-Pacheco, J.M. A novel chaotic system without equilibrium: Dynamics, synchronization, and circuit realization. *Complexity* **2017**, *2017*, 7871467. [CrossRef]

Article

Fractional Order Fuzzy Dispersion Entropy and Its Application in Bearing Fault Diagnosis

Yuxing Li [1,2], Bingzhao Tang [1], Bo Geng [1] and Shangbin Jiao [1,2,*]

[1] School of Automation and Information Engineering, Xi'an University of Technology, Xi'an 710048, China
[2] Shaanxi Key Laboratory of Complex System Control and Intelligent Information Processing, Xi'an University of Technology, Xi'an 710048, China
* Correspondence: jiaoshangbin@xaut.edu.cn

Abstract: Fuzzy dispersion entropy (FuzzDE) is a very recently proposed non-linear dynamical indicator, which combines the advantages of both dispersion entropy (DE) and fuzzy entropy (FuzzEn) to detect dynamic changes in a time series. However, FuzzDE only reflects the information of the original signal and is not very sensitive to dynamic changes. To address these drawbacks, we introduce fractional order calculation on the basis of FuzzDE, propose FuzzDE$_\alpha$, and use it as a feature for the signal analysis and fault diagnosis of bearings. In addition, we also introduce other fractional order entropies, including fractional order DE (DE$_\alpha$), fractional order permutation entropy (PE$_\alpha$) and fractional order fluctuation-based DE (FDE$_\alpha$), and propose a mixed features extraction diagnosis method. Both simulated as well as real-world experimental results demonstrate that the FuzzDE$_\alpha$ at different fractional orders is more sensitive to changes in the dynamics of the time series, and the proposed mixed features bearing fault diagnosis method achieves 100% recognition rate at just triple features, among which, the mixed feature combinations with the highest recognition rates all have FuzzDE$_\alpha$, and FuzzDE$_\alpha$ also appears most frequently.

Keywords: fuzzy dispersion entropy; fractional order; feature extraction; bearing fault diagnosis

1. Introduction

Entropy, as a measure of time series disorder and predictability, can evaluate the complexity of the signal [1,2]. The greater the entropy value, the higher the complexity of signal [3,4]. In recently years, entropy has been widely applied in mechanical fault diagnosis and has shown excellent performance [5–7].

Dispersion entropy (DE) divides time series into integer series by introducing different mapping criteria for the first time [8], which enables it to capture more amplitude information than permutation entropy (PE) and sample entropy (SE) [9,10]. Some scholars have made every attempt to study the improved version of DE to further enhance its performance as a complexity index. Fluctuation-based DE (FDE) and reverse DE (RDE) have also been proposed by introducing fluctuation information and distance information between time series and white noise [11–13]. In 2021, by combining the fluctuation information of FDE and the distance information of RDE [14], the reverse DE (FRDE) based on fluctuation is proposed, which has better stability and discrimination ability for different types of time series.

Fuzzy dispersion entropy (FuzzDE) is a new method proposed in 2021 [15], which combines the advantages of fuzzy entropy (FuzzEn) as well as DE by replacing the round mapping function of DE with fuzzy membership function in FuzzEn, by which the dynamic changes of time series can be retained to a greater extent and the problem of missing useful information brought about by round mapping function can be alleviated. Nevertheless, the FuzzDE still suffers from the same problem of single feature as common entropies, which cannot characterize the time series from multiple fractional orders.

To address the problem of single fractional order, in recent years, many scholars have conducted research on the application of fractional order calculation to entropy [16–18]. In

2019, the fractional fuzzy entropy algorithm was proposed and used for physiological and biomedical analysis of EEG signals [19]. In 2020, generalized refined composite multiscale fluctuation-based fractional dispersion entropy (GRCMFDE$_\alpha$) combined refined composite multiscale dispersion entropy (RCMDE) as well as fractional order calculation and was applied for bearing signal fault diagnosis with good results [20]. In 2022, fractional order calculation was introduced to slope entropy to effectively diagnose the location and severity of faults in rolling bearings [21].

Inspired by these works, we introduce fractional order calculation into FuzzDE in this paper, and fractional order FuzzDE (FuzzDE$_\alpha$) is proposed. Compared with FuzzDE, FuzzDE$_\alpha$ further considers fractional order information and measures the dynamic changes of time series from multiple fractional orders. In addition, we combine FuzzDE$_\alpha$ with other fractional order entropies and propose a mixed feature bearing fault diagnosis method. Simulated as well as real-world experiments demonstrate the sensitivity of FuzzDE$_\alpha$ to the dynamic changes of time series and the excellent performance on bearing fault diagnosis.

The rest of this paper is organized as follows: Section 2 presents the theoretical steps of FuzzDE$_\alpha$ and discusses the parameter settings; Section 3 experiments on the effectiveness of fractional order on FuzzDE through simulated signals; Section 4 validates the bearing fault diagnosis capability of FuzzDE$_\alpha$ through real-world bearing signals; Section 5 concludes the whole paper.

2. Fractional Order Fuzzy Dispersion Entropy

2.1. FuzzDE$_\alpha$

FuzzDE$_\alpha$ is the introduction of the concept of fractional order calculation on the basis of FuzzDE, for a given time series $X = \{x_1, x_2, \cdots, x_N\}$ of length N, the specific steps for FuzzDE$_\alpha$ can be expressed as follows:

Step 1: By applying the normal cumulative distribution function (NCDF) to the original time series X, $Y = \{y_1, y_2, \cdots, y_N\}$ can be derived with the interval $[-1, 1]$, where the NCDF can be expressed as follows:

$$y_i = \frac{1}{\sigma\sqrt{2\pi}} \int_{-\infty}^{x_i} e^{\frac{-(t-\gamma)^2}{2\sigma^2}} dt \ (i = 1, 2, \cdots, N)$$

where σ and γ represent the standard deviation and mean of X, respectively.

Step 2: Normalize the sequence Y by converting each element in Y to the interval $[0, 1]$:

$$s_i = \frac{y_i}{Max - Min} \ (i = 1, 2, \cdots, N)$$

in which $S = \{s_1, s_2, \cdots, s_N\}$ is the normalized sequence, Max and Min are the maximum and minimum values of the sequence Y, respectively.

Step 3: Introduce the class number c to convert the sequence S into a new sequence Z^c [15]:

$$z_i^c = cy_i + 0.5 \ (i = 1, 2, \cdots, N)$$

where each element z_i^c $(i = 1, 2, \cdots, N)$ in Z^c is in the interval $[0.5, c + 0.5]$.

Step 4: Introduce the embedding dimension m and time delay τ, reconstruct the sequence Z^c of Step 3 into $N - (m+1)\tau$ subsequences $Z_j^{m,c}$:

$$Z_j^{m,c} = \left\{z_j^c, z_{j+(1)\tau}^c, \cdots, z_{j+(m-1)\tau}^c\right\} \ (j = 1, 2, \cdots, N - (m+1)\tau) \tag{1}$$

where m determines the number of elements contained in each subsequence $Z_j^{m,c}$, and τ determines the interval between two adjacent elements in the sequence Z^c.

Step 5: Introduce the fuzzy membership function on the sequence Z^c as follows:

$$\mu_{M_1}(z_i^c) = \begin{cases} 0 & z_i^c > 2 \\ 2 - z_i^c & 1 \leq z_i^c \leq 2 \\ 1 & z_i^c < 1 \end{cases}$$

$$\mu_{M_k}(z_i^c) = \begin{cases} 0 & z_i^c > k+1 \\ k+1-z_i^c & k \leq z_i^c \leq k+1 \\ z_i^c - k + 1 & k-1 \leq z_i^c \leq k \\ 0 & z_i^c < k-1 \end{cases} (k = 2, 3, \cdots, c-1)$$

$$\mu_{M_c}(z_i^c) = \begin{cases} 1 & z_i^c > c \\ z_i^c - c + 1 & c-1 \leq z_i^c \leq c \\ 0 & z_i^c < c-1 \end{cases}$$

where k stands for the kth class, and M_k is the fuzzy membership function, $\mu_{M_k}(z_i^c)$ represents the degree of membership of z_i^c for the kth class. By the fuzzy membership function, each z_i^c will have 1 or 2 different degrees, and the value range is an integer between [1, c], which is the same as the rounding function in the DE [8], but reduces the information loss in the rounding function. Figure 1 shows the fuzzy membership function.

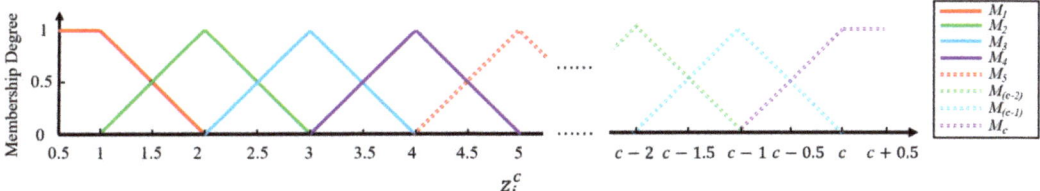

Figure 1. Fuzzy membership function.

Step 6: After the processing of the sequence Z^c in Step 5, each subsequence $Z_j^{m,c}$ can be mapped into a number of new sequences consisting of integers, and these sequences can be represented by the dispersion patterns $\pi_{v_0 v_1 \cdots v_{m-1}}$, where v_0, v_1, v_{m-1} correspond to the integer values of z_j^c, $z_{j+(1)\tau}^c$, and $z_{j+(m-1)\tau}^c$ in Equation (1) after fuzzy processing, respectively.

Step 7: Calculate the degree of membership of each $Z_j^{m,c}$ with respect to the dispersion patterns $\pi_{v_0 v_1 \cdots v_{m-1}}$ and denote as $\mu_{\pi_{v_0 v_1 \cdots v_{m-1}}}$:

$$\mu_{\pi_{v_0 v_1 \cdots v_{m-1}}}(z_j^{m,c}) = \prod_{i=0}^{m-1} \mu_{M_{v_i}}(z_{j+(i)\tau}^c)$$

in this manner, each subsequence $Z_j^{m,c}$ will correspond to multiple dispersion patterns accompanied by different membership degrees. For an example, given a subsequence $Z_1^{2,3} = [1.149, 2.306]$, all the member ship degrees can be organized as follows:

$$\begin{cases} \mu_{M_1}(z_1^3) = 0.851 \\ \mu_{M_2}(z_1^3) = 0.149 \\ \mu_{M_2}(z_2^3) = 0.694 \\ \mu_{M_3}(z_2^3) = 0.306 \end{cases} \rightarrow \begin{cases} \mu_{\pi_{12}}(Z_1^{2,3}) = \mu_{M_1}(z_1^3) \times \mu_{M_2}(z_2^3) = 0.5906 \\ \mu_{\pi_{13}}(Z_1^{2,3}) = \mu_{M_1}(z_1^3) \times \mu_{M_3}(z_2^3) = 0.2604 \\ \mu_{\pi_{22}}(Z_1^{2,3}) = \mu_{M_2}(z_1^3) \times \mu_{M_2}(z_2^3) = 0.1034 \\ \mu_{\pi_{23}}(Z_1^{2,3}) = \mu_{M_2}(z_1^3) \times \mu_{M_3}(z_2^3) = 0.0456 \end{cases}$$

Step 8: The frequency of each dispersion pattern $p\left(\pi_{v_0,v_1,\ldots,v_{m-1}}\right)$ can be calculated:

$$p\left(\pi_{v_0,v_1,\ldots,v_{m-1}}\right) = \frac{\sum_{j=1}^{N-(m-1)d} \mu_{\pi_{v_0 v_1 \cdots v_{m-1}}}\left(\mathbf{z}_j^{m,c}\right)}{N-(m-1)\tau}$$

Step 9: For writing convenience, we define $p\left(\pi_{v_0,v_1,\ldots,v_{m-1}}\right)$ as P_j. Then the fractional order calculation is applied, and the FuzzDE$_\alpha$ can be expressed as [20]:

$$\text{FuzzDE}_\alpha(X,m,c,\tau) = \sum_j P_j\left\{-\frac{P_j^{-\alpha}}{\Gamma(\alpha+1)}\left[\ln P_j + \psi(1) - \psi(1-\alpha)\right]\right\}$$

where α is the order of fractional derivative. $\Gamma(\cdot)$ and $\psi(\cdot)$ denote the gamma function and digamma function respectively.

Step 10: The normalized form NFuzzDE$_\alpha$ of FuzzDE$_\alpha$ can be computed as:

$$\text{NFuzzDE}_\alpha(X,m,c,\tau) = \frac{\text{FuzzDE}_\alpha(X,m,c,\tau)}{\ln(c^m)}$$

2.2. Parameter Selection

In this subsection, we mainly focus on the discussion of the parameter selection for FuzzDE$_\alpha$. For the parameter comparison experiments, 50 separate groups of pink noises, white noises and blue noises are selected [20], each with 2048 sample points. Where white noise consists of a homogeneous mixture of signals of different frequencies, with a variety of frequencies in a haphazard manner. Pink noise enhances the sound intensity of low frequency signals and weakens the intensity of high frequency signals compared to white noise, while blue noise, in contrast, enhances the sound intensity of the high frequency signal on top of the white noise. Using the control variables method, the effects of three FuzzDE$_\alpha$ parameters, namely the number of classes c, the embedding dimension m and the mapping method, on the mean as well as the standard deviation of the selected noise signals are explored as shown in Figures 2–4, respectively.

To begin with, we conduct comparative experiments on the effects of c, and the interval is set to an integer between 2 and 5 (m = 3, mapping as NCDF), Figure 2 shows the means and standard deviations of different class number c at different fractional orders.

Comparing the four images, it can be seen that for the average of the entropy values of the three noises, the trend when m equals 3 and c equals 2 is different from the other three in that it has a slope from large to small, while the others are from small to large. However, the general trend is that it increases with the increase of α. For the standard deviation of the entropy values of the three noise entropy values, the standard deviation of the pink noise is larger, and the others are smaller, and as α increases, the value of the standard deviation also increases, which is especially evident in the pink noise. In summary, changes in c have an impact on the magnitude of entropy value, but the overall trend in entropy value and the ability to discriminate between different noises does not change as the fractional order changes.

We next discuss the effect of m, with the interval set to an integer between 3 and 6 (c = 3, mapping as NCDF), Figure 3 is means and standard deviations of different embedding dimensions m at different fractional orders.

Observing the four subplots, for the average of the FuzzDE$_\alpha$ values of the three noises, all four cases of taking values show a similar upward trend. For the standard deviation of the entropy values of the three noises, there is only a difference between the exact values and the overall trend is almost the same. Thus, it is clear that the effect of m has a greater impact on the magnitude of the entropy value compared to c, but the overall trend and the ability to distinguish between different noises does not change.

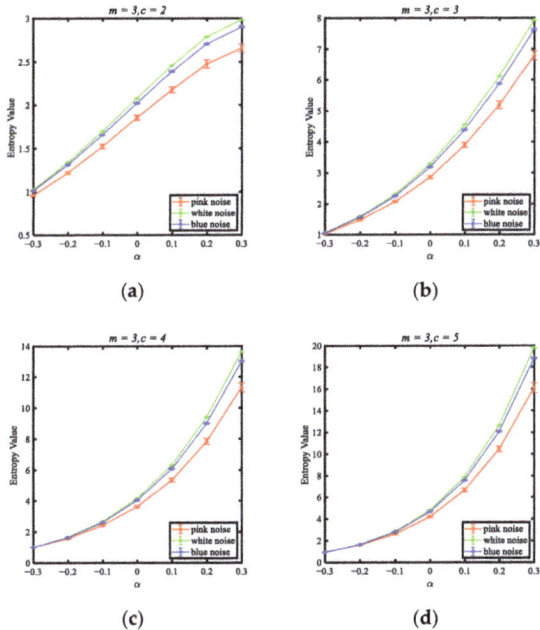

Figure 2. Means and standard deviations of different class number c at different fractional orders. (**a**) $c = 2$; (**b**) $c = 3$; (**c**) $c = 4$; (**d**) $c = 5$.

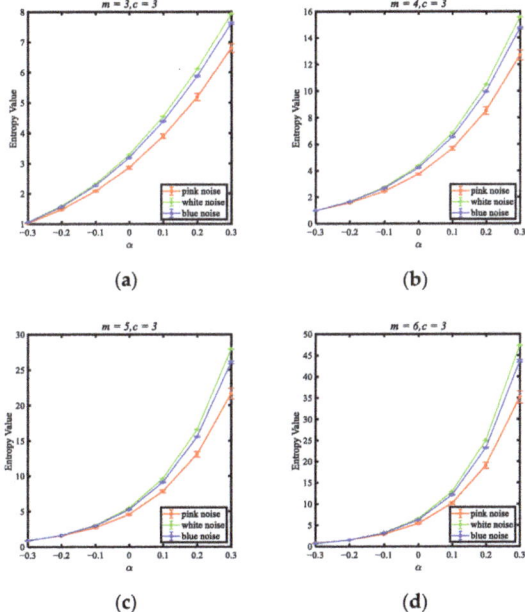

Figure 3. Means and standard deviations of different embedding dimensions m at different fractional orders. (**a**) $m = 3$; (**b**) $m = 4$; (**c**) $m = 5$; (**d**) $m = 6$.

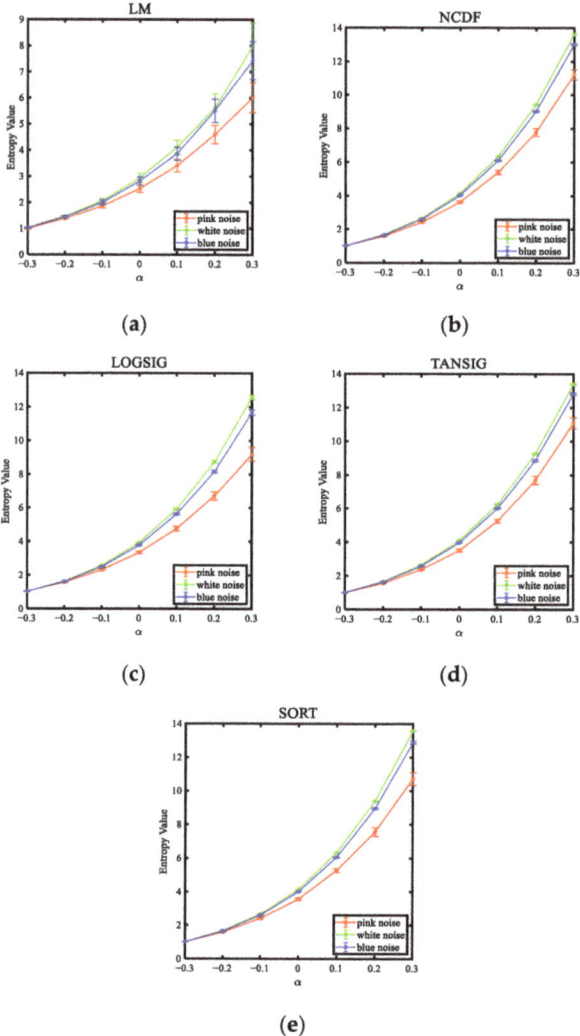

Figure 4. Means and standard deviations of different mapping approaches at different fractional orders. (**a**) LM; (**b**) NCDF; (**c**) LOGISG; (**d**) TANSIG; (**e**) SORT.

Finally, we discuss the effect of the mapping method, which is also an important influencing factor, so we choose different mapping methods for comparison. Figure 4 shows the means and standard deviations of different mapping approaches at different fractional orders, among which the mapping methods include linear mapping (LM), normal cumulative distribution function (NCDF), tangent sigmoid (TANSIG), logarithm sigmoid (LOGSIG), and sorting method (SORT) respectively ($c = 3$, $m = 3$) [8–11].

According to Figure 4, the overall trends of the five mapping methods are very similar, but when using the LM mapping method, the standard deviation of the various noise entropy values is significantly larger, accompanied by the condition that the various noise entropy values overlap each other, which indicates that when the selected mapping method is LM, the stability of FuzzDE$_\alpha$ after mapping is relatively weak, and it is difficult to distinguish the three types of noise. While the standard deviation of other mapping methods is relatively small. Therefore, it is concluded that NCDF, LOGISG, TANSIG or SORT are the recommended mapping approaches.

In conclusion, m and c have little effect on the experiment, but a large m is more likely to lead to an increase in FuzzDE$_\alpha$ values compared to c. Among all mapping methods, only LM is not stable. Therefore, we recommend that m be set to 3–6, c to 2–5 and the mapping method be NCDF, LOGISG, TANSIG or SORT. In the later simulations and the real-world signal experiments, we choose m = 3, c = 4 and the mapping method to be NCDF.

3. Experiments on Simulated Signals

In this section, we focus on demonstrating the usefulness of fractional order calculations on FuzzDE by simulated signals, mainly including noise signals, chirp signal and MIX signal.

3.1. Noise Signals Experiment

In order to verify the effectiveness of fractional order calculation on FuzzDE, pink noise, white noise and blue noise are selected for comparative experiments, and the fractional orders change from -0.5 to 0.5 with interval 0.1. 100 independent pink noises, white noises and blue noises are created to prove the discrimination ability of fractional order. The means and standard deviations of these 100 FuzzDE$_\alpha$. values are calculated respectively as displayed in Figure 5.

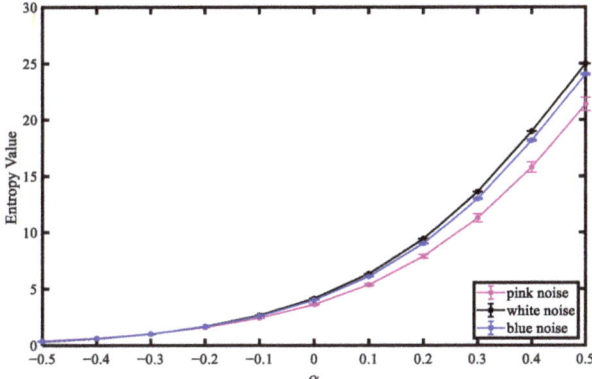

Figure 5. Means and standard deviations of different fractional order entropies under noise signals.

As shown in Figure 5, the FuzzDE$_\alpha$ value of the three kinds of noise signals has a similar upward trend with the increase of fractional order; when the fractional order is less than -0.1, the mean characteristics of the three noise signals are mixed together; when the fractional order is greater than -0.1, the difference of mean characteristics of the three noise signals gradually increases, and the FuzzDE$_\alpha$ value of white noise is the largest, with the smallest standard deviation and the most stable FuzzDE$_\alpha$ value. Experiments show that as the fractional order increases (when the fractional order is greater than -0.1), FuzzDE$_\alpha$ has a better distinguishing effect on pink noise, white noise and blue noise.

3.2. Chirp Signal Experiment

Chirp signal is a typical unstable signal, and frequency of chirp signal will change over time [22,23]. In order to better show the feature extraction effect of FuzzDE$_\alpha$ at different fractional orders, chirp signal is used for simulated experiments. Chirp signal can be expressed as:

$$x(t) = e^{(j2\pi(f_0 t + \frac{1}{2}kt^2))}$$

where f_0 is the initiation frequency and is taken as 20 Hz, k is the modulation frequency and is taken as 3, we can understand that the frequency increases from 20 Hz to 80 Hz. The chirp signal lasts 20 s with a sampling frequency of 1000 Hz (20,000 sampling points).

We take the length of the sliding window as 1000 sampling points, and slide backward from the first sampling point with 90% overlap to obtain 190 samples. FuzzDE$_\alpha$ for chirp signal of each sample are calculated. Chirp signal (top) and the corresponding different entropy curves (bottom) are shown in Figure 6.

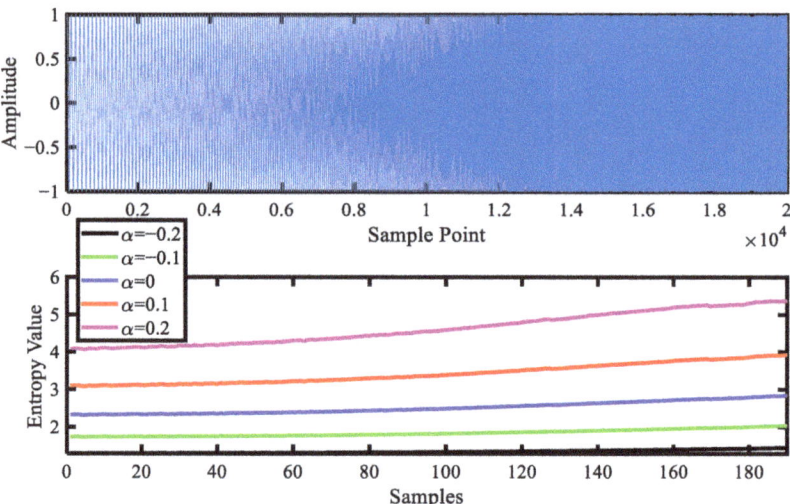

Figure 6. Chirp signal (**top**) and the corresponding different entropy curves (**bottom**).

It can be observed from Figure 6 that the waveform of the chirp signal gradually becomes denser as the number of sampling points increases, and the higher the fractional order, the larger the FuzzDE$_\alpha$ value as well as the rate of increase of the curve. In a word, the experimental results show that the higher the fractional order of FuzzDE$_\alpha$, the better performance of FuzzDE$_\alpha$ in chirp signal feature extraction.

3.3. MIX Signal Experiment

In order to study the influence for fractional order of FuzzDE$_\alpha$ on the effect of feature extraction, we select MIX signal for simulated experiments. MIX signal describes a stochastic sequence that progressively turns into a periodic time series [24,25], which can be expressed as:

$$\begin{cases} MIX(t) = (1-Z) \times X(t) + Z \times Y(t) \\ X(t) = \sqrt{2}\sin\frac{2\pi t}{12} \end{cases}$$

where $X(t)$ is a periodic signal, the value of $Y(t)$ is uniformly distributed from $-\sqrt{3}$ to $\sqrt{3}$, and Z is a random number taking 1 or 0 with probabilities P and $1-P$, respectively, and decreasing linearly from 0.99 at the beginning to 0.01 at the end. The sampling frequency of mix signal is 1000 Hz, with a total of 20 s. We take the length of sliding window as 1000 sampling points, and slide backward from the first sampling point with 90% overlap to obtain 190 samples. MIX signal (top) and the corresponding different entropy curves (bottom) are shown in Figure 7.

As can be seen from Figure 7, the MIX signal changes from dense to sparse as the number of sampling points increases; the value of FuzzDE$_\alpha$ decreases as the number of sampling points increases; the higher the fractional order, the larger the FuzzDE$_\alpha$ value and the rate of decline of the curve also increases. Therefore, we can conclude that an increase in fractional order can better reflect the complexity of the MIX signal.

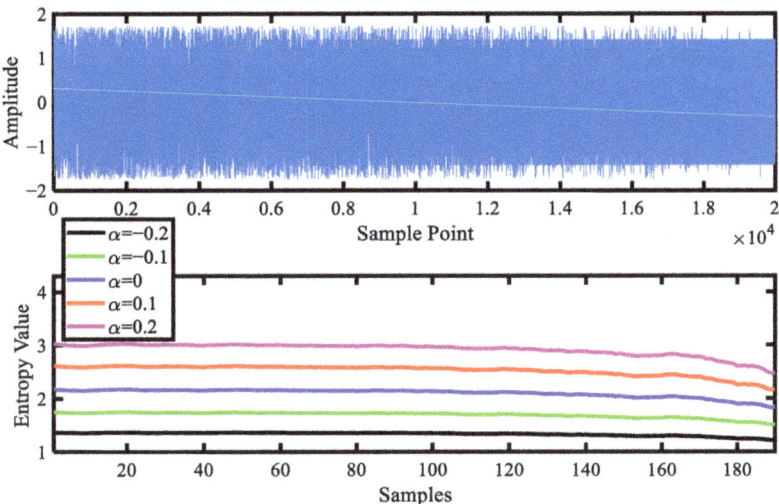

Figure 7. MIX signal (**top**) and the corresponding different entropy curves (**bottom**).

4. Experiments on Bearing Fault Diagnosis

In this section, we focus on the bearing fault diagnosis, and achieve early prevention in order to avoid economic losses and even personal safety due to different bearing faults. Since entropy can be used to detect changes in the dynamics of weak time series, the higher the entropy value, the more unstable the time series and vice versa. At the same fault size, different faults have similar amplitude-frequency features, but their bearing fault complexity and dynamics changes are different, and these changes can be reflected in successive subsequences, for which entropy features can be extracted for fault diagnosis of the bearing signals. The experiments in this section are mainly to verify the effectiveness of FuzzDE$_\alpha$ for bearing fault diagnosis, and the proposed mixed features bearing fault diagnosis method experimental flow chart is shown in Figure 8, with the following steps:

Step 1: Input the real-world bearing signals of ten different classes.

Step 2: Segment the input signals into M samples, each with N sample points, by which way, we receive a total of M samples for each class of signal.

Step 3: For each sample, calculate their FuzzDE$_\alpha$ values at different fractional orders. For the purpose of contrast, we also introduce fractional order DE (DE$_\alpha$), fractional order PE (PE$_\alpha$) and fractional order FDE (FDE$_\alpha$) for comparison, with fractional orders of -0.2, -0.1, 0, 0.1, and 0.2 respectively.

Step 4: Mix the 20 features obtained in Step 3 and set the number of selected features to K (initialized to 2), by which way we can acquire a total of C_{20}^K combinations.

Step 5: Calculate the recognition rate of all C_{20}^K combinations and select the combination with the highest recognition rate.

Step 6: Determine the direction of the process by the number of features selected, and if $K < 5$, skip to Step 7; otherwise, output the combination of 5 features with the highest recognition rate and the corresponding recognition rate, as a way to avoid the increased computational consumption when the recognition rate has reached the threshold.

Step 7: Determine the direction of the process by the highest recognition rate among K feature combinations. If the recognition rate reaches 100%, then output these feature combinations; otherwise, let $K = K + 1$ and back to Step 5.

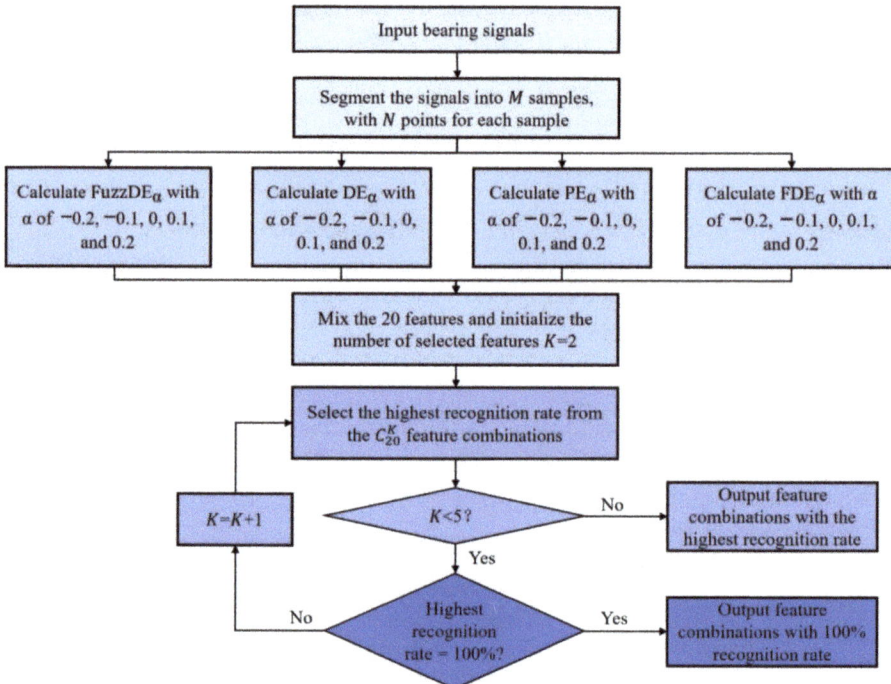

Figure 8. Flow chart of the proposed mixed features bearing fault diagnosis method.

4.1. Analysis of Experiment Data

This section employs the bearing signal obtained from Case Western Reserve University (CWRU) [26] to verify the effectiveness of the proposed FuzzDE$_\alpha$. The bearing under test is a deep groove ball bearing type SKF6205 (CWRU, Cleveland, America) with a motor speed set to 1730 r/min and a load of 3 hp. The original bearing signal is acquired by collecting the acceleration sensor installed at the driving end, and the sampling frequency is 12 kHz. Depending on the states of the bearing and the diameters of the failure, there are 10 different types of bearing signals marked NORM, IR1, BE1, OR1, IR2, BE2, OR2, IR3, BE3 and OR3, all damage is caused by electro discharge machining as a single point of damage. The details of the selected bearing signals are shown in Table 1. For each class of bearing signal, the length of sample points is 120,000, and Figure 9 shows the time domain distribution of ten classes of bearing signals.

Table 1. Details of the selected bearing signals.

Class	Label	Fault Size (mm)	Selected Data
Normal	NORM	0	100_normal_3
Inner race fault	IR1	0.1778	108_IR007_3
Balling element fault	BE1	0.1778	121_B007_3
Outer race fault	OR1	0.1778	133_OR007@6_3
Inner race fault	IR2	0.3556	172_IR014_3
Balling element fault	BE2	0.3556	188_B014_3
Outer race fault	OR2	0.3556	200_OR014@6_3
Inner race fault	IR3	0.5334	212_IR021_3
Balling element fault	BE3	0.5334	225_B021_3
Outer race fault	OR3	0.5334	237_OR021@6_3

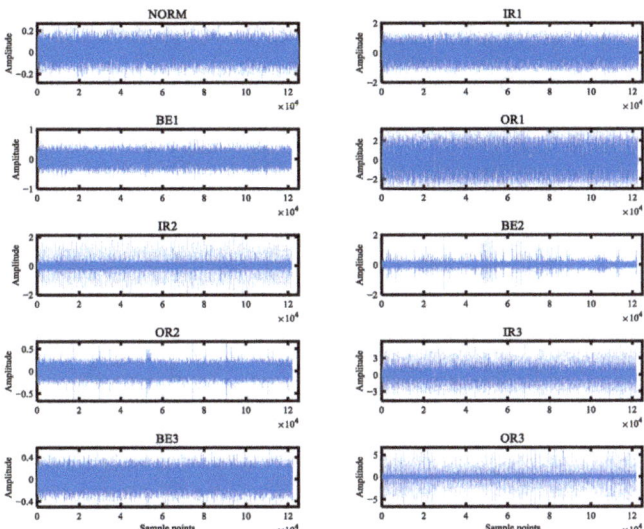

Figure 9. Time domain distribution of ten classes of bearing signals.

4.2. Single Feature Extraction and Classification

The ten classes of bearing signals are used as the object of the experiment for single feature extraction. There are 50 samples for each type of bearing signal, and each sample contains 2048 sample points. While calculating the FuzzDE$_\alpha$ of the bearing signal, the DE$_\alpha$, PE$_\alpha$, and FDE$_\alpha$ are calculated respectively as comparative analysis. The parameter settings are as follows: embedding dimension m is 3, class number c is 4, and the range of fractal order α is from -0.2 to 0.2 with interval 0.1. For other fractional entropies, the parameter settings are the same as FuzzDE$_\alpha$. The Distribution of fractional entropy features of different classes of bearing signals are exhibited in Figure 10.

From Figure 10, for the four types of fractional entropies, it is difficult to completely distinguish all ten types of bearing signals under different fractional order; for FuzzDE$_\alpha$, DE$_\alpha$, and FDE$_\alpha$, there is always some standard deviation of fractional entropy values close to each other for bearing signals; in addition, the standard deviation of fractional entropy values are significantly higher than that of PE$_\alpha$ under different fractional order, for PE$_\alpha$, the standard deviations of fractional entropy values for ten classes of bearing signals are all very close, which is difficult to distinguish. Furthermore, we employ KNN to classify the ten classes of bearing signals, in which there are 50 samples for each type of bearing signal, the first 25 samples are training samples, and the rest samples are test samples. Table 2 illustrates the classification recognition rate of different entropies at various fractional orders.

Table 2. Classification recognition rate of different entropies at various fractional orders.

Entropy	Recognition Rates (%)				
	$\alpha=-0.2$	$\alpha=-0.1$	$\alpha=0$	$\alpha=0.1$	$\alpha=0.2$
FuzzDE$_\alpha$	82.8	81.6	74	68.4	67.6
DE$_\alpha$	76.4	79.6	76.4	71.2	66.0
PE$_\alpha$	59.6	56.8	58.4	56.8	54.0
FDE$_\alpha$	79.2	82.8	78.4	77.6	80.4

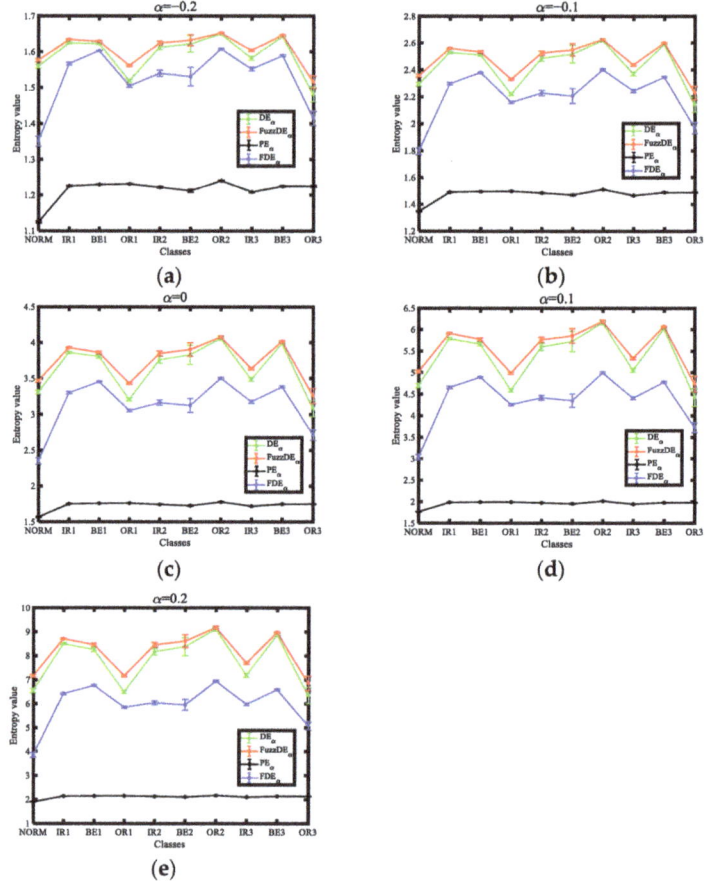

Figure 10. Distribution of fractional entropy features of different classes of bearing signals. (**a**) $\alpha = -0.2$; (**b**) $\alpha = -0.1$; (**c**) $\alpha = 0$; (**d**) $\alpha = 0.1$; (**e**) $\alpha = 0.2$.

It can be seen from Table 2, for four classes of fractional entropies, the recognition rates of bearing signals are all lower than 85% under different fractional orders, and the recognition effect is poor. Therefore, it is difficult to distinguish ten classes of signals with one feature.

4.3. Double Features Extraction and Classification

In order to improve recognition performance and demonstrate the effectiveness of the mixed feature extraction method proposed in this paper, we choose different entropy-based feature extraction methods, extract any two fractional orders with the same entropy and choose the best combinations of fractional orders. Since fractional order α has 5 values, a total of C_5^2 combinations can be obtained by each entropy-based feature extraction method. In addition, we use the mixed feature extraction method proposed in this paper to calculate the highest recognition rate, with a total of C_{20}^2 combinations. Table 3 demonstrate the highest classification recognition rates for each feature extraction method when double features are selected.

Table 3. Highest classification recognition rates for each feature extraction method (double features).

Feature Extraction Methods	Combinations	Recognition Rate (%)
$FuzzDE_\alpha$-based	$FuzzDE_{\alpha=0}$ & $FuzzDE_{\alpha=0.2}$	91.6
DE_α-based	$DE_{\alpha=0}$ & $DE_{\alpha=0.2}$	88.4
PE_α-based	$PE_{\alpha=-0.2}$ & $PE_{\alpha=0.1}$	58.4
FDE_α-based	$FDE_{\alpha=-0.1}$ & $FDE_{\alpha=0}$	90.0
Proposed method	$FuzzDE_{\alpha=0.1}$ & $FDE_{\alpha=0.1}$ (1 of 3)	99.6

In Table 3, $FuzzDE_{\alpha=0}$ & $FuzzDE_{\alpha=0.2}$ represents $FuzzDE_\alpha$ when fractional order α is 0 and 0.2 respectively, other combinations of entropy are the same for $FuzzDE_{\alpha=0}$ & $FuzzDE_{\alpha=0.2}$. As can be observed in Table 3, $FuzzDE_\alpha$-based feature extraction method has the best classification effect among the four entropy-based feature extraction methods, but the highest recognition rate is only 91.6%, which cannot fully recognize the bearing signals. Nevertheless, the mixed feature extraction method proposed in this paper can reach a maximum classification rate of 99.6%, significantly higher than the 91.6% of $FuzzDE_\alpha$-based feature extraction method, and there are three combinations in total, namely $FuzzDE_{\alpha=0.1}$ & $FDE_{\alpha=0.1}$, $FuzzDE_{\alpha=-0.1}$ & $FDE_{\alpha=0.1}$ and $FuzzDE_{\alpha=0.1}$ & $FDE_{\alpha=-0.1}$. It is noteworthy that when reaching the highest recognition rate, the three combinations all contain $FuzzDE_\alpha$, which further proves the importance of $FuzzDE_\alpha$ in bearing fault diagnosis recognition. Figure 11 shows the distribution of the highest classification recognition rate of mixed double features.

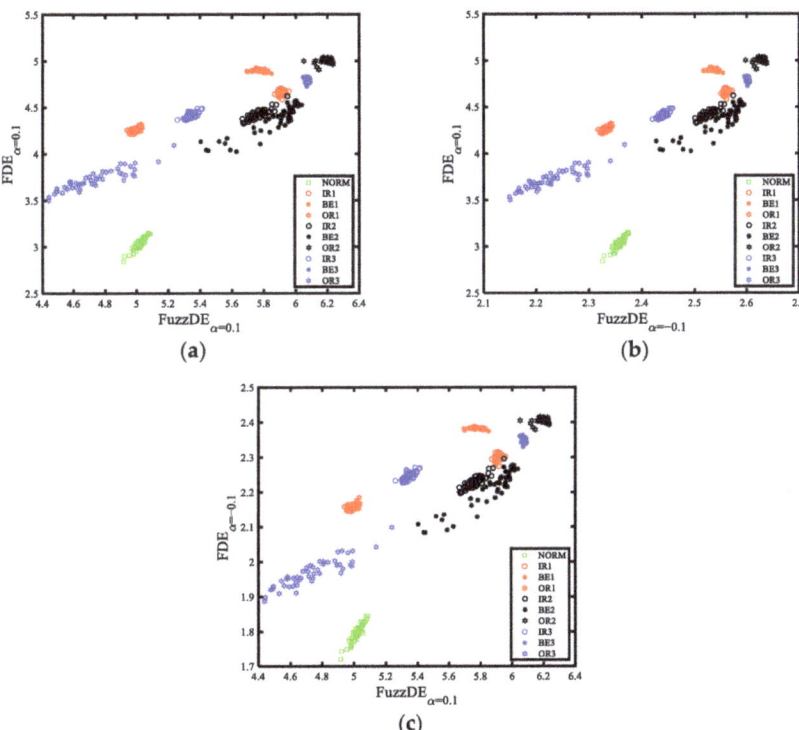

Figure 11. Distribution of the highest classification recognition rate of mixed double features. (**a**) $FuzzDE_{\alpha=0.1}$ & $FDE_{\alpha=0.1}$; (**b**) $FuzzDE_{\alpha=-0.1}$ & $FDE_{\alpha=0.1}$; (**c**) $FuzzDE_{\alpha=0.1}$ & $FDE_{\alpha=-0.1}$.

As can be seen from Figure 11, under the mixed double features, the distribution of each type of bearing signal is relatively concentrated, and the overlapping part is very small. However, there are few samples that are not completely distinguishable, for example, a small percentage of IR1 and IR2 samples are mixed. In summary, compared with the entropy-based feature extraction methods, the mixed feature extraction method proposed in this paper further improves the recognition rate and can better distinguish the ten classes of bearing signals. To sum up, mixed double features extraction method can well distinguish the ten classes of bearing signals.

4.4. Triple Features Extraction and Classification

In order to further improve the recognition rate of bearing fault diagnosis, we set the number of selected features H to 3. The rest of the steps are the same as Section 4.3, and Table 4 shows the highest classification recognition rates for each feature extraction method when triple features are selected.

Table 4. Highest classification recognition rates for each feature extraction method (triple features).

Feature Extraction Methods	Combinations	Recognition Rate (%)
FuzzDE$_\alpha$-based	FuzzDE$_{\alpha=-0.1}$ & FuzzDE$_{\alpha=0}$ & FuzzDE$_{\alpha=0.2}$	92
DE$_\alpha$-based	DE$_{\alpha=-0.1}$ & DE$_{\alpha=0}$ & DE$_{\alpha=0.2}$	92
PE$_\alpha$-based	PE$_{\alpha=-0.2}$ & PE$_{\alpha=0}$ & PE$_{\alpha=0.1}$	58
FDE$_\alpha$-based	FDE$_{\alpha=-0.2}$ & FDE$_{\alpha=-0.1}$ & FDE$_{\alpha=0}$	91.6
Proposed method	FuzzDE$_{\alpha=-0.1}$ & PE$_{\alpha=-0.2}$ & FuzzDE$_{\alpha=0.1}$ (1 of 15)	100

From Table 4, it can be seen that as the number of features increases, the recognition rates of the feature extraction methods based on FuzzDE$_\alpha$, DE$_\alpha$ and FDE$_\alpha$ all improved, but the fault diagnosis performance is still much less than that of the mixed double features in Table 3, which indicates that different fractional order features with the same entropy still have certain limitations. Furthermore, we can also observe from Table 4 that the mixed feature extraction method proposed in this paper achieves a recognition rate of 100% for 15 combinations when triple features are selected, further demonstrating the excellent performance of the mixed feature extraction method for bearing fault diagnosis. To visualize the specific details of these 15 combinations, Table 5 shows the number of occurrences of each feature in the combinations with 100% recognition rate.

Table 5. Number of occurrences of each feature in the combination of the mixed triple features with 100% recognition rate.

Feature	Appear Times
FuzzDE$_{\alpha=-0.1}$	11
FuzzDE$_{\alpha=-0.2}$	4
PE$_{\alpha=-0.2}$	2
PE$_{\alpha=-0.1}$	3
PE$_{\alpha=0}$	3
PE$_{\alpha=0.1}$	4
PE$_{\alpha=0.2}$	3
FDE$_{\alpha=-0.1}$	6
FDE$_{\alpha=0}$	5
FDE$_{\alpha=0.1}$	4

It is clear from Table 5 that FuzzDE$_{\alpha=-0.1}$ has the highest number of occurrences at 11, far more than any other features, which proves the efficiency of FuzzDE$_\alpha$ in bearing fault diagnosis. In addition, among the feature combinations with 100% recognition rate, only DE$_\alpha$ is absent, which is due to the fact that FuzzDE is an improvement on DE, further validating the conclusion that FuzzDE is more differentiable than DE. We can also find that although the PE$_\alpha$ has a low recognition rate on bearing fault diagnosis, it can accurately classify some samples that cannot be correctly classified by other entropies. Hence, we can also conclude that different entropies can distinguish different signal classes, and following the mixed feature extraction method proposed in this paper, while selecting mixed fractional order entropies simultaneously can effectively improve the performance of bearing fault diagnosis.

Figure 12 depicts the distribution of the triple features at 100% recognition rate with the combination of FuzzDE$_{\alpha=-0.1}$, PE$_{\alpha=-0.2}$ and FDE$_{\alpha=0.1}$. Compared to Figure 11, we can intuitively find that Figure 12 can perfectly distinguish between IR1 as well as IR2, which are two different sizes of the same fault class, and it is obvious that the mixed double features distribution cannot achieve such results.

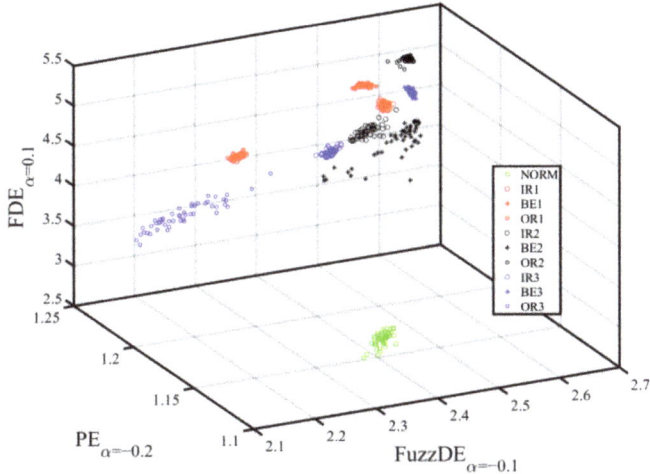

Figure 12. Distribution of the mixed triple features at 100% recognition rate (FuzzDE$_{\alpha=-0.1}$, PE$_{\alpha=-0.2}$, FDE$_{\alpha=0.1}$).

5. Conclusions

In this paper, a new non-linear dynamic parameter is proposed, and a mixed features extraction method is put forward based on this new parameter. The main conclusions are as follows.

1. Fractional order calculation is introduced on the basis of fuzzy dispersion entropy (FuzzDE), and a new entropy called fractional order FDE (FuzzDE$_\alpha$) is proposed. Simulated experiments have shown that compared with FuzzDE, FuzzDE$_\alpha$ can provide more features of greater sensitivity to changes in the dynamics of the time series.
2. FuzzDE$_\alpha$ is combined with DE$_\alpha$, PE$_\alpha$ as well as FDE$_\alpha$ to present a mixed features extraction method. For ten classes of bearing signals, the proposed mixed features fault diagnosis method achieves 100% recognition rate at only triple features.
3. Regardless of how many features are selected, the FuzzDE$_\alpha$ proposed in this paper is the most effective in fault diagnosis compared to the other three fractional order entropies, where FuzzDE$_{\alpha=-0.1}$ appears a total of 11 times in the combination of the triple features with the recognition rate of 100%

Author Contributions: Formal analysis, B.T.; funding acquisition, Y.L.; methodology, B.G.; project administration, B.G.; visualization, S.J.; writing—original draft, B.T.; writing—review and editing, Y.L. All authors have read and agreed to the published version of the manuscript.

Funding: This research was funded by [National Natural Science Foundation of China] grant number [61871318], [Natural Science Foundation of Shaanxi Province] grant number [2022JM-337].

Institutional Review Board Statement: Not applicable.

Informed Consent Statement: Not applicable.

Data Availability Statement: The data used to support the findings of this study are available from the corresponding author upon request.

Conflicts of Interest: The authors declare no conflict of interests.

Nomenclature

FuzzDE	Fuzzy Dispersion Entropy
FuzzDE$_\alpha$	Fractional order fuzzy dispersion entropy
PE	Permutation entropy
PE$_\alpha$	Fractional order permutation entropy
DE	Dispersion entropy
DE$_\alpha$	Fractional order dispersion entropy
FDE	Fluctuation-based dispersion entropy
FDE$_\alpha$	Fractional order fluctuation-based dispersion entropy
NCDF	Normal cumulative distribution function
SE	Sample entropy
FRDE	Fluctuation-based reverse dispersion entropy
RDE	Reverse dispersion entropy
FuzzEn	Fuzzy entropy
RCMDE	Refined composite multiscale dispersion entropy
GRCMFDE$_\alpha$	Generalized refined composite multiscale fluctuation-based fractional dispersion entropy
LM	Linear mapping
TANSIG	Tangent sigmoid
LOGSIG	Logarithm sigmoid
SORT	Sorting method

References

1. Berger, A.L.; Della Pietra, V.J.; Della Pietra, S.A. A maximum entropy approach to natural language processing. *Comput. Linguist.* **1996**, *22*, 39–71.
2. Martyushev, L.M.; Seleznevb, V.D. Maximum entropy production principle in physics, chemistry and biology. *Phys. Rep.* **2006**, *426*, 1–45. [CrossRef]
3. Rostaghi, M.; Khatibi, M.M.; Ashory, M.R.; Azami, H. Bearing Fault Diagnosis Using Refined Composite Generalized Multiscale Dispersion Entropy-Based Skewness and Variance and Multiclass FCM-ANFIS. *Entropy* **2021**, *23*, 1510. [CrossRef] [PubMed]
4. Zhang, X.; Liang, Y.; Zhou, J.; Zang, Y. A novel bearing fault diagnosis model integrated permutation entropy, ensemble empirical mode decomposition and optimized SVM. *Measurement* **2015**, *69*, 164–179. [CrossRef]
5. Yan, R.; Liu, Y.; Gao, R. Permutation entropy: A nonlinear statistical measure for status characterization of rotary machines. *Mech. Syst. Signal Process.* **2012**, *29*, 474–484. [CrossRef]
6. Zhang, X.; Wang, H.; Ren, M.; He, M.; Jin, L. Rolling Bearing Fault Diagnosis Based on Multiscale Permutation Entropy and SOA-SVM. *Machines* **2022**, *10*, 485. [CrossRef]
7. Ying, W.; Tong, J.; Dong, Z.; Pan, H.; Liu, Q.; Zheng, J. Composite Multivariate Multi-Scale Permutation Entropy and Laplacian Score Based Fault Diagnosis of Rolling Bearing. *Entropy* **2022**, *24*, 160. [CrossRef]
8. Rostaghi, M.; Azami, H. Dispersion Entropy: A Measure for Time Series Analysis. *IEEE Signal Process. Lett.* **2016**, *23*, 610–614. [CrossRef]
9. Gu, C.; Qiao, X.; Li, H. Misfire Fault Diagnosis Method for Diesel Engine Based on MEMD and Dispersion Entropy. *Shock Vib.* **2021**, *5*, 1–14. [CrossRef]
10. Azami, H.; Fernandez, A.; Escudero, J. Multivariate Multiscale Dispersion Entropy of Biomedical Times Series. *Entropy* **2017**, *21*, 913. [CrossRef]
11. Azami, H.; Escudero, J. Amplitude- and Fluctuation-Based Dispersion Entropy. *Entropy* **2018**, *20*, 210. [CrossRef] [PubMed]
12. Li, Y.; Gao, X.; Wang, L. Reverse Dispersion Entropy: A New Complexity Measure for Sensor Signal. *Sensors* **2019**, *19*, 5203. [CrossRef] [PubMed]
13. Li, Y.; Jiao, S.; Gao, X. A novel signal feature extraction technology based on empirical wavelet transform and reverse dispersion entropy. *Def. Technol.* **2021**, *17*, 1625–1635. [CrossRef]
14. Jiao, S.; Geng, B.; Li, Y. Fluctuation-based reverse dispersion entropy and its applications to signal classification. *Appl. Acoust.* **2021**, *175*, 107857. [CrossRef]

15. Rostaghi, M.; Khatibi, M.M.; Ashory, M.R.; Azami, H. Fuzzy Dispersion Entropy: A Nonlinear Measure for Signal Analysis. *IEEE Trans. Fuzzy Syst.* **2022**, *30*, 3785–3796. [CrossRef]
16. Ali, K. Fractional order entropy: New perspectives. *Opt.-Int. J. Light Electron Opt.* **2016**, *127*, 9172–9177.
17. Ingo, C.; Magin, R.L.; Parrish, T.B. New Insights into the Fractional Order Diffusion Equation Using Entropy and Kurtosis. *Entropy* **2014**, *16*, 5838–5852. [CrossRef] [PubMed]
18. Zunino, L.; Pérez, D.G.; Martín, M.T. Permutation entropy of fractional Brownian motion and fractional Gaussian noise. *Phys. Lett. A* **2008**, *372*, 4768–4774. [CrossRef]
19. He, S.; Sun, K. Fractional fuzzy entropy algorithm and the complexity analysis for nonlinear time series. *Eur. Phys. J. Spec. Top.* **2018**, *227*, 943–957. [CrossRef]
20. Zheng, J.; Pan, H. Use of generalized refined composite multiscale fractional dispersion entropy to diagnose the faults of rolling bearing. *Nonlinear Dyn.* **2021**, *101*, 1417–1440. [CrossRef]
21. Li, Y.; Mu, L. Particle Swarm Optimization Fractional Slope Entropy: A New Time Series Complexity Indicator for Bearing Fault Diagnosis. *Fractal Fract.* **2022**, *6*, 345. [CrossRef]
22. Azami, H.; Escudero, J. Improved multiscale permutation entropy for biomedical signal analysis: Interpretation and application to electroencephalogram recordings. *Biomed. Signal Process. Control* **2016**, *23*, 28–41. [CrossRef]
23. Azami, H.; Fernandez, A.; Escudero, J. Refined Multiscale Fuzzy Entropy based on Standard Deviation for Biomedical Signal Analysis. *Med. Biol. Eng. Comput.* **2017**, *55*, 2037–2052. [CrossRef] [PubMed]
24. Wu, G.; Baleanu, D. Chaos synchronization of the discrete fractional logistic map. *Signal Process.* **2014**, *102*, 96–99. [CrossRef]
25. Li, Y.; Liu, F.; Wang, S. Multi-scale Symbolic Lempel-Ziv: An Effective Feature Extraction Approach for Fault Diagnosis of Railway Vehicle Systems. *IEEE Trans. Ind. Inform.* **2021**, *17*, 199–208. [CrossRef]
26. Case Western Reserve University. Available online: http://csegroups.case.edu/bearingdatacenter/pages/download-data-file (accessed on 1 July 2022).

Article

Global Bifurcation Behaviors and Control in a Class of Bilateral MEMS Resonators

Yijun Zhu and Huilin Shang *

School of Mechanical Engineering, Shanghai Institute of Technology, Shanghai 201418, China
* Correspondence: shanghuilin@sit.edu.cn

Abstract: The investigation of global bifurcation behaviors the vibrating structures of micro-electromechanical systems (MEMS) has received substantial attention. This paper considers the vibrating system of a typical bilateral MEMS resonator containing fractional functions and multiple potential wells. By introducing new variations, the Melnikov method is applied to derive the critical conditions for global bifurcations. By engaging in the fractal erosion of safe basin to depict the phenomenon pull-in instability intuitively, the point-mapping approach is used to present numerical simulations which are in close agreement with the analytical prediction, showing the validity of the analysis. It is found that chaos and pull-in instability, two initial-sensitive phenomena of MEMS resonators, can be due to homoclinic bifurcation and heteroclinic bifurcation, respectively. On this basis, two types of delayed feedback are proposed to control the complex dynamics successively. Their control mechanisms and effect are then studied. It follows that under a positive gain coefficient, delayed position feedback and delayed velocity feedback can both reduce pull-in instability; nevertheless, to suppress chaos, only the former can be effective. The results may have some potential value in broadening the application fields of global bifurcation theory and improving the performance reliability of capacitive MEMS devices.

Keywords: global bifurcation; MEMS resonator; homoclinic orbit; heteroclinic orbit; chaos; fractal; safe basin; pull-in instability; delayed feedback

1. Introduction

Electrostatic microresonators have attracted significant attention thanks to their wide applications in micro-electromechanical systems (MEMS) such as micro sensors [1], micro filters [2], and energy harvesters [3]. To maintain their normal work performance, harmonic vibration is desirable. However, due to nonlinearities in the driven force, stiffness, damping [4] and structural geometry [5], the vibrating structures of MEMS resonators do not necessarily undergo periodic responses. During these decades, sufficient works have studied the conditions for achieving stable periodic responses. Hajjaj et al. [6] investigated different types of internal resonances of an electrostatic MEMS arch resonator via the theory of local bifurcation and experiments. Ali and Ardeshir [7] modeled a dielectric elastomer resonator as a sandwiched Euler-Bernoulli microbeam and presented multiple periodic responses induced by subcritical bifurcations. Zhu and Shang [8] discussed the phenomenon jump among coexisting multiple periodic attractors in an electrostatic bilateral microresonator. It has been realized that even if MEMS resonators finally vibrate periodically, the phenomenon jump among coexisting multiple periodic attractors is unwanted as it leads to unreliability of work performance of the micro devices.

Apart from multistability, there are some other initial-sensitive dynamic behaviors of micro resonators, for instance, chaos and pull-in instability. The former is well-known in nonlinear dynamic systems [9–11], whereas the latter is a unique phenomenon of electric-actuated capacitive micro devices. The phenomenon pull-in instability is related to but different from the behavior pull in. The latter describes a movable electrode collapsing to a rigid one [12] thus implying an unbounded or escape solution of the corresponding dynamic systems [13]. It is unfavorable in MEMS resonators for causing the failure of their performance. Pull-in instability means that a subtle disturbance of initial state causes a sudden change of dynamic behavior from bounded dynamic responses to pull in. It is similar to the phenomenon of frequency jump. It is also an unwanted dynamic behavior since it implies the loss of global integrity and performance reliability of the concerned MEMS devices [14,15].

For chaos and its control of MEMS resonators, there have been significant works in recent years. Fu and Xu [16] considered the application of a single-side MEMS resonator in pressure detecting and numerically studied critical conditions for multi-field parameters for inducing chaos. For a single-side arch micro/nano resonator, Liu et al. [17] introduced delayed velocity feedback to restrain frequency jump as well as chaos and discussed the control effect numerically. For double-side micromechanical resonators, as there are multiple potential wells in their vibrating systems, chaos is easily triggered by homoclinic bifurcations [18–20]. Luo et al. [18] studied the observer-based adaptive stabilization issue of the fractional-order chaotic MEMS resonator with uncertain functions via numerical simulations. Haghighi and Markazi [19] predicted the transient chaos of another type of bilateral MEMS resonator by the approximately analytical criterion of homoclinic bifurcation and then proposed a robust adaptive fuzzy control algorithm to suppress it. Siewe and Hegazy [20] found that chaos could be induced by both homoclinic and heteroclinic bifurcation which was confirmed by numerical simulations of basins of attraction and bifurcation diagrams. Due to the electrostatic-driven forces of MEMS resonators, the dynamic systems of these MEMS resonators contain fractional functions, which cause the difficulty of analyzing homoclinic bifurcation by classical bifurcation theory. In most studies, homoclinic bifurcation is discussed by expanding the fractal functions approximately in Taylor's series as third-order [19] or fifth-order [20] polynomials, thus it has some limitations in the values of system parameters such as DC voltage. When it comes to heteroclinic bifurcation, this theoretical method cannot work.

The phenomenon pull-in instability is still relatively little considered in the literature. For the vibrating system of a single-side MEMS resonator, Alsaleem et al. [21] applied the erosion of safe basin to depict pull-in instability numerically, proposed delayed feedback to suppress this phenomenon, and studied the control effect experimentally and numerically. On this basis, Shang [22] studied the mechanism of pull-in instability and its control in this system and found that it is induced by homoclinic bifurcation, and that the two types of delayed controllers were both useful for a positive coefficient of the gain and a short delay. For the MEMS resonator actuated by two-sided electrodes, Gusso et al. numerically illustrated its rich nonlinear dynamics such as multistability, pull-in instability and chaos [23].

As shown in the above research, chaos and pull in instability are both global bifurcation behaviors. Two questions are raised: Is there any relationship between chaos and pull-in instability? Can a control strategy reduce both of them? To answer these questions, we considered a typical bilateral MEMS resonator containing multiple potential wells [8,19], and investigated the mechanisms behind chaos and pull-in instability of MEMS resonators as well as the mechanisms of control strategies on reducing them. The rest of the paper is arranged as follows. In Section 2, the dynamic model of the MEMS resonator and its static bifurcation is discussed. In Section 3, global bifurcation and induced behaviors are analyzed. In Section 4, two control strategies, namely, delay position feedback and delay velocity feedback, are applied to the original system respectively; and their control mechanisms and effect on the global bifurcation behavior are studied in detail. Section 5 contains the discussion.

2. Mathematical Model and Unperturbed Dynamics

The schematic diagram of a typical bilateral MEMS resonator is depicted in Figure 1. The MEMS resonator consists of the movable electrode and nonlinear electrostatic forces on each side [8,19]. In this system, an external driving force on the resonator is applied by means of electrical driving voltages. According to the Second Law of Newton, the governing differential equation of motion for this MEMS resonator can be expressed as

$$m\frac{d^2z}{dt^2} + c\frac{dz}{dt} + k_1 z + k_3 z^3 = F_e^u + F_e^l, \quad (1)$$

where F_e^u and F_e^l are the electrostatic forces from the upper and the lower capacitor in Figure 1, respectively. As they are driven by the combined voltage, which is made up of a DC bias voltage and an AC voltage, they can be described as [12,19]

$$F_e^u = \frac{A_0}{2(d-z)^2}(V_b + V_{AC}\sin\Omega t)^2, \quad F_e^l = -\frac{A_0 V_b^2}{2(d+z)^2}. \quad (2)$$

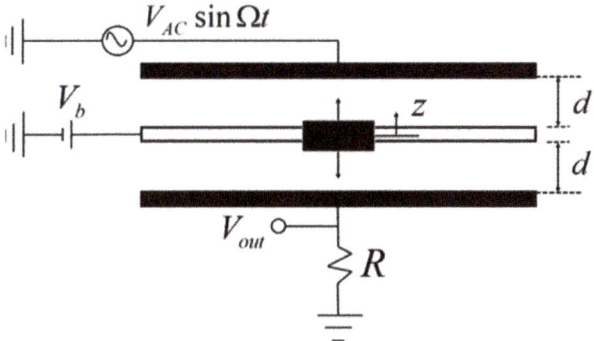

Figure 1. Simplified diagram of a bilateral electrostatic micro resonator.

The nomenclatures of the system parameters in Equations (1) and (2) are presented in Table 1.

Table 1. Parameters of systems (1) and (5).

Parameter	Symbol
Equivalent mass of the proof mass (kg)	m
Viscous damping coefficient in the high vacuum environment (N·s/m)	c
Linear stiffness coefficient (N/m)	k_1
Cubic stiffness term (N/m^3)	k_3
Capacitance of each parallel plate at rest (Fm)	A_0
Initial gap width between the two neighboring parallel plates (m)	d
DC bias voltage (V)	V_b
Frequency of AC voltage (HZ)	Ω
Amplitude of AC voltage (V)	V_{AC}
Time	t
Displacement of the proof mass at time t	z

By introducing the dimensionless time $T = \omega_0 t$ where $\omega_0 = \sqrt{\frac{k_1}{m}}$, and the variable $x(T) = \frac{z}{d}$, the dimensionless form of Equation (1) can be expressed by

$$x''(T) + \mu x'(T) + x + \alpha x^3 = \frac{\beta}{(1-x)^2}(1+\gamma\sin(\omega T))^2 - \frac{\beta}{(1+x)^2}. \quad (3)$$

where

$$\omega = \frac{\Omega}{\omega_0}, \mu = \frac{c}{m\omega_0}, \alpha = \frac{k_3 d^2}{m\omega_0^2}, \beta = \frac{A_0 V_b^2}{2k_1 d^3}, \gamma = \frac{V_{AC}}{V_b} \quad (4)$$

Denoting $x(T) \triangleq x$, $x'(T) \triangleq \dot{x}$, $x''(T) \triangleq \ddot{x}$ in Equation (3) yields the following dimensionless system

$$\ddot{x} + \mu \dot{x} + x + \alpha x^3 = \frac{\beta}{(1-x)^2}(1 + \gamma \sin(\omega T))^2 - \frac{\beta}{(1+x)^2}. \tag{5}$$

The variable x in Equation (5) should satisfy $|x| \leq 1$. Note that $|x| = 1$ shows the gap width between the movable electrode and one of its neighboring fixed electrodes being zero, thus creating the phenomenon pull in. Since the viscous-damping coefficient c is tiny, and $V_{AC} \ll V_b$, the parameters μ and β in Equation (5) are both small, the concerned terms can be considered as the perturbed ones. Thus, the unperturbed system of Equation (5) is

$$\dot{x} = y, \quad \dot{y} = -x - \alpha x^3 + \frac{\beta}{(1-x)^2} - \frac{\beta}{(1+x)^2} \tag{6}$$

which is a Hamiltonian system with the Hamiltonian [19]

$$H(x, y) = \frac{1}{2}x^2 + \frac{1}{2}y^2 + \frac{\alpha}{4}x^4 - \frac{\beta}{1-x} - \frac{\beta}{1+x} + 2\beta. \tag{7}$$

According to Equations (6) and (7), the existence, shapes and positions of potential wells as well as the number of equilibrium points are determined by the parameters α and β.

Theorem 1. *If α and β satisfy $\beta > \frac{1}{4}$ and $\beta > \frac{(\alpha+1)^3}{27\alpha^2}$, then the trivial $O(0, 0)$ will be the only equilibrium and the saddle point of the system (6).*

Proof of Theorem 1. Setting

$$F(u) = -u - \alpha u^3 + \frac{\beta}{(1-u)^2} - \frac{\beta}{(1+u)^2}, \quad G(u) = \frac{F(u)}{u} = -1 - \alpha u^2 + \frac{4\beta}{(1-u^2)^2}. \tag{8}$$

If $\beta > \frac{1}{4}$, then $G(0) > 0$, and $\lim_{u \to \pm 1} G(u) = +\infty$. If $\beta > \frac{1}{4}$ and $\alpha < 2$, there will be no equilibria in the equation $G'(u) = 0$; and $G'(u) > 0$ when $u \in (-1, 1)$. Due to the monotony of the function $G(u)$, there will be no non-trivial solutions in the equation $G(u) = 0$. When $\beta > \frac{(\alpha+1)^3}{27\alpha^2}$ and $\alpha \geq 2$, one may have $\beta > \frac{1}{4}$. Then there will be only one equilibrium of the equation $G'(u) = 0$ satisfying $u \in (0, 1)$, i.e., $u_p = \sqrt{1 - 2\sqrt[3]{\frac{\beta}{\alpha}}}$. Since

$$G(u_p) = -(1 + \alpha) + 3\sqrt[3]{\alpha^2 \beta} > 0 \tag{9}$$

$G(u)$ will always be more than 0 when $u \in (-1, 1)$, which shows that there are no non-trivial equilibria in the equation $G(u) = 0$. When $\beta > \frac{1}{4}$, the eigenvalues of the equilibrium $O(0, 0)$ of the system (6) are $\lambda = \pm\sqrt{4\beta - 1}$, showing that one eigenvalue is positive and the other negative. Thus, the trivial equilibrium is a saddle point of the system (6). □

Theorem 2. *When $\beta < \frac{1}{4}$, there will be three equilibria in the system (6) where the trivial $O(0, 0)$ is a center, and the other two are saddle points.*

Proof of Theorem 2. If $\beta < \frac{1}{4}$, then $G(0) < 0$ and $G(\pm 1) > 0$. Due to the symmetry and continuity of the function $G(u)$, there must be a pair of solutions $\pm x_s$ for $G(u) = 0$ as well as $F(u) = 0$ in the ranges $(0, 1)$ and $(-1, 0)$. According to Equation (10), when $\beta < \frac{1}{4}$, there is a pair of pure imaginary eigenvalues for the system (6), i.e., $\lambda = \pm\sqrt{1 - 4\beta}i$, showing that $O(0, 0)$ is a center. For the two nontrivial equilibriums of the system (6), i.e., $S_{\pm}(\pm x_s, 0)$, the corresponding characteristic equation is

$$\lambda^2 + \frac{2x_s^2(\alpha - 2 - 3\alpha x_s^2)}{1 - x_s^2} = 0 \qquad (10)$$

It follows from Equation (10) that $\alpha - 2 - 3\alpha x_s^2 < 0$ if $\beta < \frac{1}{4}$ and $\alpha \leq 2$. If $\beta < \frac{1}{4}$ and $\alpha > 2$, then $\beta < \frac{(\alpha+1)^3}{27\alpha^2}$; setting $u_0 = \sqrt{\frac{\alpha-2}{3\alpha}}$, we can derive that $0 < u_0 < 1$, and

$$G(u_0) = \frac{-1-\alpha}{3} + \frac{9\alpha^2\beta}{(\alpha+1)^2} < \frac{-1-\alpha}{3} + \frac{\alpha+1}{3} = 0 \qquad (11)$$

showing the positive root of the equation $G(u) = 0$, i.e., x_s will surely be within the range $(u_0, 1)$. We also have

$$\alpha - 2 - 3\alpha x_s^2 < \alpha - 2 - 3\alpha u_0^2 = 0 \qquad (12)$$

implying that $S_\pm(\pm x_s, 0)$ are saddle points as there will be a positive and a negative eigenvalue for them that can be solved from Equation (10). Therefore, when $\beta < \frac{1}{4}$, the equilibria $S_\pm(\pm x_s, 0)$ are saddle points. □

Theorem 3. *When the parameters α and β satisfy $\frac{1}{4} < \beta < \frac{(\alpha+1)^3}{27\alpha^2}$ and $\alpha > 2$, there will be five equilibria in the system (6) where three equilibriums are saddle points, and the other two are centers.*

Proof of Theorem 3. Since $F(0) = 0$, the origin $(0,0)$ will be an equilibrium and a saddle point of the system (6) if $\beta > \frac{1}{4}$. In this case, we also have

$$G(0) > 0, \ G(1) > 0 \qquad (13)$$

If $\frac{1}{4} < \beta < \frac{(\alpha+1)^3}{27\alpha^2}$ and $\alpha > 2$, we can get

$$1 > 1 - \sqrt[3]{\frac{8\beta}{\alpha}} > \frac{\alpha-2}{3\alpha} > 0 \qquad (14)$$

Considering $u_0 = \sqrt{\frac{\alpha-2}{3\alpha}}$, we will obtain

$$G(u_0) = \frac{27\alpha^2\beta - (\alpha+1)^3}{3(\alpha+1)^2} < 0 \qquad (15)$$

According to Equations (13) and (15) as well as the continuity of the function $G(u)$ when $u \in (-1, 1)$, there will be two pairs of real solutions $\pm x_c$ and $\pm x_s$ for $G(u) = 0$ satisfying

$$0 < x_c < \sqrt{\frac{\alpha-2}{3\alpha}} < x_s < 1. \qquad (16)$$

Therefore, there will be five equilibria of the system (6), i.e., $O(0,0)$, $C_1(x_c, 0)$, $C_2(-x_c, 0)$, $S_1(x_s, 0)$ and $S_2(-x_s, 0)$ when $\frac{1}{4} < \beta < \frac{(\alpha+1)^3}{27\alpha^2}$ and $\alpha > 2$. For each nontrivial equilibrium, the eigenvalues at these equilibria can be solved from the characteristic equation

$$\lambda^2 = \frac{2\tilde{u}^2}{3\alpha(1 - \tilde{u}^2)}(\tilde{u}^2 - \frac{\alpha-2}{3\alpha}) \qquad (17)$$

where $\tilde{u}$ represents the horizontal coordinate of each equilibrium. Due to the condition (16), when $\beta < \frac{(\alpha+1)^3}{27\alpha^2}$, we have $\lambda^2 > 0$ at $S_1(x_s, 0)$ and $S_2(-x_s, 0)$, implying that the two equilibria are saddle points; similarly we get $\lambda^2 < 0$ at $C_1(x_c, 0)$ and $C_2(-x_c, 0)$, showing that they are centers. □

According to Theorems 1–3, the parameter plane α-β can be separated into three regions I, II and III, respectively, as depicted in Figure 2. With the help of the Hamilton function (7), the trajectories under different values of the parameters α and β are also classified, as shown in the following three cases.

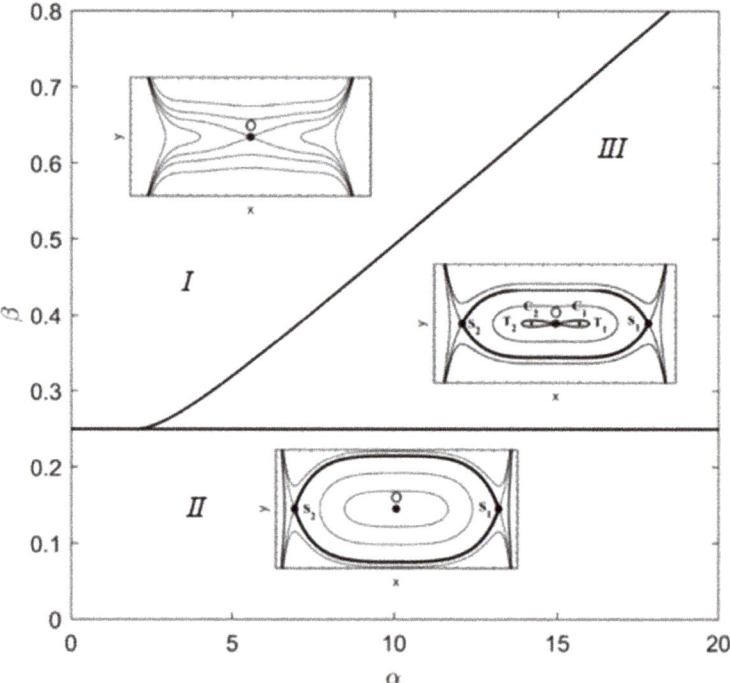

Figure 2. Orbits of the unperturbed system (6) under different values of α and β.

Case 1: the values of α and β chosen in the region I. There will be one equilibrium and no potential well in the unperturbed system (6), meaning that each orbit will be unbounded for different values of the Hamiltonian $H(x,y) = E$. In this case, the phenomenon of pull in, namely static pull-in, will be unavoidable. Returning the conditions of the parameters α and β in Theorem 1 to the original system parameters, we can get the threshold of DC bias voltage for static pull-in

$$V_b > V_b^{Pull-in} = \max\left\{\sqrt{\frac{k_1 d^3}{2A_0}}, \frac{(k_3 d^2 + m\omega_0^2)^{\frac{3}{2}}}{3\omega_0 k_3}\sqrt{\frac{2k_1}{3mA_0 d}}\right\}, \quad (18)$$

illustrating that the increase in DC bias voltage V_b may lead to static pull-in [12]. Comparatively, the orbits in the other two regions are unnecessary to be unbounded, showing that for the parameter values in the regions II and III, pull in may be led by initial conditions rather than the system parameters. It is a so-called dynamic pull in [14,21].

Case 2: the values of the parameters α and β in the region II. There will be two saddle points crossing which there are heteroclinic orbits to surround a single potential well. Here the heteroclinic orbits are determined by $H(x,y) = H(x_s, 0)$.

Case 3: the values of the parameters α and β in the region III. There will be two potential well centers $C_1(x_c, 0)$ and $C_2(-x_c, 0)$ surrounded by homoclinic orbits $H(x,y) = 0$; outside of the homoclinic orbits, there are heteroclinic orbits determined by $H(x,y) = H(x_s, 0)$ and crossing two saddle points $S_1(x_s, 0)$ and $S_2(-x_s, 0)$. Hence, the unperturbed system (6) contains homoclinic and heteroclinic orbits as well as multiple potential wells.

To discuss homoclinic bifurcation and heteroclinic bifurcation in the system, we focus on Case 3. Based on the same physical properties of the bilateral MEMS resonator in Refs. [8,19], in the following parts, some invariable parameters of the dimensionless system (5) can be calculated as:

$$\alpha = 12, \beta = 0.338, \mu = 0.01, \omega = 0.5. \tag{19}$$

The dimensionless AC-voltage amplitude γ in the dimensionless system (5) will be changed to study the influence mechanism of dynamic response characteristics.

3. Global Bifurcations and Complex Dynamics

Since the dimensionless system (5) is a time-periodic perturbation of a Hamiltonian system, we may use the Melnikov method [19,20] to describe how the heteroclinic/homoclinic orbits break up in the presence of the perturbation. To begin with, homoclinic and heteroclinic orbits should be expressed as explicit functions of the time variable T. Note that the unperturbed system (6) contains fractional functions. Thus, these orbits cannot be written as the explicit functions of T. To tackle this problem, we will introduce new variables to express both the orbits and the time variable T explicitly. Then by substituting the explicit functions of new variables into the Melnikov functions, we can employ the Melnikov method smoothly.

3.1. Homoclinic Bifurcation Behavior

According to the Hamiltonian $H(x, y) = 0$, the coordinates x_{homo} and y_{homo} of homoclinic orbits of the system (6) satisfy

$$y_{homo} = x_{homo} \sqrt{\frac{4\beta}{1 - x_{homo}^2} - 1 - \frac{\alpha}{2} x_{homo}^2} \tag{20}$$

The intersection points between the orbits and the x axis are expressed as $T_1(x_e, 0)$ and $T_2(-x_e, 0)$ (see Figure 2), thus satisfying

$$x_e = \sqrt{\frac{\alpha - 2 - \eta_1}{2\alpha}} \tag{21}$$

where $\eta_1 = \sqrt{(\alpha + 2)^2 - 32\alpha\beta}$. By introducing a new time transformation $\varphi(T)$ of the form [24]

$$\frac{d\varphi(T)}{dT} = \Phi(\varphi) = \Phi(\varphi + 2\pi), \tag{22}$$

we assume at the saddle point $O(0,0)$ that

$$\varphi(\infty) = \pi, \ \varphi(-\infty) = 0. \tag{23}$$

It follows from Equations (20)–(23), the homoclinic orbits can be expressed by φ as

$$x_{homo}(\varphi) = x_e \sin \varphi, \ y_{homo} = x_e^2 \sin \varphi \cos \varphi \sqrt{\frac{\eta_1 - \alpha x_e^2 \sin^2 \varphi}{2(1 - x_e^2 \sin^2 \varphi)}}. \tag{24}$$

As shown in Figure 3, homoclinic orbits expressed by Equation (20) and the explicit functions of φ are in complete agreement with each other, which shows the validity of the explicit functions. Also, we have

$$T = \frac{\sqrt{2}\text{sign}(\cos \varphi)}{\sqrt{\alpha} x_e^2 x_0} (E_1(\phi_1, \frac{\eta_1}{\alpha x_0}) + E_3(\frac{x_0 \eta_1}{\alpha x_e^2}, \phi_1, \frac{\eta_1}{\alpha x_0})) \tag{25}$$

in which $x_0 = \sqrt{1-x_e^2}$ and $\phi_1 = -\text{arcsinh}(\frac{\alpha x_e^4 |\cos \varphi|}{\sqrt{2(4+\alpha x_e^2)}})$; the functions E_1 and E_3 are the elliptic integrals of the first kind and the third kind, respectively.

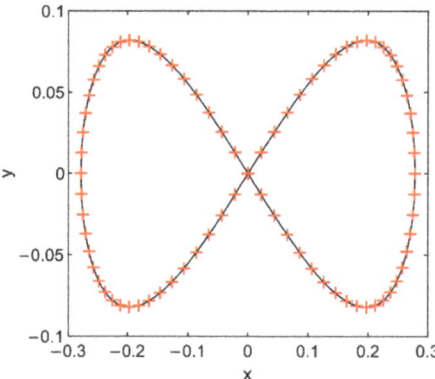

Figure 3. Comparison of homoclinic orbits of the system (6) where the solid curve represents the exact model based on Hamiltonian and the sign + shows the orbits in explicit functions of φ.

As well known, the Melnikov function [25–28] is a signed measure of the distance between the stable and un-stable manifolds for a perturbed system. If there are simple zeros in it, there will be intersection of homoclinic/heteroclinic orbits, corresponding to homoclinic/heteroclinic bifurcation. Assuming small parameters μ and γ of the dimensionless system (5) as $\mu = \varepsilon \widetilde{\mu}$, $\gamma = \varepsilon \widetilde{\gamma}$, and neglecting second-order terms of ε in Equation (5) yield

$$\ddot{x} + x + \alpha x^3 + \frac{\beta}{(1+x)^2} - \frac{\beta}{(1-x)^2} = -\varepsilon \widetilde{\mu} \dot{x} + \frac{2\varepsilon \beta \widetilde{\gamma} \sin(\omega T)}{(1-x)^2}. \quad (26)$$

By substituting Equations (24) and (25) into the corresponding Melnikov function of the system (26), and returning the parameters into $\widetilde{\mu}$ and $\widetilde{\gamma}$ to μ and γ, respectively, we have

$$M_{homo}(T_0) = -\mu I_1 + 2\beta \gamma x_e \cos(\omega T_0) I_2 + 2\beta \gamma x_e \sin(\omega T_0) I_3. \quad (27)$$

where

$$I_1 = \sqrt{\alpha} x_e^3 \int_{-1}^{1} x^2 \sqrt{\frac{(3\eta_1 - \alpha + 2) + (\alpha - 2 - \eta_1)x^2}{(\alpha + 2 + \eta_1) + (\alpha - 2 - \eta_1)x^2}} dx$$
$$= (\frac{(2+\alpha x_e^2)x_0\sqrt{2\eta_1}}{24\alpha} - \frac{4}{x_e^4}) E_2(\text{arccsch}(\frac{x_0}{x_e}), -\frac{\alpha x_0^2}{\eta_1}) - \frac{4x_0}{x_e^3 \sqrt{1-2x_e^2}} + \frac{4}{x_e^2} E_1(\text{arccsch}(\frac{x_0}{x_e}), -\frac{\alpha x_0^2}{\eta_1}) > 0, \quad (28)$$
$$I_2 = \int_0^\pi \frac{\cos \varphi \sin(\omega T(\varphi))}{(1-x_e \sin \varphi)^2} d\varphi, \quad I_3 = \int_0^\pi \frac{\cos \varphi \cos(\omega T(\varphi))}{(1-x_e \sin \varphi)^2} d\varphi;$$

the functions E_1 and E_2 are the elliptic integrals of the first kind and the second kind, respectively. In Equation (28), the integrals I_2 and I_3 can be evaluated numerically [29]. If $2\beta \gamma x_e \sqrt{I_2^2 + I_3^2} > \mu I_1$, namely,

$$V_{AC} > V_{AC}^{homo0} = \frac{\mu V_b I_1}{2\beta x_e \sqrt{I_2^2 + I_3^2}}. \quad (29)$$

there will be a real number of T_0 satisfying $M_{homo}(T_0) = 0$ and $M_{homo}'(T_0) \neq 0$. It indicates that the equilibria of Equation $M_{homo}(T_0) = 0$ are simple, enabling the existence of the transverse homoclinic orbits, i.e., homoclinic bifurcation. As homoclinic bifurcation usually triggers transient chaos [18–20], it follows from Equation (29) that the increase in AC voltage amplitude may induce transient chaos. Here, it can be calculated that $V_{AC}^{homo0} = 0.15$ V.

In order to verify the accuracy of the theoretical prediction, we numerically simulate the solutions of Equation (5). In this paper, we utilize the fourth-order Runge-Kutta approach via MATLAB. For the ordinary differential Equation (5), the software package ODE45 is applied. Poincaré map [30], a commonly used method for investigating continuous time nonlinear systems, is employed to display the bifurcation process and rich dynamic behaviors. By setting $\omega = 0.5$ and initial conditions $x(0) = 0$ and $\dot{x}(0) = 0$, the bifurcation diagram for the system (5) with the increase in AC voltage amplitude V_{AC} is shown in Figure 4. Here, the points on the Poincaré map are collected from a cross-section at $y = 0$ in the sufficiently long time interval $5000 \leq T \leq 7000$. As can be observed in Figure 4, there are periodic doubling windows and chaotic windows, implying that the MEMS resonator will undergo complex dynamics as V_{AC} grows. Note that when V_{AC} is higher than the threshold $V_{AC}^{homo0} = 0.15$ V (see the red dashing line in Figure 4), chaos occurs. For instance, when $V_{AC} = 0.16$ V, the phase portrait and the Poincaré map in Figure 5 depict the chaotic motion clearly. The numerical results closely match the analytical prediction of Equation (29), showing the validity of the analysis. It follows that the increase in V_{AC} can induce homoclinic bifurcation, thus triggering chaos of the bilateral MEMS resonator.

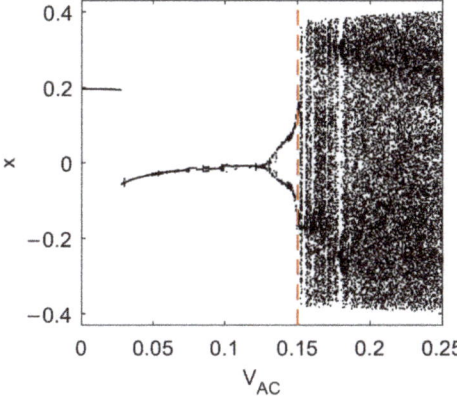

Figure 4. Bifurcation diagram of the dimensionless system (5) when $\omega = 0.5$.

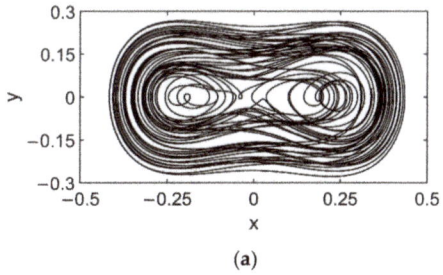
(a)

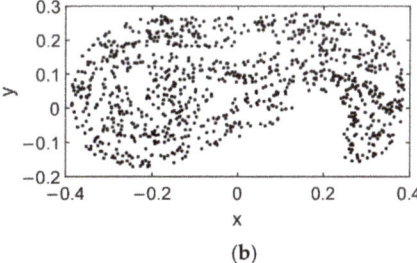
(b)

Figure 5. Dynamic behavior of the system (5) for $V_{AC} = 0.16$ V, $V_b = 3.8$ V, $\omega = 0.5$: (a) phase portrait; (b) Poincáre map.

3.2. Heteroclinic Bifurcation Behavior

Similarly, we introduce a new variable ψ to express the heteroclinic orbits of the unperturbed system (6) that satisfies

$$\frac{d\psi}{dT} = \Psi(\psi) = \Psi(\psi + 2\pi). \tag{30}$$

The heteroclinic orbits crossing the saddle points $S_1(x_s, 0)$ and $S_2(-x_s, 0)$ can be set as $x_0(\psi) = \pm x_s \cos \psi$ [24]. Here x_s as the horizontal coordinate of a saddle point of the unperturbed system (6) can be solved from the following equation

$$4\beta = (1 + \alpha x_s^2)(1 - x_s^2)^2. \tag{31}$$

Based on Equations (7) and (31), the coordinates x_{hetero} and y_{hetero} of the heteroclinic orbits can be expressed as

$$x_{hetero}(\psi) = \pm x_s \cos \psi, \quad y_{hetero}(\psi) = \mp x_s^2 \sin^2 \psi \sqrt{\frac{\eta_2 + \alpha x_s^2 \cos^2 \psi}{2(1 - x_s^2 \cos^2 \psi)}}. \tag{32}$$

where $\eta_2 = 2\alpha x_s^2 - \alpha + 2$. And the time variable T can be expressed by ψ as

$$T = -\sqrt{\frac{2}{\eta_2}} \text{sign}(\cos \psi)(E_1(\psi_1, \frac{\alpha}{\eta_2}) + \frac{1 - x_s^2}{x_s^2} E_3(\frac{1}{x_s^2}, \psi_1, \frac{\alpha}{\eta_2})) \tag{33}$$

where $\psi_1 = \arcsin(x_s|\cos \psi|)$. The comparison of the orbits in both implicit functions $H(x,y) = H(x_s, 0)$ and the explicit form (32) are presented in Figure 6. The complete agreement between them shows that the expression of heteroclinic orbits expressed by explicit functions of ψ is accurate. Then, substituting heteroclinic orbits (32) and Equation (32) into the Melnikov function of the approximate system (26) yields

$$M_{hetero}(t_0) = -2\mu J_1 \mp 2\beta\gamma x_s \sin(\omega T_0) J_2 \mp 2\beta\gamma x_s \cos(\omega T_0) J_3, \tag{34}$$

where

$$J_1 = \int_0^{\frac{\pi}{2}} \sin^3 \varphi \sqrt{\frac{2\beta(2x_s^2 - 1 + x_s^2 \cos^2 \varphi)}{(1 - x_s^2)^2 (1 - x_s^2 \cos^2 \varphi)} + \frac{1}{2}} d\varphi$$
$$= \frac{x_s}{3} \sqrt{\frac{(\eta_2 + \alpha x_s^2)(1 - x_s^2)}{2}} - \frac{2 + \alpha(1 - x_s^2)^2}{6\alpha(1 - x_s^2)^2} \sqrt{2\eta_2} E_2\left(\arcsin x_s, \frac{\alpha}{\eta_2}\right) + \frac{(1 + \alpha x_s^2)(1 - x_s^2)}{3\alpha x_s^2} \sqrt{2\eta_2} E_1\left(\arcsin x_s, \frac{\alpha}{\eta_2}\right) > 0, \tag{35}$$
$$J_2 = \int_0^{\pi} \frac{\sin \psi \cos(\omega T(\psi))}{(1 - x_s \cos \psi)^2} d\psi, \quad J_3 = \int_0^{\pi} \frac{\sin \psi \sin(\omega T(\psi))}{(1 - x_s \cos \psi)^2} d\psi.$$

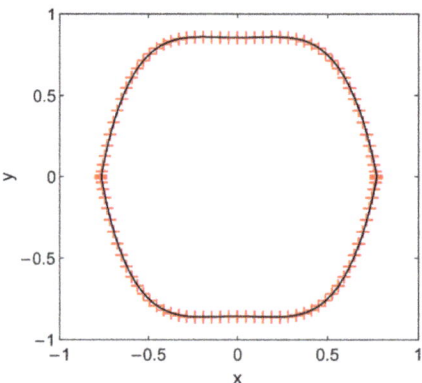

Figure 6. Comparison of heteroclinic orbits of the system (6) where the solid curve represents the exact model based on Hamiltonian and the sign + shows the orbits in explicit functions of ψ.

When $\beta \gamma x_s \sqrt{J_2^2 + J_3^2} \geq \mu J_1$, i.e.,

$$V_{AC} > V_{AC}^{Hetero0} = \frac{\mu V_b J_1}{\beta x_s \sqrt{J_2^2 + J_3^2}}. \tag{36}$$

there will be a simple equilibrium of the Melnikov function (34), enabling the existence of the transverse heteroclinic orbits, and the dimensionless system (5) may undergo a type of initial-sensitive motion. Here, it can be calculated that $V_{AC}^{hetero0} = 0.25$ V, much higher than the threshold for homoclinic-bifurcation chaos $V_{AC}^{homo0} = 0.15$ V (see last section), indicating that complex dynamic behavior induced by heteroclinic bifurcation will be different from chaos. Since heteroclinic bifurcation in nonlinear systems is usually the mechanism responsible for triggering fractal erosion of safe basin [13,21,31], for V_{AC} higher than the threshold $V_{AC}^{hetero0}$, erosion of safe basin of the dimensionless system (5) will be expected. In Equation (5), the escape solution $x = 1$ or -1 means pull in to the upper electrode or the lower one, respectively. All the initial conditions leading to pull in construct the basin of attraction of pull-in attractors, which can be considered as dangerous basin [21]. In contrast, for bounded solutions satisfying $|x(T)| < 1$, the union of their basins of attraction is defined as safe basin. The intermingle of safe basin and dangerous basin implies that a subtle disturbance of initial conditions may change the dynamics of the system (5), for instance, from a bounded motion to pull in. it can intuitively depict the phenomenon pull-in instability.

In order to verify the criterion obtained in this section, numerical simulations are carried out. The 4th Runge-Kutta approach and the point-mapping method [22,23] are employed to describe safe basin. In this paper, safe basin is drawn in the sufficiently large space region defined as $-1.2 \leq x(0) \leq 1.2$, $-1.0 \leq y(0) \leq 1.0$ by generating a 200 × 200 array of initial conditions for each of those starting points. The escaping set for infinite time is approximated with good accuracy by a study of 1000 excited circles. The time step is taken as 0.01. The white region represents the numerical approximation to basin of pull-in attractors, and the black region is safe basin.

The variation of safe basin with the increase in V_{AC} is given in Figure 7. It can be noticed that when there is no AC voltage in the vibrating system (see Figure 7a), the boundary of safe basin is nearly the same as the region surrounded by heteroclinic orbits. When V_{AC} increases to 0.15 V (see Figure 7b), namely the threshold for homoclinic bifurcation, safe basin becomes smaller, but its boundary is still smooth. When V_{AC} reaches 0.3 V (see Figure 7c), higher than the threshold $V_{AC}^{hetero0}$, the fractal fingers occur on the basin boundary, which is in agreement with our theoretical prediction. As V_{AC} continue to increase, the fractality of safe basin becomes more and more visible (see Figure 7d,e). Finally, when V_{AC} grows to 1.05 V, the whole initial-condition plane is eroded to be white (see Figure 7f), meaning that pull in of the MEMS resonator is unavoidable, i.e., static pull-in. It shows that in the dynamic system of the bilateral MEMS resonator, heteroclinic bifurcation induces pull-in instability.

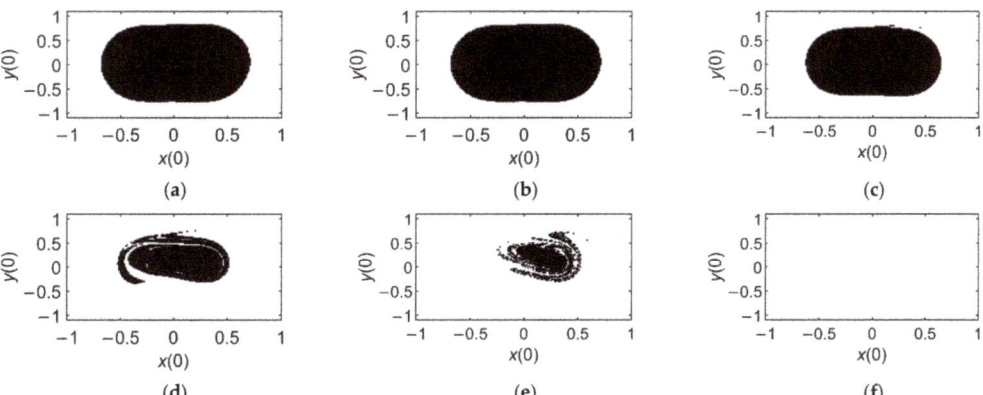

Figure 7. Safe basins of the system (5) under different values of AC voltage amplitude: (**a**) $V_{AC} = 0$ V; (**b**) $V_{AC} = 0.15$ V; (**c**) $V_{AC} = 0.30$ V; (**d**) $V_{AC} = 0.50$ V; (**e**) $V_{AC} = 0.70$ V; (**f**) $V_{AC} = 1.05$ V.

4. Control of Complex Dynamics via Delayed Feedback

In this section, two types of linear-delayed feedback controllers, i.e., delayed-position feedback and delayed-velocity feedback, are applied on the DC voltage source to stabilize the micro resonator. The corresponding control diagram is schemed in Figure 8 where w represents the position $z(t)$ or the velocity $\frac{dz}{dt}$. The governing controlled system can be expressed as

$$m\frac{d^2z}{dt^2}+c\frac{dz}{dt}+k_1z+k_3z^3=\frac{A_0}{2(d-z)^2}(V_b+G(w(t-\tilde{\tau})-w)+V_{AC}\sin\Omega t)^2-\frac{A_0}{2(d+z)^2}(V_b+G(w(t-\tilde{\tau})-w))^2, \quad (37)$$

where $\tilde{\tau}$ is time delay, and G the gain of the feedback controller. G and $\tilde{\tau}$ are independent parameters. When $\tilde{\tau}=0$, the controlled term becomes that $G(w(t-\tau)-w(t))=0$, and then the controlled system becomes the original system (1). Setting

$$g_p=\frac{Gd}{V_b},\quad g_v=\frac{\omega_0 Gd}{V_b},\quad \tau=\omega_0\tilde{\tau}, \quad (38)$$

and substituting Equation (4) into the controlled system (37), we will have

$$\ddot{x}+\mu\dot{x}+x+\alpha x^3=\frac{\beta}{(1-x)^2}(1+g_p(x(T-\tau)-x)+\gamma\sin\omega T)^2-\frac{\beta}{(1+x)^2}(1+g_p(x(T-\tau)-x))^2, \quad (39)$$

for $w(t)=x(t)$, and

$$\ddot{x}+\mu\dot{x}+x+\alpha x^3=\frac{\beta}{(1-x)^2}(1+g_v(\dot{x}(T-\tau)-\dot{x})+\gamma\sin\omega T)^2-\frac{\beta}{(1+x)^2}(1+g_v(\dot{x}(T-\tau)-\dot{x}))^2, \quad (40)$$

for $w(t)=\frac{dx(t)}{dt}$. Considering the engineering application, we do not discuss the periodic characteristics of the dimensionless time delay τ but restrict that $0\leq\tau<2\pi$. Since there is no signal that can be returned to the delayed-feedback control system (37) before $t=0$, the initial conditions for the controlled system can be supposed as $x(t)=0$ and $x'(t)=0$ for $-\tau\leq t<0$ [23,32]. Then the initial-condition space of the delayed system can be projected onto the initial-phase plane $x(0)-x'(0)$. It means that we can set $x(T)=y(T)=0$ for $-\tau\leq t<0$ in the dimensionless controlled systems (39) and (40), and still depict safe basin in the initial-state plane $x(0)-y(0)$, the same as the original system (5). To be different from Section 3, the software package applied in this section is DDE23, as the controlled systems (39) and (40) are delayed differential equations rather than ordinary differential ones.

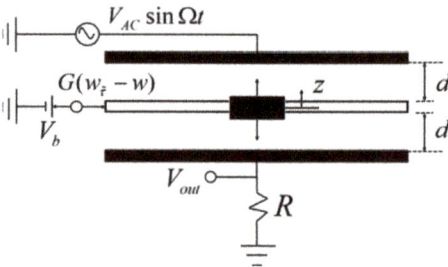

Figure 8. Schematic diagram of the delayed-feedback-control bilateral MEMS resonator.

4.1. Delayed Position Feedback

To study the control mechanism of chaos and pull-in instability in the delayed system via the Melnikov method conveniently, the precondition is that the delayed-position feedback $g_p(x(T-\tau)-x)$ can be treated as a perturbed term of the controlled system (39). In other words, we should ensure that the value of time delay τ will not exceed the first stability switch of equilibria in a linearized system [23,32]. In this situation, we can expand the delayed feedback of the system (39) into Taylor's series so as to obtain an approximately ordinary different equation. On this basis, similar to the last section, the Melnikov method can be applied to discuss critical conditions for chaos and pull-in instability.

Since $\mu > 0$ and $\alpha - 2 - 3\alpha x_c^2 > 0$, in the linearized system of the uncontrolled system (5), the two equilibria $C_1(x_c, 0)$ and $C_2(-x_c, 0)$ are stable. Thus, we should present the linear-stability analysis in the vicinity of the two equilibria. The position x is set as

$$x = \pm x_c + \varepsilon u + O(\varepsilon^2), \tag{41}$$

where $u = O(1)$. Substituting (41) into the delayed system (39), expanding the terms $\frac{\beta}{(1-x)^2}$ and $\frac{\beta}{(1+x)^2}$ in Taylor's series and neglecting ε terms and higher-order terms of ε yield, the following delayed-linear system

$$\ddot{u} + \mu \dot{u} = \frac{2x_c^2(2-\alpha+3\alpha x_c^2)}{1-x_c^2}u + 2(1+\alpha x_c^2)x_c g_p(u(T-\tau)-u) \tag{42}$$

Its characteristic equation can be written by

$$\lambda^2 + \mu\lambda + \rho - 2x_c(1+\alpha x_c^2)g_p(e^{-\lambda\tau}-1) = 0 \tag{43}$$

where $\rho = \frac{2x_c^2(\alpha-2-3\alpha x_c^2)}{1-x_c^2} > 0$. Substituting $\lambda = iv$ into Equation (43), separating the imaginary and real parts, and eliminating the triangular functions yield

$$v^4 + v^2(-2\rho - 4x_c(1+\alpha x_c^2)g_p + \mu^2) + \rho(\rho + 4x_c(1+\alpha x_c^2)g_p) = 0 \tag{44}$$

According to Equation (44), if the gain g_p satisfies

$$4x_c(1+\alpha x_c^2)g_p > \mu^2 + 2\mu\sqrt{\rho}, \tag{45}$$

there will be two different positive solutions of Equation (44) expressed as v_+ and v_-. And the critical value of time delay for the stability switch of the two equilibria $C_1(x_c, 0)$ and $C_2(-x_c, 0)$ can be expressed as

$$\tau_+(0) = \frac{1}{v_+}(2\pi - \arccos(1 + \frac{\rho - v_+^2}{2x_c(1+\alpha x_c^2)g_p})) \tag{46}$$

Thus, the delayed position feedback can be considered as the perturbed term when $0 < \tau < \tau_+(0)$. Fixing $g_p = 0.2$, it can be calculated from Equation (46) that $\tau_+(0) \approx 1.53$. When applying the delayed position feedback suppressing global bifurcation behaviors, it is better to ensure the delay τ less than $\tau_+(0)$.

4.1.1. Control of Chaos

In the delayed-position-feedback controlled system (39), for $0 < \tau < \tau_+(0)$, rescaling that $\tau = \varepsilon\hat{\tau}$, expanding the delayed feedback $g_p(x(T-\tau) - x$ in Taylor's series, neglecting ε^2 terms and higher-order terms of ε, and then returning to the non-dimensional variables, we can approximate Equation (39) as the following ordinary differential equation

$$\ddot{x} + x + \alpha x^3 + \frac{\beta}{(1+x)^2} - \frac{\beta}{(1-x)^2} = -\mu\dot{x} + \frac{2\beta\gamma \sin \omega T}{(1-x)^2} - \frac{8\beta g_p \tau x\dot{x}}{(1-x^2)^2} \tag{47}$$

The similar as the uncontrolled system (5), based on homoclinic orbits (24) and Equation (25), the Melnikov function of the system (47) can be written as

$$M_{homo-P}(t_0) = -\mu I_1 \pm 2\beta\gamma(I_2 \cos(\omega T_0) + I_3 \sin(\omega T_0)) - \beta g_p \tau I_p \tag{48}$$

where

$$I_p = \frac{(\alpha - 2 - \eta_1)^2 \sqrt{\eta_1}}{2\sqrt{2}\alpha^2} \int_0^\pi \sin^2 2\varphi \sqrt{\frac{1 - \frac{\alpha-2-\eta_1}{2\eta_1}\sin^2\varphi}{\left(1 - \frac{\alpha-2-\eta_1}{2\alpha}\sin^2\varphi\right)^5}} d\varphi > 0 \quad (49)$$

The integral I_p in the above equation can be evaluated numerically. When $2\beta\gamma\sqrt{I_2^2 + I_3^2} > \mu I_1 + \beta g_p \tau I_p$, namely

$$V_{AC} > V_{AC}^{Homo-P} = V_{AC}^{Homo0} + \frac{g_p \tau V_b I_p}{2\sqrt{I_2^2 + I_3^2}}. \quad (50)$$

there will be a simple zero in the Melnikov function. Accordingly, the threshold of V_{AC} for homoclinic bifurcation of the system is V_{AC}^{Homo-P} of the above equation. It follows from Equation (50) that for $g_p > 0$, the threshold of V_{AC} for homoclinic bifurcation in the delayed-position-feedback controlled system will become higher than in the uncontrolled system. It illustrates the mechanism of delayed-position feedback on controlling chaos.

Given $g_p = 0.2$, the change of V_{AC} threshold with the increase in the delay τ is depicted in Figure 9. Here τ ranges from 0 to 0.25, satisfying $\tau \ll \tau_+(0)$. The numerical results of V_{AC}^{Homo-P} are obtained under which the transient chaos occurs. Each numerical value of V_{AC}^{Homo-P} has two decimal places. In Figure 9, the numerical results for V_{AC}^{Homo-P} are in substantial agreement with the analytical ones. It demonstrates that the threshold of AC voltage amplitude for transient chaos increases monotonically with the delay τ for a positive gain and a small τ. For example, setting V_{AC} = 0.16 V, one can observe the evolution of dynamics with time delay in Figure 10. As shown in the bifurcation diagram of Figure 10a, with the increase in time delay, the transient chaos is reduced effectively. For example, when τ = 0.13, it becomes a periodic attractor (see Figure 10b). It shows that the delayed position feedback can be used to suppress chaos of the micro resonator effectively.

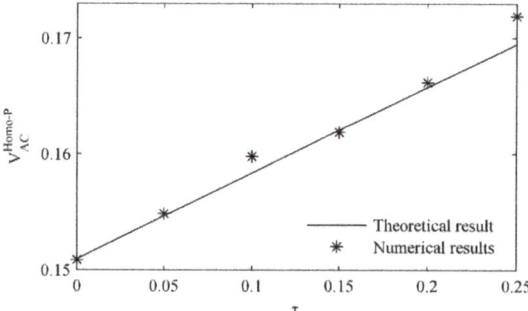

Figure 9. Variation of V_{AC} threshold for homoclinic bifurcation with τ when $g_p = 0.2$.

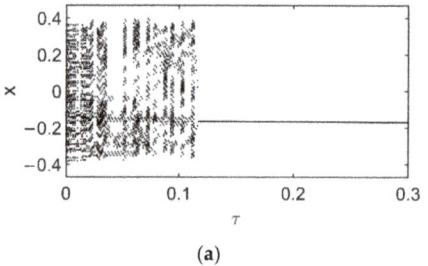

(a)

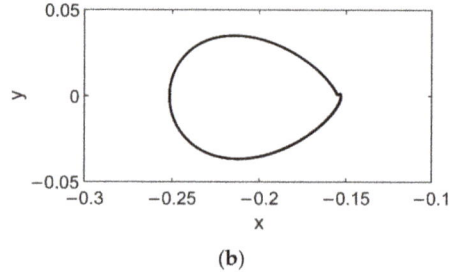

(b)

Figure 10. Dynamic behavior of the delayed system (39) when $g_p = 0.2$ and $V_{AC} = 0.16$ V (**a**) Bifurcation with τ in Poincáre map (**b**) Phase map when τ = 0.12.

4.1.2. Control of Pull-In Instability

Similar to last section, we can also employ the Melnikov method to obtain the critical condition for heteroclinic bifurcation of the controlled system (47). Substituting heteroclinic orbits (31) and Equation (32) into the Melnikov function of Equation (47) yields

$$M_{hetero-P}(T_0) = -2\mu x_s^2 J_1 \mp 2\beta\gamma x_s (J_2 \sin(\omega T_0) + J_3 \cos(\omega T_0)) - 8\sqrt{2\beta} x_s \tau g_p J_p, \quad (51)$$

where

$$J_p = \frac{\sqrt{\alpha x_s^2 + \eta_2}(x_s^2 + 3x_s^2\beta + \beta - 1) - \sqrt{\eta_2}(x_s^2 + 3x_s^2\beta + 3\beta - 1)}{3(1 - x_s^2)^{\frac{3}{2}}} + \sqrt{\alpha\beta}(\operatorname{arcsinh}\frac{2\sqrt{\alpha}x_s}{\sqrt{1 + \alpha x_s^2}} - \operatorname{arcsinh}\frac{\sqrt{2\alpha}x_s}{\sqrt{1 + \alpha x_s^2}}) > 0. \quad (52)$$

For $\beta\gamma\sqrt{J_2^2 + J_3^2} > \mu x_s J_1 + 4\sqrt{2\beta}g_p \tau J_p$, namely

$$V_{AC} > V_{AC}^{Hetero-P} = V_{AC}^{Hetero0} + \frac{4\sqrt{2}g_p \tau V_b J_p}{\sqrt{\beta(J_2^2 + J_3^2)}} \quad (53)$$

according to the global bifurcation theory [25–28], there will be a simple equilibrium of the above Melnikov function, implying heteroclinic bifurcation. It shows in Equation (53) that the increase in V_{AC} in the delayed-position-feedback controlled system can also trigger heteroclinic bifurcation, similar as in the uncontrolled system. For $g_p > 0$, one has $V_{AC}^{Hetero-P} > V_{AC}^{Hetero0}$, showing that for a positive gain, heteroclinic bifurcation will occur under a higher AC voltage amplitude in the controlled system than in the uncontrolled system. It shows the control mechanism of heteroclinic-bifurcation behavior.

In light of the theoretical predictions, we present numerical examples to verify their validity. As shown in Figure 11, the theoretical results for $V_{AC}^{Hetero-P}$ increase monopoly with the dimensionless delay τ for $g_p = 0.2$. The numerical values of $V_{AC}^{Hetero-P}$ are obtained at the point which the boundary of safe basin begins to be unsmooth. In other words, if V_{AC} is less than the numerical results of $V_{AC}^{Hetero-P}$, the boundary of safe basin will still be smooth. It can be seen in Figure 11 that the numerical results match the theoretical ones well, which illustrates that under a positive gain, the delayed position feedback can be used to control pull-in instability.

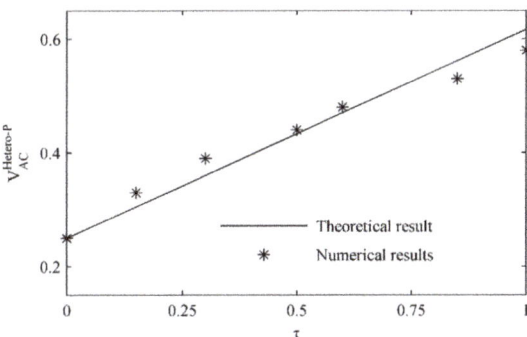

Figure 11. Variation of V_{AC} threshold for heteroclinic bifurcation with τ for $g_p = 0.2$.

To depict the effect of delayed position feedback on controlling pull-in instability in details, the evolution of safe basin with the increase in τ is presented in Figure 12 where the delay is short, satisfying $\tau << \tau_+(0)$. When $\tau = 0$ (see Figure 12a,d,g), safe basins mean those of the uncontrolled system, which contain fractal boundaries, illustrating pull-in instability. With the increase in the delay τ, the fractal extent, namely the probability of pull-in instability, is obviously lessened, and the basin area enlarged, which can be observed in each line of Figure 12. When $\tau = 0.55$, the basin boundary under $V_{AC} = 0.46$ V becomes smooth (see Figure 12b), and the other two basins are enlarged whose boundaries are still fractal (see Figure 12e,h). When $\tau = 0.81$, the basin boundary under $V_{AC} = 0.52$ V becomes smooth too (see Figure 12f). Even though safe basin in Figure 12i still has a fractal boundary, the situation is much better than in the uncontrolled system: at least the vicinity of the origin is black, showing that dynamic pull-in will not occur in the initial-condition region.

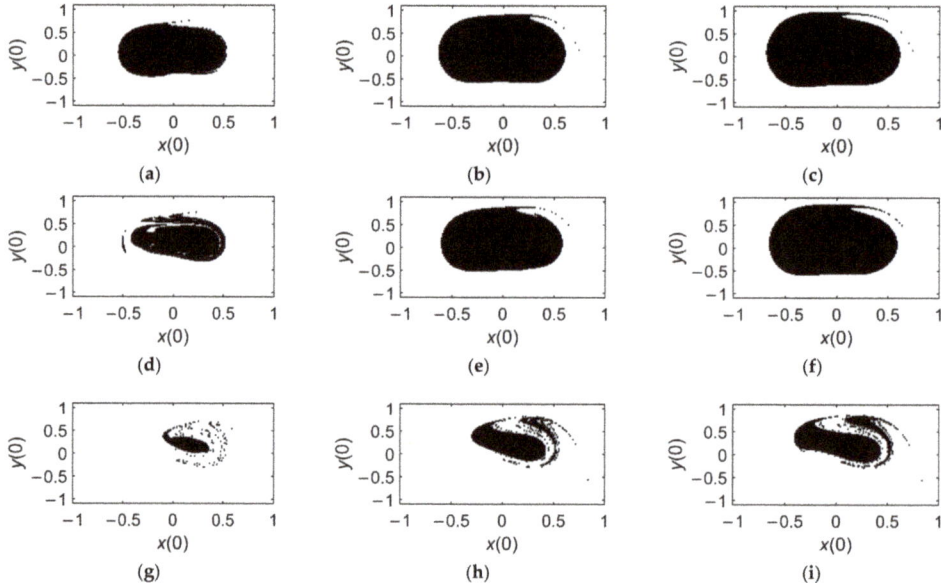

Figure 12. Safe basins of the controlled system (39) under different values of V_{AC} and τ: (a) $V_{AC} = 0.46$ V, $\tau = 0$; (b) $V_{AC} = 0.46$ V, $\tau = 0.55$; (c) $V_{AC} = 0.46$ V, $\tau = 0.75$; (d) $V_{AC} = 0.52$ V, $\tau = 0$; (e) $V_{AC} = 0.52$ V, $\tau = 0.55$; (f) $V_{AC} = 0.52$ V, $\tau = 0.75$; (g) $V_{AC} = 0.81$ V, $\tau = 0$; (h) $V_{AC} = 0.81$ V, $\tau = 0.55$; (i) $V_{AC} = 0.81$ V, $\tau = 0.75$.

4.2. Delayed Velocity Feedback

Similar to delayed-position feedback, we also expect to treat the delayed velocity feedback as a perturbed term so as conveniently to discuss the global bifurcation of the controlled system. Thus, the value of time delay τ should be kept less than the first stability switch of equilibria in the linearized system. Based on the linearized system in the vicinity of the stable equilibria of the uncontrolled system (5) and the corresponding characteristic equation, the critical condition for the stability switch is that there exists a purely imaginary eigenvalue $\lambda = iv$ satisfying

$$-v + (\frac{1+3x_c^2\alpha}{v} - \frac{4\beta(1+3x_c^2)}{v(1-x_c^2)^2}) = \frac{8\beta g_v x_c}{(1-x_c^2)^2}\sin v\tau, \quad \mu + \frac{8\beta x_c g_v}{(1-x_c^2)^2} = \frac{8\beta g_v x_c}{(1-x_c^2)^2}\cos v\tau \quad (54)$$

For a positive gain g_v, since $\mu > 0$, it is easy to conclude that there is no real root of v in Equation (54). It implies that the stability of the two equilibria will not be changed by the delayed velocity feedback under a positive g_v.

4.2.1. Suppression of Chaos

Now expressing a short time delay τ as $\varepsilon\widetilde{\tau}$, expanding $g_v(\dot{x}(T-\tau) - \dot{x})$ in Taylor's series, neglecting higher-order terms of ε, and returning the parameters to the non-dimensional parameters, we approximate the delayed-velocity-feedback controlled system as

$$\ddot{x} + x + \alpha x^3 + \frac{\beta}{(1+x)^2} - \frac{\beta}{(1-x)^2} = -\mu\dot{x} + \frac{2\beta\gamma \sin \omega T}{(1-x)^2} - \frac{8\beta g_v \tau x \ddot{x}}{(1-x^2)^2} \quad (55)$$

Substituting homoclinic orbits (24) and Equation (25) into the Melnikov function of the above ordinary differential-equation yields

$$M_{homo-V}(T_0) = -\mu I_1 \pm 2\beta\gamma(I_2 \cos(\omega T_0) + I_3 \sin(\omega T_0) - 2g_v \tau \beta \int_{-\infty}^{+\infty} (\frac{1}{(1-x_{homo})^2} - \frac{1}{(1+x_{homo})^2}) y_{homo} dy_{homo}(\varphi) \quad (56)$$

Since $\int_{-\infty}^{+\infty} (\frac{1}{(1-x_{homo})^2} - \frac{1}{(1+x_{homo})^2}) y_{homo} dy_{homo}(\varphi) = 0$, one has $M_{homo-V}(T_0) = M_{homo}(T_0)$. Accordingly, $V_{AC}^{Homo-V} = V_{AC}^{Homo0}$. It indicates that the delayed velocity feedback cannot work for reducing transient chaos. It can also be verified by the numerical bifurcation diagram in Figure 13 for $g_v = 0.2$. As depicted in Figure 13, with the variation of the delay τ, the dynamic behavior is still complex.

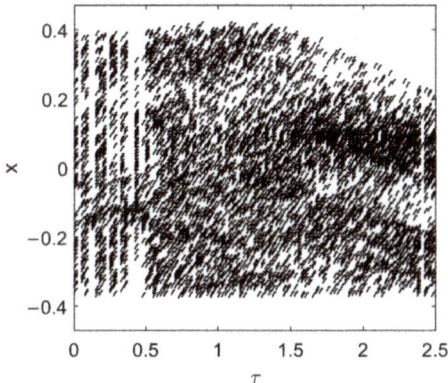

Figure 13. Bifurcation of the delayed-velocity-feedback controlled system (40) with τ in Poincaré map for $g_v = 0.2$ and $V_{AC} = 0.16$ V.

4.2.2. Suppression of Pull-In Instability

Similarly, by substituting heteroclinic orbits (31) and Equation (32) into the Melnikov function of Equation (55), we can the Melnikov function as follows

$$M_{hetero-V}(T_0) = -2\mu J_1 \mp 2\beta\gamma x_s \sin(\omega T_0) J_2 \mp 2\beta\gamma x_s \cos(\omega T_0) J_3 - 8\beta g_v \tau J_v \quad (57)$$

where

$$J_v = \frac{3}{x_s^3} - \frac{\beta(72 - 51x_s^2 - 8x_s^4 + 3x_s^6)}{6x_s^3(1-x_s^2)^{\frac{3}{2}}} + \frac{(4+\beta-6\alpha+6\alpha x_s^2)}{2x_s^2}\text{arctanh}(x_s) > 0 \quad (58)$$

According to the theory of global bifurcation, the critical condition for heteroclinic bifurcation is $\beta\gamma x_s \sqrt{J_2^2 + J_3^2} > \mu J_1 + 4\beta g_v \tau J_v$. Expressing it by the original parameters V_{AC} and V_b yields

$$V_{AC} > V_{AC}^{Hetero-V} = V_{AC}^{Hetero0} + \frac{4g_v \tau V_b J_v}{x_s\sqrt{J_2^2 + J_3^2}}. \quad (59)$$

In Equation (59), $V_{AC}^{Hetero-V}$ means the threshold of AC voltage amplitude for pull-in instability in the delayed-velocity-feedback controlled system. It follows that $V_{AC}^{Hetero-V} >$

$V_{AC}^{Hetero0}$ for $g_v > 0$, demonstrating that under a positive gain, the delayed velocity feedback can be useful to control heteroclinic bifurcation behavior.

The effectiveness of the delayed-velocity feedback control can be verified by the comparison of the theoretical thresholds and the numerical ones for pull-in instability in Figure 14 for $g_v = 0.2$. Furthermore, the sequences of safe basin with the increase in time delay are depicted in detail (see Figure 15). It follows from the comparison of safe basins under the same values of V_{AC} and different values of τ that under a positive gain g_v, the delayed-velocity feedback can restrict the extent of pull-in instability and dynamic pull in successfully (see each row of Figure 15). When $\tau = 0$, the delayed system becomes the uncontrolled one; thus, for V_{AC} higher than 0.25 V ($V_{AC}^{Hetero0}$), safe basin is fractal (see the first column of Figure 15), showing the occurrence of pull-in instability. With the increase in time delay τ, the fractal extent of safe basin will be reduced. When $\tau = 1.6$, the basin boundary under $V_{AC} = 0.46$ V turns smooth (see Figure 15b). When τ reaches 2.0, the basin boundary under $V_{AC} = 0.52$ V also becomes smooth, as shown in Figure 15f. Comparing with the uncontrolled safe basin in Figure 15g, although safe basin in Figure 15i is still fractal, the vicinity of the point O(0, 0) and $C_1(x_c, 0)$ becomes black, showing that in this region, the MEMS resonator under the delayed velocity feedback will not undergo pull-in, thus having a more stable performance.

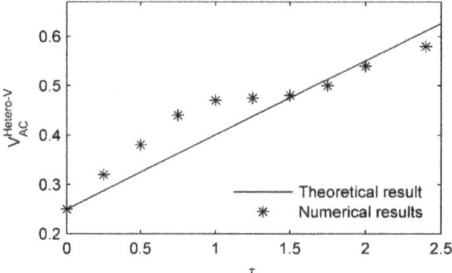

Figure 14. Variation of AC voltage threshold for heteroclinic bifurcation with τ when $g_v = 0.2$.

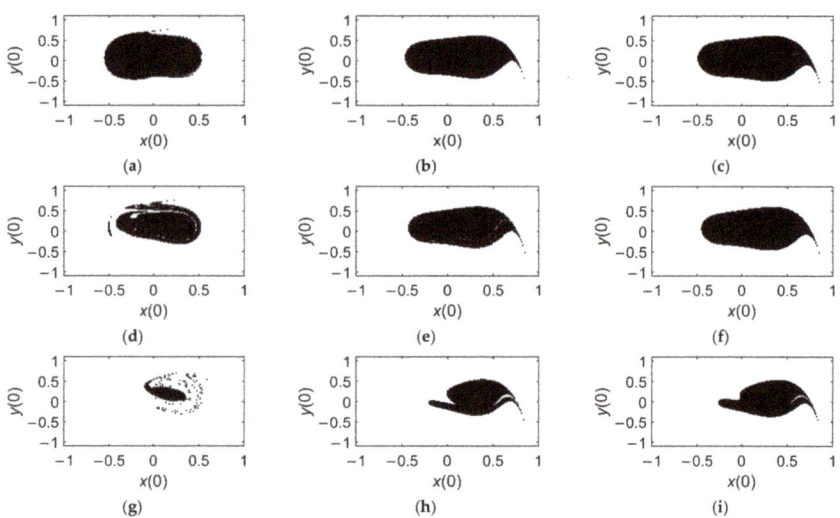

Figure 15. Safe basins of velocity-feedback-controlled system (40) under different V_{AC} and τ: (a) $V_{AC} = 0.46$ V, $\tau = 0$; (b) $V_{AC} = 0.46$ V, $\tau = 1.6$; (c) $V_{AC} = 0.46$ V, $\tau = 2$; (d) $V_{AC} = 0.52$ V, $\tau = 0$; (e) $V_{AC} = 0.52$ V, $\tau = 1.6$; (f) $V_{AC} = 0.52$ V, $\tau = 2$; (g) $V_{AC} = 0.81$ V, $\tau = 0$; (h) $V_{AC} = 0.81$ V, $\tau = 1.6$; (i) $V_{AC} = 0.81$V, $\tau = 2.0$.

5. Discussion

In the dynamic systems of MEMS resonators, initial-sensitive dynamic behaviors such as chaos and pull-in instability are unfavorable for causing the loss-of-performance reliability of these devices. It is known that initial-sensitive dynamic behaviors are usually attributed to global bifurcations. To understand their mechanisms adequately and to propose effective control strategies, we consider a typical bilateral MEMS resonator and discuss its global bifurcation behaviors analytically and numerically.

First, the ordinary differential equation governing the vibrating system of the MEMS resonator is made dimensionless. The static bifurcation of equilibria is investigated for the unperturbed system. The bifurcation sets of the equilibria in parameter space are constructed to demonstrate that the number and shapes of potential wells depend on DC bias voltage. The increase in DC bias voltage may lead to static pull-in of the micro resonator. In a certain range of DC bias voltage, the unperturbed system contains both homoclinic orbits and heteroclinic orbits, implying the possibility of rich complex dynamics.

Next, by fixing the physical parameters of the micro resonator and varying the AC voltage amplitude, the case of coexisting homoclinic orbits and heteroclinic ones is discussed in detail. The Melnikov method is employed to provide analytical critical conditions for global bifurcations. It is worth mentioning that this vibrating system contains fractional terms which constitute an obstacle for expressing the unperturbed orbits in explicit functions of time variable. Thus, the Melnikov method cannot be applied conveniently. To tackle this problem, new variables are introduced to express both the orbits and the time variable explicitly so as to detect the analytical criteria for global bifurcations via the Melnikov method.

Furthermore, the analytical results are verified by the numerical simulations in the form of phase maps, safe basins, bifurcation diagrams and Poincaré maps. Fractal erosion of safe basin is induced to depict pull-in instability intuitively. It is found that chaos and pull-in instability are different initial-sensitive phenomena attributed to homoclinic and heteroclinic bifurcation, respectively. The increase in AC voltage amplitude may trigger chaos and pull-in instability of this MEMS resonator successively.

Consequently, delayed-position feedback and delayed-velocity feedback are applied to the DC-voltage source to stabilize the micro resonator, respectively. To study the control mechanisms for chaos and pull-in instability in the delayed system conveniently, we treat the two types of delayed feedback as perturbed terms by expanding them in Taylor's series so as to transform these delayed systems to ODEs. To this end, we discuss the first stability switch of equilibria in linearized controlled systems to make sure the delay is much less than the original system, thus it will not change the original stability of equilibria. On this basis, the similar as the original system, critical conditions for global bifurcation under control are discussed and confirmed by the numerical simulations. It shows that the two types of delayed feedback applied on DC bias voltage can both reduce pull-in instability effectively. The control mechanism behind is that under a positive gain coefficient, the AC voltage amplitude threshold of heteroclinic bifurcation increases with time delay. For suppressing chaos, only delayed-position feedback under a positive gain can be effective.

This work presents a detailed analysis of pull-in instability and chaos of a typically MEMS resonator as well as their control, which may provide some potential applications for the design and control of relevant MEMS devices. It should be pointed out that the results are limited to the fixed physical properties of this MEMS resonator. We have not yet discussed the effect of physical properties on triggering complex responses. For a better performance reliability of MEMS resonators, these should be taken into account in theoretical study as well as experiment, which will be included in our future work.

Author Contributions: Conceptualization, H.S.; methodology, H.S.; software, Y.Z.; validation, H.S.; formal analysis, H.S.; investigation, Y.Z. and H.S.; resources, H.S.; data curation, Y.Z.; writing—original draft preparation, Y.Z. and H.S.; writing—review and editing, H.S.; visualization, Y.Z.; supervision, H.S.; project administration, H.S.; funding acquisition, H.S. All authors have read and agreed to the published version of the manuscript.

Funding: This research was funded by the National Natural Science Foundation of China, grant number 11472176.

Data Availability Statement: The datasets generated during the current study are available from the corresponding author on reasonable request.

Acknowledgments: The authors acknowledge the support of the National Natural Science Foundation of China under grant number 11472176. The authors are grateful for the valuable comments of the reviewers.

Conflicts of Interest: The authors declare no conflict of interest.

References

1. Amer, T.S.; Galal, A.A.; Abady, I.M.; Elkafly, H.F. The dynamical motion of a gyrostat for the irrational frequency case. *Appl. Math. Modeling* **2021**, *89*, 1235–1267. [CrossRef]
2. Ilyas, S.; Jaber, N.; Younis, M.I. A MEMS coupled resonator for frequency filtering in air. *Mechatronics* **2018**, *56*, 261–267. [CrossRef]
3. Zorlu, Ö.; Külah, H. A MEMS-based energy harvester for generating energy from non-resonant environmental vibration. *Sens. Actuators A Phys.* **2013**, *202*, 124–134. [CrossRef]
4. Zaitsev, S.; Shtempluck, O.; Buks, E.; Gottlie, O. Nonlinear damping in a micromechanical oscillator. *Nonlinear Dyn.* **2012**, *67*, 859–883. [CrossRef]
5. Gusso, A. Nonlinear damping in double clamped beam resonators due to the attachment loss induced by the geometric nonlinearity. *J. Sound Vib.* **2016**, *372*, 255–265. [CrossRef]
6. Hajjaj, A.Z.; Jaber, N.; Hafiz, M.A.A.; Ilyas, S.; Younis, M.I. Mulitple internal resonances in MEMS arch resonators. *Phys. Lett. A* **2018**, *382*, 3393–3398. [CrossRef]
7. Ali, A.; Ardeshir, K.M. Nonlinear dynamics and bifurcation behavior of a sandwiched micro-beam resonator consist of hyperelastic dielectric film. *Sens. Actuators A Phys.* **2020**, *312*, 112113.
8. Zhu, Y.; Shang, H. Multistability of the vibrating system of a micro resonator. *Fractal Fract.* **2022**, *6*, 141. [CrossRef]
9. Barceló, J.; Rosselló, J.L.; Bota, S.; Segura, J.; Verd, J. Electrostatically actuated microbeam resonators as chaotic signal generators: A practical perspective. *Commun. Nonlinear Sci. Numer. Simulat.* **2016**, *30*, 316–327. [CrossRef]
10. Alemansour, H.; Miandoab, E.M.; Pishkenari, H.N. Effect of size on the chaotic behavior of nano resonators. *Commun. Nonlinear Sci. Numer. Simulat.* **2017**, *44*, 495–505. [CrossRef]
11. Dantas, W.G.; Gusso, A. Analysis of the chaotic dynamics of MEMS/NEMS double clamped beam resonators with two-sided electrodes. *Int. J. Bifurc. Chaos* **2018**, *28*, 1850122. [CrossRef]
12. Zhang, S.; Zhang, J. Fatigue-induced dynamic pull-in instability in electrically actuated microbeam resonators. *Int. J. Mech. Sci.* **2021**, *195*, 106261. [CrossRef]
13. Rega, G.; Settimi, V. Dynamical integrity and control of nonlinear mechanical oscillators. *J. Vib. Control* **2008**, *14*, 159–179. [CrossRef]
14. Xi, W.; Elsinawi, A.; Guha, K.; Karumuri, S.R.; Shaikh-Ahmad, J. A study of the effect of transient stresses on the fatigue life of RF MEMS switches. *Int. J. Numer. Model.* **2019**, *32*, 2570. [CrossRef]
15. Zhang, W.M.; Yan, H.; Peng, Z.K.; Meng, G. Electrostatic pull-in instability in MEMS/NEMS: A review. *Sens. Actuators A Phys.* **2014**, *214*, 187–218. [CrossRef]
16. Fu, X.; Xu, L. Multi-field coupled chaotic vibration for a micro resonant pressure sensor. *Appl. Math. Model.* **2019**, *72*, 470–485. [CrossRef]
17. Liu, C.; Yan, Y.; Wang, W. Resonances and chaos of electrostatically actuated arch micro/nano resonators with time delay velocity feedback. *Chaos Solitons Fractals* **2020**, *131*, 109512. [CrossRef]
18. Luo, S.; Li, S.; Tajaddodianfar, E.; Hu, J. Observer-based adaptive stabilization of the fractional-order chaotic MEMS resonator. *Nonlinear Dyn.* **2018**, *92*, 1079–1089. [CrossRef]
19. Haghighi, S.H.; Markazi, H.D.A. Chaos prediction and chaos in MEMS resonators. *Commun. Nonlinear Sci. Numer. Simulat.* **2010**, *15*, 3091–3099. [CrossRef]
20. Siewe, S.M.; Hegazy, H.U. Homoclinic bifurcation and chaos control in MMES resonators. *Appl. Math. Modeling* **2011**, *35*, 5533–5552. [CrossRef]
21. Alsaleem, F.M.; Younis, M.I. Stabilization of electrostatic MEMS resonators using a delayed feedback controller. *Smart Mater. Struct.* **2010**, *19*, 035016. [CrossRef]
22. Shang, H. Pull-in instability of a typical electrostatic MEMS resonator and its control by delayed feedback. *Nonlinear Dyn.* **2017**, *90*, 171–183. [CrossRef]

23. Gusso, A.; Viana, L.R.; Mathias, C.A.; Caldas, L.I. Nonlinear dynamics and chaos in micro/nanoelectromechanical beam resonators actuated by two-sided electrodes. *Chaos Solitons Fractals* **2019**, *122*, 6–16. [CrossRef]
24. Cao, Y.Y.; Chung, K.W.; Xu, J. A novel construction of homoclinic and heteroclinic orbits in nonlinear oscillators by a perturbation-incremental method. *Nonlinear Dyn.* **2011**, *64*, 221–236. [CrossRef]
25. Zhang, D.; Li, F. Chaotic Dynamics of Non-Autonomous Nonlinear System for a Sandwich Plate with Truss Core. *Mathematics* **2022**, *10*, 1889. [CrossRef]
26. Litak, G.; Borowiec, M.; Dąbek, K. The Transition to Chaos of Pendulum Systems. *Appl. Sci.* **2022**, *12*, 8876. [CrossRef]
27. Zhou, B.; Jin, Y.; Xu, H. Global dynamics for a class of tristable system with negative stiffness. *Chaos Solitons Fractals* **2022**, *162*, 112509. [CrossRef]
28. Zheng, H.; Xia, Y.; Pinto, M. Chaotic motion and control of the driven-damped Double Sine-Gordon equation. *Discret. Contin. Dyn. Syst. -Ser. B* **2022**, *27*, 7151–7167. [CrossRef]
29. Tékam, G.T.O.; Kuimy, C.K.; Woafo, P. Analysis of tristable energy harvesting system having fractional order viscoelastic material. *Chaos* **2015**, *25*, 191–206.
30. Stephen, W.; David, M. Introduction to applied nonlinear dynamical systems and chaos. *Comput. Phys.* **1990**, *4*, 563.
31. Qin, B.; Shang, H.; Jiang, H. Initial-Sensitive Dynamical Behaviors of a Class of Geometrically Nonlinear Oscillators. *Shock Vib.* **2022**, *10*, 6472678. [CrossRef]
32. Mondal, J.; Chatterjee, S. Controlling self-excited vibration of a nonlinear beam by nonlinear resonant velocity feedback with time delay. *Int. J. Non-Linear Mech.* **2021**, *131*, 103684. [CrossRef]

Article

Fractal Analysis and Time Series Application in ZY-4 SEM Micro Fractographies Evaluation

Maria-Alexandra Paun [1,2], Vladimir-Alexandru Paun [3] and Viorel-Puiu Paun [4,5,*]

[1] School of Engineering, Swiss Federal Institute of Technology (EPFL), 1015 Lausanne, Switzerland
[2] Division Radio Monitoring and Equipment, Section Market Access and Conformity, Federal Office of Communications OFCOM, 2501 Bienne, Switzerland
[3] Five Rescue Research Laboratory, 75004 Paris, France
[4] Department of Physics, Faculty of Applied Sciences, University Politehnica of Bucharest, 060042 Bucharest, Romania
[5] Academy of Romanian Scientists, 050094 Bucharest, Romania
* Correspondence: viorel.paun@physics.pub.ro or viorel_paun2006@yahoo.com

Abstract: SEM microfractographies of Zircaloy-4 are studied by fractal analysis and the time-series method. We first develop a computer application that associates the fractal dimension and lacunarity to each SEM micrograph picture, and produce a nonlinear analysis of the data acquired from the quantitatively evaluated time series. Utilizing the phase space-embedding technique to reconstruct the attractor and to compute the autocorrelation dimension, the fracture surface of the Zircaloy-4 samples is investigated. The fractal analysis method manages to highlight damage complications and provide a description of morphological parameters of various fractures by calculating the fractal dimension and lacunarity.

Keywords: fractal dimension; lacunarity; time series; phase space; attractor; correlation dimension; Zircaloy-4

Citation: Paun, M.-A.; Paun, V.-A.; Paun, V.-P. Fractal Analysis and Time Series Application in ZY-4 SEM Micro Fractographies Evaluation. *Fractal Fract.* **2022**, *6*, 458. https://doi.org/10.3390/fractalfract6080458

Academic Editor: António Lopes

Received: 29 July 2022
Accepted: 19 August 2022
Published: 21 August 2022

Publisher's Note: MDPI stays neutral with regard to jurisdictional claims in published maps and institutional affiliations.

Copyright: © 2022 by the authors. Licensee MDPI, Basel, Switzerland. This article is an open access article distributed under the terms and conditions of the Creative Commons Attribution (CC BY) license (https://creativecommons.org/licenses/by/4.0/).

1. Introduction

Zirconium, the chemical element with atomic number 40, is an interesting material in the nuclear domain especially because it is crystallized in the cubic lattice with the densest packing and due to the good neutron absorption properties proven.

The best known of its alloys, Zircaloy-2 and Zircaloy-4, are used for reactor components such as cladding, spacers, and shroud or guide tubes. The effects of alloy composition, grain size, and cold work on the terminal solubility and thermodynamic activity of hydrogen in the alpha phase of zirconium, Zircaloy-2, and Zircaloy-4 are well appreciated in nuclear power.

Nowadays, Canadian and all Romanian power reactor fuels in activity/operation utilize Zircaloy-4 (in short Zy-4) [1–3]. Of large importance are the thin-walled Zy-4 pipes, which are occasionally subjected to cyclic loadings that can start/produce and transmit meaningful fatigue cracks. The cracks are usually initiated at flaws or stress concentrations. Metal alloy fatigue cracks are initiated commonly from the surface area of a component structure, when the fatigue damage commences as scissors cracks on crystallographic slip planes. The surface of the deteriorated object, in particular the slip planes, is highlighted in the first place as packed intrusions and extrusions.

One major direction of mechanical comportment study of structural materials is fracture surface analysis and intrinsic cracking. As such, entire fracture surface and crack localization can ensure important indications regarding the legitimate source and damage advancement in time.

Based on the latest progress in statistical inference techniques for continuous chaotic systems and with the conceptualization of spatio-temporal chaos, we present a deterministic approach to the microscopic study of Zy-4 sample fracture surface [4].

This paper produces an assessment of Zy-4 scanning electron microscope (SEM) micrographs by application of fractal analysis and non-linear time series, a natural development of a preceding study [5]. It also performs a fractal analysis of morphological parameters.

Considering the microstructural behavior of solid materials, the fractal analysis method makes it possible to solve the problems of recognizing and highlighting the morphological characteristics of various phases, not only in metal and metal alloys, but also in complex metallic compound structures and classes of nano-composites. Thus, this method can be used both for realizing a complete analysis of the image and for determining parameters such as the configuration and repartition of separate constitutional components and phases, which is unfeasible by classical methods.

However, apart from the many proven advantages of the method, it also touches on some justified inconveniences, among which is also the fact that the fractal analysis results heavily depend both on the outside action on the investigated objects and on the pictures' inner "content," which was analyzed. Therefore, an important direction of development of the fractal analysis method of material structures pictures is advised. This involves taking into account not only the fractal dimension and lacunarity, but also alternative non-fractal-specific features together with the associated fractal type (still) in a perfect complete analysis.

The paper is structured in four parts. Besides the introduction, which sets up the background and state of the art regarding the use of zirconium in the nuclear domain, the work continues with a presentation of the theoretical considerations, including mathematical notions about the fractal dimension, lacunarity, time series, phase-space reconstruction, and SEM image evaluation. The third part of the present work is devoted to highlighting the results obtained and to discussing them. Finally, the paper concludes in the fourth part, which is devoted to the conclusions.

2. Theoretical Part

2.1. Fractal Dimension

The technical grid-type algorithm has more scanning schemes, through which it sets the mode on how the data will be aggregated, or in other words, how the grid will be displaced during the time that the image has been scanned. A classical scheme is a fixed survey, based on a multiple grip-position, where the grid cells are not overlapped and are not superimposed on the position occupied ahead [6,7]. Much more, the activity carried out is reiterated until the entire image zone is scanned. The most easy and normal type of fractal analysis of pictures is the box-counting method, also known as the network method or grid method. This method consists of collected data analysis and splitting a picture in a cell network of successively changing size. Data collection or exploring occurs in several phases, and the cell size increase is evaluated in various stages. The image fractal specific feature highlighted here is the fractal dimension, conditioned by the following formula:

$$D = \lim_{\varepsilon \to 0} \left(\frac{\ln N}{\ln \varepsilon} \right) \qquad (1)$$

where N is the cell number and ε is the cell size.

2.2. Lacunarity

The microfractures and free space distribution in the structure of the material, in the total quantity of Zy-4 metal alloy matrix, is globally signaled by lacunarity, measured as a modified value density of the integral image. The lower the gap value (named lacunarity) is, the more lacunae there are, or the more numerous the interstices are in the picture, it can be assumed that the alloy distribution is even more unequal, too. To specify the fractal dimension of a picture, it is sufficient to examine the inclusion partitions/segregations in time, which is a necessary step to estimate the lacunae distribution, which is essential to produce a complete analysis of the entire picture [8]. The numerical lacunarity value is computed in accordance with the formula:

$$\Lambda = \left(\frac{\sigma}{\mu}\right)^2 \qquad (2)$$

when σ is the standard deviation of the mass and μ is also the average value of the mass of the total picture. To estimate the fractal dimension, it is necessary to compose a graphic, and to calculate the lacunarity afresh, the graphical algorithm of least squares must be utilized. Now, it must be said that the tendency line inclination (mathematical slope) is determined through a special formula other than the one presented above:

$$\Lambda = \left(\frac{\sigma}{\mu}\right)^2 + 1 \qquad (3)$$

The latter expression/relationship is utilized to determine the tendency direction slope and to avoid "unsafe" calculations due to some homogeneous images. An ordinary picture is taken into account as being homogeneous only when the pixel number in the brick/aggregate is not modified during distinct scanning stages. In other words, if $\sigma = 0$, then (and) therefore, $\Lambda = 0$.

2.3. Time Series

A sui-generis definition of time series refers to an important aspect that is an observation selection/collection of well-ascertained elements realized by frequent amplitude measurements (regardless of the measured object), made into time. For a simple understanding, we provide below some classic examples such as measuring the retail sales value every day or month in a whole year, ocean tide elevations, sunspot counts on a given surface, and electrocardiograms (ECGs)—heart-activity monitoring, each being a conclusive example of time series. This is because the size of these events/categories is quantitatively defined and consequently measured to evenly distanced time intervals. Instead, the intermittently collected facts or highlighted ones cannot be considered representative time series, under any circumstances.

The common definition of time series may be as follows: "A well-ordered sequence, established from diverse values of a variable scale, measured at evenly spaced time interludes".

Stationary and non-stationary time series happen when we focus attention on industrial, economical, biological, and scientific experimental data. At present, one more significant practice of this technique, developed in the article, is quantitative Zy-4 SEM microfractography evaluation. As for analyzing the time series, this refers to the statistical procedure aimed at investigating/assessing the time series facts and pulling the important statistics and parameters regarding the data in discussion.

To achieve the aim of the study, we further present a brief mathematical appreciation for the time series in discussion. Let us consider $(S, +)$ as a semigroup together with X, a nonempty set of states (we shall suppose that X is a metric space dotted with a function d, called the "metric function", otherwise considered a "distance function"). Lastly, a dynamical system, in the area of mathematics, is considered as a possible constitutive map $T: S \times X \to X$, so

$$(i)\ T(0,x) = x, \text{ for every } x \in X\ (ii)\ T(t, T(s,x)) = T(t+s, x), \text{ for every } t, s \in S \text{ and } x \in X \qquad (4)$$

In this context, a map with real values $F: X \to R$ is understood as a state space measurement. If t, $\tau \in S$ are fixed (τ is the time delay and $x \in X$), then a measurement sequence

$$F(x), F(T(t+\tau, x)), F(T(t+2\tau, x)), F(T(t+3\tau, x)), \ldots, F(T(t+(d-1)\tau, x)) \qquad (5)$$

can be denominated as a time series directly related to T, which takes starts from the bipoint (t,x).

Time series behavior (meaning of the series randomness) can be examined by calculating the autocorrelation function, which is a measure of the effect/influence of past situations in suite, concerning the present/current state of the series member [9]. To one discrete dynamical system T, introduced by an isomorphism map $f : M \to M$, the autocorrelation function related to the time series

$$F(x), F(f(x)), \ldots, F(f^p(x)) \qquad (6)$$

is calculated with

$$C(n) = \frac{\sum_{i=0}^{p-n}(ZF \circ f^i - m_t)(x) \cdot (F \circ f^{i+n} - m_t)(x)}{\sum_{i=0}^{p-n}(F \circ f^i)^2(x)} \qquad (7)$$

where m_t, called the time average, is determined by

$$m_t = \frac{\sum_{i=0}^{p}(F \circ f^i)(x)}{p+1} \qquad (8)$$

The autocorrelation function graphic is significant only within a certain time range $n \in [0, m]$, wherein $m \ll p$ (much smaller).

The range of values $C(n)$ of the correlation function is between 0 and 1; thus, $C(n) = 1$ indicates a strong correlation (maximum) and a value of $C(n) = 0$ suggests no kind of correlation. To be able to compare two time series suitable/calculated for two distinct initial values $\{F(f^i(x))\}$ and $\{F(f^i(y))\}$, the correlation function may be utilized, represented by

$$K(n) = \frac{\sum_{i=0}^{p-n}(F \circ f^i - m)(x) \cdot (F \circ f^{i+n} - m)(y)}{\sqrt{\sum_{i=0}^{p-n}(F \circ f^i(x) - m_x)^2 \sum_{i=0}^{p-n}(F \circ f^i(y) - m_y)^2}} \qquad (9)$$

wherein m_x signifies a time mean of $\{F(f^i(x))\}$ and m_y signifies the time mean of $\{F(f^i(y))\}$.

The correlation function graphic is important only within a certain time range, wherein $m \ll p$ (much smaller).

2.4. Phase Space Reconstruction

A large number of mathematic notional studies attempt to give response to a major question as regards the time series theory. The demand put, however, is as simple as possible. It is about, in experimental scrutiny, how we know which physical quantities, and how many of them, need to be determined to correctly comprehend the system asymptotic behavior. The amazing response to this question is that it is more than sufficient to measure one physical quantity (only one). In other words, the infinite time series corresponding to the measurement of one right suitable physical quantity for only one initial state must be known. In substance, Takens' embedding theorem presumes total information concerning an infinite time series and about the attractor box dimension [10,11]. Nearly all retardation times τ are hypothetically good, but it turns out that this undertaking does not always work in real practice (true world). More than likely, experimental data arrive still in the format of finite time series. Since the box dimension and correlation dimension are numerically close to each other, the latter could be utilized successfully for embedding dimension evaluation, because it is again acceptable to calculate in this manner [12].

2.5. SEM Image Evaluation

Chaotic behavior or generally disordered behavior has been proven in numerous chemical, physical, economical, and biological complex systems. As philosophical foundations, two notions/attitudes about systemic chaos are today unanimously accepted. The first concept refers to the temporal chaos definition, for which the functions defined in phase space are considered only time dependent. The second concept, called the spatial chaos conceptualization, denotes a veritable disorder situation in relation to spatial coordinates. These speculative theoretical clarifications open/start the successful accession of nonlinear deterministic techniques to spatio-temporal virtual phenomena [6,7].

In spite of the fact that the cardinal principles of thermo-mechanical behavior of various materials (especially our metal alloys) are familiar to us, the nature, number, and interaction of chemical, physical, and geometric variables implicated in an effective microstructure engendering cannot be accurately expressed. In addition, however, it seems legitimate to adopt a functional viewpoint and believe that the image textures are like "black boxes," being caused either by a stochastic process (in an extensive sense) or by a deterministic chaos process [6–8].

The study of Zy-4 SEM pictures was realized by a original software implementation that creates a time series associated with the image, and afterwards restores the attractor and calculates its autocorrelation dimension. The procedure to analyze the SEM images begins by loading a bitmap version of the micrographs in our computational application. The chosen path in our investigation was to generate the weighted fractal dimensions map (WFDM), which emphasizes the potential modified formations (conforming to preceding articles [4,5,13,14]). To generate a time series (in reality, a spatial series) starting from an selected image area, we did the following: The initial picture was sectioned into pieces of about 12–16 pixels in altitude; by placing together all these pieces, we procured an entire strip. The spatial series, noted with $s(t)$, was acquired by calculating the gray-level mean value for each of the pixels' procession from within the formed strip. The nonlinear analysis of these data series started with the attractor reconstruction by first embedding the spatial series in a higher dimensional phase space, repeating the procedures until the appropriate dimension was obtained. We did not forget to introduce a certain time delay $\tau > 0$, compared to the measured standard time.

For an established embedding dimension d, the next mathematical set was considered

$$s(t), s(t+\tau), \ldots, s(t+2\tau), \ldots, s(t+(d-1)\tau) \tag{10}$$

which can be assimilated to a point in pseudo-phase space. Ultimately, the desired attractor can be obtained by linking these items accordingly to the evidence of their succession.

Note. In the general situation of finite data embedding, a difference needs to be made among the dynamical system dimension that generates input data and provides a suitable embedding dimension for this and of the restored mathematical object that the data depicts [12].

Technically speaking, the autocorrelation integral of the attractor, $C(r)$, is the presumption of the likelihood that two points of the phase space may be separated (isolated) by a Euclidian distance less or equal to a standard distance r. In consequence, this means that $C(r)$ is a power function of r, with the exponent D, which is also the actual autocorrelation dimension. The regression line slope in direct correlation to C®estimates D [13,14]). The methodology is reproduced again for diverse values of the embedding dimension d, each time at a difference equal to one unit. Finally, it is recommended to draw the graph (figure) of the autocorrelation dimension that is a function of the embedding dimension, from which the regression line slope is calculated [15].

3. Results and Discussion

The microstructure influence study of the mechanical properties of Zy-4 claddings is of crucial relevance in CANDU fuel behavior prevision during nuclear reactor operation. In this paragraph we put into application a new technique and suitable algorithms to detect major failure in a number of Zy-4 specimens, which were tested until the final stage of rupture. Alpha-crystallized Zy-4 high-temperature deformation textures are not explained here, and the classical system of mechanical deformation suffered by nuclear fuel shells (exterior cladding) [3] during normal operation in the reactor is not discussed on this occasion. The only analyses performed were related to the microcracks suffered and the careful observation of the break produced in the structure of the sealing material: the tubes of Zy-4.

We will highlight one method of SEM micro-fractography investigation of the Zy-4 specimens, deteriorated and altered by the rupture process [16–18]. We will also say from the beginning that we selected only the micrographs of the modified areas, which were subsequently prepared and produced separately by a new method of the weighted fractal dimensions map, (WFDM) [4]. Let us start now with the image analysis from the SEM micro-fractographs obtained on the samples from Zy-4 by studying the time series (space series) produced [19] by the entire image contained in Figure 1, the area delimited with a yellow contour.

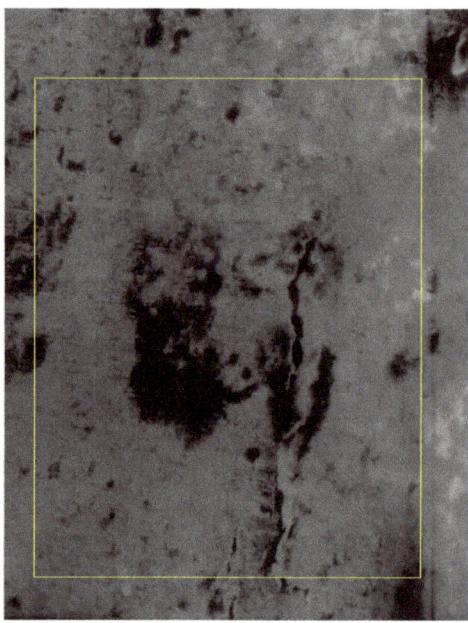

Figure 1. Original image and a selected area.

Figure 2 shows the attractor reconstruction [20] for the rectangle with yellow sides of the normal area along with a considerable area with microcracks and prominent breakage, conformable to Figure 1. Both attractor reconstructions are presented. In embedding dimension 2 some points were observed, and in embedding dimension 3 some broken lines were noticed. Suitable to Figure 1, we exhibit in Figure 3 the time series (spatial series) produced by the entire area, contained in the yellow frame. Thus, the selected area exhibited every surface morphological modification, due to the presence both of the intact, unaffected areas and of the material zones assailed by fracture.

A slow, slightly steep slope at the time series start, sprinkled with uniform matched values of the entire period, followed by a tendency of mediation in the sawtooth (see solid blue line), is observed in Figure 3. The horizontal green line represents the average value of the series over the entire period considered.

For the second pitch we will investigate the image part that contains the modified area with obvious cracks, selected from the entire available image. Thus, we can say that Figure 4 contains the modified area in total agreement with the WFDM procedure. The choice made was limited to the area with yellow edges and was due to the visual aspect, which was different from the unaffected parts of the material, with the rest remaining in the whole picture.

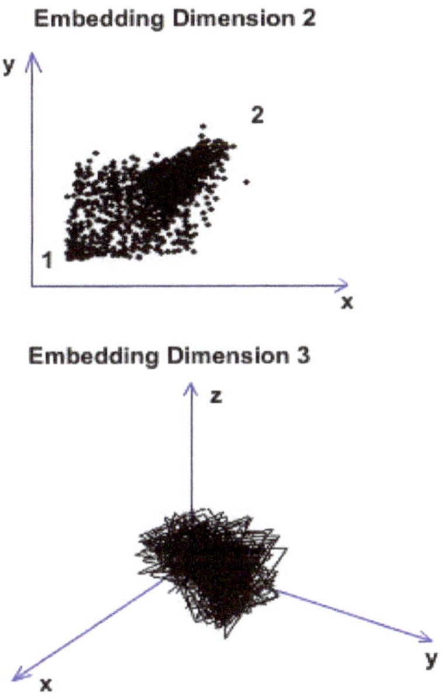

Embedding Dimension 2

Embedding Dimension 3

Figure 2. Attractor reconstruction from Figure 1.

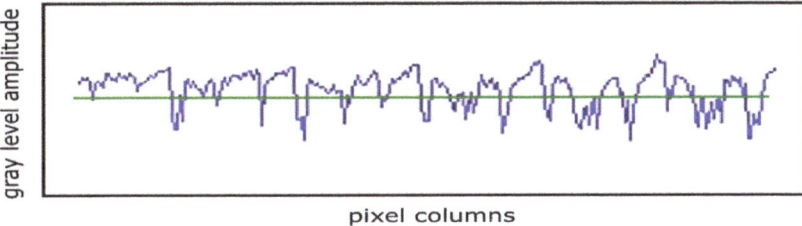

Figure 3. The time series generated by the selected area.

Figure 4. The selection of the modified area.

Figure 5 shows the attractor reconstruction for the rectangle with yellow sides of the normal area, conformable to Figure 4. Both attractor reconstructions are presented. In embedding dimension 2, some points were observed and in embedding dimension 3 some broken lines were noticed [11]. Suitable to Figure 4, we exhibit in Figure 6 the time series (spatial series) produced by the modified area, a material zone attacked/assailed by fracture. In Figure 6 is presented the time series associated with the selected modified area. A steep slope at the time series beginning with the highest value of entire period, followed by a tendency of mediation in sawtooth (see solid blue line), was observed. The horizontal green line represents the average value of the series over the entire period considered.

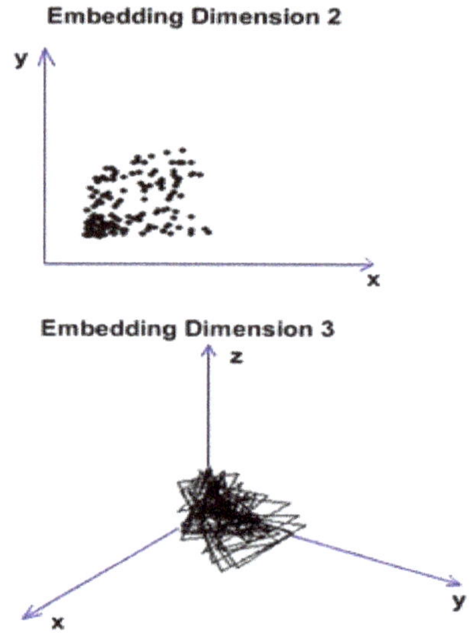

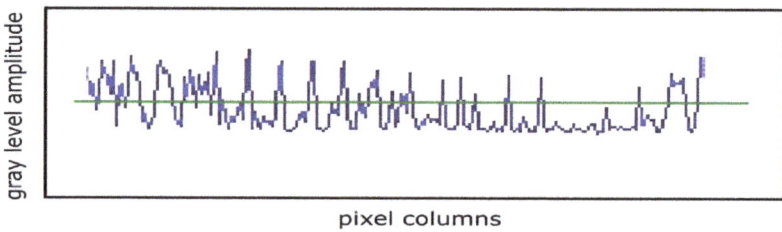

Figure 5. Attractor reconstruction from Figure 4.

Figure 6. The time series associated with the selected modified area.

The graphic of the modified area autocorrelation in Figure 7, representing the correlation dimension (CorDim) versus the embedding dimension (EmbDim), shows the slope computation. The (CorDim) versus (EmbDim) slope was 0.2213. The equation of the regression line is $y = 0.2213x + 0.4525$. R^2 (R-Squared or coefficient of determination) was equal to 0.9994, representing that the very good data fit the regression model used.

Figure 8 introduces the original image of the affected/modified area in the yellow border. Figure 9 introduces the binary version of the image in the yellow box. Figure 10 introduces the process of applying the mask to the image, for lacunarity calculation. The blue box represents the area of interest.

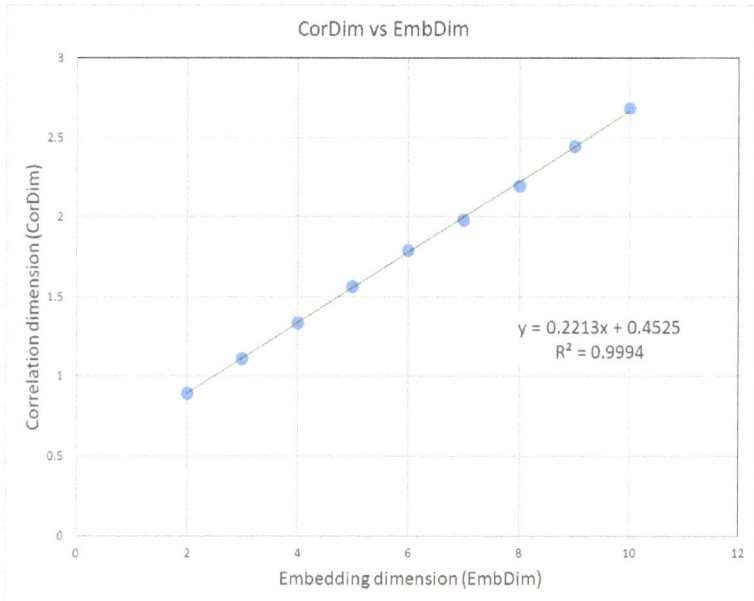

Figure 7. The slope of the autocorrelation dimension versus the embedding dimension for the modified area.

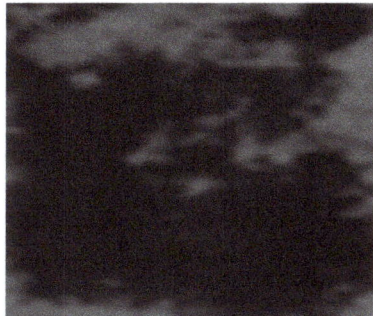

Figure 8. The original image of the affected/modified area in the yellow border.

Figure 9. The binary version of the image in the yellow box.

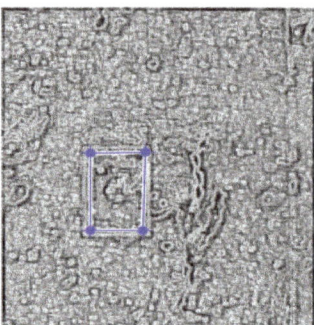

Figure 10. Applying the mask for lacunarity calculation.

Following the numerical evaluations with the appropriate software of the image to affected/modified area, the values of fractal dimension $D = 1.7411$, standard deviation $s = \pm\sqrt{\sigma^2} = \pm 0.4568$, and lacunarity $\Lambda = 0.0688$ were obtained.

Figure 11 shows the verification of the image in the affected/modified area with the Harmonic and Fractal Image Analyzer Demo software version 5.5.30 [21] of the fractal dimension of the area for various ruler scales r.

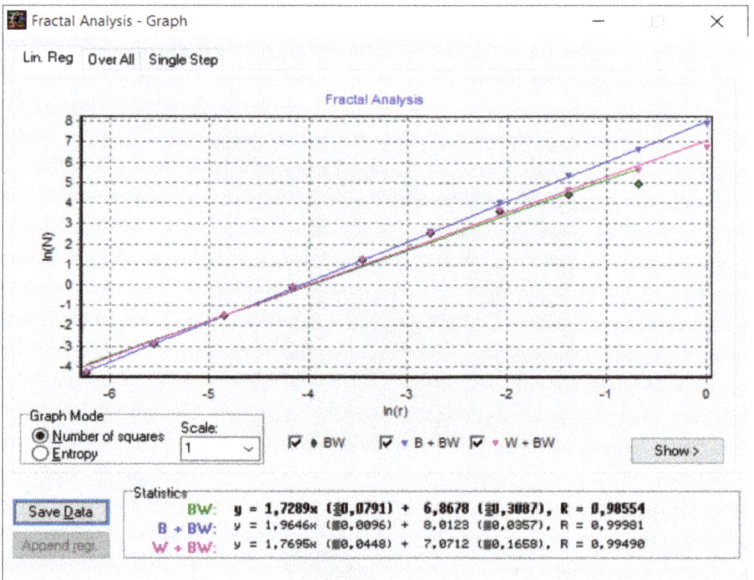

Figure 11. Graphic of the fractal dimension for the affected/modified area.

Figure 12 represents the three-dimensional graph of the voxel representation of the image in the affected/modified area.

The last studied area of the SEM image of Zy-4, in fact the third zone, is the one that refers to the area considered normal—more precisely, the area that remained undeformed and was prepared according to the WFDM protocol. Figure 13, which consists of a sector framed in the yellow rectangle, represents the structure that was considered/remained normal by comparison with the parts affected by microcracks.

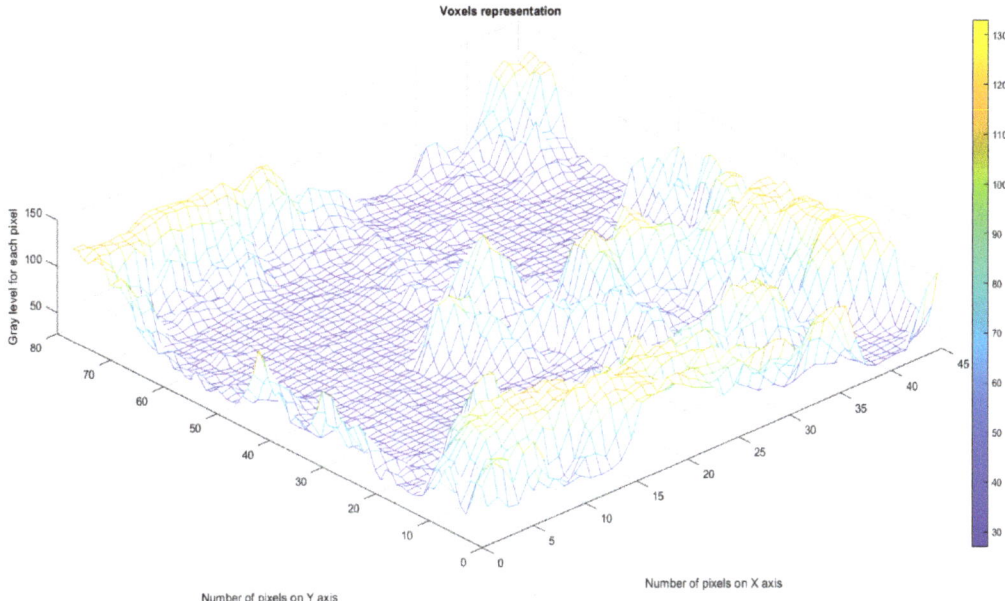

Figure 12. Voxel representation of the image in the affected/modified area.

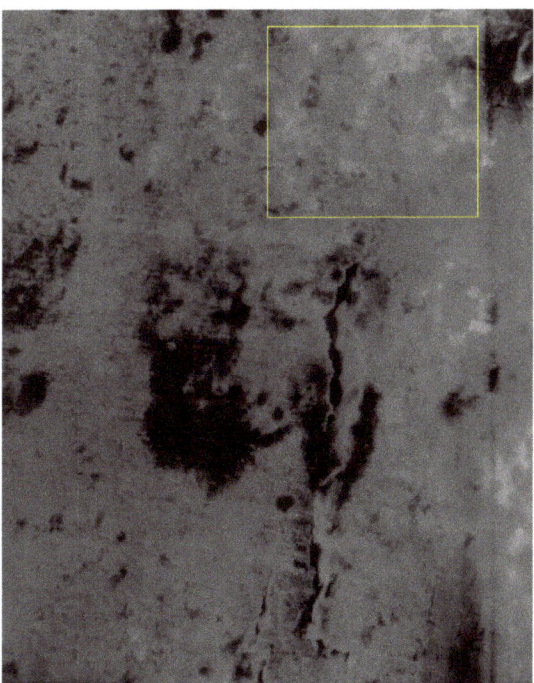

Figure 13. The selection of a normal area.

Figure 14 shows the attractor reconstruction for the rectangle with yellow sides of the normal area, conformable to Figure 13. Both attractor reconstructions are presented. In embedding dimension 2 some points were observed, and in embedding dimension 3 some broken lines were noticed. Suitable to Figure 13, we exhibit in Figure 15 the time series (spatial series) produced by the normal (unaffected) area, a material zone considered intact.

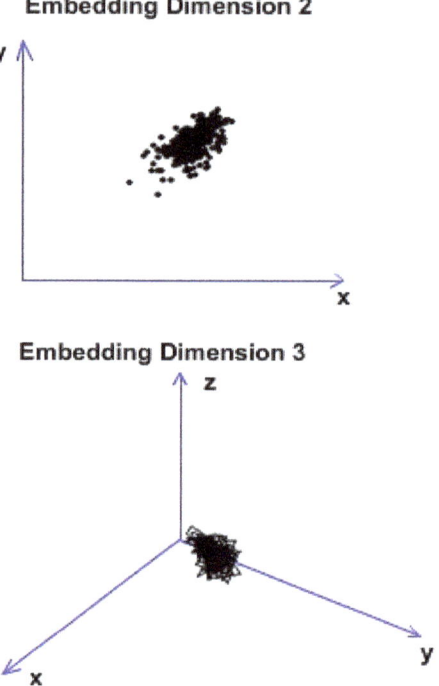

Figure 14. Attractor reconstruction from Figure 13.

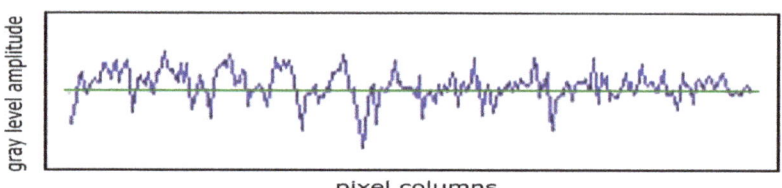

Figure 15. Time series associated with a normal area.

A steep slope at the time series throughout the entire period accompanied by the tendency to average the peaks and a mediation propensity in sawtooth (see solid blue line) was observed. The horizontal green line represents the average value of the series over the entire period considered.

The graphic of the normal area autocorrelation in Figure 16, representing the correlation dimension (CorDim) versus the embedding dimension (EmbDim), shows the slope computation. The CorDim versus EmbDim slope was 0.1479. The equation of the regression line is $y = 0.148x + 0.815$. R^2 (R-Squared or coefficient of determination) was equal to 0.9842, representing that the very good data fit the regression model used.

Figure 17 introduces the original image of the unaffected area in the yellow border. Figure 18 introduces the binary version of the image in the yellow box. Figure 19 introduces the process of applying the mask to the image, for lacunarity calculation. The blue box represents the area of interest.

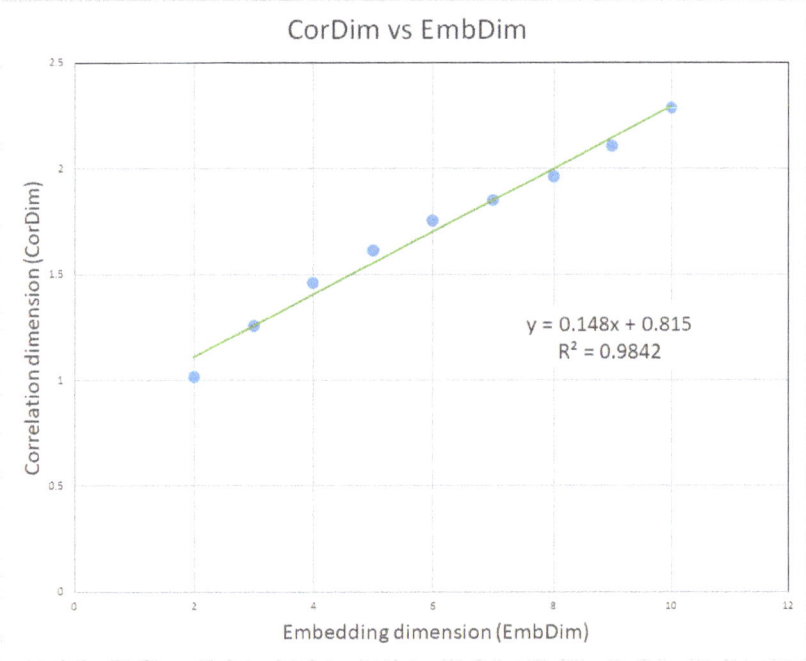

Figure 16. The slope of the autocorrelation dimension versus the embedding dimension for the normal area.

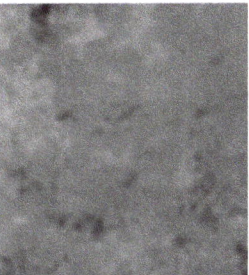

Figure 17. The original image of the unaffected area in the yellow border.

Figure 18. The binary version of the image in the yellow box.

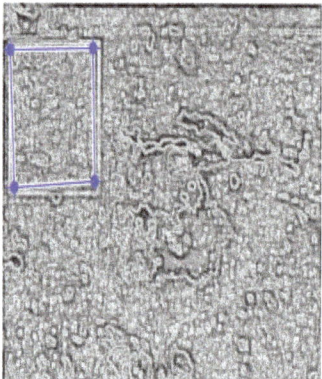

Figure 19. Applying the mask for lacunarity calculation.

Following the numerical evaluations with the appropriate software of the image to unaffected area, the values of fractal dimension $D = 1.8422$, standard deviation $s = \pm\sqrt{\sigma^2} = \pm 0.3278$, and lacunarity $\Lambda = 0.0317$ were obtained.

Figure 20 represents the three-dimensional graph of the voxel representation for the image in the unaffected area [19,22].

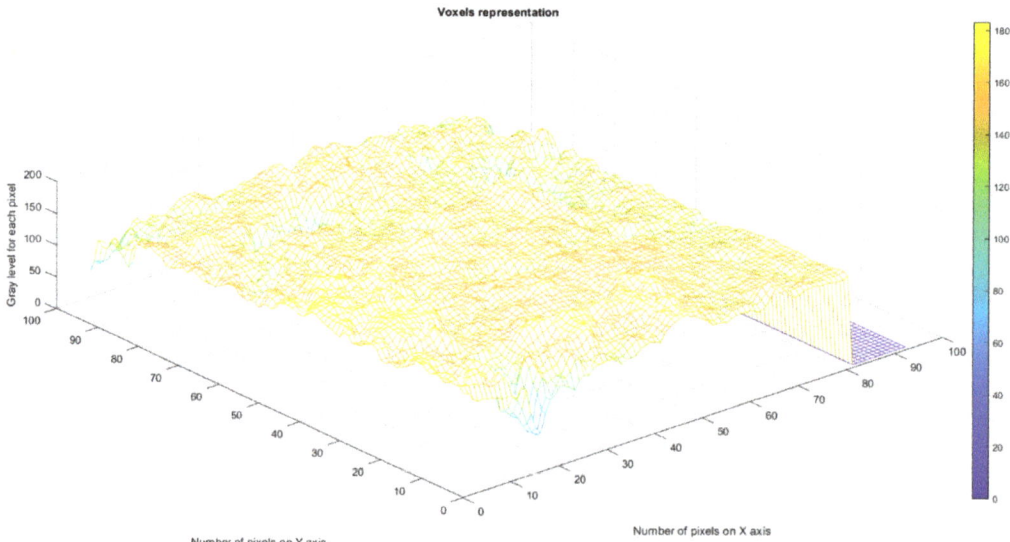

Figure 20. Voxels representation of the image in the unaffected area.

Figure 21 shows the verification of the image in the unaffected area with the Harmonic and Fractal Image Analyzer Demo software version 5.5.30 of the fractal dimension of the area for various ruler scales r.

The carefully conducted research was carried out on 20 SEM images, microfractographs of some samples that presented either the original unmodified area or the modified area. Two distinct areas were selected from each picture, one with a distinct portion that included an area with a normal original structure (unaffected) and another zone with a modified structure affected by microfractures [23].

The conclusive results obtained are presented in the format of a histogram in Figure 22. We thus drew a histogram graphic (a bar data representation) for the correlation dimension function versus the embedding dimension slopes [24,25], with the slopes of the calculated regression lines in the domain between the values/range [0.08, 0.32].

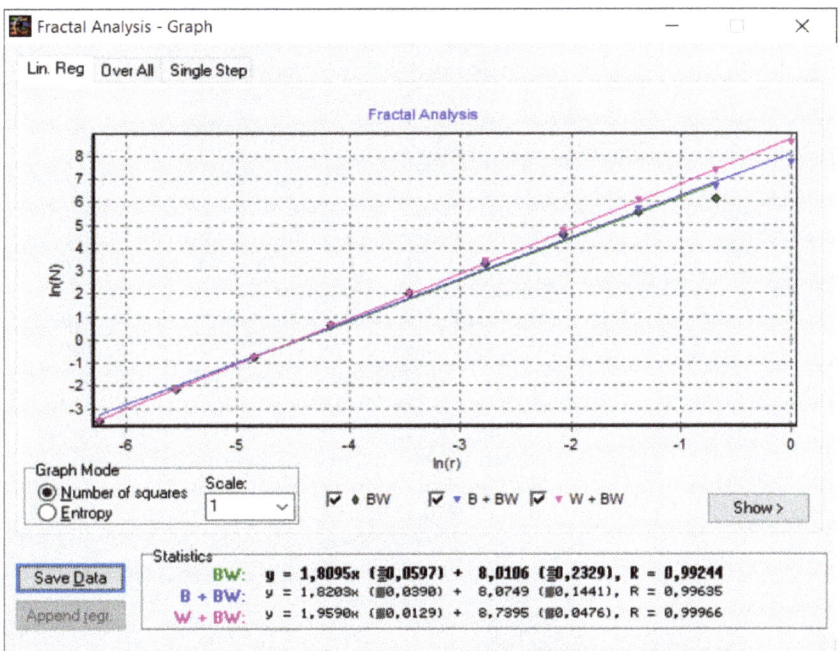

Figure 21. Graphic of the fractal dimension for the unaffected area.

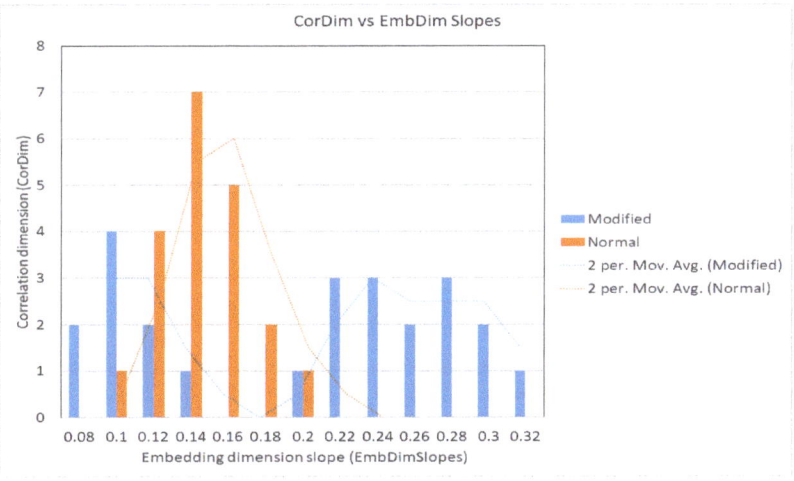

Figure 22. The histogram of the CorDim vs. EmbDim slopes.

4. Conclusions

This work pursues and completes the complex research initiated in preceding papers, where pictures of the fracture surface of SEM Zy-4 samples are considered by employment of the fractal analysis method and the time-series technique. The fractal analysis method manages to resolve the damage complications and finally to ascertain the morphological parameters of various fractures, documented in SEM images in metal alloys and in Zy-4 SEM pictures. For the Zy-4 SEM picture investigation, we developed a computer software practice that generates a time series (spatial series) associated with the picture, then restores the attractor and calculates its autocorrelation dimension.

Considering the analyzed Figure 1, Figure 4, and Figure 13, we proved that obtaining fractal compositions (organizations) in Zy-4 SEM images (microfractographies) is a reasonable and pragmatic assumption. In addition, the application of fractal analysis to the SEM images of Zy-4 samples and the calculation of fractal dimension and lacunarity was a success of this study.

The fractal numerical valuations of the affected/modified area image of Zy-4 samples were achieved, and the values of fractal dimension $D = 1.7411 \pm 0.4568$ and lacunarity $\Lambda = 0.0688$ were obtained. In the same conditions, regarding the Zy-4 image for the unaffected area, values of fractal dimension $D = 1.8422 \pm 0.3278$ and lacunarity $\Lambda = 0.0317$ were achieved.

The results performance, acquired from the topical investigation provided, lead to the conclusions listed below. Thus, the attractors in embedding dimensions 2 and 3 of the entire picture had three connected components, one corresponding to the entire picture, another to the normal (unaffected) area, and the last to the modified (affected) area. The role of these graphic representations is to provide the researcher with notable clues about the anomalies contained in each investigated image.

The CorDim versus EmbDim slope was 0.1479 for the graphic of the normal area autocorrelation and 0.2213 for the modified area autocorrelation. The autocorrelation dimension average for the normal areas was 0.1587, following a normal distribution on the interval [0.11, 0.24] determined on the abscissa. There are no obvious conclusions on the autocorrelation dimension for the modified (affected) areas. As one can see in the histograms diagram, it covered a rather broad interval with two peaks, one between [0.08, 0.18] and the other between [0.19, 0.32], with both intervals being determined on the abscissa. The correlation dimension function versus the embedding dimension slopes had slopes of the calculated regression lines in the domain between the values/range [0.08, 0.32].

Author Contributions: Conceptualization, V.-P.P. and M.-A.P.; methodology, V.-P.P.; software, V.-A.P.; validation, V.-P.P., M.-A.P. and V.-A.P.; formal analysis, V.-P.P., M.-A.P. and V.-A.P.; investigation, V.-A.P. and M.-A.P.; resources, V.-A.P. and M.-A.P.; data curation, V.-A.P.; writing—original draft preparation, V.-P.P.; writing—review and editing, M.-A.P. and V.-P.P.; visualization, V.-A.P.; supervision, V.-P.P.; project administration, V.-P.P. All authors have read and agreed to the published version of the manuscript.

Funding: This research received no external funding.

Institutional Review Board Statement: Not applicable.

Informed Consent Statement: Not applicable.

Data Availability Statement: The data used to support the findings of this study cannot be accessed due to commercial confidentiality.

Acknowledgments: The co-authors M.-A.P., V.-A.P. and V.-P.P. would like to thank Jenica Paun, for her continuous kind support.

Conflicts of Interest: The authors declare no conflict of interest.

References

1. Moan, G.D.; Rudling, P. *Zirconium in the Nuclear Industry, 13th International Symposium*; ASTM-STP 1423; American Society for Testing & Materials: West Conshohocken, PA, USA, 2002; pp. 673–701.
2. Kaddour, D.; Frechinet, S.; Gourgues, A.F.; Brachet, J.C.; Portier, L.; Pineau, A. Experimental determination of creep properties of Zirconium alloys together with phase transformation. *Scr. Mater.* **2004**, *51*, 515–519. [CrossRef]
3. Brenner, R.; Béchade, J.L.; Bacroix, B. Thermal creep of Zr–Nb1%–O alloys: Experimental analysis and micromechanical modelling. *J. Nucl. Mater.* **2002**, *305*, 175–186. [CrossRef]

4. Olteanu, M.; Paun, V.P.; Tanase, M. Fractal analysis of zircaloy-4 fracture surface, Conference on Equipments, Installations and Process Engineering. *Rev. Chim.* **2005**, *56*, 97–100.
5. Takens, F. Detecting strange attractors in turbulence. *Lect. Notes Math.* **1981**, *898*, 366–381.
6. Takens, F. On the Numerical Determination of the Dimension of an Attractor. In *Dynamical Systems and Bifurcations*; Braaksma, B.L.J., Broer, H.W., Takens, F., Eds.; Springer: Berlin/Heidelberg, Germany, 1985; pp. 99–106.
7. Xu, L.; Shi, Y. Notes on the Global Attractors for Semigroup. *Int. J. Mod. Nonlinear Theory Appl.* **2013**, *2*, 219–222. [CrossRef]
8. Sauer, T.; Yorke, J.; Casdagli, M. Embedology. *J. Stat. Phys.* **1991**, *65*, 579–616. [CrossRef]
9. Mandelbrot, B.B.; Passoja, D.E.; Paullay, A.J. Fractal character of fracture surfaces of metals. *Nature* **1984**, *308*, 721–722. [CrossRef]
10. Mandelbrot, B. *Fractal Geometry of Nature*; Freeman: New York, NY, USA, 1983; pp. 25–57.
11. Passoja, D.E.; Psioda, J.A. *Fractography in Materials Science*; ASTM STP: American Society for Testing & Materials: West Conshohocken, PA, USA, 1981; pp. 335–386.
12. Mattfeldt, T. Nonlinear deterministic analysis of tissue texture: A stereological study on mastopathic and mammary cancer tissue using chaos theory. *J. Microsc.* **1997**, *185*, 47–66. [CrossRef] [PubMed]
13. Peitgen, H.-O.; Jurgens, H.; Saupe, D. Chaos and Fractals. In *New Frontiers of Science*; Springer: Berlin/Heidelberg, Germany, 1992.
14. Thompson, J.M.T.; Stewart, H.B. *Nonlinear Dynamics and Chaos*; John Wiley and Sons: Hoboken, NJ, USA, 1986.
15. Available online: https://www.mathworks.com/matlabcentral/answers/how-to-estimate-correlation-integrals-and-local-slopes-for-embedding-dimension (accessed on 7 March 2022).
16. Datseris, G.; Kottlarz, I.; Braun, A.P.; Parlitz, U. Estimating the fractal dimension: A comparative review and open source implementations. *arXiv* **2021**, arXiv:2109.05937v1.
17. Falconer, K. *Fractal Geometry: Mathematical Foundations and Applications*, 3rd ed.; John Wiley & Sons, Ltd.: Chichester, UK, 2014.
18. Paun, V.P. Fractal surface analysis of Zircaloy-4 SEM micrographs using the time-series method. *Cent. Eur. J. Phys.* **2009**, *7*, 264–269. [CrossRef]
19. Nichita, M.V.; Paun, M.A.; Paun, V.A.; Paun, V.P. Fractal Analysis of Brain Glial Cells. Fractal Dimension and Lacunarity. *Univ. Politeh. Buchar. Sci. Bull. Ser. A Appl. Math. Phys.* **2019**, *81*, 273–284.
20. Bordescu, D.; Paun, M.A.; Paun, V.A.; Paun, V.P. Fractal Analysis of Neuroimagistics. Lacunarity Degree, a Precious Indicator in the Detection of Alzheimer's Disease. *Univ. Politeh. Buchar. Sci. Bull. Ser. A Appl. Math. Phys.* **2018**, *80*, 309–320.
21. Available online: https://astronomy.swin.edu.au/~{}pbourke/fractals/fracdim/index.html (accessed on 3 September 2021).
22. Nichita, M.V.; Paun, M.A.; Paun, V.A.; Paun, V.P. Image Clustering Algorithms to Identify Complicated Cerebral Diseases. Description and Comparaisons. *IEEE Access* **2020**, *8*, 88434–88442. [CrossRef]
23. Rempe, M.; Mitchell, T.M.; Renner, J.; Smith, S.A.F.; Bistacchi, A.; Di Toro, G. The relationship between microfracture damage and the physical properties of fault-related rocks: TheGole Larghe Fault Zone, Italian SouthernAlps. *J. Geophys. Res. Solid Earth* **2018**, *123*, 7661–7687. [CrossRef]
24. Scott, D.W. *Statistics: A Concise Mathematical Introduction for Students, Scientists, and Engineers*; John Wiley & Sons, Inc.: Hoboken, NJ, USA, 2020.
25. Michalak, K.P. Estimating correlation dimension of high-dimensional signals—Quick algorithm. *AIP Adv.* **2018**, *8*, 105201. [CrossRef]

 *fractal and fractional*

Article

Minkowski's Loop Fractal Antenna Dedicated to Sixth Generation (6G) Communication

Maria-Alexandra Paun [1,2], Mihai-Virgil Nichita [3], Vladimir-Alexandru Paun [4] and Viorel-Puiu Paun [5,6,*]

1. School of Engineering, Swiss Federal Institute of Technology (EPFL), 1015 Lausanne, Switzerland; maria_paun2003@yahoo.com
2. Division Radio Monitoring and Equipment, Section Market Access and Conformity, Federal Office of Communications OFCOM, 2501 Bienne, Switzerland
3. Doctoral School, Faculty of Applied Sciences, University Politehnica of Bucharest, 060042 Bucharest, Romania; mihai_nichita9@yahoo.com
4. Five Rescue Research Laboratory, 75004 Paris, France; vladimir.alexandru.paun@ieee.org
5. Department of Physics, Faculty of Applied Sciences, University Politehnica of Bucharest, 060042 Bucharest, Romania
6. Academy of Romanian Scientists, 050094 Bucharest, Romania
* Correspondence: viorel.paun@physics.pub.ro or viorel_paun2006@yahoo.com

Abstract: In this study, we will discuss the engineering construction of a special sixth generation (6G) antenna, based on the fractal called Minkowski's loop. The antenna has the shape of this known fractal, set at four iterations, to obtain maximum performance. The frequency bands for which this 6G fractal antenna was designed in the current paper are 170 GHz to 260 GHz (WR-4) and 110 GHz to 170 GHz (WR-6), respectively. The three resonant frequencies, optimally used, are equal to 140 GHz (WR-6) for the first, 182 GHz (WR-4) for the second and 191 GHz (WR-4) for the third. For these frequencies the electromagnetic behaviors of fractal antennas and their graphical representations are highlighted.

Keywords: fractal dimension; fractal geometry; Minkowski's loop; fractal antenna; 6G communication

1. Introduction

The commencement history of the 6G activity is quite recent in time. In the USA, the Federal Communications Commission (FCC) has thus begun to provide tentative 6G frequency band licenses, starting with the year 2019. By its statute, the FCC organization will offer innovative engineers a minimum ten-year authorization to test the established frequency spectrum of new sixth generation industrial objects and utilities. As for the appointment with the appellative 6G, this is the abbreviation of the new generation, in fact the sixth era of wireless networks, declared as the descendant of 5G technics. Ultimately, as a successor to previous generations, the new 6G generation is expected to amplify the existing qualities of the 5G generation.

This study of the subject in question is ready to host excellent information, such as 6G radio-frequency domain, and frequency bands and ultimately expose 6G technics [1–3]. In short, the frequency spectral range, falling in the 95 GHz (gigahertz) to 3 THz (terahertz) domain, will be experimentally initiated for utilization to allow technicians reverie of the next radio-wireless descendent and outset new activity. However, it is self-evident that the frequency band being considered superfluous to the original purpose could deliver an extra rapid Internet exploitation for ascensive data practice, such as extra determination computer imaging and sensing signal appliances.

First, we talk about what 6G is, how it is possible to achieve 6G communications (about frequencies, especially) and how current this requirement is. One of the potential purposes of it is to substitute or operate together with those known as 5G networks and be superior to them [4]! Moreover, as the first major advantage, it can be stated that it can afford meaningfully more dynamic propagation, at a signal velocity of approximately 95 Gbit/s, taken as the reference speed in our case. Thus, in the distributed communications area, the so-called 6G is evidently the sixth engendering standard for wireless transmission technics in radio natural networks (see frequency bands used).

The present paper is organized by comprising the six following chapters/sections. In Section 1, the first work section, a brief general introduction is presented. After the introductory remarks, in Section 2, the essential notions about fractal geometry are mentioned, with the specification of some Minkowski fractal characteristics. In Section 3, a review of the Minkowski fractal antenna designs inspired by mutual fractal patterns is made. In Section 4, the impact of performances in the utilization of fractal antenna are reported. At this point, important results such as the charge and current distribution of fractal island antenna, electric and magnetic fields 3D distribution, Minkowski fractal antenna pattern radiation and overlay, signal magnitude versus frequency for Minkowski fractal antenna, impedance versus frequency as well as signal magnitude versus frequency for VSWR are obtained and discussed. In Section 5, a comparison of Horn antenna versus Minkowski fractal antenna, mostly among operating parameters, is highlighted. At the end, in Section 6, the last work section, the conclusions of this study are drawn.

2. Fractal Antennas, Fractals Geometry, Minkowski Fractal Characteristics

2.1. About the Fractal Antennas

From the beginning, we can say that the fractals idea has motivated the electrical engineering collectivity to do a thorough investigation about the fact that the fractal geometries could serve in employment at the special antennas design, subsequently named fractal antennas. Thus, in this sense, our work is intending now to highlight the involvement of fractals in fractal antenna technology. The novel research pursuit has as a result obtained extremely spectacular miniature devices, of great perspective, considered basic bricks in the development of professional antennas.

The fractal type antenna has applications in the military area, in particular, as well as the economical-commercial zone, wherein by projecting the device, it controls its advisable ownerships, such as:

- Compact/short dimension;
- Reduced perimeter;
- Multi-band frequency;
- Conformal typology.

Some fractal type antenna shortcomings are the following:

- Antenna gain losing;
- Complicated composition;
- Smaller benefits in dimension according to early recurrence.

Fractal antennas are welcome to be studied as being able to support frequencies in the 6G spectrum, obviously after determining the corresponding fractal geometric shape and the iteration required for the established frequency.

The 6G Radio Frequency

The frequency bands for which this 6G antenna was designed are presented in Table 1 [5].

Table 1. 6G radio frequency.

Band	Frequency	WR-Size
D	110 GHz to 170 GHz	WR-6
G	140 GHz to 220 GHz	WR-5
G	170 GHz to 260 GHz	WR-4
G	220 GHz to 325 GHz	WR-3

Among the bidder fractal objects, the most popular are fractal curves such as the fractal curve type, for example, the Koch Curve (1.2618), Sierpinski Triangle (1.5848), Sierpinski Carpet (1.8928), Koch Snowflake (1.2618) and Minkowski Curve (1.465), with fractal dimensions written in parentheses. For this study, we found that the Minkowski Curve meets our requirements [6], more precisely Minkowski's loop, which is justified to do this research.

2.2. About the Fractal Character: Minkowski's Loop

This section introduces a few considerations about the fractal character of the Minkowski's loop and Minkowski fractal antenna. Let us briefly discuss the effects of using the Minkowski fractal figure on each side of the square area antenna in certain recurrences, through which to find its ideal shape, to be used in the design of the corresponding fractal antenna. First of all, we are interested in how the fractal shape is realized from a geometric point of view and the iterative process that is necessary to obtain the fractal figure considered ideal for the proposed purpose [7].

Currently, by employing the Minkowski procedure, this can be resumed, and the n-th reiteration is accomplished by sharing a linear section a_{n-1} into five subsections $r_n - c_n - b_n - c_n - r_n$ and repeating it over and over again. Between the values of the five segments is the following constitutive relation $a_{n-1} = 2r_n + b_n$, in which c_n is the fractal deep of the generator in the n-th Minkowski recurrent relation (we start from a straight line, and we obtain the step generator, height/indentation equal to r_n), Figure 1, baseline. Another indicator used, named δ_n, is the iteration factor in the respective iteration and is noted as $\delta_n = C_n/B_n$. Both values of equality, respectively C_n and δ_n at the n-th iteration, are adaptable and will be optimized based on the design performances of the developed antenna.

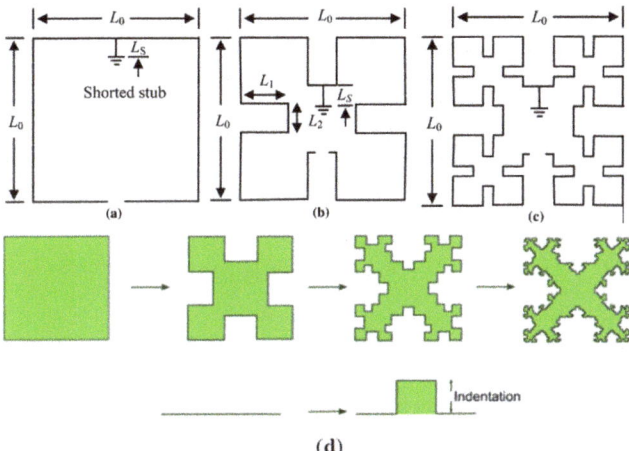

Figure 1. A drawing with the four iterations made (**a**–**d**), starting from the Minkowski initiator. (**a**) the initial start (square ring); (**b**) the 1st iteration; (**c**) the 2nd iteration; (**d**) the initial start (square ring) plus the first three iterations.

The measure D of fractal characteristics can be decided by a logarithmic rapport. The general equation is $s = p^D$, a power type law, as in the calculus formula for D

$$s = p^D, \log s = \log p^D = D\log p, D = \frac{\log s}{\log p} = \frac{\ln s}{\ln p} \quad (1)$$

where s is the number of self-similar segments obtained from one portion after every repetition and p is the number of parts obtained from one segment of every repetition [7,8].

Conformable to Formula (1), the computed fractal measure, named fractal dimension, is equal to 1.465 [7]. The fractal dimension D of a fractal curve is an indication of superior achievement of space-addition (or filling) for the fractal in cause [9]. Yet, some fractal curves cannot be utilized in the fractal antenna design practice. However, several fractal geometries have been successfully employed in the projection of different antennas.

In Figure 1a–c, the steps of growth of the modified Minkowski fractal structure are shown, respectively, as (a) the square ring, (b) the 1st iteration and (c) the 2nd iteration. In Figure 1d, the first three iterations of Minkowski's loop are introduced, together with the linear generator consisting of five segments. More precisely, in the outline above, we start from the initial appearance (one single figure), named the Minkowski initiator and arrive through three iterations to the fourth complex figure (last figure). This is the fractal figure used in making the fractal antenna in our study.

Suitable to Falconer [10], the amended variant of the Minkowski fractal geometry is called multi-fractal or fractal geometry with above one ratio in the generator, such as a_1 and a_2. In this situation, the fractal dimension, D, can be achieved, as in the solution of the next equation:

$$2\left(\frac{1-a_1}{2}\right)^D + 2a_2^D + a_1^D = 1 \qquad (2)$$

where $a_1 = L_1/Lo$, respectively, $a_2 = L_2/Lo$, Figure 1b.

In Figure 2, the variation of the fractal dimensions D of the modified Minkowski fractal, with the $a_1 = x$ (on ox axis) and $a_2 = y$ (on oy axis) functioning as independent variables is presented. The value of D is greater than 1 and less than 2 (in our chart less than 1.99, to be exact).

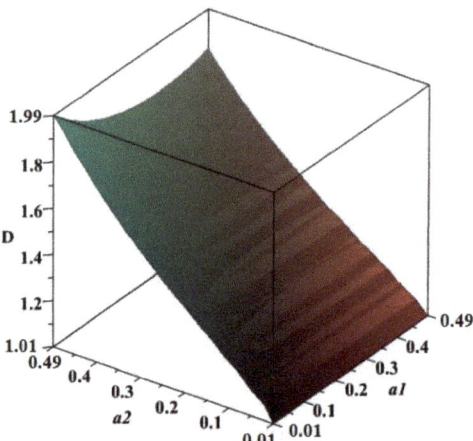

Figure 2. The 3D graphical representation of the fractal dimension D, depending on the variables a_1 and a_2.

3. Minkowski Fractal Antenna

The fractal island object named the Minkowski's loop geometric figure was used to develop a fractal type antenna, more precisely to make a professional antenna. As is known, the fractal antenna is the profitable beneficiary of a self-similarity project able to increase to the maximum lengthiness, to grow the contour of a physical entity, which emits electromagnetic waves in space, or to be in receipt of electromagnetic waves within a circumscribed area, or rather into a surface, respectively volume restricted [11]. The chosen fractal antenna has the shape of a "Minkowski's loop", with four iterations placed above a ground plane antenna (electrical conductance area) [12].

For printed circuit boards, a ground plane is a large area of copper foil on the board, which is connected to the ground terminal of the power supply and serves as a return path for the current from various components on the board; therefore, it seems the most appropriate definition [13].

In Figure 3, the antenna corresponding to the drawn fractal is graphically described. The power supply/current alimentation to the antennas is normal [9]. For the template in the figure above, there have been set in the simulation environment titled Antenna Designer offered by MATLAB R2021a, the following values:

- Length = 0.03 m; Width = 0.028 m; StripLineWidth = 0.0008 m; SlotLength = 0.004 m;
- SlotWidth = 0.00585 m; Height = 0.001 m; GroundPlaneLength = 0.05 m;
- GroundPlaneWidth = 0.03 m; FractalCenterOffset (m) = [0 0]; Tilt (deg) = 0; TiltAxis = [1 0 0].

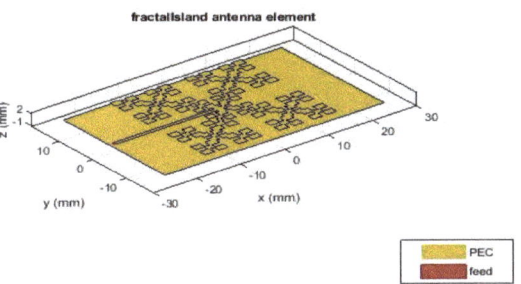

Figure 3. Fractal island antenna element (for third iteration).

The dielectric used is air, with a value of relative dielectric permittivity ε_r (air) =1 and which is present in a layer of 0.00004 m. The absolute dielectric permittivity of the classical vacuum is $\varepsilon_0 = 8.8541 \times 10^{-12}$ F·m^{-1}.

The favorable frequency bands for which this 6G Minkowski fractal antenna (four iterations) was here designed, are 110 GHz to 170 GHz (WR-6), respectively, 170 GHz to 260 GHz (WR-4) [5]. The strips were chosen according to the indications on the website https://www.miwv.com/what-is-6g (accessed on 11 June 2022).

The Revised Minkowski Geometry Figure of Fractal

The particular standard used in the fractal figure choice, as far as that goes in the radiation circuit of minimum measure, is without question its size. With the increase in the fractal size, the fractal figure replenishes the suitable domain much better than usual. To achieve the antenna able to work in the planned frequency range, we benefit from the Minkowski type fractal decomposition scheme to the quadratic area, first of all for the enlargement of lengthiness of the actual effluent route and thereby diminution of the device physical dimension. The fundamental Minkowski type fractal item, presented in detail in Figure 3, is utilized for the enhancement of the actual running lengthiness, named to be the depth of the fractal. The Minkowski type fractal item can be included into the composition as a structure one after the other, added to every part developed of the Minkowski fractal process, at a precedent recurrence step. In this way, it is the obtained/realized enlargement of actual route lengthiness, and it minimized the antenna dimension for a certain frequency of resonance.

4. Results and Discussion

Antenna sketch and project are generally easy to accomplish, but all component parts, which are incorporated in the final project, are frequently the more exciting ones.

By definition, the so-called antennas as parts of a circuit deal with the reception or transmission of electromagnetic waves in the environment. In this context, project managers are concerned with priority in obtaining appropriate performances, especially for the gain, and in the directivity of the designed antennas.

Thus, we will continue to speak about the radiation patterns, power gain and power dissipation of a fractal Minkowski antenna, completed on this occasion. The charge distribution simulation (Figure 4), and respectively the current distribution simulation (Figure 5) of fractal island antenna, are made only for the resonance frequency equal to 140 GHz, (WR-6). In Figures 6 and 7, the antennas corresponding to the drawn fractal are graphically described. The power supply/current alimentation to the antennas is normal (Figures 3 and 4), and in Figures 6 and 7, is lateral.

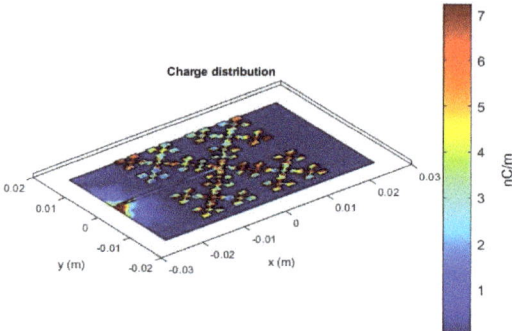

Figure 4. Charge distribution of fractal island antenna.

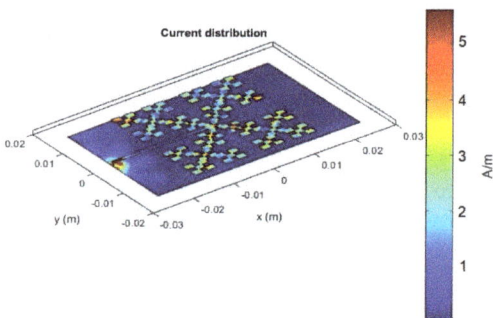

Figure 5. Current distribution of fractal island antenna (normal alimentation).

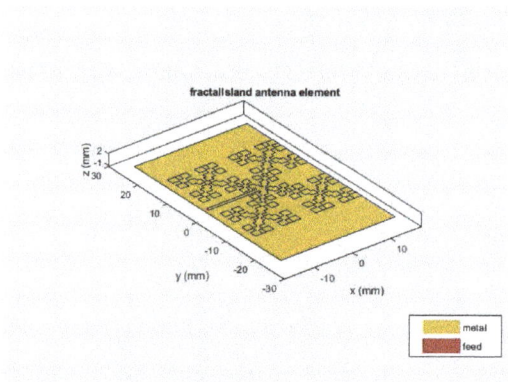

Figure 6. Fractal island antenna element (for fourth iteration).

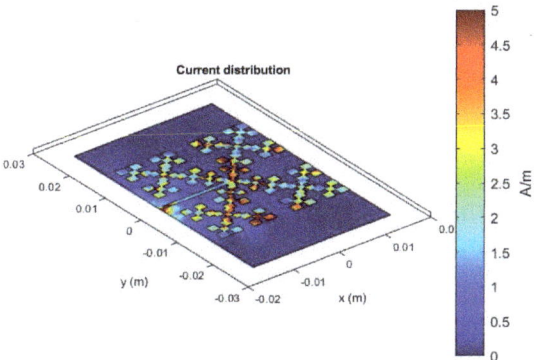

Figure 7. Current distribution of fractal island antenna (lateral alimentation).

Two more interesting frequencies are discovered where the Minkowski fractal antenna resonates (182 GHz and 191 GHz), (WR-4).

In Figures 8 and 9, current distribution simulations of fractal island antenna are made only for the resonance frequencies equal to 182 GHz and 191 GHz, respectively. Power supply/current bias to the antennas is normally made in the figure on the left, and in the figure on the right, is laterally made!

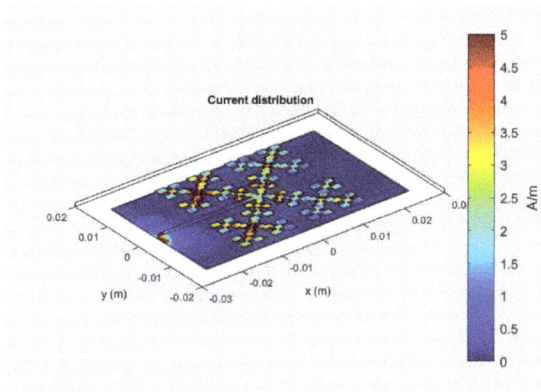

Figure 8. Fractal island normal antenna at 191 GHz.

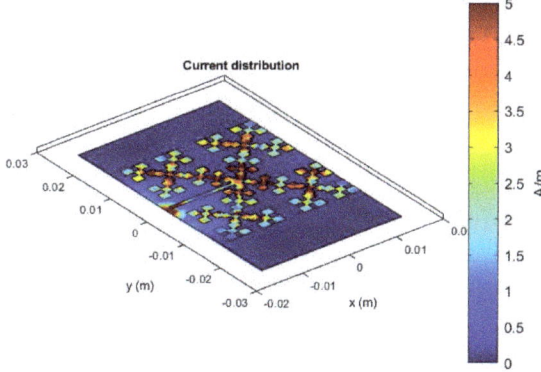

Figure 9. Fractal island lateral antenna at 182 GHz.

In Figure 10, the Azimuth pattern of the Minkowski fractal antenna, respectively signal directivity, at 140 GHz resonance frequency, is presented. In Figure 11 are graphically represented the Electric (blue) and Magnetic (red) Fields 3D Distribution, for normally powered antenna [14]. It is a sphere uniformly distributed with the vectors of the two fields, E and H, but with a higher density in the area of the two geographical poles. In the left corner of the sketch is the Minkowski flat fractal antenna, designed for the fourth iteration.

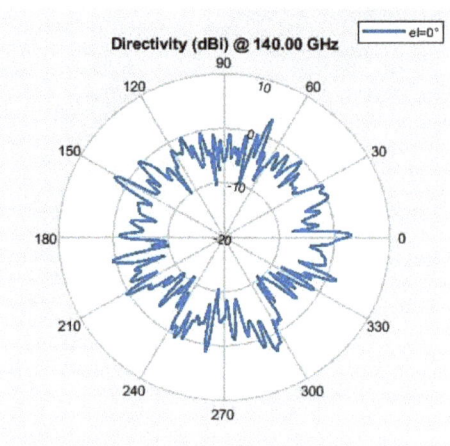

Figure 10. Azimuth pattern of Minkowski fractal antenna.

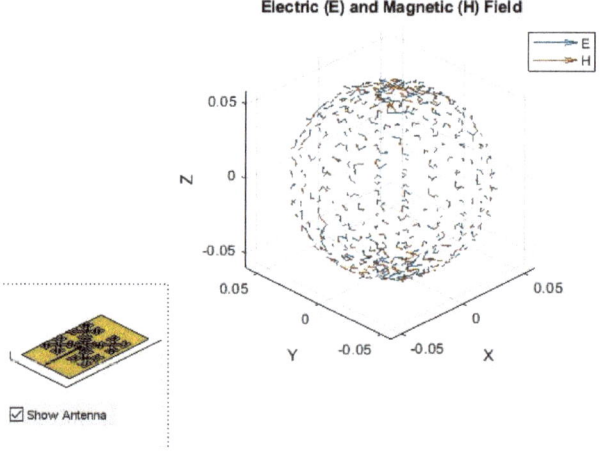

Figure 11. Electric and Magnetic Fields 3D Distribution.

Figures 12 and 13 are figures with 3D (spatial) representation. These are made to indicate the behavior of the Minkowski fractal antenna pattern radiation, having a colored band on the right, graded in dBi. Unlike the known units named dB (decibels), the dBi (isotropic decibels) units, they are also decibels, but in relation to an isotropic radiator device.

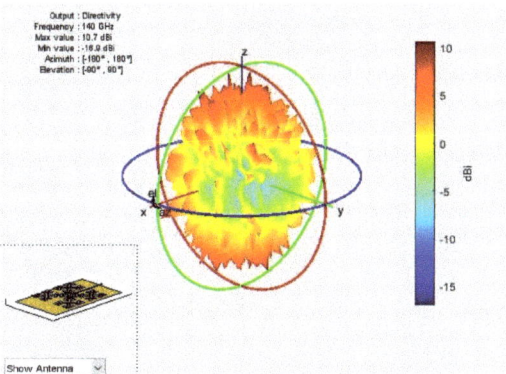

Figure 12. Minkowski fractal antenna pattern radiation.

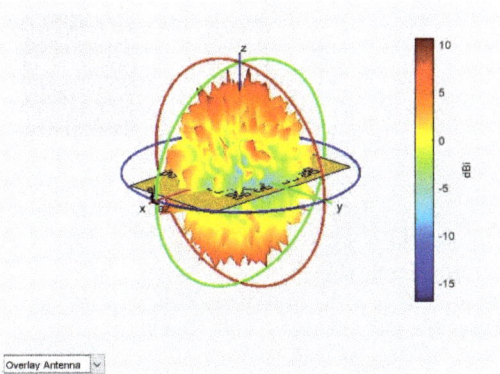

Figure 13. Fractal antenna pattern radiation overlay.

Figure 14 presents impedance versus frequency, in two distinct curves. The first curve is resistance (blue) and the second is reactance (red). These are almost horizontal variations curves, except for the end-of-scale effects [15].

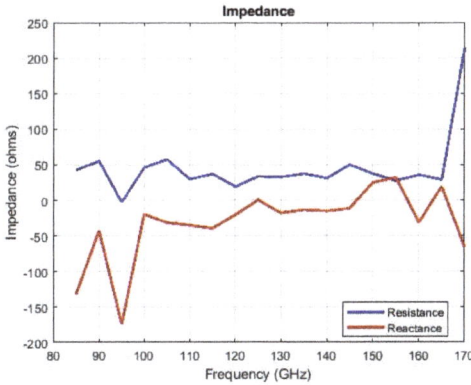

Figure 14. Impedance versus frequency.

Figure 15 shows the signal magnitude (dB) versus frequency (GHz) (blue line) for the Minkowski fractal antenna, where the last listed refers to the Voltage Standing Wave Ratio (VSWR) [16].

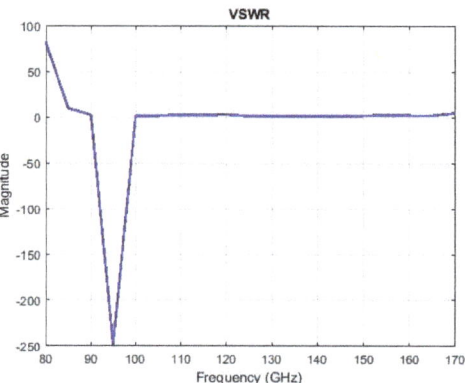

Figure 15. Signal magnitude versus frequency for VSWR.

Such that a radio device (which emits or receives electromagnetic waves) must be able to provide energy to its antenna, the radio total impedance and emission circuits line impedance must be well tuned according to the antenna's effective resistance. The impedance is thus the actual resistance of an integral electric circuit or the constituent in an alternative current, which results from both ohmic resistance and reactance mixed effects [16,17]. The parameter Voltage Standing Wave Ratio (VSWR) is the physical degree that numerically depicts how well the antenna is coupled to the impedance provided of the radio line or emission line to which it is related. The VSWR is a service of the numerical reflection factor, which describes the energy reflected from the device used to transmit or receive electromagnetic signals.

In Figures 16–18 of the Minkowski fractal antenna for two, three, and respectively, four iterations, the self-reflection coefficient S_{11} and return loss graphics are presented.

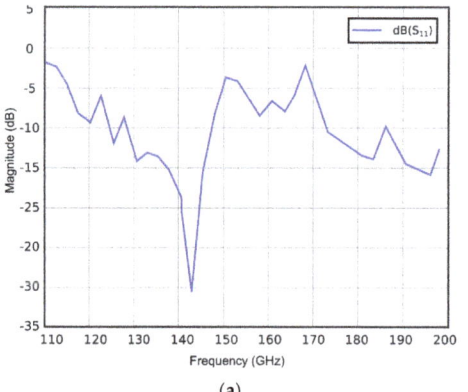
(a)

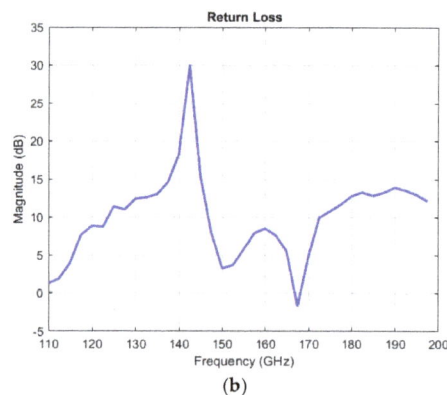
(b)

Figure 16. Minkowski fractal antenna for 2 iterations: (**a**) Self-reflection coefficient S_{11}, (**b**) Return loss.

Figures 16–18 show the graphs for (a) the self-reflection coefficient (S_{11}), and respectively, the return loss for (b), of the Minkowski type fractal antennas for two, three and four iterations.

Now, it can be said that S-parameters sometimes get used interchangeably with the return loss, insertion loss and reflection coefficient, and often without discernment. In particular, there seems to be the casual strong confusion around the dissimilarity between the return loss versus the reflection coefficient, as well as because these associate to (S_{11}). These mistaking overlaps do occur, however, from the fact that these quantities defined above all describe the reflection of a wave propagating from a reference pack, either that it is a terminal transmission line or that it is a grid of preset circuits, ultimately.

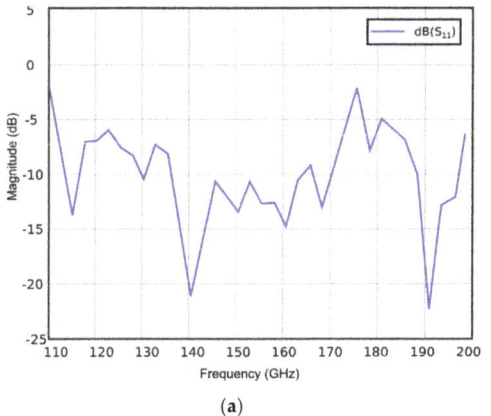
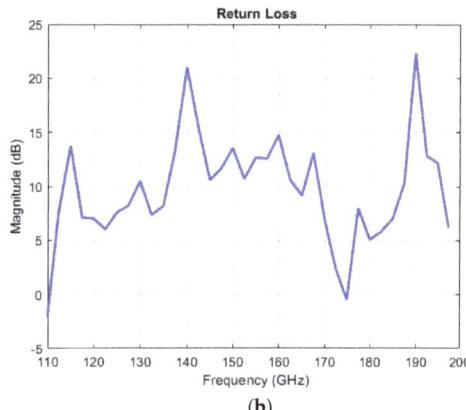

Figure 17. Minkowski fractal antenna for 3 iterations: (**a**) Self-reflection coefficient S_{11}, (**b**) Return loss.

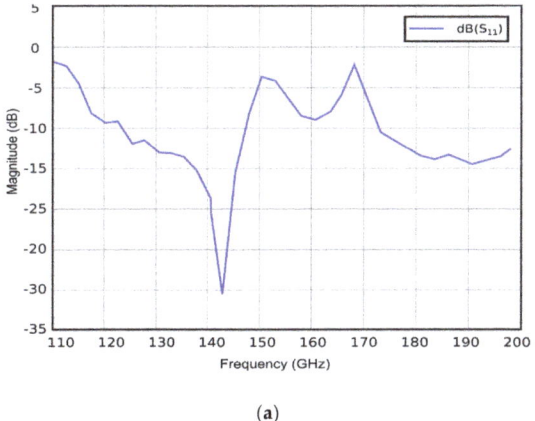
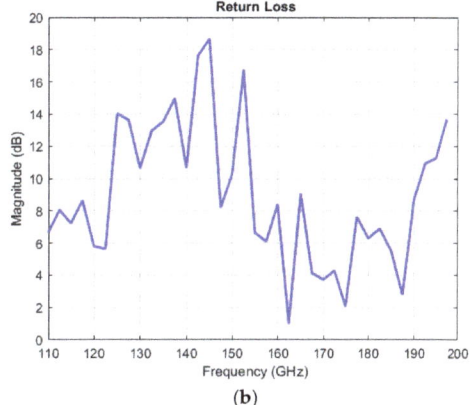

Figure 18. Minkowski fractal antenna for 4 iterations: (**a**) Self-reflection coefficient S_{11}, (**b**) Return loss.

Fractal Antenna Measurements

According to a number of relevant simulations and measurements on Minkowski's loop-based fractal configurations, the optimum one is presented in the following figure. In such an iterative procedure, an initial structure is replicated countless times at different scales, positions and directions, to obtain the final fractal structure. In Figure 19, the photography of a fabricated antenna from a fractal curve scheme of the Minkowski's loop third iteration can be noted.

The modeling and design process of the antenna are completed in MATLAB with the help of the AntennaDesigner toolbox: (https://www.mathworks.com/help/antenna/ref/antennadesigner-app.html (accessed on 11 June 2022)). The toolbox first asks for the frequency for which one wants to design the antenna. Once this value is entered, a prototype is made which can then be adjusted until the simulations suit the designer. We modify certain dimensions of the fractal until we obtain the desired values for impedance, VSWR, etc. All graphs are obtained with this program. The iterative process is performed up to the third iteration. The Rogers 4350 0.8 mm thick material is used for the dielectric having the relative permittivity of ε_r = 4.4. The fractal antenna is fed from the normal position by coaxial cable having the inner and outer diameters of the SMA connector. The scale factor of antennas is 1/3 and the stage of iteration is n = 3. The size of the substrate and the patch are the same. At the end of the modeling, the Gerber files are generated, useful for printing the antenna wiring on the dielectric material (the PCB design has to be completed with a specialized device to strictly observe the fractal dimensions). In the measurements effectuated with the fractal antenna obtained, the VDI - Erickson Power Meters (PM5B) were used. This power meter, covering both analog and digital carriers, is a calibrated calorimeter-style power meter for 75 GHz to >3 THz applications. It offers power measurement ranges from 1 µW up to 200 mW. The PM5B is the de facto standard for frequency > 100 GHz power measurement and can be used in measurements such as VSWR for antenna and cable, antenna return loss and cable return loss to measure forward power and measure reflected power.

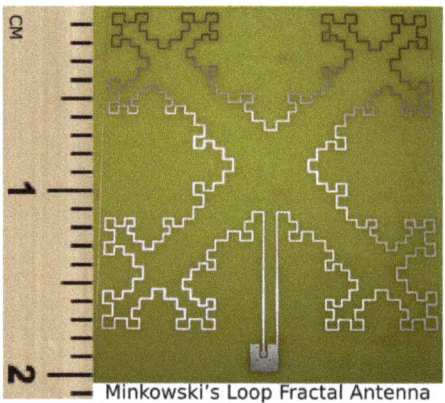

Figure 19. Fabricated antenna photography from a Minkowski fractal curve scheme.

From the investigation of the graph representations, a good match of the experimental results with the simulated ones is observed. An excellent overlap, between simulated and measured impedance, is presented in Figure 20. The graph in Figure 21 shows that we have low, reduced VSWR values. This is gratifying, because the lower the VSWR, the better the antenna is impedance-matched to the transmission line and the higher the power delivered to the antenna. Furthermore, a small VSWR reduces reflections from the antenna.

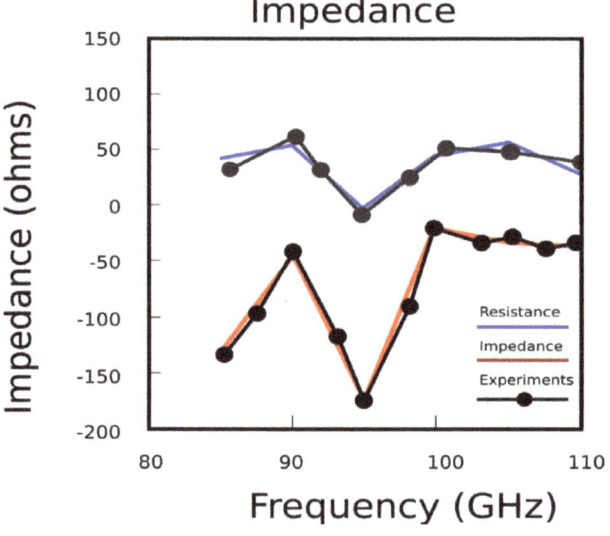

Figure 20. Graphical representation of simulated and measured impedance.

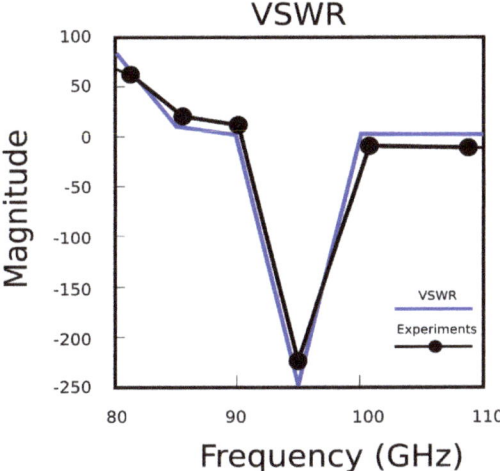

Figure 21. Graphical representation of simulated and measured VSWR.

5. Horn Antenna versus Minkowski Fractal Antenna

The Minkowski fractal antenna and the classic Horn antenna were discussed, for example [14]. In both representations, the constituent elements of the antennas in the plates present in the perpendicular plane *y0z* (black drawing on an olive background) are passed, generically called the anisotropic fractal meta-surface and, respectively, the dual-band printed Horn antenna.

Figure 22 shows two distinct antennas operating in the same frequency band specific to the 6G communications frame, in order to make a direct comparison of the quality of the emission factors. From our assumptions, this concept is among primal designs for a meta-surface applied to a dual-band antenna with contrary beams. In a positive vision, the proposed meta-surface-based fractal antenna concept may present novel opportunities in the projection of multi-functional antennas [18].

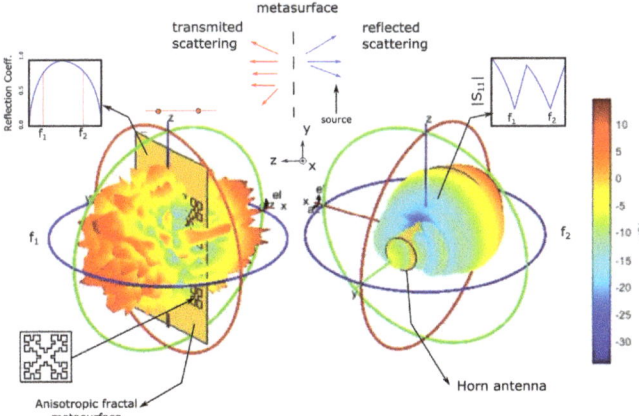

Figure 22. Direct comparison between Minkowski fractal antenna and Horn antenna.

As can be seen from the graphical representations, the Minkowski's loop fractal antenna is better in terms of pattern radiation overlay, having the signal strength close to 10 dBi (after the dark red color that appears in the figure on the left), being present on a larger surface such as emissivity [15].

Regarding the directivity and gain of the two compared types of antennas, we present two graphs in Figures 23 and 24, both at the resonant frequency of 140 GHz. The gains are different from each other, with values of 14.63 dB for the Horn antenna and 3.133 dB for the Minkowski fractal antenna, the fourth iteration. Figures 23 and 24 highlight the directivity qualities and the gain associated to the individual antenna, graphically represented in 2D, each separately [16]. Thus, we have the main directivity θ = 295° at a gain G = 3.13 dB for the fractal Minkowski antenna, and a main directivity θ = 270° at a gain G = 14.6 dB for the Horn antenna.

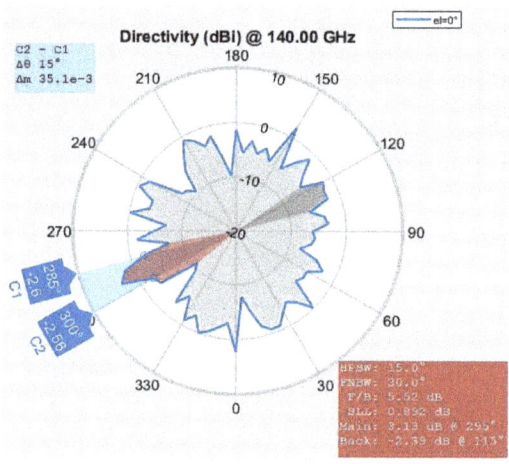

Figure 23. Azimuth pattern (directivity) of Minkowski fractal antenna.

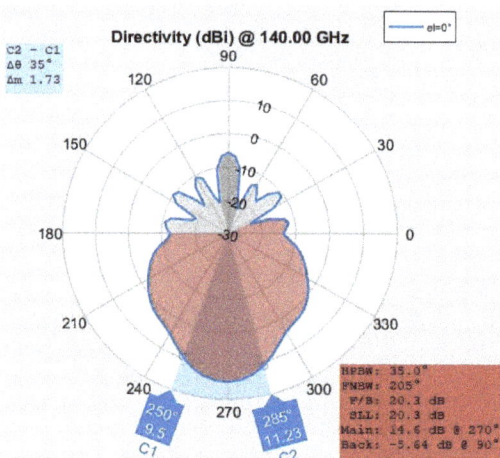

Figure 24. Azimuth pattern (directivity) of Horn antenna.

Finally, we mention that in the graphical representations proposed in this paper we used the software programs initiated in *Image Clustering Algorithms to Identify Complicated Cerebral Diseases*, in a medical article [19].

6. Conclusions

In this paper, the engineering construction of a special Sixth Generation (6G) antenna has been presented, based on the fractal geometry called Minkowski's loop. The antenna has the shape of this known fractal, set finally at four iterations, to obtain a maximum electromagnetic performance.

The frequency bands for which this 6G fractal antenna was projected in the article are 170 GHz to 260 GHz (WR-4), and 110 GHz to 170 GHz (WR-6), respectively. The three resonant frequencies, optimally used, are equal to 140 GHz (WR-6) for the first, 182 GHz (WR-4) for the second and 191 GHz (WR-4) for the third. For these frequencies, the electromagnetic behaviors of fractal antennas are well shown.

Our review highlighted qualities of fractal geometry in the antenna's design, made a classical analysis of the Minkowski fractal antenna, and calculated and graphically represented the electric and magnetic parameters such as charge and current distribution, electric and magnetic fields 3D distribution, impedance, radiation efficiency, Azimuth pattern and directivity, radiation pattern and VSWR.

It is immediately noticeable that, as with most fractal antennae, the radiation pattern, and consequently, the detection efficiency and quality of the emission factors, do not fluctuate umpteen with respect to frequency, mathematically speaking.

The antenna gain is reasonable compared to other fractal antennas, namely, we have a gain equal to G = 3.13 dB at an angle of main directivity equal to θ = 295°, for the fractal Minkowski's loop antenna (the three iterations). A good match of the experimental results with the simulated ones is observed.

Author Contributions: Conceptualization, V.-P.P. and M.-A.P.; methodology, V.-P.P.; software, M.-V.N. and V.-A.P.; validation, V.-P.P., M.-A.P. and V.-A.P.; formal analysis, V.-P.P., M.-A.P. and V.-A.P.; investigation, V.-A.P. and M.-A.P.; resources, V.-A.P. and M.-A.P.; data curation, M.-V.N. and V.-A.P.; writing—original draft preparation, V.-P.P.; writing—review and editing, M.-A.P. and V.-P.P.; visualization, V.-A.P. and M.-V.N.; supervision, V.-P.P.; project administration, V.-P.P. All authors have read and agreed to the published version of the manuscript.

Funding: This research received no external funding.

Institutional Review Board Statement: Not applicable.

Informed Consent Statement: Not applicable.

Data Availability Statement: The data used to support the findings of this study cannot be accessed due to commercial confidentiality.

Acknowledgments: The co-authors M.-A.P., V.-A.P. and V.-P.P. would like to thank Jenica Paun for her continuous kind support.

Conflicts of Interest: The authors declare no conflict of interest.

References

1. Hajiyat, Z.; Ismail, A.; Sali, A.; Hamidon, M.N. Antenna in 6G Wireless Communication System: Specifications, Challenges, and Research Directions. *Optik* **2021**, *231*, 166415. [CrossRef]
2. Sa'don, S.N.H.; Kamarudin, M.R.; Dahri, M.H.; Ashyap, A.Y.I.; Seman, F.C.; Abbasi, M.I.; Abidin, Z.Z. The Review and Analysis of Antenna for Sixth Generation (6G) Applications. In Proceedings of the 2020 IEEE International RF and Microwave Conference (RFM), Kuala Lumpur, Malaysia, 14–16 December 2020.
3. Wu, Y.; Singh, S.; Taleb, T.; Roy, A.; Dhillon, H.S.; Kanagarathinam, M.R.; De, A. (Eds.) *6G mobile Wireless Networks*; Springer: Cham, Switzerland, 2021.
4. Nichita, M.V.; Paun, M.A.; Paun, V.A.; Paun, V.P. On the 5G Communications: Fractal-Shaped Antennas for PPDR Applications. *Complexity* **2021**, *2021*, 9451730. [CrossRef]
5. Kato, Y.; Omori, K.; Sanada, A. D-Band Perfect Anomalous Reflectors for 6G Applications. *IEEE Access* **2021**, *9*, 157512–157521. [CrossRef]
6. Prakriti, S. Application of Fractal Antennas with advantages and disadvantages. *Int. J. Creat. Res. Thoughts* **2018**, *6*, 551–554.
7. Mandelbrot, B. *Fractal Geometry of Nature*; Freeman: New York, NY, USA, 1983; pp. 25–57.
8. Paun, V.P.; Agop, M.; Chen, G.; Focsa, C. Fractal-Type Dynamical Behaviors of Complex Systems. *Complexity* **2018**, *2018*, 8029361. [CrossRef]
9. Nichita, M.V.; Paun, M.A.; Paun, V.A.; Paun, V.P. Fractal Analysis of Brain Glial Cells. Fractal Dimension and Lacunarity. *Univ. Politeh. Buchar. Sci. Bull.-Ser. A-Appl. Math. Phys.* **2019**, *81*, 273–284.
10. Falconer, K. *Fractal Geometry: Mathematical Foundations and Applications*, 3rd ed.; John Wiley & Sons, Ltd.: Chichester, UK, 2014.

11. Lapidus, M.L.; Pearse, E.P.J.; Winter, S. Minkowski measurability results for self-similar tilings and fractals with monophase generators. In *Fractal Geometry and Dynamical Systems in Pure and Applied Mathematics, I. Fractals in Pure Mathematics*; Carfi, D., Lapidus, M.L., Pearse, E.P.J., Frankenhuysen, M.V., Eds.; Contemporary Mathematics American Mathematical Society: Providence, RI, USA, 2013; Volume 600, pp. 185–203.
12. Ziboon, H.T.; Ali, J.K. Minkowski Fractal Geometry: An Attractive Choice of Compact Antenna and Filter Designs. *ARPN J. Eng. Appl. Sci.* **2018**, *13*, 8548–8553.
13. Chiu, C.-Y.; Cheng, C.-H.; Murch, R.D.; Rowell, C.R. Reduction of Mutual Coupling between Closely-Packed Antenna Elements. *IEEE Trans. Antennas Propag.* **2007**, *55*, 1732–1738. [CrossRef]
14. Tupik, V.A.; Potapov, A.A.; Margolin, V.I. Some features of the interaction of electromagnetic radiation with complex fractal objects. *J. Phys. Conf. Ser.* **2019**, *1348*, 012016. [CrossRef]
15. Paun, M.A.; Paun, V.A. High Frequency Three-dimensional Model for the Study of Antennas in Cochlear Implants. *IEEE J. Trans. Compon. Packag. Manuf. Technol.* **2018**, *8*, 1135–1140. [CrossRef]
16. Sankaralingam, S.; Dhar, S.; Bag, A.K.; Kundua, A.; Gupta, B. Use of Minkowski Fractal Geometry for the Design of Wearable Fully Fabric Compact. *J. Phys. Sci.* **2014**, *18*, 7–13.
17. Gupta, A.; Chawla, P. Review on Fractal Antenna: Inspiration through Nature. *Int. J. Sci. Eng. Appl. Sci. (IJSEAS)* **2015**, *1*, 508–514.
18. Anguera, J.; Andújar, A.; Jayasinghe, J.; Sameer Chakravarthy, V.V.S.S.; Chowdary, P.S.R.; Pijoan, J.L.; Ali, T.; Cattani, C. Fractal antennas: An historical perspective. *Fractal Fract.* **2020**, *4*, 3. [CrossRef]
19. Nichita, M.V.; Paun, M.A.; Paun, V.A.; Paun, V.P. Image Clustering Algorithms to Identify Complicated Cerebral Diseases. Description and Comparaisons. *IEEE Access* **2020**, *8*, 88434–88442. [CrossRef]

Article

Particle Swarm Optimization Fractional Slope Entropy: A New Time Series Complexity Indicator for Bearing Fault Diagnosis

Yuxing Li [1,2], Lingxia Mu [1,2] and Peiyuan Gao [1,*]

1. School of Automation and Information Engineering, Xi'an University of Technology, Xi'an 710048, China; liyuxing@xaut.edu.cn (Y.L.); mulingxia@xaut.edu.cn (L.M.)
2. Shaanxi Key Laboratory of Complex System Control and Intelligent Information Processing, Xi'an University of Technology, Xi'an 710048, China
* Correspondence: 2210320082@stu.xaut.edu.cn

Abstract: Slope entropy (SlEn) is a time series complexity indicator proposed in recent years, which has shown excellent performance in the fields of medical and hydroacoustics. In order to improve the ability of SlEn to distinguish different types of signals and solve the problem of two threshold parameters selection, a new time series complexity indicator on the basis of SlEn is proposed by introducing fractional calculus and combining particle swarm optimization (PSO), named PSO fractional SlEn (PSO-FrSlEn). Then we apply PSO-FrSlEn to the field of fault diagnosis and propose a single feature extraction method and a double feature extraction method for rolling bearing fault based on PSO-FrSlEn. The experimental results illustrated that only PSO-FrSlEn can classify 10 kinds of bearing signals with 100% classification accuracy by using double features, which is at least 4% higher than the classification accuracies of the other four fractional entropies.

Keywords: fractional order; slope entropy; time series complexity; permutation entropy; dispersion entropy

1. Introduction

Entropy is a measure of the complexity of time series [1–5], among which the entropies based on Shannon entropy [6] are the most widely used, including permutation entropy (PE) [7], dispersion entropy (DE) [8], etc. The definition of PE is based on the sequential relationship among the time series. Moreover, the concept of PE is simple, and its calculation speed is fast [9], but its stability is not very good. Therefore, as an improved algorithm of PE, dispersion entropy (DE) is proposed, which has the advantages of little influence by burst signals and good stability [10]. These two kinds of entropies and their improved entropies have shown good results in various fields [11–13].

PE is one of the most commonly used time series complexity estimators. PE has clearly proved its usefulness in mechanical engineering, mainly in the field of fault diagnosis. Taking the research on fault diagnosis for rolling bearing as an example, the advantage of PE is that it is not limited by the bearing signals and the length of permutation samples [14]. However, PE does not take the difference between the amplitude values. In order to consider the amplitude information of time series, the complexity of time series is analyzed by weighted permutation entropy (WPE) [15]. It is concluded that WPE not only has the same advantages as PE, but also can detect the complexity of dynamic mutation by quantifying amplitude information. Concurrently, other application fields of PE and WPE have also received great attention [16–19].

As an improved algorithm of PE, DE also introduces amplitude information, and has the advantage of distinguishing different types of signals easily and calculating fast. Regarding the applications of DE, it has been used widely in bearing signals classification. In the feature extraction experiment of bearing fault diagnosis, DE can classify bearing faults through short data, and has high recognition accuracy in the case of small samples [20].

However, DE is impossible to evaluate the fluctuation of time series. Thus, the fluctuation information is combined with DE to obtain fluctuating dispersion entropy (FDE) [21]. FDE takes into account the fluctuation of time series, which can discriminate deterministic from stochastic time series. And relative to DE, FDE reduces all possible dispersion modes to speed up the calculation of entropy. After that, DE and FDE have also made great achievements in the fields of medicine and underwater acoustics [22,23]. In order to make the feature of DE more significant, fractional calculus is proposed to combine with DE [24], where fractional calculus can introduce fractional information into entropy [25]. Similarly, there is the existence of fractional fuzzy entropy (FE), which is the combination of fractional calculus and FE [26].

Slope entropy (SlEn) is a new time series complexity estimator proposed in recent years. Its concept is simple, which is only based on the amplitude of time series and five modules. Since it was proposed, it has been used in the fields of medical, hydroacoustics, and fault diagnosis. In 2019, SlEn was first proposed by David Cuesta-Frau, and successively applied it to the classification of electroencephalographic (EEG) records and electromyogram (EMG) records [27], classify the activity records of patients with bipolar disorder [28], and the features extraction of fever time series [29]. Then SlEn is also used to extract the features of ship radiated noise signals [30] and bearing fault signals [31].

SlEn has proven to have strong superiority as features. However, SlEn has not received the attention it deserves. A big factor that leads to this situation is the influence of the two threshold parameter settings on its effect. Therefore, in order to solve this problem, we introduce particle swarm optimization (PSO) algorithm to optimize these two threshold parameters. Another factor is that there is still room for improvement in the basic SlEn. Therefore, in order to improve the significance of features, we combine fractional calculus with SlEn. Finally, a new algorithm named PSO fractional SlEn (PSO-FrSlEn) is proposed in this paper, which is an improved time series complexity indicator of SlEn.

The structure of this paper is divided as follows. Section 2 introduces the algorithm steps of the proposed method in detail. Section 3 exhibits the experimental process of this paper briefly. Sections 4 and 5 demonstrate the experiment and analysis of single feature extraction and double feature extraction separately. Finally, the innovations of this paper and the conclusions of the experiments are drawn in Section 6.

2. Algorithms

2.1. Slope Entropy Algorithm

For a given time series $S = \{s_i, i = 1, 2, 3, \ldots, n\}$, SlEn is calculated according to the following steps.

Step 1: set an embedding dimension m, which can divide the time series into $k = n - m + 1$ subsequences, where m is greater than two and much less than n. The disintegrate form is as follows:

$$S_k = \{s_k, s_{k+1}, \ldots, s_n\} \quad (1)$$

Here, all subsequences $S_1, S_2, \ldots, S_k$ contain m elements, such as $S_1 = \{s_1, s_2, \ldots, s_m\}$.

Step 2: subtract the latter of the two adjacent elements in all the subsequences obtained in Step 1 from the former to obtain k new sequences. The new form is as follows:

$$T_k = \{t_k, t_{k+1}, \ldots, t_{n-1}\} \quad (2)$$

Here, the element $t_k = s_{k+1} - s_k$, and all sequences $T_1, T_2, \ldots, T_k$ contain $m - 1$ elements, such as $T_1 = \{t_1, t_2, \ldots, t_{m-1}\}$.

Step 3: lead into the two threshold parameters η and ε of SlEn, where $0 < \varepsilon < \eta$, and compare all elements in the sequences obtained from Step 2 with the positive and negative values of these two threshold parameters. The positive and negative values of these two threshold parameters $-\eta, -\varepsilon, \varepsilon$ and η serve as the dividing lines, they divide the number field into five modules $-2, -1, 0, 1,$ and 2. If $t_k < -\eta$, the module is -2; if $-\eta < t_k < -\varepsilon$, the module is -1; if $-\varepsilon < t_k < \varepsilon$, the module is 0; if $\varepsilon < t_k < \eta$, the module is 1; if $-\varepsilon < t_k < \varepsilon$, the module is 0; if $t_k > \eta$, the module is 2. The intuitive module division principle is shown by the coordinate axis in Figure 1 below:

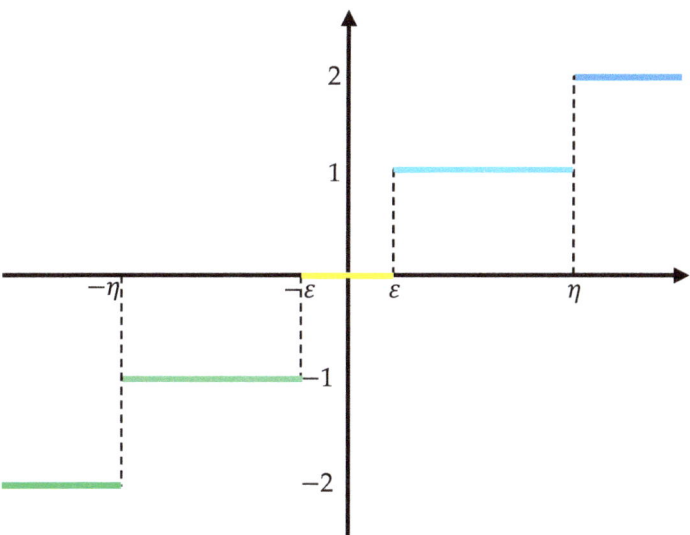

Figure 1. Module division principle.

The form of the sequences is below:

$$E_k = \{e_k, e_{k+1}, \ldots, e_{n-1}\} \quad (3)$$

Here, each element in E_k is $-2, -1, 0, 1,$ or 2, and there will be the exactly the same sequence.

Step 4: the number of modules is 5, so all types of the sequences E_k are counted as $j = 5^{m-1}$. Such as when m is 3, there will be at most 25 types of E_k, which are $\{-2, -2\}, \{-2, -1\}, \ldots, \{0, 0\}, \{0, 1\}, \ldots, \{2, 1\}, \{2, 2\}$. The number of each type records as $r_1, r_2, \ldots, r_j$, and the frequency of each type is calculated as follows:

$$R_j = \frac{r_j}{k} \quad (4)$$

Step 5: based on the classical Shannon entropy, the formula of SlEn is defined as follows:

$$SlopeEn(m, \eta, \varepsilon) = -\sum_j R_j \ln R_j \quad (5)$$

2.2. Fractional Slope Entropy Algorithm

In this paper, the concept of fractional order is introduced into SlEn for the first time, and the calculation formula of the improved algorithm of SlEn (FrSlEn) is obtained through the following steps.

Step 1: Shannon entropy is the first entropy to consider fractional calculus, and its generalized expression is as follows:

$$ShannonEn_\alpha = \sum_j p_i \left\{ -\frac{p_i^{-\alpha}}{\Gamma(\alpha+1)} [\ln p_i + \psi(1) - \psi(1-\alpha)] \right\} \quad (6)$$

Here, α is the order of fractional derivative, $\Gamma\ (\cdot)$ and $\psi\ (\cdot)$ are the gamma and digamma functions.

Step 2: extract the fractional order information of order α from Equation (6):

$$I_\alpha = -\frac{p_i^{-\alpha}}{\Gamma(\alpha+1)} [\ln p_i + \psi(1) - \psi(1-\alpha)] \quad (7)$$

Step 3: combine the fractional order with SlEn, which is to replace $-\ln R_j$ with Equation (7). Therefore, the formula of FrSlEn is defined as follows:

$$SlopeEn_\alpha(m, \eta, \varepsilon) = \sum_j R_j \left\{ -\frac{R_j^{-\alpha}}{\Gamma(\alpha+1)} [\ln R_j + \psi(1) - \psi(1-\alpha)] \right\} \quad (8)$$

2.3. Particle Swarm Optimization and Algorithm Process

In order to get a better effect of FrSlEn, we use particle swarm optimization (PSO) algorithm to optimize the two threshold parameters η and ε of SlEn. Considering all the above algorithm steps and conditions, the algorithm flowchart of SlEn and three kinds of improved SlEn is as follows in Figure 2:

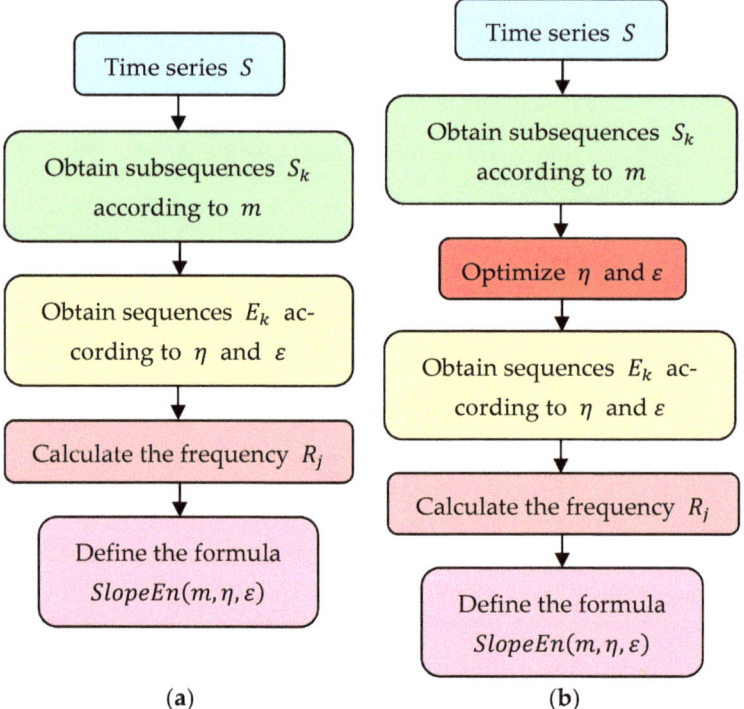

Figure 2. Cont.

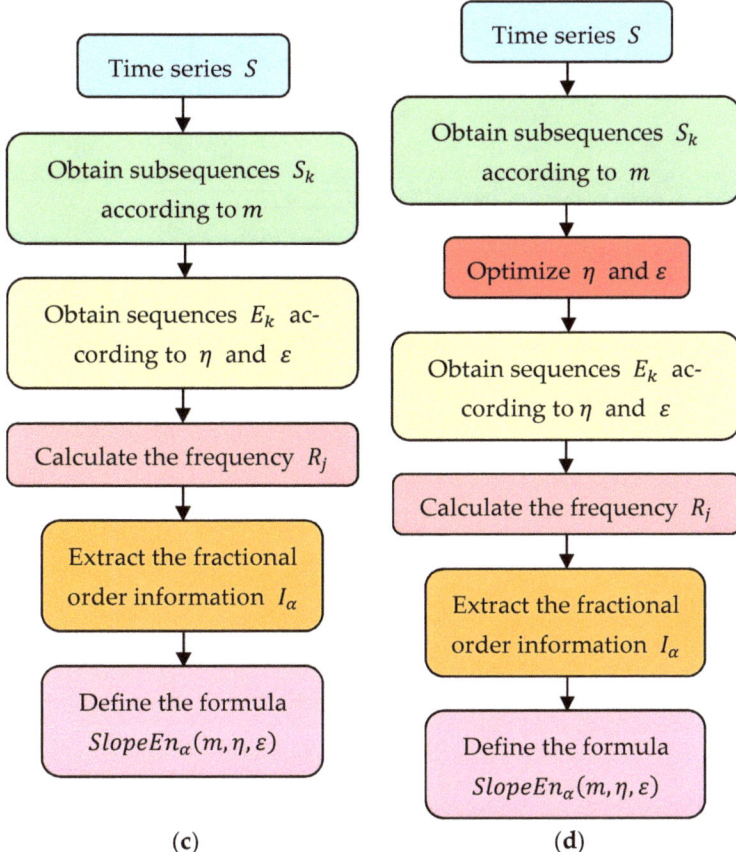

Figure 2. Algorithm flowchart: (**a**) SlEn; (**b**) PSO-SlEn; (**c**) FrSlEn; (**d**) PSO-FrSlEn.

3. Proposed Feature Extraction Methods

The experiment of this paper is divided into two parts: single feature extraction and double feature extraction. The specific experimental process of single feature extraction is as follows.

Step 1: the 10 kinds of bearing signals are normalized, which can make the signals neat and regular, the threshold parameters η and ε less than 1, where ε is less than 0.2 in most cases.

Step 2: the five kinds of single features of these 10 kinds of normalized bearing signals are extracted separately under seven different fractional orders.

Step 3: the distribution of the features is obtained and the hybrid degrees between the feature points are observed.

Step 4: these features are classified into one of the 10 bearing signals by K-Nearest Neighbor (KNN).

Step 5: the classification accuracies of the features are calculated.

The experimental process of double feature extraction is roughly the same as that of single feature extraction. In the Step 2 of double feature extraction, combine any two different fractional orders of the seven fractional orders as double features, which can obtain 21 double feature combinations. The experimental process flowchart is as follows in Figure 3:

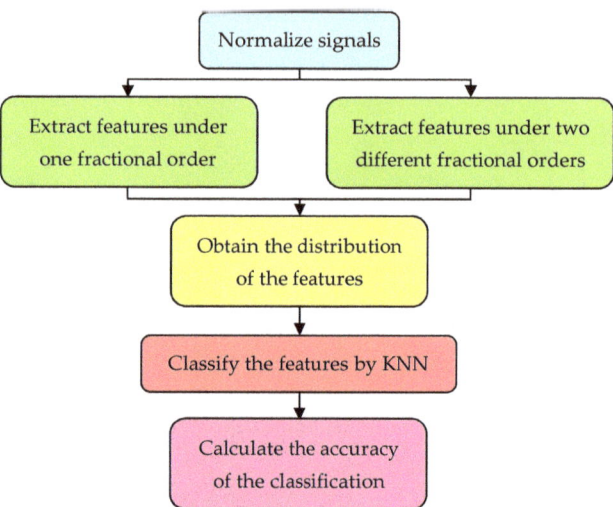

Figure 3. The flowchart of the proposed feature extraction methods.

4. Single Feature Extraction

4.1. Bearing Signals

The object of this paper is bearing signal. Ten kinds of bearing signals with different faults and fault diameter sizes under the same working state are randomly selected and downloaded for this paper, and the 10 kinds of bearing signals come from the same website [32].

The signal data are measured when the motor load is three horsepower. First of all, it is essential to have a normal bearing signal, which is coded as N-100. Then, the bearing fault signals are divided into three types: inner race fault signals, ball fault signals and outer race fault signals, where for the outer race fault signals, the relative position coincidence area of the outer race is the central direction (six o'clock direction). Finally, there are three kinds of fault diameter sizes, which are 0.007 in, 0.014 in, and 0.021 in. According to the three different types of faults and the three different sizes of fault diameter, the fault signals are divided into nine categories, and they are coded as IR-108, B-121, OR-133, IR-172, B-188, OR-200, IR-212, B-225, and OR-237.

The data files are in MATLAB format, and each file contains the acceleration time series data of drive end, fan end and base. The drive end acceleration time series data are chosen as the experimental data in this paper. The signals data are normalized, and the normalized signals are shown in Figure 4.

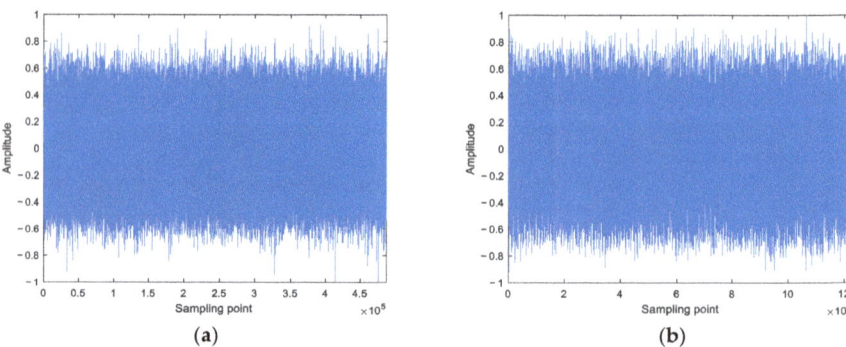

Figure 4. *Cont.*

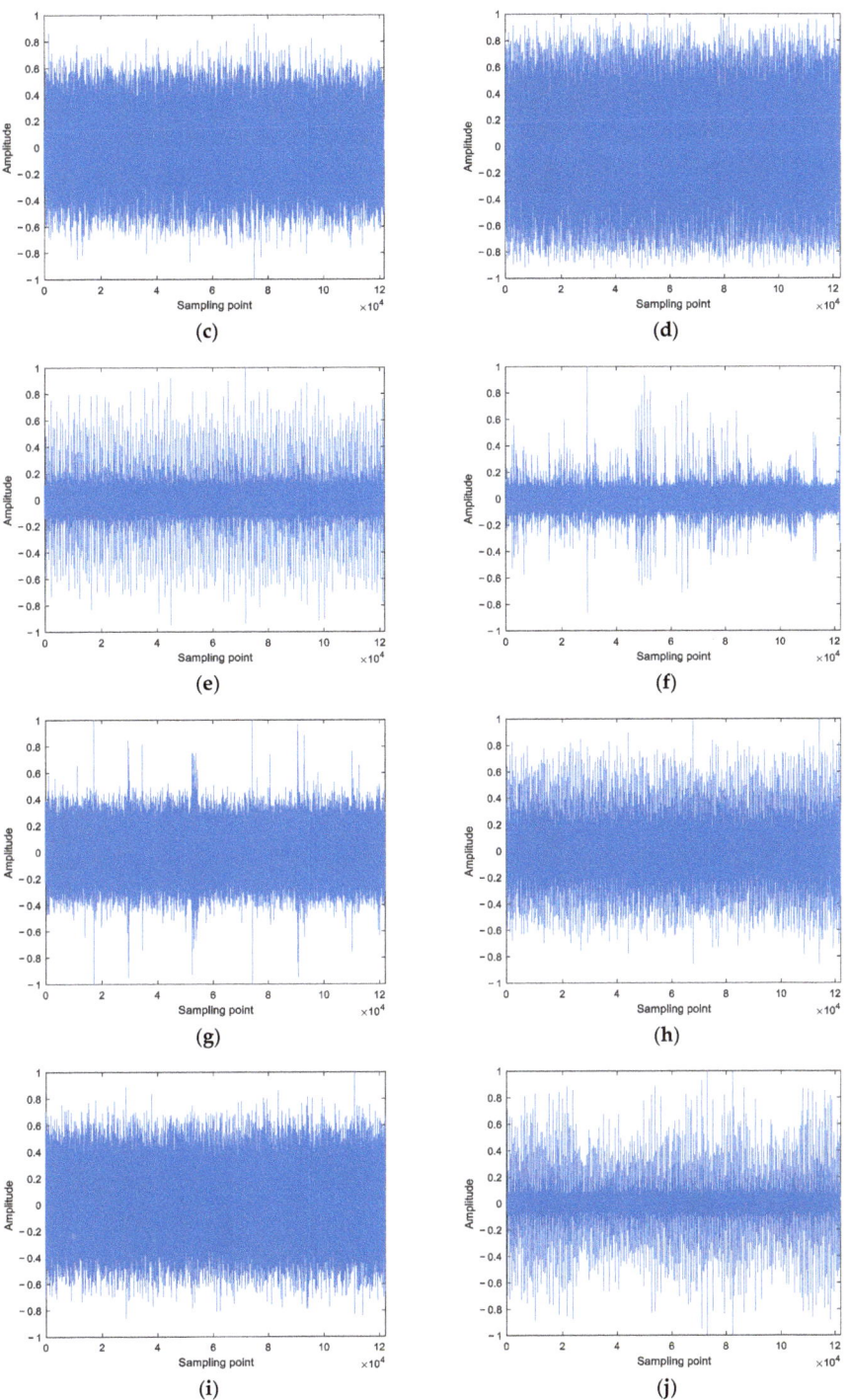

Figure 4. The normalized 10 bearing signals: (**a**) N-100; (**b**) IR-108; (**c**) B-121; (**d**) OR-133; (**e**) IR-172; (**f**) B-188; (**g**) OR-200; (**h**) IR-212; (**i**) B-225; (**j**) OR-237.

4.2. Feature Distribution

In this paper, five kinds of entropies based on Shannon entropy are selected as the features of the above 10 bearing signals for feature extraction. The five kinds of entropies are PE, WPE, DE, FDE, and SlEn, which are renamed FrPE, FrWPE, FrDE, FrFDE, and FrSlEn after combining with the fractional orders.

The parameters shared by different entropies are necessary to be set to the same value. There are three parameters of FrPE and FrWPE, five parameters of FrDE and FrFDE, and four parameters of FrSlEn, where the two same parameters of them are embedding dimension (m) and fractional order (α). So set all the m as 4, and take all the α from -0.3 to 0.3, where $\alpha = 0$ is the case without fractional order. The same parameter of FrPE, FrWPE, FrDE, and FrFDE is time lag (τ), and all the τ are set as 1. The two proprietary parameters of FrDE and FrFDE are number of classes (c) and mapping approach, we set the c of them as 3 and the mapping approach of them is normal cumulative distribution function (NCDF). There are two threshold parameters of FrSlEn are proprietary, which are large threshold (η) and small threshold (ε). They are non-negative and optimized by PSO in this paper, so FrSlEn is renamed as PSO-FrSlEn.

According to the sampling point lengths of the above signals, most of which are just more than 1.2×10^5, every 4000 sample points are taken as one sample, so there are 30 samples for each kind of bearing signals. Combined with all the parameter settings mentioned above, the single features of the 30 samples of each kind of signals are extracted. PSO-FrSlEn under different α is taken as an example, the feature distribution of PSO-FrSlEn is shown in Figure 5 below:

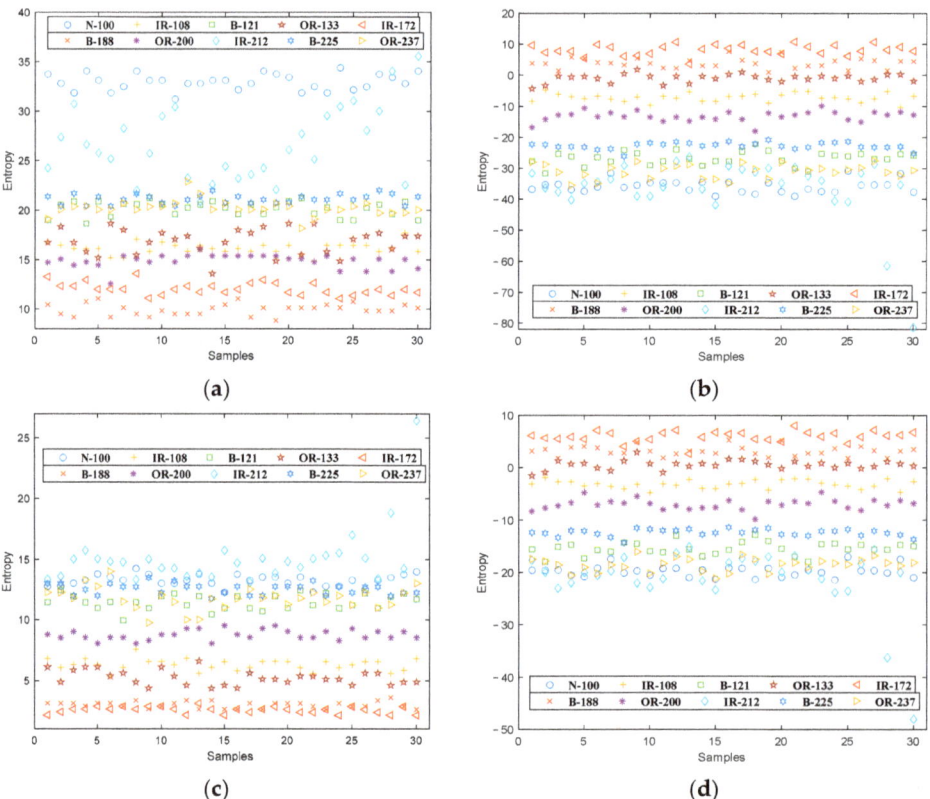

Figure 5. *Cont.*

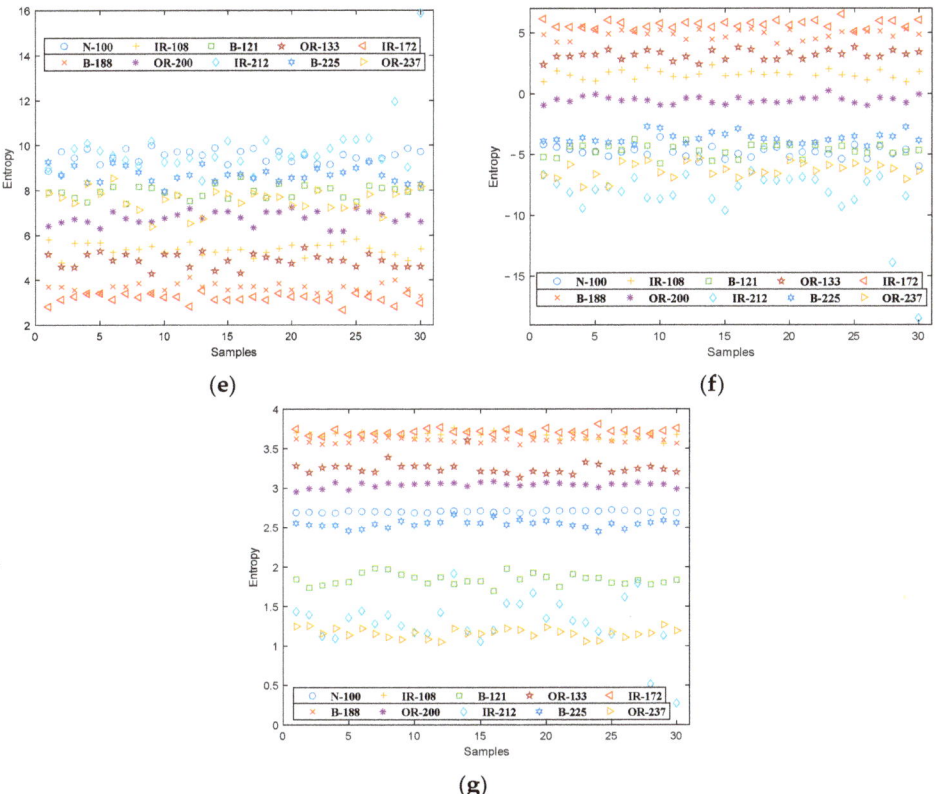

Figure 5. Single feature distribution of PSO-FrSlEn: (**a**) $\alpha = -0.3$; (**b**) $\alpha = 0.3$; (**c**) $\alpha = -0.2$; (**d**) $\alpha = 0.2$; (**e**) $\alpha = -0.1$; (**f**) $\alpha = 0.1$; (**g**) $\alpha = 0$.

As can be seen from Figure 5, the feature points of B-121, B-225, and OR-237 are obviously mixed under $\alpha = -0.3$; under $\alpha = 0.1$, $\alpha = 0.2$, and $\alpha = 0.3$, the feature points of N-100, B-121, IR-212, B-225, and OR-237 are mixed with each other; all feature points except those of OR-200 are mixed to varying degrees under $\alpha = -0.2$ and $\alpha = 0$; under $\alpha = -0.1$, no kind of feature points is isolated. According to the distribution and confusion degree of these kinds of feature points, we can judge whether each entropy under different α is a notable feature of the signals. In order to intuitively show whether the features are distinguishing, we also undertake classification experiments.

4.3. Classification Effect Verification

KNN is selected as a classifier for the features, which can classify all the features into the corresponding positions of the signals after being trained. The number of nearest samples *k* is set as 3, and 15 samples are taken as training samples and 15 as test samples from the 30 samples of each type of the signals. Also take PSO-FrSlEn as an example. The final classification results and distribution of PSO-FrSlEn are shown in Figure 6 below:

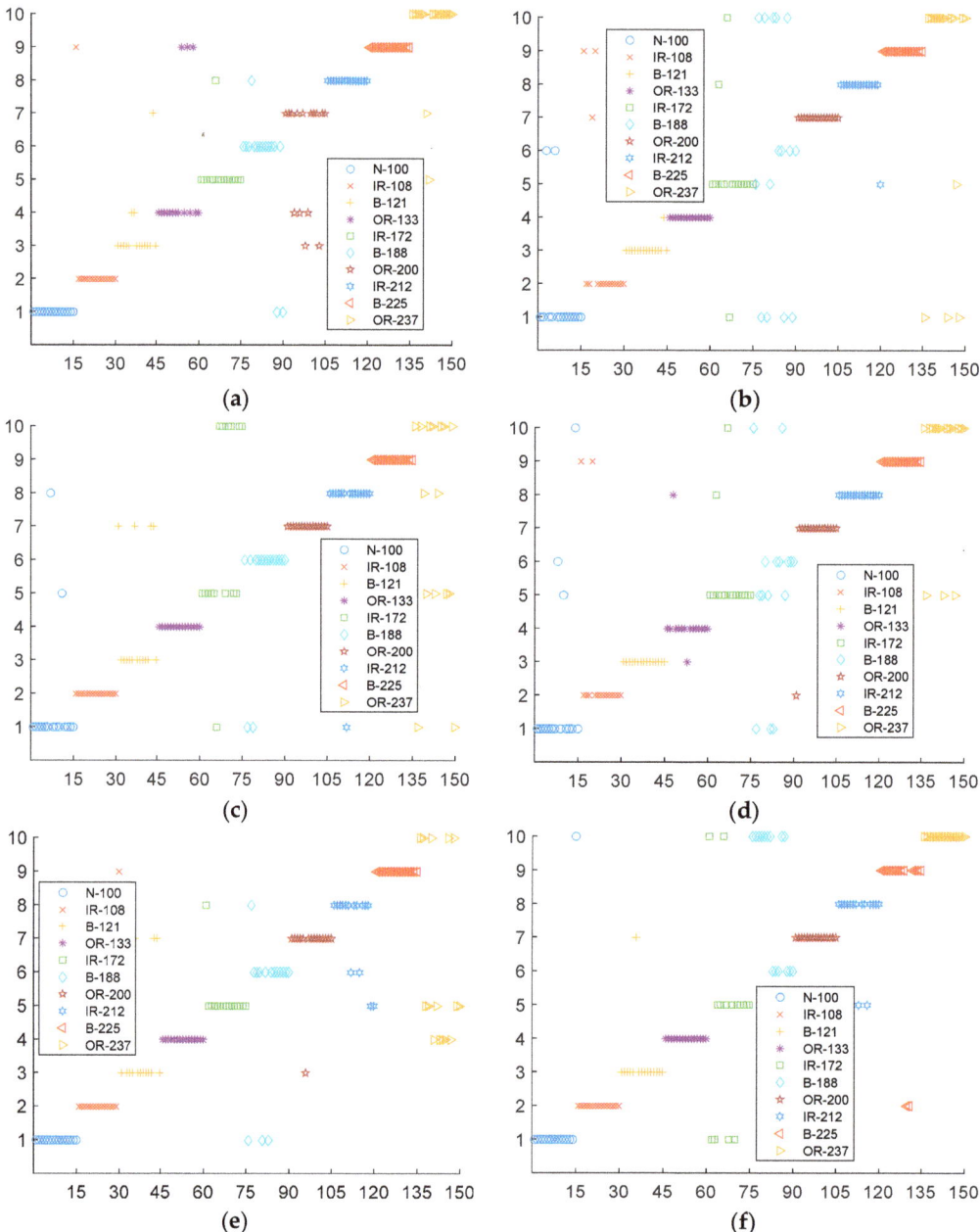

Figure 6. *Cont.*

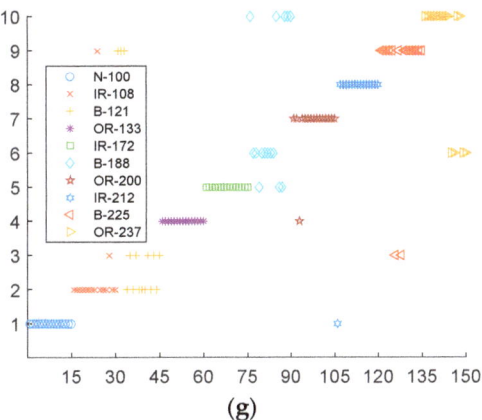

(g)

Figure 6. Classification results and distribution of PSO-FrSlEn: (**a**) $\alpha = -0.3$; (**b**) $\alpha = 0.3$; (**c**) $\alpha = -0.2$; (**d**) $\alpha = 0.2$; (**e**) $\alpha = -0.1$; (**f**) $\alpha = 0.1$; (**g**) $\alpha = 0$.

It can be seen from the distribution of sample points in Figure 6, for N-100, IR-108, OR-133, OR-200, IR-212, and B-225, at most five sample points are misclassified; for B-121, more than half of the sample points are misclassified when $\alpha = 0$, but at most only four sample points are misclassified when the α is another value, and the classification is completely correct when $\alpha = 0.2$; for IR-172, most of the sample points are misclassified when $\alpha = -0.2$ and $\alpha = 0.1$, but the classification is basically correct when the α is another value; for B-188, the classification effect of sample points is very poor no matter what value α takes except when $\alpha = -0.2$; for OR-237, all sample points can be classified correctly when $\alpha = 0.1$. It can be concluded that the classification ability of the same entropy is different under different values of α.

The classification accuracies of each entropy under different fractional orders are obtained after calculation. All the accuracies obtained are recorded in the Table 1 below, and a line graph is drawn in Figure 7 for comparison.

Table 1. The classification accuracy of each entropy under different fractional orders.

Figure	FrPE Accuracy (%)	FrWPE Accuracy (%)	FrDE Accuracy (%)	FrFDE Accuracy (%)	PSO-FrSlEn Accuracy (%)
−0.3	64.67	46.67	82.67	77.33	88
−0.2	78.67	60.67	81.33	73.33	84
−0.1	76.67	66.67	80.67	79.33	83.33
0	76.67	69.33	69.33	79.33	81.33
0.1	75.33	69.33	80	79.33	86
0.2	75.33	69.33	82	80.67	85.33
0.3	66	72.76	82.67	80	83.33

The following information can be obtained from Table 1 and Figure 7, all the classification accuracies are less than 90%; the classification accuracies of PSO-FrSlEn under any fractional orders are greater than those of other arbitrary entropies, and are greater than 80%; the classification accuracies of DE and SlEn with fractional orders are higher than those without fractional orders, which proves that fractional order can make entropy have higher classification accuracy. In order to further improve the classification accuracy and prove the superiority of PSO-FrSlEn, we add a double feature extraction experiment.

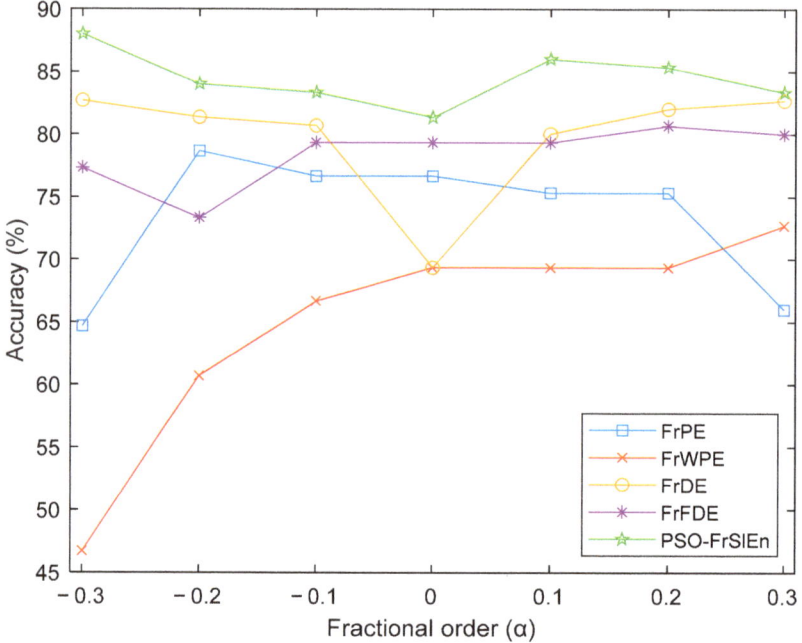

Figure 7. The classification accuracies under different fractional orders.

5. Double Feature Extraction

5.1. Feature Distribution

There are 7 values of α, and the classification accuracies of the sample points vary greatly under different α. Therefore, combine any two different α of the same entropy as a fractional order combination. Each entropy can get 21 groups of fractional order combinations. Define the 21 groups of fractional order combinations as 21 double feature combinations, which are $-0.3\&-0.2$, $-0.3\&-0.1$, $-0.3\&0$, ..., $0.1\&0.3$, $0.2\&0.3$. There are also 30 samples for each signal in the double feature extraction experiment. Each entropy has 21 double feature combinations, so there are 105 double feature combinations in total. Double feature distribution of the nine highest classification accuracies is shown in Figure 8, in which there is only one highest classification accuracy for FrPE, FrWPE, FrDE, and FrFDE, while there are five highest classification accuracy for PSO-FrSlEn.

We can obtain the following information from Figure 8, for FrPE, most feature points of IR-108, OR-133, IR-172, B-188, B-225, and OR-237 are mixed together; for FrWPE, the feature points of each signal are mixed with each other expect those of N-100, OR-200, and IR-212; for FrDE, only a few feature points of IR-108, IR-172, and B-188 have mixed phenomenon, most feature points of the other signals are connected into lines and parallel to each other; for FrFDE, only the feature points of B-121, IR-172, and B-188 are mixed, but the degree of the mixing is great; for PSO-FrSlEn, only one or two feature points of IR-172 are mixed into the feature points range of B-188, and those of other signals are in their respective own piles and not mixed into the others' range.

The mixing degree and the kind number of the feature points determine whether these features are significant. The greater the mixing degree of feature points or the more kinds of mixed feature points, the less significant the features are. Therefore, it can be concluded from the above information, the features of FrWPE are the least significant, and those of PSO-FrSlEn are the most significant. In order to confirm this conclusion, we carried out feature classification experiment to verify.

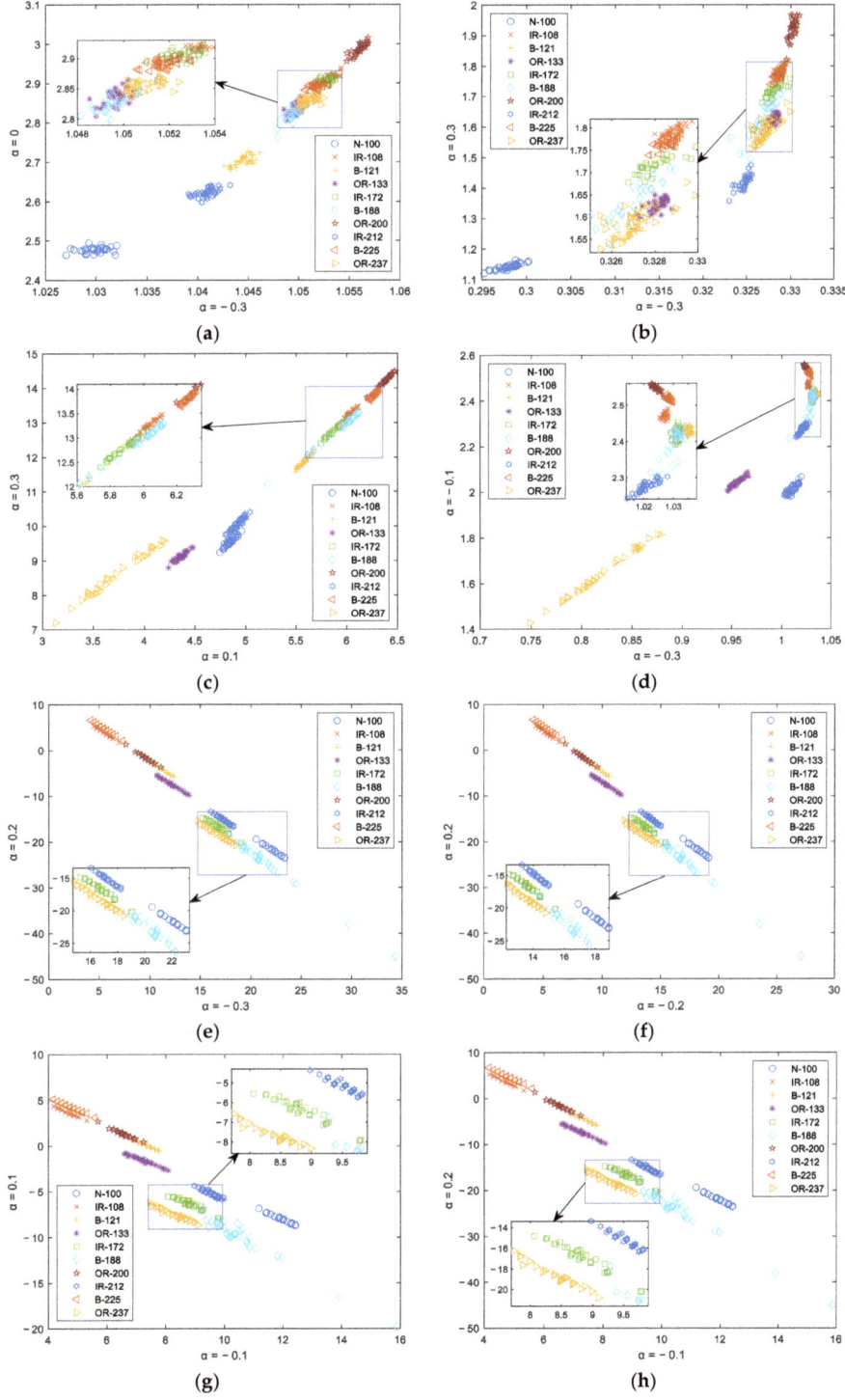

Figure 8. *Cont.*

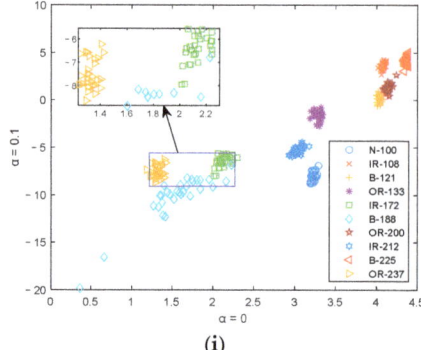

(i)

Figure 8. Double feature distribution of the nine highest classification accuracies: (**a**) FrPE, $\alpha = -0.3\&0$; (**b**) FrWPE, $\alpha = -0.3\&0.3$; (**c**) FrDE, $\alpha = 0.1\&0.3$; (**d**) FrFDE, $\alpha = -0.3\&-0.1$; (**e**) PSO-FrSlEn, $\alpha = -0.3\&0.2$; (**f**) PSO-FrSlEn, $\alpha = -0.2\&0.2$; (**g**) PSO-FrSlEn, $\alpha = -0.1\&0.1$; (**h**) PSO-FrSlEn, $\alpha = -0.1\&0.2$; (**i**) PSO-FrSlEn, $\alpha = 0\&0.1$.

5.2. Classification Effect Verification

KNN is used as a classifier to classify these double features, and the parameter settings are the same as those in the single feature experiment. The highest classification accuracy of each entropy calculated by the program is shown in Table 2 below. A line graph is drawn in Figure 9 for comparison, where 1 to 21 on the abscissa axis represent the double feature combinations from $-0.3\ \&\ 0.2$ to $0.2\ \&\ 0.3$ respectively.

Table 2. The highest accuracy of each entropy under different double feature combinations.

Entropy	Fractional Order Combinations	Accuracy (%)
FrPE	$-0.3\&0$	78.67
FrWPE	$-0.3\&0.3$	72.67
FrDE	$0.1\&0.3$	96
FrFDE	$-0.3\&-0.1$	89.33
PSO-FrSlEn	$-0.3\&0.2$	100
	$-0.2\&0.2$	100
	$-0.1\&0.1$	100
	$-0.1\&0.2$	100
	$0\&0.1$	100

As can be seen from the data in Table 2, there are five double feature combinations of PSO-FrSlEn, which can make the feature classification accuracy up to be the highest, and the highest accuracy is 100%; the highest classification accuracy of the other four kinds of entropies is only 96% of FrDE, and the lowest one is 72.67% of FrWPE. The line graph in Figure 9 shows that most double feature combinations of PSO-FrSlEn has higher classification accuracy than the other kinds of entropies. These conclusions are sufficient to prove that the features of PSO-FrSlEn are the most significant to distinguish the 10 kinds of bearing signals.

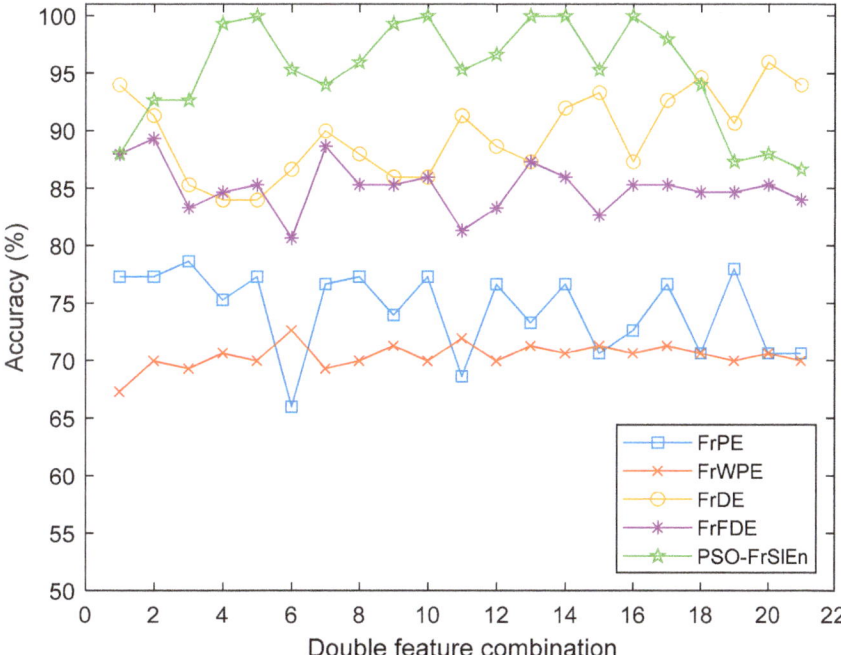

Figure 9. The classification accuracies under different double feature combinations.

6. Conclusions

In this paper, the fractional order is combined with the five kinds of entropies, which are PE, WPE, DE, FDE and SlEn, and the features of these five kinds of entropies are extracted for the 10 kinds of bearing signals. Single feature experiment and double feature experiment are carried out respectively. KNN is used to classify these features to verify the significant degree of various features. The main innovations and experimental comparison results are as follows:

(1) As an algorithm proposed in 2019, SlEn has not been proposed any improved algorithm. It is proposed for the first time to combine the concept of fractional information with SlEn, and get an improved algorithm of SlEn named FrSlEn.

(2) In order to solve the influence of the two threshold parameters of SlEn on feature significance, PSO is selected to optimize the two threshold parameters, which assists FrSlEn to make the extracted features more significant.

(3) In the experiment of single feature extraction, under any values of α, the classification accuracies of PSO-FrSlEn are the highest. The classification accuracies of PSO-FrSlEn are higher than that of PSO-SlEn, where 88% is the highest classification accuracy of PSO-FrSlEn under $\alpha = -0.3$. The highest classification accuracy of PSO-FrSlEn is at least 5.33% higher than FrPE, FrWPE, FrDE, and FrFDE.

(4) In the experiment of double feature extraction, the classification accuracies of PSO-FrSlEn under five double feature combinations are 100%. The highest classification accuracies of FrPE, FrWPE, FrDE, and FrFDE are at least 4% less than PSO-FrSlEn, where the highest classification accuracy of FrWPE is 27.33% less than PSO-FrSlEn.

Author Contributions: Conceptualization, Y.L.; Data curation, L.M.; Formal analysis, Y.L.; Methodology, Y.L.; Project administration, L.M.; Resources, Y.L.; Supervision, P.G.; Validation, Y.L.; Writing—review & editing, P.G. All authors have read and agreed to the published version of the manuscript.

Funding: This research was funded by [the National Natural Science Foundation of China] grant number [61903297], [Young Talent Fund of University Association for Science and Technology in Shaanxi] grant number [20210114], [Natural Science Foundation of Shaanxi Province] grant number [2022JM-337].

Institutional Review Board Statement: Not applicable.

Informed Consent Statement: Not applicable.

Data Availability Statement: The data used to support the findings of this study are available from the corresponding author upon request.

Conflicts of Interest: The authors declare no conflict of interests.

Nomenclature

PE	Permutation entropy
WPE	Weighted permutation entropy
DE	Dispersion entropy
FDE	Fluctuation dispersion entropy
SlEn	Slope entropy
PSO-SlEn	Particle swarm optimization slope entropy
FrPE	Fractional permutation entropy
FrWPE	Fractional weighted permutation entropy
FrDE	Fractional dispersion entropy
FrFDE	Fractional fluctuation dispersion entropy
FrSlEn	Fractional slope entropy
PSO-FrSlEn	Particle swarm optimization fractional slope entropy
α	Fractional order
m	Embedding dimension
τ	Time lag
c	Number of classes
NCDF	Normal cumulative distribution function
η	Large threshold
ε	Small threshold
N-100	Normal signals
IR-108	Inner race fault signals (fault diameter size: 0.007 inch)
B-121	Ball fault signals (fault diameter size: 0.007 inch)
OR-133	Outer race fault signals (fault diameter size: 0.007 inch)
IR-172	Inner race fault signals (fault diameter size: 0.014 inch)
B-188	Ball fault signals (fault diameter size: 0.014 inch)
OR-200	Outer race fault signals (fault diameter size: 0.014 inch)
IR-212	Inner race fault signals (fault diameter size: 0.021 inch)
B-225	Ball fault signals (fault diameter size: 0.021 inch)
OR-237	Outer race fault signals (fault diameter size: 0.021 inch)
KNN	K-Nearest Neighbor

References

1. Tsallis, C. Possible generalization of Boltzmann-Gibbs statistics. *J. Stat. Phys.* **1988**, *52*, 479–487. [CrossRef]
2. Rényi, A. On measures of entropy and information. *Virology* **1985**, *142*, 158–174.
3. Yin, Y.; Sun, K.; He, S. Multiscale permutation Rényi entropy and its application for EEG signals. *PLoS ONE* **2018**, *13*, 0202558. [CrossRef]
4. Richman, J.S.; Moorman, J.R. Physiological time-series analysis using approximate entropy and sample entropy. *Am. J. Physiol.-Heart Circ. Physiol.* **2000**, *6*, 2039–2049. [CrossRef]
5. Zair, M.; Rahmoune, C.; Benazzouz, D. Multi-fault diagnosis of rolling bearing using fuzzy entropy of empirical mode decomposition, principal component analysis, and SOM neural network. *Proc. Inst. Mech. Eng. Part C* **2019**, *233*, 3317–3328. [CrossRef]
6. Lin, J.; Lin, J. Divergence measures based on the Shannon entropy. *IEEE Trans. Inf. Theory* **1991**, *37*, 145–151. [CrossRef]
7. Bandt, C.; Pompe, B. Permutation entropy: A natural complexity measure for time series. *Phys. Rev. Lett.* **2002**, *88*, 174102. [CrossRef]

8. Rostaghi, M.; Azami, H. Dispersion Entropy: A Measure for Time Series Analysis. *IEEE Signal Process. Lett.* **2016**, *23*, 610–614. [CrossRef]
9. Tylová, L.; Kukal, J.; Hubata-Vacek, V.; Vyšata, O. Unbiased estimation of permutation entropy in EEG analysis for Alzheimer's disease classification. *Biomed. Signal Process. Control.* **2018**, *39*, 424–430. [CrossRef]
10. Rostaghi, M.; Ashory, M.R.; Azami, H. Application of dispersion entropy to status characterization of rotary machines. *J. Sound Vib.* **2019**, *438*, 291–308. [CrossRef]
11. Qu, J.; Shi, C.; Ding, F.; Wang, W. A novel aging state recognition method of a viscoelastic sandwich structure based on permutation entropy of dual-tree complex wavelet packet transform and generalized Chebyshev support vector machine. *Struct. Health Monit.* **2020**, *19*, 156–172. [CrossRef]
12. Azami, H.; Escudero, J. Improved multiscale permutation entropy for biomedical signal analysis: Interpretation and application to electroencephalogram recordings. *Biomed. Signal Process. Control.* **2016**, *23*, 28–41. [CrossRef]
13. Zhang, W.; Zhou, J. A Comprehensive Fault Diagnosis Method for Rolling Bearings Based on Refined Composite Multiscale Dispersion Entropy and Fast Ensemble Empirical Mode Decomposition. *Entropy* **2019**, *21*, 680. [CrossRef] [PubMed]
14. Feng, F.; Rao, G.; Jiang, P.; Si, A. Research on early fault diagnosis for rolling bearing based on permutation entropy algorithm. In Proceedings of the IEEE Prognostics and System Health Management Conference, Beijing, China, 23–25 May 2012; Volume 10, pp. 1–5.
15. Fadlallah, B.; Chen, B.; Keil, A. Weighted-permutation entropy: A complexity measure for time series incorporating amplitude information. *Phys. Rev. E* **2013**, *87*, 022911. [CrossRef] [PubMed]
16. Xie, D.; Hong, S.; Yao, C. Optimized Variational Mode Decomposition and Permutation Entropy with Their Application in Feature Extraction of Ship-Radiated Noise. *Entropy* **2021**, *23*, 503. [CrossRef]
17. Li, D.; Li, X.; Liang, Z.; Voss, L.J.; Sleigh, J.W. Multiscale permutation entropy analysis of EEG recordings during sevoflurane anesthesia. *J. Neural Eng.* **2010**, *7*, 046010. [CrossRef]
18. Deng, B.; Cai, L.; Li, S.; Wang, R.; Yu, H.; Chen, Y. Multivariate multi-scale weighted permutation entropy analysis of EEG complexity for Alzheimer's disease. *Cogn. Neurodyn.* **2017**, *11*, 217–231. [CrossRef]
19. Zhenya, W.; Ligang, Y.; Gang, C.; Jiaxin, D. Modified multiscale weighted permutation entropy and optimized support vector machine method for rolling bearing fault diagnosis with complex signals. *ISA Trans.* **2021**, *114*, 470–480.
20. Li, R.; Ran, C.; Luo, J.; Feng, S.; Zhang, B. Rolling bearing fault diagnosis method based on dispersion entropy and SVM. In Proceedings of the International Conference on Sensing, Diagnostics, Prognostics, and Control (SDPC), Beijing, China, 15–17 August 2019; Volume 10, pp. 596–600.
21. Azami, H.; Escudero, J. Amplitude- and Fluctuation-Based Dispersion Entropy. *Entropy* **2018**, *20*, 210. [CrossRef]
22. Zami, H.; Rostaghi, M.; Abásolo, D.; Javier, E. Refined Composite Multiscale Dispersion Entropy and its Application to Biomedical Signals. *IEEE Trans. Biomed. Eng.* **2017**, *64*, 2872–2879.
23. Li, Z.; Li, Y.; Zhang, K. A Feature Extraction Method of Ship-Radiated Noise Based on Fluctuation-Based Dispersion Entropy and Intrinsic Time-Scale Decomposition. *Entropy* **2019**, *21*, 693. [CrossRef] [PubMed]
24. Zheng, J.; Pan, H. Use of generalized refined composite multiscale fractional dispersion entropy to diagnose the faults of rolling bearing. *Nonlinear Dyn.* **2021**, *101*, 1417–1440. [CrossRef]
25. Ali, K. Fractional order entropy: New perspectives. *Opt.-Int. J. Light Electron Opt.* **2016**, *127*, 9172–9177.
26. He, S.; Sun, K. Fractional fuzzy entropy algorithm and the complexity analysis for nonlinear time series. *Eur. Phys. J. Spec. Top.* **2018**, *227*, 943–957. [CrossRef]
27. Cuesta-Frau, D. Slope Entropy: A New Time Series Complexity Estimator Based on Both Symbolic Patterns and Amplitude Information. *Entropy* **2019**, *21*, 1167. [CrossRef]
28. Cuesta-Frau, D.; Dakappa, P.H.; Mahabala, C.; Gupta, A.R. Fever Time Series Analysis Using Slope Entropy. Application to Early Unobtrusive Differential Diagnosis. *Entropy* **2020**, *22*, 1034. [CrossRef]
29. Cuesta-Frau, D.; Schneider, J.; Bakštein, E.; Vostatek, P.; Spaniel, F.; Novák, D. Classification of Actigraphy Records from Bipolar Disorder Patients Using Slope Entropy: A Feasibility Study. *Entropy* **2020**, *22*, 1243. [CrossRef]
30. Li, Y.; Gao, P.; Tang, B. Double Feature Extraction Method of Ship-Radiated Noise Signal Based on Slope Entropy and Permutation Entropy. *Entropy* **2022**, *24*, 22. [CrossRef]
31. Shi, E. Single Feature Extraction Method of Bearing Fault Signals Based on Slope Entropy. *Shock. Vib.* **2022**, *2022*, 6808641. [CrossRef]
32. Case Western Reserve University. Available online: https://engineering.case.edu/bearingdatacenter/pages/welcome-case-western-reserve-university-bearing-data-center-website (accessed on 17 October 2021).

Article

Sensitivity of Uniformly Convergent Mapping Sequences in Non-Autonomous Discrete Dynamical Systems

Yongxi Jiang [1], Xiaofang Yang [1,*] and Tianxiu Lu [1,2,*]

[1] College of Mathematics and Statistics, Sichuan University of Science and Engineering, Zigong 643000, China; jyx970817@163.com

[2] The Key Laboratory of Higher Education of Sichuan Province for Enterprise Informationalization and Internet of Things, Zigong 643000, China

* Correspondence: yxf_suse@163.com (X.Y.); lubeeltx@163.com (T.L.); Tel.: +86-134-0813-8464 (X.Y.)

Abstract: Let H be a compact metric space. The metric of H is denoted by d. And let $(H, f_{1,\infty})$ be a non-autonomous discrete system where $f_{1,\infty} = \{f_n\}_{n=1}^{\infty}$ is a mapping sequence. This paper discusses infinite sensitivity, m-sensitivity, and m-cofinitely sensitivity of $f_{1,\infty}$. It is proved that, if $f_n(n \in \mathbb{N})$ are feebly open and uniformly converge to $f : H \to H$, $f_i \circ f = f \circ f_i$ for any $i \in \{1, 2, \ldots\}$, and $\sum_{i=1}^{\infty} D(f_i, f) < \infty$, then (H, f) has the above sensitive property if and only if $(H, f_{1,\infty})$ has the same property where $D(\cdot, \cdot)$ is the supremum metric.

Keywords: sensitivity; uniformly converge; non-autonomous discrete systems

MSC: 54H20; 37B45

Citation: Jiang, Y.; Yang, X.; Lu, T. Sensitivity of Uniformly Convergent Mapping Sequences in Non-Autonomous Discrete Dynamical Systems. *Fractal Fract.* **2022**, *6*, 319. https://doi.org/10.3390/fractalfract6060319

Academic Editor: Viorel-Puiu Paun

Received: 16 April 2022
Accepted: 30 May 2022
Published: 7 June 2022

Publisher's Note: MDPI stays neutral with regard to jurisdictional claims in published maps and institutional affiliations.

Copyright: © 2022 by the authors. Licensee MDPI, Basel, Switzerland. This article is an open access article distributed under the terms and conditions of the Creative Commons Attribution (CC BY) license (https://creativecommons.org/licenses/by/4.0/).

1. Introduction

Chaos, as a universal motion form of topological dynamical systems, is one of the core contents of the research for dynamical systems. At present, fruitful results of chaos theory have been obtained in autonomous discrete dynamical systems. However, many complex systems in real life, such as medicine, biology, and physics, are difficult to describe by autonomous systems. Therefore, it is necessary to use other models (for example, non-autonomous discrete systems). Since 1996, chaos of non-autonomous discrete dynamical systems (for convenience, we abbreviate it to NDDS) has began to be studied [1]. In recent years, the discussion about the chaotic properties in NDDS has been active. Si [2] gives some sufficient conditions for NDDS to have asymptotically stable sets. Lan and Peris [3] showed the relation between the weak stability of an NDDS and its induced set-valued system. Li, Zhao, and Wang [4] studied stronger forms of sensitivity and transitivity for NDDS by using the Furstenberg family. Meanwhile, under the condition $\lim_{n \to \infty} d_\infty(g_m^m, g^m) = 0$, a necessary and sufficient condition for g to be $\mathcal{F}$-mixing is established in [5]. Vasisht and Das [6] discussed the difference between $\mathcal{F}$-sensitivity and some other stronger forms of sensitivity by some examples. Salman and Das [7] proved that on a compact metric space, every finitely generated NDDS which is topologically transitive and has a dense set of periodic points is thickly syndetically sensitive. Vasisht and Das [8] proved that if the rate of convergence at which (f_n) converges to f is "sufficiently fast", then various forms of sensitivity for the autonomous system (X, f) and the NDDS $(X, f_{1,\infty})$ coincide. For the chaoticity of other maps in NDDS, see [9–12] and other literature.

This paper further studies the chaotic properties in the sense of sensitivity. The basic definitions of chaos are given in Section 2. In Section 3, under the conditions of that, $f_n : H \to H(n \in \mathbb{N})$ are feebly open and uniformly converge to $f : H \to H$, $f_i \circ f = f \circ f_i$ for any $i \in \{1, 2, \ldots\}$, and $\sum_{i=1}^{\infty} D(f_i, f) < \infty$. This paper proves that (H, f) is $\mathcal{Q}$-sensitive if and only if $(H, f_{1,\infty})$ is $\mathcal{Q}$-sensitive where $D(\cdot, \cdot)$ is the supremum metric (see Section 3),

Q-sensitive denotes one of the four properties: accessible, infinitely sensitive, m-sensitive, and m-cofinitely sensitive.

2. Preliminaries

For any initial value $x_0 \in H$, the orbit of x under $f_{1,\infty}$ is denoted by $\{f_n \circ f_{n-1} \circ \cdots \circ f_1(x_0) : n \in \mathbb{N}\}$.

A subset K of $\mathbb{N}$ is *cofinite* [4,5] if there exists a $N \in \mathbb{N}$ such that $[N, +\infty] \subset K$.

A system $(H, f_{1,\infty})$ (or maps sequence $\{f_n\}_{n \in \mathbb{N}}$) is called "feebly open" [4,5] if for any nonempty open subset V of H, $int(f_n(V)) \neq \phi$ for any $n \in \mathbb{N}$. Where $int A$ denotes the interior of set A.

A pair (x, y) is proximal [13] for $(H, f_{1,\infty})$ if for any $x \in H$, $\liminf\limits_{n \mapsto \infty} d(f_1^n(x), f_1^n(y)) = 0$.

Definition 1 ([14]). *A system $(H, f_{1,\infty})$ is "spatio-temporal chaotic" if for any $x \in H$ and each neighborhood V of x, there is a $y \in V$ such that $\limsup\limits_{n \mapsto \infty} d(f_1^n(a), f_1^n(b)) > 0$ but $\liminf\limits_{n \mapsto \infty} d(f_1^n(a), f_1^n(b)) = 0$.*

Definition 2 ([4,5]). *A system $(H, f_{1,\infty})$ is called "sensitive dependent on initial condition" if there exists an $\eta > 0$ such that for any $x \in H$ and $\varepsilon > 0$, there exists a $y \in B(x, \varepsilon)$ and an $n \in \mathbb{N}$ such that $d(f_1^n(x), f_1^n(y)) > \eta$.*

Definition 3 ([7,8]). *A system $(H, f_{1,\infty})$ is called "infinitely sensitive" if there exists an $\eta > 0$ such that, for any $x \in H$ and $\varepsilon > 0$, one can find a $y \in B(x, \varepsilon)$ and an $n \in \mathbb{N}$ such that $\limsup\limits_{n \to \infty} d(f_1^n(x), f_1^n(y)) \geq \eta$.*

Definition 4 ([15]). *A system $(H, f_{1,\infty})$ is called "accessible" if for any $\varepsilon > 0$ and any two nonempty open subsets $U_1, U_2 \subset H$, there are two points $x \in U_1$ and $y \in U_2$ such that $d(f_1^n(x), f_1^n(y))) < \varepsilon$ for some integer $n > 0$.*

For convenience, write

$$A(U, m, n) = \min\{d(f_1^n(x_i), f_1^n(y_j)) : x_i, y_j \in U, i, j \in \{1, 2, \ldots, m\}, i \neq j\}$$

and

$S_{f_{1,\infty}, m}(U, \lambda) = \{n \in \mathbb{N}: \text{there is } x_i, y_j \in U \ (i, j \in \{1, 2, \ldots, m\}, i \neq j) \text{ such that } A(U, m, n) \geq \lambda\}$,

where $m, n \in \mathbb{N}$, U is an arbitrary nonempty open subset in X.

Definition 5 ([16]). *Given an integer m with $m \geq 2$. The system $(H, f_{1,\infty})$ is called "m-sensitive", if there is a real number $\lambda > 0$ such that for any nonempty open subset U of H, there are $2m$ points $x_1, x_2, \ldots, x_m; y_1, y_2, \ldots, y_m \in U$ such that $S_{f_{1,\infty}, m}(U, \lambda)$ is nonempty.*

Definition 6 ([16]). *Given an integer m with $m \geq 2$. The system $(H, f_{1,\infty})$ is called "m-cofinitely sensitive", if there is a real number $\lambda > 0$ such that for any nonempty open subset U of H, there are $2m$ points $x_1, x_2, \ldots, x_m; y_1, y_2, \ldots, y_m \in U$ such that $S_{f_{1,\infty}, m}(U, \lambda)$ is a cofinite set.*

3. The Relation of Chaoticity between $f_{1,\infty}$ and Its Limit Map f

Let $\mathcal{C}(H)$ be the set of all continuous self-maps on (H, d). For any $f, g \in \mathcal{C}(H)$, the supremum metric (see [4]) is defined by $D(f, g) = \sup\limits_{x \in H} d(f(x), g(x))$. This section will give equivalence of chaotic properties between $(H, f_{1,\infty})$ and (H, f).

Lemma 1 ([5]). *Let $(H, f_{1,\infty})$ be an NDDS on a nontrivial compact metric space (H, d) and $f \in C(H)$. If $f_i \circ f = f \circ f_i$ for any $i \in \{1, 2, \dots\}$, then for any $x \in H$, any integer $q \geq 1$ and any integer $p \geq 1$ one has*

$$d(f_1^{q+p}(x), f^q(f_1^p(x))) \leq \sum_{j=p+1}^{q+p} D(f_j, f).$$

Theorem 1. *If $f_n (n \in \mathbb{N})$ are a feebly open mapping sequence which uniformly converges to f, $f_i \circ f = f \circ f_i$ for any $i \in \{1, 2, \dots\}$, and $\sum_{i=1}^{\infty} D(f_i, f) < \infty$, then (H, f) is accessible if and only if $(H, f_{1,\infty})$ is accessible.*

Proof. Suppose that (H, f) is accessible. Given $\varepsilon > 0$, let U, V are two nonempty open subsets in H. Because $f_i \circ f = f \circ f_i$ for any $i \in \{1, 2, \dots\}$, by Lemma 1, for the above $\varepsilon > 0$, $d(f_1^{p^0+q}(x), f^q(f_1^{p^0}(x))) < \sum_{j=p_0+1}^{q+p_0} D(f_j, f)$ for any $x \in H$ and any integer $p^0, q \geq 1$. Moreover, because $\sum_{i=1}^{\infty} D(f_i, f) < \infty$, then there is an integer $S_0 \geq 1$ such that $\sum_{j=s}^{\infty} D(f_j, f) < \frac{1}{3}\varepsilon$ for any $s \geq s_0$. Combine with the arbitrariness of p_0, q, one can get that $d(f_1^{p^0+q}(x), f^q(f_1^{p^0}(x))) < \frac{\varepsilon}{3}$. Because $f_i (i \in \{1, 2, \dots\})$ are feebly open, the interiors of $f_1^{p^0}(U)$ and $f_1^{p^0}(V)$ are nonempty sets. Let U', V' be the interiors of $f_1^{p^0}(U)$ and $f_1^{p^0}(V)$, respectively.

Because (H, f) is accessible, for the above $\varepsilon > 0$, there are $x \in U'$ and $y \in V'$ such that $d(f^q(x), f^q(y)) < \frac{\varepsilon}{3}$ for some $q > 0$. Then, there exist $x' \in U, y' \in V$ satisfying $x = f_1^{p^0}(x')$, $y = f_1^{p^0}(y')$. Thus, $d(f^q(f_1^{p^0}(x')), f^q(f_1^{p^0}(y'))) < \frac{\varepsilon}{3}$. Noting that $d(f_1^{q+p^0}(x), f^q(f_1^{p^0}(x))) < \frac{\varepsilon}{3}$ for $x \in H$, by triangle inequality, one has that

$$\begin{aligned}
d(f_1^{p^0+q}(x'), f_1^{p^0+q}(y')) &\leq d(f_1^{p^0+q}(x'), f^q(f_1^{p^0})(x')) + d(f^q(f_1^{p^0})(x'), f^q(f_1^{p^0})(y')) \\
&\quad + d(f_1^{p^0+q}(y'), f^q(f_1^{p^0})(y')) \\
&\leq \frac{\varepsilon}{3} + \frac{\varepsilon}{3} + \frac{\varepsilon}{3} \\
&= \varepsilon.
\end{aligned}$$

Hence, $(H, f_{1,\infty})$ is accessible.

Now, suppose that $(H, f_{1,\infty})$ is accessible. For a given $\varepsilon > 0$, let $U, V \subset H$ be nonempty and open. Because $\sum_{i=1}^{\infty} D(f_i, f) < \infty$, by Lemma 1, there is an integer $p^0 \geq 1$ such that for the above $\varepsilon > 0$, $x \in H$, $d(f_1^{p^0+q}(x), f^q(f_1^{p^0}(x))) < \frac{\varepsilon}{3}$ for any integer $q \geq 1$. Because $f_i (i \in \{1, 2, \dots\})$ are feebly open, then the interiors of $f_1^{p^0}(U)$ and $f_1^{p^0}(V)$ are nonempty sets. Let U', V' be the interiors of $f_1^{p^0}(U)$ and $f_1^{p^0}(V)$, respectively.

Because $(H, f_{1,\infty})$ is accessible for the above $\varepsilon > 0$, there are $x \in U$ and $y \in V$ such that $d(f_1^{q+p^0}(x), f_1^{q+p^0}(y)) < \frac{\varepsilon}{3}$ for some $q > 0$. Then, there exist $x' \in U', y' \in V'$ satisfying $x' = f_1^{p^0}(x), y' = f_1^{p^0}(y)$. Noted that $d(f_1^{q+p^0}(x), f^q(x')) < \frac{\varepsilon}{3}$, by triangle inequality,

$$d(f^q(x'), f^q(y'))$$
$$\leq d(f^q(x'), f^{q+p^0}(x)) + d(f^{q+p^0}(x), f^{q+p^0}(y)) + d(f^q(y'), f^{q+p^0}(y)) < \varepsilon.$$

Hence, (H, f) is accessible. □

Theorem 2. *If $f_n (n \in \mathbb{N})$ is a feebly open mapping sequence which uniformly converges to f, $f_i \circ f = f \circ f_i$ for any $i \in \{1, 2, \dots\}$, and $\sum_{i=1}^{\infty} D(f_i, f) < \infty$, then (H, f) is infinitely sensitive if and only if $(H, f_{1,\infty})$ is infinitely sensitive.*

Proof. Suppose that (H, f) is infinitely sensitive with $\lambda > 0$ as an infinitely sensitive constant. Let $\varepsilon > 0$, $U \subset H$ is a nonempty open set. Because $\sum_{i=1}^{\infty} D(f_i, f) < \infty$, by Lemma

1, there is an integer $p \geq 1$ such that $d(f_1^{p+q}(x), f^q(f_1^p(x))) < \varepsilon$ for any integer $q \geq 1$, $x \in H$ and the above $\varepsilon > 0$. Taking an integer $k \in \{1, 2, \dots\}$ satisfying $k > \frac{4}{\lambda}$. Then, there is an integer $p^0 \geq 1$ such that $d(f_1^{p^0+q}(x), f^q(f_1^{p^0}(x))) < \frac{1}{k}$ for any integer $q \geq 1$ and $x \in H$. Because f_i is feebly open ($i \in \{1, 2, \dots\}$), then the interior of $f_1^{p^0}(U)$ is nonempty. Let U' be the interior of $f_1^{p^0}(U)$. Because (H, f) is infinitely sensitive with infinitely sensitive constant $\lambda > 0$, then there is a $y \in U'$ such that $\limsup_{q \to \infty} d(f^q(x), f^q(y)) > \lambda$. Because

$$x = f_1^{p^0}(x'), y = f_1^{p^0}(y'), \limsup_{q \to \infty} d(f^q(f_1^{p^0}(x')), f^q(f_1^{p^0}(y'))) > \lambda,$$

and because

$$d(f_1^{p^0+q}(x'), f^q(f_1^{p^0}(x'))) < \tfrac{1}{k} \quad \text{and} \quad d(f_1^{p^0+q}(y'), f^q(f_1^{p^0}(y'))) < \tfrac{1}{k}$$

for any integer $q \geq 1$. By triangle inequality,

$$d(f_1^{p^0+q}(x'), f_1^{p^0+q}(y')) > \lambda - \frac{2}{k} > \frac{1}{2}\lambda.$$

Taking the upper limit of both sides of the inequality, one has that

$$\limsup_{q \to \infty} d(f^{q+p^0}(x'), f^{q+p^0}(y')) > \tfrac{1}{2}\lambda.$$

Therefore, $(H, f_{1,\infty})$ is infinitely sensitive.

Conversely, let $(H, f_{1,\infty})$ be infinitely sensitive with $\lambda > 0$ as an infinitely sensitive constant. Let $\varepsilon > 0$, $U \subset H$ be a nonempty open set. Because $\sum_{i=1}^{\infty} D(f_i, f) < \infty$, by Lemma 1, there is an integer $p \geq 1$ such that $d(f_1^{p+q}(x), f^q(f_1^p(x))) < \varepsilon$ for any integer $q \geq 1$, $x \in H$, and the above $\varepsilon > 0$. Taking an integer $k \in \{1, 2, \dots\}$ satisfying $k > \frac{4}{\lambda}$. Then, there is an integer $p^0 \geq 1$ such that $d(f_1^{p^0+q}(x), f^q(f_1^{p^0}(x))) < \frac{1}{k}$ for any integer $q \geq 1$ and $x \in H$. Because f_i is feebly open ($i \in \{1, 2, \dots\}$), the interior of $f_1^{p^0}(U)$ is nonempty. Let U' be the interior of $f_1^{p^0}(U)$. Because $(H, f_{1,\infty})$ is infinitely sensitive with $\lambda > 0$ as a sensitive constant, then there is a $y \in U'$ such that $\limsup_{q \to \infty} d(f_1^{q+p^0}(x), f_1^{q+p^0}(y)) > \lambda$. So, there exist $x', y' \in U$ such that $x' = f_1^{p^0}(x), y' = f_1^{p^0}(y)$. Noted that

$$d(f_1^{p^0+q}(x), f^q(f_1^{p^0}(x))) < \tfrac{1}{k} \quad \text{and} \quad d(f_1^{p^0+q}(y), f^q(f_1^{p^0}(y))) < \tfrac{1}{k}$$

for any integer $q \geq 1$, then

$$d(f_1^{p^0+q}(x), f^q(x')) < \tfrac{1}{k} \quad \text{and} \quad d(f_1^{p^0+q}(y), f^q(y')) < \tfrac{1}{k}$$

for any integer $q \geq 1$. By triangle inequality, one has that

$$d(f^q(x'), f^q(y')) > \lambda - \tfrac{2}{k} > \tfrac{1}{2}\lambda.$$

Taking the upper limit of both sides of the inequality, one has that $\limsup_{q \to \infty} d(f^q(x'), f^q(y'))) > \tfrac{1}{2}\lambda$. Consequently, (H, f) is infinitely sensitive. □

Theorem 3. *If $f_n(n \in \mathbb{N})$ is a feebly open mapping sequence which uniformly converges to f, $f_i \circ f = f \circ f_i$ for any $i \in \{1, 2, \ldots\}$, and $\sum_{i=1}^{\infty} D(f_i, f) < \infty$, then (H, f) is m-sensitive if and only if $(H, f_{1,\infty})$ is m-sensitive.*

Proof. Suppose that (H, f) is m-sensitive with m-sensitive constant $\lambda > 0$. Let $\varepsilon > 0$ and a open set $U \subset H : U \neq \phi$. Because $\sum_{i=1}^{\infty} D(f_i, f) < \infty$, by Lemma 1, there is an integer $p \geq 1$ such that $d(f_1^{p+q}(x), f^q(f_1^p(x))) < \varepsilon$ for any integer $q \geq 1$, $x \in H$, and the above $\varepsilon > 0$. Taking $m \in \{1, 2, \ldots\}$ with $m > \frac{4}{\lambda}$. Then, there is an integer $p^0 \geq 1$ such that $d(f_1^{p^0+q}(x), f^q(f_1^{p^0}(x))) < \frac{1}{m}$ for any integer $q \geq 1$ and $x \in H$. Because f_i is feebly open for all $i \in \{1, 2, \ldots\}$, the interior of $f_1^{p^0}(U)$ is nonempty. Let U' be the interior of $f_1^{p^0}(U)$. Because (H, f) is m-sensitive with m-sensitive constant $\lambda > 0$, there are m points $x_1, x_2, \ldots, x_m \in U'$ and a $q \in \mathbb{N}$ such that

$$\min\{d(f^q(x_i), f^q(x_j)) : i, j \in \{1, 2, \ldots, m\} i \neq j\} \geq \lambda.$$

Because $x_1, x_2, \ldots, x_m \in f_1^{p^0}(U)$, there are $x'_1, x'_2, \ldots, x'_m \in U$ satisfying $x_1 = f_1^{p^0}(x'_1)$, $x_2 = f_1^{p^0}(x'_2), \ldots, x_m = f_1^{p^0}(x'_m)$ and

$$\min\{d(f^q(f_1^{p^0}(x'_i)), f^q(f_1^{p^0}(x'_j))) : i, j \in \{1, 2, \ldots, m\} i \neq j\} \geq \lambda.$$

And because $d(f_1^{p^0+q}(x'_i), f^q(f_1^{p^0}(x'_i))) < \frac{1}{m}$ for any $i = 1, 2, \ldots, m$. By triangle inequality,

$$\min\{d(f_1^{p^0+q}(x'_i), f_1^{p^0+q}(x'_j)) : i, j \in \{1, 2, \ldots, m\} i \neq j\} \geq \lambda - \frac{2}{m} > \frac{1}{2}\lambda.$$

This implies $(H, f_{1,\infty})$ is m-sensitive.

Conversely, let $\varepsilon > 0$ and $U \subset H : U \neq \phi$ be an open set. Because $\sum_{i=1}^{\infty} D(f_i, f) < \infty$, by Lemma 1, there is an integer $p \geq 1$ such that $d(f_1^{p+q}(x), f^q(f_1^p(x))) < \varepsilon$ for any integer $q \geq 1$ $x \in H$, and the above $\varepsilon > 0$. Taking $m \in \{1, 2, \ldots\}$ with $m > \frac{4}{\lambda}$. Then, there is an integer $p^0 \geq 1$ such that $d(f_1^{p^0+q}(x), f^q(f_1^{p^0}(x))) < \frac{1}{m}$ for any integer $q \geq 1$ and $x \in H$. Because f_i is feebly open for all $i \in \{1, 2, \ldots\}$, the interior of $f_1^{p^0}(U)$ is nonempty. Let U' be the interior of $f_1^{p^0}(U)$. Because $(H, f_{1,\infty})$ is m-sensitive with $\lambda > 0$ as a sensitive constant, there are m points $x_1, x_2, \ldots, x_m \in U'$ and $p^0 > 0$ such that $\min\{d(f_1^q(x_i), f_1^q(x_j)) : i \neq j \in \{1, 2, \ldots, m\}\} > \lambda$ for any integer $q > 0$. Because $x_1, x_2, \ldots, x_m \in U'$, then there are $x'_1, x'_2, \ldots, x'_m \in U$ satisfying $x_1 = f_1^{p^0}(x'_1), x_2 = f_1^{p^0}(x'_2), \ldots, x_m = f_1^{p^0}(x'_m)$. And because $d(f_1^{p^0+q}(x'_i), f^q(f_1^{p^0}(x'_i))) < \frac{1}{m}$ for any $i \in \{1, 2, \ldots, m\}$, then $d(f_1^{p^0+q}(x'_i), f^q(x_i)) < \frac{1}{m}$ for any $i \in \{1, 2, \ldots, m\}$. By triangle inequality, one has that

$$\min\{d(f^q(x'_i), f^q(x'_j)) : i \neq j \in \{1, 2, \ldots, m\}\} > \lambda - \frac{2}{m} > \frac{1}{2}\lambda.$$

Hence, (H, f) is m-sensitive with $\frac{1}{2}\lambda$ as an m-sensitive constant. □

Theorem 4. *If $f_n(n \in \mathbb{N})$ is a feebly open mapping sequence which uniformly converge to f, $f_i \circ f = f \circ f_i$ for any $i \in \{1, 2, \ldots\}$, and $\sum_{i=1}^{\infty} D(f_i, f) < \infty$, then (H, f) is m-cofinitely sensitive if and only if $(H, f_{1,\infty})$ is m-cofinitely sensitive.*

Proof. This proof is similar to that of Theorem 1, and hence is omitted. □

Example 1. *Let H be the compact interval [0,1] and g, h be defined by $g(x) = x$ for any $x \in [0, 1]$ and*

$$h(x) = \begin{cases} 2x + \dfrac{1}{3} & for \quad x \in [0, \dfrac{1}{3}] \\ -3x + 2 & for \quad x \in [\dfrac{1}{3}, \dfrac{2}{3}] \\ x - \dfrac{2}{3} & for \quad x \in [\dfrac{2}{3}, 1] \end{cases}.$$

In fact, for any nonempty open subset V of H, $int(h(V)) \neq \phi$. Then $h(x)$ is feeble open. It is easy to know that, for any $x_1, x_2 \in [0,1] : x_1 \neq x_2$ (without loss of generality, $x_1 < x_2$), the following conclusions are held.

If $x_1, x_2 \in [0, \frac{1}{3}]$ or $x_1, x_2 \in [\frac{1}{3}, \frac{2}{3}]$ or $x_1, x_2 \in [\frac{2}{3}, 1]$, one can get that

$$| h(x_1) - h(x_2) | \geq | x_1 - x_2 |.$$

If $x_1 \in [0, \frac{1}{3}], x_2 \in [\frac{1}{3}, \frac{2}{3}]$, one has

$$| h(x_1) - h(x_2) | = | 2x_1 + \dfrac{1}{3} - (-3x_2 + 2) | = | 2x_1 + 3x_2 - \dfrac{5}{3} | > | x_1 + \dfrac{3}{2}x_2 - \dfrac{5}{6} |.$$

If $x_1 \in [\frac{1}{3}, \frac{2}{3}], x_2 \in [\frac{2}{3}, 1]$, one has

$$| h(x_1) - h(x_2) | = | -3x_1 + 2 - (x_2 - \dfrac{2}{3}) | = | 3x_1 + x_2 - \dfrac{8}{3} | > | x_1 + \dfrac{1}{3}x_2 - \dfrac{8}{9} |.$$

If $x_1 \in [0, \frac{1}{3}], x_2 \in [\frac{2}{3}, 1]$, one has

$$| h(x_1) - h(x_2) | = | 2x_1 + \dfrac{1}{3} - (x_2 - \dfrac{2}{3}) | = | 2x_1 - x_2 + 1 | > | x_1 - \dfrac{1}{2}x_2 + \dfrac{1}{2} |.$$

Write

$$\Delta_1 = \{| x_1 - x_2 | : x_1, x_2 \in [0, \dfrac{1}{3}]\}; \quad \Delta_2 = \{| x_1 - x_2 | : x_1, x_2 \in [\dfrac{1}{3}, \dfrac{2}{3}]\};$$

$$\Delta_3 = \{| x_1 - x_2 | : x_1, x_2 \in [\dfrac{2}{3}, 1]\}; \quad \Delta_4 = \{| x_1 + \dfrac{3}{2}x_2 - \dfrac{5}{6} | : x_1 \in [0, \dfrac{1}{3}], x_2 \in [\dfrac{1}{3}, \dfrac{2}{3}]\}$$

$$\Delta_5 = \{| x_1 + \dfrac{1}{3}x_2 - \dfrac{8}{9} | : x_1 \in [\dfrac{1}{3}, \dfrac{2}{3}], x_2 \in [\dfrac{2}{3}, 1]\};$$

$$\Delta_6 = \{| x_1 - \dfrac{1}{2}x_2 + \dfrac{1}{2} | : x_1 \in [0, \dfrac{1}{3}], x_2 \in [\dfrac{2}{3}, 1]\}.$$

Taking $\delta = inf(\cup_{i=1}^{6} \Delta_i)$. Then, for any $n \in \mathbb{N}$, $| h^n(x_1) - h^n(x_2) | \geq \delta$. This implies that the map $h : [0,1] \to [0,1]$ is sensitive-dependent on initial condition. The computer simulation with explanation of chaotic behavior is provided in Figure 1. The red dots and the green dots represent the trajectories of initial value $x_1 = 0.3556$ and $x_2 = 0.3557$ iterate for 3000 times, respectively. It can be seen that, after iteration, the orbit of x_1 (or x_2) is ergodic and disorder (see red dots or green dots). And with little difference between initial values x_1 and x_2, there is a big gap between the iterative values after 1995 times (see $h^{1995}(x_1) = 0.0803$, $h^{1995}(x_2) = 0.9032$). This means that h is sensitive-dependent on initial condition.

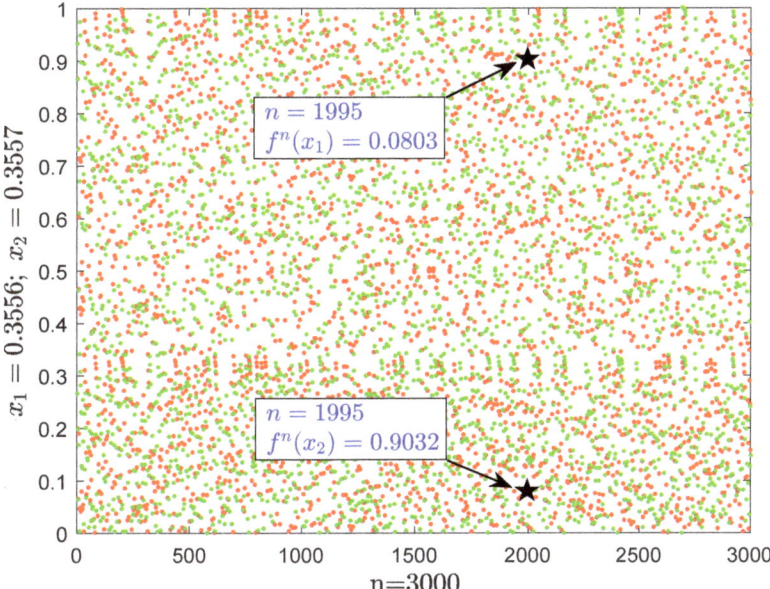

Figure 1. Chaotic behaviors of h in Example 1 with the initial data $x_1 = 0.3556$, $x_2 = 0.3557$ and $n = 3000$.

Then, it can be proved that the system (H, h) is infinitely sensitive, m-sensitive, and m-cofinitely sensitive.

Now, let $f_n(x) = g(x)(n = 2k+1, k \in \mathbb{N})$ and $f_n(x) = h(x)(n = 2k, k \in \mathbb{N})$. Then the family (f_n) consists of feebly open mappings converging uniformly to h. Obviously, $(H, f_{1,\infty})$ is also infinitely sensitive, m-sensitive, and m-cofinitely sensitive. Thus, the system $(H, f_{1,\infty})$ is conform to the assumption of Theorems 1–4.

Example 2. *Defining*

$$p(x) = 25\,saw(x) + \cos(x^2(1-x)), x \in H = \mathbb{R},$$

where, $saw(x)$ is the sawtooth function defined by

$$saw(x) = (-1)^m(x - 2m), 2m - 1 \leq x \leq 2m + 1, m \in \mathbb{Z}.$$

One can prove that the map $p(x)$ satisfies the definitions of chaos in Section 2. The computer simulation with explanation of chaotic behavior is provided in Figure 2. The red dots and the green dots represent the trajectories of initial value $x_1 = 0.3556$ and $x_2 = 0.3557$ iterate for 6000 times, respectively. And with little difference between initial values x_1 and x_2, there is a big gap between the iterative values after 4123 times (see $p^n(x_1) = 18.3449$, $p^n(x_2) = -24.1185$).

Now, let $f_n(x) = p(x)(n \in \mathbb{N})$. Then $f_n(n \in \mathbb{N})$ are feebly open mappings which uniformly converge to p. Similar to Example 1, $(H, f_{1,\infty})$ is infinitely sensitive, m-sensitive, and m-cofinitely sensitive.

Remark 1. *The above discussion tells us that under some conditions, studying the effect of a series of disturbances on the system can be simplified to studying the effect of a single map (i.e., the limit map) on the system.*

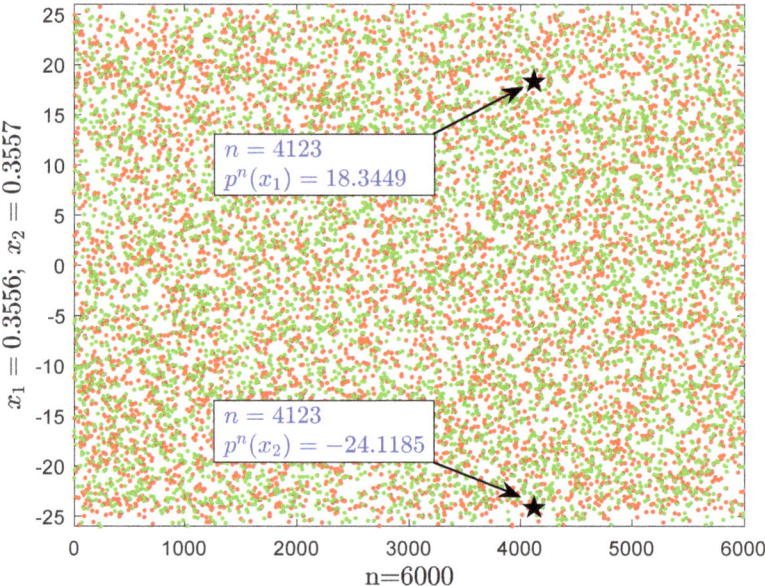

Figure 2. Chaotic behaviors of p in Example 2 with the initial data $x_1 = 0.3556$, $x_2 = 0.3557$ and $n = 6000$.

4. Some Supplements

In NDDS, is there any connection between the chaos in the sense of proximity and sensitivity? The following theorem answers this question in part.

Theorem 5. *Let H be a compact metric space and $(H, f_{1,\infty})$ be a proximal non-autonomous system, then $(H, f_{1,\infty})$ is spatio-temporal chaotic if and only if $(H, f_{1,\infty})$ is sensitive.*

Proof. (Sufficiency) $(H, f_{1,\infty})$ be a proximal system, i.e., for any $x, y \in H$, $\liminf_{n \to \infty} d(f_1^n(x), f_1^n(y)) = 0$. Because $(H, f_{1,\infty})$ is sensitive with sensitive constant $\delta > 0$, then for any $x \in H$ and any neighborhood U of x, there exist a $y \in U$ and an $n \in \mathbb{N}$ such that $d(f_1^n(x), f_1^n(y)) > \delta$.

First, we prove that $(H, f_{1,\infty})$ is infinitely sensitive. This is similar to the proof of Theorem 2.1 in Ref. [17].

Given any $N \in \mathbb{N}$, set $\mathcal{D}_N = \{(x,y) : \rho(f_1^n(x), f_1^n(y)) \leq \frac{\eta}{4}\}$ for an $\eta > 0$. It is clear that $\mathcal{D}_N$ is a closed set. And we can claim that $\text{int}\mathcal{D}_N = \phi$ for any $N \in \mathbb{N}$. In fact, if there are some $N \in \mathbb{N}$ such that $\text{int}\mathcal{D}_N \neq \phi$, then there exist nonempty open sets $U, V \in H$ such that $U \times V \subset \mathcal{D}_N$. Thus, for any pair $(x,y) \in U \times V$, $\rho(f_1^n(x), f_1^n(y)) \leq \frac{\eta}{4}$ holds for any $n > N$. So for arbitrary two points $x_1, x_2 \in U$ and any $n > N$,

$$\rho(f_1^n(x_1), f_1^n(x_2)) \leq \rho(f_1^n(x_1), f_1^n(y)) + \rho(f_1^n(y), f_1^n(x_2)) \leq \frac{\eta}{2}.$$

It is easy to prove that, there exists a nonempty open set $U^* \subset U$ such that for any points pair $x_1, x_2 \in U^*$ and any $0 \leq m \leq N$, $\rho(f_1^m(x_1), f_1^m(x_2)) \leq \frac{\eta}{2}$. Hence, for any points pair $x_1, x_2 \in U^*$ and any $n \in \mathbb{N}$, $\rho(f_1^m(x_1), f_1^m(x_2)) \leq \frac{\eta}{2}$, which contradicts the sensitivity of $(H, f_{1,\infty})$. So $\text{int}\mathcal{D}_N = \phi$ for any $N \in \mathbb{N}$. It follows that set $\mathcal{D} = \cup_{N \in \mathbb{N}} \mathcal{D}_N$ is a first category set in $H \times H$. Then, the set

$$(H \times H) \setminus \mathcal{D} = \{(x,y) : \forall N \in \mathbb{N}, \exists n > N \text{ such that } \rho(f_1^n(x), f_1^n(y)) > \frac{\eta}{4}\}$$

is residual in $X \times X$.

Assume that $(H, f_{1,\infty})$ is not infinitely sensitive, then there exist an $x_0 \in H$ and a $\zeta > 0$ such that $\limsup_{n\to\infty} \rho(f_1^n(x_0), f_1^n(y)) \leq \frac{\eta}{16}$ for any $y \in B(x_0, \zeta)$. Noting the fact that $(H \times H) \setminus \mathcal{D}$ is residual in $H \times H$, it follows that there exists a pair $(y_1, y_2) \in [B(x_0, \zeta) \times B(x_0, \zeta)] \cap [(H \times H) \setminus \mathcal{D}]$. Then for any $n \in \mathbb{N}$,
$$\rho(f_1^n(y_1), f_1^n(y_2)) \leq \rho(f_1^n(y_1), f_1^n(x_0)) + \rho(f_1^n(x_0), f_1^n(y_2)) \leq \frac{\eta}{8}.$$
So,
$$\limsup_{n\to\infty} \rho(f_1^n(y_1), f_1^n(y_2)) \leq \frac{\eta}{8},$$
which contradicts to $(y_1, y_2) \in H \times H \setminus \mathcal{D}$.

Hence, $(H, f_{1,\infty})$ is infinitely sensitive. That is to say, there exists an $\eta^* > 0$ such that $\limsup_{n\to\infty} \rho(f_1^n(x), f_1^n(y)) \geq \eta^*$. Then, it is easy to get that (H, f) is spatio-temporal chaotic.

(Necessity) It is clearly held, and hence is omitted.

The proof is completed. □

Corollary 1. *Let H be a compact metric space and (H, f) be a proximal system, then (H, f) is spatio-temporal chaotic if and only if (H, f) is sensitive.*

Remark 2. *In fact, there are some other relationships among chaotic properties in non-autonomous discrete systems. For example, topologically weak mixing implies sensitive, dense δ-chaos implies sensitive, generic δ-chaos implies sensitive, and Li-Yorke sensitive is equivalent to sensitive under the condition that $\bigcap_{k=1}^{\infty} \bigcup_{n=1}^{\infty} f_1^{-n}(\{y \in H : d(f_1^n(x), y) < \frac{1}{k}\}) = H$. These results are in [18–21].*

5. Conclusions

For a mapping sequence $f_{1,\infty} = (f_n)_{n=1}^{\infty}$, this paper gives four hypotheses. That is, (1) $f_n(n \in \mathbb{N})$ are feebly open; (2) $f_n(n \in \mathbb{N})$ uniformly converge to f; (3) $f_i \circ f = f \circ f_i$ for any $i \in \{1, 2, \dots\}$; and (4) $\sum_{i=1}^{\infty} D(f_i, f) < \infty$. It is proved that, under the conditions of (1)–(4), accessible or sensitivity between $f_{1,\infty}$ and its limit map f is coincide. Then, the natural problems rise. Can the above (1)–(4) be reduced? Do other chaotic properties, such as transitive, mixing, or distributional chaos, have similar conclusions? These are topics worth studying in the future.

Author Contributions: Conceptualization, Y.J.; validation, Y.J., X.Y. and T.L.; formal analysis, Y.J. and X.Y.; investigation, Y.J.; writing original draft, Y.J.; writing review and editing, X.Y. and T.L.; supervision, T.L.; funding acquisition, T.L. All authors have read and agreed to the published version of the manuscript.

Funding: This work was funded by the Project of the Department of Science and Technology of Sichuan Provincial (No. 2021ZYD0005), the Opening Project of the Key Laboratory of Higher Education of Sichuan Province for Enterprise Informationalization and Internet of Things (No. 2020WZJ01), the Scientific Research Project of Sichuan University of Science and Engineering (No. 2020RC24), and the Graduate Student Innovation Fund (No. y2021100).

Institutional Review Board Statement: Not applicable.

Informed Consent Statement: Not applicable.

Data Availability Statement: Data will be made available on reasonable request.

Acknowledgments: Many thanks to experts.

Conflicts of Interest: The authors declare no conflict of interest regarding the publication of this paper.

References

1. Kolyada, S.; Snoha, L. Topological entropy of nonautonomous dynamical systems. *Random Comput. Dynam.* **1996**, *4*, 205–233.
2. Si, H. On ω-limit sets of non-autonomous discrete dynamical system. *Adv. Fixed Point Theory* **2016**, *6*, 287–294.
3. Lan, Y.; Peris, A. Weak stability of non-autonomous discrete dynamical systems. *Topol. Appl.* **2018**, *1*, 53–60. [CrossRef]
4. Li, R.; Zhao, Y.; Wang, H.; Liang, H. Stronger Forms of Transitivity and Sensitivity for Nonautonomous Discrete Dynamical Systems and Furstenberg Families. *J. Dyn. Control Syst.* **2020**, *26*, 109–126. [CrossRef]

5. Li, R.; Lu, T.; Chen, G.; Liu, G. Some stronger forms of topological transitivity and sensitivity for a sequence of uniformly convergent continuous maps. *J. Math. Anal. Appl.* **2020**, 124443. [CrossRef]
6. Vasisht, R.; Das, R. A note on $\mathcal{F}$-sensitivity for non-autonomous systems. *J. Differ. Equ. Appl.* **2019**, *25*, 1–12. [CrossRef]
7. Salman, M.; Das, R. Multi-sensitivity and other stronger forms of sensitivity in non-autonomous discrete systems. *Chaos Soliton. Fract.* **2018**, *115*, 341–348. [CrossRef]
8. Radhika, V.; Das, R. On stronger forms of sensitivity in non-autonomous systems. *Taiwan J. Math.* **2018**, *22*, 230–245.
9. Fedeli, A.; Donne, A. A note on the uniform limit of transitive dynamical systems. *Bull. Belg. Math. Soc.-Sim.* **2009**, *16*, 59–66. [CrossRef]
10. Salman, M.; Das, R. Multi-transitivity in non-autonomous discrete systems. *Topol. Appl.* **2020**, *278*, 107237. [CrossRef]
11. Yang, X.; Lu, T.; Anwar, W. Chaotic properties of a class of coupled mapping lattice induced by fuzzy mapping in non-autonomous discrete systems. *Chaos Soliton. Fract.* **2021**, *148*, 110979. [CrossRef]
12. Jiang, Y.; Lu, T.; Pi, J.; Anwar, W. The retentivity of four kinds of shadowing properties in non-autonomous discrete dynamical systems. *Entropy* **2022**, *24*, 397. [CrossRef] [PubMed]
13. Murinova, E. Generic chaos in metric space. *Acta Univ. Matthiae Belii Ser. Math.* **2000**, *8*, 43–50.
14. Snoha, L. Dense chaos. *Comment. Math. Univ. Ca.* **1992**, *33*, 747–752.
15. Wu, X.; Wang, J. A remark on accessibility. *Chaos Soliton. Fract.* **2016**, *91*, 115–117. [CrossRef]
16. Zhang, C. Some Studies on M-Sensitivity Dependence in Topological Dynamical Systems. Master's Thesis, Nanchang University, Nanchang, China, 2016. (In Chinese)
17. Wu, X.; Zhu, P. Dense chaos and densely chaotic operators. *Tsukuba J. Math.* **2012**, *36*, 367–375. [CrossRef]
18. He, L.; Yan, X.; Wang, L. Weak-mixing implies sensitive dependence. *J. Math. Anal. Appl.* **2014**, *299*, 300–304. [CrossRef]
19. Balibrea, F.; Oprocha, P. Weak mixing and chaos in non-autonomous discrete systems. *Appl. Math. Lett.* **2012**, *25*, 1135–1141. [CrossRef]
20. Shao, H.; Shi, Y.; Zhu, H. Relationships among some chaotic properties of non-autonomous discrete dynamical systems. *J. Differ. Equ. Appl.* **2018**, *24*, 1055–1064. [CrossRef]
21. Zhu, H.; Shi, Y.; Shao, H. Devaney chaos in non-autonomous discrete systems. *Int. J. Bifurcat. Chaos* **2016**, *26*, 1650190. [CrossRef]

Article

Hidden and Coexisting Attractors in a Novel 4D Hyperchaotic System with No Equilibrium Point

Chengwei Dong * and Jiahui Wang *

Department of Physics, North University of China, Taiyuan 030051, China
* Correspondence: dongchengwei@tsinghua.org.cn (C.D.); wangjiahui2021wuli@163.com (J.W.)

Abstract: The investigation of chaotic systems containing hidden and coexisting attractors has attracted extensive attention. This paper presents a four-dimensional (4D) novel hyperchaotic system, evolved by adding a linear state feedback controller to a 3D chaotic system with two stable node-focus points. The proposed system has no equilibrium point or two lines of equilibria, depending on the value of the constant term. Complex dynamical behaviors such as hidden chaotic and hyperchaotic attractors and five types of coexisting attractors of the simple 4D autonomous system are investigated and discussed, and are numerically verified by analyzing phase diagrams, Poincaré maps, the Lyapunov exponent spectrum, and its bifurcation diagram. The short unstable cycles in the hyperchaotic system are systematically explored via the variational method, and symbol codings of the cycles with four letters are realized based on the topological properties of the trajectory projection on the 2D phase space. The bifurcations of the cycles are explored through a homotopy evolution approach. Finally, the novel 4D system is implemented by an analog electronic circuit and is found to be consistent with the numerical simulation results.

Keywords: hyperchaos; hidden attractor; coexisting attractors; bifurcation; circuit implementation

1. Introduction

The research of chaotic systems has been a topic of interest due to their many engineering applications [1,2]. In 1979, Rössler put forward the concept of hyperchaos and proposed the hyperchaotic Rössler system [3]. As we know, for an autonomous dynamical system, the minimum dimension of the phase space to produce hyperchaos should be at least four. Hyperchaotic systems have two or more positive Lyapunov exponents; thus, they have extensive application values and more complex dynamic behaviors than ordinary chaotic systems [4]. The investigation of hyperchaotic systems has attracted much attention and achieved fruitful results [5,6]. A 4D hyperchaotic system was proposed by adding a nonlinear controller to the first equation of the Lorenz chaotic system [7], and hyperchaos can also be generated from the generalized Lorenz Equation [8]. A hyperchaotic system constructed from the Lü system was found to produce many kinds of scroll chaotic attractors [9]. A 5D hyperchaotic system based on a modified generalized Lorenz system with three positive Lyapunov exponents was reported [10]. An effective method to construct hyperchaotic systems with multiple positive Lyapunov exponents was formulated [11]. A 7D hyperchaotic system with five positive Lyapunov exponents was constructed, which can exhibit complex dynamical behaviors [12].

Recent research has involved categorizing periodic and chaotic attractors as either self-excited or hidden [13]. Most famous chaotic and hyperchaotic systems, such as the classical Lorenz, Chen, Lü, and Sprott systems [14–17], have more than one equilibrium point, and their chaotic attractors with typical parameter values are self-excited. The basin of attraction of a self-excited attractor is known to intersect with small neighborhoods of unstable equilibria, whereas that of a hidden attractor intersects with no open neighborhoods of equilibria. Chaotic systems without equilibrium points [18–22], with only stable equilibria [23,24], and with an infinite number of equilibria [25–27] have hidden chaotic attractors.

Citation: Dong, C.; Wang, J. Hidden and Coexisting Attractors in a Novel 4D Hyperchaotic System with No Equilibrium Point. *Fractal Fract.* **2022**, *6*, 306. https://doi.org/10.3390/fractalfract6060306

Academic Editor: Viorel-Puiu Paun

Received: 5 May 2022
Accepted: 27 May 2022
Published: 31 May 2022

Publisher's Note: MDPI stays neutral with regard to jurisdictional claims in published maps and institutional affiliations.

Copyright: © 2022 by the authors. Licensee MDPI, Basel, Switzerland. This article is an open access article distributed under the terms and conditions of the Creative Commons Attribution (CC BY) license (https://creativecommons.org/licenses/by/4.0/).

The first hidden chaotic attractor with stable equilibria was investigated in a generalized Chua system [28]. Since then, different types of chaotic and hyperchaotic systems with hidden attractors have been reported on extensively. A quadratic hyperjerk system with no equilibrium was introduced, which can produce hidden chaotic attractors [29]. Hidden hyperchaotic attractors with three positive Lyapunov exponents were generated in a 5D hyperchaotic Burke–Shaw system with only one stable fixed point [30]. A 5D system with self-excited attractors and two types of hidden attractors with the variation of parameters was proposed [31]. A 6D coupled hidden attractor system was introduced, and the basins of attraction were analyzed [32].

Many complex dynamical systems have complicated characteristics of coexisting attractors, which is referred to as multistability. A nonlinear dynamical system with such behaviors can produce two or more attractors at the same time according to the initial values of the system. Recent research indicates that the multistability of a dynamical system is related to the existence of hidden attractors. Coexisting attractors and multistability have been widely studied in the literature. A 3D chaotic system with multiple attractors was found, the complex dynamical behaviors of the system were derived, and the circuit to realize the chaotic attractor of the system was given [33]. Furthermore, a 4D chaotic system with a plane as the equilibrium and coexisting attractors was analyzed [34]. A 4D system including chaotic or hyperchaotic attractors with no equilibrium point, a line of equilibrium points, and unstable equilibrium points, was constructed [35] and was found to exhibit multistability between different attractors. Multistability and coexisting attractors was discovered in a 4D chaotic system with only one unstable equilibrium [36] and multiple unstable equilibrium points [37]. An extended Lü system containing coexisting chaotic, periodic, and point attractors for different initial values was introduced [38]. Complex coexisting attractors can also be generated in a 4D chaotic laser system [39], a cyclic symmetry chaotic system [40], and a 4D memristor chaotic system [41].

As mentioned in the above literature, there are few examples of hyperchaotic systems which have both hidden and coexisting attractors. This paper proposes a 4D system which can generate a hidden hyperchaotic attractor when it has no equilibrium point and five types of coexisting attractors for different initial values. The short unstable periodic orbits embedded in the hidden hyperchaotic attractor are encoded and calculated systematically, and the cycles whose period changes with the parameter values are explored through the homotopy evolution approach. The proposed system is implemented by an analog electronic circuit, and the results are in good agreement with the phase portraits from the numerical simulation, which testifies to its feasibility. It should be noted that, compared to previous hyperchaotic systems with no equilibria, the proposed 4D system has richer and more complex dynamic characteristics; the most salient features are its multiple coexisting attractors and multistability. It is obvious that our proposed hyperchaotic system with coexisting hidden attractors and riddled basins exhibits some behaviors previously unobserved, which satisfies the relevant criteria put forward by Sprott for the publication of a new chaotic system [42].

The rest of this paper is organized as follows. Section 2 describes the mathematical model of the new 4D hyperchaotic system and shows some of its basic dynamical properties. In Section 3, the complex dynamical structure of the proposed hyperchaotic system is further revealed by common nonlinear analysis tools, and various types of coexisting attractors are discussed. A periodic orbit analysis for the new system using the variational method is presented in Section 4. A corresponding analog circuit for the implementation of the novel 4D system is designed in Section 5. Section 6 presents the conclusions and recommendations for future work.

2. The Novel 4D Hyperchaotic System

Consider a 3D chaotic system [24],

$$\begin{aligned}
\frac{dx}{dt} &= a(y-x) + kxz \\
\frac{dy}{dt} &= -cy - xz \\
\frac{dz}{dt} &= -b + xy,
\end{aligned} \quad (1)$$

where a, b, c, and k are parameters. When $(a, b, c, k) = (10, 100, 11.2, -0.2)$, the system has a hidden chaotic attractor with two stable equilibrium points. The dynamical properties, periodic orbit analysis, and circuit realization of the 3D chaotic system have been investigated [24].

Based on the method for constructing new 4D hyperchaotic systems proposed by Li et al. [43], we can make the original 3D system become 4D by adding a linear state feedback controller to the first equation of system (1) so as to meet the minimal dimension required for generating hyperchaos. This creates the opportunity to possess two positive Lyapunov exponents along with one zero and one negative Lyapunov exponent. Thus, we obtain a 4D autonomous system,

$$\begin{aligned}
\frac{dx}{dt} &= a(y-x) + kxz + w \\
\frac{dy}{dt} &= -cy - xz \\
\frac{dz}{dt} &= -b + xy \\
\frac{dw}{dt} &= -my,
\end{aligned} \quad (2)$$

where x, y, z, and w are state variables, and a, b, c, k, and m are the real parameters. Setting the right side of each equation of system (2) to zero, the equilibrium points can be easily calculated. Obviously, when $b \neq 0$, system (2) has no equilibrium point, and Hopf, pitchfork, or homoclinic bifurcations that usually take place in dynamical systems with equilibrium points will not occur. When $b = 0$, system (2) has two lines of equilibria, $(0, 0, z, 0)$ and $(\frac{w}{a}, 0, 0, w)$. System (2) has no equilibrium point when $b \neq 0$, and the basin of attraction of the hyperchaotic attractor does not intersect with small neighborhoods of equilibria. However, system (2) has infinite equilibria when $b = 0$, although the basin of attraction of the chaotic attractor may intersect with the equilibrium points in some regions in this situation, and an infinite number of the other equilibrium points are located outside the basin of attraction. Thus, system (2) belongs to the new category of hidden attractors, which is unique because of the existence of two different types of hidden attractors. We discuss the new system with no equilibrium point.

When the parameters of system (2) are taken as $(a, b, c, k, m) = (10, 100, 2.7, -0.2, 1)$ and the initial conditions (x_0, y_0, z_0, w_0) are set as $(1, 1, 1, 1)$, the system has a hidden hyperchaotic attractor, with phase portraits as depicted in Figure 1. The corresponding four Lyapunov exponents can be calculated using the method of Ramasubramanian et al. [44]: $L_1 = 0.7796, L_2 = 0.1058, L_3 = 0, L_4 = -12.7177$, as shown in Figure 2. The Kaplan–Yorke dimension is characterized by its Lyapunov exponents, $D_{KY} = 3 + (L_1 + L_2 + L_3)/|L_4| = 3.0696$, which indicate that the hidden hyperchaotic attractor has a fractal dimension. Figure 3 also displays different sections of 2D Poincaré maps for system (2) under the current parameters.

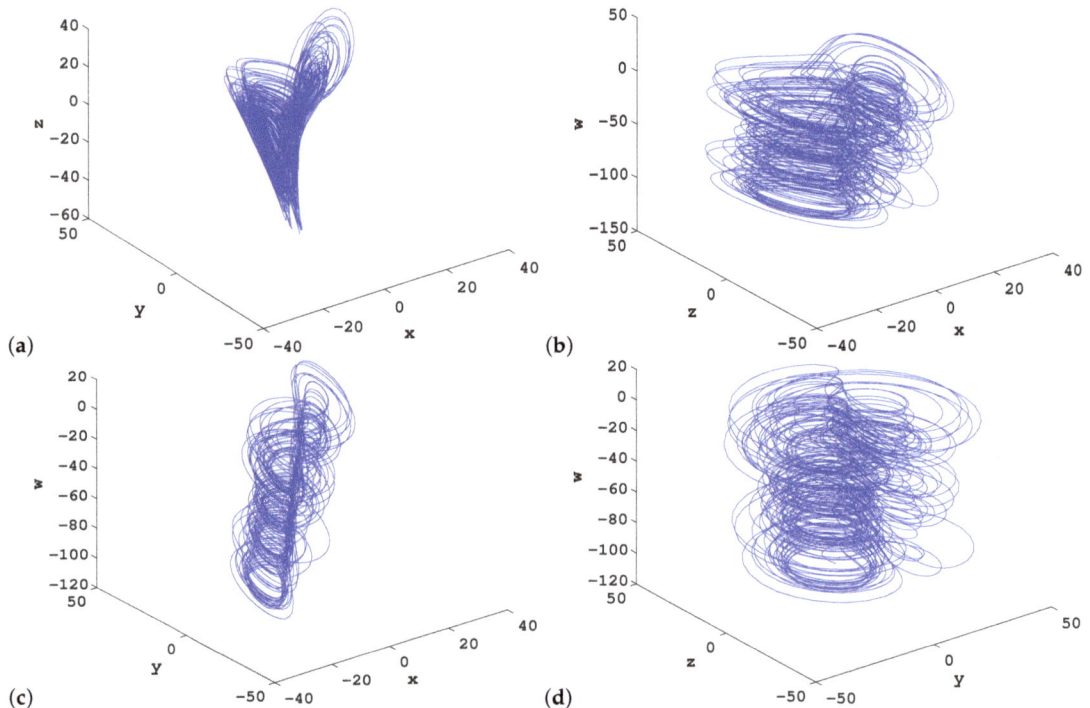

Figure 1. Three-dimensional projections of the hyperchaotic attractor of system (2): $(a, b, c, k, m) = (10, 100, 2.7, -0.2, 1)$. (**a**) x-y-z phase space; (**b**) x-z-w phase space; (**c**) x-y-w phase space; (**d**) y-z-w phase space.

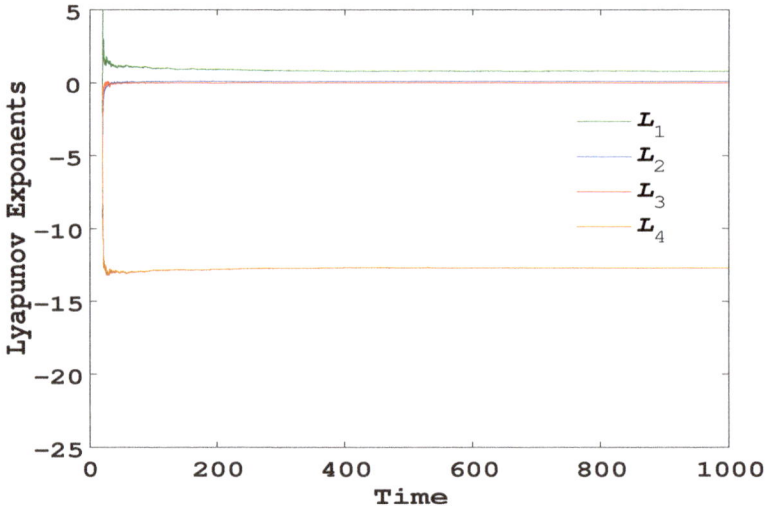

Figure 2. Four Lyapunov exponents of system (2) for $(a, b, c, k, m) = (10, 100, 2.7, -0.2, 1)$.

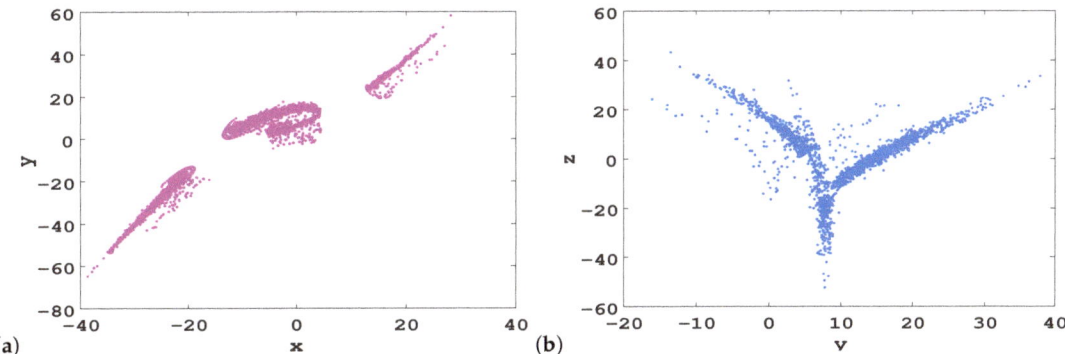

Figure 3. Two-dimensional Poincaré maps of the hyperchaotic attractor of system (2); $(a, b, c, k, m) = (10, 100, 2.7, -0.2, 1)$; (**a**) on section $z = 0$; (**b**) on section $x = 0$.

The dynamical properties of system (2) can be examined as follows:

(1) Symmetry and invariance. System (2) is invariant under the coordinate transformation $(x, y, z, w) \to (-x, -y, z, -w)$, i.e., it has rotational symmetry around the z-axis, which means that any orbit that is not itself invariant under the transformation must have its conjugate orbit;

(2) Since the divergence of system (2) is defined as

$$\nabla \cdot V = \frac{\partial \dot{x}}{\partial x} + \frac{\partial \dot{y}}{\partial y} + \frac{\partial \dot{z}}{\partial z} + \frac{\partial \dot{w}}{\partial w} = -a + kz - c, \quad (3)$$

the system is dissipative under the condition $-a + kz - c < 0$. Consequently, each volume containing the trajectory of the system eventually converges to zero at an exponential rate $-a + kz - c$;

(3) A well-known prominent characteristic of hyperchaotic dynamics is its sensitive dependence on initial values. When the parameters of system (2) are fixed at $(a, b, c, k, m) = (10, 100, 2.7, -0.2, 1)$ and the initial values change slightly, the time-series diagram of the system generated from two very close initial values within the simulation time $t = 200$ is as plotted in Figure 4.

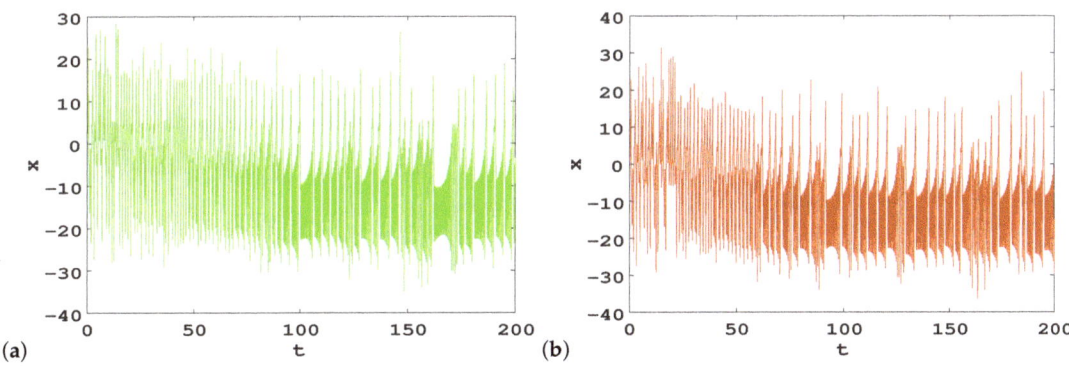

Figure 4. Cont.

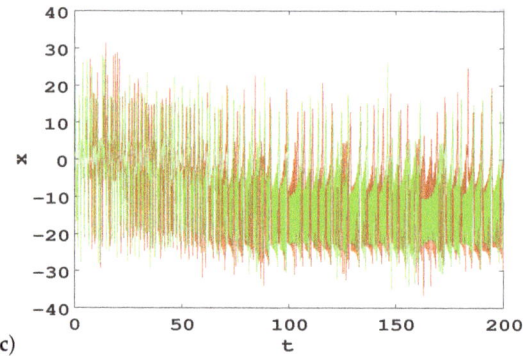

Figure 4. Time-sequence diagrams of system (2); $(a, b, c, k, m) = (10, 100, 2.7, -0.2, 1)$: (**a**) $(x_0, y_0, z_0, w_0) = (1, 1, 1, 1)$; (**b**) $(x_0, y_0, z_0, w_0) = (1.001, 1, 1, 1)$; (**c**) green and brown represent initial values of (**a**,**b**), respectively.

3. Complex Dynamical Structure of the Proposed Hyperchaotic System

The new system (2) exhibits abundant complicated dynamical characteristics in a wide range of parameters, which can be explored by numerical analysis. We fixed parameters a, c, k, and m while varying b. Using nonlinear analysis tools such as phase diagrams, Lyapunov exponents, and bifurcation diagrams, the system can show periodic solutions, quasi-periodic solutions, chaos, and hyperchaos for different parameters. Coexisting attractors refer to the multistability phenomena for certain parameter values, where different attractors exist depending on different initial conditions. Interestingly, compared with similar chaotic systems, when taking different parameters and initial values, system (2) can display various types of coexisting attractors.

3.1. Lyapunov Exponents, Bifurcation Diagram, and C_0 Complexity Analysis

To explore the influence of b on the dynamics of the new 4D system, we fixed parameters $(a, c, k, m) = (10, 2.7, -0.2, 1)$, and varied b in the interval $[0, 120]$. As we know, the main dynamical properties of system (2) can be analyzed by its Lyapunov exponent spectrum and bifurcation diagram. We took the initial values as $(x_0, y_0, z_0, w_0) = (1.67610, -0.37856, 3.69140, 1.45851)$. Figure 5a,b show the changes of four Lyapunov exponents with the increase of b, and Figure 5c gives the corresponding bifurcation diagram with respect to b. It can be observed that the Lyapunov exponent spectrum well coincides with the bifurcation diagram. It can be clearly seen from Figure 5 that system (2) indeed produces hyperchaotic attractors with two positive Lyapunov exponents for a wide range of b. Three-dimensional projections of attractors for some typical values of b, are shown in Figure 6, and the corresponding Lyapunov exponents and fractal dimensions are tabulated in Table 1, from which the intricate topological structure and abundant hyperchaotic dynamic properties of system (2) can be seen.

Table 1. Lyapunov exponents and Kaplan–Yorke dimension of system (2) with $a = 10$, $c = 2.7$, $k = -0.2$, and $m = 1$.

b	L_1	L_2	L_3	L_4	D_{KY}	Dynamics
10	0	−0.0377	−0.4173	−11.6842	1.0	Periodic
20	0.0483	0	−0.2258	−11.9110	2.24	Chaos
38	0	−0.0227	−0.0243	−12.0242	1.0	Periodic
42	0	0	−0.1340	−11.9278	2.0	Quasi-periodic
50	0.0182	0	−0.2922	−11.7656	2.06	Chaos
120	0.9302	0.0850	0	−12.8638	3.08	Hyperchaos

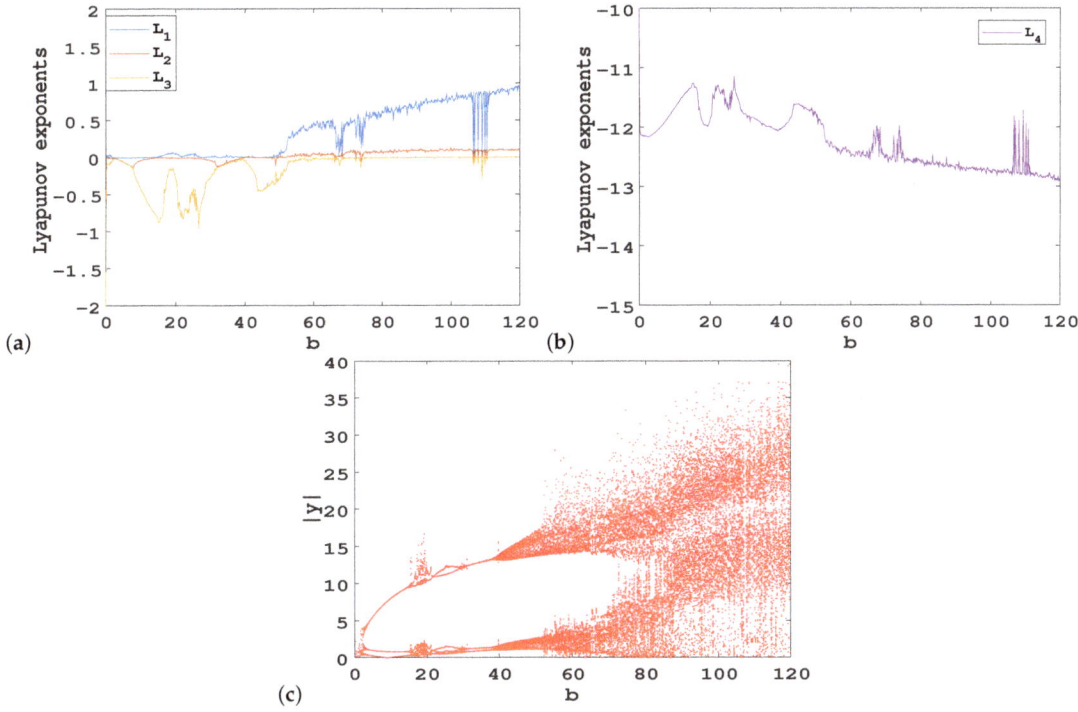

Figure 5. Dynamics of system (2) versus parameter $b \in [0, 120]$ with $(a, c, k, m) = (10, 2.7, -0.2, 1)$: (**a**,**b**) Lyapunov exponent spectrum; (**c**) bifurcation diagram.

The C_0 complexity analysis relating to different parameters in new system (2) was also investigated, as shown in Figure 7. Compared with Figure 5, we can see that when the system is in a periodic state, the value of the C_0 complexity is small, whereas when the system is in a chaotic state or hyperchaotic state, the value of C_0 fluctuates between 0.1 and 0.4, which is significantly larger than that of the periodic state. Therefore, there is a positive correlation between the C_0 complexity measure and Lyapunov exponents, which can reflect the dynamic characteristics and complexity of the system.

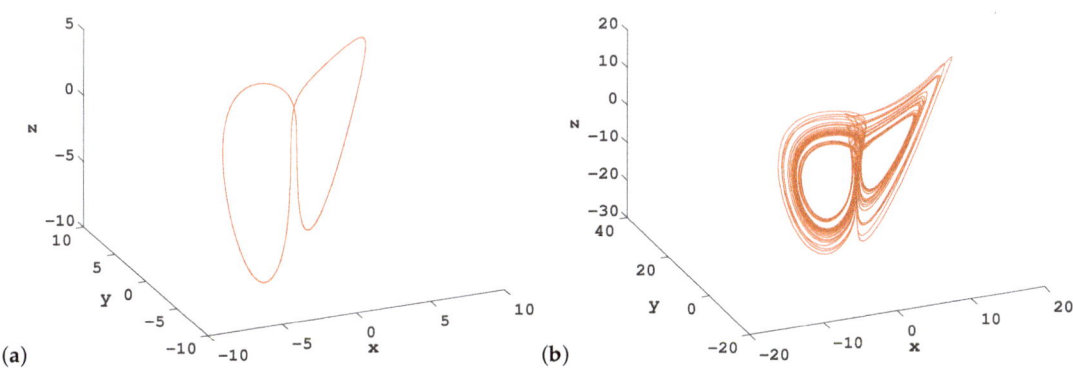

Figure 6. *Cont.*

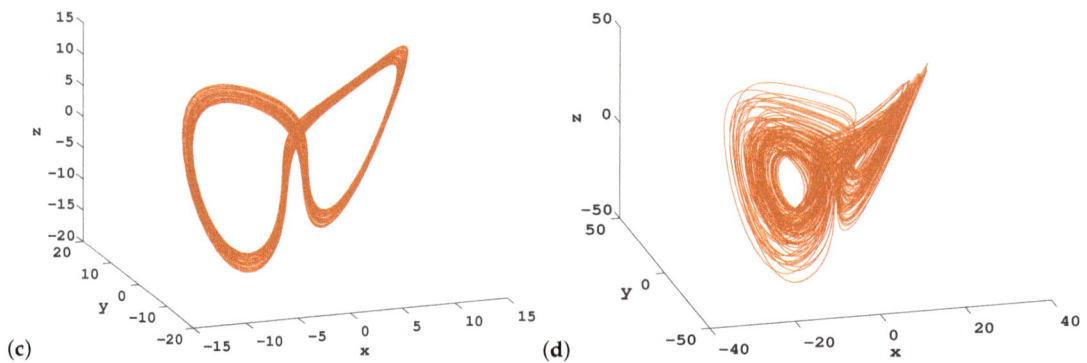

Figure 6. Some representative dynamical behaviors of system (2) with parameters $(a, c, k, m) = (10, 2.7, -0.2, 1)$ and different values of b: (**a**) $b = 10$; (**b**) $b = 20$; (**c**) $b = 42$; (**d**) $b = 120$.

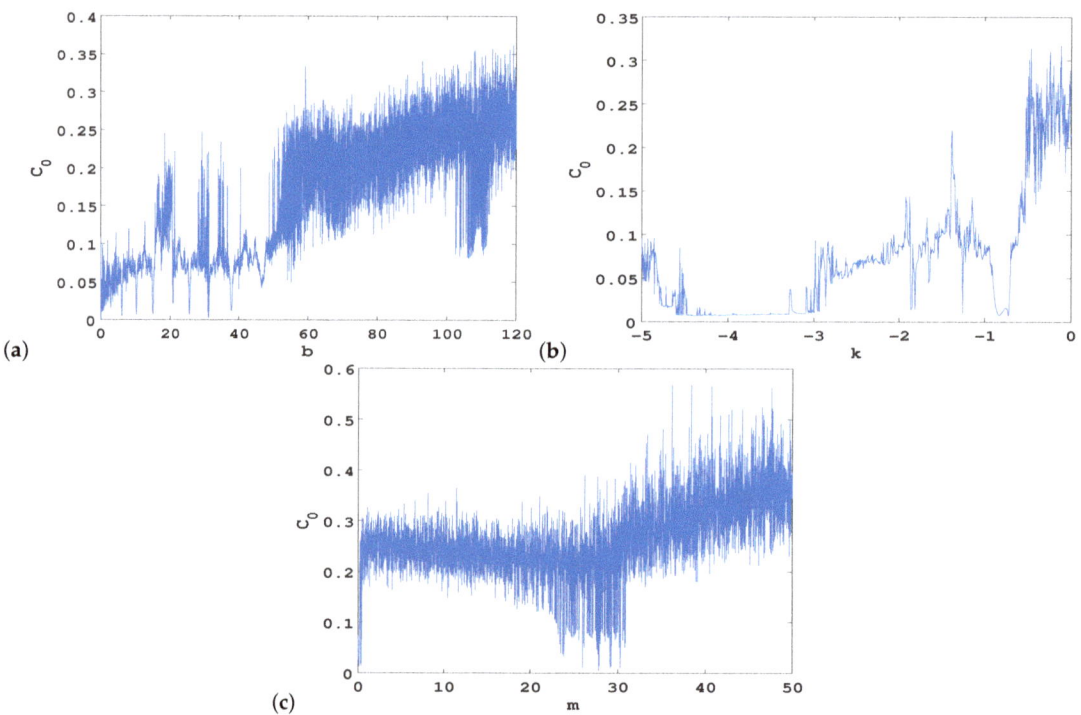

Figure 7. C_0 complexity curve of the new system (2). (**a**) Versus b for $a = 10$, $c = 2.7$, $k = -0.2$, $m = 1$; (**b**) versus k for $a = 10$, $b = 100$, $c = 2.7$, $m = 1$; (**c**) versus m for $a = 10$, $b = 100$, $c = 2.7$, $k = -0.2$. The initial values were set as $(1.67610, -0.37856, 3.69140, 1.45851)$.

3.2. Coexisting Attractors

As discussed above, system (2) shows many complex dynamics, such as hyperchaos, chaos, and quasi-periodic and periodic motions. Several coexisting attractors of system (2) will be present under some appropriate parameters, indicating that hidden multistability emerges. A system with coexisting attractors is very sensitive to the initial values, noise, and system parameters. Importantly, under sudden disturbance, the state of the system can easily change and switch from an ideal state to another state that may be undesirable. However, multistability can make systems more flexible without adjusting parameters, and can be used with the correct control strategy to induce switching between various coexistence states. The coexisting attractors of system (2) satisfying different initial values may exhibit various dynamical behaviors.

3.2.1. Coexistence of Chaotic and Periodic Attractors

When we take the parameters $(a, b, c, k, m) = (10, 12, 2.7, -0.2, 1)$, the dynamic behavior of system (2) may change greatly in the long run:

(a) For initial values $(x_0, y_0, z_0, w_0) = (1, 1, 1, 1)$, the Lyapunov exponents can be calculated as $L_1 = 0.037, L_2 = 0, L_3 = -0.2098$, and $L_4 = -11.9386$, and the fractal dimension of the system is estimated to be 2.1765. A hidden chaotic attractor with no equilibrium point can be revealed, whose 2D phase portrait is shown in Figure 8a;

(b) For initial values $(x_0, y_0, z_0, w_0) = (-0.9, -1, -8, -1.7)$, the trajectory of the system converges to a stable periodic orbit, as shown in Figure 8b. The Lyapunov exponents of the system are found to be $L_1 = 0, L_2 = -0.0144, L_3 = -0.6047$, and $L_4 = -11.5121$, and the Kaplan–Yorke dimension is 1.0.

Hence, for parameters $(a, b, c, k, m) = (10, 12, 2.7, -0.2, 1)$, system (2) has intricate dynamics with coexisting chaotic and periodic attractors, as shown in Figure 8c.

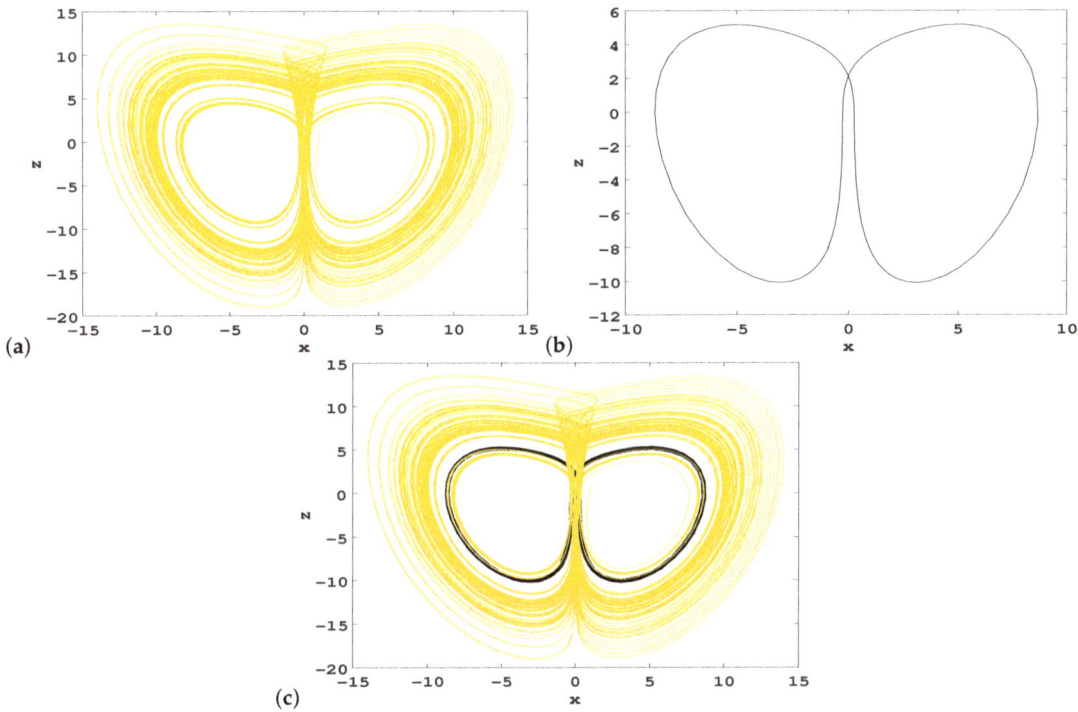

Figure 8. Two coexisting hidden attractors of system (2); $(a, b, c, k, m) = (10, 12, 2.7, -0.2, 1)$; (**a**) chaotic attractor; (**b**) periodic attractor; (**c**) coexisting attractors. The yellow line represents chaotic attractor and the black line represents periodic attractor.

3.2.2. Coexistence of Quasi-Periodic and Periodic Attractors

When we take the parameters $(a, b, c, k, m) = (10, 24, 2.7, -0.2, 1)$ and change the initial values, the dynamic behavior of system (2) may produce different coexisting attractors:

(a) For initial values $(x_0, y_0, z_0, w_0) = (0.885798, 0.890960, -7.338199, 1.357681)$, the Lyapunov exponents of system (2) are calculated as $L_1 = 0, L_2 = 0, L_3 = -0.7809$, and $L_4 = -11.3183$, and the Kaplan–Yorke dimension of the system can be estimated as 2.0.

Because there are two zeros and two negative Lyapunov exponents, system (2) experiences dynamical motion, which is called a quasi-periodic attractor, as depicted in Figure 9a;

(b) For initial values $(x_0, y_0, z_0, w_0) = (-0.8, -0.8, -6.8, -1.8)$, the trajectory of the system converges to a periodic orbit, as shown in Figure 9b. The Lyapunov exponents are found to be $L_1 = 0, L_2 = -0.004, L_3 = -0.5976$, and $L_4 = -11.4953$, and the Kaplan–Yorke dimension is 1.0.

Hence, for parameters $(a, b, c, k, m) = (10, 24, 2.7, -0.2, 1)$, quasi-periodic and periodic attractors of system (2) coexist, as shown in Figure 9c.

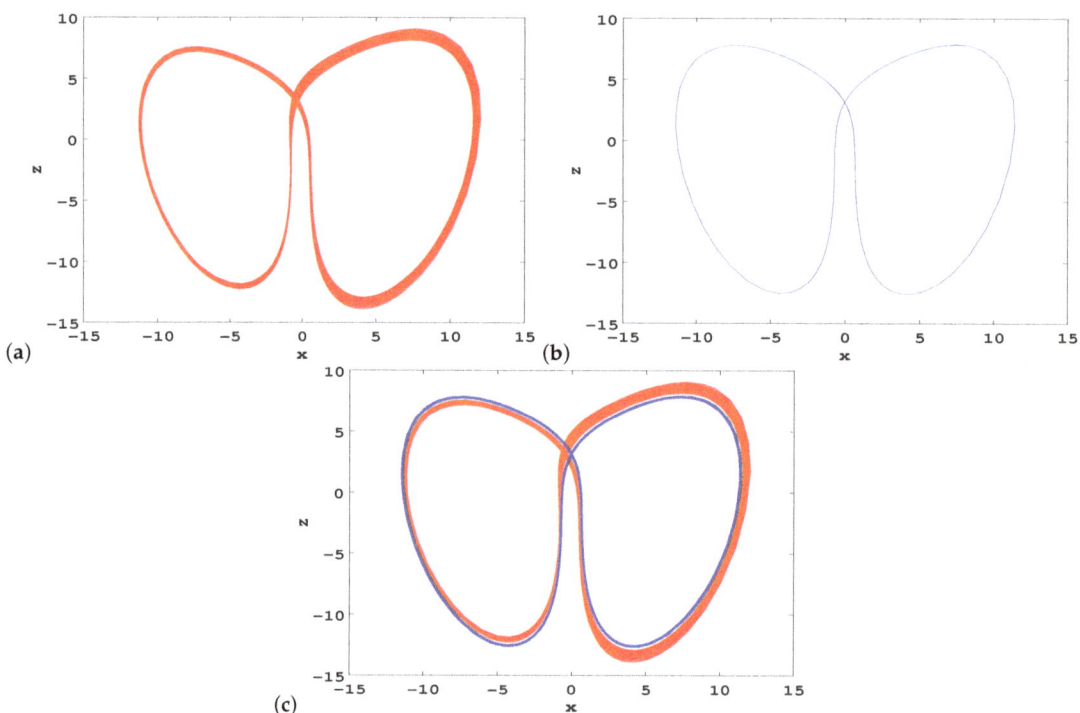

Figure 9. Two coexisting hidden attractors of system (2); $(a, b, c, k, m) = (10, 24, 2.7, -0.2, 1)$; (**a**) quasi-periodic attractor; (**b**) periodic attractor; (**c**) coexisting attractors. The red line represents quasi-periodic attractor and the blue line represents periodic attractor.

3.2.3. Coexistence of Chaotic and Quasi-Periodic Attractors

Let the parameters $(a, b, c, k, m) = (10, 40, 2.7, -0.2, 2)$ and choose initial values $(1, 2, 5.2, 1)$. The corresponding Lyapunov exponents are $L_1 = 0.0177, L_2 = 0, L_3 = -0.1730$, and $L_4 = -11.9126$, which means the attractor is chaotic. The corresponding fractal dimension is 2.0876. The projection of this chaotic attractor onto the 2D phase space is presented in Figure 10a.

Choosing the same parameter values and taking initial values $(1, 1, 1, 1)$, the four Lyapunov exponents are $L_1 = 0, L_2 = 0, L_3 = -0.1686$, and $L_4 = -11.9045$, which implies that system (2) has a quasi-periodic attractor, whose projection onto the 2D phase space is presented in Figure 10b.

Thus, for parameters $(a, b, c, k, m) = (10, 40, 2.7, -0.2, 2)$, system (2) has complex dynamics with coexisting chaotic and quasi-periodic attractors, as illustrated in Figure 10c.

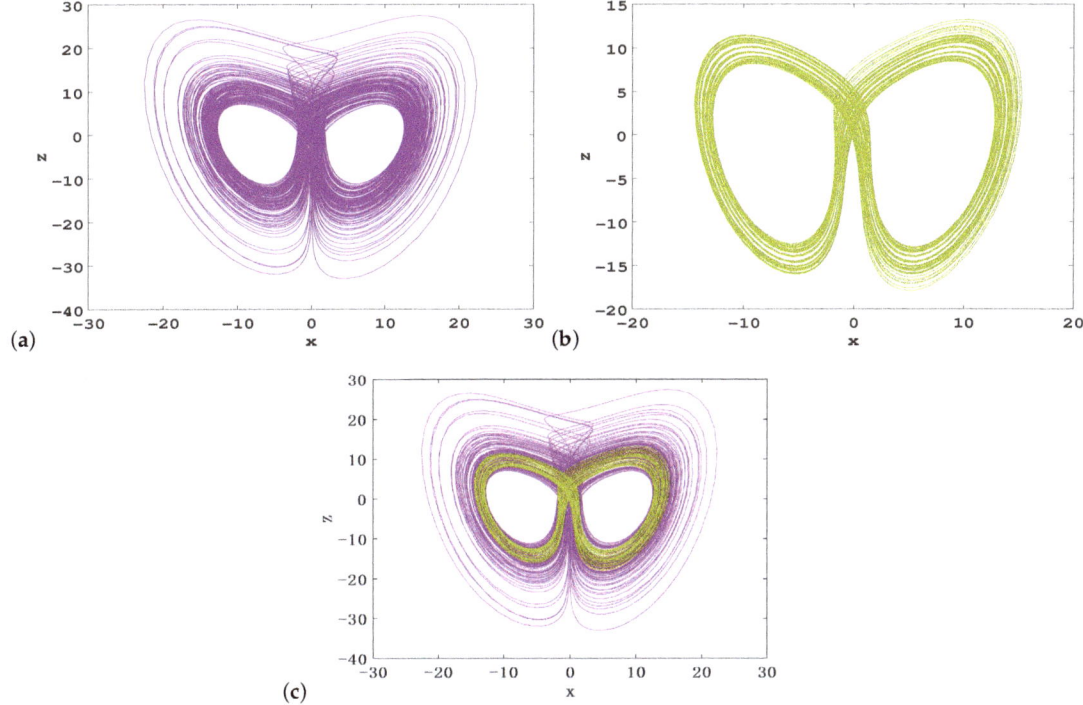

Figure 10. Two coexisting hidden attractors of system (2); $(a, b, c, k, m) = (10, 40, 2.7, -0.2, 2)$; (**a**) chaotic attractor; (**b**) quasi-periodic attractor; (**c**) coexisting attractors. The purple line represents chaotic attractor and the yellow line represents quasi-periodic attractor.

3.2.4. Coexistence of Hidden Periodic Attractors

Fixing the parameters $(a, b, c, k, m) = (10, 10, 2.7, -0.2, 2)$ and choosing initial values $(-0.05, 0.15, -0.04, -3.77)$, system (2) has a periodic attractor with projection onto the x–z plane, as presented in Figure 11a. The four Lyapunov exponents are $L_1 = 0$, $L_2 = -0.0688, L_3 = -0.0699$, and $L_4 = -12.0132$.

Choosing initial values $(-0.61, -0.38, -1.33, -0.79)$, one obtains the corresponding Lyapunov exponents $L_1 = 0, L_2 = -0.0234, L_3 = -0.0245$, and $L_4 = -12.1119$, which also implies a periodic attractor. The projection of the periodic attractor onto the 2D phase space is displayed in Figure 11b and has a different topology from the periodic attractor in Figure 11a.

Thus, we can conclude that two periodic attractors in system (2) coexist with parameters $(a, b, c, k, m) = (10, 10, 2.7, -0.2, 2)$, as depicted in Figure 11c.

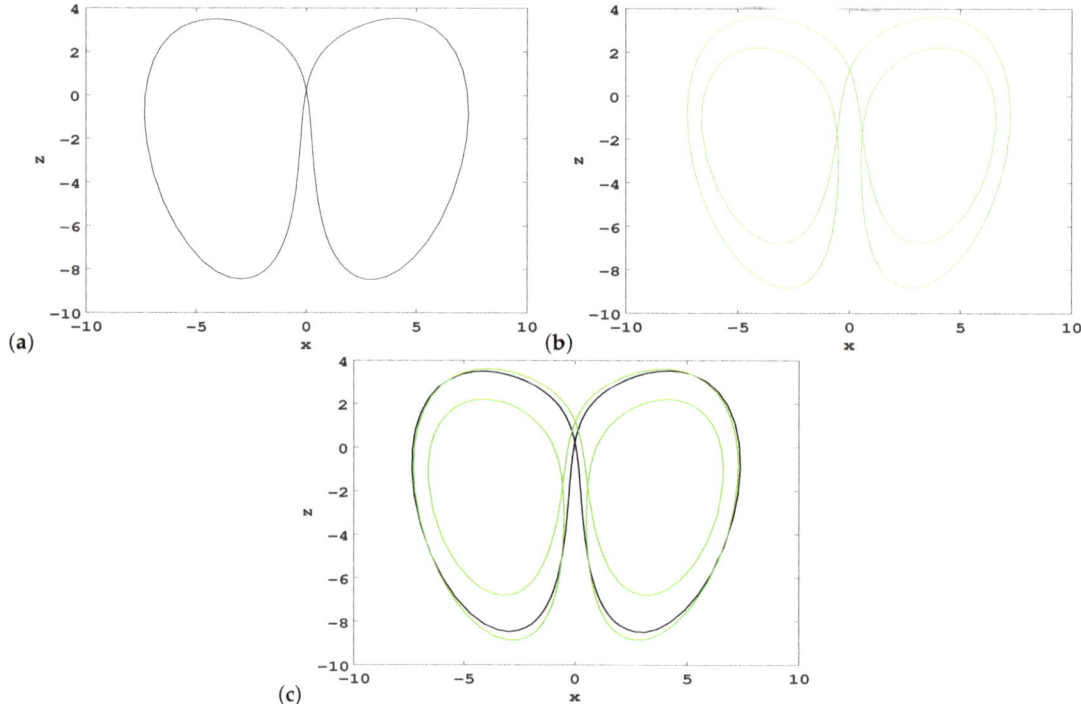

Figure 11. Two coexisting hidden periodic attractors of system (2); $(a, b, c, k, m) = (10, 10, 2.7, -0.2, 2)$; (a) periodic attractor; (b) another periodic attractor; (c) coexisting periodic attractors. The black line and the green line correspond to the periodic attractor shown in (a,b), respectively.

3.2.5. Coexistence of Hidden Hyperchaotic Attractors

Fixing the parameters $(a, b, c, k, m) = (10, 70, 2.7, -0.2, 5)$ and taking the initial values $(1, -1, 1, 4)$, system (2) has an asymmetrical hidden hyperchaotic attractor with projection onto the x–z plane, as shown in Figure 12a. The four Lyapunov exponents are $L_1 = 0.2069$, $L_2 = 0.1033$, $L_3 = -0.1665$, and $L_4 = -12.0257$. The corresponding fractal dimension is 3.0119.

Based on the symmetry about the z-axis of system (2), if we choose initial values $(-1, 1, 1, -4)$, the other asymmetrical hidden hyperchaotic attractor can be obtained, whose 2D phase portrait is shown in Figure 12b. The two attractors have the same Lyapunov exponents and fractal dimension.

Choosing the same parameters and taking initial values $(1, 1, 1, 1)$, the four Lyapunov exponents are $L_1 = 0.4159$, $L_2 = 0.2456$, $L_3 = 0$, and $L_4 = -12.6681$, and the Kaplan–Yorke dimension is 3.0521. A symmetrical hidden hyperchaotic attractor can be found, whose projection onto the 2D phase space is presented in Figure 12c.

Through the above analysis, we can observe that system (2) simultaneously has three coexisting hidden hyperchaotic attractors under parameters $(a, b, c, k, m) = (10, 70, 2.7, -0.2, 5)$, as shown in Figure 12d. The basins of attraction of three coexisting hidden hyperchaotic attractors can also be calculated, as shown in Figure 13, where the yellow area denotes the basin of attraction of a symmetrical hyperchaotic attractor, while the red and blue areas represent the basin of attraction of an asymmetrical hyperchaotic attractor presented in Figure 12a,b, respectively. Riddled basins can be observed in Figure 13, which means that the dynamical behaviors of the proposed 4D system are extremely sensitive to the initial values.

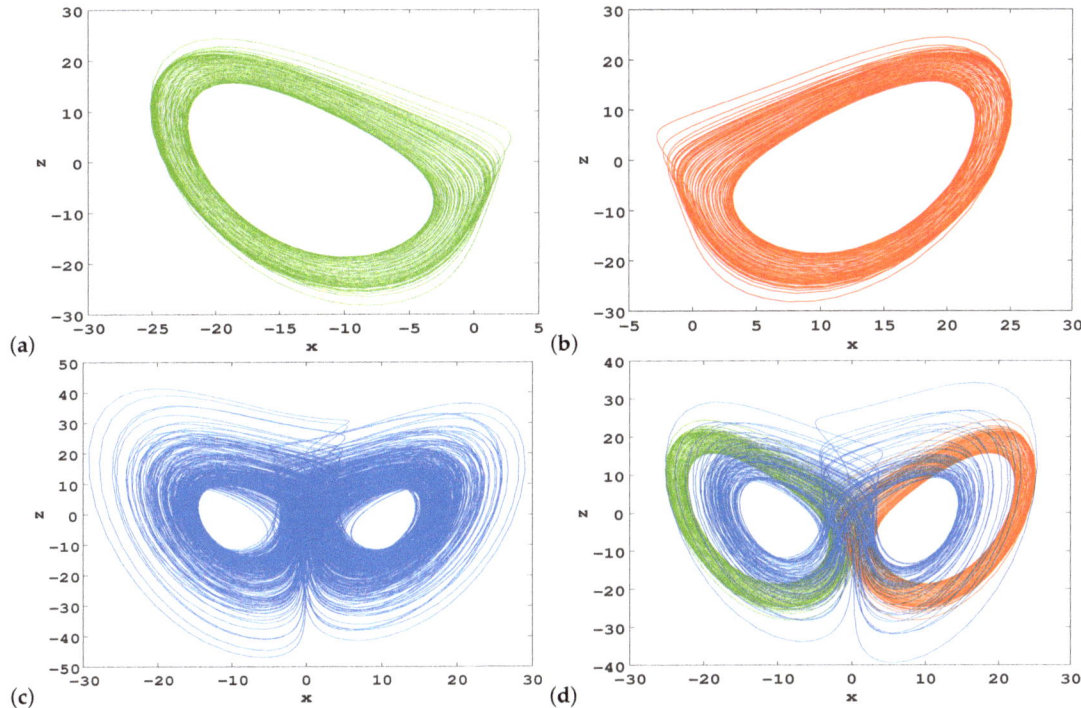

Figure 12. Three coexisting hidden hyperchaotic attractors of system (2); $(a, b, c, k, m) = (10, 70, 2.7, -0.2, 5)$; (**a**) asymmetrical hyperchaotic attractor; (**b**) the other asymmetrical hyperchaotic attractor; (**c**) symmetrical hyperchaotic attractor; (**d**) coexisting hyperchaotic attractors. The green line, the red line and the blue line correspond to the hyperchaotic attractor shown in (**a**–**c**), respectively.

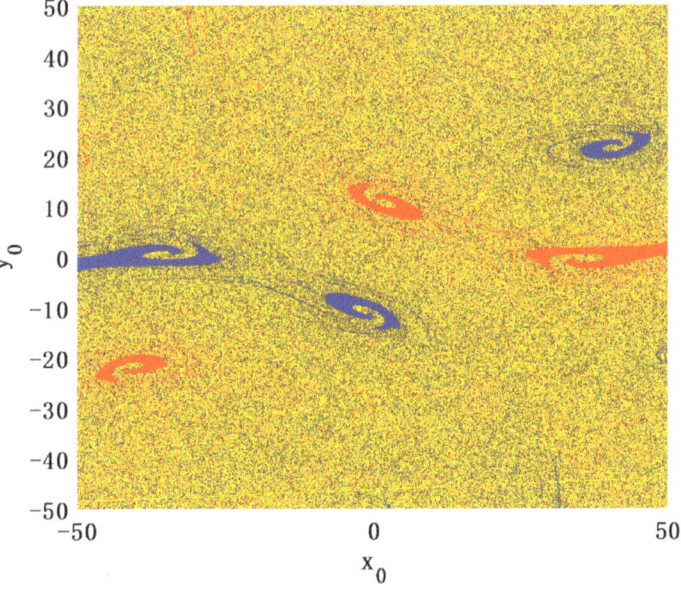

Figure 13. Basins of attraction in the $x(0)$–$y(0)$ initial plane with $z(0) = w(0) = 0$.

4. Analysis of Unstable Cycles for New 4D Hyperchaotic System via Variational Approach

In this section, we employ the variational calculation approach for the unstable periodic orbit search and establish an appropriate symbolic encoding for the found cycles. We also analyze the continuous deformations of cycles by the homotopy evolution method, which shows applicable flexibility under different circumstances. We aim to accurately find the encircling way of the orbit in the new 4D hyperchaotic system and develop an effective way to classify periodic orbits. Several short periodic orbits in system (2) are located, and the evolution law of the period of cycle alteration with parameters is discussed, which indicates that the proposed method is effective at analyzing unstable periodic orbits.

4.1. Variational Method for Calculations

Strange attractors in hyperchaotic systems are densely covered by countless unstable periodic orbits. Therefore, extracting unstable cycles usually has an important influence on understanding their properties. Many numerical methods are employed to extract the periodic orbits of various systems [45]. We utilized the variational method in this paper, which has shown its reliability and efficiency [46]. The basic physical idea is to make an initial loop guess about the shape of the periodic orbit, and then gradually evolve it into a real periodic orbit. Initialization is important in the variational calculations, as it determines whether the calculated periodic orbit is the one of interest, and it can be implemented by various means [47].

Using the variational method to locate periodic orbits, a discretization equation,

$$\begin{pmatrix} \hat{A} & -\hat{v} \\ \hat{a} & 0 \end{pmatrix} \begin{pmatrix} \delta \tilde{x} \\ \delta \lambda \end{pmatrix} = \delta \tau \begin{pmatrix} \lambda \hat{v} - \tilde{v} \\ 0 \end{pmatrix}, \qquad (4)$$

can be derived to solve for $\delta \tilde{x}$ and $\delta \lambda$, so as to achieve the location of the cycle and period [46]. Compared to other numerical methods, as a result of the use of a continuum of points, the variational method has the advantage of numerical stability. Furthermore, we do not need to choose a Poincaré section beforehand. The variational method can be used to calculate the stable or unstable periodic orbits of various systems [48–50]. In addition, the continuous deformation of cycles with the variation of parameters can be studied based on the variational method, and the bifurcation phenomenon can be observed by analyzing whether the number or stability of cycles has changed. Next, we use the variational method to extract the unstable cycles in system (2).

4.2. Extracting Unstable Cycles in a Hidden Hyperchaotic Attractor

We calculated the unstable cycles embedded in a hidden hyperchaotic attractor with parameters $(a, b, c, k, m) = (10, 100, 2.7, -0.2, 1)$ by the variational method. Symbols were used to encode them for cycles with different topological structures, so that all of the cycles could be located without duplication or being missing based on symbolic dynamics [51]. When utilizing the variational method for initialization, the segments of trajectories with similar shapes were obtained through numerical integration, and they were manually connected to close, so as to become a loop. By this approach, several cycles with different complexity were found. Figure 14 shows two periodic orbits with the simplest topology; they have certain symmetry with each other and the shortest periods of the same size. Figure 15 shows four more intricate periodic orbits, which are composed of two building blocks of periodic orbits with different topologies.

Motivated by this observation, we marked the cycles in Figure 15a,b as 03 and 12, respectively; thus, the cycle in Figure 14a is cycle 2, and that in Figure 14b is cycle 3. We did not find cycle 0 or 1, which means that they were pruned. With the help of four basic orbital segments, longer periodic orbits can also be encoded and calculated. Figure 16 shows six cycles with topological length 3. In total, we found 18 periodic orbits within topological length 3, which are listed in Table 2. It is worth noting that the symmetry of system (2) can also be seen from Table 2. The two cycles of commutative symbols 0 and 1, or 2 and 3, are conjugate to each other, and they have the same periods.

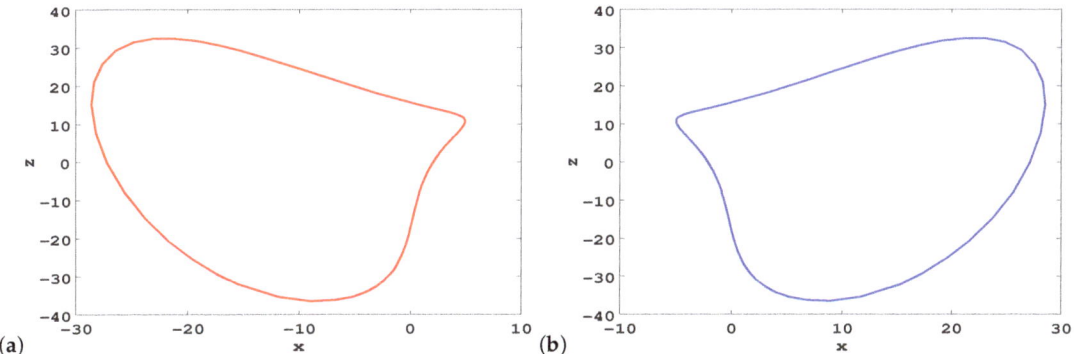

Figure 14. Two shortest periodic orbits in system (2) for parameters $(a, b, c, k, m) = (10, 100, 2.7, -0.2, 1)$; (**a**) cycle 2; (**b**) cycle 3.

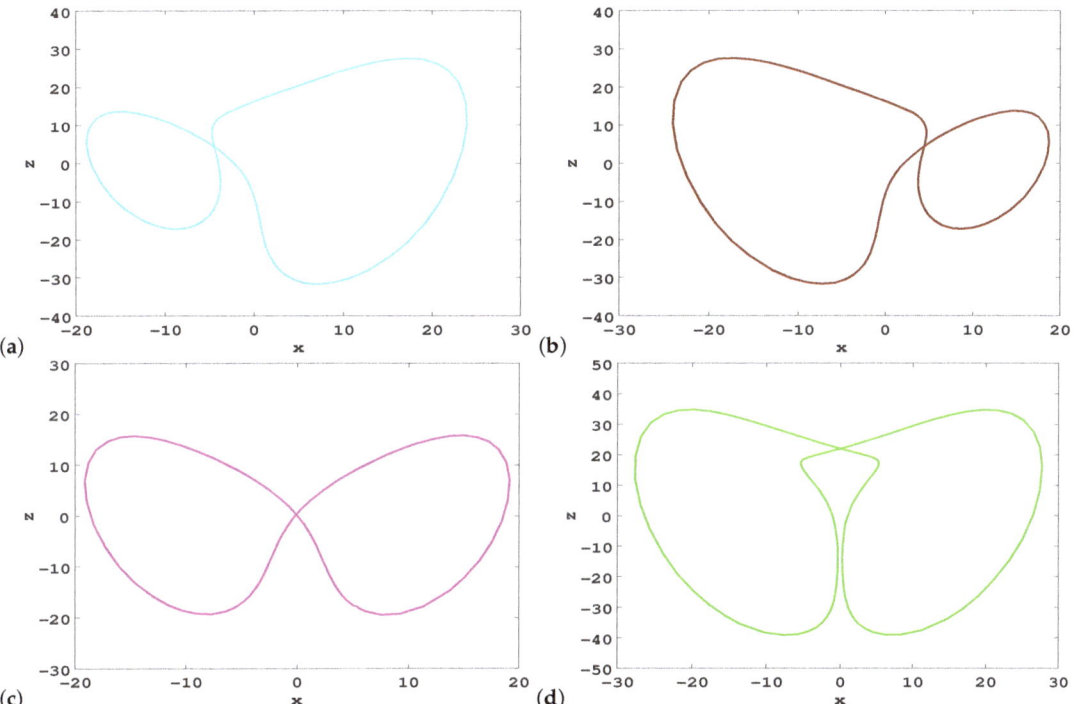

Figure 15. Four periodic orbits with topological length 2 in system (2) for parameters $(a, b, c, k, m) = (10, 100, 2.7, -0.2, 1)$; (**a**) cycle 03; (**b**) 12; (**c**) 01; (**d**) 23.

According to the above encoding rules, other complex long periodic orbits can also be calculated as follows. We generated the initial loop guess based on the symbol sequence corresponding to the cycle, and employed the variational method to verify whether the cycle existed. Figure 17 shows an unstable cycle with a topological length of 8, with corresponding symbol encoding 02130101. The successful search of such complex periodic orbits also shows the effectiveness of our encoding method in calculating various periodic orbits embedded in a hidden hyperchaotic attractor.

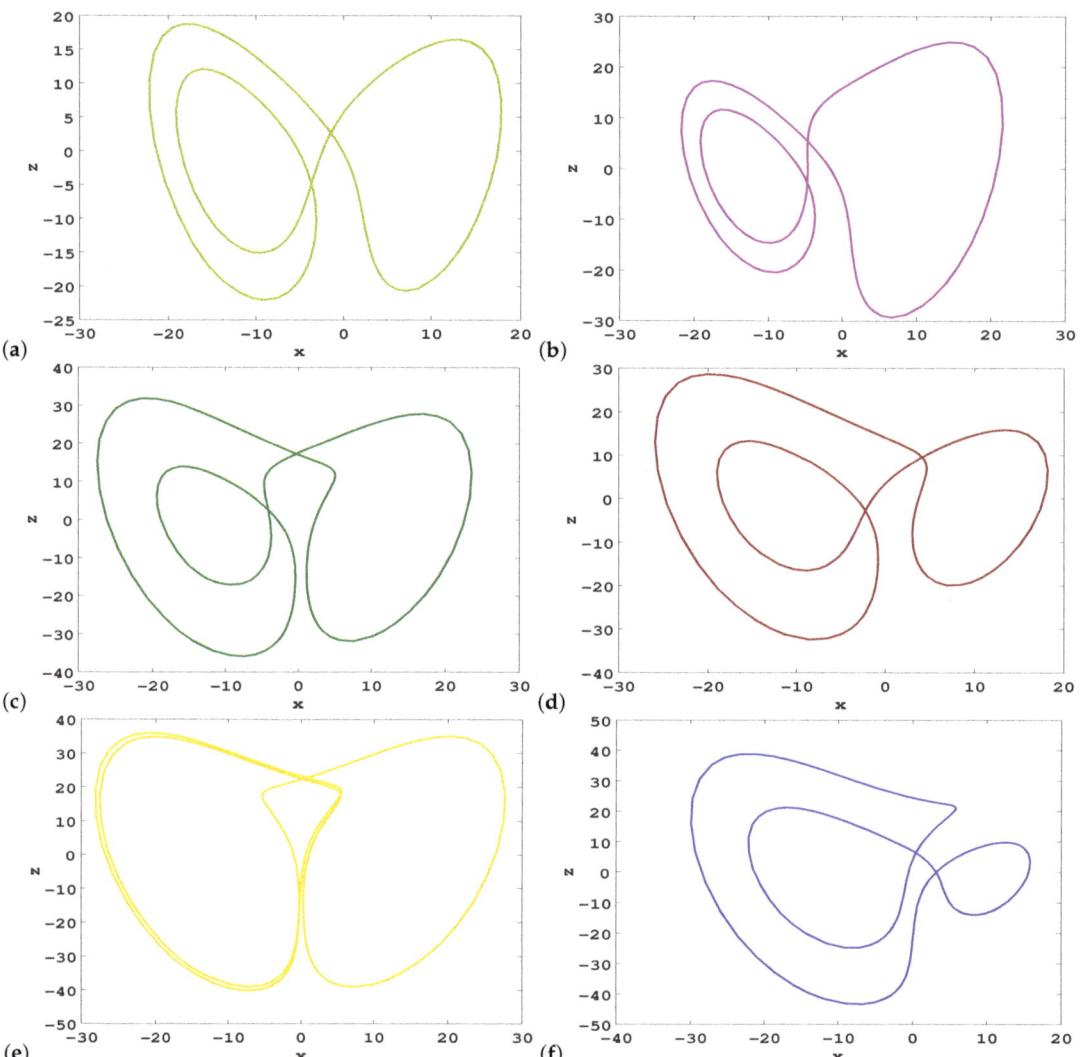

Figure 16. Unstable cycles with topological length 3 in system (2) for parameters $(a, b, c, k, m) = (10, 100, 2.7, -0.2, 1)$; (**a**) cycle 001; (**b**) 003; (**c**) 023; (**d**) 021; (**e**) 223; (**f**) 012.

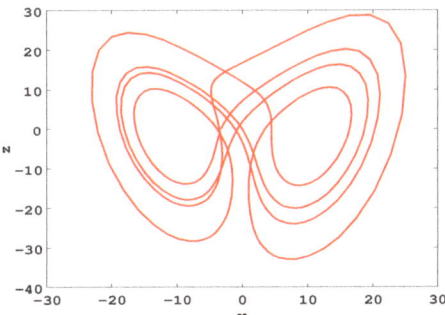

Figure 17. Cycle 02130101 with topological length 8 in system (2) for parameters $(a, b, c, k, m) = (10, 100, 2.7, -0.2, 1)$.

Table 2. Eighteen unstable periodic orbits embedded in the hidden hyperchaotic attractor of system (2) for $(a, b, c, k, m) = (10, 100, 2.7, -0.2, 1)$; listed are the topological length, itinerary p, period T_p, and four coordinates of a point on the cycle.

Length	p	T_p	x	y	z	w
1	2	0.858233	0.851259	3.599482	−8.032931	−39.656931
	3	0.858233	−0.851259	−3.599482	−8.032931	39.656931
2	03	1.362034	−4.076805	−1.813737	1.109695	−14.135359
	12	1.362034	4.076805	1.813737	1.109695	14.135359
	01	1.194275	5.206540	7.525051	−17.639962	1.385740
	23	1.830597	0.626331	−0.321247	−4.302274	1.490707
3	001	1.732553	−5.282481	3.245260	0.268165	−34.418329
	011	1.732553	5.282481	−3.245260	0.268165	34.418329
	003	1.821191	−4.653735	2.777113	−2.962048	−38.837657
	112	1.821191	4.653735	−2.777113	−2.962048	38.837657
	132	2.211630	11.320228	14.639216	−16.413004	25.186818
	023	2.211630	−11.320228	−14.639216	−16.413004	−25.186818
	021	1.968277	−6.298304	3.295041	5.572765	−20.401797
	013	1.968277	6.298304	−3.295041	5.572765	20.401797
	223	2.766255	1.453074	−0.422130	2.547336	1.463103
	233	2.766255	−1.453074	0.422130	2.547336	−1.463103
	012	2.207939	4.137109	5.676602	−5.643553	−9.306008
	031	2.207939	−4.137109	−5.676602	−5.643553	9.306008

4.3. Homotopy Evolution of Cycle Variation with Different Parameters

With the change of different parameters, the number of periodic orbits and their stability can undergo changes, which means that bifurcations may occur [52]; the variational approach is convenient to study various bifurcation behaviors. We studied the evolution of unstable cycles of system (2) when parameters were altered, and the homotopy evolution method could be conveniently used for the initialization [53]. For a dynamical system, when the parameters alter little, most short cycles experience slight deformation unless bifurcation occurs. Therefore, the periodic orbits previously calculated with given parameters could be taken as the initial loop guess for the next calculations. Initializing in this way, the calculations of cycles were very efficient.

First, the bifurcations of periodic orbits were investigated by varying a while fixing $b = 100$, $c = 2.7$, $k = -0.2$, and $m = 1$. We used the previously calculated cycle 2 as the initial loop guess to calculate cycle 2 for the next a value. Figure 18a illustrates the homotopy evolution cases. We found that when $a < 5$ or $a > 20$, the calculation of cycle 2 by the variational method was no longer convergent. Thus, we can conclude that the system experiences periodic orbit bifurcations at $a = 5$ and $a = 20$.

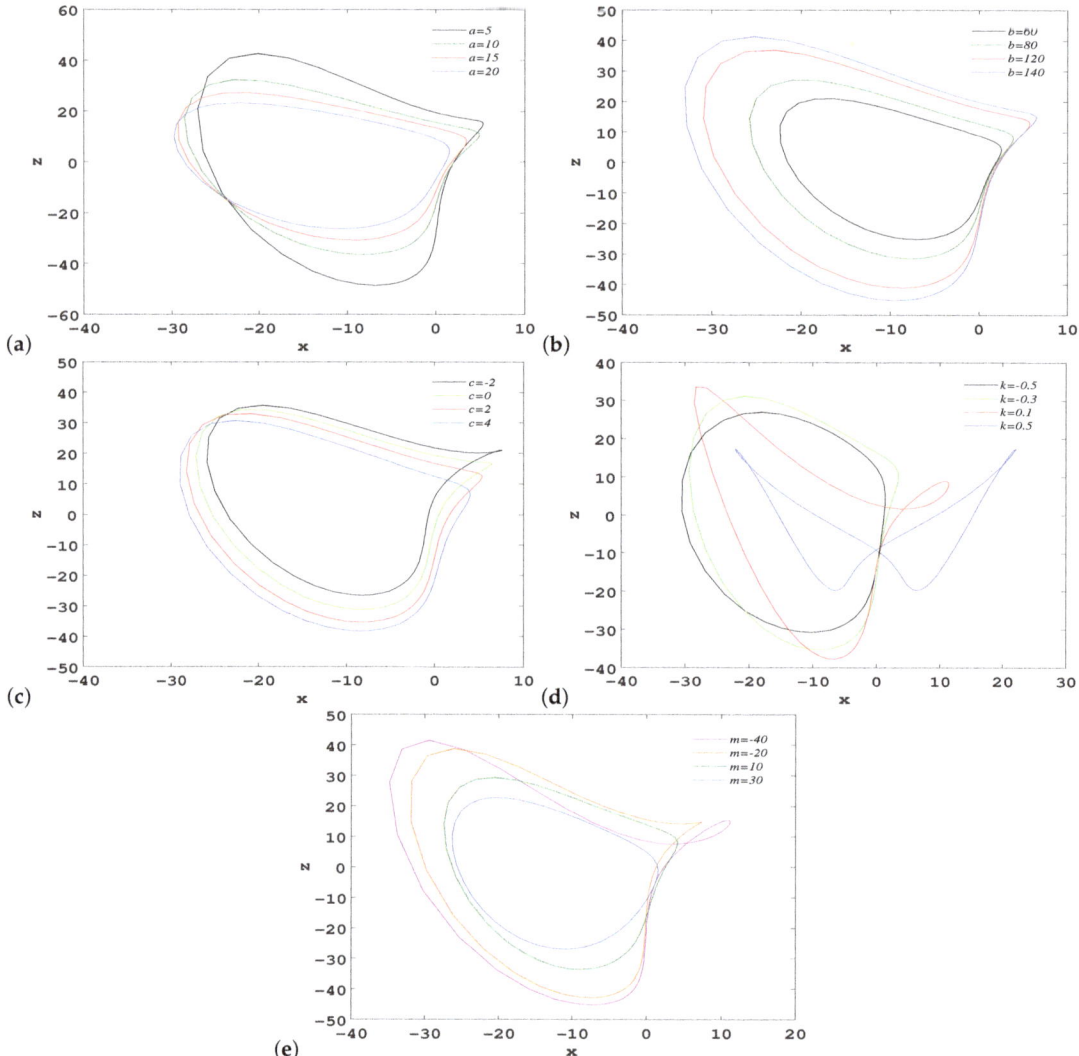

Figure 18. Homotopy evolution of cycle 2 with respect to different parameters: (**a**) four a values; (**b**) b values; (**c**) c values; (**d**) k values; (**e**) m values.

Then, we studied the continuous deformation of cycle 2 with respect to the b value in the same way, fixing $a = 10$, $c = 2.7$, $k = -0.2$, and $m = 1$. Figure 18b shows the deformation of cycle 2 with the b value. We also found that the periodic orbit bifurcations occurred when $b = 52$. Similarly, we changed c, k, and m, respectively, and fixed the remaining parameters to study the continuous deformation of cycle 2; the homotopy evolution processes are shown in Figure 18c–e. Table 3 lists the periods T_p of cycle 2 at different parameter values. By symmetry, it is obvious that cycle 3 has a similar deformation as the variation of parameters. The above discussion demonstrates that if we take a new set of parameters, new periodic orbits corresponding to the new period will appear, and some of the periodic orbits in Table 2 will no longer exist due to periodic orbit bifurcations.

Finally, we explored the evolution rule between the orbital period and different parameters. From Table 3, it can be concluded that the larger the parameters a, b, c, and m, the smaller the periods, and as k increases, the period becomes larger. We confirm that this conclusion is applicable to all of the other short cycles calculated in system (2).

Table 3. Periods T_p of cycle 2 for different parameters.

a	T_p	b	T_p	c	T_p	k	T_p	m	T_p
5	1.082797	60	0.953492	-2	0.880703	-0.5	0.705715	-40	0.996271
10	0.858233	80	0.911549	0	0.873372	-0.3	0.821457	-20	0.968155
15	0.729400	120	0.811395	2	0.864607	0.1	0.964986	10	0.799075
20	0.610639	140	0.771540	4	0.833397	0.5	1.140899	30	0.611363

5. Circuit Design and Realization of New System

The circuit implementation can verify the feasibility and validity of a new chaotic system. The electronic synthesis of a novel antimonotic hyperjerk system was proposed based on an analog computing approach [54]. We employed Multisim simulation software to build a circuit. We selected four channels, corresponding to four state variables of the new system, to observe whether the results of the phase diagrams were consistent with the output of the actual circuit. The main task was to design and implement the hyperchaotic system and verify the circuit that realized the coexistence of chaotic and periodic attractors. Since the state variables of system (2) were beyond the dynamic range of the device, a proportional transformation was required to set the amplitude scaling factor to 10, where $X = \frac{1}{10}x$, $Y = \frac{1}{10}y$, $Z = \frac{1}{10}z$, and $W = \frac{1}{10}w$. Therefore, system (2) was rewritten as

$$\begin{aligned} \dot{X} &= a(Y-X) + 10kXZ + W \\ \dot{Y} &= -cY - 10XZ \\ \dot{Z} &= -0.1b + 10XY \\ \dot{W} &= -mY. \end{aligned} \quad (5)$$

We implemented a time-scale transformation of Equation (5), with the time scale factor set to $\tau_0 = \frac{1}{R_0 C_0} = 1000$. A new time variable τ was used instead of t, and $t = \tau_0 \tau$. As shown in Figure 1, a hyperchaotic attractor exists under the parameters $(a, b, c, k, m) = (10, 100, 2.7, -0.2, 1)$. The proposed circuit design is depicted in Figure 19, in which three analog multipliers (the output gain was 0.1) were used to realize 3 nonlinear terms, 12 AD712AH operational amplifiers, 4 capacitors, and 25 resistances to realize the addition, integration, and inversion operations. The power supply voltage was ± 18 V. Based on Kirchhoff's law, the corresponding circuit equations can be derived as

$$\begin{aligned} \dot{X} &= \frac{R_5}{R_2 R_6 C_1} Y - \frac{R_5}{R_1 R_6 C_1} X - \frac{R_5}{R_3 R_6 C_1} 0.1 XZ + \frac{R_5}{R_4 R_6 C_1} W \\ \dot{Y} &= -\frac{R_{11}}{R_9 R_{12} C_2} Y - \frac{R_{11}}{R_{10} R_{12} C_2} 0.1 XZ \\ \dot{Z} &= \frac{R_{17}}{R_{16} R_{18} C_3} V_1 + \frac{R_{17}}{R_{15} R_{18} C_3} 0.1 XY \\ \dot{W} &= -\frac{R_{22}}{R_{21} R_{23} C_4} Y. \end{aligned} \quad (6)$$

The values of each device in the circuit can be obtained by comparing Equations (5) and (6); we set $V1 = -1$ V, $R_3 = 5$ kΩ, $R_9 = 37.037$ kΩ, $C_i = 100$ nF (i =1,2,3,4), $R_i = 10$ kΩ ($i = 1, 2, 6, 7, 8, 12, 13, 14, 16, 18, 19, 20, 23, 24, 25$), $R_j = 100$ kΩ ($j = 4, 5, 11, 17, 21, 22$), and $R_k = 1$ kΩ ($k = 10, 15$). The results obtained by Multisim 14.0 with initial conditions $(X(0), Y(0), Z(0), W(0)) = (1 \text{ V}, 1 \text{ V}, 1 \text{ V}, 1 \text{ V})$ are shown in Figure 20, and it can be clearly seen that the results are consistent with the phase diagrams from the numerical simulation.

When the system parameters change to $a = 10$, $b = 12$, $c = 2.7$, $k = -0.2$, and $m = 1$, system (2) has coexisting chaotic and periodic attractors. We implemented a scale transformation of z, reducing it by a factor of 5, to obtain

$$\begin{aligned}
\dot{X} &= a(Y - X) + 5kXZ + W \\
\dot{Y} &= -cY - 5XZ \\
\dot{Z} &= -0.2b + 0.2XY \\
\dot{W} &= -mY.
\end{aligned} \quad (7)$$

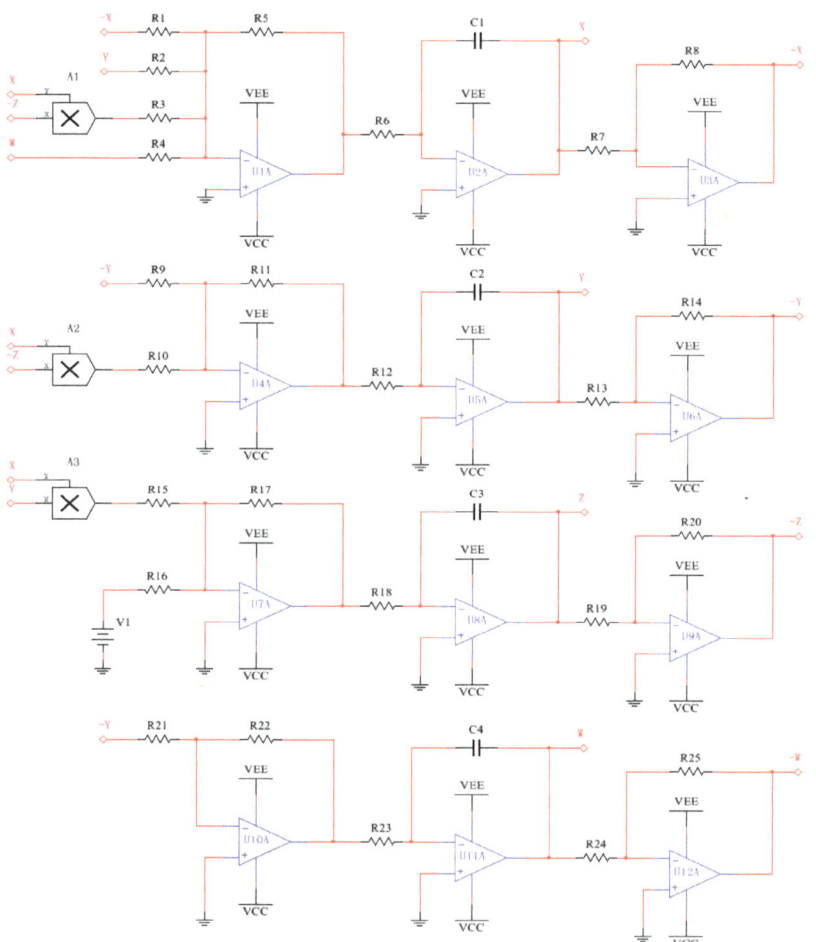

Figure 19. Circuit diagram of the implementation of system (2).

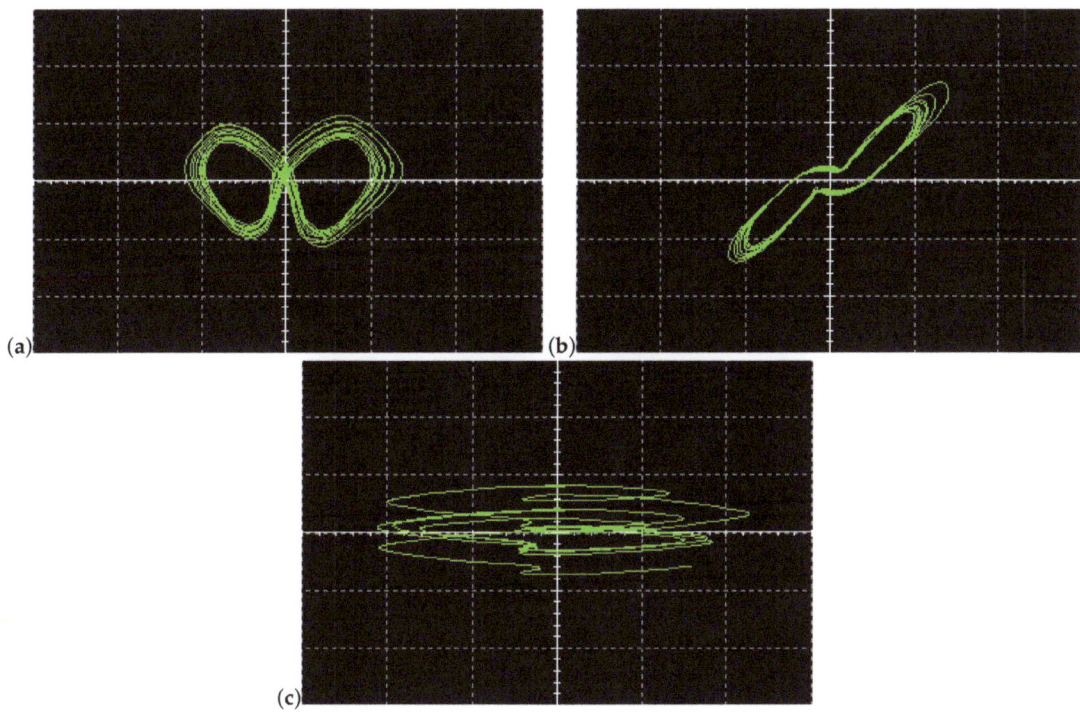

Figure 20. Two-dimensional phase portraits of the new system in Multisim of the circuit with $a = 10$, $b = 100$, $c = 2.7$, $k = -0.2$, and $m = 1$: (**a**) X–Z plane; (**b**) X–Y plane; (**c**) Y–W plane.

We modified the values of several resistors, $R_3 = 10$ kΩ, $R_{10} = 2$ kΩ, $R_{15} = 60$ kΩ, $R_{16} = 50$ kΩ, and $R_{17} = 120$ kΩ, while keeping the other devices in the circuit unchanged; two coexisting attractors can now be observed with initial conditions $(X(0), Y(0), Z(0), W(0)) = (1 \text{ V}, 1 \text{ V}, 1 \text{ V}, 1 \text{ V})$ and $(X(0), Y(0), Z(0), W(0)) = (-0.9 \text{ V}, -1 \text{ V}, -8 \text{ V}, -1.7 \text{ V})$, as illustrated in Figure 21. Obviously, the circuit modeling findings are in good agreement with Figure 8, which shows the validity and practicability of the proposed system.

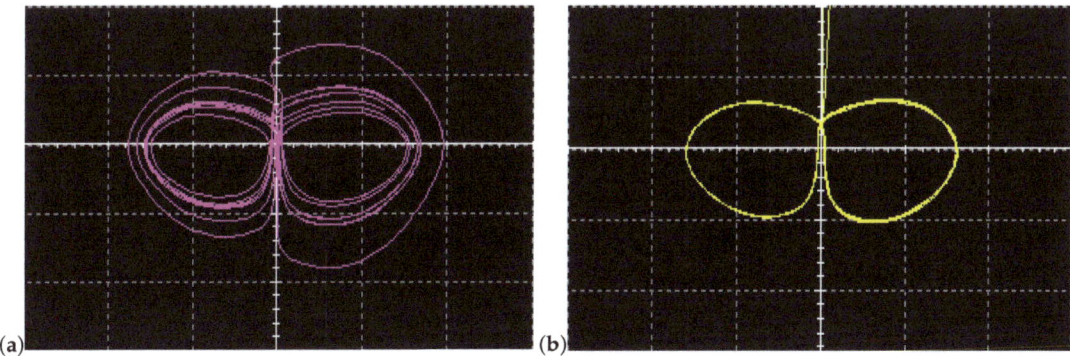

Figure 21. Phase portraits of coexisting attractors in Multisim of the circuit with $a = 10$, $b = 12$, $c = 2.7$, $k = -0.2$, and $m = 1$: (**a**) hidden chaotic attractor; (**b**) hidden periodic attractor. Scales of horizontal and vertical axes are 5 and 2 V/div, respectively.

6. Conclusions

In this study, we constructed a novel 4D hyperchaotic system by linearly adding a new state variable to a new hidden chaotic system with two stable equilibrium points. The proposed system could generate hidden hyperchaotic attractors and various types of coexisting attractors, depending on the choice of parameters and initial values; this showed the diversity and complexity of the dynamical behavior of the system. The numerical analyses of phase diagrams, time-sequence diagrams, basins of attraction, Lyapunov exponents, and bifurcation diagrams were also been discussed, further confirming the coexistence of these attractors and riddled basins. The C_0 complexity analysis related to the main parameters of the new system was also explored, which identified the dynamic characteristics and complexity of the system. In addition, by using the variational method, the unstable cycles embedded in the hidden hyperchaotic attractor were calculated and encoded accordingly. The periodic orbit bifurcations were analyzed based on the continuous deformation of cycles. The feasibility of the novel 4D hyperchaotic model was verified by an analog circuit, which was in good qualitative agreement with the results obtained by numerical simulations.

Although the four-letter encoding of unstable periodic orbits embedded in the hidden hyperchaotic attractor was presented in this paper, the symmetric reduction of a given dynamical system is still an interesting problem to investigate, and may reduce the number of letters used to encode periodic orbits. In addition, the analysis of the dynamics and various attractors of the newly proposed 4D system with two lines of equilibria is also worthy of further research. More mathematical investigations, including other types of bifurcations and periodic orbits of the new system, will be carried out in our future work. We believe that this kind of autonomous 4D system with hidden hyperchaotic attractors and many coexisting attractors have potential application in physics and engineering, such as in lasers, robotics, secure communications, control systems, random signal generation, and information encryption. The research in this paper could provide some enlightenment for the more systematic study of 4D hyperchaotic systems.

Author Contributions: C.D.: conceptualization, methodology, formal analysis, software, investigation, supervision, writing—original draft, writing—review and editing. J.W.: software, methodology, validation, investigation, writing—original draft, writing—review and editing. All authors have read and agreed to the published version of the manuscript.

Funding: This work is supported by the National Natural Science Foundation of China (grant nos. 11647085 and 11647086), the Shanxi Province Science Foundation for Youths (grant no. 201901D211252), and the Scientific and Technological Innovation Programs of Higher Education Institutions in Shanxi (grant nos. 2019L0505 and 2019L0554).

Institutional Review Board Statement: Not applicable.

Informed Consent Statement: Not applicable.

Data Availability Statement: The data used to support the findings of this study are available from the corresponding author upon request.

Acknowledgments: We thank the anonymous reviewers for their many insightful comments and suggestions, which have improved our manuscript substantially.

Conflicts of Interest: The authors declare no conflict of interest.

References

1. Strogatz, S.H. *Nonlinear Dynamics and Chaos: With Applications to Physics, Biology, Chemistry, and Engineering*; Perseus Books: Reading, MA, USA, 1994.
2. Cvitanović, P. *Universality in Chaos*, 2nd ed.; Bristol: Adam Hilger, UK, 1989.
3. Rössler, O.E. An equation for hyperchaos. *Phy. Lett. A* **1979**, *71*, 155–156. [CrossRef]
4. Wang, X.; Kuznetsov, N.V.; Chen, G. (Eds.) *Chaotic Systems with Multistability and Hidden Attractors*; Emergence, Complexity and Computation; Springer: Cham, Switzerland, 2021; Volume 40, pp. 149–150.
5. Gao, T.; Chen, Z.; Yuan, Z.; Chen, G. A hyperchaos generated from Chen's system. *Int. J. Mod. Phys. C* **2011**, *17*, 471–478. [CrossRef]

6. Wang, F.Q.; Liu, C.X. Hyperchaos evolved from the Liu chaotic system. *Chin. Phys.* **2006**, *15*, 963–968.
7. Wang, X.; Wang, M. A hyperchaos generated from Lorenz system. *Physica A* **2008**, *387*, 3751–3758. [CrossRef]
8. Li, Y.; Tang, W.; Chen G. Hyperchaos evolved from the generalized Lorenz equation. *Int. J. Circ. Theor. Appl.* **2005**, *33*, 235–251. [CrossRef]
9. Bao, B.; Xu, J.; Liu, Z.; Ma, Z. Hyperchaos from an augmented Lü system. *Int. J. Bifurcat. Chaos* **2010**, *20*, 3689–3698. [CrossRef]
10. Yang, Q.; Bai, M. A new 5D hyperchaotic system based on modified generalized Lorenz system. *Nonlinear Dyn.* **2017**, *88*, 189–221. [CrossRef]
11. Shen, C.; Yu, S.; Lü, J.; Chen, G. Generating hyperchaotic systems with multiple positive Lyapunov exponents. In Proceedings of the 9th Asian Control Conference (ASCC), Istanbul, Turkey, 23–26 June 2013; pp. 1–5.
12. Yang, Q.; Zhu, D.; Yang, L. A New 7D hyperchaotic system with five positive Lyapunov exponents coined. *Int. J. Bifurcat. Chaos* **2018**, *28*, 1850057. [CrossRef]
13. Leonov, G.A.; Kuznetsov, N.V. Hidden attractors in dynamical systems. From hidden oscillations in Hilbert-Kolmogorov, Aizerman, and Kalman problems to hidden chaotic attractor in Chua circuits. *Int. J. Bifurcat. Chaos* **2013**, *23*, 1330002. [CrossRef]
14. Lorenz, E.N. Deterministic nonperiodic flow. *J. Atmos. Sci.* **1963**, *20*, 130–141. [CrossRef]
15. Chen, G.R.; Ueta, T. Yet another chaotic attractor. *Int. J. Bifurcat. Chaos* **1999**, *9*, 1465–1466. [CrossRef]
16. Lü, J.; Chen, G. A new chaotic attractor coined. *Int. J. Bifurcat. Chaos* **2002**, *12*, 659–661. [CrossRef]
17. Sprott, J.C. Some simple chaotic flows. *Phys. Rev. E* **1994**, *50*, 647–650. [CrossRef]
18. Wei, Z.; Wang, R.; Liu, A. A new finding of the existence of hidden hyperchaotic attractors with no equilibria. *Math. Comput. Simulat.* **2014**, *100*, 13–23. [CrossRef]
19. Cao, H.Y.; Zhao, L. A new chaotic system with different equilibria and attractors. *Eur. Phys. J. Spec. Top.* **2021**, *230*, 1905–1914. [CrossRef]
20. Lai, Q.; Wan, Z.; Kuate, P. Modelling and circuit realisation of a new no-equilibrium chaotic system with hidden attractor and coexisting attractors. *Electron. Lett.* **2020**, *56*, 1044–1046. [CrossRef]
21. Pham, V.T.; Volos, C.; Jafari S.; Wei, Z.; Wang, X. Constructing a novel no-equilibrium chaotic system. *Int. J. Bifurcat. Chaos* **2014**, *24*, 1450073. [CrossRef]
22. Azar, A.T.; Volos, C.; Gerodimos, N.A.; Tombras, G.S.; Pham, V.T.; Radwan, A.G.; Vaidyanathan, S.; Ouannas, A.; Munoz-Pacheco, J.M. A novel chaotic system without equilibrium: Dynamics, synchronization, and circuit realization. *Complexity* **2017**, *2017*, 7871467. [CrossRef]
23. Yang, Q.; Wei, Z.; Chen, G. An unusual 3d autonomous quadratic chaotic system with two stable node-foci. *Int. J. Bifurcat. Chaos* **2010**, *20*, 1061–1083. [CrossRef]
24. Dong, C. Dynamics, periodic orbit analysis, and circuit implementation of a new chaotic system with hidden attractor. *Fractal Fract.* **2022**, *6*, 190. [CrossRef]
25. Pham, V.T.; Jafari, S.; Kapitaniak T. Constructing a chaotic system with an infinite number of equilibrium points. *Int. J. Bifurcat. Chaos* **2016**, *26*, 1650225. [CrossRef]
26. Wang, X.; Chen, G. Constructing a chaotic system with any number of equilibria. *Nonlinear Dyn.* **2013**, *71*, 429–436. [CrossRef]
27. Yang, Q.; Qiao, X. Constructing a new 3D chaotic system with any number of equilibria. *Int. J. Bifurcat. Chaos* **2019**, *29*, 1950060. [CrossRef]
28. Kuznetsov, N.V.; Leonov, G.A.; Vagaitsev, V.I. Analytical-numerical method for attractor localization of generalized Chua's system. In Proceedings of the IFAC Proceedings Volumes (IFAC-Papers Online), Antalya, Turkey, 26–28 August 2010.
29. Ren, S.; Panahi, S.; Rajagopal, K.; Akgul, A.; Pham, V.T. A new chaotic flow with hidden attractor: The first hyperjerk system with no equilibrium. *Z. Naturforsch. A* **2018**, *73*, 239–249. [CrossRef]
30. Wei, Z.; Rajagopal, K.; Zhang, W.; Kingni, S.T.; Akgül, A. Synchronisation, electronic circuit implementation, and fractional-order analysis of 5D ordinary differential equations with hidden hyperchaotic attractors. *Pramana–J. Phys.* **2018**, *90*, 50. [CrossRef]
31. Yang, Q.; Yang, L.; Ou, B. Hidden hyperchaotic attractors in a new 5D system based on chaotic system with two stable node-foci. *Int. J. Bifurcat. Chaos* **2019**, *29*, 1950092. [CrossRef]
32. Cui, L.; Luo, W.; Ou, Q. Analysis of basins of attraction of new coupled hidden attractor system. *Chaos Soliton. Fract.* **2021**, *146*, 110913. [CrossRef]
33. Lai, Q.; Akgul, A.; Li, C.; Xu, G.; Cavusoglu, U. A new chaotic system with multiple attractors: Dynamic analysis, circuit realization and S-Box design. *Entropy* **2017**, *20*, 12. [CrossRef]
34. Bayani, A.; Rajagopal, K.; Khalaf, A.J.M.; Jafari, S.; Leutcho, G.D.; Kengne, J. Dynamical analysis of a new multistable chaotic system with hidden attractor: Antimonotonicity, coexisting multiple attractors, and offset boosting. *Phys. Lett. A* **2019**, *383*, 1450–1456. [CrossRef]
35. Nazarimehr, F.; Rajagopal, K.; Kengne, J.; Jafari, S.; Pham, V.T. A new four-dimensional system containing chaotic or hyper-chaotic attractors with no equilibrium, a line of equilibria and unstable equilibria. *Chaos Soliton. Fract.* **2018**, *111*, 108–118. [CrossRef]
36. Lai, Q.; Chen, C.; Zhao, X.W.; Kengne, J.; Volos, C. Constructing chaotic system with multiple coexisting attractors. *IEEE Access* **2019**, *7*, 24051–24056. [CrossRef]
37. Ma, C.; Mou, J.; Xiong, L.; Banerjee, S.; Liu, T.; Han, X. Dynamical analysis of a new chaotic system: asymmetric multistability, offset boosting control and circuit realization. *Nonlinear Dyn.* **2021**, *103*, 2867–2880. [CrossRef]

38. Lai, Q.; Norouzi, B.; Liu, F. Dynamic analysis, circuit realization, control design and image encryption application of an extended Lü system with coexisting attractors. *Chaos Soliton. Fract.* **2018**, *114*, 230–245. [CrossRef]
39. Natiq, H.; Said, M.; Al-Saidi, N.; Kilicman, A. Dynamics and complexity of a new 4D chaotic laser system. *Entropy* **2019**, *21*, 34. [CrossRef]
40. Rajagopal, K.; Akgul, A.; Pham, V.T.; Alsaadi, F.E.; Nazarimehr, F.; Alsaadi, F.E.; Jafari, S. Multistability and coexisting attractors in a new circulant chaotic system. *Int. J. Bifurcat. Chaos* **2019**, *29*, 1950174. [CrossRef]
41. Lai, Q.; Wan, Z.; Kuate, P.; Fotsin, H. Coexisting attractors, circuit implementation and synchronization control of a new chaotic system evolved from the simplest memristor chaotic circuit. *Commun. Nonlinear Sci. Numer. Simul.* **2020**, *89*, 105341. [CrossRef]
42. Sprott, J.C. A proposed standard for the publication of new chaotic systems. *Int. J. Bifurcat. Chaos* **2011**, *21*, 2391–2394. [CrossRef]
43. Li, Y.; Tang, W.K.S; Chen, G.R. Generating hyperchaos via state feedback control. *Int. J. Bifurcat. Chaos* **2005**, *15*, 3367–3375. [CrossRef]
44. Ramasubramanian, K.; Sriram, M.S. A comparative study of computation of Lyapunov spectra with different algorithms. *Physica D* **2000**, *139*, 72–86. [CrossRef]
45. Cvitanović, P.; Artuso, R.; Mainieri, R.; Tanner, G.; Vattay, G. *Chaos: Classical and Quantum*; Niels Bohr Institute: Copenhagen, Denmark, 2012; pp. 131–133.
46. Lan, Y.; Cvitanović, P. Variational method for finding periodic orbits in a general flow. *Phys. Rev. E* **2004**, *69*, 016217. [CrossRef]
47. Dong, C.; Jia, L.; Jie, Q.; Li, H. Symbolic encoding of periodic orbits and chaos in the Rucklidge system. *Complexity* **2021**, *2021*, 4465151. [CrossRef]
48. Dong, C.; Liu, H.; Li, H. Unstable periodic orbits analysis in the generalized Lorenz–type system. *J. Stat. Mech.* **2020**, *2020*, 073211. [CrossRef]
49. Dong, C.; Lan, Y. Organization of spatially periodic solutions of the steady Kuramoto–Sivashinsky equation. *Commun. Nonlinear Sci. Numer. Simul.* **2014**, *19*, 2140–2153. [CrossRef]
50. Dong, C.; Liu, H.; Jie, Q.; Li, H. Topological classification of periodic orbits in the generalized Lorenz-type system with diverse symbolic dynamics. *Chaos Soliton. Fract.* **2022**, *154*, 111686. [CrossRef]
51. Hao, B.L.; Zheng, W.M. *Applied Symbolic Dynamics and Chaos*; World Scientic: Singapore, 1998; pp. 11–13.
52. Guckenheimer J.; Holmes, P. *Nonlinear Oscillations, Dynamical Systems, and Bifurcations of Vector Fields*; Springer: New York, NY, USA, 1983.
53. Dong, C. Topological classification of periodic orbits in the Yang-Chen system. *EPL* **2018**, *123*, 20005. [CrossRef]
54. Zambrano-Serrano, E.; Anzo-Hernández, A. A novel antimonotic hyperjerk system: Analysis, synchronization and circuit design. *Physica D* **2021**, *424*, 132927. [CrossRef]

Article

Boundary Layer via Multifractal Mass Conductivity through Remote Sensing Data in Atmospheric Dynamics

Dragos-Constantin Nica [1], Marius-Mihai Cazacu [2], Daniel-Eduard Constantin [3], Valentin Nedeff [4], Florin Nedeff [5], Decebal Vasincu [6], Iulian-Alin Roșu [2,7,*] and Maricel Agop [2,8]

[1] Department of Geography, Faculty of Geography and Geology, "Alexandru Ioan Cuza" University of Iași, 700505 Iași, Romania; dragos.nica@uaic.ro
[2] Department of Physics, "Gheorghe Asachi" Technical University of Iași, 700050 Iași, Romania; marius.cazacu@tuiasi.ro (M.-M.C.); magop@tuiasi.ro (M.A.)
[3] Faculty of Sciences and Environment, "Dunărea de Jos" University of Galati, 800008 Galați, Romania; daniel.constantin@ugal.ro
[4] Department of Industrial Systems Engineering and Management, Faculty of Engineering, "Vasile Alecsandri" University of Bacău, 600115 Bacau, Romania; vnedeff@ub.ro
[5] Department of Environmental Engineering and Mechanical Engineering, Faculty of Engineering, "Vasile Alecsandri" University of Bacău, 600115 Bacau, Romania; florin_nedeff@ub.ro
[6] Department of Biophysics, Faculty of Dental Medicine, "Grigore T. Popa" University of Medicine and Pharmacy, 700115 Iași, Romania; decebal.vasincu@umfiasi.ro
[7] Faculty of Physics, "Alexandru Ioan Cuza" University of Iași, 700506 Iași, Romania
[8] Romanian Scientists Academy, 010071 Bucharest, Romania
* Correspondence: alin.iulian.rosu@gmail.com

Abstract: In this manuscript, multifractal theories of motion based on scale relativity theory are considered in the description of atmospheric dynamics. It is shown that these theories have the potential to highlight nondimensional mass conduction laws that describe the propagation of atmospheric entities. Then, using special operational procedures and harmonic mappings, these equations can be rewritten and simplified for their plotting and analysis to be performed. The inhomogeneity of these conduction phenomena is analyzed, and it is found that it can fluctuate and increase at certain fractal dimensions, leading to the conclusion that certain atmospheric structures and phenomena of either atmospheric transmission or stability can be explained by atmospheric fractal dimension inversions. Finally, this hypothesis is verified using ceilometer data throughout the atmospheric profiles.

Keywords: atmosphere; multifractal; conductivity; ceilometer

1. Introduction

Often, to describe atmospheric dynamics, models must be constructed with combinations of physical theories and computer simulation [1–5]. If such descriptions imply simulations based on specific algorithms, this development in relation to physical theories relies on two classes of models [4–7]:

(i) Based on typical conservation laws developed on integer-dimensional spaces, also known as differentiable models [1–3];
(ii) Based on conservation laws developed on non-integer-dimensional spaces, or non-differentiable models (fractal or multifractal) [6,7].

It is a recent development that new models based on Scale Relativity Theory have appeared, either using monofractal dynamics or multifractal dynamics, as with the Multifractal Theory of Motion [8–10]. In both situations, presupposing that the atmosphere is both structurally and functionally assimilated to multifractal objects, atmospheric dynamics can be described through the motions of such multifractal structural units on continuous and non-differentiable curves, also known as multifractal curves. Because, for a large temporal scale resolution, with respect to the inverse of the highest Lyapunov exponent trajectories, these structural units can be replaced with collections of potential trajectories; it is then possible to replace the notion of "deterministic definite trajectory" with that of a probability density [11,12].

2. Hydrodynamic Multifractal Scenario Conservation Laws

In the description of complex system dynamics through a hydrodynamic multifractal scenario, it is possible to find the involvement of the specific multifractal impulse conservation law [13,14]:

$$\partial_t v^i + v^l \partial_l v^i = -\partial^i Q, \ i = 1,2,3 \quad (1)$$

and that of the conservation law of the multifractal states density:

$$\partial_t \rho + \partial^l \left(\rho v^l \right) = 0 \quad (2)$$

where:

$$\begin{aligned}
&\partial_t = \tfrac{\partial}{\partial t}, \partial_l = \tfrac{\partial}{\partial x^l} \\
&\rho = \psi \overline{\psi}, \ \psi = \sqrt{\rho} e^{is} \\
&Q = 2\lambda^2 (dt)^{[\frac{4}{f(\alpha)}]-2} \frac{\partial_l \partial^l \sqrt{\rho}}{\sqrt{\rho}} = \frac{u_i u^i}{2} + \lambda (dt)^{[\frac{2}{f(\alpha)}]-1} \partial^l u_l \\
&\partial_t \rho + \partial_x (\rho v) = 0
\end{aligned} \quad (3)$$

In the above relations, the given measures have the following physical meanings:

- t is nonmultifractal time, an affine parameter of movement curves of the entities found in the complex system;
- x^l is the multifractal spatial coordinate;
- v^i is the velocity field at a differentiable scale resolution;
- u^i is the velocity field at a non-differentiable scale resolution;
- dt is the scale resolution;
- λ is a constant coefficient associated with the multifractal-nonmultifractal scale transition;
- ρ is the state density;
- ψ is the state function with the amplitude $\sqrt{\rho}$ and phase s;
- Q is the scalar specific multifractal potential which quantifies the multifractalization degree of the movement curves in the complex system;
- f(α) is the singularity spectrum of order α = α(D_F) where D_F is the fractal dimension of movement curves of the complex system entities. This spectrum allows the identification of universality classes in the complex system dynamics, even when attractors have different aspects, and it also allows the identification of areas in which the dynamics can be characterized by a specific fractal dimension.

Because of its nonlinearity, Equations (1) and (2) admit analytical solutions only in special, particular cases. Such a case is dictated by the one-dimensional dynamics of the complex system entities through the following:

$$\begin{aligned}
&\partial_t v + v \partial_x v = 2\lambda^2 (dt)^{[\frac{4}{f(\alpha)}]-2} \frac{\partial_{xx} \sqrt{\rho}}{\sqrt{\rho}} \\
&\partial_t \rho + \partial_x (\rho v) = 0
\end{aligned} \quad (4)$$

with the initial and boundary constraints:

$$\begin{aligned}
&v(x, t=0) = v_0, \ \rho(x, t=0) = \rho_0 e^{-(\frac{x}{a})^2} \\
&v(x = ct, t) = v_0, \ \rho(x = -\infty, t) = \rho(x = +\infty, t) = 0
\end{aligned} \quad (5)$$

The following solution is found:

$$v_0 a^2 + \left[\frac{\lambda(dt)^{\left[\frac{2}{f(\alpha)}\right]-1}}{a}\right]^2 xt \tag{6}$$
$$\overline{}$$
$$a^2 + \left[\frac{\lambda(dt)^{\left[\frac{2}{f(\alpha)}\right]-1}}{a}\right]^2 t$$

and:

$$\rho = \frac{\pi^{-\frac{1}{2}}}{\left\{a^2 + \left[\frac{\lambda(dt)^{\left[\frac{2}{f(\alpha)}\right]-1}}{a}\right]^2 t\right\}^{\frac{1}{2}}} \cdot e^{\left\{-\frac{(x-v_0 t)^2}{a^2 + \left[\frac{\lambda(dt)^{\left[\frac{2}{f(\alpha)}\right]-1}}{a}\right]^2 t}\right\}} \tag{7}$$

This solution, through the nondimensional variables is:

$$\frac{v}{v_0} = \overline{v}, \quad \rho\sqrt{\pi}a = \overline{\rho}, \quad \frac{x}{v_0 \tau} = \xi, \quad \frac{t}{\tau} = \eta \tag{8}$$

and through the nondimensional parameters,

$$\theta = \frac{\lambda(dt)^{\left[\frac{2}{f(\alpha)}\right]-1} \tau}{a^2}, \quad \mu = \frac{v_0 \tau}{a} \tag{9}$$

can be rewritten as:

$$\overline{v} = \frac{1 + \theta^2 \xi \eta}{1 + \theta^2 \eta^2} \tag{10}$$

and:

$$\overline{\rho} = \frac{1}{\sqrt{1 + \theta^2 \eta^2}} \cdot e^{\left[-\mu^2 \frac{(\xi-\eta)^2}{1+\theta^2 \eta^2}\right]} \tag{11}$$

Through Equation (3), the solutions in Equations (6) and (7) allow us to construct the following set of variables:
- The velocity field at a non-differentiable scale:

$$u = 2\lambda(dt)^{\left[\frac{2}{f(\alpha)}\right]-1} \cdot \frac{(x - v_0 t)}{a^2 + \left[\frac{\lambda(dt)^{\left[\frac{2}{f(\alpha)}\right]-1}}{a}\right]^2 t} \tag{12}$$

- The specific multifractal force field:

$$f = -\partial_x Q = 2\lambda(dt)^{\left[\frac{4}{f(\alpha)}\right]-2} \cdot \frac{(x - v_0 t)}{\left\{a^2 + \left[\frac{\lambda(dt)^{\left[\frac{2}{f(\alpha)}\right]-1}}{a}\right]^2 t\right\}^2} \tag{13}$$

This set of variables employs the notations:

$$\frac{u}{2v_0} = \overline{u}, \quad \frac{f\tau}{2v_0} = \overline{f} \tag{14}$$

Considering Equations (8) and (9) they become:

$$\overline{u} = \theta \frac{\xi - \eta}{1 + \theta^2 \eta^2} \tag{15}$$

respectively:
$$\bar{f} = \theta^2 \frac{\xi - \eta}{\left(1 + \theta^2 \eta^2\right)^2} \tag{16}$$

Then, let us assume the functionality, in nondimensional coordinates, of a relation of the form:
$$\bar{j} = \bar{\sigma}\bar{f} \tag{17}$$

where $\bar{j}$ is a mass current density, $\bar{f}$ is the nondimensional specific multifractal force field, and $\bar{\sigma}$ is a mass conductivity, which then allows us to define the following conductivity types:

- Conductivity at differentiable scale resolutions:

$$\overline{\sigma_D} = \frac{\overline{\rho v}}{\bar{f}} = \sqrt{1 + \theta^2 \eta^2} \frac{1 + \theta^2 \xi \eta}{\theta^2 (\xi - \eta)} e^{\left[-\mu^2 \frac{(\xi-\eta)^2}{1+\theta^2\eta^2}\right]} \tag{18}$$

- Conductivity at non-differentiable scale resolutions:

$$\overline{\sigma_F} = \frac{\overline{\rho u}}{\bar{f}} = \sqrt{1 + \theta^2 \eta^2} \left(\frac{\mu}{\theta}\right)^2 e^{\left[-\mu^2 \frac{(\xi-\eta)^2}{1+\theta^2\eta^2}\right]} \tag{19}$$

- Conductivity at global scale resolutions:

$$\bar{\sigma} = \frac{\overline{\rho(\bar{v} + i\bar{u})}}{\bar{f}} = \overline{\sigma_D} + i\overline{\sigma_F} = \sqrt{1 + \theta^2 \eta^2} \left[\frac{1 + \theta^2 \xi \eta}{\theta^2 (\xi - \eta)} + i\left(\frac{\mu}{\theta}\right)^2\right] e^{\left[-\mu^2 \frac{(\xi-\eta)^2}{1+\theta^2\eta^2}\right]} \tag{20}$$

In this context, since the θ parameter is a measure of the multifractality degree, then $\varepsilon = \frac{1}{\theta}$ will function as a measure of an ordering degree. Then, the conductivity species in Equations (18)–(20) change as:

- Conductivity at differentiable scale resolutions:

$$\overline{\sigma_D} = \sqrt{\varepsilon^2 + \eta^2} \frac{\varepsilon^2 + \xi \eta}{\varepsilon(\xi - \eta)} e^{\left[-(\mu\varepsilon)^2 \frac{(\xi-\eta)^2}{\varepsilon^2+\eta^2}\right]} \tag{21}$$

- Conductivity at non-differentiable scale resolutions:

$$\overline{\sigma_F} = \sqrt{\varepsilon^2 + \eta^2} \varepsilon \mu^2 e^{\left[-(\mu\varepsilon)^2 \frac{(\xi-\eta)^2}{\varepsilon^2+\eta^2}\right]} \tag{22}$$

- Conductivity at global scale resolutions:

$$\bar{\sigma} = \sqrt{\varepsilon^2 + \eta^2} \left[\frac{\varepsilon^2 + \xi \eta}{\varepsilon(\xi - \eta)} + i\varepsilon\mu^2\right] e^{\left[-(\mu\varepsilon)^2 \frac{(\xi-\eta)^2}{\varepsilon^2+\eta^2}\right]} \tag{23}$$

From the dependencies of these conductions, the following is found:

- Conduction in complex systems is performed through specific mechanisms dependent on the scale resolution. As a consequence, we make the distinction between differentiable conduction $\overline{\sigma_D}$, non-differentiable conduction $\overline{\sigma_F}$ and global conduction $\bar{\sigma}$;
- Conduction mechanisms at the two types of scale resolutions are simultaneous and reciprocally conditional. Thus, the values of $\overline{\sigma_D}$ and $\overline{\sigma_F}$ increase along with the increase of the ordering degree (synchronous type conductions) and with the increase of the multifractalization degree $\overline{\sigma_D}$ values increase and $\overline{\sigma_F}$ values decrease (asynchronous type conductions).

3. Non-Manifest Dynamic States through Harmonic Mappings

Taking into consideration Equation (3), in what follows, it will be seen that non-manifest dynamic states through these complex systems can be generated through metrics of the Lobachevsky plane. Indeed, we admit the functionality of:

$$x^2 + y^2 = 1 \tag{24}$$

where:

$$\Psi = A + iB, \quad x = \frac{A}{\sqrt{\rho}}, \quad y = \frac{B}{\sqrt{\rho}} \tag{25}$$

Here, the Lobachevski plane metric can be produced in the form of a Cayleyan metric of a Euclidean plane, whose absoluteness is a circle of unit radius, as seen in Equation (24). In this manner, the Lobachevski plane is placed in a bi-univocal correspondence with the given circle's interior. This general procedure of metrization of a Cayleyan space starts with the definition of the metric as an anharmonic ratio [15,16]. Thus, we suppose that the absoluteness is given by the quadratic form $\Omega(X,Y)$ where X denotes any vector. The Cayleyan metric is then given by the differential quadratic form:

$$\frac{-ds^2}{k^2} = \frac{\Omega(dX, dX)}{\Omega(X, X)} - \frac{\Omega^2(X, dX)}{\Omega^2(X, X)} \tag{26}$$

In Equation (26), $\Omega(X,Y)$ is in fact the duplication of $\Omega(X,X)$ and k is a constant that is connected to the given space curvature.

In the case of the Lobachevsky plane, the following is found:

$$\begin{aligned}\Omega(X, X) &= 1 - x^2 - y^2 \\ \Omega(X, dX) &= -xdx - ydy \\ \Omega(dX, dX) &= -dx^2 - dy^2\end{aligned} \tag{27}$$

which produces:

$$\frac{-ds^2}{k^2} = \frac{(1-y^2)dx^2 + 2xydxdy + (1-x^2)dy^2}{(1-x^2-y^2)^2} \tag{28}$$

By performing the coordinate transformation:

$$x = \frac{h\bar{h} - 1}{h\bar{h} + 1}, \quad y = \frac{h + \bar{h}}{h\bar{h} + 1} \tag{29}$$

The metric found in Equation (28) becomes the Lobachevsky metric:

$$\frac{-ds^2}{k^2} = -4\frac{dhd\bar{h}}{(h-\bar{h})^2} \tag{30}$$

Then, one can observe that the absoluteness $1 - x^2 - y^2 = 0$ tends to the straight line $Im(h) = 0$. In this case, the straight lines of the Euclidean plane tend to be circles with centers located on the real axis of the complex plane (h). Now, let it be considered that these complex system dynamics are described by the variables (Y^j), for which the following multifractal metric is found:

$$h_{ij} dY^i dY^j \tag{31}$$

In an ambient space of multifractal metrics, the previous equation can be rewritten as:

$$\gamma_{\alpha\beta} dX^\alpha dX^\beta \tag{32}$$

In this situation, the field equations of the complex system dynamics are derived from a variational principle connected to the multifractal Lagrangian:

$$L = \gamma^{\alpha\beta} h_{ij} \frac{dY^i dY^j}{\partial X^\alpha \partial X^\beta} \tag{33}$$

In the current case, Equation (31) is given by Equation (30), the field multifractal variables being h and $\bar{h}$ or, equivalently, the real and imaginary part of h. Therefore, if the variational principle:

$$\delta \int L \sqrt{\gamma} d^3 x \tag{34}$$

is accepted as a starting point where $\gamma = |\gamma_{\alpha\beta}|$, the main purpose of the complex system dynamics research would be to produce multifractal metrics of the multifractal Lobachevsky plane (or relate to them) [17]. In such a context, the multifractal Euler equations corresponding to the variational principle in Equation (34) are:

$$\begin{aligned} \left(h - \bar{h}\right) \nabla (\nabla h) &= 2(\nabla h)^2 \\ \left(h - \bar{h}\right) \nabla \left(\nabla \bar{h}\right) &= 2\left(\nabla \bar{h}\right)^2 \end{aligned} \tag{35}$$

which admits the solution:

$$h = \frac{\left[\cosh\left(\frac{X}{2}\right) - \sinh\left(\frac{X}{2}\right)\right] e^{-i\alpha}}{\left[\cosh\left(\frac{X}{2}\right) + \sinh\left(\frac{X}{2}\right)\right] e^{-i\alpha}}, \quad \alpha \in \mathbb{R} \tag{36}$$

where α is real and arbitrary, and for a $\left(\frac{X}{2}\right)$ the solution is a Laplace-type equation for the free space, so that $\nabla^2\left(\frac{X}{2}\right) = 0$. For a choice of the form $\alpha = 2\omega t$, in which case, a temporal dependency was introduced in the complex system dynamics, Equation (36) becomes:

$$h = \frac{i\left[e^{2X} \sin(2\omega t) - \sin(2\omega t) - 2i\, e^X\right]}{e^{2X} [\cos(2\omega t) + 1] - \cos(2\omega t) + 1} \tag{37}$$

Now, Equation (37) can be rewritten as:

$$h = \frac{1 + ie^{2X} \tan(\omega t)}{e^X + i \tan(\omega t)} \tag{38}$$

In order to actually perform any analysis and plot of this function, the parameters found here must be elucidated. We shall see that a concrete connection between the states' function and h exists, which implies that h is a function of t and x; given the fact that $\nabla^2\left(\frac{X}{2}\right) = 0$, it is more than fair to assume that $\chi = x$, which not only easily satisfies the condition but creates a spatial connection to h, as imposed. For ω, it can be considered a given constant for each specific simulation.

The following plots show the behavior and spatio-temporal dependencies of h, in which x, ω and t are dimensionless parameters (Figures 1 and 2).

These plots show that oscillatory components can exist in the complex systems at all scales; interestingly, h manifests ordered predictable peaks whose intensity tends to slightly increase in time, but only if ω is an odd integer (Figures 1 and 2). Otherwise, other plotting instances show relatively disordered and unpredictable distributions of these peaks. It can be interpreted that an undulatory-corpuscular duality can be observed through this behavior, with odd integer ω representing the damping oscillatory behavior and all other cases producing corpuscular behavior (Figures 1 and 2). We note that in the behavior manifested in Figures 1 and 2, discontinuities are induced by the interactions between the complex system entities (more precisely, through the interaction strength between the complex system entities).

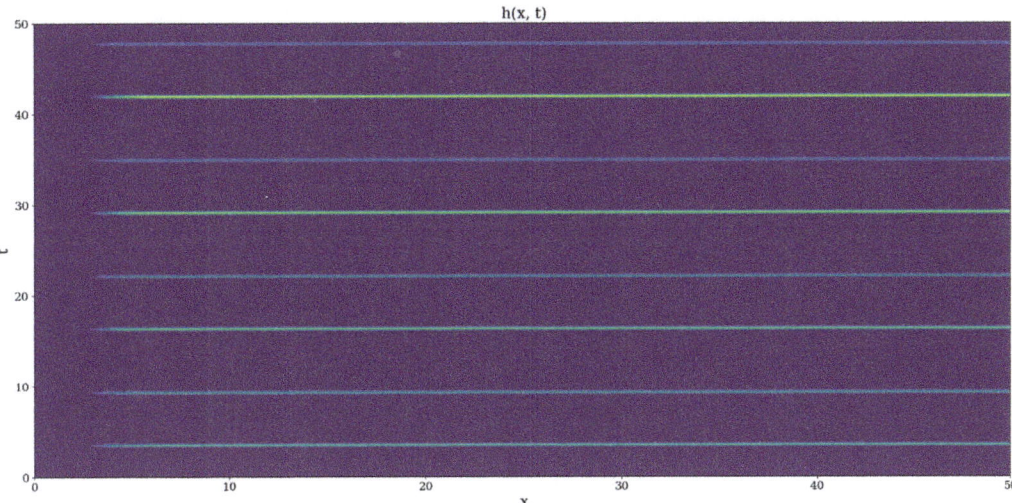

Figure 1. Example plot of h(x,t); ω constant.

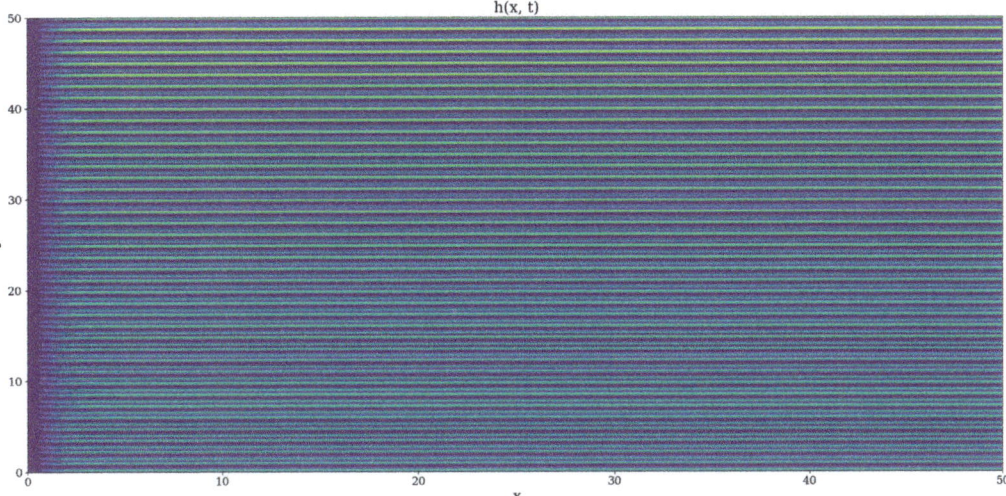

Figure 2. Example plot of h(x,t); ω constant odd integer.

Now, for in-phase coherences of the complex system entities, for example: $e^{is} = 1$ which implies $s = 2\pi n$, $n \in \mathbb{Z}$, ψ becomes:

$$\psi = \sqrt{\rho}\frac{h\overline{h} - 1}{h\overline{h} + 1} \qquad (39)$$

The produced plots show instances of the states function manifesting in a sporadic and periodic manner, with varying spatial dimensions (Figures 3 and 4). Given the fact that, at this point, the only control parameter of ψ is ω, no other constant will affect the behavior of the function of the state; furthermore, even the choice of this parameter does not seem to fundamentally affect the dynamical regime of ψ, which manifests multifractal states of varying length fluctuating in time (Figures 3 and 4). These fluctuations show the spontaneous and periodic occurrence of multifractal structures in the given multifractal flow. Worth noting, however, is the fact that the areas of the plot that manifest no color at all are in fact not areas where the states function is zero, but are areas where the ψ calculation yields cases of non-determination, and thus these are regions where it is absolutely impossible for states to exist. Moreover, a completely different fine structure exists at small scales compared to large scales, wherein vanishing states are manifested, and the appearance of these intense negative fluctuations manifests absolutely no periodicity (Figures 3 and 4).

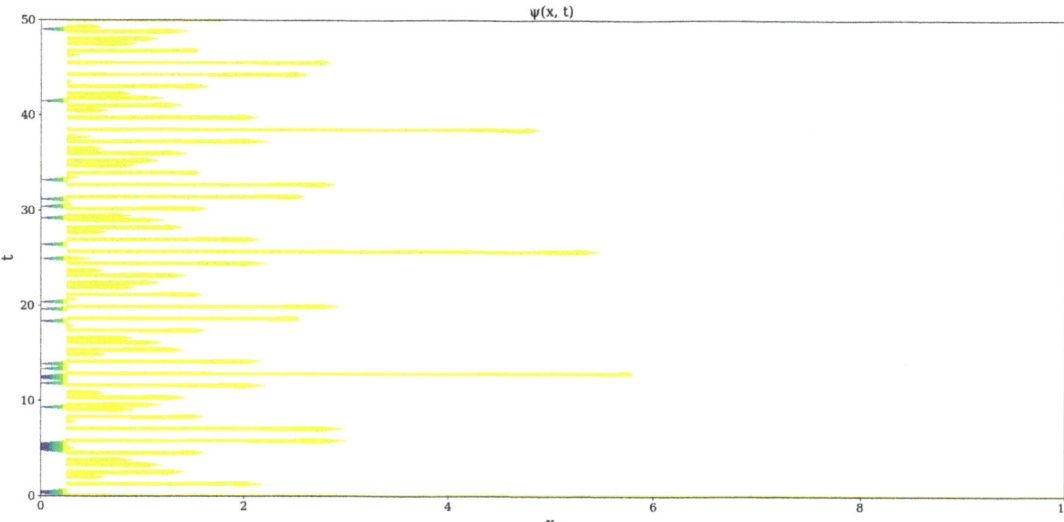

Figure 3. Example plot of ψ(x,t); ω constant.

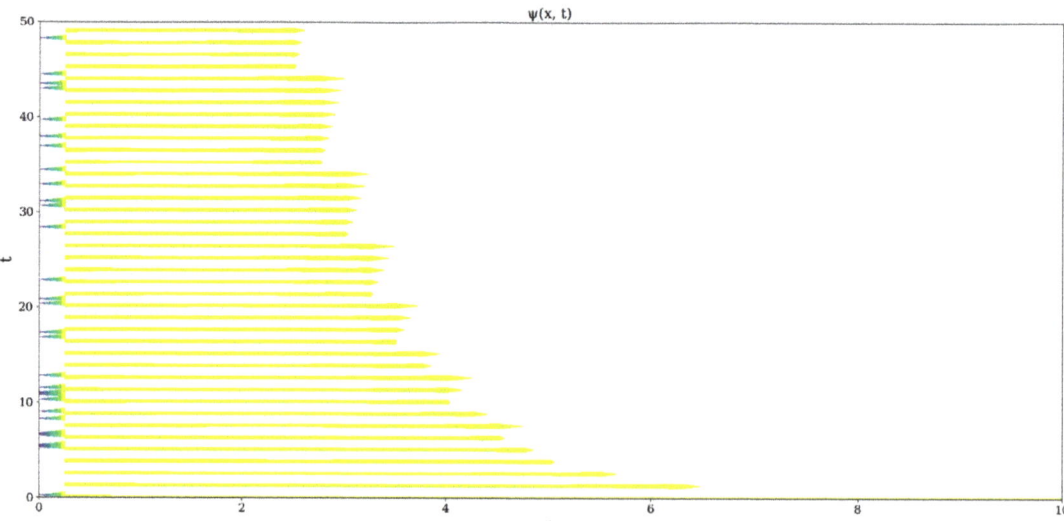

Figure 4. Example plot of ψ(x,t); ω constant odd integer.

In performing the first step of our analysis, the inhomogeneity map of the multifractal non-differentiable mass conduction needs to be performed. By definition, the total inhomogeneity of any parameter in a given volume V of atmospheric fluid is [18]:

$$G = \frac{1}{2} \int \langle \vartheta'^2 \rangle dV \qquad (40)$$

Given a non-strict dependency on spatial conditions, and the non-dimensionality entailed throughout much of the previous analysis, it will suffice to perform $\langle |\overline{\sigma_F}|^{'2} \rangle$. Through a Reynolds decomposition, the following is obtained [18,19]:

$$\langle |\overline{\sigma_F}|^{'2} \rangle = \langle (|\overline{\sigma_F}| - \langle |\overline{\sigma_F}| \rangle)^2 \rangle \tag{41}$$

This can then be iterated across the fractal dimension in a bifurcation map, where we have noted $x \equiv \theta, t \equiv \eta$ (Figures 5–12).

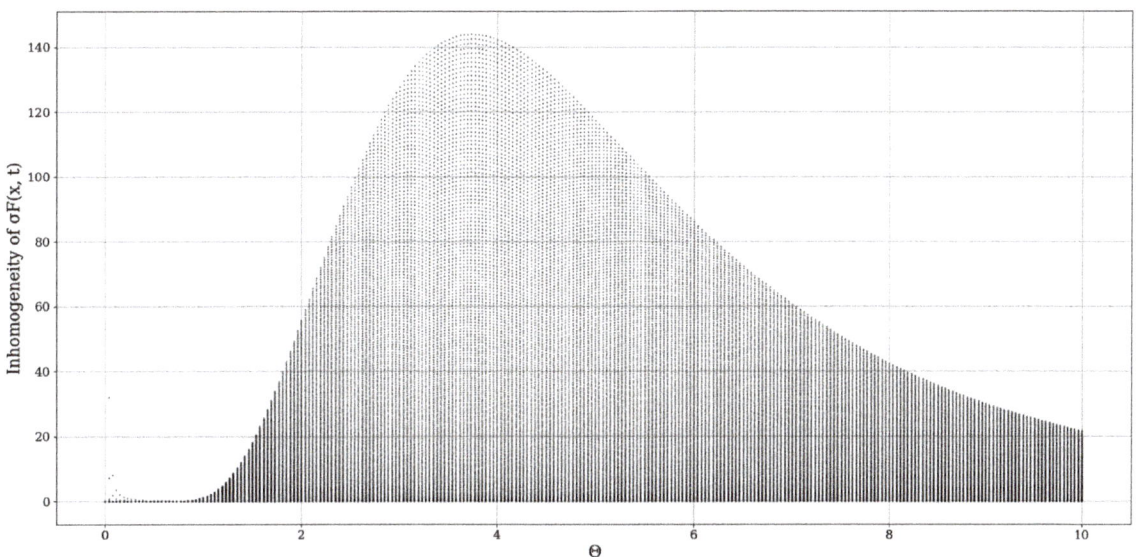

Figure 5. $\langle |\overline{\sigma_F}|^{'2} \rangle$ example plot with θ as control parameter; $\xi = 0.5$; $\mu = 1$.

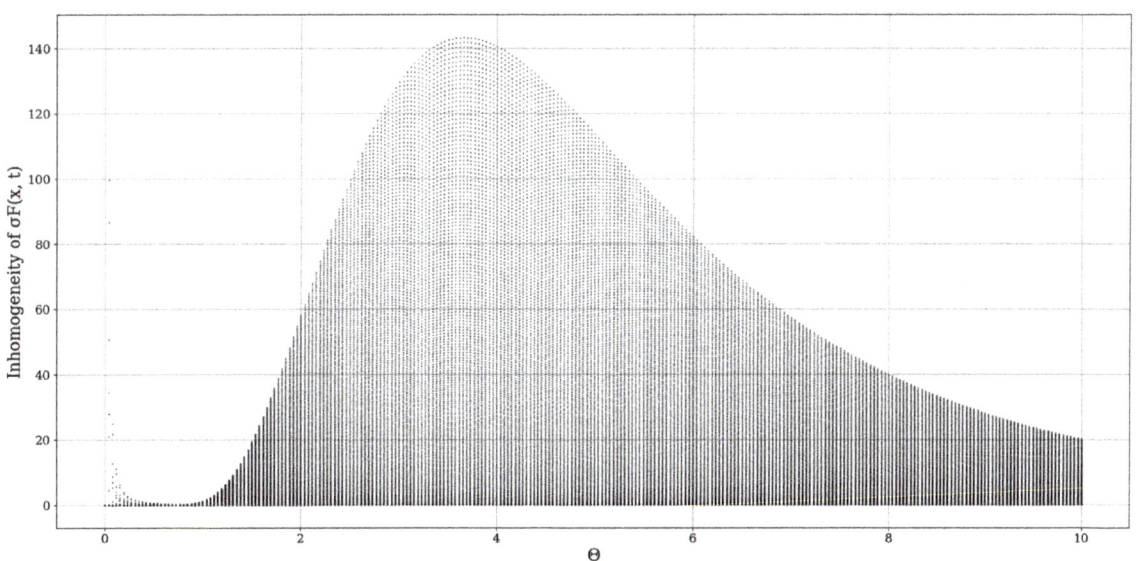

Figure 6. $\langle |\overline{\sigma_F}|^{'2} \rangle$ example plot with θ as control parameter; $\xi = 3$; $\mu = 1$.

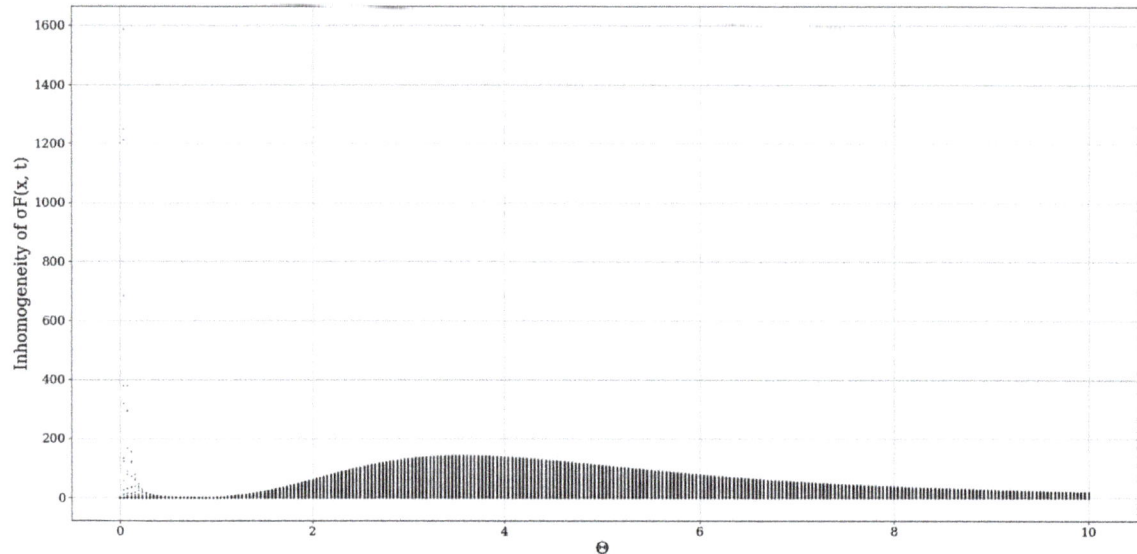

Figure 7. $\langle |\overline{\sigma_F}|'^2 \rangle$ example plot with θ as control parameter; ξ = 6; μ = 1.

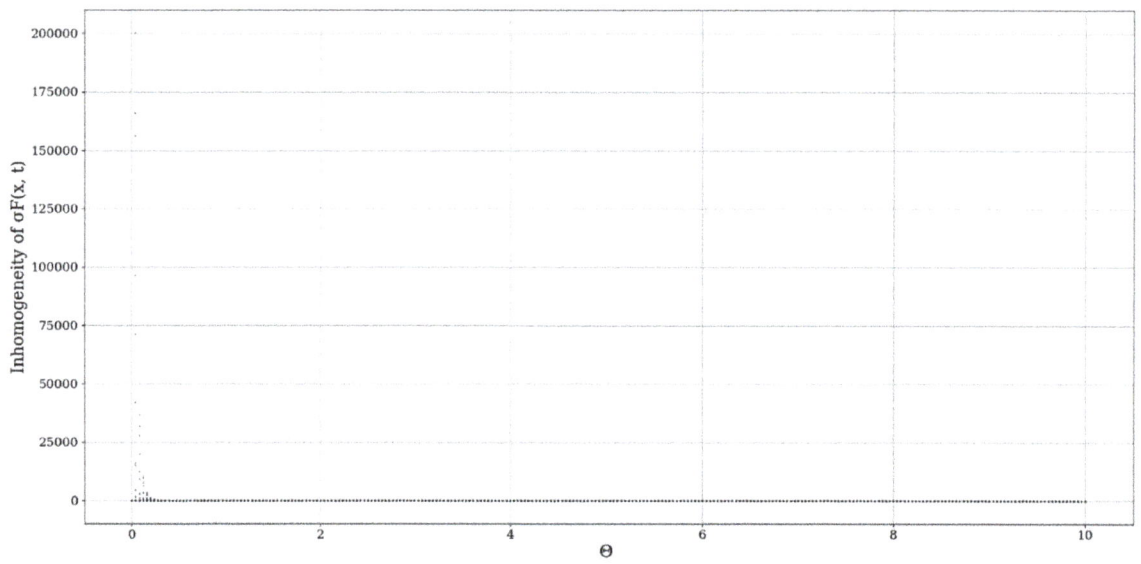

Figure 8. $\langle |\overline{\sigma_F}|'^2 \rangle$ example plot with θ as control parameter; ξ = 9; μ = 1.

It seems that ξ plays the role of a spatial limiting factor, dictating the conduction band intensity, and it is to be expected that a constant inversely proportional to the initial value of the differentiable velocity field would play an important role here (Figures 5–8).

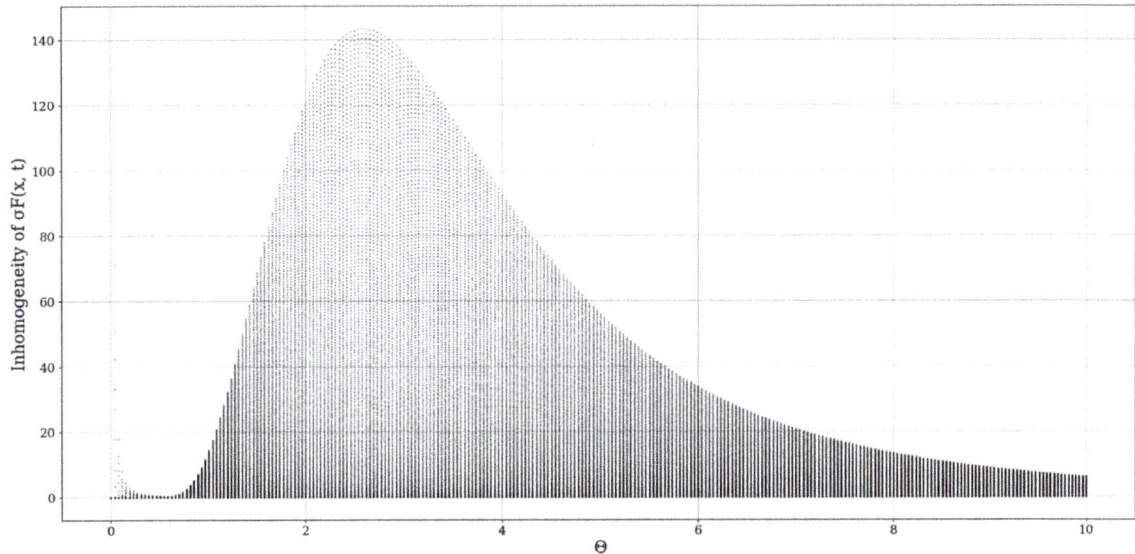

Figure 9. $\langle |\overline{\sigma_F}|'^2 \rangle$ example plot with θ as control parameter; ξ = 3; μ = 0.5.

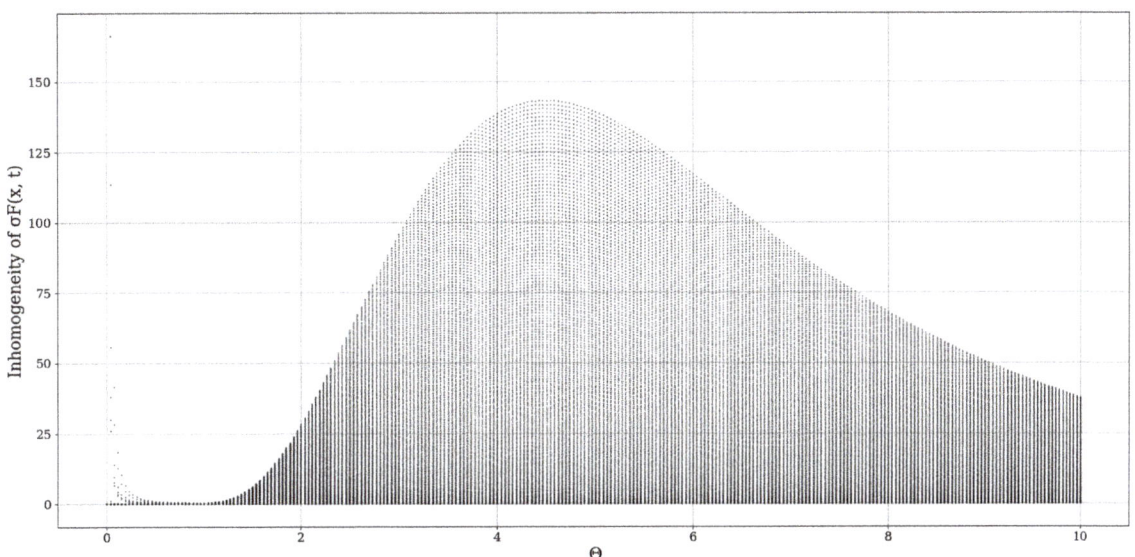

Figure 10. $\langle |\overline{\sigma_F}|'^2 \rangle$ example plot with θ as control parameter; ξ = 3; μ = 3.

Modifying the multifractal-nonmultifractal scale transition constant μ appears to have relatively similar effects to the inhomogeneity map; however, it affects not only the intensity but also the relative shape of the conduction bands (Figures 9–12). All cases exhibit what are practically two peak-like structures; one of them found at low values of θ, which shows a very high value variability and unpredictability. Otherwise, the exact value of τ does not seem to affect the dynamic regime of the modeled behavior.

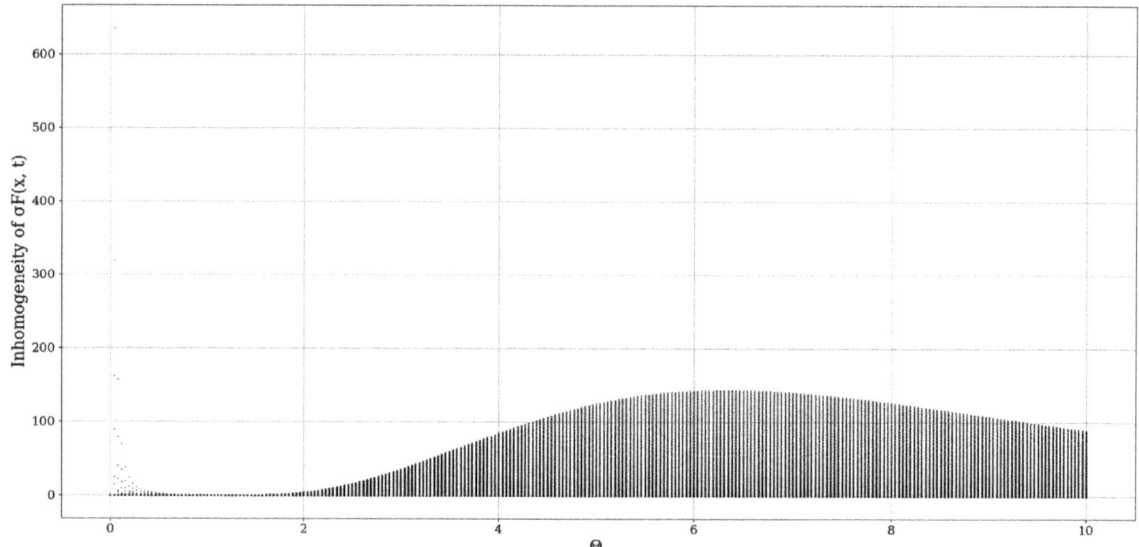

Figure 11. $\langle |\overline{\sigma_F}|'^2 \rangle$ example plot with θ as control parameter; ξ = 3; μ = 6.

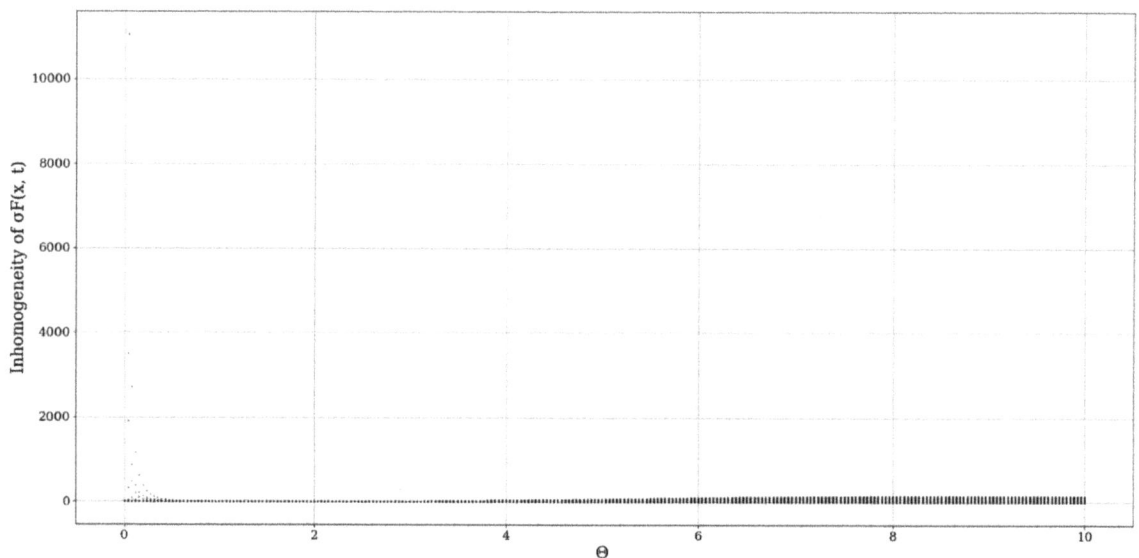

Figure 12. $\langle |\overline{\sigma_F}|'^2 \rangle$ example plot with θ as control parameter; ξ = 3; μ = 9.

4. Results

In any case, it seems that the inhomogeneity analysis points to very dynamic behavior, however, a constant aspect is that indifferent to the values being chosen, one or more inhomogeneity peaks always appear at certain values of θ, and thus, at certain fractal dimensions. While this peak can apparently be shifted or modified, it almost always exists, pointing to the existence of certain dimensions, at certain atmospheric parameters, that entail high unpredictability and values of conduction. This then means that, if certain conditions are fulfilled, inversions of fractal dimensions might lead to unpredictability and high values of multifractal non-differentiable mass conduction. The exact values of the fractal dimension would not be important here, however, jumps or inversions of the atmospheric fractal dimension would imply special behaviors of atmospheric conduction, which would then either create stability or instability as a function of the fractal dimension.

For parallels to be drawn between theory and experimental data, experimental ceilometer data must be produced. This data shall be used to calculate the initial and final turbulent scales in order for the atmospheric fractal dimension profile to be obtained, and for this, the structure coefficient of the refraction index profile $C_N^2(L)$ is obtained by [18,20]:

$$\sigma_I^2(L) = 1.23\ C_N^2(L) k^{\frac{7}{6}} L^{\frac{11}{6}} \quad (42)$$

in which we have named σ_I^2 the scintillation of a source of light observed from a distance represented by the optical path L. In this case, the source of light itself is the point in the optical path at which ceilometer light is being backscattered. Meanwhile, I refers to the intensity of the backscattered range-corrected lidar signal at a particular point in the optical path, or the RCS (range-corrected signal) intensity, which will be used to find σ_I^2 [13,14,18,20]. In past studies, it has been deemed and proved sufficient to employ three RCS profiles in the averaging process. After the C_N^2 profile has been determined, it is now possible to calculate the length scales with various approximations. The inner scale profile is linked to scintillation:

$$\sigma_I^2(L) \cong 0.615\ C_N^2(L) L^3 l_d(L)^{\frac{-7}{3}} \quad (43)$$

and the outer scale can be connected to the C_N^2 profile:

$$C_N^2(z) = L_0(z)^{\frac{4}{3}} (\nabla \langle n(z) \rangle)^2 \quad (44)$$

For atmospheric turbulent eddies in the inertial subrange, the following approximation is possible:

$$n(z) \cong n_0 - \sqrt{C_N^2(z) z^{\frac{2}{3}}} \quad (45)$$

which can then be used to extract the outer scale profile. This method is well-referenced in our studies and has been already used successfully multiple times.

When introducing the ceilometer data plots, technical details must be presented; the platform used to produce this data is described in the following segment. The platform utilized in this study is a CHM15k ceilometer operating at a 1064 nm wavelength, positioned in Galați, Romania, at the UGAL–REXDAN facility found at the coordinates 45.435125N, 28.036792E, 65 m ASL, which is a part of the "Dunărea de Jos" University of Galați. The instrument itself has been chosen so as to conform to the standards imposed by the ACTRIS community. From a computational perspective, the necessary calculations are performed through code written and operated in Python 3.6.

These sets of ceilometer data were profiled on the 22nd and 23nd of December 2021, starting right before noon. Many typical features of the atmosphere, including aerosol plumes, clouds and the PBL, along with its variation, can be observed in the RCS data (Figures 13–16). Despite the presence of many cloud-type structures, the lower part of the time series is generally unaffected and can be analyzed. The start of the time series shows a convective mixed layer typical of noon conditions, and in the latter stages of the time series, the stratified structure of the stable boundary layer (SBL) and the residual layer (RL)—the gap between them, which we shall name "the double layer"—is delineated by the region of low RCS intensity [21,22] (Figures 13–16).

The C_N^2 profile can be commonly used as an indicator of atmospheric turbulence strength; it can be also used to more accurately quantify the PBL altitude, and to identify regions of atmospheric calm or extreme turbulence (Figures 17–20) [13,14]. The region of delineation between the SBL and the RL can also be seen, and while the RCS indicated a region of lower intensity and thus of a lower concentration of atmospheric components, C_N^2 time series shows higher activities, especially at the limits of the SBL and RL itself (Figures 17–20). Higher C_N^2 implies higher degrees of turbulence, which implies greater mixing. However, C_N^2 reduces abruptly beyond the boundary between the SBL and the

RL, which indicates that this increased mixing, which is limited only to the interior of the apparent boundary layer, implies that the atmospheric matter found in the boundary layer is being shifted upwards and downwards into the SBL and the RL. This, then explains why fewer backscatterings of atmospheric matter can be found, and why the RCS intensity is lower in that region (Figures 17–20).

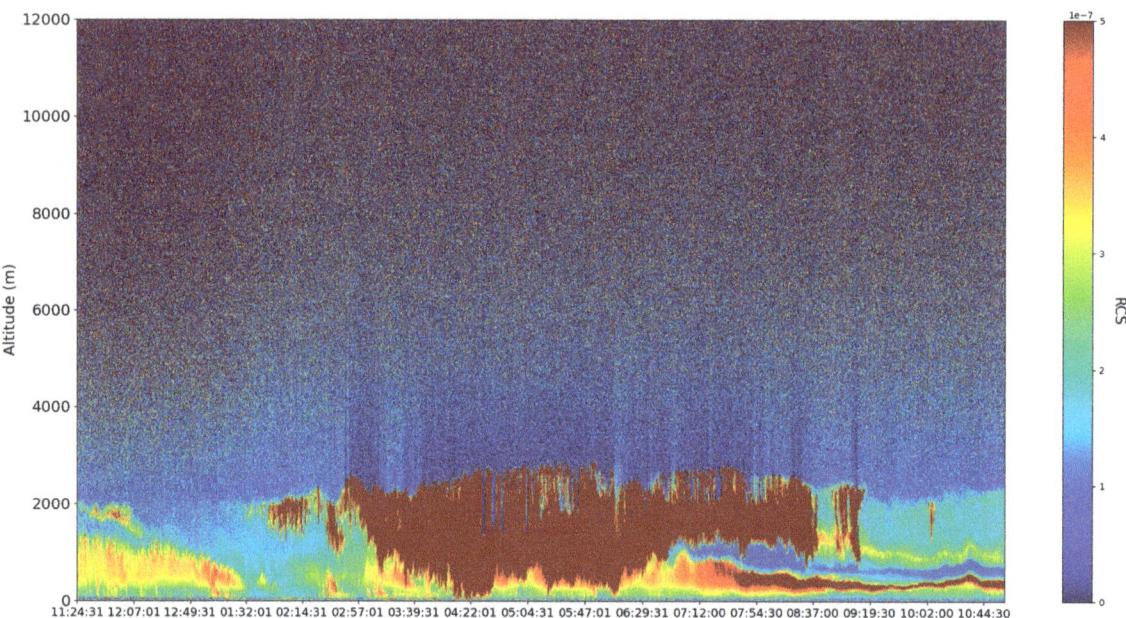

Figure 13. RCS time series, λ = 1064 nm, Galați, Romania, 23 December 2021.

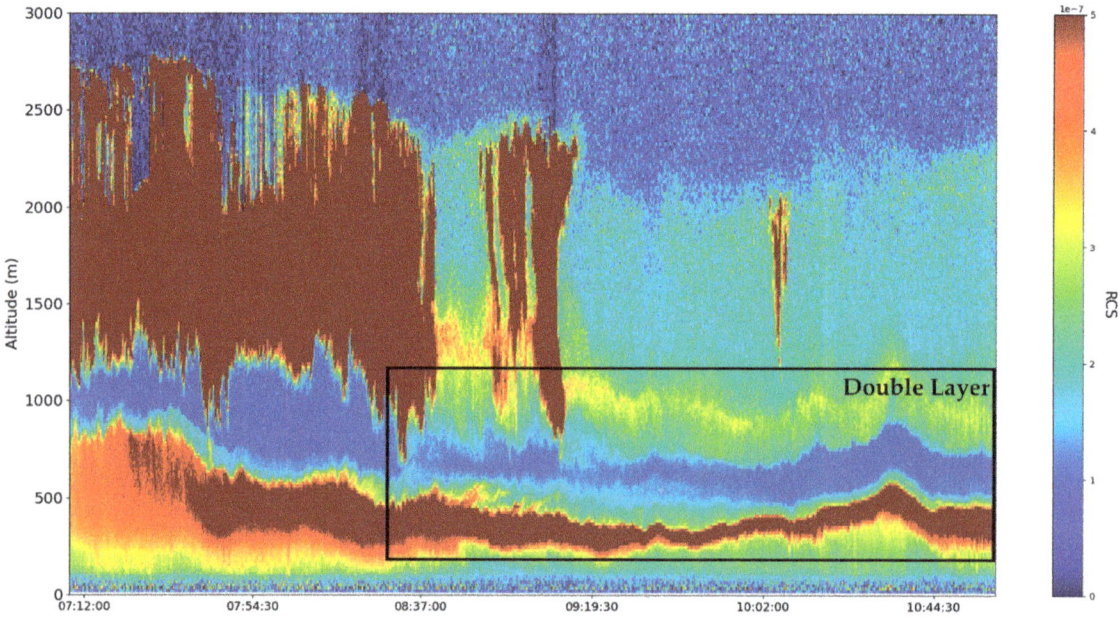

Figure 14. Zoomed-in (region of interest) RCS time series, λ = 1064 nm, Galați, Romania, 23 December 2021.

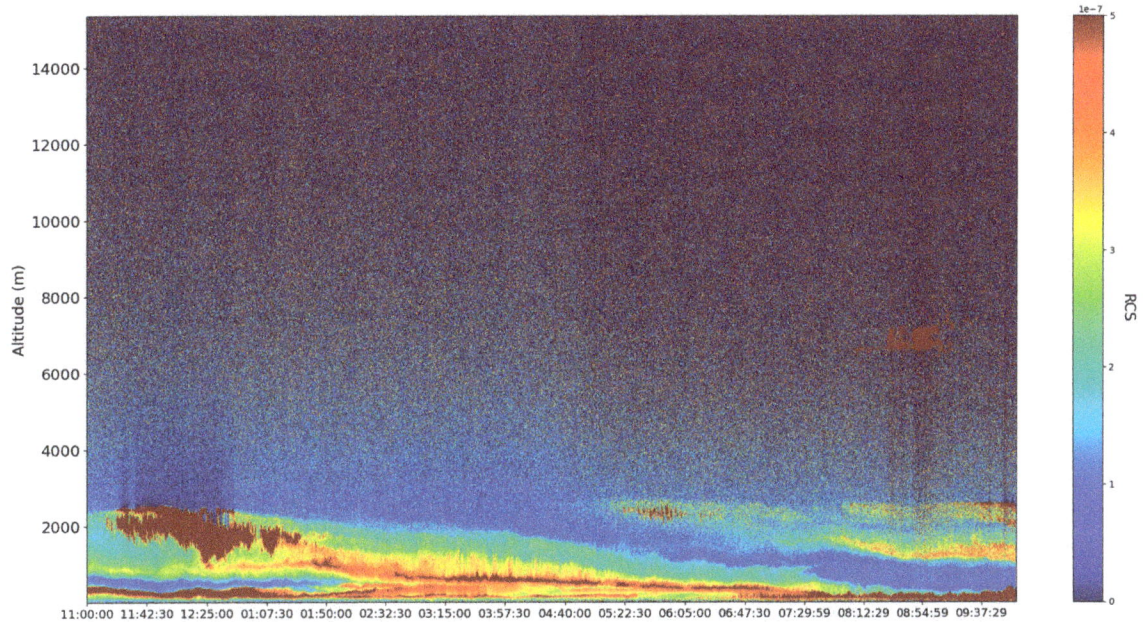

Figure 15. RCS. time series, λ = 1064 nm, Galați, Romania, 22 December 2021.

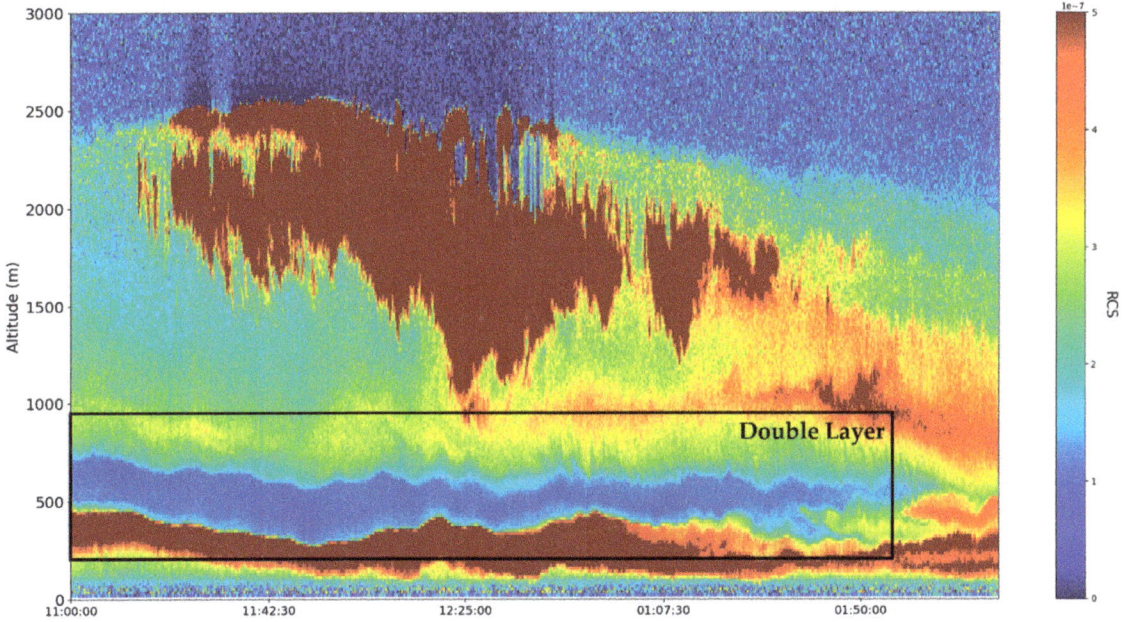

Figure 16. Zoomed-in (region of interest) RCS time series, λ = 1064 nm, Galați, Romania, 22 December 2021.

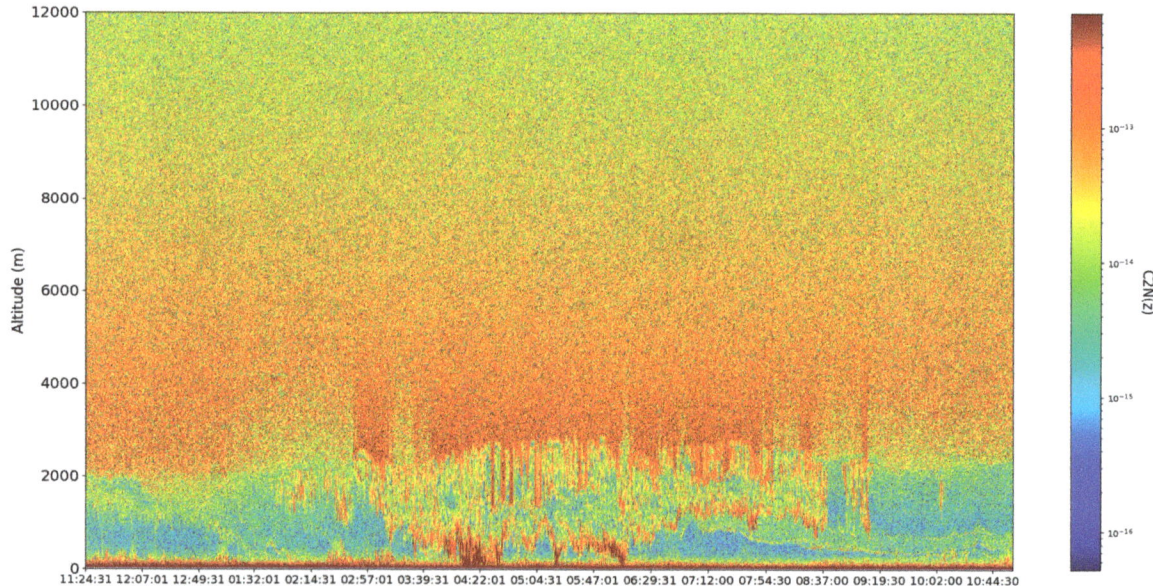

Figure 17. C_N^2 time series, λ = 1064 nm, Galați, Romania, 23 December 2021.

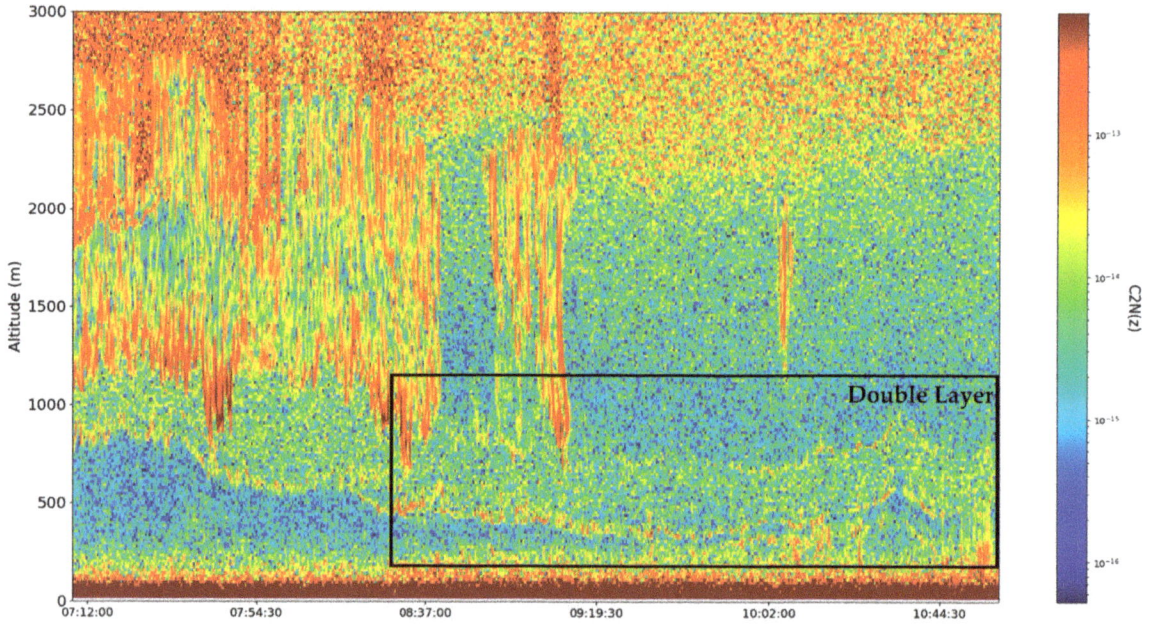

Figure 18. Zoomed-in (region of interest) C_N^2 time series, λ = 1064 nm, Galați, Romania, 23 December 2021.

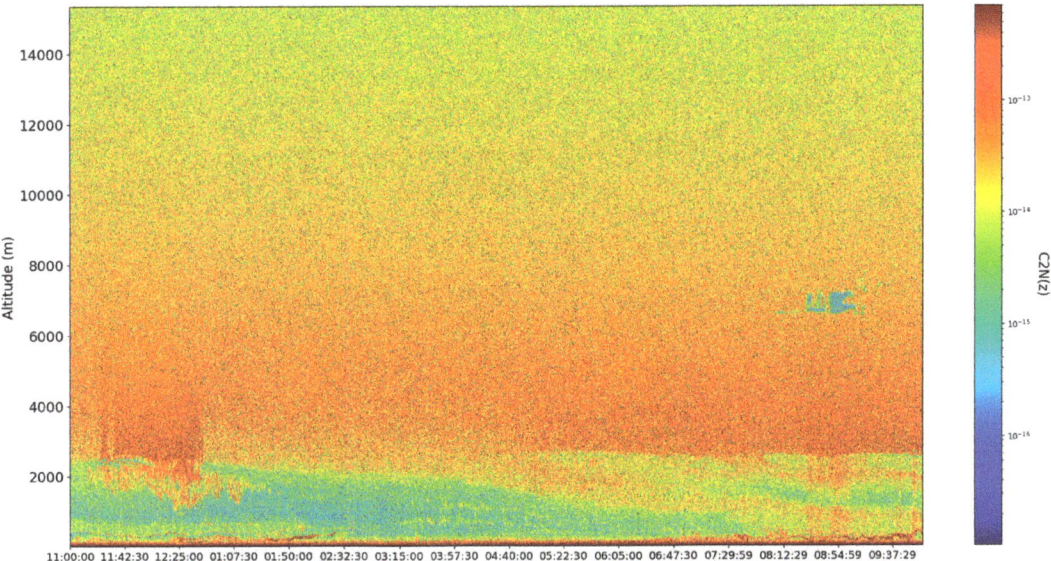

Figure 19. C_N^2 time series, λ = 1064 nm, Galați, Romania, 22 December 2021.

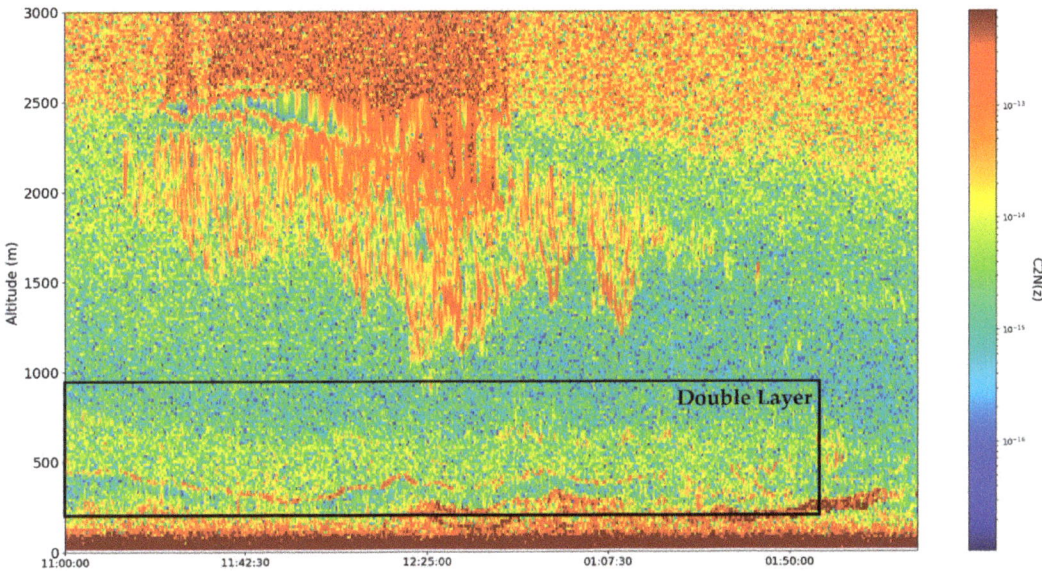

Figure 20. Zoomed-in (region of interest) C_N^2 time series, λ = 1064 nm, Galați, Romania, 22 December 2021.

Since the minimal fractal dimension of atmospheric turbulent vortices, in general, is logically 2 since vortices are by definition at least two-dimensional, and the maximal fractal dimension of atmospheric turbulent vortices is 3, it can be entirely expected for the average of these vortices, as plotted in Figures 21–24, to be quite close to 3 because such dimensions rapidly increase asymptotically towards 3 in the turbulent cascade [14]. In any case, lower fractal dimensions, especially sudden spatial decreases of fractal dimensions, point towards ordering and autostructuring—this is partially confirmed by the fact that the atmospheric cloud structure present in the time series manifests sudden and markedly-lower transitions of fractal dimensions, as expected for relatively orderly atmospheric structures, such as clouds (Figures 21–24). This autostructuring then also entails the existence of the boundaries between the SBL and the RL, because, for the boundary to exist, it must be stable—however, this seems to be a type of "dynamic stability", one marked by higher turbulence and mass transfer from the boundary area to the SBL and the RL. Furthermore, we have previously determined that inversions of fractal dimensions might lead to unpredictability and high values of multifractal non-differentiable mass conduction, and these inversions are exactly what we see at the boundary edges between the SBL and the RL, thus confirming the conduction theory presented in this study.

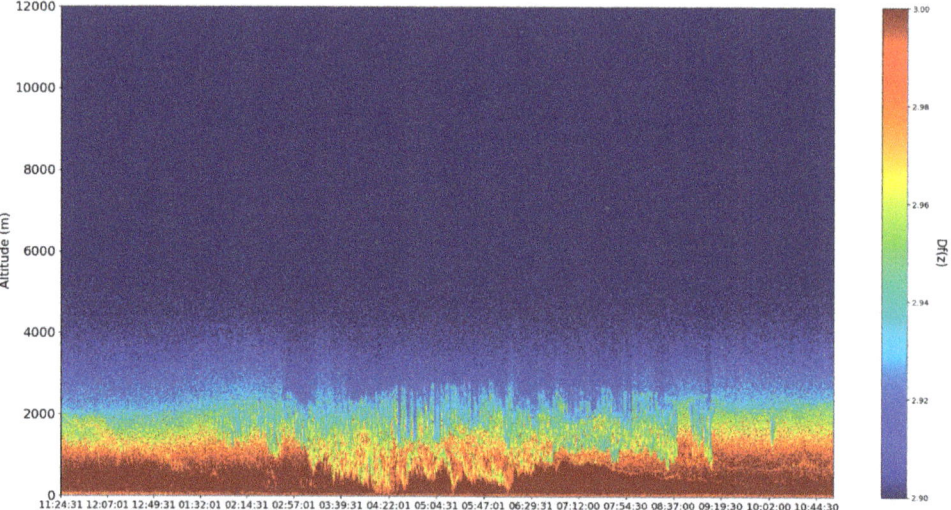

Figure 21. D_f time series, λ = 1064 nm, Galați, Romania, 23 December 2021.

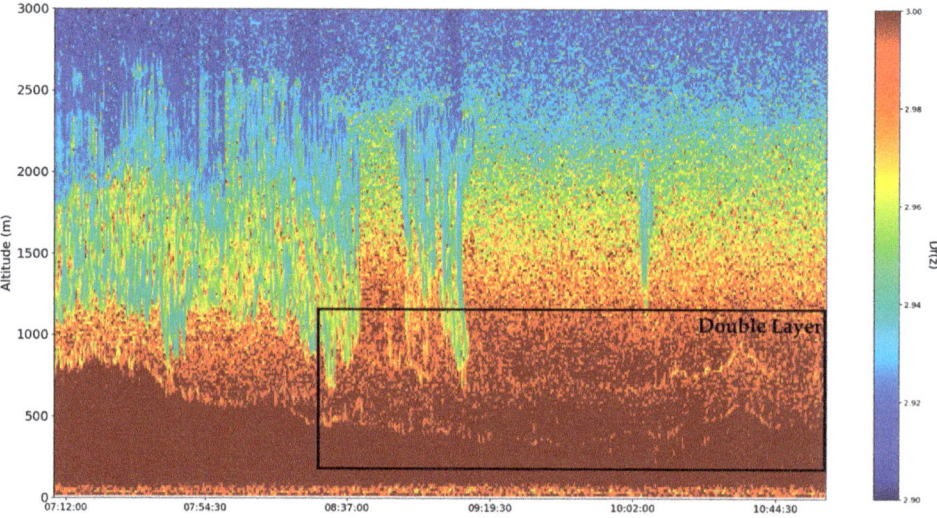

Figure 22. Zoomed-in (region of interest) D_f time series, λ = 1064 nm, Galați, Romania, 23 December 2021.

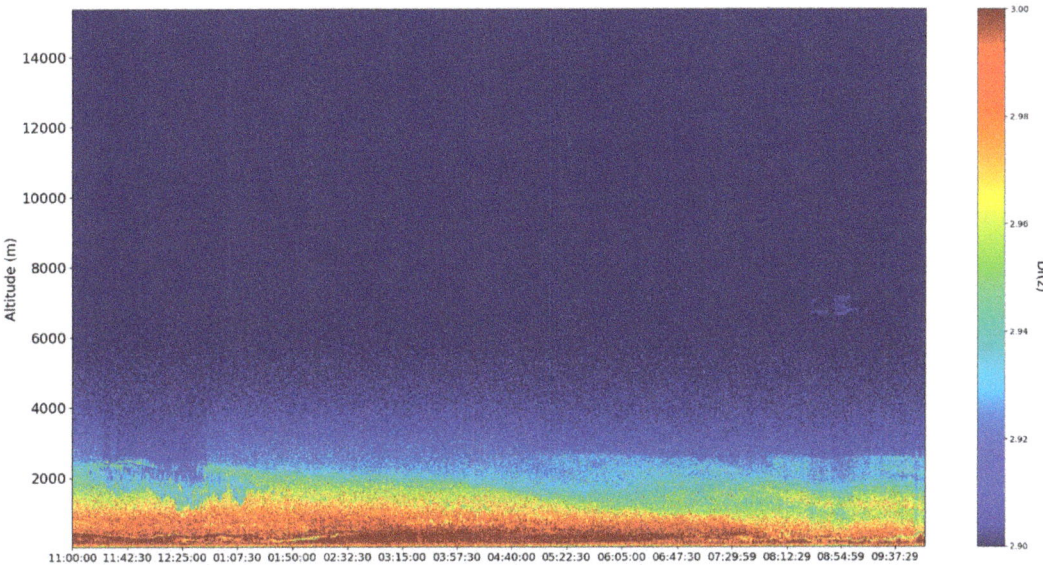

Figure 23. D_f time series, $\lambda = 1064$ nm, Galați, Romania, 22 December 2021.

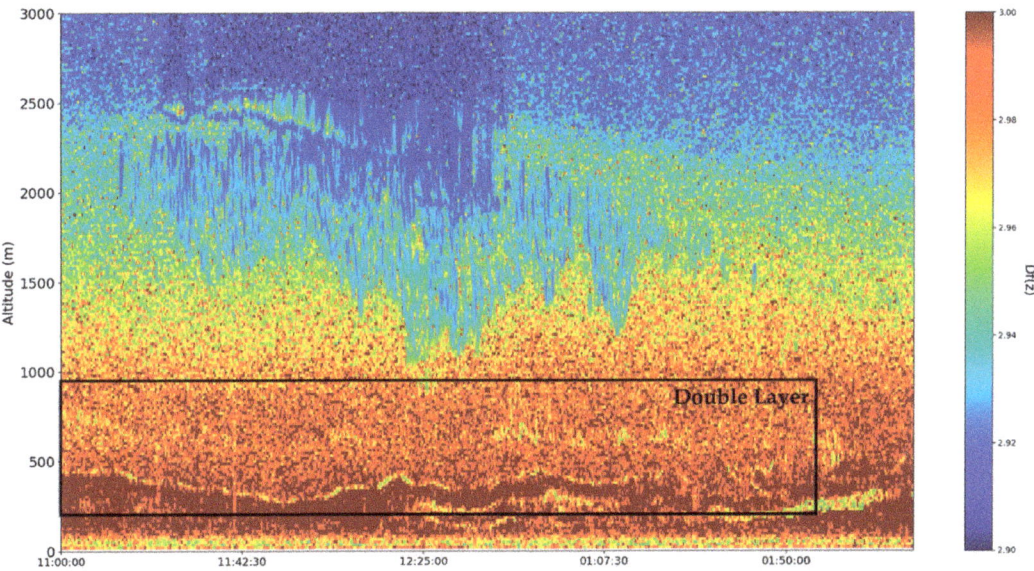

Figure 24. Zoomed-in (region of interest) D_f time series, $\lambda = 1064$ nm, Galați, Romania, 22 December 2021.

5. Conclusions

Applying the multifractal theory of motion to atmospheric entities through a hydrodynamic multifractal scenario, a multifractal conservation law that leads to differentiable and non-differentiable velocity fields is found; this then implies, through various nondimensionalizations, the existence of a specific multifractal force field that drives non-differentiable interactions between the atmospheric multifractal entities. Supposing then, that there exists a mass current density-type relation regarding these entities, then multifractal atmospheric mass conduction is found at differentiable, non-differentiable and global resolutions. In order for the exact form of this conduction to be found, a Lobachevsky plane metric is employed to find a component of the state function described by the multifractal conservation law. The inhomogeneity of the non-differentiable conduction is then analyzed regarding the fractal dimension variation, and it is found that there exist certain fractal dimensions where the non-differentiable conduction can present large fluctuations and values.

This then implies that, at fractal dimension inversions, intense non-differentiable conduction phenomena can occur, leading to vertical mass conduction and the formation of certain stable atmospheric features. Finally, ceilometer data is introduced, and this data is used in order to construct various time series profiles, including time series of the atmospheric fractal dimension. Fractal dimension inversions are observed in connection to the SBL and RL boundaries, which then validates that such inversions can lead to phenomena of mass conduction and atmospheric structure stability. There are possible limitations to the employed method, mainly regarding rapid aerosol intrusions—generally speaking, the associated multifractal and ceilometer theory works best only in relatively calm conditions, without the appearance of unexpected cloud or aerosol concentrations. Further studies could include further theoretical and practical validation that employs climatic models, such as ALARO or WRF, and such studies could also utilize larger batches of ceilometer data.

Author Contributions: Conceptualization, D.-C.N. and I.-A.R.; methodology, D.-E.C., D.V., M.-M.C. and I.-A.R.; software, I.-A.R.; validation, D.-C.N., M.-M.C. and M.A.; formal analysis, D.-C.N., M.-M.C. and I.-A.R.; investigation, D.-C.N., M.-M.C. and I.-A.R.; resources, D.-C.N., V.N. and F.N.; data curation, M.-M.C. and D.-E.C.; writing—original draft preparation, D.-C.N., I.-A.R. and M.A.; writing—review and editing, D.-C.N., M.-M.C. and M.A.; visualization, D.V. and I.-A.R.; supervision, D.-C.N. and M.A.; project administration, D.-C.N., V.N., F.N., D.V. and M.A.; funding acquisition, D.-C.N., V.N., F.N. and M.A. All authors have read and agreed to the published version of the manuscript.

Funding: This work was supported by a grant from the Romanian Ministry of Education and Research, CNCS-UEFISCDI, project number PN-III-P1-1.1-TE-2019-1921, within PNCDI III. Furthermore, the present research/article/study was also supported by the project, An Integrated System for the Complex Environmental Research and Monitoring in the Danube River Area, REXDAN, SMIS code 127065, co-financed by the European Regional Development Fund through the Competitiveness Operational Programme 2014-2020; contract no. 309/10.07.2020.

Institutional Review Board Statement: Not applicable.

Informed Consent Statement: Not applicable.

Data Availability Statement: Not applicable.

Acknowledgments: The authors acknowledge the RADO (Romanian Atmospheric 3D research Observatory) and the UGAL cloud remote sensing station, part of the ACTRIS–RO (Aerosol, Clouds and Trace gases Research InfraStructure-Romania) for providing ceilometer data used in this study. The authors also acknowledge the Faculty of Engineering of the "Vasile Alecsandri" University of Bacău for the financial support offered for the publication of this study.

Conflicts of Interest: The authors declare no conflict of interest.

References

1. Bar-Yam, Y.; McKay, S.R.; Christian, W. Dynamics of Complex Systems (Studies in Nonlinearity). *Comput. Phys.* **1998**, *12*, 335–336. [CrossRef]
2. Mitchell, M. *Complexity: A Guided Tour*; Oxford University Press: Oxford, UK, 2009.
3. Badii, R.; Politi, A. *Complexity: Hierarchical Structures and Scaling in Physics*; Cambridge University Press: Cambridge, UK, 1999; p. 6.
4. Flake, G.W. *The Computational Beauty of Nature: Computer Explorations of Fractals, Chaos, Complex Systems, and Adaptation*; MIT Press: Cambridge, MA, USA, 1998.
5. Țîmpu, S.; Sfîcă, L.; Dobri, R.V.; Cazacu, M.M.; Nita, A.I.; Birsan, M.V. Tropospheric Dust and Associated Atmospheric Circulations over the Mediterranean Region with Focus on Romania's Territory. *Atmosphere* **2020**, *11*, 349. [CrossRef]

6. Baleanu, D.; Diethelm, K.; Scalas, E.; Trujillo, J.J. *Fractional Calculus: Models and Numerical Methods*; World Scientific: Singapore, 2012; Volume 3.
7. Ortigueira, M.D. *Fractional Calculus for Scientists and Engineers*; Springer Science & Business Media: Berlin, Germany, 2011; Volume 84.
8. Nottale, L. *Scale Relativity and Fractal Space-Time: A New Approach to Unifying Relativity and Quantum Mechanics*; Imperial College Press: London, UK, 2011.
9. Merches, I.; Agop, M. *Differentiability and Fractality in Dynamics of Physical Systems*; World Scientific: Singapore, 2015.
10. Mandelbrot, B.B. *The Fractal Geometry of Nature*; WH Freeman: San Francisco, CA, USA, 1982.
11. Jackson, E.A. *Perspectives of Nonlinear Dynamics*; CUP Archive: Cambridge, UK, 1989; Volume 1.
12. Cristescu, C.P. *Nonlinear Dynamics and Chaos. Theoretical Fundaments and Application*; Romanian Academy Publishing House: Bucharest, Romania, 1987.
13. Roşu, I.A.; Cazacu, M.M.; Ghenadi, A.S.; Bibire, L.; Agop, M. On a multifractal approach of turbulent atmosphere dynamics. *Front. Earth Sci.* **2020**, *8*, 216. [CrossRef]
14. Roşu, I.A.; Cazacu, M.M.; Agop, M. Multifractal Model of Atmospheric Turbulence Applied to Elastic Lidar Data. *Atmosphere* **2021**, *12*, 226. [CrossRef]
15. Mazilu, N.; Agop, M. *Skyrmions: A Great Finishing Touch to Classical Newtonian Philosophy*; World Philosophy Series; Nova: New York, NY, USA, 2012.
16. Mazilu, N.; Agop, M.; Merches, I. *Scale Transitions as Foundations of Physics*; World Scientific: Singapore, 2021.
17. Xin, Y. *Geometry of Harmonic Maps (Vol. 21)*; Springer Science & Business Media: Heidelberg, Germany, 1996.
18. Tatarski, V.I. *Wave Propagation in a Turbulent Medium*; Courier Dover Publications: New York, NY, USA, 2016.
19. Alfonsi, G. Reynolds-averaged Navier–Stokes equations for turbulence modeling. *Appl. Mech. Rev.* **2009**, *62*, 040802. [CrossRef]
20. Rosu, I.A.; Cazacu, M.M.; Prelipceanu, O.S.; Agop, M. A Turbulence-Oriented Approach to Retrieve Various Atmospheric Parameters Using Advanced Lidar Data Processing Techniques. *Atmosphere* **2019**, *10*, 38. [CrossRef]
21. Busch, N.E. The surface boundary layer. *Bound. Layer Meteorol.* **1973**, *4*, 213–240. [CrossRef]
22. Haeffelin, M.; Angelini, F.; Morille, Y.; Martucci, G.; Frey, S.; Gobbi, G.P.; Lolli, S.; O'Dowd, C.D.; Sauvage, L.; Xueref-Rémy, I.; et al. Evaluation of mixing-height retrievals from automatic profiling lidars and ceilometers in view of future integrated networks in Europe. *Bound. Layer Meteorol.* **2012**, *143*, 49–75. [CrossRef]

Article

Dynamics, Periodic Orbit Analysis, and Circuit Implementation of a New Chaotic System with Hidden Attractor

Chengwei Dong

Department of Physics, North University of China, Taiyuan 030051, China; dongchengwei@tsinghua.org.cn

Abstract: Hidden attractors are associated with multistability phenomena, which have considerable application prospects in engineering. By modifying a simple three-dimensional continuous quadratic dynamical system, this paper reports a new autonomous chaotic system with two stable node-foci that can generate double-wing hidden chaotic attractors. We discuss the rich dynamics of the proposed system, which have some interesting characteristics for different parameters and initial conditions, through the use of dynamic analysis tools such as the phase portrait, Lyapunov exponent spectrum, and bifurcation diagram. The topological classification of the periodic orbits of the system is investigated by a recently devised variational method. Symbolic dynamics of four and six letters are successfully established under two sets of system parameters, including hidden and self-excited chaotic attractors. The system is implemented by a corresponding analog electronic circuit to verify its realizability.

Keywords: hidden attractor; unstable periodic orbit; symbolic dynamics; electronic circuit

1. Introduction

Chaos theory, which is regarded as the third scientific theory revolution in the 20th century, has been extensively and intensively studied since the meteorologist Lorenz discovered chaotic phenomena for three-dimensional (3D) autonomous quadratic systems in 1963 [1]. As chaotic states in nonlinear dynamic systems are extremely sensitive to initial values, a large amount of research work shows that chaos is closely related to engineering technology, with wide application in fields such as circuit control [2], image encryption [3], secure communications [4], and neural networks [5].

Many chaotic systems have been constructed [6–9] that include both self-excited and hidden attractors [10]. Self-excited attractors have a basin of attraction related to the unstable equilibrium, whereas those of hidden attractors do not intersect with small neighborhoods of any equilibria [11,12]. Most well-known dynamical systems have self-excited chaotic attractors [13–15]. As hidden attractors cannot be calculated from the initial conditions in the neighborhood of the equilibrium point, they were not introduced until recently, and there are some new studies on how to locate them [16,17]. Hidden attractors have attracted great interest in recent years due to their considerable importance in both theory and engineering, because they allow unexpected and potentially catastrophic responses to structural disturbances such as to bridges or aircraft wings. It has been shown that attractors in a dynamical system with stable equilibria [18–20], an infinite number of equilibria [21–23], or no equilibrium points [24–29] are hidden attractors. These are also represented in a 3D continuous dynamical system with only one unstable node as the equilibrium point [30].

Hidden attractors have been broadly investigated in the literature. Wang and Chen constructed a chaotic system with only one stable equilibrium via a constant control parameter added to the Sprott E system [31]. Wei found a new chaotic system with no equilibrium by adding a simple constant to the Sprott D system [32]. Two modified Sprott systems that have only stable node-focus points with hidden chaotic attractors were

analyzed [33]. The generalized Sprott C system with two stable equilibrium points was proposed [34], and its chaotic and complex dynamic behaviors in the parametric space were investigated. Hidden chaos and hyperchaos have been found in the jerk system [35–37], meminductor-based chaotic system [38], extended Rikitake system [39], 4D Rabinovich system [40], 4D modified Lorenz-Stenflo system [41], and 5D homopolar disc dynamo [42]. Self-excited and hidden attractors can also be generated in a modified Chua's circuit and in a 3D memristive Hindmarsh–Rose neuron model [43,44]. Moreover, some 3D dynamical systems with three different families of hidden attractors have been discovered [45–47]. A 4D autonomous chaotic system that has two types of hidden attractors with a line of equilibria or no equilibria was derived [48]. A 5D chaotic system with both hidden attractors and extreme multistability was introduced [49], and coexisting self-excited and hidden attractors in a Lorenz-like system with two equilibria were found [50].

This paper proposes a hidden chaotic attractor system with two stable fixed points. With the change of parameters, its complex dynamical behaviors are analyzed using multiple dynamical tools, such as phase portraits, time sequence, power spectrum, and Lyapunov exponents. We establish two symbolic dynamics in the system, and classify the unstable periodic orbits embedded in hidden and self-excited chaotic attractors topologically for two sets of parameters. The electronic circuit of the system is designed and simulated by Multisim software, which proves the existence of chaos. Compared to the above contributions in the literature, the novelty of the work lies in the unstable periodic orbits of the new system showing a complexity of significant differences with different parameter values. For the system with hidden chaotic attractors, which is determined by four parameters, the complexity is relatively simple; however, the system with self-excited chaotic attractors, which contains only two parameters, unexpectedly has more complex dynamics.

The rest of this paper is arranged as follows. Section 2 introduces the mathematical model of the system, and its nonlinear dynamic characteristics are investigated. In Section 3, observation of chaotic and complex dynamics in the system is implemented by varying different parameters. To locate the unstable cycles in the system, we review the variational method in Section 4, which can be effectively utilized in calculations. We systematically calculate all short unstable cycles of the new system under two parameters. To establish appropriate symbolic dynamics, one needs four letters, and the other needs six. Section 5 presents a circuit implementation of the system to validate its feasibility. Section 6 discusses our conclusions.

2. The New System and Its Dynamic Characteristics

Inspired by the chaotic system proposed by [51], a new system can be easily constructed by adding a nonlinear term of cross-product kxz to the first equation,

$$\begin{aligned} \frac{dx}{dt} &= a(y-x) + kxz \\ \frac{dy}{dt} &= -cy - xz \\ \frac{dz}{dt} &= -b + xy, \end{aligned} \quad (1)$$

where x, y, and z are state variables, and a, b, c, and k are the control parameters. Note that adding a cross-product nonlinear term is not a general method to realize chaos in a 3D quadratic system. In addition, the proposed system (1) has three nonlinear terms, where notably each equation has one single cross-product term, so it certainly does not belong to algebraic simple chaotic flows, but is suitable for practical implementation as an electronic circuit. When the parameters of system (1) are assigned as $(a, b, c, k) = (10, 100, 11.2, -0.2)$, and the initial values (x_0, y_0, z_0) are set as $(1, 1, 1)$, a fourth-order Runge–Kutta method is adopted in the numerical integration, which reveals the chaotic behaviors characterized by strange attractors, as shown in Figure 1a–c, and the power spectrum with continuous broadband characteristics (Figure 1d) verifies the emergence of chaos. Correspondingly, the Lyapunov exponents are calculated based on the Wolf algorithm [52], which gives $LE_1 = 0.7457, LE_2 = -0.0057, LE_3 = -26.8144$ (see Figure 2). The positive Lyapunov exponent indicates that the phase volume of the system is expanding and folding in a certain direction, which means that the system is in a chaotic state. The Kaplan–Yorke dimension is $D_{KY} = 2 + (LE_1 + LE_2)/|LE_3| = 2.0276$, which also verifies the chaoticity of system (1).

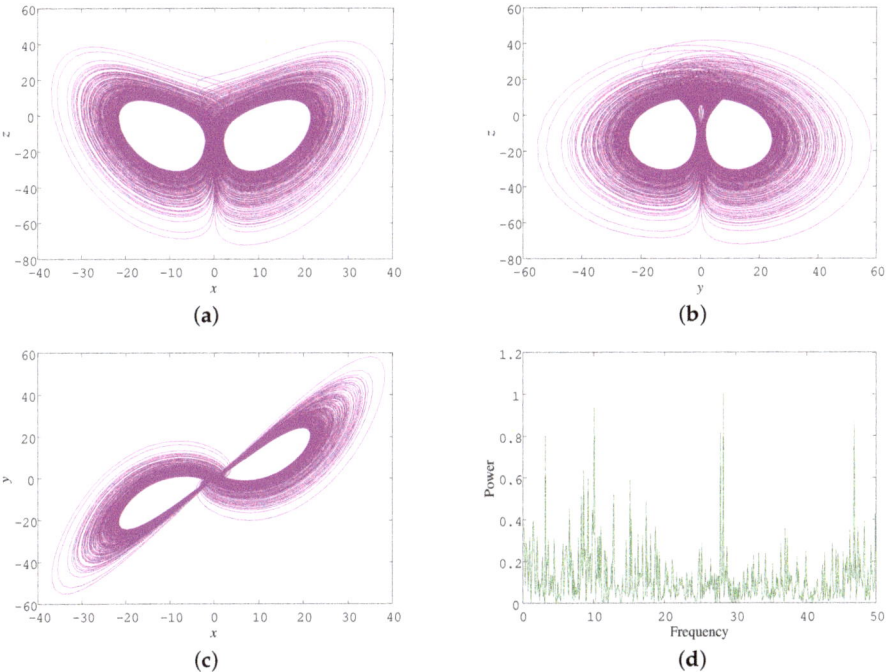

Figure 1. Projections of chaotic attractor onto various planes at time $t = 200$: (**a**) x–z phase space; (**b**) y–z phase space; (**c**) x–y phase space; (**d**) continuous broadband frequency spectrum.

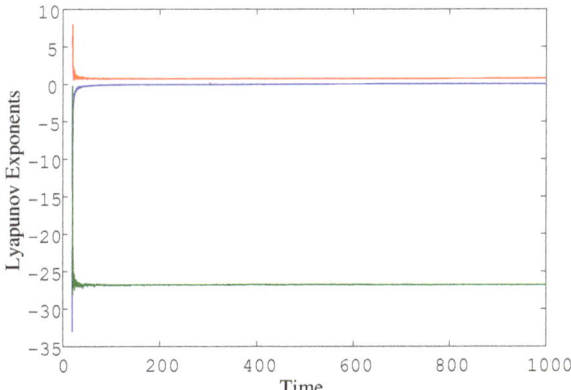

Figure 2. Lyapunov exponent spectrum of system (1) for $(a, b, c, k) = (10, 100, 11.2, -0.2)$.

The new system has the following fundamental dynamic properties:
(1) System (1) is rotationally symmetric versus the z-axis, which is invariant under the coordinate transformation $(x, y, z) \to (-x, -y, z)$. Any attractors are either a symmetric pair or symmetric under a 180-degree rotation around the z-axis;
(2) Since the divergence of system (1) is

$$\nabla \cdot V = \frac{\partial \dot{x}}{\partial x} + \frac{\partial \dot{y}}{\partial y} + \frac{\partial \dot{z}}{\partial z} = -a + kz - c, \quad (2)$$

under the condition $-a + kz - c < 0$, it is dissipative and can converge to a set of zero measure in exponential form,

$$\frac{dV}{dt} = e^{-a+kz-c}; \quad (3)$$

(3) System (1) possesses two equilibrium points:

$$E_1 : \left(-\sqrt{\frac{ab-bck}{a}}, -\frac{b}{\sqrt{\frac{ab-bck}{a}}}, \frac{ac}{ck-a}\right),$$

$$E_2 : \left(\sqrt{\frac{ab-bck}{a}}, \frac{b}{\sqrt{\frac{ab-bck}{a}}}, \frac{ac}{ck-a}\right). \quad (4)$$

Linearizing the system gives the Jacobian matrix

$$A = \begin{pmatrix} -a+kz & a & kx \\ -z & -c & -x \\ y & x & 0 \end{pmatrix}. \quad (5)$$

For the parameters $(a, b, c, k) = (10, 100, 11.2, -0.2)$, the Jacobian eigenvalues at E_1 and E_2 can be calculated by solving the corresponding characteristic equations, and they have the same values: $\lambda_1 = -18.7413$, $\lambda_{2,3} = -0.314 \pm 11.424i$. From the eigenvalues, we can see that E_1 and E_2 are both stable node-focus points.

Since the new system can generate strange attractors, it is implied that system (1) under current parameters has hidden chaotic attractors. Figure 3a displays the coexistence of chaotic motion and stable node-foci in 3D phase space. We can see clearly that the trajectory starting from initial conditions $I_1 = (1, 1, 1)$ becomes a disordered state; however, orbits starting from initial conditions $I_2 = (-20, -10, -10)$ and $I_3 = (20, 10, -10)$ spirally converge to E_1 and E_2, respectively. Figure 3b displays the time-domain waveform diagram for initial conditions I_1, I_2, and I_3; an apparently chaotic waveform of $x(t)$ illustrates that hidden chaotic attractors exist in system (1). To avoid transient chaos, we also confirmed the existence of a hidden chaotic attractor, since the orbit remains on it for $t = 10^6$.

The graphics of the basin of attraction, which is defined as the initial condition set that the orbits converge to a given attractor, can clearly exhibit the initial point distributions of different attractors. To further check whether the chaotic attractor in Figure 3 is hidden, a section $z = -9.1503$, including E_1 and E_2, is selected, and the initial condition regions of coexisting attractors are explored, as shown in Figure 4. Three types of basins of attraction on the cross section are colored yellow, blue, and red. Yellow areas with black stripes represent the basin of attraction of a chaotic attractor and the Poincaré section concerning the chaotic attractor with two wings, while blue and red areas denote that the movement from these initial conditions will converge to equilibria E_1 and E_2, respectively. From Figure 4, we find that the basin of attraction has the expected symmetric similarity and a smooth boundary. Moreover, in view of the topology of basins in Figure 4, the basins of attraction of chaotic attractors do not intersect with small neighborhoods of stable equilibrium points E_1 and E_2, which also illustrates that there is a hidden chaotic attractor in system (1).

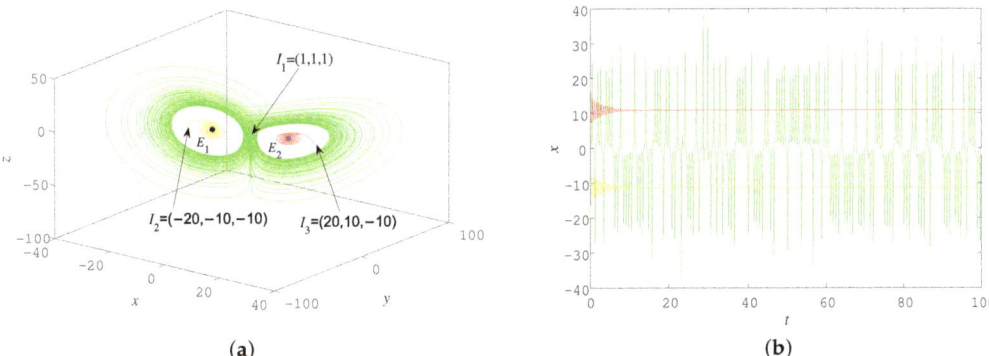

Figure 3. (**a**) 3D phase portrait of system (1) for $(a,b,c,k) = (10, 100, 11.2, -0.2)$. Initial conditions I_1 lead to hidden chaotic attractor, and initial conditions I_2, I_3 lead to asymptotically converging behaviors to equilibrium point E_1 and E_2, respectively; (**b**) coexisting time series diagram of $x(t)$.

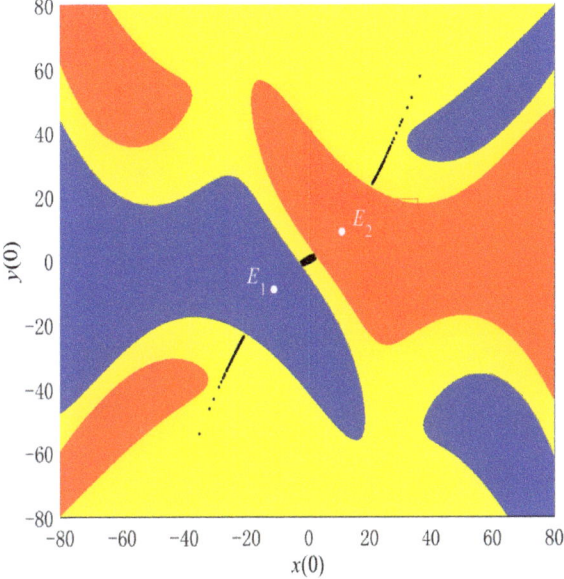

Figure 4. Basins of attraction for system (1) at $z = -9.1503$. Blue and red basins represent attractors of two stable node-focus points E_1 and E_2, yellow region denotes basin of chaotic attractor, and black stripes denote crossing trajectories of chaotic attractor.

3. Chaotic and Complex Dynamics in New System

The system parameters can significantly influence the dynamics, and the qualitative or topological variety in the behavior of dynamic systems means that a bifurcation occurs [53]. We discuss the chaotic and complex dynamics of the proposed system (1) through varying the parameters, taking the initial values as $(x_0, y_0, z_0) = (1, 1, 1)$. The bifurcation diagram, largest Lyapunov exponent, and division diagram are adopted as tools to observe the impacts of parameters.

3.1. Fix $a = 10, c = 11.2, k = -0.2$ and Vary b

To investigate the effect of the parameters on the dynamics of system (1), we first take parameters $(a, c, k) = (10, 11.2, -0.2)$ and vary $b \in [10, 140]$. When altering b, the system shows many complex dynamic behaviors that can be explored in the parameter space. The typical Benettin method is employed to calculate the maximum Lyapunov exponent spectrum, and the corresponding bifurcation diagram versus parameter b is displayed in Figure 5. Obviously, a positive maximum Lyapunov exponent implies that the system is chaotic over a wide range of parameters. It is clear that the bifurcation diagram with the variation of parameter b matches well with the largest Lyapunov exponent spectrum. We can see that the state of system (1) becomes chaotic through pitchfork and period-doubling bifurcations, then periodic, and chaotic again. The bifurcation diagram in Figure 5b demonstrates that the system evolves smoothly from a periodic solution to a chaotic region through a typical period-doubling route; hence, no clear boundary exists between a periodic phase portrait and chaos. When b is in the interval $[125, 140]$, the largest Lyapunov exponent quickly becomes negative, and the corresponding bifurcation diagram suddenly changes to no cutoff points, which both mean that the trajectory of system (1) finally converges to a fixed point. More details are presented through the 3D projections of phase portraits of system (1) at different b values, as shown in Figure 6.

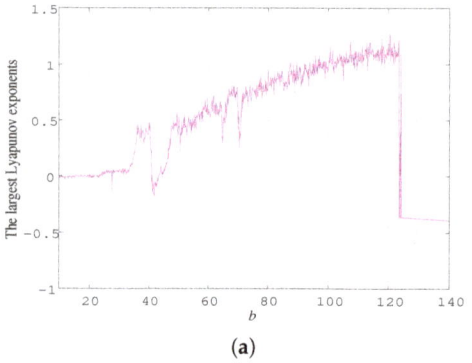

(a)

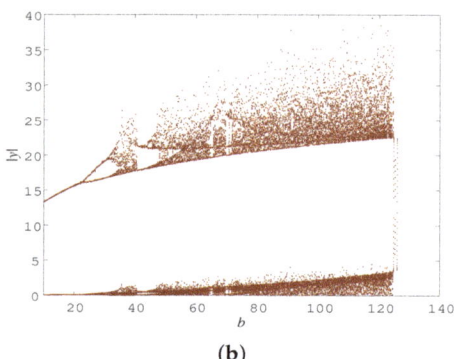

(b)

Figure 5. Largest Lyapunov exponent spectrum (**a**) and bifurcation diagram (**b**) of system (1) versus b, where $a = 10, c = 11.2, k = -0.2$.

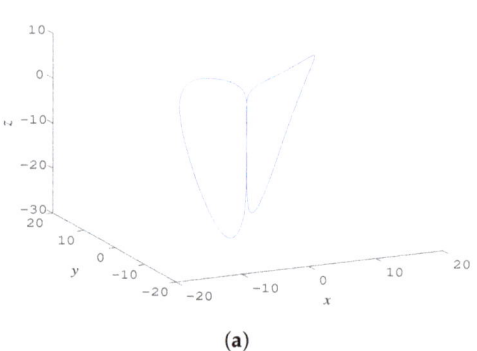

(a)

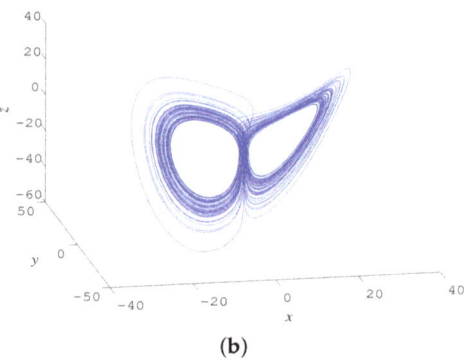

(b)

Figure 6. Cont.

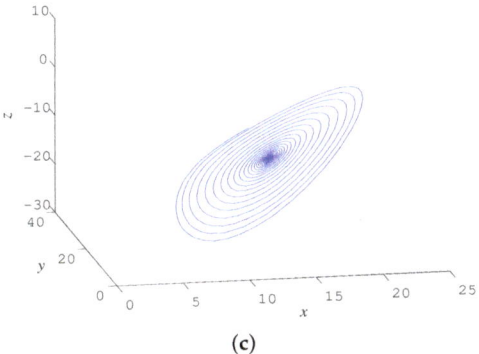

(c)

Figure 6. 3D view of phase portraits of system (1), where $a = 10, c = 11.2, k = -0.2$: (**a**) $b = 20$, (**b**) $b = 80$, (**c**) $b = 130$.

3.2. Fix $b = 100, c = 11.2, k = -0.2$ and Vary a

Now, we fix $(b, c, k) = (100, 11.2, -0.2)$ and vary $a \in [6, 20]$ and explore the dynamical evolution of system (1). Figure 7a shows the largest Lyapunov exponent spectrum with respect to a, and Figure 7b displays the bifurcation diagram of the whole evolution process. As can be seen from Figure 7, these results are consistent with each other and demonstrate that the dynamical behaviors vary when a undergoes change. Obviously, when a is in the interval $[6, 9.7]$, the system converges to one stable equilibrium, as shown in Figure 8a, where $a = 7$. When $a \in (9.7, 12.1]$, the system has a chaotic status. Near $a = 12.2$, the largest Lyapunov exponent is about zero, which implies that system (1) is periodic in a small parameter range, as demonstrated in Figure 8b, where $a = 12.2$. However, the system becomes chaotic again when a is in the interval $[12.6, 13.7]$ (see Figure 8c). Then, when $a > 13.7$, the system experiences an inverse period-doubling bifurcation process with the increase of a, and eventually becomes periodic again. Figure 8d displays the 3D phase diagram for $a = 20$.

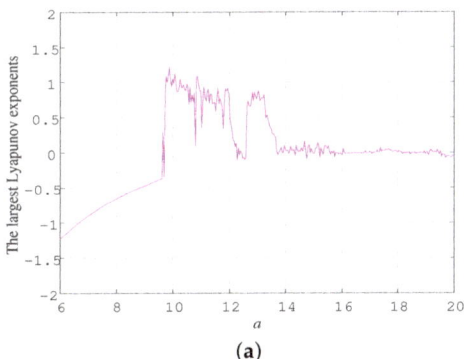

(a)

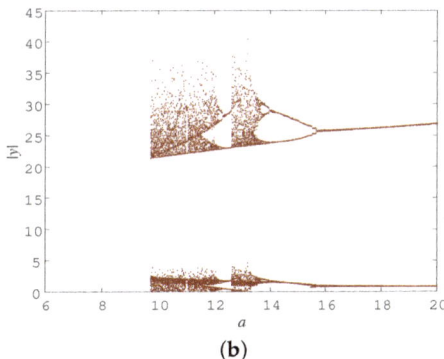

(b)

Figure 7. Parameter values $(b, c, k) = (100, 11.2, -0.2)$, largest Lyapunov exponent spectrum (**a**), and bifurcation diagram (**b**) of system (1) for $a \in [6, 20]$.

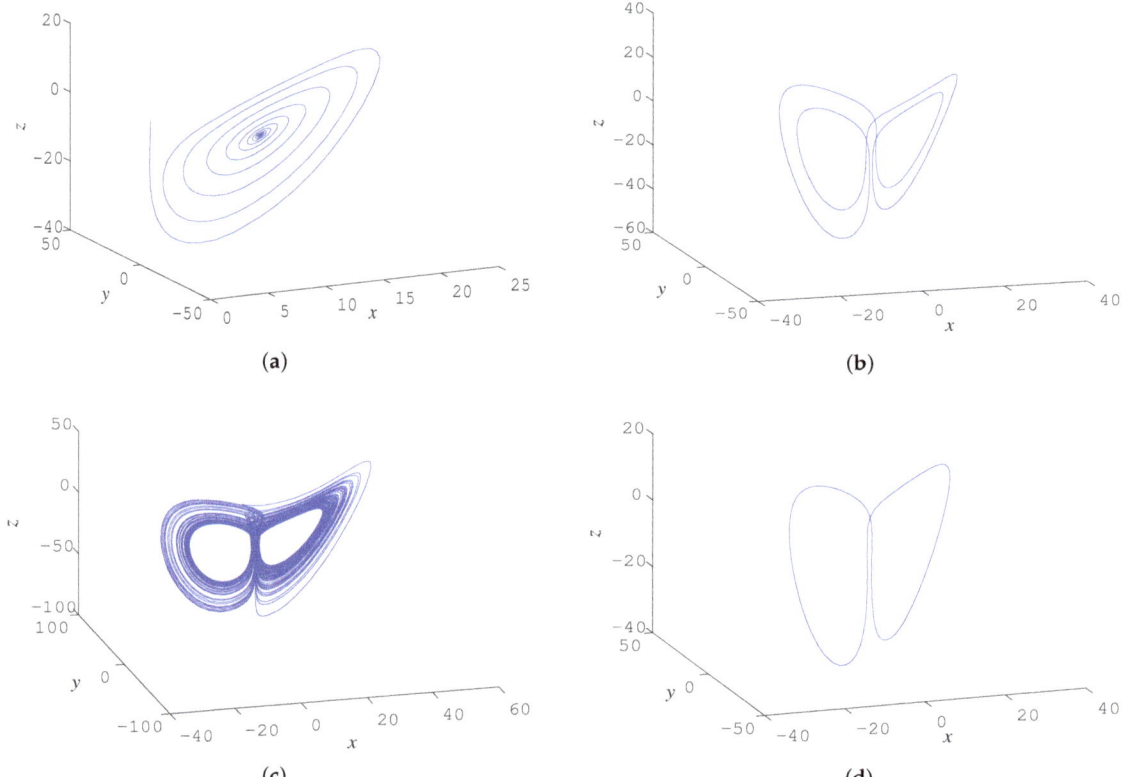

Figure 8. 3D view of phase portraits of system (1), $b = 100, c = 11.2, k = -0.2$: (**a**) $a = 7$; (**b**) $a = 12.2$; (**c**) $a = 13$; (**d**) $a = 20$.

3.3. Fix $a = 10, b = 100, k = -0.2$ and Vary c

Here, we fix the parameters $a = 10, b = 100, k = -0.2$, and vary c. The Lyapunov exponent spectrum and bifurcation diagram presented in Figure 9 reveal that the limit cycle, chaos, and equilibrium point appear alternately as c increases from -30 to 20. We can see that the system shows complex dynamic behavior in this region, and generates chaos via period-doubling bifurcation. Moreover, periodic windows exist in such a parameter region. An attractor of system (1) becomes a limit cycle from chaos through a process of reverse period-doubling bifurcations, then becomes chaotic again through period-doubling bifurcations, and finally converges to a stable equilibrium point. With initial values $(x_0, y_0, z_0) = (-1, -1, 1)$, the system will undergo the same bifurcation process, and the orbits in the phase space will eventually converge toward another stable fixed point.

When the parameters $a = 10, b = 100, k = -0.2$, the emergence of a hidden chaotic attractor is dependent on the value of $c > 0$. When we take $c \in [-10.7, 0]$, the system generates a self-excited chaotic attractor. It is worth noting that the periodic regions do not share the same dynamical characteristics; diverse limit cycles appear in four periodic regions, as shown in Figure 10.

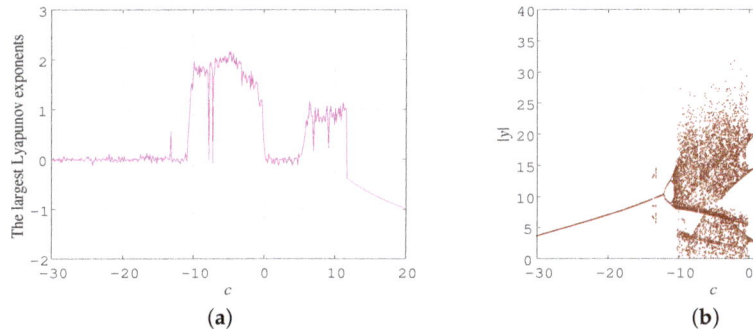

Figure 9. Parameter values $(a, b, k) = (10, 100, -0.2)$, largest Lyapunov exponent spectrum (**a**) and bifurcation diagram (**b**) of system (1) for $c \in [-30, 20]$.

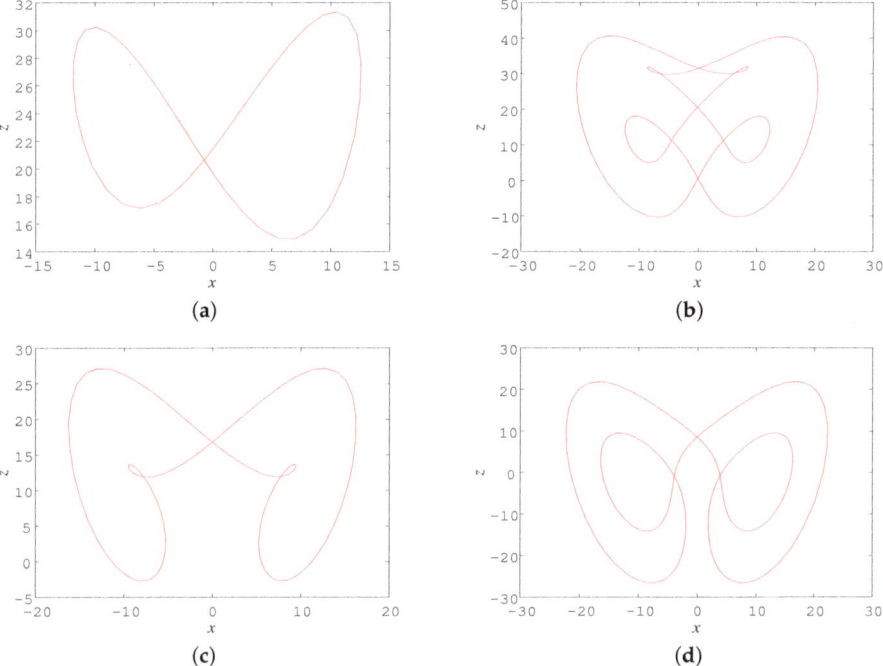

Figure 10. 2D view of different limit cycles of system (1), $a = 10, b = 100, k = -0.2$: (**a**) $c = -12$; (**b**) $c = -7.74$; (**c**) $c = -7.2$; and (**d**) $c = 3$.

3.4. Fix $a = 10, b = 100, c = 11.2$ and Vary k

The Lyapunov exponent spectrum and bifurcation diagram shown in Figure 11 reveal that equilibrium point and chaotic orbit appear alternately with k increasing gradually from -2 to 0.9. When we take parameters $(a, b, c, k) = (10, 100, 11.2, 0)$, system (1) becomes the system with a hidden chaotic attractor in Ref. [51]. As shown in Figure 11, when k becomes slightly positive or negative, chaotic attractors can still be generated. However, the type of chaotic attractors will depend on the positive or negative value of k; these are the new structures that have emerged. As required by the Routh–Hurwitz stability criterion, when we take parameters $(a, b, c) = (10, 100, 11.2)$, hidden chaotic attractors can exist if the following inequalities are satisfied: $a + c - \frac{ack}{ck-a} > 0$, which requires $k < 0$ or $k > 1.69$. Hence, when k is slightly positive, the chaotic attractor is self-excited, while when

k is slightly negative, it generates a hidden chaotic attractor with two stable node-foci. It is noteworthy that, with k increasing in the range $k > 0.9$, the orbit finally leads to infinity.

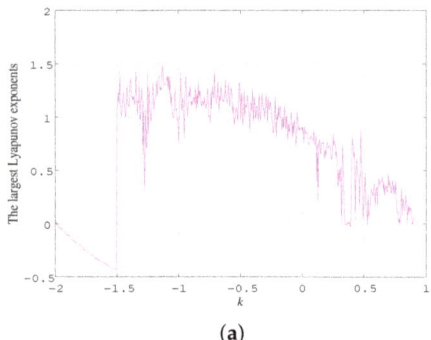
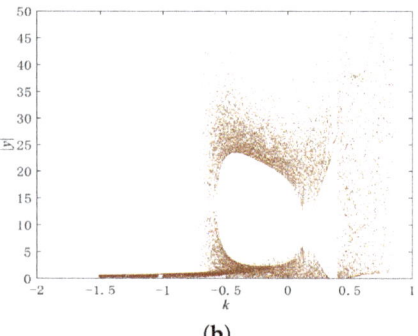

Figure 11. Largest Lyapunov exponent spectrum (**a**) and bifurcation diagram (**b**) of system (1) versus k, where $a = 10, b = 100, c = 11.2$.

3.5. Fix $a = 10, b = 100$ and Vary k and c

We draw a division diagram to capture different kinds of dynamical modes of system (1) with respect to parameters k–c. Varying k and c within the region of $k \in [-4, 0]$, $c \in [0, 25]$, by calculating the largest Lyapunov exponents, we obtain a pseudo-colored map on a 300×250 grid of parameters (k, c) (see Figure 12a). Colors correspond to magnitudes of the largest Lyapunov exponents, where green and blue imply equilibrium, yellow indicates a limit cycle, and red represents a state of chaos. It can be observed from Figure 12a that the dynamical mode of system (1) evolves as k and c change. To more clearly show the evolution of chaos, we fix $k = -0.2$, take $c \in [5, 15]$, and plot a vertical line A–B–C, presented in Figure 12a for $A = 5, B = 10, C = 15$. The rich dynamics of the evolution process in the division diagram are shown in Figure 9. Starting with the periodic region A, as c increases, the chaos degenerates through period-doubling bifurcations in line A–B, and the system abruptly changes to one equilibrium through the chaotic status in line B–C. Similarly, we plot a horizontal line, D–E, fix c at 11.2, and take $k \in [-2, -1]$. The system changes from one stable equilibrium to a chaotic state at $k = -1.5$.

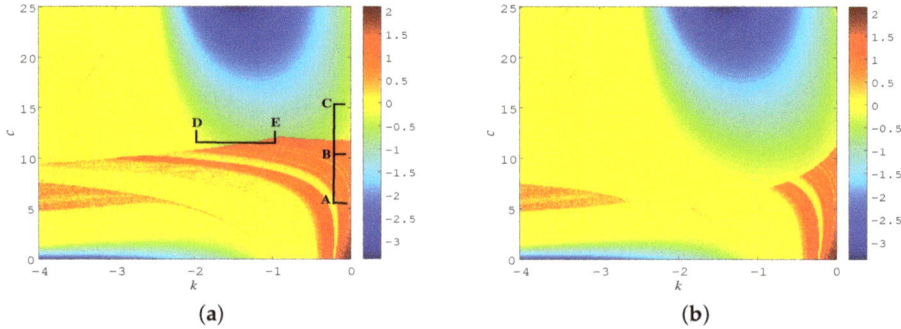

Figure 12. Division of parameters k and c with different initial conditions: (**a**) $(x_0, y_0, z_0) = (1, 1, 1)$; (**b**) $(x_0, y_0, z_0) = (1, 10, 1)$.

Taking initial conditions $(x_0, y_0, z_0) = (1, 10, 1)$, the numerical results in Figure 12b illustrate that the other initial conditions have an impact on the division diagram, leading to expansion of the regions of stable equilibrium. The original chaotic state regions become an equilibrium state, indicating the existence of a hidden attractor in the corresponding parameters. If the regions remain in a chaotic state, a self-excited attractor might exist under the corresponding parameters, as the regions may become one equilibrium at other initial values.

Inspired by the k–c division diagram, it is clear that the parameter values $k = 0$ and $c = 0$ at the lower-right corner are dark red, which means the chaos is most complex. As will be discussed shortly, system (1) has a self-excited chaotic attractor at parameter values $(a, b, c, k) = (10, 64, 0, 0)$.

4. Diverse Symbolic Dynamics for Unstable Periodic Orbits

We employ the variational method for the cycle search in system (1) and establish appropriate symbolic dynamics for the found periodic orbits. We first introduce the variational method, which can be effectively used in the calculations. After that, we aim to accurately find the surrounding mode of the orbit in system (1), and develop a universal approach for the symbolic encodings of cycles. We select two sets of parameters, one corresponding to the hidden chaotic attractor, and the other to the self-excited chaotic attractor. The symbolic encoding method based on orbit topology will enable us to analyze periodic orbits by establishing diverse symbolic dynamics.

As shown in Figure 1, the strange attractor of system (1) is composed of numerous unstable periodic orbits. The 3D continuous flow can be transformed to a 2D discrete mapping by an appropriate Poincaré section. The idea is to select a section properly in a high-dimensional phase space, on which a pair of conjugate variables are fixed; then, the information about the motion characteristics can be obtained by observing the intersection points of the motion trajectory and cross section. Figure 13a shows the first return map of system (1) for $(a, b, c, k) = (10, 100, 11.2, -0.2)$. When we choose a special Poincaré section $z = -9.1503$, the initial values are $[1, 1, 1]$, where a dense point with a four-branch structure is presented under these parameters, which indicates the necessity to encode all short cycles by symbolic dynamics with four letters. For the parameters $(a, b, c, k) = (10, 64, 0, 0)$, which also correspond to a chaotic state, the first return map with a Poincaré section $z = 0$ with the same initial values is shown in Figure 13b. We can see more branches in this case, which means that more symbols are needed to encode the periodic orbits, and demonstrates better complexity in the topological structure of periodic orbits. To the best of our knowledge, investigations of such complex unstable cycles in the chaotic attractor have rarely been reported. The Lyapunov exponents under the parameters $(a, b, c, k) = (10, 64, 0, 0)$ are also calculated, which gives $LE_1 = 1.4456$, $LE_2 = 0.0017$, and $LE_3 = -11.4473$ (see Figure 14). Correspondingly, the Kaplan–Yorke dimension is $D_{KY} = 2.1264$. Compared with the largest Lyapunov exponent, i.e., 0.7457, under the parameters $(a, b, c, k) = (10, 100, 11.2, -0.2)$, the largest Lyapunov exponent becomes larger, which indicates that the chaotic characteristics of the system are more complex for the parameters $(a, b, c, k) = (10, 64, 0, 0)$.

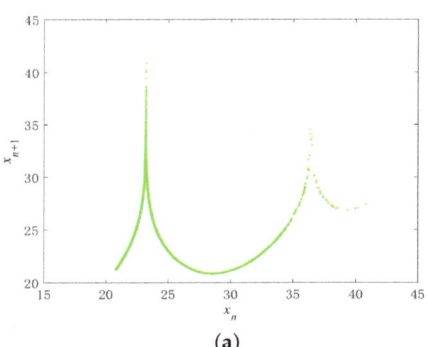
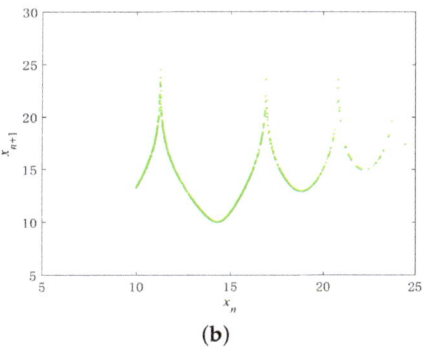

Figure 13. First return map of system (1) under different parameters: (**a**) Poincaré section $z = -9.1503$, $(a, b, c, k) = (10, 100, 11.2, -0.2)$; (**b**) Poincaré section $z = 0$, $(a, b, c, k) = (10, 64, 0, 0)$.

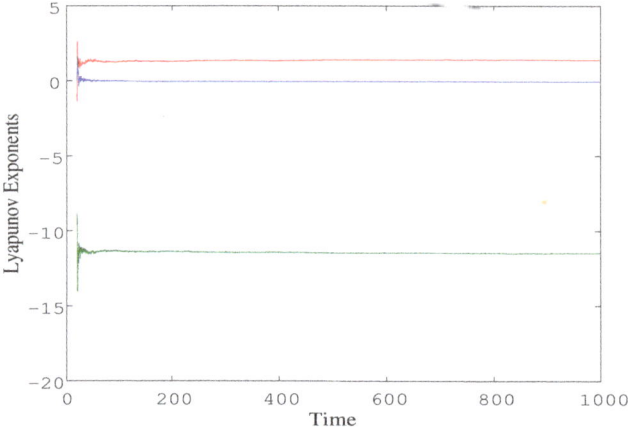

Figure 14. Lyapunov exponent spectrum of system (1) for $(a, b, c, k) = (10, 64, 0, 0)$.

4.1. Variational Method

Periodic orbits play important roles in physical and engineering applications. It is relatively easy to locate the unstable cycles in low-dimensional chaotic systems in general [54]. When we locate them in a high-dimensional state space, because the topological structure of the dynamical system is difficult to perceive, even if points on the cycle are guessed, the shooting method may fail. This problem can be solved by initializing a complete orbit with similar topology, and making it gradually evolve into a real cycle. This is also the basic idea for the variational method to calculate unstable periodic orbits of dynamical systems. For the calculations of unstable cycles, a discretization equation was derived as [55]

$$\begin{pmatrix} \hat{A} & -\hat{v} \\ \hat{a} & 0 \end{pmatrix} \begin{pmatrix} \delta \tilde{x} \\ \delta \lambda \end{pmatrix} = \delta \tau \begin{pmatrix} \lambda \hat{v} - \tilde{v} \\ 0 \end{pmatrix}, \tag{6}$$

where τ is the virtual time related to iteration times. We use λ to adjust the period, which has the relationship with the period $T = 2\pi\lambda$ when the periodic orbit converges. We want to match the vector fields $\hat{v} = (v_1, v_2, \ldots, v_N)^t$, $\tilde{v} = (\tilde{v}_1, \tilde{v}_2, \ldots \tilde{v}_N)^t$ everywhere along the loop, and v and $\tilde{v}$ represent the flow velocity and loop velocity vector, respectively. $\hat{a}$ is an Nd-dimensional row vector that restricts coordinate alterations. $\hat{A} = \hat{D} - \lambda \text{diag}[A_1, A_2, \ldots, A_N]$, where $A_{ij} = \frac{\partial v_i}{\partial x_j}$, is the gradient matrix of the velocity field, and the five-point approximation matrix is

$$\hat{D} = \frac{N}{24\pi} \begin{pmatrix} 0 & 8 & -1 & & & & 1 & -8 \\ -8 & 0 & 8 & -1 & & & & 1 \\ 1 & -8 & 0 & 8 & -1 & & & \\ & & & \cdots & & & & \\ & & & 1 & -8 & 0 & 8 & -1 \\ -1 & & & & 1 & -8 & 0 & 8 \\ 8 & -1 & & & & 1 & -8 & 0 \end{pmatrix}, \tag{7}$$

where each matrix element is $d \times d$ dimensional, and blanks are filled with zeros. The $[(Nd + 1) \times (Nd + 1)]$ matrix on the left side of Equation (6) must be inverted to solve for $\delta \tilde{x}$ and $\delta \lambda$, and the banded lower-upper decomposition method for accelerated computing and the Woodbury formula are adopted. In addition, because the virtual time steps are sometimes not significant, we may choose larger time steps for numerical integration, so as to effectively search the real periodic orbit.

To utilize the variational method, as a first step, a loop guess which is fit to the cycle calculations is a prerequisite, and the loop guess can be initialized in many ways in the numerical calculations [55]. For example, we can use a fast Fourier transform of a nearly closed orbital fragment obtained from the numerical integration, keep only the lowest-frequency components, and use a reverse fast Fourier transform back to the phase space, in which emerges a glossy loop guess that can be used to initialize. We can also easily construct the initial loop guess by utilizing the homotopy evolution method [56]. We mention other initialization methods below.

The flexibility of the variational method for cycle searching has been verified by many examples [57–59], including conservative systems and low- or high-dimensional dissipative systems. The method can also locate other invariant sets in dynamical systems with proper modification [60,61]. The method cannot only find cycles with fixed parameters, but can be used to study the deformations of cycles when changing some parameters, i.e., to investigate the bifurcation behaviors of a dynamical system [62,63]. Hence, this approach can be used to study the generation or disappearance of periodic orbits and the change of cycle stability.

4.2. Unstable Cycles Embedded in Hidden Chaotic Attractor for $(a, b, c, k) = (10, 100, 11.2, -0.2)$

The unstable periodic orbits in system (1) when $(a, b, c, k) = (10, 100, 11.2, -0.2)$ are investigated based on the variational method. In the process, establishing appropriate symbolic dynamics is important for locating all short cycles without missing any [64]. To obtain the topological shape of the periodic orbit to be calculated, we perform numerical simulations, intercepting part of the simple orbital fragment to construct the initial loop guess. Several short periodic orbits with uncomplicated topological structures are found, as shown in Figure 15. Figure 15a shows a periodic orbit that revolves one turn around the left equilibrium E_1 with an elliptical shape, which has a relatively small extension in the z-axis with shortest period $T = 0.635920$. We mark it as cycle 0. Figure 15b shows a cycle that rotates once around the right equilibrium E_2 with an elliptical shape, and mark it as cycle 1. It can be seen that the two periodic orbits are symmetric to each other. Similarly, we mark the cycle with a wing shape rotating around the fixed point on the left once as cycle 2, as shown in Figure 15c, and its symmetric cycle with reasonably large extension in the z orientation is denoted as cycle 3 (see Figure 15d). The above four cycles can be regarded as the building blocks, and other periodic orbits can be calculated systematically by the symbolic dynamics of four letters.

There are four situations in which an orbit revolves one turn both around the left and right fixed points, and they are the cycles with topological length 2, as listed in Figure 16a–d. The rotationally symmetric property of system (1) implies the exchange symmetry 0 and 1 or 2 and 3 of the symbol sequence. Consequently, it is shown that the symmetry partner of cycle 12 is 03, and they have the same period. Cycles 01 or 23 are conjugated with themselves, so that no other orbit has the same period. Figure 16e–h display four cycles with topological length 3. Utilizing symbolic dynamics, we can calculate the cycles up to any topological length, i.e., we first construct the loop guess of the corresponding symbol sequence, and use the variational technique to verify its existence. Altogether, we found 20 periodic orbits with topological length 3, as listed in Table 1.

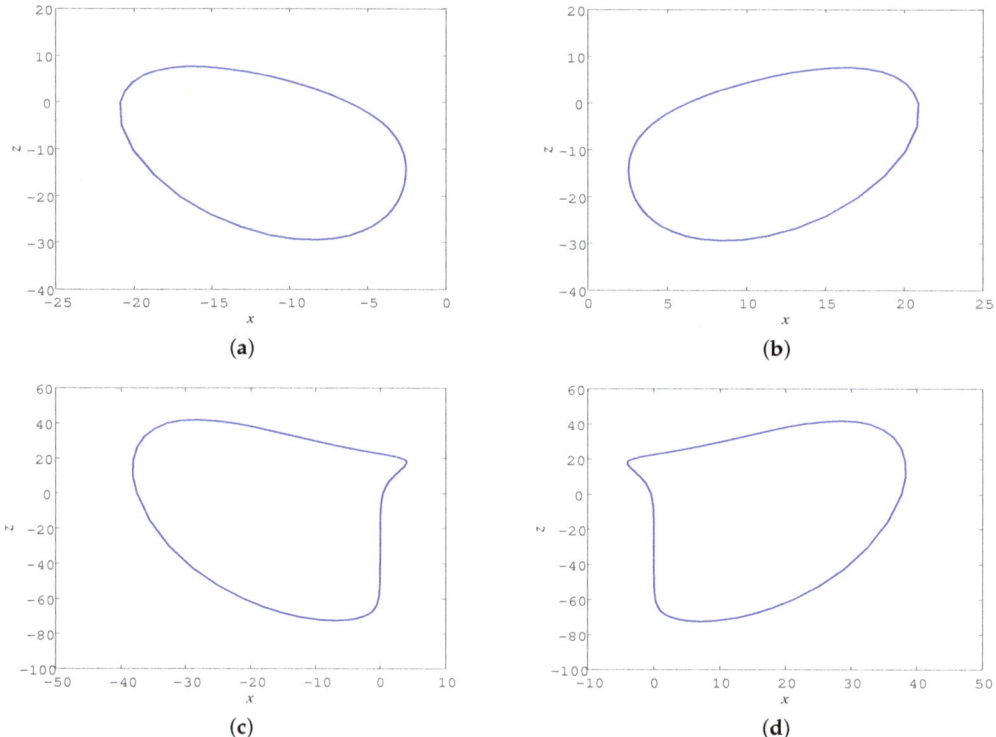

Figure 15. Four basic building blocks in system (1) for parameters $(a, b, c, k) = (10, 100, 11.2, -0.2)$: (**a**) cycle 0; (**b**) cycle 1; (**c**) cycle 2; and (**d**) cycle 3.

Table 1. Twenty unstable periodic orbits embedded in hidden chaotic attractor of system (1) for $(a, b, c, k) = (10, 100, 11.2, -0.2)$, showing topological length, itinerary p, period T_p, and three coordinates of a point on the periodic orbit.

Length	p	T_p	x	y	z
1	0	0.635920	−7.028076	0.430355	1.092913
	1	0.635920	7.028076	−0.430355	1.092913
	2	1.192933	2.544434	12.123766	20.650672
	3	1.192933	−2.544434	−12.123766	20.650672
2	12	1.752388	2.807407	6.313538	12.146665
	03	1.752388	−2.807407	−6.313538	12.146665
	01	1.467965	0.100280	1.271667	−7.073590
	23	2.383824	−14.090307	17.922194	33.086632
3	001	2.174153	−7.214950	4.081725	7.082844
	011	2.174153	7.214950	−4.081725	7.082844
	003	2.361334	−1.162938	−0.669254	−14.983886
	112	2.361334	1.162938	0.669254	−14.983886
	132	2.940945	−2.570910	−0.291669	11.591391
	023	2.940945	2.570910	0.291669	11.591391
	021	2.554559	−0.016908	−0.016629	−31.681837
	013	2.554559	0.016908	0.016629	−31.681837
	033	2.946229	0.291076	0.540818	−60.155264
	122	2.946229	−0.291076	−0.540818	−60.155264
	223	3.954898	−5.509519	−11.111451076	−71.906347
	233	3.954898	5.509519	11.111451076	−71.906347

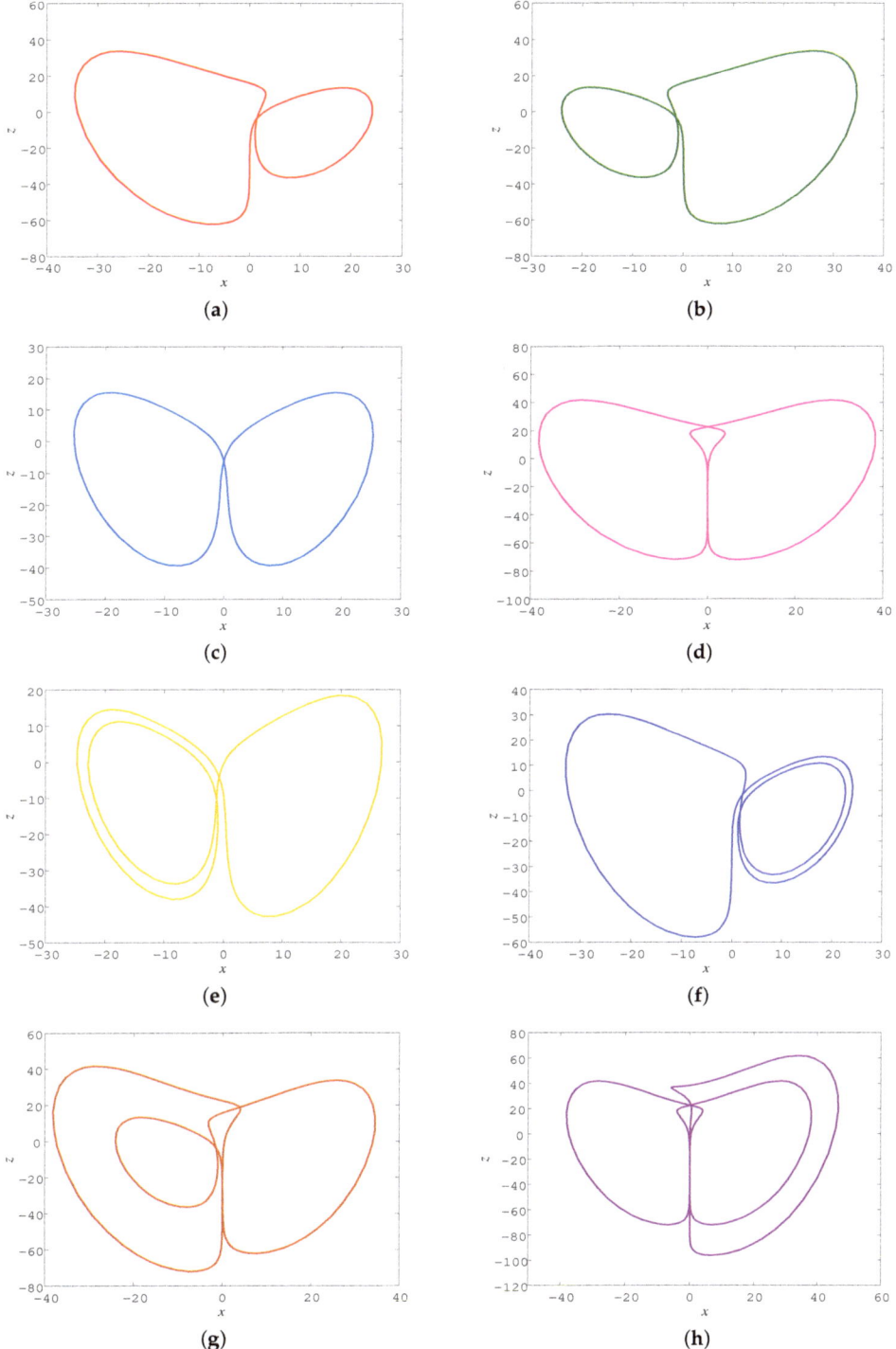

Figure 16. Unstable cycles in system (1) under parameters $(a, b, c, k) = (10, 100, 11.2, -0.2)$: (**a**) cycle 12; (**b**) 03; (**c**) 01; (**d**) 23; (**e**) 001; (**f**) 112; (**g**) 023; and (**h**) 233.

4.3. Unstable Periodic Orbits Embedded in Self-Excited Chaotic Attractor for $(a, b, c, k) = (10, 64, 0, 0)$

If we make the third and fourth parameters in the chosen set (a, b, c, k) zero, according to the Routh–Hurwitz stability criterion, $a^2b^2 < 0$ must be satisfied, so there is no solution, which means that there will be no hidden chaotic attractors in the system. Only when c and k are not zero is it possible to satisfy the Routh–Hurwitz stability criterion and a hidden chaotic attractor with stable equilibrium points can exist. When we take another set of parameters, $(a, b, c, k) = (10, 64, 0, 0)$, system (1) becomes a dynamical system with only five terms and also exhibits the existence of a chaotic state. As with some simple chaotic flows, namely the Sprott system, listed in Ref. [15], system (1) is simpler, but it has more complex dynamics, which is worthy of further research. For these parameter values, the two equilibrium points yield $E_1 = (-\sqrt{b}, -\sqrt{b}, 0)$ and $E_2 = (\sqrt{b}, \sqrt{b}, 0)$, and three eigenvalues of the fixed points $E_{1,2}$ are $\lambda_{1,2} = 1.4034 \pm 9.8983i$ and $\lambda_3 = -12.8068$. Since $E_{1,2}$ are two saddle-foci, system (1) has a self-excited chaotic attractor under current parameters.

We locate the unstable periodic orbits via the variational method, which brings great convenience. Here, we numerically integrate Equation (1) and extract approximate closed trajectories with different shapes, then artificially connect them so as to initialize the search. Figure 17 displays our calculated results for some short periodic orbits. We can also record the cycle swirling around the left fixed point E_1 once with a wing shape in Figure 17a by cycle 2, and its symmetric partner in Figure 17b with cycle 3. However, we did not find cycle 0 and cycle 1 to exist. The cycles in Figure 17c,d both have a knot, which indicates that they have a self-linking number of 1, which can conveniently be calculated [65]. We mark them as cycle 4 and cycle 5, respectively. Noting that they are symmetric to each other, the commutative symmetry 4 and 5 of the symbol sequence is satisfied.

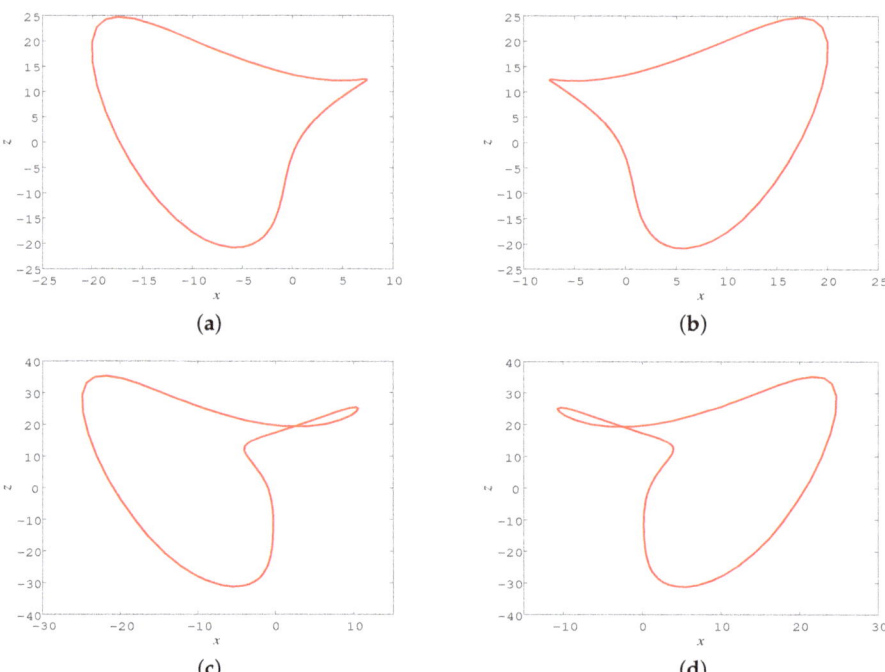

Figure 17. Four building blocks in system (1) for parameters $(a, b, c, k) = (10, 64, 0, 0)$: (**a**) cycle 2; (**b**) cycle 3; (**c**) cycle 4; (**d**) cycle 5.

We can use the above cycles as building blocks to find more complicated cycles, and the symbolic dynamics is established successfully. Figure 18 shows part of the found cycles together with equilibria E_1 and E_2. According to the symbolic dynamics, we find 41 unstable cycles with topological lengths up to 3, and sort them in Table 2. A total of 14 cycles are pruned, e.g., cycles 02, 002, and 123. Compared with the two sets of parameters, for the same periodic orbits, the cycles embedded in the hidden chaotic attractor have longer periods than those embedded in the self-excited chaotic attractor. The unstable cycles of system (1), as discussed under current parameters, must invoke symbolic dynamics for six letters, which is usually complicated. The topological classification approach used here indicates its flexibility. Additionally, although the symbolic dynamics of six letters can produce many symbol sequences within the topological length of 3, it is found that the 2 and 3 building blocks can be combined with all the other building blocks, while the 0 and 1 building blocks cannot be combined with the 4 or 5 building blocks. These behaviors are surely unusual. Therefore, the number of cycles actually allowed by the symbol sequence is greatly reduced. Whether this empirical pruning rule is applicable to longer periodic orbits is an open problem worthy of further investigation.

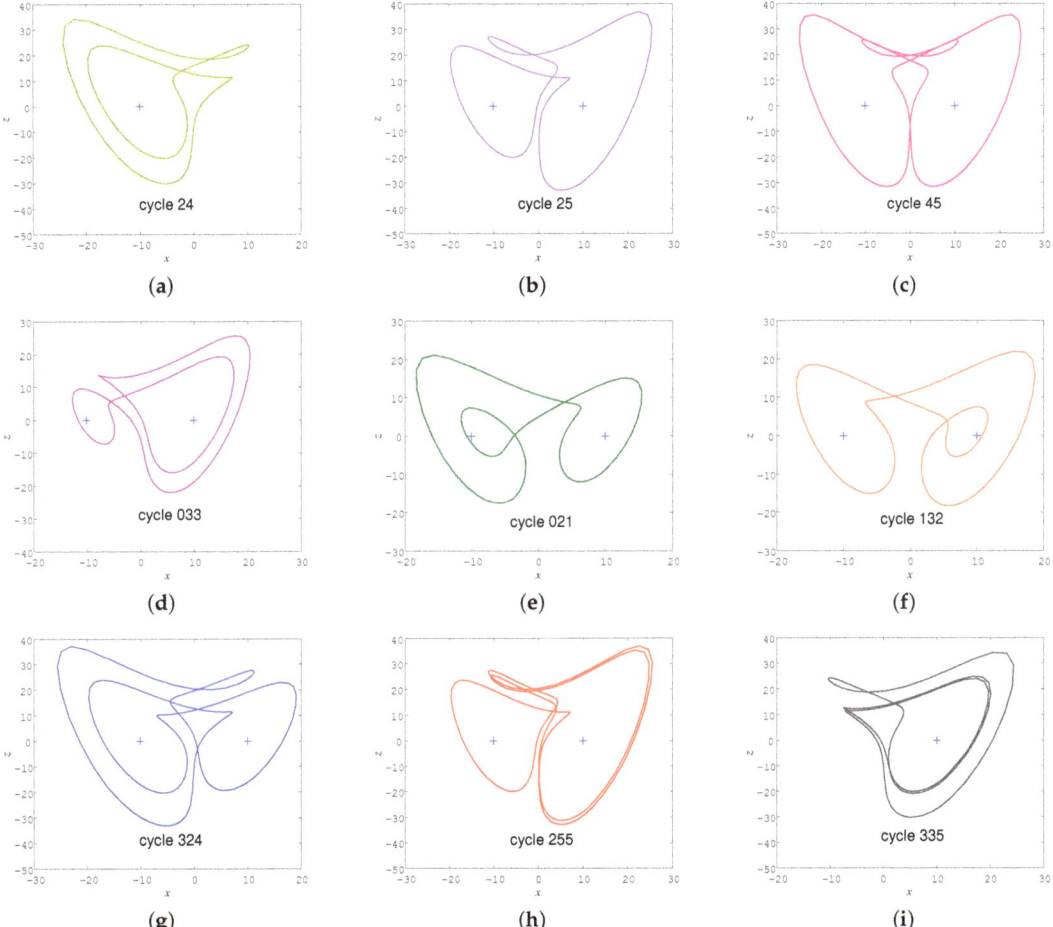

Figure 18. *Cont.*

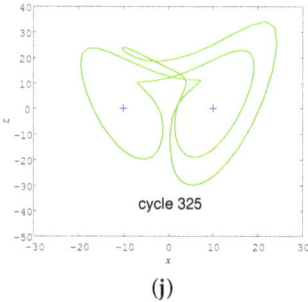 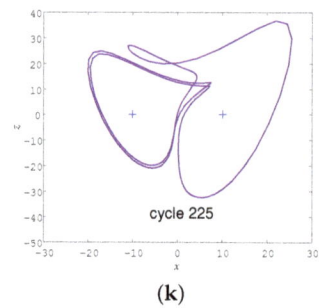 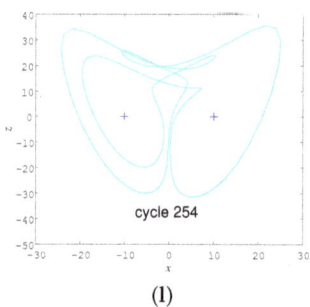

Figure 18. Unstable periodic orbits in system (1) for parameters $(a, b, c, k) = (10, 64, 0, 0)$. Two equilibria are marked with "+". (**a**) cycle 24; (**b**) cycle 25; (**c**) cycle 45; (**d**) cycle 033; (**e**) cycle 021; (**f**) cycle 132; (**g**) cycle 324; (**h**) cycle 255; (**i**) cycle 335; (**j**) cycle 325; (**k**) cycle 225; (**l**) cycle 254.

Table 2. Forty-one unstable periodic orbits embedded in self-excited chaotic attractor of system (1) for $(a, b, c, k) = (10, 64, 0, 0)$.

Length	p	T_p	Self-Linking	Length	p	T_p	Self-Linking	p	T_p	Self-Linking
1	2	1.016946	0	3	223	2.994130	0	031	2.447450	2
	3	1.016946	0		233	2.994130	0	012	2.447450	2
2	01	1.358438	1		033	2.609712	2	132	2.505368	0
	23	1.965825	1		122	2.609712	2	023	2.505368	0
	12	1.587528	1		021	2.323226	0			
	03	1.587528	1		013	2.323226	0			
1	4	1.312552	1		445	4.235720	3	354	3.955079	2
	5	1.312552	1		455	4.235720	3	234	3.263831	1
2	24	2.289914	2		344	3.667897	1	325	3.263831	1
	25	2.354458	0		255	3.667897	1	225	3.367249	1
	34	2.354458	0		335	3.312270	1	334	3.367249	1
	35	2.289914	2		224	3.312270	1	254	3.606269	3
	45	2.642183	1		244	3.600833	3	345	3.606269	3
3	235	3.349139	1		355	3.600833	3			
	324	3.349139	1		245	3.955079	2			

Regarding the system's overall dynamical complexity from the two sets of parameters chosen in the study, we can draw the following conclusions:

(1) The proposed system (1) with two parameters has more complex dynamics than the system with four parameters.

(2) The system with a self-excited attractor has more complex dynamics than the system with a hidden attractor.

(3) The system with periodic orbits containing building blocks of self-linking number 1 has more complex dynamics than that containing building blocks of self-linking number 0.

5. Circuit Simulation

We discuss the circuit implementation of system (1) to confirm the realizability of the mathematical model. Because all the values of state variables (x, y, z) in system (1) are out of the dynamic range, they should be scaled down to avoid problems during simulation. We set the amplitude scaling factor to 10, where $X = \frac{1}{10}x$, $Y = \frac{1}{10}y$, and $Z = \frac{1}{10}z$. The time scale factor is set to $\tau_0 = \frac{1}{R_0 C_0} = 2500$ to better match the system, a new time variable τ is defined instead of t, and $t = \tau_0 \tau$. As a result, system (1) after scale transformation is described as

$$\begin{aligned} R_0 C_0 \dot{X} &= a(Y - X) + 10kXZ \\ R_0 C_0 \dot{Y} &= -cY - 10XZ \\ R_0 C_0 \dot{Z} &= -\frac{b}{10} + 10XY, \end{aligned} \quad (8)$$

where $a = 10, b = 100, c = 11.2$, and $k = -0.2$.

The proposed circuit design is depicted in Figure 19, in which X, Y, and Z are the voltages at the outputs of operational amplifiers U2, U5, and U8, respectively. The circuit consists of nine AD811AN operational amplifiers, whose supply voltage is ± 18 V; three multipliers with an output coefficient of 0.1; three capacitors; and 19 resistors. Based on Kirchhoff's law, we can get

$$\begin{aligned} \dot{X} &= \frac{R_4}{R_2 R_5 C_1} Y - \frac{R_4}{R_1 R_5 C_1} X - \frac{R_4}{R_3 R_5 C_1} 0.1 XZ \\ \dot{Y} &= -\frac{R_{10}}{R_8 R_{11} C_2} Y - \frac{R_{10}}{R_9 R_{11} C_2} 0.1 XZ \\ \dot{Z} &= \frac{R_{16}}{R_{15} R_{17} C_3} V_1 + \frac{R_{16}}{R_{14} R_{17} C_3} 0.1 XY. \end{aligned} \quad (9)$$

Comparing Equation (8) with Equation (9), we select all the capacitors $C_i = 40$ nF ($i = 1, 2, 3$) and $V1 = -1$ V. The resistors $R_9 = R_{14} = 1$ kΩ, $R_3 = 5$ kΩ, $R_8 = 8.93$ kΩ, $R_i = 10$ kΩ ($i = 1, 2, 5, 6, 7, 11, 12, 13, 15, 17, 18, 19$), and $R_i = 100$ kΩ ($i = 4, 10, 16$). We used NI Multisim 14.0 to simulate the circuit, as shown in Figure 20. It can be seen that the circuit well emulates the proposed system, which is in good agreement with the numerical results in Figure 1. Therefore, we can conclude that system (1) can be realized in physical experiments.

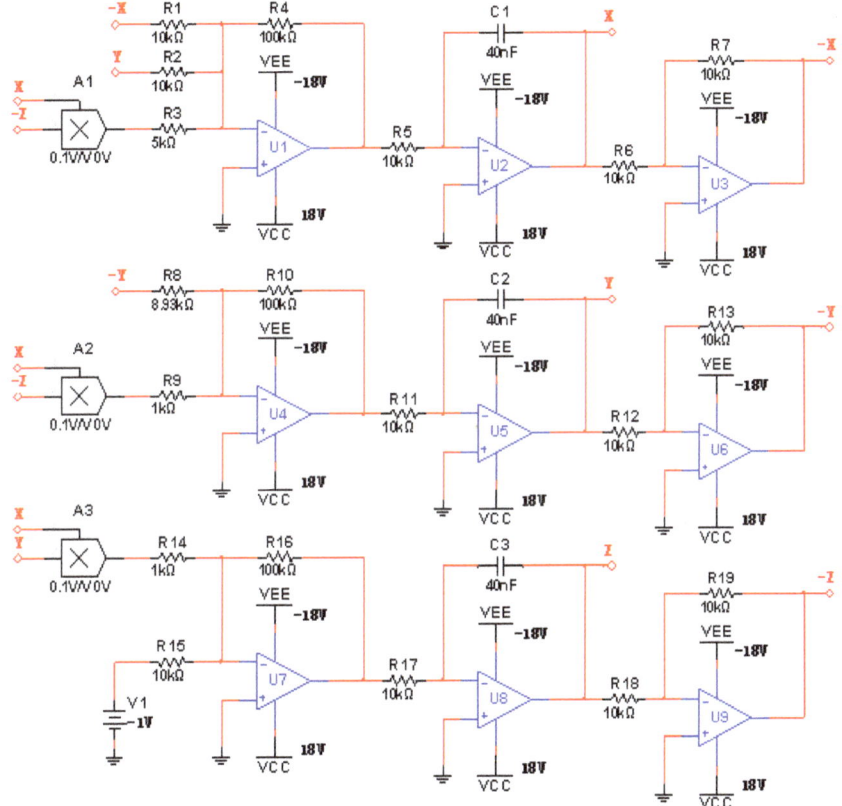

Figure 19. Schematic of circuit.

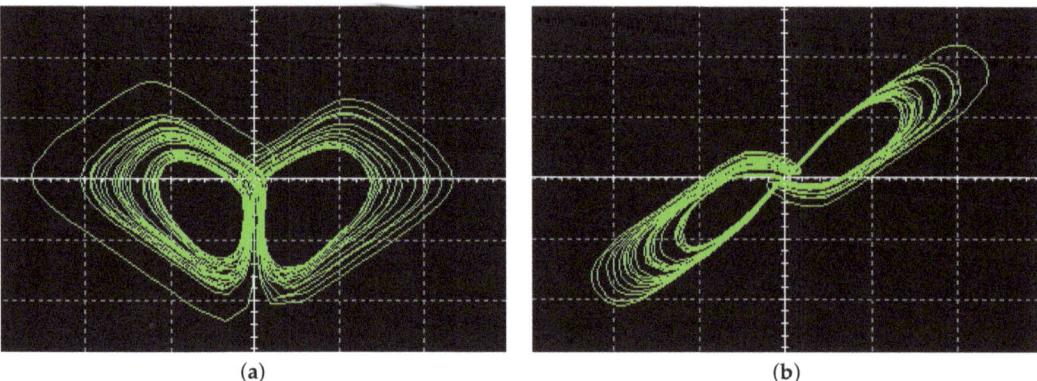

Figure 20. Phase portraits in Multisim of circuit: (**a**) X–Z plane; (**b**) X–Y plane.

6. Conclusions and Discussion

We constructed a new 3D autonomous chaotic system with coexisting self-excited and hidden attractors, in which the generation of different types of attractors depends on its parameters. The complex dynamics of the system were analyzed by different tools, and it was proved to be chaotic in the sense of having a fractional Kaplan–Yorke dimension, a phase portrait of a strange attractor, and a period-doubling route to chaos. Moreover, an applicable generic procedure for topological classification of unstable cycles in the proposed system was addressed. Guessing an entire orbit, we utilized the variational method for the calculation of cycles, and the initial conjecture loop could be gradually evolved into a real cycle. Diverse symbolic dynamics based on orbital topology was successfully established in the phase space, including four and six letters, corresponding to hidden and self-excited chaotic attractors. Periodic orbits up to certain topological lengths were found accordingly, which indicates the utility of the topological classification approach in the periodic orbit taxonomy. A Multisim circuit simulation of the system was implemented to further verify the mathematical model.

The symbolic encoding method employed here could also be applied to discrete dynamical systems, such as the memristive Rulkov neuron model [66], discrete memristor hyperchaotic maps [67], 2D memristive hyperchaotic maps [68], and 2D sine map [69]. Quotienting symmetries of a given dynamical system prior to the symbolic dynamics analysis is an attractive research direction. Symmetry reduction could not only reduce the multiple-letter symbolic encodings of periodic orbits to a single letter, but could visualize self-linking in the symmetry-reduced state space, which requires further investigation. The new system still contains rich and complex dynamic behavior, and its topology requires comprehensive and deep exploration. Moreover, as the system proposed in Ref. [51], the newly proposed system (1) is a mathematical model at present and does not correspond to any physical phenomena. It is hoped that more detailed theoretical analysis and application investigations will be carried out in the future.

Funding: This research was funded by National Natural Science Foundation of China (Grant Nos. 11647085 and 11647086), Shanxi Province Science Foundation for Youths (Grant No. 201901D211252), and the Scientific and Technological Innovation Programs of Higher Education Institutions in Shanxi (Grant Nos. 2019L0505 and 2019L0554).

Institutional Review Board Statement: Not applicable.

Informed Consent Statement: Not applicable.

Data Availability Statement: Not applicable.

Acknowledgments: I thank the anonymous reviewers for their many insightful comments and suggestions, which have improved our manuscript substantially.

Conflicts of Interest: The author declares no conflict of interest.

References

1. Lorenz, E.N. Deterministic nonperiodic flow. *J. Atmos. Sci.* **1963**, *20*, 130–141. [CrossRef]
2. Fu, S.; Liu, Y.; Ma, H.; Du, Y. Control chaos to different stable states for a piecewise linear circuit system by a simple linear control. *Chaos Solitons Fractals* **2020**, *130*, 109431. [CrossRef]
3. Gong, L.H.; Luo, H.X.; Wu, R.Q.; Zhou, N.R. New 4D chaotic system with hidden attractors and self-excited attractors and its application in image encryption based on RNG. *Physica A* **2022**, *591*, 126793. [CrossRef]
4. Hassan, M.F. Synchronization of uncertain constrained hyperchaotic systems and chaos-based secure communications via a novel decomposed nonlinear stochastic estimator. *Nonlinear Dyn.* **2016**, *83*, 2183–2211. [CrossRef]
5. Sangiorgio, M.; Dercole, F. Robustness of lstm neural networks for multi-step forecasting of chaotic time series. *Chaos Solitons Fractals* **2020**, *139*, 110045. [CrossRef]
6. Zhou, L.; You, Z.; Tang, Y. A new chaotic system with nested coexisting multiple attractors and riddled basins. *Chaos Solitons Fractals* **2021**, *148*, 111057. [CrossRef]
7. Nwachioma, C.; Pérez-Cruz, J.H. Analysis of a new chaotic system, electronic realization and use in navigation of differential drive mobile robot. *Chaos Solitons Fractals* **2021**, *144*, 110684. [CrossRef]
8. Wang, G.; Yuan, F.; Chen, G.; Zhang, Y. Coexisting multiple attractors and riddled basins of a memristive system. *Chaos* **2018**, *28*, 013125. [CrossRef]
9. Ly, A.; Qy, A.; Gc, B. Hidden attractors, singularly degenerate heteroclinic orbits, multistability and physical realization of a new 6D hyperchaotic system. *Commun. Nonlinear Sci. Numer. Simul.* **2020**, *90*, 105362.
10. Dudkowski, D.; Jafari, S.; Kapitaniak, T.; Kuznetsov, N.V.; Leonov, G.A.; Prasad, A. Hidden attractors in dynamical systems. *Phy. Rep.* **2016**, *637*, 1–50. [CrossRef]
11. Jafari, S.; Sprott, J.C.; Nazarimehr, F. Recent new examples of hidden attractors. *Eur. Phys. J. Spec. Top.* **2015**, *224*, 1469–1476. [CrossRef]
12. Pham, V.T.; Kapitaniak, T.; Volos, C. *Systems with Hidden Attractors: From Theory to Realization in Circuits*; Springer: Berlin, Germany, 2017; pp. 11–13.
13. Chen, G.R.; Ueta, T. Yet another chaotic attractor. *Int. J. Bifurc. Chaos* **1999**, *9*, 1465–1466. [CrossRef]
14. Qi, G.; Chen, G.; Du, S.; Chen, Z.; Yuan, Z. Analysis of a new chaotic system. *Physica A* **2005**, *352*, 295–308. [CrossRef]
15. Sprott, J.C. Some simple chaotic flows. *Phys. Rev. E* **1994**, *50*, 647–650. [CrossRef] [PubMed]
16. Guan, X.; Xie, Y. Connecting curve: A new tool for locating hidden attractors. *Chaos* **2021**, *31*, 113143. [CrossRef] [PubMed]
17. Kuznetsov, N.V.; Leonov, G.A.; Mokaev, T.N.; Prasad, A.; Shrimali, M.D. Finite-time lyapunov dimension and hidden attractor of the rabinovich system. *Nonlinear Dyn.* **2018**, *92*, 267–285. [CrossRef]
18. Deng, Q.; Wang, C. Multi-scroll hidden attractors with two stable equilibrium points. *Chaos* **2019**, *29*, 093112. [CrossRef] [PubMed]
19. Yang, T. Multistability and hidden attractors in a three-dimensional chaotic system. *Int. J. Bifurc. Chaos* **2020**, *30*, 2050087. [CrossRef]
20. Molaie, M.; Jafari, S.; Sprott, J.C.; Golpayegani, S.M.R.H. Simple chaotic flows with one stable equilibrium. *Int. J. Bifurc. Chaos* **2013**, *23*, 1350188. [CrossRef]
21. Huang, L.; Wang, Y.; Jiang, Y.; Lei, T. A novel memristor chaotic system with a hidden attractor and multistability and its implementation in a circuit. *Math. Probl. Eng.* **2021**, *2021*, 7457220. [CrossRef]
22. Wang, X.; Viet-Thanh, P.; Christos, V. Dynamics, circuit design, and synchronization of a new chaotic system with closed curve equilibrium. *Complexity* **2017**, *2017*, 7138971. [CrossRef]
23. Jafari, S.; Sprott, J.C.; Pham, V.T.; Volos, C.; Li, C. Simple chaotic 3d flows with surfaces of equilibria. *Nonlinear Dyn.* **2016**, *86*, 1349–1358. [CrossRef]
24. Zhang, X.; Tian, Z.; Li, J.; Wu, X.; Cui, Z. A hidden chaotic system with multiple attractors. *Entropy* **2021**, *23*, 1341. [CrossRef] [PubMed]
25. Li, C.; Sprott, J.C. Coexisting hidden attractors in a 4-D simplified lorenz system. *Int. J. Bifurc. Chaos* **2014**, *24*, 1450034. [CrossRef]
26. Jafari, S.; Sprott, J.C.; Mohammad Reza Hashemi Golpayegani, S. Elementary quadratic chaotic flows with no equilibria. *Phys. Lett. A* **2013**, *377*, 699–702. [CrossRef]
27. Zhou, W.; Wang, G.; Shen, Y.; Yuan, F.; Yu, S. Hidden coexisting attractors in a chaotic system without equilibrium point. *Int. J. Bifurc. Chaos* **2018**, *28*, 1830033. [CrossRef]
28. Zuo, J.L.; Li, C.L. Multiple attractors and dynamic analysis of a no-equilibrium chaotic system. *Optik* **2016**, *127*, 7952–7957. [CrossRef]
29. Maaita, J.O.; Volos, C.K.; Kyprianidis, I.M.; Stouboulos, I.N. The dynamics of a cubic nonlinear system with no equilibrium point. *J. Nonlinear Dyn.* **2015**, *2015*, 257923. [CrossRef]
30. Sprott, J.C.; Jafari, S.; Pham, V.T.; Hosseinib, Z.S. A chaotic system with a single unstable node. *Phys. Lett. A* **2015**, *379*, 2030–2036. [CrossRef]
31. Wang, X.; Chen, G.R. A chaotic system with only one stable equilibrium. *Commun. Nonlinear Sci. Numer. Simul.* **2012**, *17*, 1264–1272. [CrossRef]
32. Wei, Z. Dynamical behaviors of a chaotic system with no equilibria. *Phys. Lett. A* **2011**, *376*, 102–108. [CrossRef]

33. Yang, Y.; Huang, L.; Xiang, J.; Bao, H.; Li, H. Generating multi-wing hidden attractors with only stable node-foci via non-autonomous approach. *Phys. Scr.* **2021**, *96*, 125220. [CrossRef]
34. Wei, Z.; Yang, Q. Dynamical analysis of the generalized sprott C system with only two stable equilibria. *Nonlinear Dyn.* **2012**, *68*, 543–554. [CrossRef]
35. Tian, H.; Wang, Z.; Zhang, P.; Chen, M.; Wang, Y. Dynamic analysis and robust control of a chaotic system with hidden attractor. *Complexity* **2021**, *2021*, 8865522 . [CrossRef]
36. Wang, Z.; Sun, W.; Wei, Z.; Zhang, S. Dynamics and delayed feedback control for a 3D jerk system with hidden attractor. *Nonlinear Dyn.* **2015**, *82*, 577–588. [CrossRef]
37. Wei, Z.; Zhang, W.; Yao, M. On the periodic orbit bifurcating from one single non-hyperbolic equilibrium in a chaotic jerk system. *Nonlinear Dyn.* **2015**, *82*, 1251–1258. [CrossRef]
38. Qi, A.; Muhammad, K.; Liu, S. Dynamical analysis of the meminductor-based chaotic system with hidden attractor. *Fractals* **2021**, *29*, 2140020. [CrossRef]
39. Wei, Z.; Zhang, W.; Wang, Z.; Yao, M. Hidden attractors and dynamical behaviors in an extended Rikitake system. *Int. J. Bifurc. Chaos* **2015**, *25*, 1550028. [CrossRef]
40. Wei, Z.; Yu, P.; Zhang, W.; Yao, M. Study of hidden attractors, multiple limit cycles from Hopf bifurcation and boundedness of motion in the generalized hyperchaotic Rabinovich system. *Nonlinear Dyn.* **2015**, *82*, 131–141. [CrossRef]
41. Wei, Z.; Zhang, W. Hidden hyperchaotic attractors in a modified Lorenz–Stenflo system with only one stable equilibrium. *Int. J. Bifurc. Chaos* **2014**, *24*, 1450127. [CrossRef]
42. Wei, Z.; Moroz, I.; Sprott, J.C.; Akgul, A.; Zhang, W. Hidden hyperchaos and electronic circuit application in a 5D self-exciting homopolar disc dynamo. *Chaos* **2017**, *27*, 033101. [CrossRef] [PubMed]
43. Wang, N.; Zhang, G.; Kuznetsov, N.V.; Bao, H. Hidden attractors and multistability in a modified Chua's circuit. *Commun. Nonlinear Sci. Numer. Simul.* **2021**, *92*, 105494. [CrossRef]
44. Bao, H.; Hu, A.; Liu, W.; Bao, B. Hidden bursting firings and bifurcation mechanisms in memristive neuron model with threshold electromagnetic induction. *IEEE Trans. Neural Netw. Learn. Syst.* **2020**, *31*, 502–511. [CrossRef] [PubMed]
45. Wu, Y.; Wang, C.; Deng, Q. A new 3d multi-scroll chaotic system generated with three types of hidden attractors. *Eur. Phys. J. Spec. Top.* **2021**, *230*, 1863–1871. [CrossRef]
46. Wei, Z.; Li, Y.; Sang, B.; Liu, Y.; Zhang, W. Complex dynamical behaviors in a 3D simple chaotic flow with 3D stable or 3D unstable manifolds of a single equilibrium. *Int. J. Bifurc. Chaos* **2019**, *29*, 1950095. [CrossRef]
47. Kingni, S.T.; Jafari, S.; Pham, V.T.; Woafo, P. Constructing and analyzing of a unique three-dimensional chaotic autonomous system exhibiting three families of hidden attractors. *Math. Comput. Simul.* **2017**, *132*, 172–182. [CrossRef]
48. Zhang, S.; Zeng, Y.; Li, Z.; Wang, M.; Le, X. Generating one to four-wing hidden attractors in a novel 4D no-equilibrium chaotic system with extreme multistability. *Chaos* **2018**, *28*, 013113. [CrossRef] [PubMed]
49. Jafari, S.; Ahmadi, A.; Khalaf, A.; Abdolmohammadi, H.R.; Pham, V.T.; Alsaadi, F.E. A new hidden chaotic attractor with extreme multi-stability. *AEU—Int. J. Electron. C.* **2018**, *89*, 131–135. [CrossRef]
50. Cang, S.; Yue, L.; Zhang, R.; Wang, Z. Hidden and self-excited coexisting attractors in a lorenz-like system with two equilibrium points. *Nonlinear Dyn.* **2019**, *95*, 381–390. [CrossRef]
51. Yang, Q.; Wei, Z.; Chen, G. An unusual 3d autonomous quadratic chaotic system with two stable node-foci. *Int. J. Bifurc. Chaos* **2010**, *20*, 1061–1083. [CrossRef]
52. Wolf, A.; Swift, J.B.; Swinney, H.L.; Vastano J.A. Determining Lyapunov exponents from a time series. *Physica D* **1985**, *16*, 285–317. [CrossRef]
53. Strogatz, S.H. *Nonlinear Dynamics and Chaos: With Applications to Physics, Biology, Chemistry, and Engineering*; Perseus Books: Reading, MA, USA, 1994; pp. 44–45.
54. Cvitanović, P.; Artuso, R.; Mainieri, R.; Tanner, G.; Vattay, G. *Chaos: Classical and Quantum*; Niels Bohr Institute: Copenhagen, Denmark, 2012; pp. 131–133.
55. Lan, Y.; Cvitanović, P. Variational method for finding periodic orbits in a general flow. *Phys. Rev. E* **2004**, *69*, 016217. [CrossRef]
56. Dong, C.; Jia, L.; Jie, Q.; Li, H. Symbolic encoding of periodic orbits and chaos in the Rucklidge system. *Complexity* **2021**, *2021*, 4465151. [CrossRef]
57. Lan, Y.; Cvitanović, P. Unstable recurrent patterns in Kuramoto–Sivashinsky dynamics. *Phys. Rev. E* **2008**, *78*, 026208. [CrossRef] [PubMed]
58. Dong, C.; Liu, H.; Li, H. Unstable periodic orbits analysis in the generalized Lorenz-type system. *J. Stat. Mech.* **2020**, *2020*, 073211. [CrossRef]
59. Dong, C. Topological classification of periodic orbits in the kuramoto–sivashinsky equation. *Mod. Phys. Lett. B* **2018**, *32*, 1850155. [CrossRef]
60. Lan, Y.; Chandre, C.; Cvitanović, P. Newton's descent method for the determination of invariant tori. *Phys. Rev. E* **2006**, *74*, 046206. [CrossRef]
61. Dong, C.; Lan, Y. A variational approach to connecting orbits in nonlinear dynamical systems. *Phys. Lett. A* **2014**, *378*, 705–712. [CrossRef]
62. Dong, C.; Lan, Y. Organization of spatially periodic solutions of the steady Kuramoto–Sivashinsky equation. *Commun. Nonlinear Sci. Numer. Simul.* **2014**, *19*, 2140–2153. [CrossRef]

63. Dong, C.; Liu, H.; Jie, Q.; Li, H. Topological classification of periodic orbits in the generalized Lorenz-type system with diverse symbolic dynamics. *Chaos Solitons Fractals* **2022**, *154*, 111686. [CrossRef]
64. Hao, B.L.; Zheng, W.M. *Applied Symbolic Dynamics and Chaos*; World Scientic: Singapore, 1998; pp. 11–13.
65. Ray, A.; Ghosh, D.; Chowdhury, A.R. Topological study of multiple coexisting attractors in a nonlinear system. *J. Phys. A-Math. Theor.* **2009**, *42*, 385102. [CrossRef]
66. Li, K.; Bao, H.; Li, H.; Ma, J.; Hua, Z.; Bao, B. Memristive Rulkov neuron model with magnetic induction effects. *IEEE Trans. Ind. Inform.* **2022**, *18*, 1726–1736. [CrossRef]
67. Bao, H.; Hua, Z.; Li, H.; Chen, M.; Bao, B. Discrete memristor hyperchaotic maps. *IEEE Trans. Circuits—I* **2021**, *68*, 4534–4544. [CrossRef]
68. Li, H.; Hua, Z.; Bao, H.; Zhu, L.; Chen, M.; Bao, B. Two-dimensional memristive hyperchaotic maps and application in secure communication. *IEEE Trans. Ind. Electron.* **2021**, *68*, 9931–9940. [CrossRef]
69. Bao, H.; Hua, Z.; Wang, N.; Zhu, L.; Chen, M.; Bao, B. Initials-boosted coexisting chaos in a 2-D Sine map and its hardware implementation. *IEEE Trans. Ind. Inform.* **2021**, *17*, 1132–1140. [CrossRef]

MDPI
St. Alban-Anlage 66
4052 Basel
Switzerland
Tel. +41 61 683 77 34
Fax +41 61 302 89 18
www.mdpi.com

Fractal and Fractional Editorial Office
E-mail: fractalfract@mdpi.com
www.mdpi.com/journal/fractalfract

www.ingramcontent.com/pod-product-compliance
Lightning Source LLC
LaVergne TN
LVHW070510100526
838202LV00014B/1826